Black, White, and in Color

D1598242

Black, White, and in Color

ESSAYS ON

AMERICAN LITERATURE

AND CULTURE

Hortense J. Spillers

The University of Chicago Press
Chicago and London

2003

Hortense J. Spillers is the Frederick J. Whiton Professor of English at Cornell University. She is the editor of *Comparative American Identities: Race, Sex, and Nationality in the Modern Text* and coeditor of *Conjuring: Black Women, Fiction, and Literary Tradition*.

The University of Chicago Press, Chicago 60637
The University of Chicago Press, Ltd., London
© 2003 by The University of Chicago
All rights reserved. Published 2003
Printed in the United States of America
12 11 10 09 08 07 06 05 04 03   5 4 3 2 1

ISBN (cloth): 0-226-76979-8
ISBN (paper): 0-226-76980-1

Credits for prior publication are included with the notes to individual chapters.

Library of Congress Cataloging-in-Publication Data

Spillers, Hortense J.
    Black, white, and in color : essays on American literature and culture / Hortense J. Spillers.
        p.   cm.
    Includes index.
    ISBN 0-226-76979-8 (cloth) — ISBN 0-226-76980-1 (pbk.)
    1. American literature—African American authors—History and criticism.   2. American literature—20th century—History and criticism.   3. African Americans in literature. 4. Human skin color in literature.   5. Race relations in literature.   6. Whites in literature. 7. Racism in literature.   8. Race in literature.   I. Title.
    PS153.N5 S67   2003
    810.9′896073′00904—dc21

                                                                        2002014268

⊗ The paper used in this publication meets the minimum requirements of the American National Standard for Information Sciences—Permanence of Paper for Printed Library Materials, ANSI Z39.48-1992.

FOR IRA AND "MISS PETIE"

AND ALL THE LOST LOVES:

DAD, BROTHER, GRAYLING,

AND MICHAEL

(IN MEMORIAM)

Contents

Preface

This collection of essays exists because colleagues and students urged it.[1] I finally had to concede myself that writings scattered over years and venues would stand a better crack at survival and continuity between two covers. But the additional bonus in this case is that these essays sprang up in response to two concurrent curricular developments that have played a dramatic role in altering the humanities academy, and that was the post-nineteen sixties emergence of "Black Studies," on the one hand, and "Women's Studies," on the other. It is fair to say that both of these curricular objects, taking cue from their respective and overlapping historic occasions, at once wrecked my travel plans and defined them. In other words, they have configured my professional career (and given me a splendid life so far), replete with the agonies of beginnings. I had fully *intended* to write something else twenty years ago, including fiction (even though I have been informed in certain quarters that the latter is what I have in fact produced), but the "pull of the occasional," in the words of my colleague, Professor Roger Gilbert, effectually mobilized my initial plans to an ever-vanishing horizon. (At one time hot on the trail of William Blake's poetry and the theoretical intricacies of the English Romantics, I almost did not pursue scholarship at all, having in mind, before an encounter with Blake's Prophetic Books, a career in broadcast journalism, or law and politics—at thirteen, I wanted to be president of the United States, thinking that I could do the job at least as well as Eisenhower, and if not that, then the work of a junior senator from the state of Tennessee. I was told by my wonderful father, which earnest remark inadvertently awakened a feminist interest in my imagination, that if I did not become president myself, then I'd likely have a son who would.) But the route that I discovered on the tangential course could not have been more suitable.

The prevailing logic of the occasion is that it will end, or perhaps transmute into something more permanent, but anyone paying close attention to the rhythms and punctualities of the new field specifications might have observed the following: a field, never given in the fullness of its time, finds and situates itself on its feet, on the occasions of *practice* and *performance,* inasmuch as it depends on discursive positions staked out against the apparently more settled terrain, moment by uncertain moment. If we think of the new field as a yawning in the chain of historical necessity,[2] then its appearance is neither guaranteed, on the one hand, nor foreclosed, on the other, but answers to certain conditions that cannot be predicted beforehand. The charges leveled against Black Studies and Women's Studies, especially the former, in the initial period of their instauration—that the subject(s) were "unresearched," among other indictments—were blind to a material fact of discursive production—discourses do not spontaneously appear, but as writing, as an intellectual technology, they will follow the path and the tide of generation; that is to say, books and articles beget their like only after a sufficient density of differentiated objects are available to an articulation of elements. An investigator will not "find" what he or she is looking for, but will have to partially "create" the differentiations against the stubbornness of tradition. Starting with a "hermeneutic demand," which had already been formulated in political movement, as well as the saturated inquiries related to modernist critical/theoretical postures, the new studies were not at all bound to come about, but discovered their urgency of moment in the very alignments of procedure that had assumed their impossibility. The questions broached by the new itineraries could be posed because the intransigent (and arbitrary) borders of the canonical were fragile to start with, predicated, as they were, on the reified properties of "race" and "gender." Paradoxically, the curricular objects that emerged in the late sixties and beyond drew attention to the emphases, the texts, the propositions that had been excluded by the traditional configurations of humanistic inquiry, but both Black Studies and Women's Studies must now go beyond what was perceived as their historic mission in order to escape the frozen postures of closure that actually substitute for knowledge.

Called upon to hit the ground, already running, the new procedures were compelled to *establish* the game and *play* it at once. The essays gathered here were motivated, then, by exactly such urgency, the awful need to respond in the moment, on point. Most of the essays were commissioned by occasions related to the new niche markets in publishing and the sudden explosion of readerly demand linked to the new curricular objects, but the yet-to-be-written histories of African-American and Women's Studies, respectively, will show uneven and asymptotic development over the decades, despite the fact that neither constituency could boast any substantial institutional attachment to the long-standing and prestigious protocols that belonged to the repertoire of human sciences, and indeed, one set of actants in the matter might as well have been—as far as higher education in predominantly white institutions across the United States was concerned—two-legged creatures from planet Mars. In the academic year 1973–74, when I began my post-doctoral teaching career at Wellesley College in the hostile climate of the institution's English Department, Black Studies there were virtually months old; as a joint appointment in the two fields, I believe that I intuitively understood what the assignment was and had to trust it, insofar as few of my collegial elders, if any, offered much of any kind of professional guidance to the cadre of six newly minted Ph.D.'s on the staff, and sure enough, we were each, in time, given the boot, with a swift right-hand blow thrown in for good measure. The arts of eldering here were impoverished indeed, as it is perhaps no longer a very well-kept secret that blushing humanists do not always practice what they preach, or is it that they practice exactly what they do preach, insofar as humanistic study, in some quarters, has little to do with the others? By the time it was my turn to be slapped, I had completed 8 to 10 of the essays, all of them on aspects of African-American writing, and had been awarded the National Magazine Award for fiction for a short story, "Isom," appearing in *Essence Magazine*.[3] Between 1971, when my first writing was published by *Black Scholar* on Martin Luther King's pulpit style,[4] and the fall of 1982, when Carole Vance invited me to Barnard College's "Feminist and Scholar Conference #9," which eventuated in "Interstices," I had completed pieces of writing on Jean Toomer, Gwendolyn Brooks, Ralph Ellison, James Baldwin, Toni Morrison, Zora Neale Hurston, and Margaret Walker (which appear in this volume, with the exception of the pieces on Toomer and Baldwin)[5] and conducted my first foray onto the terrain of "theory," here represented in "Formalism Comes to Harlem." The latter, alongside "A Hateful Passion, A Lost Love: Three Women's Fiction," both written c. 1977–78, cooled their heels at a journal in the Midwest for three or four years, until Professor Rachel Blau DuPlessis, then editor of *Feminist Studies,* selected one of them for the new women's studies initiative, and Dean Joel Weixelman, then editor of *Black American Literature Forum* (now the *African-American Review*), was courageous enough to run the other. To DuPlessis and Weixelman, as well as Professor Robert Chrisman, executive editor and publisher of *The Black Scholar,* and Professors Sandra Gilbert and Susan Gubar, co-editors of *Shakespeare's Sisters,* where "Gwendolyn, the Terrible" first appeared, I owe inestimable gratitude because they honored my efforts early on and without question.

Anyone looking back at the nineteen-seventies from the vantage of the new millennium might possibly be puzzled that the word "courageous" was evoked in the preceding paragraph, when, today, even dissertations on African-American themes and/or gender studies are accorded nearly instantaneous recognition. But I should note that despite the fact that publishers and editors were scouting the horizon for work in Black Studies by the mid- to latter end of the decade, I recall that it was simply hell trying to lay down discourse on aspects of African-American life and thought that did not conform to and replicate certain deeply held convictions regarding the sound and sense of language generated in this field, and if the writer were female, then she had best be prepared to clear yet one more hurdle. I can think of no other reason that would explain why the suppressed essays were put on hold for so long a time, or why an editor at a major university press withdrew interest in my dissertation manuscript (which he had solicited) on the rhetoric of black sermons (joined by no fewer than twelve other press editors, I think I remember, including ones at a prestigious black university press), if it were not rabid fear and revulsion—exercised with the consistency and unconsciousness of automatic reflex action, the jerk of a knee, the bat of an eyelash—toward ideas and a perplexed response to them in association with black life that would make "racism," as we usually think we mean it, look like a Sunday picnic. Bear in mind that we are talking about *cultivated* subjects here, not unintelligent ones in a Klansman's clown suit or gestapo headpiece. I would say, then, as a result of this vicious epiphenomenon, which we have not yet understood, that my career, by way of the essays collected in this volume, has been profoundly touched by a peculiar combination of passions that I would call "racist" and "sexist" only if I were caught in a fit of impatience, which acts have been redeemed by a handful of others who had no idea what good offices they were performing. I should hope that by way of this volume they will know now.

I have waited a quarter of a century for a plank to fall out of the ceiling and give me a *name*—a "strategy," Kenneth Burke called it—for a situation that we need a name for, still. And that is, the name for the segregation and separation of the *Word,* which outcome marks, on its lower frequencies, a concentration of infested elements. The social arrangements that I am attempting to describe, as painful as they have been for me and even though they have exacted a personal and professional toll, should not be dismissed as a single practitioner's "experience" alone; if that were all, they could be deservedly forgotten as an anomalous feature of her biography. But, rather, what I believe I mean in reference to the proximity denied between ideas and black life has to do with the shadow that falls over the Word as it approaches some supposed dread subject/object, imagined to inhabit a territory of power and danger. From that angle, the nameless phenomenon that eludes the grasp, but which we know the instant it appears, has no more to do with single individuals than a given pathogen, moving along a path of attack in its historic signature; rather, it touches generations of social formations both over time (transhistorical and memorial) and in time (historical and material). I have attempted in several of these essays to pin it down, most notably in "Interstices," "Mama's Baby, Papa's Maybe," "The Permanent Obliquity of an In(pha)llibly Straight," "Notes on an Alternative Model—Neither/Nor," and "Moving on Down the Line." In fact, I believe that the single common conceptual feature, if not obsession, of all the essays from "Interstices," on, might be put down to an effort to wrestle this particular segment of political economy, for I am convinced that material values engender symbolic and discursive ones (and vice-versa) in perfect synecdochic harmony. The institutions of enslavement and colonization were established, in part, by greed, while historiographical projects have no taxonomies for that class of substance abuse, let's call it, that would include such a thing, in addition to "love," "envy," and "desire." But to call greed one of the culprits here glibly begs the question, insofar as it seems that material gain and collective and individual self-interest actually do not penetrate the picture far enough to provide sufficient motivation and explanation over the centuries. This *other,* which theorists have designated "epistemic violence," nearly dissolves into the hidden recesses of psychoanalytic inquiry, but we would be content to be able to identity that portion that we imagine is detectable: the languages and discourses of publicly sanctioned and operative powers in the laws and the whole cultural domain. (In that regard, today's politics are too obvious and vulgar as the massive and undemocratic buyout by moneyed interests and, as an extension of the entertainment industry in the United States now, too superficial to offer much guidance in an analysis of the ways and means of power precisely because nothing in it is hidden any longer.) We must look *everywhere else,* then, in order to see how the society signs itself, from the choice of love objects, to the symptoms of piety and their plethora of displacements, to the decisions that move mass markets and items of popular culture, to the kinds of faces and voices that deliver our daily news products and dictate fantasy mechanisms, from fashion, to movies, to sports, to the unrelenting celebration of corporate values (if the latter formulation is not an oxymoron) in its stunning now transglobal avatar. What must be brought to heel, I think, is the way that discourses precisely conjugate the social relation, for the Word and its discriminating punctualities are at play there.

Barnard College's "Feminist and Scholar Conference" on female sexuality perhaps marked a tangential route for me that became the way, so to speak, inasmuch as it opened onto questions of power, which, in turn, incited my sustained interest in slavery and its links to cultural studies. "Notes on an Alternative Model—Neither/Nor," an investigation into the vagaries of the mulatto figure in literature, and "Mama's Baby, Papa's Maybe," an attempt to locate the bodies of African women in the Atlantic Slave Trade and the massive consequences attendant upon it, as well as other essays of the late eighties—"Changing the Letter: The Yokes, the Jokes of Discourse" and "Moving on Down the Line," among them—are all directly related to that inquiry whose major thrust was aimed at scrutinizing positions in discourse and the elements that enter into their semiotic calculus. My current work in progress, *In the Flesh: A Situation for Feminist Inquiry*, elaborates the protocol unfolded in "Mama's Baby, Papa's Maybe."

One of the most important collaborative projects that engaged my critical efforts was the work completed on *Conjuring: Black Women, Fiction, and Literary Tradition*, which I co-edited with good friend and colleague, Professor Marjorie Pryse.[6] Published in the mid-eighties, *Conjuring*, alongside other critical anthologies on black women writers, not only appeared at an opportune time, but was one of the first cross-racial critical projects, aligned with feminist perspectives, to offer sustained readings of this community of writers. The editorial apparatus of the work reflected our contrastive views on the critical mission, as we parceled out our respective positions across the Introduction and the Afterword. My own contribution to the anthology proper, an essay on Paule Marshall's *Chosen Place, Timeless People*, pays tribute to one of the finest writers in the African Diaspora the last half century. "Some Figurations on the New World" attempts to highlight the geopolitical orchestrations of this persistently forceful novel, just as "Black, White, and in Color, or Learning How to Paint," which appears in this volume, aims at drawing out the subversive psychoanalytic underpinnings that drone across it in powerful surges. The only writer represented here with two essays is Gwendolyn Brooks, whose exquisite writing life crosses several decades of black American letters, from the lapidary sonnets of the fifties, to the exhortative poetic witness of the nineties; Brooks's "Maud Martha," in its subtle lyrical formulations, is taken up here in "An Order of Constancy."

As chairman of the English Institute board for a period of time during the early nineties, I was quite literally instructed by Professor Barbara Hernnstein Smith to edit a series of Institute essays that would be entitled *Comparative American Identities: Race, Sex, and Nationality in the Modern Text*.

My not balking at the assignment is a measure of my profound respect for Professor Smith, but the hidden advantage in the project, which serendipity I only understood, like the Monday morning quarterback (after it was all over), was that it introduced me to a systematic engagement with texts and propositions that border the post-colonial field and that may be summed up in the felicitous formulations initiated by Professor Mary Louise Pratt as studies in the "contact zone."[7] Called upon to find a strategy for editing a collection of writings, divergent in focus and manner of treatment, I decided that it could be done by altering the figurative valence of the "United States" in relationship to other elements in the repertoire. "Who Cuts the Border?"—which title was based on a private household joke at the time—opened up to my understanding a new dimension of reading both "America" and the "Diaspora." By way of William Faulkner's *Absalom, Absalom!* and José Martí's "Our America," the geopolitical situation and symbolicity of the United States of America looks quite a bit different than without them. "Faulkner Adds Up," completed during the summer of 1999, subsequent to my address to the 1998 annual Faulkner Conference, revisits the theme with a slightly different twist. Both essays appear in this collection.

Increasingly troubled over the last few years that what I was attempting to theorize was, to an uncomfortable extent, quite a lot closer than I would have imagined to what I actually observe in the field of post-sixties social relations, I have been rather surprised (to put it mildly) that black critics, for the most part, appear less concerned about *intramural critique* than I think we should be. Some things in the academic zone are clearer now than they were a quarter century ago, among them, that gender differences and inequalities, under certain historical circumstance, are not only figments of imagination, but refract light, most probably, from the symbolic economies that must be rooted in New World slavery. The Black Studies movement, now over, has eventuated in the installation of this curriculum, by various other names, across the United States, and while I can offer no definitive assessment of those programs, my impression is that they have quite literally settled down into routine institutional existence that more or less resembles the surround; from one point of view, implantation, in some quarters, appears to signal stagnated growth and the pursuit of continuity toward personal, if not always corrupt, ends. Perhaps the black "creative intellectual," as Harold Cruse named it, is, by definition, the locus of "crisis," but the pressures of late capital development have thrown the entire engine of black intellectual work out of kilter and rhythm not least because the intellectual himself/herself is situated in a radically different place since *Crisis of the Negro Intellectual* appeared. "Crisis of the Negro Intellectual: A

Post-Date" was written in response not only to that particular problematic, but as an outcry in the face of a movement now mired in a retrogressive, male-centered, uncritical synthesis. The "movement" to which I refer is not only, or not simply, Black Studies per se, but the African-American Studies ensemble, wherever it might be situated on the academic map. If the simple arrival on predominantly white campuses of America was the destination, as it appears to have been, rather than the point of departure, as it ought to be, then I have entirely misunderstood the program. In case I have not, I systematically advance in "Crisis" a set of questions appropriate to a dilemma that must be solved if our membership in the academy is going to have, at last, any redemptive value.

And what is the "dilemma"? "'All the Things You Could Be By Now, If Sigmund Freud's Wife Was Your Mother': Race and Psychoanalysis" attempts to formulate just this question; it contends that outer-directed forces are not definitive, although they have been, in the case of diasporic African communities, unrelenting and overwhelming. What must be done at the place of the speaking subject, in light of all "I" know now, and what is its *name?* This essay does not offer a "solution," just as its "relatives" in this volume, but, rather, finds and circumlocutes certain static in a field of force. Doing so may be preferable, after all, to the false certainty of solutions. Here they are: sixteen (un)easy pieces (plus one) that began their journey in a Boston brownstone once upon a time . . .

Ithaca, N.Y.
April 2000

Acknowledgments

As an occasional victim of my own stubbornness—quite possibly an outgrowth of my nativity under the earth sign of Taurus—I will not advance one step until I am convinced that every hair is in place, or more precise to the matter at hand, not until the work is as perfect as the idea of it in my mind. This conviction, if carried far enough, will result in unconscionable delays, but the value of friendship is that it breaks the thrall, socializes fear, and brings us back to the place where we live—in the context of imperfection, personal and otherwise, and change, which stops for nothing. Several friends and colleagues have spoken in my closest ear words of encouragement concerning the value of this collective witness when I doubted it. In fact, a couple of people have been insistent and loud, and I am grateful to them for timely impatience: to Leslie Sanders and "Skip" Gates, who were tiring of all those loose leaves, to Moira Ferguson, who virtually jumped up and down, to Michael Cobb, for threatening to put together his own Reader of these essays if I did not, to Jackie Goldsby, whose lapidary measure of things is a genuine gift to her friends, to Dwight McBride, Michael Awkward, Lindon Barrett, Paul Bové, Jonathan Arac, Elliott Butler Evans, Charles Rowell, Colin McCabe, W. J. T. Mitchell, Anthony Monteiro, Don Rose, Winfried Siemerling, Dave Bartholomae, Herman Beavers, and Wilfred "Pepye" Samuels, whose intelligent sympathy and unstudied generosity renew my faith in the possibility that academic men and women can live together, to Farah Griffin, Saidiya Hartman, Sharon Holland, Jennifer Brody, and Gina Dint, who give me more credit than I think I deserve, to Wahneema Lubiano, Cheryl Wall, Nahum Chandler, Mae Henderson, Michele Wallace, and Ron Judy, who always know what in the world I am trying to say, to Mary Jacobus for an enthusiasm that puts the wind to my sails and hurries me up, and to Kristin Breen and Gabrielle McIntire for friendship, gentle humor, and "Just a Taste," I owe more than thanks. Special acknowledgments are due to Vicky Brevetti and Darlene Flint of the English Department staff at Cornell University for more good offices than I will ever be able to compensate. Without them, this project, would not have seen the light of day.

To Alan Thomas at the University of Chicago Press and two superb readers I am profoundly indebted.

And to an ancient friend, still as good as gold, I thank H. D. "Peter" Briggs, whose culinary adroitness inspired the original title of this book, and for the unfailing humor and loving respect that he has accorded me over the years. To a new friend and colleague, Tommy Lott, and two first friends, Lucius Outlaw and Phillip Kimball, for a special kind of shrewdness that makes their soul-mates work even harder, I am sending a heartfelt zaftig laugh. One never gets very far without her mother—and if I am not mistaken, Evelyn Taylor Spillers will take great delight in this book, although her copy, at some point, will likely go the way of all my diplomas—"lost" in the caverns of 2478.

Introduction

Peter's Pans: Eating in the Diaspora

I

When I think on the stunning alimentation of an egg, I come face to face with one of the miracles of human existence; after all, I started out that way (and so did you) and grew and grew. . . . A deep appreciation for the simple elegance of beginnings, or *appreciation* of any kind, for that matter, does not belong to the postmodern's repertoire of gestures, but inasmuch as I am not one, I invite you to consider this: the brilliant food that makes "omelettes, and cake and custard and soufflés and poaching and frying and boiling and baking"[1] was manipulated by someone, either silly or perspicacious, who wondered what would happen if he or she "slowly trickled oil on to egg yolks and then gone ahead and tried" out the mother of mayonnaise.[2] One commentator even goes so far as to suggest an angelic authorship for that recipe of the supplement—the left-over whites and their translation into the exquisite delicacy of *meringue*. Said to be "frightfully good" with anchovies, an egg can assume so many different shapes and contexts that we might think of the stuff as a form of mimicry. An egg, for instance, that one wants half-scrambled and half-up at once must be prepared in a very hot pan, with a spit of bacon fat, and if the pan is smoking, the egg will yield a "flash in the pan," anywhere from five to ten seconds over a gas-burning flame. But the miracle of the egg is its total usefulness; even its non-comestible features might complement other organic arrangements: eggshells, I understand, make excellent soup clarifiers, as well as good water filters, we suppose, around the roots of roses.[3] If the egg's perfect oval inspires, like the rose, a varied artistic flight, then its connection with the idea of the celebratory links Waterford and Fabergé to a time-honored sequence of sumptuary extravagance—the following tale does not appear in Scripture or myth, but it ought to. A narrative of counting and excess, it carries the delicious lying appeal of the unverifiable, even though history has recorded it: in the first half of the first millennium, the neo-Assyrian monarch, Assurnasirpal II, threw a magnificent feast to celebrate the completion of the royal palace at Kalhu. The feast lasted over a week, with 69,574 reported guests from all the districts of the kingdom and apparently from all the kingdom's classes, since some 40,000 of them were conscripted laborers who had built the place. For the occasion were numbered "1,000 plump oxen, 14,000 sheep, 1,000 lambs, several hundred deer of various kinds, 20,000 pigeons . . . 10,000 fish, 10,000 jerboa, 10,000 eggs,"[4] and jugs of beer and skins of wine, all appropriately apocryphal in feel. The feast of Cana and the Good Lord's feeding the multitude, spinning no small wonders Himself with those two little fish and five loaves of bread, actually have nothing on the bash at Kalhu.

A comparable plenty is concocted in Ralph Ellison's *Juneteenth*,[5] when, on the fictitious occasion of the celebration of black Jubilee, the sheer abundance and proliferation of food take on even nauseating superfluity, which drives the visual, as well as the gustatory, savor into riot. If Ellison's gourmands experienced potato salad on that day, then there would have been bushels of it in a wreck of potatoes, eggs, and mayonnaise. This cross-Atlantic cousin of *salade niçoise* is one of the premier moments of the egg in the New World, which figurative resonance lends Ike McCaslin his vision of the whole world of human and property relations.[6] Could we say, then, that in a very real sense, our world is an egg? The quintessential maker of makers?

I should like to poach on precisely that figurative wealth here as an introductory vehicle to this volume of essays—on "literature" and "culture"—and as my own initial approach to the conduct of the foodway and the culinary. My hope is that "Peter's Pans," for all its quirkiness of conception, will take its place among these essays that have sought, in the first instance, to work the cultural ground between "African" and "American" in a particular historical juncture. Written between 1975 and 2001, these essays, not entirely unlike the ingredients in a new-world callaloo, return over and over again to certain thematic and stylistic signatures. The point, however, is the *blend,* or that point at the boil where the discretion of contents disappears into the mix. My sense of how the concatenation works makes up one of the lines of inquiry that I pursue here.

II

"Ellison's Usable Past: Toward a Theory of Myth" is not only the first of the essays in this collection to be published, but also marks an attempt at a systematic articulation of the conundrum that has hounded an entire generation of investigators with a persistence by no means dissipated in the new century; though redirected, perhaps, the puzzle remains how an oxymoron, with an actual and material dimension, is to be expressed, when it lays hold of a cultural semantics rather than a locality of sentences. Even if we grasp a general economy of practices all at once, it can still only be "said" bit by bit and part by part. At any given moment, theories about African-American culture and its manifold contents are partial and incomplete. We never surpass some things, or get over them, insofar as their opaqueness bears down on the imagination with a clarity of refusal that must be confronted. In other words, the culture, because it locates a synthesis, as well as a symptom of resistance, shows all the instabilities of definition and practice. But I am not convinced that the perception of the unstable rests, in this case, in the beholder alone. It seems to be given, as it were, with the American hyphen. Not caught on one side of it or the other, African-American life and thought has had the bar passing through it. From the late nineteen-sixties on, "Black Studies" in the American academy was itself yet another manifestation of the paradox of the oxymoron.

Suddenly a curricular object, "Black Studies" was the name in the morning of a set of impulses that had been called the "movement" only the night before. It is not customary that a studies protocol discloses either its provenance or its whereabouts. By the time it reaches us, it has already acquired the sanction of repetition, the authority of repression, and the blessings of time and mimesis so that, effactually, such a protocol now belongs to the smooth natural order of the cultural. In the astonishing instance of "Black Studies" (and shortly thereafter, "Women's Studies" on a very similar basis), this new "cognizable object," with its conceptual "home" in "Negro History,"[7] among other confluential elements and as curricular matter, lost its mystical qualities. Now it no longer seemed, like hot water, to come from God, but, rather, like the arts of plumbing, a gamble predicated on the laws of gravity and the soundness of an underground circuit of conductors—so many liquid volumes of pressure poised in piping only a thumb's thickness away from a great little flood. (Nothing mysterious here and a far distance from the glamour of unruffled "tradition.") I believe that the transformation was unforgettable—between street protest and the podium, the interface was porous and the door a swinging one, while the discourse, from one locus to the other, spoke the same rhetorical accents and timbres. But what did it mean to talk *that* talk in *that* place? For the next decade and a half, the question and the frameworks through which it would unfold defined the paradox—of a "schizoid" (ambiguous) form; that is, a politically defined activism that not only "remembers" itself as such, but "remembers" itself as such through the filter of the historical, now compelled to meditate on its reasons. Even though it seemed that there was only slight difference between the subject(s) of "activism" and the subject(s) of meditation/mediation, there actually yawned enough of a spatio-temporal *beance* or break between one and another to give birth to anxieties of displacement and misorientation simultaneously emergent with the event itself. And in a sense, it would not be wrong to say that an aspect of the curricular event *was* the nimbus of anxiety that shadowed it and still does. Brought over with the curricular object to the "scene of instruction," the anxiety itself was a sure sign that we were somewhere else. After a few decades of schooling, I had seen nothing quite like the moment we entered, neither in the quality of intelligent response that it mandated, nor in the degree of canny defamiliarization that one was called upon to engage (as a result) right away.

But that historical moment—albeit vivid—was merely one of a sequence of occurrences that demarcate the historical apprenticeship of African community in the New World. Ralph Ellison's *Invisible Man*—the transumptive and revisionary text published in the nineteen-fifties—had anticipated the moment that we had entered by going farther than any imaginative writing to chart the transitional flows of a "tremendous striving," DuBois had called it. But because of the transumptive ratio[8] of a fiction that predates and trumps what comes before it and to my mind, what, so far, has come after it, *Invisible Man* exceeded its era: what was so remarkable about the Ellisonian project was its double translation—once, into the figural economy of fiction from the texts of the historical and the mythical, then again, into *psychic* figures of a symbolic economy that one could employ in a comprehensive survey of *memorial* material. The genial achievement of the novel's translative modes is that the protagonist and his content are interpenetrative and dialectical. "Ellison's Usable Past" offered a conceptual narrative, in turn, of the workings of Ellison's fictive dialectics.

While generalizations tend to be useless, I would venture one that appears to stick—black writers, whatever their location and by whatever projects and allegiances they are compelled, must retool the language(s) that they inherit. The work of logological refashioning not only involves the dissipation of the poisons of cliché and its uncritical modalities but it also takes a stab at the pulsating infestations that course through the grammars of "race," on "blackness" in particular. Ellison, therefore, had few models before him in overturning the discursive decisions that had arrested notions of "blackness" in retrograde rhetorical behaviors. Another way to put it is to say that the examples before him were endless. *His* problem was to slay them. By revising and correcting "blackness" into a *critical* posture, into a preeminent site of the "multicultural," long before the latter defined a new politics and polemic, and by distinguishing it from a sign called the "American Negro" (and we can make any substitution here that might be appropriate, i.e., "black," "Afro-American," "African-American," as more or less the same lady and gentleman), Ellison harnessed "blackness" to a symbolic program of philosophical "disobedience" (a systematic skepticism and refusal) that would make the former available to *anyone,* or more pointedly, *any* posture, that was willing to take on the formidable task of *thinking* as a willful act of imagination and invention. In other words, *Invisible Man* made "blackness" a *process,* a *strategy,* of culture critique, rather than a condition of physiognomy and/or the embodiment of the *auto-bios-graphe;* we had come a considerable distance in layering "blackness" as subject possibility. Under the "laws" of this novel, the game of "blackness" was no longer captive to the auspices of dominance, somewhere "out there" beyond the veil, but came home, as it were, right between the ears, as the glittering weapon of an "invisible" field of choice. With the "world" in his head now, invisible man quite literally and figuratively "contained" the wealth that white philanthropy had alienated in the first place as its own to proffer.

The critical act that I engaged in response to the novel was not only bent on reading its scrupulous disseminations, but tried, as well, to anticipate a discursive posture that would be apposite to the unsettled terrain of new propositions and occasions on which the unwonted curricular object was unfolding. If Ellison had forged a repertory of fictional alternatives that would make it virtually impossible to perceive either U.S. literary history or practice in the ways that it had been worked when Robert Spiller et al. set out their study of the nation's literary culture,[9] and if Ellison had opened a space of intervention that would interrupt the elegant narratives of F. O. Matthiessen's "American Renaissance"[10] and its future, then the criticism would have to keep abreast. It would take a couple of decades, however, for it to do so, as the reviews contemporaneous with the publication of *Invisible Man* and the status of the study of the "Negro novel" in general suggest a fairly bleak critical landscape that only began to burst with sunlight in the researches of Darwin T. Turner, J. Saunders Redding, and Charles T. Davis,[11] to name a few of our most illustrious predecessors in the breach before the advent of structuralist/post-structuralist critical readings altered the field.[12] These latter-day formalists, coming from the campuses of historically black institutions, to the University of Iowa, Cornell, and Yale, respectively, were engendering a commitment to reading texts by black writers against the powerful orthodoxies of both neo-Marxist and sociological schools of criticism in which case the literary document stood for (or "against") the formidable symptoms of other textual programs, conceding little to its field of provenance. At the same time, cultural black nationalist critique was dismantling the very notion of the "aesthetic"[13] as a realm of practice separate from the "political," as currents of continental criticism and philosophy[14] were exciting severe patterns of weather across the North Atlantic. In this maelstrom of forces, one forgot her hairdo and learned to wear a hat and a good, warm cashmere scarf—in short, to go toward a critical practice that was sensitive to nationalist aims, alert to the materialist and aesthetic dimensions of a convergent cultural problematics, and informed in the emergent critico-theoretical languages of the day. "Formalism Comes to Harlem" offers just such an attempt to position one's practice in the very midst of contending overlapping claims.

I have always regarded my membership in my natal community as an ethical obligation. In brief, not to assume it, but to *tend* and *attend* it with a most careful eye; but every membership is not natal—in fact, most of them are not—so that the *difference* to the latter must be comprehended as a genuine possibility. In an examination of William Gaddis's *Recognitions,* I was not as clear then as I am now that "the most serviceable of the alien figures-of-thought" was a beneficial name for *détente* between my cohort, the new university subject, and the resisting academy. In drawing comparisons in "Formalism Comes to Harlem" between aspects of modernist and black fiction (not that fiction cannot be both at the same time, as *Invisible Man* must surely demonstrate), I wanted to understand at the level of the sentence the contrast between the word as "an act of reciprocity, and address which anticipates reply," and the word as self-reflexive opacity. But in order to do so, I had to read "Harlem" across the grain of its own biases, as if modernism were its own reinvention. In short, textual formalism, originating decades ago in some other neighborhood of the culture map, was fairly comfortably situated in a context of other valences, even though the modern innovator of jazz/blues had already laid down an example of *subject trained on the object.* The idea of "Harlem" as both demographic locus and the "location" of an imaginary rounds out its significatory thrust as symbolic/geography. As figure and field, "Harlem" stood in for the moment of reconciliation between supposedly binary dispositions; in this case, I was far less wed to formalist methods of reading than to *reading* as a method, period. "Formalism Comes to Harlem" in that regard was itself metaphorical of a repertory of attitudes committed to the discursive and the semiotic analysis, though at the time that I wrote the essay, neither "discourse," nor "semiotic" was available to me as a figure of thought. At the suggestion of one of my most formidable teachers, J. V. Cunningham, I was trying to learn to write "idiomatically," according to what he had called the "abiding centrality of the word," and to my mind, that meant the creation of sentences that could *not* be anticipated, that violated the rules within the sights of grammar. What, for me, would a sentence sound and "feel" like that was not *oratorical?* For one who had grown up listening to the rich rhetorical babble of southern black Baptist preaching and still admire it, Cunningham's idea was a most peculiar one to me both in the ear and off the tongue.

The stylistic elements of the idiomatic were (and remain) for me a *political* choice, inasmuch as I have wanted, as a critico-theoretical practitioner, to *surprise* the most blatant of the racist presumptions that invade every field of discourse, from advertising and its slick manipulations of the word-image, to the languages of learning and criticism, for, as I observed in the Preface, the *materiality of discourse* is as solid an aspect of political economy as the Gross Domestic Product, and its far-flung subtleties and evasions, its coded displacements and well-choreographed insinuations, decidedly more pernicious as the missile that hides its hand. To spot it by preventing, or warding off, its closures, *on its own terrain,* with its own weapons, defines the "war," as I have understood it. And indeed, my perception that I was embattled turned out to be utterly right. Within six years of Gayatri C. Spivak's "Derrida,"[15] which, among a handful of other texts, altered critical practice in the humanities academy forever, one of my tenure referees would actually write the words that Wellesley's harshly reactionary English department would put to good use—in effect, the idea that the "cause" of "Black Studies" could best be served by writing that was "clear" coded the notion that there was nothing afoot in the literary and cultural studies that it engendered that was not already known; in other words, why make a mountain out of a mole-hill, since everybody and his mama knew that this "stuff" wasn't "about" much?

For lack of a better word, I have called this massive conviction "idea bigotry," and when it carries on the pulse of the race-driven nerve, its virulence defies description. We actually have no vocabulary to explain it, even though I have conjectured that Melanie Klein's bundle of attitudes identified as "envy"[16] gets us on its track. I have also regretted over the ensuing years that, with few exceptions (and I have also had the good fortune to experience a couple of the exceptional sites as well), I believe that this nest of malicious feeling, of diseased disregard, becomes the special property of the academy's English Department precisely because its objects are so elusive.

In the absence, then, of a Burkean "strategy" for an explanation that is still pressing, I attempted to go through the disorder in order to arrive at a position and disposition *in writing* that would be responsive to the strong emergence of the intellectual technologies that were making it new. In that regard, these early essays might be thought of as "experiments," or short, pointed five-finger exercises designed tendentiously—to respond to a single "problem" that had either been butchered by the inherited orthodoxies, both from my natal community and other formations, or advanced by a willful stupidity, or that needed addressing, in my view. "A Hateful Passion, A Lost Love: Three Women's Fiction" initiated my dialogue with interlocutors in "Women's Studies" and what was not quite yet "feminist literary criticism." I should note here with a degree of more than casual interest that the essays I had written up to that moment had focused on male culture work, beginning with the pulpit style of Martin Luther King. But with "Hateful Passion" and "Gwendolyn, the Terrible: Propositions on Eleven Poems," the right turn that I took (or perhaps it was left!) had the force of a perpendicular.

Some of the wonder of the work of Toni Morrison, Toni Cade Bambara, and Paule Marshall is that we have had the keen pleasure of watching it in the respective unfolding. It is fair to say that Morrison's *Sula* was the plank that fell out of my ceiling, and the eventuality of it was so crucial to my sense of a "happening," of a transitional moment, that "Hateful Passion" sprang directly from it. While Margaret Walker's *Jubilee* and Zora Neale Hurston's *Their Eyes Were Watching God* are both considerable achievements, three decades apart, it also seemed to me that each one, in its own way, reenforced what I have called elsewhere the "habit of pathos." But a way had to be found to say so without devaluing their moment, inasmuch as Sula Peace had changed the topic and radically reoriented the sociological regimen that had invented "the black woman" as "the black woman" in the first place. This essay that compares the three writers actually wanted to hustle in a "message" through the back door about genuine political insurgency and women under the colors of literary criticism, as it seemed that an actantial inquiry[17] would get it done. Sula's pursuit of a *negative* freedom and a morality called "ad hoc" in the essay broke the compact that society had made with black female subjects—that is to say, the agreement to go hungry (on all the registers)—to demand nothing of anyone, to slay desire—in clear sight of a state-sponsored munificence, public and private. That the cost of "disobedience" in this case is death marked an unavoidable rupture with the powerful thematics of "overcoming" that "adventures in blackness" had inscribed as its own mythos. There is, therefore, a dimension of the forbidden to this quiet, thus treacherous, storm of a text that does not flinch. Because I regarded the novel as a "sharply discontinuous" move away from the "dominant traditions of Afro-American literature," I grasped its gestures as doubly interventional: on the one hand, its precise "ex-centricity"—several chapters elapse before the appearance of Sula—described another way to manage a genealogy of character, while on the other, the character of Sula itself suggested that questions of identity were neither automatic nor unfraught, but were, instead, shot through with regimes of difference. The latter could only mean, for the reader, at least, that the "not-me," the unalterable projection outward and otherward, had to be understood anew as her own product. In a sense that could only be called oblique, *Sula* stated what *Invisible Man* had acted—if she had had the "discipline"[18] of the strings, say, or a "metaphor" for her "tremendous curiosity" marked the subjunctive attitude that Ellison's character had engaged as an act called a "novel." In other words, Sula was in search of a project, which eventuality invisible man had already landed. For character, thus, to arise out of the context of a misorientation, or a displacement that had failed, was light years away from the literary (and otherwise) requirements of abjection. To have to recognize the Sula-part, so to speak, of predication would return for me as an aspect of a dialectics that African-American culture theory had not yet articulated, and it was manifestly linked to the entire cultural problematic that African presence in the West had engendered. By way of "Hateful Passion," what would evolve for me as a full-blown (not always friendly) contradiction later on was incipiently rendered.

"Gwendolyn, the Terrible: Propositions on Eleven Poems" tracked my encounter with Gwendolyn Brooks's poetry. The lapidary concision and the sharp geometric elegance of this canon signaled a collision course with lingering high modernist formulae because Brooks's speakers remained ironically poised toward modernism's silences, early and late, at the same time that they assert its stylistic signatures. The application of those modalities to fictions of the ordinary and the quotidian added up to splendid revolt, but it was precisely within Brooks's difference to modernistic tendencies that her poetry was so gracile an instance of their regimen. Her example, situated between Harlem Renaissance poetry on one side and that of the Black Arts Movement of the sixties on the other, struck an allegiance to both historical particularity and aesthetic claims. In fact, by effecting rapproachment between them, Brooks becomes one of few black writers to advance an *interested* aesthetics. "Gwendolyn, the Terrible" and the propositions that it offered on select poems of the writer's work across the decades attempted to situate Brooks's moment as a unique juncture between American and African-American traditions of writing. Never a sentimentalist, Brooks was a craftsman of the line, which delighted in subverting, at every turn, the substitution of feeling for the "hard precision of thought." The essay was designed to express my response to a project that is consistently stunning, but it also had an eye poised on the complicated grammar and weave of motives that these poems orchestrate. Customarily, fields of discourse place "black poetry" and "poetry" at odds, but the power of Brooks's workshop, as it were, was the staging of their collapse; in effect, the newer modes of African-American culture critique would need to venture analogous redefinitions, and the latter were especially pressing in an era dogmatically tied to false oppositions and ill-defined rhetorical posing. Brooks's project advanced a paradigm for an interpenetrative protocol along varied lines of stress, if only a translation could be effected.

The World of Gwendolyn Brooks ably dislodges embedded ways of *thinking* black culture by breaking through the "perpetual cramp" contused around it.[19] Perhaps there is no more powerful instance of undoing than Brooks's tale of one Maud Martha Brown, which novelette apparently surfaced without much ado in the early nineteen-fifties.[20] A Chicago housewife, subjected to all the dreary disorder and decay of urban living for "children of the poor,"[21] Maud Martha manages, nevertheless, to impose "an order of constancy" on a crammed living space by the sheer act of indulgent imagination—perhaps we could even say *willful*—that borrows its colorings from a playful and sustained attentiveness to world's things, from crystal and fine linen, to cloud formations and bursting splendid spring weather. The reader, however, does not come away with the sense that this act of capable imagination is simply compensatory, but that Maud Martha deploys it as a weapon in her own behalf. That domestic space here and its association with the feminine contravert the traditional values assigned to its precincts gives way exactly to the unexpected. "'An Order of Constancy': Notes on Brooks and the Feminine" examines this proposition in alignment with the contrarieties that I had mapped in "Gwendolyn the Terrible." And the whole cluster of contrary, contradistinctive, and contradictory movements, reposing in complex figures of paradox—irony, double entendre, catechresis, oxymoron, ambiguity, ambivalence—answered for me a conceptual theme whose resources would be worked and elaborated across a wide swath of cultural phenomena; through Ellison and Brooks, it appeared that I had arrived at a provisional reading of DuBois's "double consciousness," except that the outcome would conduce to the eternal play of oppositions and not their closure. The logic of the hyphen, if we could say so, rests in the movement *between* punctualities so that its elements are always coming and going in the "contact zone"[22] of mutually incommensurable contents.

Though it took awhile for me to perceive the constancy of my own conceptual narrative and that aspects of it were replicative from one essay to another, I inchoately followed a protocol of inquiries, fast on the track of the "problem" that had vexed African-American critical theory and practice for several generations of practitioners. It seemed to me that it was woefully insufficient to a clarification of the "problem" to simply attach "black" to a line-up of emergent epistemologies—"structuralism," "post-structuralism," "feminism," "postmodernism," to name a few—but that we had rather go into the formation itself to determine what it had missed in drawing its borders, which inevitably excluded "black" from its accounting procedures. In effect, we were given the peculiar occasion to observe the troubling effects of a kind of intellectual and theoretical gerrymander that maintained, that staged the prerogatives of apartheid with which we were well familiar from the political arena. Rather than provide a figure of supplement to the dominant intellectual technologies, "blackness" had to be cast as their "blindness" in the field of vision that enabled their "insight" as a tool of speech performance.[23] There were, then, two possibilities of encounter: (1) the contradictory and interstitial character of Africanity in the West, with U.S. society as one of the leading paradigms of the problematic, and (2) the scotomatous effects of "tradition," which was quite capable of repressing its "other" and without which it could not have appeared in the first instance. The trick that one had not anticipated, however, was the porous nature of this interstitial—in other words, it moved, as well, across the terrain of intramural black life. From about the mid-eighties on, these flashes of the discontinuous—like a blinding light that reveals its whereabouts only intermittently and deceptively—pointed the landscape that we did not know we were already crossing.

"Interstices: A Small Drama of Words" was the first of these essays going toward that different light. Not set down in the field of literary criticism per se, "Interstices," as most of the essays that followed it, would rely on the heuristic tools brought over from it. I regard this piece of writing as crucially transitional for that reason, but the essay also brings into focus a join, or joint, that I had wanted to avoid: my ambivalence at the time regarding academic feminism and its critico-theoretical practices, hinted in certain sentences of the essay, has never been fully resolved, although I recognize that it is one of few sites available—perhaps the only one—to the "subject of feminism"[24] in its most rounded recurrences. I have had no difficulty at all accepting and strongly endorsing the political protocols of the U.S.

women's movement at mid-century; there were virtually no aspects of its programs with which I disagreed. We must also restate the obvious: without such a movement and its subsequent development along the sociopolitical/cultural spectrum, the entire question of global justice for women's transnational community would look very different here at the turn of the century. My discomfort remains lodged, however, in academic feminism's shaky relationship to "race" matters, or more specifically, the truncation of its sense of social justice across the boundaries of the provincial. The women's movement, going back to its eighteenth century roots in America, and its occasionally strained relationship to social justice movements, especially against racism, has long documentation that need not be rehearsed here. Suffice it to say that my cohort has *honestly not* escaped the slippages, and by "honestly" I mean that we know it. For that reason, I am committed to its promises as, perhaps, women's best hope in light of an entrenched status quo.

If academic feminism had difficulty stepping away from race-driven presumptions, *when they star-crossed the life-world of women,* then black community had not garnered any more superior record in its response to the "querelle de femmes." Even though, for historical reasons and no other, the rift along lines of gender was well hidden in black life and therefore has not usually extruded itself with such insistence, we know now that elements of gender division here could not have sprung from the head of Zeus all of a sudden. Exacerbated precisely by the traumas of "success," related to radical changes of public policy and certain social praxes, intramural gender tensions are today fully out in the open, as the academy and its public relations engines become one of its most privileged and expressive locations. By the mid-eighties, then, one found herself wholly locked in the perfect bind-situation—let's call it—between a rock and a hard place—between the politics of academic feminism on the one hand and the politics of the Black Studies movement on the other. "Interstices" seemed entirely appropriate for naming my own location, as these epistemes, one detected slowly, were not so much the "answer" as they were themselves among the very highlights of the "problem."

And what was the "problem"? Always shifting and elusive, it is the giant that the midget would depose. But in a word, it is the Word—both the named and that which struggles to be named, but just as emphatically, it is the never-said. The assignment that I was given to present a paper on black women and sexuality at Barnard's ninth annual "Feminist and Scholar" Conference struck me with suspicion almost instantly. Whatever the truth was about black women and sexuality would be, for all of thirty minutes or so, entirely in my hands! And I knew impeccably well what one must do: *Tell* something about "sexual experience" that would roughly equate with the suspect positioning of the "native informant" to an audience of other cultural nuance. But going on the idea that sexuality is only partially experential and "performative" and that its most salient features are not empirical at all (and perhaps even overrun narrative containment, as well), I wanted to specify those angles of it (regarding African-American women's community) that had not quite been tried before, as far as I could tell. As a result, "Interstices: A Small Drama of Words" became a provisional reading of the sexuality *concept* as discursive static in the field of black women's historicity. This view of the question, then, shifted the topic from the genre of public (im)personal confession, with its links to the traditions and habits of pathos and sentimentality, to an examination of a field of discursive objects and events; albeit sketchily accomplished in the essay, its aim anticipates a genealogy of the sexual *lexis* in reference to African-American women. In other words, before one could venture conceptualization on the sexual performative, she had to confront the entire landscape of prohibitions that literally mire its subjects in the nostalgic reiterative gestures of a frozen temporality.

Fairly convinced that both "sexuality" and "feminine sexuality" (in particular) were among the code words for a more or less smooth transition between the public and private moments of a political economy, when it does not break speed in its transferential flows, I was interested in the hindrances that rocked the sexual performative across the race/culture divide. "Sexuality" may be read either of two ways: (a) as a neutral reference to a set of practices that would circumscribe all the discriminations of gendered forms, or (b) as a class-bound narrative firmly situated in the mythemes of the "nuclear family," in which case "feminine sexuality" becomes the lack that denotes an unmarked fullness (aka masculinity/male sexuality). If (b) is the case, as Saidiya Hartman might argue that it is most emphatically not,[25] then "sexuality" belonged, first and foremost, to the idea-forms of modernism (was, perhaps, its *first* word, if we start the survey of the modernistic with the "fallen" subject of the Freudian trauma, c. 1900). Following the trail of (b), we might conclude that "sexuality," as a discursive cluster that breaks out, so to speak—rather like measles used to—all over the West only at a particular moment and not before, then it is to my mind another version of Western time, or a strategy of the historiographical. While this reading may be far too stipulative and transgressive of the normal acceptation of the term, it bears decided advantage nevertheless in messing up a neat picture, which black women, cut on the bias to the West, certainly do: sexual subject and object, simultaneously, this social formation could be read as a sexuality-to-be, insofar as its performances were thought to replicate mythic events that had never occurred in the first place. From that point of view, black woman subject demarcated a sexual limit, at which point "sexuality" did not have a name anymore. Sheer phenomena, *this* sexuality refused category, as a staging ground of the abnormal—"(im)purity" and "danger," or those "other things." Focus on this supercharged investment became the obsessive property of this essay, which wanted to say, at last, that "superwoman" had a sister with a very peculiar name, "Wedosere," or "we-don't-do-sex-here." Actually, this sister is a twin, a study of a double text that says two things the same way, except that one would not necessarily detect it.

Quiet as it's kept, the black life-world figures into the sexual universe at different velocities, even ferocities, I think we could say, but those mythemes that I am identifying are not empowered to register either nuance over time (synchrony), or intricate pulse in time (diachrony). And that absence of variation gauges precisely what I mean by the "interstitial"—those punctualities (in a linked sequence of events) that go unmarked so that the mythic view remains undisturbed. Winning the right to the *nuantial*—let's say—goes with the territory of the subjecthood, which must be *earned* for some; it is also intimately proximate to "sexuality." In order to name black women in the sexual, the investigator is obligated to back all the way up to that suspenseful chapter in the unfolding of subjecthood, which begins for Africanity in the West *not* with a body (which one sees well enough), but what that body was made to *mean* via the powerful grammars of capture: "A small drama of words" distinguishes this sexuality as a meaning, as a position in discourse. Discursive positioning became for me one of the thematic threads that opened onto an entire landscape of cognitive objects related to that perpendicular pronoun shifter named "I," except that "I," in this case, is not simply autobiographical. Even though I would approach a more systematic understanding of the puzzle in the essay, "'All the Things You Could Be By Now If Sigmund Freud's Wife Was Your Mother': Psychoanalysis and Race" (1996), what I had inchoately grasped with "Interstices" was the degree to which the paradox of "invisibility" actually pronounced a target's high visibility, and that the latter was connected with the *failures of differentiation*—or access to enough spaces that could account for a range of the varied. Even now an explanation of this principle of interrelated factors is difficult to tell concisely, but perhaps the idea might be clarified by way of parable: whatever eye regards the fall of the sparrow has certainly been mindful of my own. Said still another way, if Ellison had configured "blackness" as a series of critical postulates and the figure of "Rineheart" had staged it as a caricature of *transformational* possibilities, then radical change would consist in the time of "blackness" dispersed across predicates. (In the crudest political terms, it would mean that the spectacle of Martin Luther King, chastised because he dared to speak about American "foreign policy" and the question of the distribution of wealth, rather than stick to the script of "civil rights," was unacceptable, inasmuch as the criticism had been founded on the time-honored notion of "blackness" as constriction.) But the new university subject had to discover the ways and means to say as much in the terms of coeval critico-theoretical debate. In short, the *potential of becoming* was closely bound up with the subversion of not only the limitations of actions, but also of those impediments of speech-as-actions, which imperative had to be contested pervasively. My response to such "warfare" was a series of essays that followed "Interstices," which writings would attempt to highlight this centrality.

To return to a point that I made earlier, the investigator usually takes on more than she can manage, insofar as all the ribs in the chain of a putative social logic, seemingly joined at the hip, drop away rib by rib, if at all. If the key to Western development has been the more or less successful underdevelopment of the non-Western world, then such underdevelopment is manifest in the occasional masking of its role in an enormous puzzle. Pierre Bourdieu goes to great lengths to articulate the "science of a general economy of practices,"[26] which makes it possible to integrate the social gesture in an economic system, more narrowly defined. The spectacle of the practices of slavery in the modern world seems to offer a paradigm for just such an articulation, its layered displacements reaching deep into the whole social fabric. But for all that, the culture critique, as well as writings responsive to the complex implications of slavery's theories and practices, shows all the earmarks of cultural and formal particularity. Just as it appears that "sexuality" bears a decisive textual dimension, stretching like an invisible membrane across elements of the socius, the phenomena of enslavement have conduced to textual concatenations that interrupt at every point the narratives of national identity. One of its prime examples occurs on the American scene. In the following essays, I aimed to explore not only slavery's thematic displacements in examples drawn from literary work produced in the context of the United States, but also its dramatic cultural ramifications along multiple lines of stress: "Changing the Letter: The Yokes, the Jokes of Discourse, or Mrs. Stowe and Mr. Reed," "Mama's Baby, Papa's Maybe: An American Grammar Book," "The Permanent Obliquity of an In(pha)llibly Straight: In the Time of the Daughters and the Fathers," and "Notes on an Alternative Model—Neither/Nor" all aimed in the same direction, as it became quite clear to me only *after* the fact of their publication that they were offspring of a common parent.

The essay on Harriet Beecher Stowe's *Uncle Tom's Cabin* and Ishamel Reed's *Flight to Canada*, which revisits the "scene of the crime," so to speak, more than a full century later, but this time with the literary weapons of paronomasia and the hilarity of pastiche, owes the inspiration of its title to Ralph Ellison's "Change and Joke and Slip the Yoke."[27] In "Changing the Letter," the writing strategy is not only comparative—in crucial ways, a comparative reading of these wildly different novels is itself a kind of joke— but also interrogatory, insofar as it risks the spectre of *distance* from a topic taken to heart. In other words, if Reed could ring comic changes on a selective repertory of texts concerning the situations of enslavement—his multimedia concoction also takes in a vocabulary of extraliterary effects, from visual and aural gags, to elements of the cartoon, the comic strip, and the advertisement—then did his executions not mean that the reader could be variously positioned in her reception of the idea of slavery? Did it not mean that a century after the fact, we could adopt dispositions of reading toward the idea that brought it back home, as it were, stripped of the costumes of terror that it inhabits? *Flight to Canada* demonstrated quite successfully that slavery was also "slavery" and that the latter belonged, in part, to what William Faulkner called the "lumberroom of literature"—an artifactually transmitted commodification of elements that *re-presented* the idea of the "thing itself." The history of the iconic career of Stowe's Uncle Tom, who "morphes" into a slick "house nigger," Uncle Robin, to a dyslexic master in Reed's *Flight to Canada,* instantiates the idea of such translation with stunning clarity—the dolls and effigies and peep shows and exhibits, a veritable kitch of forms, that flare on the market in the wake of Stowe's sensational success—Lincoln is said to have been acquainted with the novel—attest quite plainly to the value of reverence as an item of exchange. From the vantage of *Flight to Canada,* "slavery" was, therefore, a selection and sifting of elements that had gained the aura of truth from the religion of exchange and certain inviolate habits of speech and gesture; it was, thus, an *arrangement* of attitudes and postures that could only be understood, in the distance, as shadows of the memorial, as indicia of the distillations of a fullness no longer available. It was, properly speaking, *mythic,* although it would be repulsively stupid to argue, like today's confederate mentality, that slavery never existed, or was simply a nominative outcome for a collection of "bad facts." The difference between Stowe and Reed, in short, broke open a closure that essentially prohibited speech about slavery that was not already pre-invested in, imbued with, *official* feeling. We could now penetrate an undifferentiated punctuality that would allow us access to these historic occasions as text and historiography, as well as psychic figures of thought that could be actively triggered.

The recognition that slavery bears a dimension of time and space that gives it ineluctable "coverage" does nothing less than rewrite the lion's view of the West. It is no longer possible to reproduce the story of Western development with slavery as supplement, but rather, as a result of researches conducted over the last six decades especially, slavery's critical agency in Western self-conceptualization, even from the perspective of the United States in its massively induced oblivion, is nothing short of foundational. At the same time, we need complementary names to distinguish instances of a spatio-temporal coverage over five global centuries, which would suggest significant deviation in a picture imagined uniform. For that reason, there cannot have been a monolithic formation called "slavery," but, rather, several versions of slavery, both simultaneous and successive, that generated series of trends of practices in the career of emergent democratic governance that would come, increasingly, to exact an equation between *skin color* and human standing. The revocation of fundamental human and social rights to black subjects, which process systematically unfolded in British North America from the latter half of the seventeenth century down to the period of federalist agitation a century later,[28] lends insight into the *making* of status as social relations, rather than an act of divine ordination. If John Hope Franklin and other historians are right, then the twenty Africans (possibly Spanish-speaking), stolen at sea and landed in a Dutch man-of-war at Jamestown, 1619,[29] were apparently victims of piratical activity (as though the entire Atlantic trade were not!), but were very likely not bonded persons; in any case, Jamestown society, with its rigid divisions of subjects into multiple categories of servitude,[30] might be taken as a model of cumulative legislative acts, which, in their dry unvarnished appearance on the page, actually mask the anxious sociologies that engendered them. From this distance, it will appear that a Virginia law of 1682, for example, which held that "any imported Negro was presumed to be a slave, no matter what his religious or national background,"[31] did not evoke any resistance or contradiction at all, and in any event, whatever the quantum of resistance to the ruling might have been was insufficient to prevail against the interests of property and the sacredly held prerogatives of greed. But the modifying clause in the citation does at least signal that religious status became a nettlesome question in a colonial society that did not flinch, at one point, from enslaving Europeans, as well as others, that would not hesitate, in the long run, to tether its developmental energies to the bloody business of coerced labor and profit.

Following the trail of legislation that accrues around colonial black subjects, we see that it took Virginia, for instance, a full century to configure and "secrete" a class of objects called "the Negro," named in the law as its negation, as the denial of what seems riddled to us now with the automatic character of divine sanction, e.g., the right to keep and bear arms, the right to trial by jury, the right to self-defense, etc. But as Edmund Morgan has argued,[32] the establishments of slavery were not simply the antitheses of freedom; they were the other of freedom in allowing it to "say" itself, to clear and claim ground for what it was not. Because slavery stands "under the bar" of freedom's signification, it is already there in the inscriptions of its meanings. Slavery, then, allows freedom, provides it enabling postulates, conditions it for social and discursive practices, just as the litotes always carries its negation. As the "invisible" portion of freedom's meanings, slavery can be said to be "defined by the visible as *its* invisible, *its* forbidden vision: the invisible is not therefore simply what is outside the visible . . . the outer darkness of exclusion—but the *inner darkness of exclusion,* inside the visible itself because defined by its structure" (emphasis added).[33] The foregoing passage from Althusser might be read as a gloss on the Marxian "symptom," which, as Žižek contends,[34] opens a fissure in the social field. The "critique of ideology," or the "symptomatic reading" "consists in detecting a point of breakdown *heterogeneous* to a given ideological field and at the same time *necessary* for that field to achieve its closure, its accomplished form" (emphasis added).[35] Insofar as every Universal—in this case, "freedom"—is "false," it is so because it "necessarily includes a specific case which breaks its unity."[36]

In "Mama's Baby, Papa's Maybe," I tried a series of inquiries designed to unpack a relay of contradictions rather like inscriptions of the "social symptom." But the stakes here were not simply naming the contradictions (as though that were somehow simple), but laying hold of an *unformulated,* which an investigator *felt,* despite, perhaps even because of, the massive archival maneuvers on the entire location of western Africanity. Nothing about the institutions of enslavement, as a leading instance, had been left unsaid, if we were only talking about the *facts* of the matter. Actually, this historiographical field might be described as an over-known, an emphatically overdetermined mode of procedure that made the subject of slavery the historian's special property—or that that could be solved through the progressive, sequential manipulation of data. These arts and sciences of the objective art, as impressive as they are in their authoritative and informing protocols, proceed as if the gold were several furlongs deep and that if the investigator is long-armed and tireless enough, he will reach the goal of the gold.[37] But what did these phenomena *mean?* How to decide what to ask? And how to formulate questions that did not only *not* have an "answer" per se, but that problematized the conditions of interrogation in the first place? In this essay, I attempted to approach the conditional horizon of inquiry on the logic and practice of dominative modes by *revisiting the obvious,* or the already known, but recasting it as a *first* question, defamiliarized as a kind of frontier-instance. I wanted to imagine primary questions, which the historians had already exhausted, but also to try to posit an "interiority" in what had been treated as an "outside" and to assign an "outside" to an "interiority," i.e., the regulation of interracial sexual congress in the Virginia colony offers a dazzling instance of the invasion of the intimate ground by the whip of the public statute, just as the public statute—with a sufficient lapse of time—would begin to "instruct" the fantasy (which then takes over the material order as its individual portion) that it can only love and dream in terms of its imagined own/same. Above all, I wanted to plant a stop sign before the glib flow of speeding traffic that knew too much about its automative machineries, but hardly enough about the roadbed and infrastructure through which it was traveling. Exactly how to do the latter eluded me— what I did start with, however, was the *doubleness of the law*—its bare-faced two-facedness—and, as a result, the shimmer of institutional ambiguity right across the spectrum of the socius when "blackness" was in question. When "female" is introduced to the arrangement, the shimmer across stabilities of meaning (although colonial law, while it appears to be so in the distance, was anything but stable; more properly speaking, it does describe a trend line of nicely determined differences and discriminations that we watch unfold like a staged performance) is instantaneously translated into crisis, e.g., motherhood incarcerated by the laws and practices of ownership, a dual patrimony that could not, either way, speak its name, woman-labor undifferentiated by type and severity, women as "men," men as "women," or the loosening the cinctures of gender, the pregnant body of the bonded woman "split" into social economy between the belly and the unborn and the penally constituted backside. One was vexed, then, by worlds of words and deeds fallen in the gaps of cliometric quantums that had come to define what human becoming was under these conditions.

If the twentieth century would witness, at the midpoint, the terrifying spectacle of the totalitarian regime, in which case *anything could happen,* as Hannah Arendt describes it,[38] then we often think of its technologies of terror adumbrated in the long centuries of unregulated violence against black people. In this case, crisis could either mean the collapse of well-enough de-fined structures of practice, or their clarification—that point at which the make-up rolls away. What began as the puzzle of the law's duplicity modu-lated along the social registers that I have defined, but their apogee, we could say, was reached in the moral and intellectual jujitsu that yielded the catechresis, person-as-property. Even though we are reading this apparent conundrum—a "category mistake," some have called it—through the lens of the modern world and its valuational grids and grammars of feeling, the question for me remains the concatenation itself—what in the nature of "property" might have provoked a sufficient enough displacement and condensation along a sequence of analogical thinking that would bring it within the scope of "human"? That the pagan Classical world had sus-tained practices of human ownership, albeit quite different from moder-nity's arrangements, was little help here because the idea that the genealogical trace might demolish a mystery installed in the social order is somewhat misleading, while there can be no doubt that several examples over vastly disparate spatio-temporal zones are better than a single one. We gratefully take what we can get. But the "chattels-personal" idea, as well as the crisis of reproductive violence in slavery, has never made sense to me, especially in light of democratic claims and processes. This failure of sense, however, marks precisely the (il)logic of the "symptom," both in its forma-tion and appearance—in the Freudian outline, what might have its source on an "inside" materializes in an "outside" as a specified break in a kinetic relay of movement. Slavery, as far as I am able to understand it, offers an analogous spectacle of successive displacements, in which case, nothing is what it appears to be, little or nothing is called by its name, precisely because the institutional order and its inhabitants on either side of the question (while the "sides" here are not moral equivalents) are trying, in-tolerably, to square a circle, or not to notice, like the Miltonic legions, that they are trying to assure their oxygen supply of the social upside down; but the mandate here was to try to stand up this anarchically inverted arrange-ment of the social in order to hear its stutter more clearly.

In both "Mama's Baby, Papa's Maybe" and "The Permanent Obliquity of an In(pha)llibly Straight," I aimed to posit a grammar of a different "subject of feminism." Inasmuch as black women's community, as I understand it, is both like and unlike other such communities (leaving aside for the mo-ment the license we take in calling "community" what must be without doubt scored by the *heterogeneous*). If that were so, then what were the speci-ficable differences? If one could "reduce" the question, then we might say that it both converges on and is summed up in the "body" in Western culture. Unlike many commentators on the latter, if I have read them justly, I would contend that the "body" is neither *given* as an uncomplicated empirical rupture on the landscape of the human, nor do we ever actually "see" it. In a very real sense, the "body," insofar as it is an analytical construct, does not exist in person at all. When we invoke it, then, we are often confusing and conflating our own momentousness as address to the world, in its layered build-up of mortal complexities, with an idea on paper, only made vivid because we invest it with living dimensionality, mimicked, in turn, across the play of significations. In the same way, "race," as the anti-essentialists have persistently misunderstood, never had much to do with *bodies*, as *skin color* (or a number of other substitutive possibilities) in all hierarchical economies that make meaning in that way, actually only *facilitates* an imperative that has emerged otherwise. When I spoke of a "hieroglyphics of the flesh" in "Mama's Baby, Papa's Maybe," I was trying to identify not only one of diasporic slavery's technologies of violence through marking, but also to suggest that "beyond" the violating hand that laid on the stigmata of a recognition that was misrecognition, or the regard that was disregard, there was a *semiosis* of procedure that had enabled such a moment in the first place. The marking, the branding, the whipping—all instruments of a terrorist regime—were more deeply *that*—to get in somebody's face in that way would have to be centuries in the making that would have had little to do, though it is difficult to believe, with the biochemistry of pigmentation, hair texture, lip thickness, and the indicial measure of the nostrils, but everything to do with those "unacknowledged legislators" of a discursive and an economic discipline. (To that extent, the critique of "identity politics" has positioned the wrong objects in its sights; it needs to ask, more precisely, how *status* is made and pay attention to *that* because *that* is the dialectic that plays here.) Just so, the "body" should be specified as a discursive and particular instance that belongs, always, to a *context*, and we must look for its import there; otherwise, we come face to face with a cypher in the dictionary, or those scary illustrations of corpus stripped down to longitudes of veins and latitudes of nerves that so grace *Gray's Anatomy*. It is interesting that from continent to continent and from language to language and from the wooly-headed to the straight, the anatomy of "body" carries right across. Now that the human genome project has been mapped—in fact, reported on during the writing of this essay—the "science" of "race," that dearly beloved fiction of all time, will now belong to the museum of man; but the fiction of differences is something else again.

Even though the "subject of feminism"[39] can only be anachronistically elaborated as a conceptual narrative with regard to the historical situatedness of bonded women, it names nevertheless the intent of the protocol that I was pursuing in "Mama's Baby, Papa's Maybe." Here, two points were critical: (1) to stress the *historic* character of bonded slavery as relations induced by material and political circumstance; in other words, to insist that the enslaved does not belong to the natural order—like flora and fauna—but that such *positionalities* are created from the complications of choice and alternative, given certain openings in the chain of necessity; in a sense, slavery's *persons* remain the hidden, shrouded agencies of a human order that has begun to think of itself as an autotelic, self-perpetuating regime. By subjecting the latter to *first* questions, it was possible to rediscover in it the human signature—in short, that porosity of motives whose direction and outcome could be reversed, in fact, demolished. By isolating a subject of gender here, we were interested in *process* and the laws by which it operated that ascribed to subjects on this stage of history their particular role and act. (2) This "grammar of motives," the subject of my long-term project in connection with this essay, commences an investigation of *gender-making* in British colonial North America. It was rather clear to me from the start that "gender," like "race," is not given, although it would appear to be counterintuitive to make such a claim: after all, the "facts" of human reproductive biology cannot be contravened. But the powerful additions of culture render such facts not simply descriptive, or differential, but, as we know, evaluative and inherent. If that is so, then it must be possible to point the switch in frames of reference from one category of narrative figurations to another; perhaps I have placed too much pressure on the laws, insofar as they arise as much from a prohibitive animus as from a permissive impulse. In the shuttle between the prohibitive and the permissive, the performing human apparently has little to choose. Clearly, "gender," as well as "race," is maneuvered between these horns of a dilemma, situated in the world of material culture, political choice, and historical contingency. But the point was to try to understand the *maneuver,* the colonial "choreography" that rendered subjects dominant and subordinate not because some were inherently better than others, but, rather, because some were *installed*—a political decision reinforced by words, words, words—over others. To break into the view, then, that what we see is transparent, or that what we see is what we get, I aimed to translate certain subjectivities back into modes of abeyance, in which case we would have to await a content, ideally, in contradistinction to arriving on the scene with one already in hand.[40]

   In "The Permanent Obliquity of an In(pha)llibly Straight: In the Time of the Daughters and the Fathers," the project that "Mama's Baby, Papa's Maybe" heads was lengthened across aspects of psychoanalytic inquiry;

just as we had decided that slavery was the massive spectacle of a public hysteria, in which event all the subject-participants bore the signature of the mark and the knowledge, I had tentatively concluded that, despite my reservations and reluctance, slavery could be thought of as a pathological field, or more precisely, one that displayed a tissue of symptomatic scars, or breaks, in the flow of the common good(s) between subject parties. In part a response to Houston Baker's powerful essay on Trueblood commerce[41] and Lynda Boose's invitation to produce some thinking on the thematics of daughters and fathers, "The Permanent Obliquity," punning on a line from Father Mapple's sermon in *Moby-Dick*,[42] staged an elaboration on the idea of *differentiating;* if the violence of slavery had been the loss of distinction— of a name, a cultural identity, factors of kinship, demographic specification, and geographical habitus, among them—then the corrective and revisionary measures that would alter the slave relations would need to be radical, and if radical, then definitive in restructuring every conceivable gesture and idea engendered in the quotidian round. Thus, who were "daughters" and "fathers," predicated on the historic instance of an "absent" father—one not actually "there," or one disabled in being "there," or one "absented" from "there," or one, who, symbolically speaking, had fallen off the orbit of paternal sanction? Well acquainted with the rhetorical pressures brought to bear on the very notion of the "black family" from all conceivable directions and wanting to circumvent their disciplines because I felt that they were practically useless, I looked at two *fictional* examples of incest and its displacements as an allegorical reading on the thematics of differentiation, or its failure. I wanted to argue that the scene of incest was not necessarily mythical in its use, but that its prohibitive character was charged with contemporary relevance, (1) insofar as its path of detour suggested that it happened daily, albeit unconsciously, within the precincts of the intimate and that (2) incest had to occur in order to be "defeated" in the preservation of *exogamous* social arrangements: one could love another only because, chiasmically, s/he had learned another to love at home. If both of the foregoing were true, then the incestuously linked characters in Ralph Ellison's *Invisible Man* and Alice Walker's "Child Who Favored Daughter"[43] were not only straddled by error, but were jettisoned, tout de suite, onto the ground of a nightmarish undifferentiation, whose leading exemplar had been diasporic slavery—in short, the failure to make the leap into contemporaneity: either time as progressive halting and puzzling, or time as the creative demarcations of what is becoming and overcoming moment by moment. The former opens a route to the reality check, the latter, to the possibilities of a philosophical self-inquiry. Because one needed to start *counting* in time, which the triumph of incestuous social practice would impede, I could see no reason to celebrate a paternal order of unusual tumescence.

Some interlocutors have questioned the exclusion of certain fictional examples here—perhaps the most popular ones—but my logic of selection was soundly based, I believe, on the notion that primary and secondary processes[44] must be assumed in an understanding of the scene of incest, even in a fictional translation of it; in short, I am not wholly persuaded that *acting* incestuously gets us much beyond the transgressive, which comes to repose in the thing itself, rather than its processes. The idea was to avoid the sensational, the melodramatic, by trying to follow an itinerary in which case the actors are *fighting* against an inclination that they are not even aware that they have—which testifies to the strength of the inhibition *and* the prohibition—but are overrun, despite themselves, by bad judgment: in Ellison's case, Trueblood *dreams* his error (which is perfectly fictional along several registers), while in Walker's case, the degrees of displacement and insinuation are so powerfully executed that it is not at all clear that the tale of the story ever happened within the deceptive frame of realism that its narrator seems to pose. One might well decide that "The Child Who Favored Daughter" is wholly fantastic as an expression of sexual guilt. In any case, incest, as far as I might understand it, does not, dare not, speak its name, but that of another—the "obliquity" that is indeed "permanent."

In both essays, I extended my inquiry into the impact of double signification—how meaning, destabilized by varied symptomatic pressure and hobbled to troubling complexity under the thumbs of context, bears the imprint of its contrary, if not always oppositional, movement. While the latter explanation comes over quite easily here from its provenance in studies in modern linguistics, its additional resources in the target culture have to do, in the historic instance, with social enactment as double exposure (e.g., in the case of the dual paternity of black children, or mothers bereft, at least in theory, of the socialities of motherhood, or black fathers denied the role of caretaker, we have, to my mind, determining instances). Going back, then, to the cluster of terms that I posed earlier, we could place "ambivalence" at the heart of a curve that veers quite sharply off the path of a single outcome, but for all that, is not rendered asymptotic to it. But the doubleness of ambivalence that I am proposing here is not at all a number, or a quantity; it is, rather, as I suggest in "Moving On Down the Line: Variations on the African-American Sermon," an "abeyance of closure," a break "in the passage of syntagmatic movement from one more or less stable property to another, as in the radical disjuncture between 'African' and 'American.'" Perhaps no spate of discourse, or even an entire social formation, shows a higher incidence of ambivalent behavior than the embrace of Christian practices in New World African communities. "Moving On Down the Line" was devoted to this whole problematic, whose contradictory angles are not yet exhausted.

Returning to the cultural thematic that I had pursued in the decade before I wrote "Moving On Down the Line," I tried to puzzle out a handful of key questions in this essay: (1) What is the black sermon (by way of a half-dozen examples, closely read in this essay, drawn from eighteenth and nineteenth century documents) "remembering" that its audience recognizes in the participatory rituals of black religious worship? (2) How are "writing" and "wounding" brought onto the same cultural ground? (One thinks here of the terrible juncture in which a line from Frederick Douglass's 1845 *Narrative* makes its appearance—in this fusion of elements, "the body's wreck and the autobiographical topic" line up: "My feet have been so cracked with the frost that the pen with which I am writing might be laid in the gashes."[45] Robert Stepto refers to Douglass's phrasing here as "syncretic."[46]) (3) In what ways is the African-American sermon paradigmatic of the structure of ambivalence that marks African apprenticeship in American/New World culture? (4) How do we theorize the hyphen as a "neither/nor" and a "both/and"? In short, was "African-American" merely descriptive, and if so, then what did it purport to describe and evaluate? It seemed to me that black sermons, in their sharply agonistic appeal, could not be isolated in any single historical moment (or else Martin Luther King's witness could not have been understood in its provocative use of modern and traditional intellectual technologies), but inscribed instead a grammar of feeling that continued to undergo transformation and redress up to the present, which I would regard as a break so formally decisive that it defies naming: until the nineteen-nineties, it seems, we could identify trends of cultural variation more or less continuous with ironical self-reflexivity (Imamu Baraka has called it the culture of a "blues people");[47] Aretha's Franklin's "Climbing High Mountains," for example, belongs to the "church" and the "world" in its hard-driving, celebratory rocking. Moreover, it proposes an untenable—that "coming up on the rough side of the mountain" can be danced and boogied on down. Examples of the syncretic nodes of black culture, from Clara Ward, to James Baldwin, to Wynton Marsalis, can be multiplied endlessly. Today, we are apparently generating forms that are *contiguous* to the syncretic/synthetic, or forms that seem to split off purposes of the "world" from those of the "church" not so much by content (religious rap, for example), but by marketing and commercial indexing. In any case, the sermon was a carrier of the music, was often itself a hybrid motion between word and music—the dissipation of syllabic contours in highly agitated layers of air, in shouts, lengthened moans and groans, etc.—and above all else, it became the "voice" that kept on talking across the long feverish nights of America's "race" dilemma. The Big Voice, the Big Mouth. If the sermon were motive amplified and enlarged to the extent that differences were effaced by its enactments, then it was the rhetorical/ social field to understand the most.

Written for a project launched by Cathy Davidson on the subject of American readerships and literacy, "Moving on Down the Line" not only picked up my doctoral dissertation where it left off, but attempted a refined understanding of the initial project in light of new critical persuasions—for instance, "writing" in its paronomastic echo. Secondarily, the essay does not exhaust, but makes a pass at, a comparative reading between the feast of the gaze (the hieratic church of history's rulers and the aristocracy) and the "gaze" of the ear (the Protestant church and its demotic trend lines). That these genres of church style inscribe radically disparate features of habitus is a kind of gloss on Henry Adams's fascination with European ecclesiastical architecture. But I certainly wanted to set the rich rhetoric of the black sermon down in its scale and context.

Jean Toomer proposed decades ago that "America" required a new vocabulary of cultural act and adjudication.[48] While he was addressing American "race," "race," in turn, became his metaphor for "culture," released from its customary moorings, as his "American" belonged to a plurality of subject-dispositions. No one could claim that this plurality had not been seen before, but their peculiar combination, which created the American social and political context, was, Toomer thought, unprecedented. "Hybridity," "ambivalence," in short, the repertory of reference to postmodernity's "undecidables," were not available as thinking tools to Toomer, but he got the point, even envisioning from it a new type of human and social order, which he explained to James Weldon Johnson in rejecting the latter's invitation to submit poems to his sample of "American Negro Poetry."[49] But the cut across the bias of the cultural fabric was hardly accomplished in Toomer's time and, for all we know now, remains an unfinished project. The American race saga clings to incoherence precisely because its official mythos—of distinct racial families—has been obliged to lie, to operate against a transparent, heterogeneous social order, increasingly unstable around the question of "race matters" since the early nineteen-sixties. The problematic of the "mulatto/a," which should have become a figure of speech for a heterogeneity of subjects, is, instead, the leftover trace of a racial "scientificity" that never quite worked its way through the culture as a firm ordering principle. In "Notes on an Alternative Model—Neither/Nor," I was concerned to highlight the "mulatta," not as a historical subject—because I reject the category as a naming strategy for actual subjects, who, by this definition, are the embodiment of a pathology—but, rather, as a symptom of the crisis of degree that effectually dissembled the failure of a Manichean reading of "race" and "culture" in the American context. In other words, because American culture was confronted with sufficient evidence that "black" and "white" were hardly substantial at the level of the eye, and, most worrisomely, difficult to always detect beyond it, the "mulatto/a" was created as a border guard between the highly disciplined precincts of a dualistic social economy. What Toomer had attempted to create in poetry, the culture work of criticism would try as critique.

But something rather odd happens in this discussion, which the essay did not know how to solve, that makes the idea of the "mulatto/a" as *cultural resonance* elusive; in brief, the idea keeps falling over into the descriptive apparatus of a physical type. And once fixated on the physiological, discourse then raids it for *ideological* purposes. The "neither/nor" of the essay attempted to check "mulatto/a" as mythical or reified property by translating it into a stage prop of the literary. The term, of course, does not originate in the New World, but as a European borrowing, was employed to supplement the work of division in the borrowed context. In its New World vocation, the term specifies mixed-race subjects, but that the latter needed some further distinction of naming signaled doubt to my mind that it was anything other than an elaborate mechanism of displacement on guard against a misnamed anxiety—the damaged pedigree of racial origin. The term garners no political work in the context of the United States, as far as I can tell—U.S. society never generated, for example, what Roberto Marquez calls a "pigmentocracy," as it has evolved in Afro-Latino-Criollo cultures,[50] but certain modifications are in order: Even though by virtue of the logic of the "one drop rule," one was certainly "black" by the least fraction of so-called "black" blood, this pathetic silliness, even when it did not go by the name of "mulatto/a," wreaked significant *intramural* havoc—"light and bright and got 'good' hair," "high yaller," "high-tone," etc., would suggest that pigment and its nuance have played a decisive *social* role among black people, if not a political one, for reasons that are not far to seek, vis-à-vis the dominative orders. (The politics of the 2000 U.S. census, however, emitted certain interesting developments: certain parties, Ward Connally supporting them, actually petitioned the authorities to create additional categories of race-naming on the census form—one was not simply "black," or other, but something else that the Census Bureau would not

have known to say.) Available, then, as a general cultural signifier, "mu-
latto/a" appears in "Toward an Alternative Model—Neither/Nor" as a
name for the interstitial, for the slippage of meaning from one lightpost to
another. But to reify "mulatto/a" as actual race-being, whatever that might
entail—as one fears is beginning to happen on the scene of the new pluralism—would amplify the "race" question, reinforce it as an implement of
political power, revivify the "black"/"white" divide, and essentially rein-
stall a sometimes ambiguous color consciousness that the late twentieth
century purports to have left behind. In any event the aim should be a
richer understanding of the workings of cultures in their local and translo-
cal range and not the uninteresting gradations of pigment and hair type. If
"Toward an Alternative Model—Neither/Nor" finds any use, perhaps it will
come in the guise of a safety patrol scout, helping to redirect traffic apparently moving ever more deeply into the hierarchies and delusions of
"race." In fact, racism today, in denying the historic effects of racial ideology (as though we could ignore them), is all the more poised, consequently,
to give it a boost.

Because the race matter has occupied so much prime time in U.S. society and occasioned such traumatic effects across its communities, we would
be right to regard it as a climactic condition. While its predictability is no
longer quite stunning, its tenacious powers of renewal and variation remain impressive—for example, "race" today is known in some circles of
American academe as an "intellectual fallacy." If one can succeed in establishing "race" as a *logical* fallacy—a "dance" performed on the surface of a
page, or the cerebral cortex—then s/he is free to retrieve the most traditional and vicious forms of racism, including, most emphatically, the inveterate behaviors of white male supremacism, since he would now be
guiltless of such charges, inasmuch as there is no such *intellectually competent* thing as "race" anyhow. This mangled reasoning would, if it could,
rewrite modern history and the role of "race" in it, which has been central.
It would render the Holocaust, for example, an event that we must now
read as the brainchild of an "intellectual fallacy" that some folk have mistaken for a fatal occurrence; that Hitler and his little helpers labored under
nothing more than intellectual incompetence is quite a charming idea, but
it does not tell one how she might have *felt* and what she might have *done*
about state policy and the "Jewish Question" had she been a contemporary
of the period, either as a witness to it, or a piece of its cannon fodder. If
"race" is *just* an "intellectual fallacy," then there is no compelling reason to
respond to it at all. By these naive lights, hardly innocent, and proceeding
by the insinuations of television, an eternal present that unfolds in the

head of an isolated and disembodied viewer, "race" is a *unilateral* error, inscribed by those who are presumed to "have" it.

But if "race" practices breed a knowledge, then what is it that is "known"? Transmitted habit? Mimetic conduct? The protocols of recognition and exclusion or inclusion that are wordlessly, unconsciously established in reality as the type of reality itself? In any case, when imaginative writers take up the matter, they occasionally do so with a degree of subtlety and indirection that matches its seductions and evasions. Among contemporary black writers, Paule Marshall, in her examination of some of the social economies of "Our America,"[51] advances one of the more complex readings of diasporic cultures and the problematics of "race" in her fiction, from the exquisite stories collected in *Soul, Clap Hands and Sing*,[52] to her most recent novel, *The Fisher King*.[53] Because a reader will not find easy solutions in this canon, Marshall's writings reward undivided attention. Both "Black, White, and in Color, or Learning How to Paint" and "Chosen Place, Timeless People: Some Figurations on the New World" represent my attempt to confront this subtle linguistic weave of textures.

The rich, moiling interior life of Marshall's characters often enough betrays the graceful literary surface that they present to the fictive world through which they move, and it is precisely that disparity between one front and another that the question of culture enables here and the conflict that stages contradictory motivation as the primary moment of subjectivity. As soon as we decide that a character or an action means one thing—Salina Boyce, Merle Kinbona, among others—it comes clear that they might well signify something else. And to watch these grammars of motivation carried out against material scenery that shuttles back and forth between background and foreground, frame and actor, figure and field is to lay hold of the complicated relationship that obtains between a geopolitical entity and an individual subject. In Marshall's case, "meteorology" might be understood along an range of timbres and registers, as settings and agents maintain an intricate calculus of interarticulations that might yield what a travel writer has called a "psychogeography." Having sketched out an initial response to these movements in "Some Figurations on the New World,"[54] I returned sometime later to the particular signatures of Marshall's *Chosen Place, Timeless People* in "Black, White, and in Color." An experimentation with reading, in part inspired by Roland Barthes's *S/Z*, this essay wanted, eventually, to discover a "protocol of reading" that would fit more than a single novel. But failing the more systematic ambition, the essay links the "mulatto/a" theme to intramural sexual violence in pursuit of an explanation—in this case, the fear and loathing of female sexuality plays directly into the historic question of color, which "returns" to the scene of Marshall's drama in a startlingly accurate psychoanalytic move. The masks and feints of love are here exposed as the wordless bloodletting that diasporic subjects wish to avoid. To my mind, the dynamics of sexuality, in its overlap with race, are brought to light in *Chosen Place, Timeless People* as a traumatic sequence of events that cannot be "discussed," although we discuss them endlessly. If black women's sexuality has traditionally been under (w)rap(s), then it seemed to me that this novel, perhaps inadvertently, is offering us a reason why—the breached prohibition on sexual congress between "black" and "white." The male psyche, in this case, does not "reason" that the historical female figure was trapped in a coercive sexual economy, but, rather, what it thinks it "knows" is that she surrendered. And couldn't we see, flowing from this conclusion, the entire repertoire of myth that surrounds the contemporary "subject of feminism"— from "castrating black bitch," to "strong black matriarch," to arms-akimbo, gum-popping black mama, to "welfare queen"? And furthermore, couldn't we see that the historical consciousness in the contemporary man, who might have "known," knew nothing of the sort?

It seemed that the entire case against "pigmentocracy" that had done so much to vex the intramural scene was here portrayed in the fictional germ of a novel. But miraculously, it had been sedimented in a context that had brought together all the relevant geopolitical questions, which symbolically positioned Europe, the United States, and the Caribbean on the terrain of power and desire, inflected by imperialist arrangements. "Black, White, and in Color" was as much an inquiry into this complex tweed of narrative and dramatic commotions as it was the tour of a psychoanalytic plot.

Anywhere that an investigator might be situated in the complex of the New World does not yield a neutrality of positions. By now a commonplace of contemporary criticism, this insight tends to be more theoretic than practical, inasmuch as any conceptual scheme at the time that it is advanced is, in fact, "reductive" on all the possible positions. I went as far as I thought it was plausible to go in drawing inferences from *The Chosen Place, The Timeless People* that might speak across diasporic junctures. If all the points along a historical sequence had a certain politics of domination in common, then what grammar could be concocted that would articulate both their difference and similarity? The post-1968 academic scene, for very well known reasons, had circumvented the treacheries of Grand Narrative, having installed instead "local," albeit strong, explanatory formulas that have yielded in effect discrete territories of "minority discourse"[55] with a shared horizon; in the field of African-American literary and cultural studies, we detect three "systems" of critico-theoretical investigation to emerge after 1980: Houston Baker's "blues" metaphor that opens onto black "expressive culture;" Henry Louis Gates's linguistic negotiations of a black signifying system, embedded in Africanity;[56] and Mae G. Henderson's dialogism/dialectic of black women writing.[57] These powerful theoretical acts, which adopt their motive, in part, from items at hand in black culture—musical "blues" forms, signifying practices, and African-American religious expression—are so positioned that they could well speak across forms and punctualities of cultural production. As Grand Narratives, however, we might question their explanatory power[58] in the particular case that is unnamed, inasmuch as the instances that the writers adduce are especially apt to the framework in which they are interpolated. But could we say that they are limited, or irreducible test cases, or expansively exemplary moments of reading? The *definitive* conceptual narrative on the African Diaspora, then, remains elusive in any case, as the new millennium forces us to rephrase the question itself. In "Who Cuts the Border? Some Readings on America," I took up the question of systematicity once again as I had attempted to do in "Mama's Baby, Papa's Maybe" and other essays.

Faced with a thankless task of having to present essays on a diversity of New World thematics, I was well aware, in 1991–92, of having few models from which to draw. Ideally, a paradigm that would adequately address Canada, the United States, Cuba, and Haiti, to say nothing of Panama, Brazil, Argentina, and the Yucatan—all moments along an enormous cultural mapping over a virtually immeasurable expanse of land and climate—would have antennae out for inevitable shifts of nuance both within language formations and among them. The future of an Africana studies, which this essay only inchoately understood, will instaurate a comparative cross-cultural, cross-linguistic reading of the Afro-Iberian-Hispanic-Native-Francophone-Luso-Brazilian-English-Dutch-Criollo life worlds that converge on this massive complex.

In anticipation of that future, we could make a start with an inquiry on the term "America" itself, as it was at least clear that this strategy of naming means different things to different viewers, depending on which border he is standing when evoking it. If the idea was to restore "America" to an interrogative posture, then the analogous point would compel us to make headway against those modes of analysis that have prevented our grasping it as a world system linked by exploitative labor practices, an economic order dominated by the United States from the tail-end of the nineteenth century, and "race" everywhere transposed into a cultural key; if America had been a European playpen for centuries, then it was also true, by the logic of the boomerang, that Europe had come to depend on America not only for its first luxury goods—coffee and tobacco, for instance—but also the violent, coercive, and lucrative regimes, underwritten by New World slavery and colonization, that had invented the first global consumer markets and offered incentive for profitable real-estate ventures to the younger sons; in fact, an Atlantic system would be put in place, from the competitive merchant navies of the respective nation-states, to the current avatars of the latter in the NATO/G-7/Bretton-Woods fraternity of governments and the birth of the International Monetary Fund. It is nothing short of fascinating than to trace the unfolding career of this squabbling circle of post-Crusade Christian states, from the Inquisition to European Union and its common currency, in their ruthless manipulation of each other, as well as the subject populations that they would exploit and pulverize on the glorious path of triumphant accumulation. Crushing much of the world under its heel, the iron boot would depend on that barbaric labor pool from across the seas to keep those shoe lasts in good working order. But the tale of America is radical change, and however uneven and precarious its development, not a single one of the old dominative modalities has endured to this day. "Who Cuts the Border?" revisits the scenes of subjection in order to make clear that this spate of history—where our own names were written—holds out, still, an unusual opportunity, if we dare, and that is to say, the chance to bring into being the radical democracies of a cultural creolité. It is not written in stone, however, that we will or even *can*.

According to the segregated protocols of the kingdom of letters, the canon of William Faulkner is not traditionally associated with New World writing; in fact, the American "South," supposed to be Faulkner's subject, is isolated as a cultural sphere from the surround as a case sui generis. But it seems that a different reading of Faulkner's work—as Gabriel Garcia Márquez performed—would yield Faulkner a widened categorical alignment. By looking closely at his 1936 novel, *Absalom, Absalom!* I attempted to link him, in "Who Cuts the Border?," to Martí's "Our America," as the figure of "Thomas Sutpen," who symbolically conjoins three New World compass points, might be thought of as Faulkner's first cosmopolite. It is difficult, nonetheless, to even imagine this fiction at home in Yoknapatawpha, Mississippi, but that might well have been one of the writer's motives—to return to the seedbed of an American politics that had rendered a Mississippi *before* the arrival of those European remnants, of which Thomas Sutpen is one, unthinkable—astonishingly, Faulkner's fictive genealogies commence with a figure of the Native American, which community, up to the era of Andrew Jackson's presidency, made up the dominant population of parts of the American South. This canon earns its powerful witness from a sustained meditation on the pretexts and antecedent deeds that come home to roost in "Our America" of the twentieth century's first half; that this project is managed with a "linguisticity," let's say, that firmly embeds itself in the tale so that there is no tale without those precise orchestrations is one of the most formidable reading and writing assignments of that century.

Because one is never quite finished with Faulkner—as a master craftsman (even when he's not so good, as in some of his last novels), as a figure of excess in many ways, and as a writer who appears to see his country quite clearly and does not flinch—I returned to the canon again only a short time ago to gaze on Thomas Sutpen some years later. In "Faulkner Adds Up," I concentrated on repetitive devices in *The Sound and the Fury* and *Absalom, Absalom!*, as it now seems to me that repetition is not only a favored stylistic signature of some of the high moderns, but perhaps a window onto the soul of this reader! As a generous reader of these essays has pointed out to me, I have been involved in repetition myself as certain elements of argument—which the reader calls my "dialectical plot"—and of style recur across these writings. I must admit that when I finished "Faulkner Adds Up," I probably knew less about the repetitive than when I started the essay, which began as an address to the 1998 annual meeting of the Faulkner-Yoknapatawpha Conference at "Ole Miss." But perhaps I can say now that repetition is *not* counting at all; that perhaps it is the having forgotten to count, which only a second or third party notices, and that it is the having forgotten (because you have no idea that you are doing it) that opens up a lesion or breach that we call *style*—a cut through the field of signification; in any event, it seemed to me that repetition in Faulkner, perhaps for any writer, is nothing less than the "system," or the reworking of decisive elements of choice, by which s/he is known. Repetition, therefore, does not have a beginning and an ending in a single text, but goes all the way down to a past too much to evoke all at once. In other words, Faulknerian repetition has a great deal to do with the psychoanalytic theme.

Not a traditional topic for African-American literary and cultural studies, perhaps for good reason, the psychoanalytic thematic, on the other hand, seems to offer resources that might help bring to light the long-buried articulations on the *interior* levels of the culture. I have suggested in this essay where some of the "hot spots" glare—black women's sexuality, family life, gender relations, slavery's impact on American institutional life, the whole of the intramural/intersubjective field, among them. My impression that certain formations of subjectivity here are captured under the sign of a prohibition remains strong, despite the fact that the post–Civil Rights era in the United States has granted access to unprecedented opportunity. The formidable range of doubt that psychoanalytic theories provoke, however, is not sufficient reason, in my view, to impede inquiry on the subject in specific reference to African-American culture. I attempted to set down my own initial responses to this problematic in " 'All the Things You Could Be By Now, If Sigmund Freud's Wife Was Your Mother': Psychoanalysis and Race." As it turned out, the essay was for me an important ground-clearing exercise, as I attempted to maintain two interlocutory positions in the writing—essentially, the same "voice" saying "yes" and "no," at once: yes, to the resources of this intellectual technology, and no, to any direct cultural application not only of the psychoanalytic but of any protocol unsubjected to scrutiny, in this case, the scrutiny of a historicization. Certain important observers, as " 'All The Things You Could Be'" points out, have had serious misgivings about the psychoanalytic vocation beyond its European provenance. But it seems—which therefore compels me toward the opposite view—that if this single subject is *verboten* in reference to black culture, then perhaps we need to find out why. Any taboo, for interesting reasons all its own, is just sitting there, ripe for violation.

In sketching those impression points which suggest that the black life world does not escape the net of the intersubjective/subjectivity, I designated, among other elements, the economies of the fetish as a fruitful ground of interrogation; in a current project, partially related to " 'All The Things You Could Be,' " I am turning over this notion in the following way: a stage in the development of the modern world, predicated on the rise and fall of the money device and the modern fiscal instrument, black culture "argues" with the West, as it is *in* and *of* it. Its expressivities are, therefore, modern, modernist, and postmodern in their frames of reference. But the question is, what is "black culture" to the "West"? And what is it to "itself," if we assume that the questions represent discrete, but overlapping, punctualities? In other words, do we assume that the questions mark an actual split in viewpoint? I believe that there is a break from one position to the other, even if the lines of pursuit are asymptotic. The culture does not read itself, I think, along the lines of the economy of the fetish, either as it is described in psychoanalytic terms, or in the terms of labor and commodities. And it is precisely the *alienated object* (which might explain the historic interconnection between a projective racist anxiety and the withheld fruits of labor), where a *self-image*—whether or not it is fantastical is beside the point—*ought* to be, *must become,* that black culture has sought to demolish.

The latter, I believe, describes both its differences from the "West" and its long-going quarrel with it. If the Freudian and Marxist problematics identify two key stops along the route of modernity, then one of the principal sites of their convergence is the stage of "black culture."

However else dominative practices might be explained, they are, to my mind, irresistibly struck by the irrational. In other words, no *reason* convincingly explains them. In that regard, perhaps the "master/slave" dialectic is penetrated by an element of the transhistorical so that particular instances alter the details, but neither the outcome, nor the configuration of motives that animate it. I am suggesting that domination as a social economy carries a register that cannot be delineated, or directly expressed, which makes the idea of the "symptom" a very fruitful one. This "refusal" is not the whole story, by any means, but it is certainly one of its enabling syntagms. The story of Harriet Jacobs/Linda Brent,[59] which gives us crucial insight into the situation of bonded women in the nineteenth century, is quite remarkable for a number of reasons, and one of them is the narration of the sexual dynamics of the slave relations. The protagonist's nocturnal encounters with her mistress—in the narrative, the wife of "Dr. Flint"—are so charged with elements of sexual frisson and the mishaps of ecstasy that we are led to believe that the wife is invigilating the young woman in her own behalf and not for the ostensible reasons that Jacobs's text brings to the surface. In any case, the powerful symptomaticity of these scenes first suggested to me—indeed, compelled me to consider—that for whatever else the slave relations might have been over those long centuries, it ineluctably sustained, in every one of them, a psychoanalytic element, and if we could conceive of an *institutional* psychoanalysis, it must then be possible to imagine it in the collective framework of entire cultures. " 'All The Things You Could Be' " was a sequential next step.

The distance between Linda Brent and Harriet Jacobs, aspects of the same *persona,* is measured in light years, which significance must not be mocked or taken for granted; in short, the subject formation on the other side of freedom does not declare the end of an emancipatory project, but as the celebrated fictional heroine of Toni Morrison's *Beloved* insinuates,[60] the latter must be radically addressed as the *moment of departure* that never ceases. Now that we are there, at that point, what next? The generations of culture workers have each proposed a set of responses to an enormous aftermath, but perhaps the single feature that carries over from one articulation to another is the concern to designate that complex of living and conceptual arrangements that would inhibit agency and to advance those that would foster it. But making such discriminations is not as easy as it might sound: Frantz Fanon, one of the systematic thinkers on the question, probably would have agreed with the philosopher of *The Use and Abuse of History* that "an excess of history hurts [life],"[61] when Fanon asserts, flat out, history does not determine one of my actions.[62] The claim is far too loud to be plausible and indeed belies the very context in which it is incorporated. At least a partial determination of what preceded Fanon is captured in the ironical portrait of the "Negro of the Antilles," who, upon arrival in the City of Light, suddenly learns that he is "white" no more. While it is likely true that one can, on occasion, choose the narratives that he will call his own, it is also undeniable that certain other narratives will choose him, whether he will or not. The question, then, is how best to *interarticulate* the varied temporalities that arrive on the space of the "now."

Writing in 1873, in the aftermath of the successful Bismarckian campaign against France, Nietzsche sought the right balance between too much history and enough of it—on the one hand, an excess of it conduces to life that is "maimed and degenerate, and is followed by the degeneration of history as well" (12). On the other, the "service of history" is distinguished from the excess and aids the "living man" in three ways: "in relation to his action and struggle, his conservatism and reverence, his suffering and desire for deliverance" (12). Though much has changed, it goes without saying, in our conceptualization of history since Bismarck and Empire, and certainly our relationship to it is so altered that we are called upon to believe that history itself is now receded, perhaps nothing attests more powerfully to its firm grip than the postmodern's belief that he is free of it. The history, then, to which I refer is dimensional along four registers: it is, according to Lacan, "the physical past whose existence is abolished," the epic past "perfected in the handiwork of memory," and the "historic past in which man finds the guarantor of his future."[63] But the past about which African-American culture critique has been virtually silent is the one "which reveals itself in repetition." The means of that one "are those of the Word, in so far as the Word confers a meaning on the functions of the individual; its domain is that of the concrete discourse, insofar as this is the field of the transindividual reality of the subject; its operations are those of history, insofar as history constitutes the emergence of Truth in the Real" (19).

What is historic about this Lacanian Word is that it was withheld for so long, in the African-American case, by the requirements of the engines of domination; it is not a matter, then, of relocating, or "remembering" something prior so much as it is *inventing* and *bringing to stand* the intersubjective formation; my view is that the psychoanalytic aim might be able to lend a hand there.

Though " 'All The Things You Could Be'" was written after "*The Crisis of the Negro Intellectual:* A Post-Date," this volume ends with the latter piece because of the currency of its topic. The essay, written, in part, to mark the thirtieth anniversary eve of the publication of Harold Cruse's *Crisis of the Negro Intellectual,*[64] reflects the situation of black culture at the moment, if we conclude that one of its principal sites is the academy; we come back now to the "curricular object" of "Black Studies," whose moment invites theorization on a scene revisited. The academy as an object of analysis always seems invested with urgency and always appears to be in a state of critical flux, but as Paul Bové explains in a recent issue of *boundary 2,* devoted to "The University,"[65] we have every reason to mourn the passing of Cardinal Newman's "Idea of the University" at the very same time that we might dare to hope for signs of intelligent life in the universe: "Much remains to be writtten about the university, even if it is only its history. Indeed, epitaphs can be long. But just as [Henry] Adams did not allow mourning to arrest his thinking, so too intelligence, we know, will find its own places to erupt. It simply seems doubtful that the university will ever again see itself as the place or time to encourage and solicit such turbulence" (6).

The notion of intelligence as turbulent eruption exactly fits the very model that we think we are missing in the U.S. academy today, either because the university here has misplaced its *intellectual* mission, or not yet found it, insofar as "a group of independent but authoritative generalists writing and interpreting for, and read within, the larger public sphere"[66] has yet to emerge in the United States. Allan Stoekl suggests as much and that the "agonies of the intellectual" in the French field might be instructive for his/her transatlantic counterpart, insofar as Stoekl marks a shift of the intellectual horizon on what he identifies as the post-Durkheim era. But it seems to me that this whole enormous question takes on a turn of the screw when black intellectual formation is introduced into it.

Ronald Judy's magisterially informed "Untimely Intellectuals and the University,"[67] appearing in Bové's *boundary 2* volume, argues that the "crisis in Black intellectual leadership" splits into two components—its "concern" of and for sociology and its dubious, or obscure "theoretical status" (121). Judy insists on the difference, noting not only that this "crisis" is as old as sociology itself but that it, in fact, demarcates "the occasion for both the articulation of sociology as a scientific field in the later half of the nineteenth century and the systematic study of what was then known as the Negro experience and condition, which over time became first Black studies, then Afro-American studies, and, recently, Africana studies" (122). While I think I understand Judy's insistence that the rise and systematization of the social scientific disciplines in the United States—certainly he means the latter, inasmuch as the discipline of "sociology" belongs to the German nineteenth century—cannot be decisively cordoned off from "the Negro experience and condition," I suspect that we might need a few more sentences to hand before we can declare the latter the material cause of the former. In "Working Notes on the Prehistory of Black Sociology: The Tuskegee Negro Conference,"[68] Paul Jefferson limns a contrastive genealogy, no less so because his narrative distinguishes a "black sociology" from an older "black sociological enterprise" and *both* from the "hybrid genealogy of mainstream academic sociology," which all resemble each other. But the collapse that Judy seems to make in "Untimely Intellectuals" would read against the grain of Jefferson's argument and violates both my sense of what took place to yield us a "Black studies" movement and what might have happened in the pointed historical sequence between the close of the Civil War and W. E. B. DuBois's second career at Atlanta University, 1933–44; while a full reading of these crucial years to the creation of a "Black Studies" agenda cannot be provided here, I do want to turn over, albeit very briefly, a couple of impression points that bear on the "crisis" that we mean.

Jefferson traces the emergence of U.S. academic sociology back to the late nineteenth century by way of "an omnibus reform movement orchestrated by the American Social Science Association" (121). Modeled, he contends, on the British Social Science Association, the American version took root in 1865, "disciplined by the trauma of the Civil War and purged of prewar sentimentalism" (121). A movement of "practical idealism," the ASSA sought " 'to create a special and unified science of human society and social welfare in the United States' " (121). The organization "not only lobbied for modernization of the traditional college curriculum, working to introduce courses in 'Social Science,' then promiscuously understood, that paved the way for the more differentiated modern social sciences proper" (122) but also midwived the American Historical Association, the American Political Science Association, and the American Economic Association, "whence ultimately derived the American Sociological Society itself in 1905" (122). Although Jefferson dates social science research interest in "people of color" as early as 1831, and the First Annual Convention of the People of Color, which convened in Philadelphia of that year, and which he would likely denominate an originary instance of the "black sociological enterprise," that "enterprise," he contends, was "not coextensive" with black sociology; the black sociological enterprise, which preceded black sociology, "animated it and afforded it an agenda" (122); the "enterprise" itself was concerned with "identifying and systematically exploiting instrumentalities of group survival and development" (122). Perhaps this moment in Judy's itinerary might be called a "pre-theoretical" moment, but nevertheless, it seems, this "pre-theoretical" breaks in on the putatively "theoretical" moment of "Black Studies" as a kind of "textual," transgenerational haunting that no amount of ghost-busting has succeeded in exorcising, and it is precisely that "pre-theoretical" moment of the "black sociological enterprise" to which the mainstream American academy was not then and is not now responsive, despite the fact of "Black Studies" and all its children. That, I believe, is exactly Professor Judy's point about the "concern" of "Black Studies" *for* sociology, but the problem is compounded for Black Studies *for* theory exactly because it is entangled with Black Studies as a problem, or concern for sociology; for this reason, Professor Jefferson suggests that the project of black sociology—and he makes no bones about calling it that—has always maintained a high degree of polyvalence, "has never been one dimensional," and that when its history is finally written, it must be constituted as a "suitably hybrid affair" (123).

The three interrelated concerns of the "black sociological enterprise" have not only hounded the project of black sociology into and out of the twentieth century, but for all intents and purposes, as Judy intimates, have fashioned and refashioned themselves as the major cultural capital of the entire Black Studies/African-American/Africana alignment, wherever the black academician might be situated as *another* bureaucratic and/or disciplinary person: (1)"Its rhetorical concern has been to use the canonical language of the day for purposes of advocacy and critique"; (2) "Its reform concern has been to organize and rehabilitate the black community, and wherever possible in doing so to press related community demands"; (3) "And its research concern has been to seek out and synthesize information in service of these other objectives" (122). It is fair to say, I believe, that Harold Cruse's *Crisis of the Negro Intellectual,* written in the transitional moment between the American Civil Rights Movement and its modulation into the "Black Power Revolt,"[69] actually rehearses the motives of the "black sociological enterprise" in other words. Cruse yearns for the "intellectual" that Stoekl claims the U.S. never quite engendered, in *any* of its communities, and for which formation Russell Jacoby (in *The Last Intellectuals*) is said to be nostalgic.[70]

In any event, when Judy offers that the "inclusion of Black Studies in the university was not as a response to external political pressure but as a moment in the university's function as a social institution responsible for the development and transmission of knowledge" (124), we must pause and read the sentence again: Nothing that he argues in this writing tells us why or how the "inclusion of Black studies" was not only precisely responsive to "external political pressure," and in a few cases around the United States, *violent* "external political pressure," as the academy would not have responded otherwise, even remotely, but also why, after decades of more or less rigidly racialized training formations in the United States, the agents of Higher Learning were suddenly cognizant of their intellectual duty to be "responsible for the development and transmission of knowledge," even where black culture was concerned. These same suddenly responsives had missed W. E. B. DuBois, with his Harvard degrees and German patina, at the University of Pennsylvania, following on its own commissioned study of *The Philadelphia Negro* (1900), had missed Carter G. Woodson, Alain Locke, Jessie Fauset, Bennie Mays, Horace Mann Bond, E. Franklin Frazier, John Hope Franklin (until the mid-sixties), and Harold Cruse (until the mid-sixties), to name a few of the more eminent examples. At best, the question splinters open down the central rib: the mainstream university, responding to "external political pressure," was *forced* to recognize the "university's function as a social institution responsible for the development and transmission of knowledge" along a range of unwelcome and turbulent emergence, from Black Studies, to Women's Studies, to Feminist Theory, and all the incredible aftermath. I realize that some of us would far rather forget what I have just described—for all its messiness and lack of loft—but we will not be able to unwrite it, even as we rewrite it, no matter how unpleasant and "untheoretical" and "unclean" these beginnings might appear to our anxious mind. The question that interests us, as far as I can tell, is what the "newcomers" in the mainstream are going to do *now* and are doing *now* with this fragmented legacy—these shards of broken desire—that yawns over the university rendered "impossible," an "imagined community" no longer where it was, and a project trapped between a "pre-theoretical" nostalgia and a theoretical moment that would "consume" it, not entirely unlike the sacrificial host; in other words, what makes our "crisis" seem so hard is the truth of its ambivalence. While I attempted in "A Post-Date" to argue for a *purer* theoretical object, I was worried everywhere in it by the properties of contagion that are interpolated in it and interpellate it. I am going to assume that this obliquity has been the problem all along.

And so, here we are, everywhere *in* it and *of* it—the world's mess, which, as Stuart Hall remarks, we attempt to redefine as a "field." What happens, he asks, when this field

which I've been trying to describe in a very punctuated, dispersed, and interrupted way, as constantly changing directions, and which is defined as a political project, tries to develop itself as some kind of coherent theoretical intervention? Or, to put the same question in reverse, what happens when an academic and theoretical enterprise tries to engage in pedagogies which enlist the active engagement of individuals and groups, tries to make a difference in the institutional world in which it is located?[71]

Even though Hall is specifically addressing the theoretical legacies of the cultural studies project in Britain and the United States, it seems to me that his interrogation finds apt analogy elsewhere; these essays, I should like to think, have been contextualized by none other than the "struggle" to intervene.

III

Back in the ole days, when going to see a movie was called going to the "picture show," the youngsters in my neighborhood did not have the least concern about the schedule of the showings; one simply turned up, parents or buddies in tow, at the middle—most usually—or at the end—it didn't matter—and left when the reel caught the place where she entered: "We came in here" returns us, in this instance, to the moment of the egg, where this writing began and a few remarks on "eating in the Diaspora." These notes actually comprise the first blush of a research protocol on this topic that began for me as a traveler's curiosity—completing, in the mid-seventies, my first meal of a fish stew with friends in Dansoman Estates, outside Accra, I tried to imagine how a cultural history of the African Diaspora and Continental Africa might proceed from the point of view of food and the foodways. The question of food as cultural expression, as a source of the deepest pleasure, and as an observation post on the range of the appetitive has struck me as a fruitful way to arrange a history of these geographical coordinates and perhaps from there, to specify zones of taste—"hot" and "mild," "sweet" and "tangy," the "sweet"/"sour" complex and the "bland," all on the model of Lévi-Strauss's "raw and cooked." This inquiry would run along cultural lines and dietary patterns, which would interrupt, quite likely, our dearest-held presumptions about who might eat what, according to what we think we understand about cultural affiliation. For, as Anthony Bourdain points out in *Kitchen Confidential*,[72] many of the food myths that we entertain are daily exploded by the actualities of the cuisine—perhaps the only territory of the social relations that ferociously melds the use value and the exchange value, where both are destined to disappear in the vanishing feast. I am a long way from completing such a study, but what is for sure is that the cuisine marks another punctuality in the African and Diasporic life-worlds in the public and private discourse—at the level of the recipe, as spectacular presentation, as a gesture of communion and renewal, of kinship and belonging, as aesthetic inscription, as long-standing cultural secrets that demarcate one cultural expression from another—a particular thing that one does, for example, with collard greens, macaroni and cheese, potato salad, barbecue, rutabaga, and a repertory not only of foodstuffs but of ways of culinary preparation that *semiotically* signify one kind of food consumption (or even food consumption at all!) and production and not another. The trick, nevertheless, is that the shadow does not always fall where we think it might. With food, then, we are both "at home" and "abroad," a product of a particular urban block or a spot of provincial countryside *and* a worldling of multi-languages and cultures. I see no need to choose. As material relations and practices that enter economies, institutions, and alimentary bodies, that cross spaces, borders, and defenses, that permeate differences, similarities, and commonalities, that show the intransigence of certain cultural values, at the same time that they exemplify porosity and change, the arts of the cuisine offer a central metaphor for the "contact zone" and our pluralist possibilities. The joining place of bread and "bread," the feast that moves but that can also be still, food always breeds a politics, a history, bears publicness as well as intimacy and representability, is visible, yet the stuff whose biochemistry, like growing life, remains somehow mysterious, and in the translation makes a body glow and glow. In the cuisine, contradiction comes home and is not unhappy.

The unfolding saga of food in the New World suggests that the thematics of "globalization" are hardly new with the turn of the millennium, however "hyped" the topics of "travel" and the "transnational" may be at the moment, but that they are inextricably woven into the very fabric of its lifestyles. In fact, the modern world, as cultural historians have long contended, comes about with the trade in luxury goods, the primary ones among them based on the palate and the craving for spice.[73] Looking for an easier, less expensive route to the *Genussmittel* through the Old World, medieval Europe "found" the New, "where it lost its way."[74] It seems, then, that the satisfaction of *addictive* craving—which moves a body down the road, or across an ocean—and the desiring—the insatiable itch, here represented in the oral lack—are joined in a calculus of motives that we call "modernity." What that calculus has wrought is quite remarkable, all the way around, especially when we consider that kinds of pepper were among the chief causes of it all.[75] But the trick here is that we jump from object to object in this strange concatenation of sensual, historical, and political forces so that pepper, of all things, will eventually nose open—it will take nearly six centuries for that to happen—the next suite of desire and the new "jones"—for sugar, coffee, chocolate, and tobacco. It is difficult for us to imagine now that these cultigens will join "the potato, the tomato, maize, avocados, pineapples, haricot, kidney and butter beans, scarlet runners, 'French' beans . . . peanuts, vanilla, red peppers and green peppers, tapioca, and the turkey, not to mention gold and silver . . . rubber, chewing gum, and quinine,"[76] to say nothing of "barbecue" (*FH*, 222–23) either, in a repertoire of culture only known at one time to Amerindian communities. Now fully installed in the habits and vocabulary of global consumption, the food stuffs on this list would come to demarcate not only decisive dietary changes, provoked by the drives of greed and envy, longing and desire, but would, in time, give on to a distinctive corridor of the global cuisine.

In food history, the American complex opens to world trade with these comestibles, but what we see in them is only the tip of the iceberg: At great human cost, this cuisinart of the modern has blood on its hands, as the pillage and enslavement of millions are implicated in its development; slavery and modernity are the hand in the glove of practices that come to define the new age:

> the growth of instrumental rationality, the rise of national sentiment and the nation-state, racialized perceptions of identity, the spread of market relations and wage labour, the development of administrative bureaucracies and modern tax systems, the growing sophistication of commerce and communication, the birth of consumer societies, the publication of newspapers, and the beginnings of press advertising, 'action at a distance,' and an individualist sensibility.[77]

It is not alone, then, the bite of the pepper and the virus of "dangerous tastes" that will eventually help set the table in the Americas and around the world, but what contextualizes these addictive preferences in a system thoroughly driven by the profit motive and the response to economic incentive.[78] If the Portuguese hold the dubious distinction of initiating the Transatlantic slave trade in the mid-fifteenth century with human commerce into Lisbon, then they are also said to have introduced maize farming to sub-Saharan Africa (specifically south central Africa) in order "to provide ships' stores for the slave trade" (*FH*, 205). In some accounts, manioc, the sweet potato, goundnuts, and French beans are said to be American transplants that "became widely established" on the Continent (205). But Diane Spivey, in *The Peppers, Cracklings, and Knots of Wool Cookbook*, argues that manioc, favored by the Olmec community on Mexico's Yucatan Peninsula, "had been cultivated and eaten on the African Continent long before European arrival," inasmuch as "there may have been an indigenous variety" of the plant.[79] Spivey's counter-narrative, in linking Olmec civilization, "diffused throughout Central American and across the Isthmus of Panama" (135), to an African root, suggests a far greater culinary affinity between Continental Africa and New World cultures than is customarily assumed. In her view, a corrected and revised historical record would assign to black African cultures a greater share in the story of crop and food evolution (126). For example, corn in this picture (as in the case of manioc) is both African and American in its origins, as inhabitants on both complexes (in the pre-Columbian period) "wrapped foods before cooking in cornhusks and banana and other large-leafed plants, then steamed it in the same liquor they used to wash it down" (127). At the very least, Spivey concludes, we can suggest that a different species of corn might have been grown on the Continent from the ones in the Americas, and that those pre-Columbian mariners (in whom researchers believe the inspiration for the impressive Olmec sculptures reposed in the first place)[80] likely brought the corn plant back to the Continent themselves (132). If the European nation-states would essentially execute the first "cold war" and the decided manipulation of state policy, pursuant to Alexander VI's dictum on the Demarcation of the world, then the food fight that the historians still carry on today had been inscribed already as its future. In any case, not an inch of the new age, as a spatio-temporal sequence, has gone uncontested, from the landfall of Christopher, to the contemporary period: the peace of the board, we might say, is subtended by the knocking of the poltergeist.

What will constitute American culinary practices, however, will differ, of course, over time and region, although the meals that Donna Gabaccia describes, on the basis of menus drawn from colonial North American cookbooks, demonstrate a surprising conceptual variety of tastes.[81] Relatedly, what Sidney Mintz elaborates as a cuisine "built on the cultivation of a particular complex carbohydrate, such as maize or potatoes or rice or millet or wheat,"[82] has largely disappeared over the last three centuries, thanks to "revolutionary pressures in food processing and consumption and by adding on new foods" (*SP*, 13). Apparently a radical change in the conception of cuisine, the central part of the meal (now, mostly fish and meat), which used to be the "edge," is quite different from what it was during the long centuries before; in his anthropological reading of "sweetness" and the industries of sucrose sugar, Mintz describes the "sedentary civilizations," based on the consumption of a single starch complex, as exemplary of the family of culinary cultures: "In these starch-based societies, usually but not always horticultural or agricultural, people are nourished by their bodily conversion of the complex carbohydrates, either grains or tubers, into body sugars" (9). Other plant foods, as well as "oils, flesh, fish, fowl, fruits, nuts, and seasonings" would be consumed in sedentary societies, "but users themselves usually view them as secondary, even if necessary, additions to the major starch" (9). From this basic component, Mintz adduces the fascinating theory of the "core complex carbohydrate" and the "flavor-fringe supplement" in a relations of "center" and "edge." This pattern of culinary consumption is so persistent and clear over time that Mintz calls it the "centricity of the complex carbohydrates" accompanied by a "contrastive periphery" (11). On the basis of this "flavor principle," anthropologists of the cuisine have concocted a "tetrahedron" of tastes, as well as "distinctive regional flavors"—exactly the kind of thing I first wondered about a couple of decades ago—that include "*nuoc mam* of Southeast Asia, the chili peppers (*Capsicum* species) of Mexico, West Africa, and parts of India and China, the *sofrito* of the Hispanic Americans and so on" (11).

There seems, then, an interesting similarity between the "pouch" foods of the Americas and of parts of the sub-Saharan Continent and the Asian Continent and those of the starch-central cuisine complexes—either a substance dipped into a commonly shared bowl of a liquid food (which describes the way I consumed my first meals in Ghana), or a softer food, wrapped in an outer shell or substance. The "pouch" food is probably a different category of food preparation/conception from the leaf-wrapped meal, but the two processes remind me of each other: Reay Tannahill, in *Food in History,* suggests that the vegetable-wrapped meat actually belongs to one of the transitional moments in human development, when cooking became "'the decisive factor leading man from a primarily animal existence into one that was more fully human'" (*FH,* 13). The stomach of the animal as a pouch for cooking food stuffs also belongs to Tannahill's outline of "food and cooking before 10,000 b.c." (15–16). The use of haggis—the sheep's stomach container—survived until the eighteenth century (16),[83] and modern haggis, a variation on the theme, or the sheep's stomach used as a "dumpling cloth," still serves in coeval Scotland. Interestingly enough, John Gilmore, writing on aspects of Caribbean cuisine, reports that the minced beef and salt pork that enter ingredients of "Barbados' Jug," or "jug-jug," is said to derive from haggis—"perhaps a tribute to those Highlanders defeated at Culloden who were exiled to [Barbados]," while other theories posit a West African origin for it.[84] The food that is built around a centrality, then, as the "pouch" might indicate, does not only mark a stage of global eating, but according to Mintz, "this picture still applies in much of Asia, Africa, and Latin America," as it typifies, still, "perhaps three-quarters of the world's population" (*SP,* 14).

Could it be said that food dispersed across a surface and manipulated with utensils belongs to a certain technological phase of social life and is not "natural" to our order of the foodways as it now appears to be? In this trend-line of movement toward the fork and preferential treatment of the "edge," what in the world is McDonald's? Does it veer toward the "pouch," where food and container constitute a single comestible item, or toward the plate and its display of this and that? Perhaps it is true that the fast-food take-out phenomenon could only have developed with the instauration of the gas and electric range, the wider dissemination of the cuisine art, encouraged by the spread of literacy, and the evolution of the restaurant, following on the tavern and the coffee house.[85] But until our late last century, mealtime in the United States was neither "fast," nor, for millions of families in these regions, customarily taken outside the home. Our notion, however, that these important semiotic signals were the clues to provincial taste is only partially true. In fact, Donna Gabaccia, in *We Are What We Eat,* argues that colonial/U.S. food offers an example of " 'creole,' or what cooks describe as a gumbo or a stew" (9), from its earliest settlements; the yoking of "creole" and "regional taste," outside New Orleans and the Caribbean, is not traditional for U.S. consumers, but Gabaccia pursues the thematic, beginning with Iroquois corn cultivation in the Northeast of the colonies and its significance in the diets of both indigenous and settler colonies, to the areas of rice cultivation along the Carolina Low Country, to the Sonoran cuisines of "El Norte" of the American Southwest, with their base in the wheat flour tortilla. By the late eighteenth century and U.S. independence, the advent of the global food marketplace assured that "all Americans ate hybrid, creole diets that blended the techniques and ingredients of two or more cultures" (25), while the creole blends themselves remained distinctive to particular colonial regions. By the close of the colonial era, U.S. inhabitants "had departed substantially from the eating habits of their ancestors" (35). So far as the culinary world is concerned, "region" more than "ethnic identity" apparently defined one's choices, as eventually even the regional cuisine would be muted in the onset of mechanized production and faster means of transportation. But if the U.S. culinary scene, with its relatively rapid telescoping of food history, from "pouch" to plate, and in the short period of a "minute" of eternal time—about four centuries—actually borrowed, promiscuously, from everywhere, is it this catholicity of tastes alone that distinguishes it?

The only original cuisine that I have ever given the nation credit for is the "soul" food developed in the southern United States and delivered at the skillful hands of the African-American chef, in season and out. But there is not one chauvinism, we might suppose, that does not begrudgingly yield to revision and correction, even of one so primordial as eating, in the light of different data. While Africana cuisine constitutes an area of what I would call a "strong" culinary poetics (over and against "moderate" and "weak"), there are other luminous areas of the American foodway as well; in fact, one might profitably wonder what "chowder," for example, and "gumbo" have to do with each other, if anything, since both are made up of "crowds" on the palate, and how both of these, for that matter, might be analogous to "bouillabaisse"? None of these dishes are actually soups (I've not heard them called such), if we measure them against any of the clear Asian concoctions, those Indian, Japanese, Chinese, and Thai soups, those exquisite pure liquids of taste that could be bits of flower petals floating on a limpid surface of water. But they are certainly more soup than barbecued ribs, or a square of buttermilk cornbread, or a coconut-coated orange cake with a thimble of rum secreted in it. These kinds of stew, which cross their wires between liquid and solid and the delicious blend of this and that might be as close as we come to the concept and execution of Everyman's *folk* food—the pepperpot, for instance, turns up in the vocabulary of Philadelphia cuisine, as well as that of Barbados,[86] and according to Bajan folklore, has been known to endure across generations! Perhaps these foods, as well as their "pouch" kin, argue, gently, for a common human ancestry, but none of the sources that I have examined here have gone that far. Nevertheless, I should like to put the question on the table.

If American foods demonstrate a kind of conceptual creolité, then we will not be very surprised that this view of the cuisine approximates the linguistic home of the theorization of creole, both in what certain foods are *called* and in what they contain. "Creole" perfectly names the linguistic "misreading" and adaptation—the humorous corruptions that yielded "Yucatan," for example[87]—that historians attribute to Atlantic creole formations,[88] from which the concept derives. The languages that sprang up from fifteenth-century trading practices between European and African operatives along the Atlantic littoral have been described by linguists and historians as creative blends that facilitated commercial relations, as William Pietz puts it, "between members of bewilderingly different cultures."[89] These meetings, in their growing significance in configuring the modern world, would, by definition, alter the foodways of social subjects directly affected by the new commerce. *The Oxford Companion to Food* suggests that creole cuisine—distinguished from "variant foods within a given tradition" and from "diaspora foods"—comes about, however, in the "conjunction of radically different food traditions" (226), which would drive the concept back many centuries—"perhaps even millennia." Even though the most well-documented creole cuisines follow the European route of expansion into modernity, the idea that the creoles are synonymous with conjunctural patterns goes a long way to explain, perhaps, their diverse savors and palates. Alan Davidson's repertory of the conjunctive scenes of creole in-ludes: Portuguese-Brazilian, Mexican, Filipino, French-Vietnamese, Nonya (Chinese-Malaysian), Chinese-Indian-European in Mauritius, British-Eastern United States, black-American Indian-English in the southern United States, Indian-Pacific Island in Fiji, and American-Japanese-Chinese-Hawaiian in Hawaii (226). The Americas, in their stunning cultural variety, "became in time a mirror of history, the names of its dishes reflecting the medley of its peoples, regions, wars, places and even occupations" (FH, 252).

If we can find the "first truly American dish" (252), then it began its journey as a bastardization. "Chowder"—both the New England and Man-hattan variety—is identified by the historians as a crack at *chaudière*, the large pots that French fishermen, in the waters south of Newfoundland, used for the making of fish or clam stews. Tannahill places this Ur-food "event," with fishermen of many countries, long before the Pilgrim estab-lishments in the East and posits a proto-Yankee fisherman," who, in his "polyglot get-togethers ashore, between fights," learned about chowder. These first chowders were without milk and potatoes, but the stores of ships did offer possibilities in the biscuit, salt pork, and onions to cook along with the fish (252). Davidson identifies the *chaudière* as an iron pot, which French settlers carried to the Maritime Provinces of Canada (*OCF*, 182), and from their encounters with the Canadian Micmac Indians, they cultivated a taste for the native clam; Davidson conjectures that this "combination of European technology with American foodstuffs was happening at many places more or less simultaneously, so that there could be no way of telling where the first real 'clam chowder' was made" (182). In any event, need be-came the mother of culinary innovation, as the latter must have traced, as well, a very thin line between eating and starvation.

What Davidson might identify as a variety of "diaspora food," in certain cases, the foods of non-coerced immigrants, introduced different national cuisines to the American kitchen—the apple pie of the English, the *koekjes* or cookies of the Dutch, their coleslaw (from *kool*, or cabbage and *sla*, or salad) and waffles (*FH*, 252). But the medley stretches through the vegetable and meat repertoire, from asparagus, to snickerdoodles, spoon bread, and hush puppies to jambalaya, Boston baked beans, Moravian sugar cake, and

Swedish meatballs (252–53). It is actually true that hominy—"ripe maize, whole or reduced to grits" (223)—was once a familiar pattern of the diet in the colonial Northeast and was not confined to the southern regions; in fact, the combination of hominy, succotash ("fresh or dried kernels cooked with beans"), and cornpone ("a thick, unleavened maize pancake") were the Easterner's "basic grain dishes" (223). But the foodway, sooner or later, breaks down virtually every presumption that we more or less entertain about culinary cartography, as French cooking influences not only infiltrated the New Orleans field following the War of Independence and the Louisiana Purchase, but were deftly wielded by black kitchen servants, who "injected an entirely new gusto into the self-conscious world of classical French cooking" (253). While the left-overs from the tables of affluence, including black-eyed peas, turnip tops, ham hock, and chitterlings, entered the culinary economy of the bonded, they would be transformed into the delicacies of "soul food." (In *Vibration Cooking,* Vertamae Smart-Grosvenor, writing one of the earliest contemporary travelogues of black cuisine,[90] relates a delightful story about eating in Paris: on an evening, friends of hers, taking her out to a fancy restaurant in the city, were "really dying" for her "to taste this enjoyable rare dish." When the food arrives—"Well thank you Jesus," she thinks—it is only chitterlings in the form of a sausage, or *andouillette.* On an evening that must have been similar in many respects to the one that Smart-Grosvenor narrates, I sat down to dinner with a good friend in Paris a few years ago and enjoyed one of the finest, most succulent pig's feet—that didn't quite look like the one from home—that I've ever eaten; I have since discovered that the Catalan board, by way of fine restaurants in Barcelona, for example, offers a version of pig trotters that drove me back to this kitchen more than once. In fact, both ventures were "up" to the "soul" kitchen, which could take, in some cases, a lesson in "packaging" from the all-dollar-conscious market—how to "Madison avenue" your product and "gussy" it up to the height of style.)

Even though one's food habits are, in certain respects, sacrosanct to her, this American variety of the board would suggest the great range of the edible: perhaps the only "law" of food that prevails is based on the "ancient cultural logic" of the "domesticated series—cattle-pigs-horses-dogs."[91] As Jack Goody explains it, "taboo is associated with inedibility to give the formula 'edibility is inversely related to humanity' . . . so that 'the food system' can be seen as a 'sustained metaphor on cannibalism'" (155). The more proximate the substance is to humanity the less edible it is. Within the parameters of this cultural logic, the colonial scene, for all its interethnic struggle and conflict, appears to have been an early "contact zone" of the culinary; the expansion of trade throughout the colonial world, writes Donna Gabaccia, "guaranteed the circulation of at least some crops and foods well beyond their geographical origins, and well beyond the cultural group most familiar with their cultivation, processing and cooking" (*WWE*, 25). These trading patterns, early on, argue that "French, English, Spanish, African, and native had ample opportunities to begin tasting and experimenting with one another's foods" (25).

John Gilmore traces similar patterns of creolité in Caribbean cuisine, which could well constitute a metaphor for pan-Caribbean cultures more widely speaking, or "the development of an intricate and uniquely Caribbean cultural pattern out of a wide range of elements, European, African, Asian, brought from other parts of the world."[92] If peanuts and hot peppers "were important in the indigenous cooking of the Caribbean," then its staple item is the cassava, "which never became as widely diffused as the potato" (163). As far as I can tell, cassava is much more widely consumed in Caribbean communities than in those of the United States, but the amazing "Hoppin John," which I first tasted in Fulham, London, awhile ago now, appears to be at least one Africana link across the Diaspora and perhaps directly to the African Continent. As I learned to prepare it from a close Jamaican friend, the dish was made up of red beans (Gabaccia reports cowpeas as a possibility) and rice. (Jessica Harris, in *The Welcome Table*, provides two separate recipes, back to back, one for "Hoppin John," which calls for black-eyed peas in her version, and one for red beans and rice.[93] Furthermore, Harris conjectures a link between "Hoppin John" and a Senegalese dish called *thiébou niébé;* prepared with beef, rather than smoked pork—as some versions include—the Dakarian *thiébou niébé* does have the peas and the rice [106].) The trick, which I have never successfully imitated, requires the most careful calibration of rice-beans-water ratios and proportions so that the rice, once done, has every grain "standing lonely." Jamaican master chefs know exactly the right moment to introduce rice to the simmering pot of beans so that the duo finishes with *both* enough moisture *and* the discretion of the rice grains. Perhaps one of the world's most beautiful dishes, it is also among the most succulent and especially savory when served up, hot and lush, with a pot of Jamaican fried chicken. Requiring two days to prepare, these cut-up slices of whole chicken, heavily flavored with salt and pepper, are left to marinate overnight in a mess of tomato, onion, and bell-pepper wedges. A stock is concocted of these cultigens in a tomato sauce (or ketchup, if you're on the run) and water, which is placed on low heat, while the cook fries the chicken pieces fairly rapidly until evenly brown, then places the pieces in the stock, now at even lower heat, for the long afternoon simmer. Because our Crookham Road flat was not equipped with refrigeration, I suddenly understood, Spring 1969, what the *practical* import of all that salt and pepper was, in addition to their flavoring value, working through all those juices—they preserved the meat at room temperature in the event that refrigeration were not available, and for the longest time in the world, in fact, for most of the time, it would not have been. So here was a genuine lesson in the late twentieth century about the uses to which salt and pepper had been put for generations of gourmands! The bonus, of course, was the rich satisfaction of this particular board.

It is quite probable that rice-cultivating districts in West Africa, from which "a significant proportion of the slaves of the Carolina Low Country came" (*WWE*, 30), disseminated their populations throughout the African Caribbean as well as the southern tier of the northern colonies. Gabaccia argues that evidence would suggest that colonial planters in North America consciously drew their labor pool from these sites, once rice cultivation was established in the Low Country during the eighteenth century. In any case, the "African techniques of sowing, flailing, and storing rice persisted into the nineteenth century" (30), as African cooks evolved the "rice kitchen" of the Georgia and Carolina coasts. The rice that appeared daily on the planter's table, however, was apparently not the "Hoppin John" of the bonded class of eaters. But if rice *pilau* and those separate grains are close in texture, then a kind of "intertextuality" was taking place here that we have not suspected before. The rice *pilaf* or *pilau* of the region was prepared by black cooks, as well as its ragouts and daubes (31, see also *OCF*). It turns out that the "standing lonely" grains of rice that appear in "Hoppin John" identify a Middle Eastern method of cooking that means "every grain remains separate," or pilaf/pilau (*OCF*, 606). This method of preparation, then, recurs, not surprisingly, across the zones of diasporic cuisine, as well as other regions of taste, but the mix will differ, as will the term itself. Davidson offers lamb and vegetables, for instance, as one of the pilau combinations.

The pepper and the peanut that Gilmore identifies as key ingredients in Caribbean cuisine apparently "returned" to New World sites, including the Low Country, by way of sub-Saharan Africa, where the crops had been transplanted and successfully cultivated. Ships' stores also brought from the Continent the "seeds of benne (sesame) and African yams and watermelons" (*WWE*, 31), all of them entering the foodways of black and white consumers in the region. Interestingly, some students of regional cooking have attributed "the coastal taste for hot, peppery flavors in local seafood dishes to the hands of generations of African-American cooks" (31). If this interpretation is plausible, as Gabaccia advances it, then it may be attributed to the fact that the English and French settlers of this region of the Americas were not aware of a particular combination of tomatoes, onions, and hot peppers (32). The combination appears to be one of the crucial signatures of Africana cuisine, variously applied to a range of dishes, from Jamaican fried chicken, to pepper pot, to the *sofrito,* which Spivey describes as "a basic sauce loaded with onions, tomatoes, peppers, herbs, spices, and meat" (*PCWK,* 222) and which is tracked, in her narrative, through Puerto Rican culinary development. But it is the *spiciness* that distinguishes this cuisine from other zones of global taste. The Asian food families, especially certain Thai and Indian cuisines and Japanese wasabi, are quite capable of tearing up the taste buds on the tip of the tongue and ventilating the nasal passages all the way up through the roots of the hair, but the Africana spiciness, at least to my palate, seems somewhat subtler and more thoroughgoing. There is, in any case, a decided difference, perhaps due to the kinds of peppers that are introduced to the dish, as well as the "dialectic" of flavors that surround and commingle with them. This signature of piquancy and hotness even gives way to a brand of humor, as among African-Americans, for example, a very funny story circulates about "the man with the hot sauce." Considered an indispensable accoutrement to "any well-set African-American table," hot sauce, writes Jessica Harris, may be prepared at home, as Caribbean and Brazilian chefs do (*WT,* 89). In Harris's estimation, "African-American cooking always uses the freshest possible ingredients and it's always oral. . . . Finally, it's got to be well-seasoned. It's not always hot, but it's always spicy" (83).

The taste tetrahedron that Sidney Mintz notes in *Sweetness and Power* (229–30) shows "salty" and "sour" at the opposing ends of the vertical axis of tastes and "sweet" and "bitter" on the opposing sides of the horizontal axis; the four primary tastes generate unmarked binary dispositions along the edges of the tetrahedron and unmarked tertiary dispositions on the surface. Exactly where "hot" or "spicy" might be interpolated within this geometry of the palate constitutes a puzzle to my mind—is it already incorporated in the four apices of Henning's tetrahedron, since it might appear as a companion to any of the tastes, or would a different diagram need to be derived in order to accommodate it? "Hot" does not always oppose "cold," since we cannot quite imagine what a "cold" food would be, inasmuch as "cold" in this context simply marks a hiatus—a dish that should be "warm" or the caloric "hot" that is no longer that. The "cold cut," of course, describes something else altogether different (the uncooked: the crudité), which could well support the mandates of any of the primary tastes, just as the counter-intuitive cold soup could be "hot" insofar as it was spicy. Because "hot" is not clearly oppositional to "sweet"/"bitter" and "sour"/"salty," it seems to pose an interesting problem for the lexicon of taste.

A combination that I rather reject (since I cannot really imagine turning away from a fine meal of any sort) as an untenable contradiction—sweet vinaigrette, for instance—easily enters the repertoire of certain Chinese and Caribbean/diasporic dishes. Devinia Sookia's *Caribbean Cooking*[94] carries, from the Grenadian kitchen, a recipe for "sweet and spicy chicken," for example, whose marvelous ingredients call for a finely chopped onion, two finely chopped scallions, one fresh hot chopped pepper, and a half table-spoon of brown sugar; the recipe also calls for one peeled and deseeded christophene (also known as cho-cho, choyote, chayote and a tropical squash), ground black pepper, and two crushed garlic cloves, etc. The brown sugar in the concoction must give the effect of a kind of sweet, spicy, barbecue sauce, which is favored in many parts of the mid-South, as in Memphis, my hometown. (For that matter, Ntozake Shange brings "bitter" and "sweet" to the same side of the culinary mix (would this combination of tastes be analogous to bittersweet chocolate?) when she suggests adding a third cup of syrup, or two tablespoons of honey, or three tablespoons of molasses to her stock for collard greens.)[95] If spiciness and pungency are hallmarks of African/diasporic cuisine, then they also recur with consider-able frequency, according to Jessica Harris's *Africa Cookbook*,[96] throughout the African Continent. If we are trying to identify cultural patterns and processes by the foodways and taste preferences, then how do we explain this seeming affection for spice, across oceans and centuries of radical change? Certainly we cannot mean that "biological imperatives," or an "ancestral predisposition," as Mintz puts it, are at work between the popu-lations of the Continent and the Diaspora, nor is it by any means settled that "culturally conventionalized norms" would obtain between these vastly disparate geopolitical coordinates, and for sure, the culinary *differences* are as substantial as the similarities. And lastly, the foodway interrupts the inevitable nexus of our late modernism between "ontology" and "epis-temology," inasmuch as the Africana/creole cuisine complex may be en-tered, as we have seen, by any other culinary community, just as the reverse of this proposition has yielded in the modern world a dynamic exchange of ideas and practices around the board. That said, it does appear, however, that we can specify, more or less, stylistic signatures of an African-Atlantic taste field that show certain consistent features of address—mutatis mutandis—to the cuisine art. In any case, working these patterns through systematically will pose a substantial challenge to the investigator.

Jessica Harris, in *The Africa Cookbook,* identifies a couple of those signals that include the deep fry and the grill, in addition to the cooking with spices and herbs (86). About her recipe for Nigerian *akara*—or the white bean fritter, which is traditional to western Nigeria—Harris notes that this food is one of "the defining dishes of the African-Atlantic world," just as "frying in deep oil, a traditional West African cooking technique, is one of the hallmarks of the food of the African-Atlantic world" (86). One of several types of akara, "the most common and best-known is the white bean and palm oil akara." The bean fritter may also be prepared with okra—the "akara awon"—with egusi (or melon seeds, used to thicken soups and stews), or the "akara Ijesha" of the Yoruba community. The basic ingredients that stretch across all the variations of this dish include onions and habañero chilis. While salads, "in the Western sense," are johnnies-come-lately to African cuisine (119), at least one of them invites pause, insofar as it might boast a global kinship, from the South of France, to the American South—Harris's "yam salad" resembles American "potato salad" resembles "salade niçoise" (121). The traditional African yam is not the New World sweet potato, or yam, but is "closer in taste" to the white potato (44). Widely consumed in various parts of the world, the yam has been cultivated on the Continent, according to archaeological record, for thousands of years; this tuber, for Ghana's Akan peoples, has engendered a species of celebration, and in Guinea, the yam is so essential a feature of the diet "that the word . . . is a synonym for the verb 'to eat'" (72–73). In its transatlantic passage, the yam appears "as the verb *nyam* among the Gullah-speaking peoples of the Sea Islands [the U.S. Low Country] and in Jamaica" (73). Harris's "yam salad" includes onions, peppers, and (homemade) mayonnaise, but may be complemented with European elements, as it usually is in the States—"minced sweet gherkins [or sweet pickles], thinly sliced celery, and chopped hard-boiled eggs" (121). The salad board—encompassing tomato and okra, beet, avocado, grapefruit, and papaya—is appearing more frequently in African cuisine and probably attests, as vividly as any other development, to the cross-cultural exchange along the foodway. The "colonial salad" speaks to another kind of African exchange (118), but one that must be taken into account in sketching the picture.

The traditional West African meal is built around a "center" so substantial that the "edge" or "periphery" is muted, often disappears, or is only fairly recently added, as in the case of salads. Harris distinguishes between "soups" here and what she calls "soupy stews," and if I am right about this,

the New World "soupy stew" appears at several culinary sites—I would offer the far-flung "clam chowder" as an uncustomary example—and qualifies as one of the most popular and inventive of the food types in the creole
complex. Harris's concoctions in this family run a gamut from the "green
mealie soup" of South Africa (123–27), to a culinary range based on the
pepper and the peanut prototypes of Nigeria. Most of these stews appear
with a variety of meat possibilities—chicken, fish, goat, mutton, game, and
organ meats—and many of them come with a recommendation: "be fiery
hot with spices" (124). The latter include peppersoup spice, peppercorns,
ground black pepper, and red chilis. The chicken groundnut soup, a favorite Ghanaian cuisine, may also be prepared with fish. The New World
gumbos, which give the appearance and the taste of a kind of food termi-
nus—"everything" comes into the mix—are precisely analogous to the
continental "soupy stew," and the ubiquitous pepperpot, from Philadelphia, to Bridgetown, to Port of Spain, is the most hilariously capacious dish
on the board.

The peppers that appear in these dishes are so crucial that Harris devotes
a whole chapter of *The Africa Cookbook* to "condiments" alone, suggesting
that the latter "are the name of the game on the continent generally, from
the harissa of Tunisia to the *pili pili* sauce of Angola to the peppersoup mix
of Nigeria" (128). The culinary range in this category is quite astonishing,
from Egypt's garlic dressing, to Ethiopia's spiced butter (or *nit'ir quibe*), to
the chili pastes of Tunisia and Algeria, the chilis of Senegal and preserved
lemons of Morocco, the *atjars* of South Africa, through the West African hot
sauces, toward the sweet end of the spectrum with *poires à l'aigre-doux*
(Tunisia's sweet and sour pears) and South Africa's apricot chutney. A West
African spice mixture, which offers a versatile dressing for stews and grilled
meats, commingles peppercorn, Nigerian ground ginger, grains of paradise,[97] red pepper flakes, and cubebs (small Indonesian berries) (149). A
peppercorn mixture calls for Tellicherry peppercorns (from India's Tellicherry pepper; 68), as well as three other varieties of peppercorn—white,
pink, and freeze-dried (150). More than one food writer recommends that
the chef, in handling "live" peppers, exercise considerable caution, even to
the point of wearing rubber gloves, and in one case, the writer even goes so
far as to suggest that the peppers may be soaked awhile (at least an hour) in
cold salted water in order to modulate the bite (Sookia, *CC*, 16). As the East,
generally, is the cradle of several varieties of pepper—from putchuk or cos-
tus, to spikenard (of biblical fame),[98] and the long pepper and the black
pepper—the cultural dialectic that these Old World cultures have evolved
with the crucial aid of these cultigens remains, as might be said, "a story

with legs." That relationship between a natural sequence of "givens" in the flora and fauna of a geographical location reveals the whole astonishing economy of the cultural operation—of "culture," grounded in the agricultural practices of cultivating and tilling, and of "culture" as what is made from what is given.[99] Perhaps the most eloquent testimony of this intricately calibrated dance is the cuisine, which makes the maker, even as it is made.

The Africana grill, in its often exquisite simplicty, probably takes this writer home, as it were, more completely than any other item on the board, especially when the fishes of the sea are at stake. It is fair to say that I have spent a number of years of my adult life looking for fillets of buffalo fish, which I have found in only one location outside my mother's Memphis kitchen, and that is Atlanta's International food mart, located in Decatur, Georgia. This first food in my memory, alongside chitterlings, Sunday chicken, homemade vanilla ice cream (my father simply called it "cream"), the perennial collard, with a vinegar dressing, black-eyed peas, ham hock, peach cobbler, etc., were not known to me, growing up, as "soul food." It was, as one of Jessica Harris's interlocutors observes, "just food." It was only as an adult, when this culinary fare were stacked up against other food cultures, that I needed to identify my own neighborhood of the cuisine. I would not be surprised to discover that my enormous appreciation for caviar and blini and for sushi/sashimi blends likely commenced with that first deep-fried buffalo wedge whose aroma I can nearly perfectly recall. Though the Memphis region of the Africana diet was not big on the fish stews, the gourmands of my first world never saw a fish that they did not like—from croakers to sardines and tuna. Fresh, grilled sardines on the Mediterranean would interest quite a few residents of my old neighborhood, not least because of their size; at El Port de Selva, Spain, for example, they run nearly as large as porgies and just as fine.

From the Continental fish cuisine, Harris concocts recipes that cut across the spectrum of the fishes, and one in particular arrests the eye—the Ivory Coast's grilled fish (whole sea bass) is placed over a wood-burning fire and is accompanied by a spicy tomato-based sauce, made up of peanut oil, hot and bird chilis, and freshly ground pepper (*AC*, 215). Other fish in this selection include variously prepared sardines, the butterfish of Senegal, Benin crab, Togo fried oysters, Senegalese gumbo, and a Senegalese rice and fish stew. Few of these recipes can be practiced by consumers who do not live near fresh-fish sources, or transportation networks that would bring such fare closer to hand, nor are they likely—for urban apartment dwellers in this case—to repeat the grill. But the food writers suggest how one might get closer to this simple good food when she must make do with frozen fish. Devinia Sookia's recommended marinades might be enlisted to the cause.

The fish combinations in which pepperpot is consumed would suggest that this fare is a quintessential candidate for oral expressive culture, because, as Alan Davidson notes, "No one recipe can be identified as 'the recipe'" (*OFC*, 596), as we suspect that quite a few dishes would fit this description; in my own experience as chef, it is true that a dish that I have made from a recipe does not come into its own until I have "forgotten" the guidelines. The recipe actually assures nothing, except that you will reach the *vicinity*, whereas the *house* that you are looking for is arrived at by skill and competent sensory equipment. I pause at the pepperpot as a special case because it (1) offers the "centrality" that a number of global cuisines demonstrate, (2) exemplifies a type of culinary economy that blends nutritive elements, pungent taste, and appealing "looks" to the gourmand, (3) articulates a repertoire of "neighbors" in the stews and gumbos that bring the flesh and/or fish, the cultigen, and the herb together in a stunning orchestration of textures and tastes, and (4) seems a perfect intersectional moment for the sociality of the board in its colloquial, improvisational, and witty insistence. If food is a politics, as it always is, this one is a democrat. Davidson identifies two types of pepperpot—one from the various Caribbean islands and one that turns up in eighteenth-century Philadelphia to which locus it might have migrated from the islands. The Philadelphia version of pepperpot early on incorporated sea turtle meat, then later on adopted tripe "as a less expensive substitute" (*OFC*, 596). Harris reports that the dish used to be called "Philadelphia Gumbo" and that it "was hawked as a restorative by African-American women whose cry was 'Peppery pot! Nice and hot! Makes backs strong, makes lives long!'" (*WT*, 259). Diane Spivey's explanation meets up with Alan Davidson's eighteenth century and both Davidson's and Harris's City of Brotherly Love, by way of Helen Bullock's *Williamsburg Art of Cookery* and a recipe, dated 1780, for something called, oddly enough, "George Washington Cake." This recipe is connected with the First President and Valley Forge and the winter of colonial discontent about which every schoolgirl learns; Washington's head chef, it is said, invented this dish, concocted of odds and ends, the scraps and left-overs—"tripe together with ground peppercorns and a few stray beans and carrots" (*PCKW*, 232–33). The aroma alone "was enough in itself to comfort the men," and when they actually consumed it, "the troops were indeed fortified" (232–33). That might have been enough right there, at the turning point in the War of Independence, for Washington to think that he had hit "cake." But in any event, he is said to have thought that the concoction was a "dish for heroes," and he was so pleased with it that he insisted that it take the name of "Philadelphia Pepper Pot" in honor of the chef's hometown (232–33). Even if the citation of the recipe for "George Washington Cake" did not identify that fabled army cook, I suspect that we know who he might have been—one of DuBois's early "Philadelphia Negro(es)," with a taste for spice; some relative, perhaps, who had come up from the islands and passed on the foodway, or perhaps the chef himself had traveled with it. Good food for a novel, Spivey's retailed story highlights, nonetheless, the kind of narrative supplement that tracks with the foodway.

All the pepperpot recipes carry a plentiful helping of oil and butter, peppers, chilis, cumin, parsley, and at least one type of fish (Spivey's recipe calls for a half pound of cod or other boneless white fish), carrots, squash, beef and chicken stock (234). Sookia's version shows three pounds of boiling chicken, a half pound of pig's trotter, three pounds of boned pork or beef, the perennial run of peppers, but adds a cinnamon stick, malt vinegar, brown sugar, and cassareep (*CC*, 23). The juice that is extracted from grated cassava and flavored with cinnamon, cloves, and brown sugar, cassareep is considered an essential ingredient of the pepperpot. Dorinda Hafner's "Okra and Seafood Gumbo,"[100] Danella Carter's "Shrimp Creole,"[101] and Ntozake Shange's "Uncle Eric's Gumbo,"[102] all demonstrate a surprising similarity of cooking method to the pepperpot, insofar as these kin dishes insist on variety in their one-stop alimentation. The gumbos are good for mixing pork, fish, and fowl, as Shange's Carolina gumbo calls for a whole chicken, a half-dozen crabs, shrimp, lobster, scallops, oysters, *and* clams, "if you like." The pepperpot, the gumbo, and other big-capacity cuisine were not invented for people "flying solo." Like the Thanksgiving turkey that lasts all year, even when one is coupled, these dishes are, by definition, a collective and shareable board; perhaps the whole notion of co-operation and participation—an essential human idea—cannot be imagined without the cuisine. We are not going to say now that "man is good"—there is too much evidence that the jury is still out on *that* one—but s/he is certainly wo/man with the cuisine and its mandated field of manners and pleasure, just as its induced withdrawal, in the tragic politics of food that besets the world, is the call to war and doom. But for now we traverse the pleasure side of the culinary axis.

Wayne Robinson's *African-American Travel Guide*[103] offers a "grand gastronomic tour" in each section of its sightings along the Africana foodway, from Los Angeles to Atlanta, from San Francisco to Halifax and Toronto. A guidebook to nineteen North American cities, Robinson's protocol is a near-loner in its field and will likely generate an even wider circumference of loci that may be of interest to students and researchers of topics in Africana/diasporic cultures. The photograph on the cover of the guide features a pan along a block of Beale Street that captures B. B. King's Blues Club in the foreground. Travelers who intimately know this block of the city of Memphis will be reminded of B. B. King's career beginnings at WDIA radio in the city, of the Elvis Presley Memorial nearby, of the Lorraine Motel, where MLK lost his life, about a ten-minute car ride from B. B. King's place, at what is now the National Civil Rights Museum, and of the Mississippi River itself, flowing just behind, about two blocks due west. Memphis is a good place to start the run, inasmuch as the traveler has easy access from it to the Deep South in one direction, to the Midwest and the West in another, and off I-40, across middle and eastern Tennessee, a sharp left turn toward the Northeast of the country. Robinson's "Soul Food" section for the Memphis area lists the Four Way Grill, and from my recall of what was, years ago, the big-easy atmosphere of this watering hole, the Four Way offered fine release from the straight lacings of proper Protestant black Memphis. The food was good, too. A "grill" in this culture zone is to this consumer what the "bistro" is in another; the cuisine of the grill tends toward the familial—smothered pork chops with gravy, meatloaf dishes, and occasionally, a nice piece of roast prime rib, with creamed potatoes and small green peas, and ample other side dishes that run the vegetable range. These days, salads are far more common in the grill genre than they used to be, as the community's dietary patterns have shifted radically, away from high-cholesterol ingestion. But perhaps the most substantial sign of the grill's historic meaning in an urban topography is the jukebox and the era of the 45 rpm. In the atmosphere of low lights and quiet talk, with a beer on draft, the young socius took a night out on the town, and in a family-centered, church-going community, such nights used to be news. In the semiotics of naming, the grill is a benchmark of tonal shifts of behavior and belief and in that regard harks back to the past. While the black-owned restaurant today shows a greater differentiation of menu, the grill constitutes one of its archaeological layers.

South out of Memphis, the drive across the state of Mississippi down to New Orleans can be accomplished in about eight to ten hours. One of the nation's most complex and fascinating sites, this city, especially if one is standing at any intersection in the old Latin Quarter, does not feel like the South at all, even the new New one, and not like most of the nation's cities. If the United States were a family, New Orleans would be the "odd" child in the mix—the one with the brilliant mind, a whimsical attitude, and an ut- terly unpredictable sartorial manner. The heir of the meaning of "creole" in its current usage, New Orleans belongs to the "strong" school of culinary poetics. Robinson's guide lists one African restaurant on its New Orleans food tour—boasting "traditional West African cuisine. Beef, chicken, lamb and seafood entrées" (190)—a couple of Caribbean restaurants that show Caribbean/creole cuisine, and in one instance, "Mediterranean, African, French, and Caribbean cuisine" (190). The longest food listings belong to the category "creole," and in the case of Dooky Chase's, the key combina- tion is expressed as "African-American, French, and Spanish entrées" (191). There are nearly as many Soul Food entries, as some of the restaurants double up as creole, as in Praline Connection and Gospel and Blues Hall (one of the most colorful monikers of the guide) that describes its fare as "creole-soul cuisine" (191). At Café Baquet, the gourmand may have "cat- fish jourdiane," though it is difficult to say what "jourdiane" is telling me. But that must be much to the point of the advertisement—one must go find out! Danella Carter's "Palatable New Orleans,"[104] in its array of fish preparations from "Barbecued Shrimp" to "Oyster Loaf," would suggest fresh fish as the primary basis of the New Orleans board, even though Robinson lists only two restaurants under the category of Seafood. The col- orful patchwork of New Orleans food simply tells me that all the foodways converge here and withstand no contradiction—in other words, "creole- soul" names the same thing, or two things that are neckbone to neckbone.

Robinson's guide tends to follow the tracks of the old migratory route from the South to the Midwest as the southern sojourner must have trav- eled decades ago.[105] The pattern was so predictable that the cities of Chi- cago and Detroit, at least for their black communities, became northern versions of Mississippi, Alabama, and Georgia. But the guide listings for restaurants in Detroit suggest new folds in the pleat of culinary manners that now encompass "Cajun," "Caribbean," and "Vegetarian/Muslim" fare, and among Detroit's Soul Food restaurants, Edmund Place lures the traveler with "soul food in restored Victorian ambiance" (*AATG*, 114). In the case of the "Caribbean," our traveling gourmand can sample "tropical dishes that include plenty of fruits and vegetables from the Dominican Republic and Honduras" (114). Truth in advertising and questions of "authenticity" take on muted relevance concerning these listings because the more interesting problem is the way that "African-American" cuisine is *imagined, imaged,* and practiced in the wider world of social commerce and exchange and the manner of its participation in the convergence of the culture zones. The funny story of "Häagen Dazs" offers an example of the kind of playfulness and inventive possibility that I mean—Donna Gabaccia provides the details (*WWE*, 168–69), and a linguist friend confirms the report, that suggest the sheer folly of this name; I am told that you cannot even get this combination of vowels (an "a" with an umlaut next to an "a") in any language, including the Danish, which the name is supposed to mimic, but the ice cream's inventor, Reuben Mattus, felt that the consumer would eat it up, as it were, if he thought that he was getting something "foreign." I am not now claiming that deception is okay; that is not at issue, but, rather, how communities ride the waves of change and what strategies they adopt in handling the medium. I am interested instead in how the culinary works as an object of semiotic contemplation, as well as the meeting place of diverse sociocultural elements. I know no better place than the foodway as a lookout on the intersection. The listings that appear in Robinson's guide and how restaurants display themselves in their advertisements are as much a "reading" on this cultural process as they are a skeletal guide to selective foodways.

Chicago, as another field of culinary interest, now boasts two African restaurants—Ethiopian and Nigerian—an array of Caribbean restaurants, as Island Bar and Grill offers Cuban and Hawaiian cuisine on its menu, and Island Delites serves a "Kingfish escobeche" (*AATG*, 82), right beside curried goat, jerk chicken, and red snapper. I paused at "escobeche" because of its aural and visual similarity to "ceviche," one of my favorite dishes from the Spanish board. Davidson is not quite convinced, however, that "ceviche" derives from "escabeche," as some food historians have suggested, but he does acknowledge their rather astonishing lookalikeness (*OFC*, 282). In any case, "escabeche," of which I would suppose that the restaurant's "escobeche" is a variation, starts out as a fried fish that "has been allowed to cool and is then soused with a hot marinade of vinegar and other ingredients" (*OFC*, 282). Etymologically, the term derives from Persian/Arabic *sikbaj*, which means vinegar stew. Harris's *Africa Cookbook* (213) offers a concoction called "Sardines en escabech" (or *escabèche; scapece* in Italian, and *scabetch* in Algerian, *OFC*, 282), from Algeria. Devinia Sookia defines still another variation on the theme with her Bajan "Escovitch" that calls for three pounds of skinned and filleted red snapper (*CC*, 41). Chicago's numerous Soul Food restaurants include Gladys's, which, alongside Boston's Bob, the Chef's, is, historically, one of the Taj Mahals of soul food cuisine in the United States. "Atmosphere" is no small part of its appeal, as is the case with Atlanta's Daddy Burton's, Manhattan's Sylvia's, and Durham's Mama Dips.

Once, when an English teacher and girls' basketball coach at Verde Valley School in Sedona, Arizona, I was one of two van drivers and chaperones for the school's annual field trip project, the trip that was headed for the Deep South and Greenville, Mississippi, among other sites, by way of New Orleans. Though I had grown up two states east of Texas, I had no vivid idea how enormous it is until I had to drive through it. Every U.S. motorist should drive through Texas *once*—two days out of Albuquerque, we were *still* in Texas so that by now I believe that I have completed my Texas "propers." But I will stop long enough here to say that eating in San Antonio is worth the visit, just as Robinson's guide suggests the restauranteur's ingenuity in the creation of Hispanic blends: Dallas's Café Geko, for example, tinges its Caribbean cuisine "with south-of-the-border Mexican flavors" and lists its speciality as "conch chowder" (*AATG*, 97). Used loosely to describe "a wide range of large, single-shell molluscs" (*OFC*, 209), the conch is found in Caribbean waters; Davidson lists *Daube de lambis aux haricots rouge* (or a conch stew with red beans) and *matete de lambis* (or rice and conch stew) as two of its traditional preparations. Among Dallas's soul food stops, the Soul Embassy Café offers fried green tomatoes and black-eyed pea soup on its menu, but the item that caught my eye in its protocol of presentation was something called the "Sunday Gospel Brunch" (*AATG*, 97). This particular variation on "brunch," already an acronym, creates yet another conceptual neologism by bringing "gospel" into the picture. Comically, a few of the restaurant listings in other cities offer a "jazz brunch" by contrast. The same strategy of naming applies in certain Los Angeles restaurants, as the lure, in this case, is star appeal: Los Angeles' Georgia, for example, is said to be "owned by Denzel Washington and Eddie Murphy, who occasionally drop by" (141), and Maurice's Snack and Chat in the city "is frequented by many of Hollywood's African-American performers" (142). Up California Route 1, San Francisco's Ethiopian Nyala offers a vegetarian buffet, as none of the advertisements for the Bay Area seem to have taken advantage of the sexy Pacific and the city's fabled wharves for dining. A stone's throw from Berkeley's Chez Panisse, the San Francisco restauranteurs might take a cue from L.A.'s cuisine hawkers by pitching to the "paparazzi" in the consumer. But subtlety, after all, has considerable appeal; one of San Francisco's entertainment sites, Slim's, for example, is tantalizingly explained: "Hours vary depending on shows," as most of the restaurant presentations here are short and spicy. As a genre of writing, the travel guide, I take it, blends self-presentation into the compiler's; it is difficult to decide if the information comes from the restaurant itself, or from a roaming intelligence, putting together a kind of cartography of places and events—but as I am reading these items, I have assumed that the "blank" authorship of the page—as if these lines of print were autotelic—is the outcome of an interlocked unit of needs that involves the guide writer and the chefs and owners in a mutually beneficial arrangement.

From California, across the continent to New York, the drive is four times Texas, but with a little help from my friends, I have accomplished the task round trip—in eight-hour bites and off for dinner and rest—within the compass of an American summer week, one way. The continental vista, from Tahoe, across the Rockies, offers a panorama of consumption of another kind, but sumptuous, nonetheless, in its sweeping appeal to the gaze. There is at least one dissertation waiting for Reno and one of the world's serious gambling cultures. Before 1996–97, I would not have believed, could not quite have imagined, that it was possible to mold the idea of a slot machine and games of chance into the very fabric of living, into the line of vision, but there is, as I say, at least one dissertation waiting for Reno. If the traveler has the time, he should stop off at Lincoln, Nebraska's Zoo Bar that used to feature (and perhaps still does) some of the nation's best Blues artists on the old 66 flat-out run, we might suppose, from coast to coast. Robinson's guide does not pick up any of these Western stops, but I would be curious to see what Robinson might make of Santa Fe and Taos, both of which present a face of complexity, comparable to New Orleans, but an altogether different flavor of a rough, unworked, and exquisite texture.

The last time I visited New York, I ate very well, but a body always eats well in the Apple, or *can*; during this particular itinerary, only weeks ago at this writing, I spent an impressive winter afternoon sampling single-malt scotches (a food stuff we've not touched on here) with a very knowledgeable and debonair interlocutor. The Aquavit was on the table that weekend, its kitchen wielded, I understand, by an Ethiopian chef, whose lamb on a sweet potato base and lobster roll are culinary marvels, rich and strange. The guide lists others, as Manhattan, not surprisingly, shows more African, Caribbean, and Soul Food locations than at any of the other sites. Well's celebrated "Chicken and Waffles" appears among the dishes, as this beloved spot, along Adam Clayton Powell Boulevard, is simply advertised as serving "traditional soul food." The African listings encompass cuisine from Nigeria to Senegal and Ethiopia, as the Caribbean spots offer a copious spread of jerks, grills, fries, curried meats, fritters, and stews, and the combos and trios of Africana culinary cultures.

From Ithaca, New York, about six hours north by west, the traveler enters the Annex, through the heart of Toronto. On the weekend that I visited this gentle city, the country was mourning the loss of one of its key political figures, Pierre Trudeau, at the same time, ironically, that Dominica's Prime Minister, Rosie Douglass, succumbed to heart failure. Antagonists in life, as

Toronto's black newspaper, *Share,* explained it, these two leaders-to-come had crossed swords in the turbulent sixties, and it is not clear to me that they were ever reconciled. In any case, it seems that Trudeau and Douglass, constantly linked in the headlines three decades ago, were destined to follow each other from beginning to end. Even though Edward Seaga, former Jamaican prime minister, was scheduled to visit the West End that Saturday, Eglington Street, the heart of it, along which course Toronto's black business district runs, showed no signs of unusual flutter and excitement. A fair number of small shops, eateries, and restaurants are located on Eglington, and one of these, Shanty's Restaurant, is listed in Robinson, as all the entries here feature African, Caribbean, and Cajun/creole cuisine. Sammy's New Orleans Creole, of the hundreds of restaurants that appear in the guide, is the only one that serves "alligator" (*AATG,* 292). We all know what an alligator is (sort of), but how does one *eat* one? Isn't that the creature of children's lore, of Disneyworld? And then I remember that there is an alligator I know, in J. M. Barrie's *Peter Pan,* the one who swallowed a clock, except that that one is a crocodile.[106] Alan Davidson enters just this confusion, as he explains that the alligator is "an animal now better known as food than its slightly larger relations, the various species of crocodile" (*OFC,* 11). The alligator is traditional to the New Orleans table and the waters of the Gulf, but fear of its extinction, Davidson points out, had given it protected status. Alligator farms now breed the species, and the meat itself is described as white and flaky, "resembling chicken or . . . flounder" (12). The advertisement for Sammy's does call the alligator a "cajun/creole," which places New Orleans right in the midst of Toronto. But even better, it connects on the vertical the South of the continent to the North of it and Peter's pans and Sammy's in a subtlety of drama that we tend to miss these times of the new that isn't always. But it seems to me that that is the way of the food— it enters the port, often unseen, unobtrusively, but like the weather, the climate, the slightest shift in the wind currents, it might well alter a mood, and what we believe and who we think we are. With the cuisine, we are "on" to something that we know like skin, as our sheer and democratic delight in it makes us each and all a congress of experts. The new cultural demographies of the African Diaspora, as we slowly, patiently map them, must always drop by the table, for here the interarticulatory logic of the *material* and the *symbolic* blends the universal and the particular at the same place—*inside* the one in the all.

1

Ellison's "Usable Past":
Toward a Theory of Myth

The occasion that invites this piece recalls for me certain decisive memories. Professor Elizabeth Phillips, my first instructor in American literature at the University of Memphis, returned one of my student themes one afternoon with this comment: "Why be content with the lightning bug when you can have the lightning?" I have no idea what I had written—lame, I suppose, in any case—but I saved the comment, might have even stored it in my dreams, and now, over three decades later, I know precisely what she meant. These notes on an American theme are written with Professor Phillips and the lightning in mind.

One of the critical strategies of that first course was to determine to what extent the American idiom had been driven toward precision since *Sister Carrie*. That nearly half a century separates Dreiser's first novel and *Invisible Man* is not so impressive an observation, except that between Dreiser and Ellison a radically new literary reality asserts itself, basically combative toward the past. Gass's notes on Borges's prose—its leanness, excision, lack of ornamental dress[1]—define in part the canon of taste that stamps modernist practice with the persistence of dogma. Accompanying these profound changes in aesthetic surface was the broader implication of shifts of angle in the very vision of art, or more precisely, the philosophical bases for a technology of text (perhaps most eloquently expressed in Borges's fictions of intangibility) conduced toward another kind of artistic performance which Ortega y Gasset locates in the theme of alienation:

> Analyzing the new style, one finds in it certain closely connected tendencies: it tends toward the dehumanization of art; to an avoidance of living forms ensuring that a work of art should be nothing but a work of art; to considering art simply as play and nothing else: to an essential irony; to an avoidance of all falsehood; and finally, towards an art which makes no spiritual or transcendental claims whatsoever.[2]

We have no exact name yet for "dehumanization" as a systematic mode of expression; perhaps "modernism" is the best we can do, but for sure, this deviant attitude toward the human problematic—this flight from it that Ortega determines as the goal of modernism—pursues a structural reality, even anticipates it, that consigns language itself to an area of the phenomenal, unprivileged among other things. If language is an act of concealment, condemned to obfuscation, then we should not be surprised, even if disappointed, that it talks to itself, about itself, imprisoned in an appropriate logological status.[3]

Ellison apparently saw what was coming at the end of the forties, when he completed *Invisible Man,* and responded in his acceptance speech of the National Book Award with characteristic rebellion. Wishing to avoid the "hard-boiled" idiomatic understatement of Hemingway—its "clipped, monosyllabic prose"—he found that, when compared to the rich babble of idiomatic expression around [him], a language full of imagery, gesture, and rhetorical canniness, it was embarrassingly austere.[4] His decision, then, to cast the grammar of the text in a mode contrastive to understatement is complemented by his refusal of the naturalist disposition:

> Thus to see America with an awareness of its rich diversity and its almost magical fluidity and freedom, I was forced to conceive of a novel unburdened by the narrow naturalism which has led after so many triumphs to the final and unrelieved despair which marks so much of our current fiction. (*NNA,* 198)

In repudiating the doctrine of naturalism, Ellison turned away from the influence of Richard Wright, the dominating presence of his apprenticeship (*NNA,* 198), and Dreiser, who had fathered the naturalist tradition among U.S. writers.

While Ellison would be the last to deny that his own literary procedure has been influenced by the dogmatizers of European modernism, he would also insist that his American experience, his Negroness, has mandated a literary form virtually unique in its portrayal of pluralistic issues. In order to capture the multiplicity of American experience, Ellison turned to the nineteenth century, toward Melville and Twain's "imaginative economy," where "the Negro symbolized both the man lowest down and the mysterious, underground aspect of human personality" (*NNA,* 201). This turning, which we view with unrelieved interest, is a remarkable decision because it reinforces a notion of the dialectical at a time when it is all but being driven out by theories of artistic objectivity. But Ellison feels too keenly, one imagines, the requirements of his own imposed alienation to raise it to an act of form and chooses, instead, the "ancestral imperative"[5] as the eminent domain of his own creative concern. The upshot is *Invisible Man* that remains, to my mind, one of the most influential American novels of the twentieth century. I can say with confidence that it would constitute a "first" on my own list of teachable subjects for reasons which, though obvious, may bear repeating: (1) Following a line of American fictions that had rendered "black" an item of sociological data or the subject of exotic assumptions, or yet, the gagline of white mischief, at best, its ambiguous "bi-play," *Invisible Man* addresses the issue as an exposition of modern consciousness. (2) Frustrating the tendency to perceive a coterminous relationship between the symbolic boundaries of black and the physical, genetic manifestation named black, *Invisible Man* recalls *Moby Dick* that stands Manichean orientation on its head. (3) Insisting that black American experience is vulnerable to mythic dilation, Ellison constructs a coherent system of signs that brings into play the entire repertory of American cultural traits. In order to do this, Ellison places the unnamed "agonist" on an historical line that reaches back through the generations and extends forward into the frontiers of the future. Thus, (4) the work withdraws from the modernist inclination to isolate issues of craft from ethical considerations. For Ellison, language does speak, and it clarifies selective experience under the auspices of certain figures-of-thought, unexpectedly applied to received opinions. My primary concern in these notes is to try to trace propositions three and four to some tentative conclusions.

Northrop Frye defined myth as "the union of ritual and dream in a form of verbal communication."[6] The term, however, has achieved such flexibility that it is menaced by meaning everything and nothing in particular, though Frye traces its origins and inflections from biblical and classical sources through the modern period (131–223). Any contemporary usage is haunted by the echo of specific mythic structures and Roland Barthes's caricature of contemporary mythologies in a dazzling display of linguistic demystification.[7] But Barthes's definition of myth as a "type of speech" releases us, at least for the moment, from certain inherited or monolithic notions of mythic form:

> Myth is not defined by the object of its message, but by the way in which it utters this message: there are formal limits to myth, there are no "substantial" ones. (109)

Myth, then, is a form of selective discourse since its life and death are governed by human history: "Ancient, or not, mythology can only have an historical foundation, for myth is a type of speech chosen by history: it cannot possibly evolve from the 'nature' of things" (110). Not confined to oral speech, myth can be constituted of other modes of signification, including written discourse, photography, cinema, reporting, sports, shows, publicity. Myth as form does not only denote the sacred object or event, but may also be viewed as the wider application of a certain linguistic status to a hierarchy of motives and mediations. Pursuing Saussure's well-known paradigm of signification (115), Barthes differentiates the semiological and ideological boundaries of myth in a way that can only be suggestive for our immediate purposes, for I am primarily concerned with *Invisible Man* as a literary countermyth of *good* intentions. Though from my own point of view, any countermyth is preferable to prevailing myth and is, therefore, good, I still emphasize the word to denote the particular difficulty there is in accepting Barthes's definition of myth as a type of speech, expressed by its intentions. Inevitably, some intentions are "more good" than others to the group wishing to appropriate them, and as Barthes's orientation leads into the ideological category of myth as an impoverishment of history, its nullification at the hands of the bourgeoisie, I would have to agree with him. Recognizing, then, the high danger of applying a term laden, a priori, with valuation that justifies it on the one hand and condemns it on the other, I can only proceed with caution.

What I find most suggestive in Barthes's argument is the distinction he enforces between the form of myth and the concept it borrows from particular historical order. We could say, following his lead, that mythic form is a kind of conceptual code, relying on the accretions of association that cling to the concept—"a past, a memory, a comparative order of facts, ideas, decisions" (117). A French army general, pinning a medal on a one-armed Senegalese, is not my idea of a joke, nor is it Barthes's, for that matter, and he uses it to illustrate an act of attenuation wherein the subject has become an item in the "store of mythical signifiers." In short, the visual image becomes a code of French imperial procedure and the biographical/historical implications of its subjects. It is a mode of shorthand in that the mythical signifier conceals as much as it reveals. In fact, in Barthes's example, the signifier cheats, for it tells far less than it shows. This spontaneous equation of form and concept occurs also in the literary myth whose extension, like the oral myth, is linear and successive. Barthes describes the process of identification:

> The elements of the form . . . are related as to place and proximity: the mode of presence of the form is spatial. The concept, on the contrary, appears in global fashion, it is a kind of nebula, the condensation, more or less hazy, of a certain knowledge. Its elements are linked by associative relations: it is supported not by an extension but by a depth

(although this metaphor is perhaps still too spatial): its mode of presence is memorial. (122)

It is this integrative paradigm of form and concept that is most interesting for specific application.

Returning to an initial metaphor which I used in one of my four propositions—Invisible Man standing on an historical line reaching back and forth—I think we can establish the central reason why the novel qualifies as myth. In Ellison's case, I would suggest that myth becomes a tactic for explanation and that the novel may be considered a discourse on the biographical uses of history. The preeminent element of form, Invisible Man's narrative unfolds through a complicated scheme of conceptual images that refer to particular historical order, but the order itself localizes in the metaphysical/personal issues of the narrative, which is then empowered to reveal both the envisioned structure of history and its fluid continuity. It seems to me that the themes of diachrony and synchrony properly apply here in that Invisible Man embodies the diachronous, spatial, continuing subject of particular historical depth or memory. In history, the individual is the key to both procedures, for he can arrest time, as the form of the novel does, and examine its related details in leisurely detachment, but he cannot escape it, either personally or historically, and is, therefore, detached only in a kind of suspended, temporary judgment. In short, through his activities, he is an image of man talking, furiously, unto death, lifting the weight of his aging flesh by the power of his tongue. Invisible Man confesses:

> So why do I write, torturing myself to put it down? Because in spite of myself I've learned some things. Without the possibility of action, all knowledge comes to one labeled "file and forget," and I can neither file nor forget. Nor will certain ideas forget me; they keep filing away at my lethargy, my complacency. Why should I be the one to dream this nightmare? Why should I be dedicated and set aside—yes, if not to at least *tell* a few people about it? There seems to be no escape. Here I've set out to throw my anger into the world's face, but now that I've tried to put it all down the old fascination with playing a role returns, and I'm drawn upward again. So that even before I finish I've failed (maybe my anger is too heavy, perhaps being a talker, I've used too many words). But I've failed. . . . I have been hurt to the point of abysmal pain. . . . And I defend because in spite of all I find that I love.[8]

Moving out of an infant inevitability toward a final one, Invisible Man embraces history as an act of consciousness. Paradoxically, history is both given to him and constructed by him, the emphatic identification of contempla-

tive and active modes, and his refusal of the historical commitment, to remember and go forward, is certain death. *Invisible Man* charts the adventures
of a black personality in the recovery of his own historical burden. This
restorative act, to get well and remember and reconstruct simultaneously, is
the dominating motif of the novel, and its various typological features support this central decision.

As the subject of recovery, Invisible Man must assume all, must take
upon himself the haunted, questioning, troubled, even self- subversive,
stance of one who insists on *telling* others. This telling fulfills a bardic task,
an oracular chore, and one would do well to refuse either, but pain compels
Invisible Man to talk. He calls it "nightmare" and essentially speaks to us
out of his own sustained bardic trance, while as an ignorant youth, he
spoke from the nightmare of others. We shall see shortly how these layers
or phases of speech work. In addition, Invisible Man is "on" to something
else in the quoted passages. The questions that he poses function on more
than one level: Rhetorically, they hustle on the ploys and motions of argument just as the interrogative formulation has done throughout the novel.
Then dramatically, the questions situate particular trouble. Uttered or held
back, they are often a symptom of pride and confusion, and Invisible Man
has had his share of both, but syntactically, the questions complement a
principle of iteration that distinguishes both the Prologue and the Epilogue, encircling the structure. This principle of iteration, if we look closely,
ratifies a decisive ambiguity beneath the surface symmetry of the text. From
the Epilogue, this passage excerpted in the initial quotation is suggestive:

> The very act of trying to put it all down has confused me and negated
> some of the anger and some of the bitterness. So it is that now I de-
> nounce and defend, or feel prepared to defend. I condemn and affirm,
> say no and say yes, say yes and say no. I denounce because though im-
> plicated and partially responsible, I have been hurt . . . to the point of
> invisibility. (*IM*, 437)

Each time a word or phrase is repeated, it comes back with a new twist of
meaning, an enhancement and echo, pursuing its ambiguity with passion.
This repetitive activity is one of "destructing," a flight from certainty toward systematic skepticism, in order to reconstruct the terrible complexity
of decision. But enhancement is an enrichment, even though it borders on
the tedious. Caring almost overmuch for linguistic entanglement, Invisible
Man threatens a vision of nausea and the love of detail as neurotic indulgence, but he recalls what he has said earlier about the "possibility of action" and determines to come out of his hole:

> Thus, having tried to give pattern to the chaos which lives within the pattern of your certainties, I must come out. I must emerge. (*IM*, 438)

I think we can take him at his literal word, though he is eloquently slippery, or conceptually athletic, with formulations in this passage. He must emerge: Spatially underground, he will come up into the light of day again with his dark-skinned self, a little more noble and fierce than when he entered. Sharp on punning, which has been called an "overpopulated phonetic space," Ellison recreates the illusion of a mind ordering its space, determining its motions, and this is the domain of invisibility.

The involvements of mind, its complicated calibrations in the heat of experience, point to the deeper structures of the text and, characteristically, pursue a pattern of interlocking image-clusters which emanate from the centrality of the underground. I would also impute to Ellison a circularity of influence that I think is at work in the depths of the text. The privileged geometrical version of modernist writers, circles have wrought miracles. There are rivers still flowing and young homeless boys still thumbing rides on the open road. What startles even more is that critics are still startled by these clever workings as though the repeat performance had imagined the thing on its own. Ellison, however, is not as enamored of his structures as his critics. As I recall, he doesn't mention circles or depths in interviews about the book,[9] confining himself to articulating its broad objectives, but Invisible Man cannily suggests how *he* wants his narrative read; reconciled to the chaos against which his "plan of living" has been conceived, he acquires a new sense of time:

> Under the spell of the reefer I discovered a new analytical way of listening to music. The unheard sounds came through, and each melodic line existed in itself, stood out clearly from all the rest, said its piece, and waited patiently for the other voices to speak. That night I found myself hearing not only in time, but space as well. I not only entered the music but descended, like Dante, into its depths. And *beneath the swiftness of the hot tempo there was a slower tempo and a cave and I entered it and looked around and heard an old woman singing a spiritual as full of Weltschmerz as flamenco.* (*IM*, 7)

The italicized passage is unquestionably explicit about direction, and in the event that anybody misses it the first time, Dante signalizes the pit as a return to traditional configurations of the underground, but the mental location of this geography of descent places these images out of public view and restores them to their initial status of private madness. In Dante, spatial appropriation is both visual and concealed, and the latter seems to be a repressed dimension. Invisible Man, by contrast, never allows us to forget that he is dreaming, reefer-induced, and abandons himself to the irresponsibility of the induced state. Playing on the notion of vision-in-dream-brought-on-by-other-power, he expresses himself in a mode akin to the enthusiastic, and the enthusiast sees whatever fantasies are brought to him. Thus, the dreaming mind is logically decentered as Invisible Man alludes to being, but there is, of course, a mind controlling all the time. The passage proliferates, foreshadowing the specific issues of heritage that come back to the narrative in a form of discourse more suitable to linear continuity.

The dream passages are "amazing" and involved, worked around patterns of transition and contrast that yoke disparate experience in contiguous order. Since the image-flow is both acoustical and visual, Invisible Man is liberated up to a phenomenology of sensory impressions that restore the state of innocence, like dreaming, a status of freedom. He is essentially disembodied as his mind empathizes ancestral time and space. It is notable, as well, that this entire passage takes place under the auspices of Louis Armstrong's music.

The architectonics at work here ensure that the points-of-transition in the dream state relate to specific historical and symbolic detail whose overriding influence is religious. The preacher's text on the "Blackness of Blackness" recalls the ritualistic patterns of enthusiastic worship. The call-and-response rhythms of the black church service entangle with a dramatization of unlocalized generational conflict that is in turn overtaken by a recent scene of political challenge and revolt. What this mental survey shows are the layers of conflict and renewal that Invisible Man must work through in a reversed order of things. Above ground, the dreaming mind, intruded upon by reality, does not dominate, except at peril to the individual. By having subconscious forces confiscate, with impunity, the normal order of differentiation and succession, Ellison suggests that the "truth" for Invisible Man is mobilized in a return to racial and cultural sources. This psychological economy of motives differentiates the interlocking elements of personality within a scene of temporal and spatial unfolding so that historical order or its illusion may be viewed as a survey of mental activity. But in order to actuate these mental resources or to possess the dream material beyond individual isolation, Invisible Man must submit to the dream censor, to gazing, quite consciously, at the crux of his motivations and their consequences: "It goes a long way back, some twenty years. All my life I had been looking for something, and everywhere I turned someone tried to tell me what it was" (IM, 13) shows not only hypotactic order and the deliberate selection of boundaries of experience that it implies. We are introduced, quickly, to the apparent orientation of his biography, but the sentences also enforce a notion of ironic detachment. In order to justify it, Invisible Man deploys the enriched details only implied from the opening lines in a systematic rehearsal of completed events. Thereafter, each syntactic gesture is a recall, increasingly full, of experience retailored in the guise of a wiser man. The first order of circularity, or return, is introduced here.

The second order is entirely memorial on the part of the "author," and we tend to forget that the place or situation of the narrative has not shifted from underground. The occasion to occupy us has been seized in an act of seduction: We were not immediately there, as the illusion suggests, when he goes over particular ground, but, instead, we have never left the scene of confession; immediacy is, therefore, borrowed and imposed for the sake of poetic complicity.

The third order of circularity, articulated through certain figures of archetype, is imposed on the second and consists of commonly identifiable symbols of authority. Maud Bodkin provides a working definition of the archetype: psychic residua inherited "in the structure of the brain, *a priori*, determinants of individual experience."[10] The specific application of Jungian theory to literary types, Bodkin's study implies the valorization of a collective unconscious which makes it possible to ascribe psychological motives of filiation and kinship to widely dispersed ancestral groups. For mythic studies, the archetype becomes an indispensable figure since the myth is ordained by a common ancestral meaning. For our immediate purposes, however, archetype may be surrounded by pairs of quotation marks, for it takes place in the midst of contrasting issues in a complementary relationship rather than a preponderant one. "Chaplain pants," Brockway, the yam-man of Harlem, and Trueblood are among the characters who conform to this general configuration, and Ellison appears to intend these "old world" characters to point to sources of a special racial gift. Even though these representatives of the archetype have receded in the dominance of urbanization and technological development, they are summoned in the narrative with the greatest clarity. This projection of folk character against an urban setting is significant: A synthesis of traditions, folk and urban, agrarian and industrial, it suggests the strategic interlarding of idioms. This mix, however, accounts for the fusion of old and relatively new patterns of culture and intellectual technologies which make up the fundamental content of *Invisible Man*.

This content is variously expressed and repeated, and one of its most eloquent significations takes the form of phases of rhetoric itself, from Invisible Man's mimicked speech as a young boy in the opening hotel scene, to the wonderful, persistent rabble of Ras in the pre-riot scenes of the ending. Along with these patterns of rhetoric, Invisible Man assumes levels of consciousness that he takes on and off as he would articles of clothing. It is important to understand how these phases articulate moments of transition and contrast in the narrative, for it seems that Invisible Man ultimately subverts these elements of former style in the acquisition of one more apposite to his new "plan of living."

Recalling what he was like as an adolescent, he notes with ironic bitterness: What powers of endurance he had. "What enthusiasm! What a belief in the rightness of things!" (*IM,* 24). In the hotel scene that repeats an elaboration of primitive consciousness, Ellison shows the spectacular array of sexual fantasy in a perverted connection with bloodlust. As one of the victims of the scene, Invisible Man determines to speak even louder when the time comes. Whatever he said, "social equality" got into it, and he is made to apologize. His audience is, by turn, uproariously amused by him and indifferent to his trying to yell above their noise. In every particular of nuance and intention, the scene is a replication of nightmare; at the end of the ordeal, he is rewarded for having been a good boy. The cowhide briefcase gift is his sendoff to college and elsewhere. Its message, which he dreams that night, reads: "To Whom It May Concern, Keep This Nigger-Boy Running" (*IM,* 26). The shade of his grandfather had already told him as much, mocking his so-called triumph. He will run, in fact, stumble, as it were, from one adventure to the next, the victim of everybody else's notions of his own identity. His victimage is complete until he learns to manipulate various signs.

The initial college year is an extension of the naive phase, and there is a lyrical insistence in its moving Barbee sermon, set in the college chapel, and descriptions of campus landscape and iconography that expose Invisible Man's susceptibility to a rhetorical style to be fully appropriated by him in Harlem. Already a student orator of considerable power, Invisible Man watches the vesper speakers gather on the platform and recalls how, as a student leader, he had " stridden and debated . . . directing my voice at the highest beams and farthest rafters, ringing them, the accents staccato upon the ridgepole and echoing back with a tinkling, like words hurled to the trees of a wilderness, or into a well of slate-gray water; more sound than sense, a play upon the resonances of buildings, an assault upon the temple of the ears" (*IM,* 87, 88). This particular quality of metaphorical speech becomes inherent in Invisible Man's logical and syntactical disposition. He will lose the key to this impulse in the underground, but its motivation will remain instructive for him, the urge that he checks in a new-found suspicion of old affections.

The master speech of this type is given by blind Homer Barbee in an evocation of the Founder, perhaps modeled, in its symbolic import, on Booker T. Washington:

> This barren land after Emancipation . . . this land of darkness and sorrow, of ignorance and degradation, where the hand of brother had been turned against brother, father against son, and son against father; where master had turned against slave and slave against master; where all was strife and darkness, an aching land. And into this land came a humble prophet, lowly like the humble carpenter of Nazareth, a slave and a son of slaves, knowing only his mother. A slave born, but marked from the beginning by a high intelligence and princely personality; born in the lowest part of this barren, war-scarred land, yet somehow shedding light upon it where'er he passed through. I'm sure you have heard of his precarious infancy, his precious life almost destroyed by an insane cousin who splashed the babe with lye and shriveled his seed and how, a mere babe, he lay nine days in a death-like coma and then suddenly and miraculously recovered. You might say it was as though he had risen from the dead or been reborn. (*IM*, 92)

The suspension of predication in this narrative, its protracted modifiers, its unrelieved nominality and apposition, are built on a principle of composition that anticipates the climactic moment of speech, and its internal agitation of feeling induces an enthusiastic response to the word. The mode of *anacoluthon,* where the predicate is essentially dissolved or forgotten in the stream of modifiers, seems appropriate to oral speech, or dramatic utterance, when the speaker pursues an exact identity between himself and the words he chooses. The lexis of the passage replicates both a generalized poetic diction and the prose of King James; Barbee selects it as a manner of presentation that elevates its subject in importance. In its transcodation of one mode of figurative perception to another, Barbee's speech demonstrates that a universe of figurative relationships and equivalences may be described. The ground of the metaphors actually shifts from Judaea to the American South and from Christ to the Founder. This transfer of images from their original ground of reference to a space quite distant from it points to the specific genius of figura[11] as a mode of historical narrative and explanation. But the key to the figurative mode is not only the way of its utterance, but also the particular world view that generates it. Essentially religious, the figurative mind perceives human history in a direct correlation with destiny: Men in their time move in a way consistent with the stars of heaven.

The inaugural, transitional, and terministic motifs of the passage inscribe a metaphorical order of language where contiguity in its passion to resolve contradiction holds sway. Whether we call Barbee's performance a speech or sermon doesn't matter, for the figures-of-perception that inform it are interchangeable along a hierarchy of forms:

> I feel, I feel suddenly that I have become more human. Do you understand? More human. Not that I have become a man, for I was born a man. But that I am more human. I feel strong, I feel able to get things done! I feel that I can see sharp and clear and far down the dim corridor of history and in it I can hear the footsteps of militant fraternity! No, wait, let me confess . . . I feel the urge to affirm my feelings. . . . I feel that here, after a long and desperate and uncommonly blind journey, I have come home. . . . Home! With your eyes upon me I feel that I've found my true family! My true people! My true country! I am a new citizen of the country of your vision, a native of your fraternal land. I feel that here tonight, in this old arena, the new is being born and the vital old revived. In each of you, in me, in us all. . . . WE ARE THE TRUE PATRIOTS! THE CITIZENS OF TOMORROW'S WORLD! WE'LL BE DISPOSSESSED NO MORE! (*IM*, 261–62)

The combination here of utopian images folded over a rhetoric of political revolution changes the content of Invisible Man's speeches from any apparent connection with a religious ground of feeling, but in their tendencies toward a visual elaboration of ideas, we could say that the imagery belongs to a figurative extension of reality. For a time, Invisible Man is convinced that his role in the Brotherhood idea is the key to a new identity. The shock, however, is that the answer for him lies in the "plunge outside history," at least to the extent that the Brotherhood attempts to define historical role for him. His final disillusionment comes with the death of his comrade, Tod Clifton, followed by his resignation from the Brotherhood and flight into the underground:

> So there you have all of it that's important. Or at least you almost have it. I'm an invisible man and it placed me in a hole—or showed me the hole I was in, if you will—and I reluctantly accepted the fact. What else could I have done? Once you get used to it, reality is as irresistible as a club, and I was clubbed into the cellar before I caught the hint. Perhaps that's the way it had to be; I don't know. Nor do I know whether accepting the lesson has placed me in the rear or in the *avant-garde*. That, perhaps, is a lesson for history, and I'll leave such decisions to Jack and his ilk while I try belatedly to study the lesson of my own life. (*IM*, 432)

Various features of exclamation and delay have disappeared from the discourse along with the immediate rush and excitement of words. Less visually energetic than earlier speeches, this belated discourse (from the Epilogue) argues its closure in a language not intent on celebrating itself. This movement from oral to written language inscribes, precisely, Invisible Man's deliberate attempt to come into control of his own "symbol-making task," not at the behest of others, but at his own command.

The incidents that lead to perception are charted as an "analogy of experience," graced with the accoutrements of "fall." Having very little idea why things turn out so badly for him, Invisible Man is virtually used by everyone with whom he has any degree of sustained contact. He is prey, then, to evil forces, or purely arbitrary ones, in the guise of moral and institutional sanction. Having, therefore, no ego requirements of his own, obeying no ambitions or passions that he himself has generated, he is embarrassed by the least evidence of his own connection to a historical collective. Literally knocked in the head in the basement of the paint factory, he is forced to consider the impoverishment of his chosen negation. Having suppressed chitterlings and yams, for example, for the last time, he verges on a new-found freedom as the panorama of Harlem spreads before him. "I yam what I am!" is not simply a humorous dislocating of Cartesian predication; it is a "re-cognitive" utterance of joy.

Invisible Man repeats the moves of the hero that Joseph Campbell illustrates in *Hero of a Thousand Faces.* Campbell's hero inhabits the center of the cycle of experience, the "nuclear unit of the monomyth," and returns to society, like Invisible Man, with a message. The contemporary hero, however, in returning with a stereo, introduces a dimension of "cool," hereafter called irony, to his return that inscribes it with more than a touch of complexity. Notably, the returned man lacks an affective dimension in the absence of women in his life, but embraces, instead, a love of people. As an orator, Invisible Man engages people as the anonymous entities of an audience. He loves them because they listen to him, but he also returns as a lover of forms, oratory included—in fact, Invisible Man meets the daimon of oratory at its source—and, somewhere along the way, he has managed to get himself some music and wire his hole for sound. Analytically, conceptually involved, he entertains himself with elaborate mental constructs, the most elaborate being the novel itself. Male, and just a little arrogant in its clutches, he is exactly "self-centered" in his world, just as Campbell's returning hero, contracted back into a status of ego.

The cycle of experience permits us to go back and forth, up and down its intersecting axes; without this versatility of motion, travel would not be possible on the globe or within the text. It is this shrewd knowledge of relationships that informs the speaker of the Prologue/Epilogue. The promise to end up somewhere other than the self compels the adventure that, for all its variety and color, leads back to the point of departure. Against this knowledge, the ideology of progression is fundamentally false and deceptive. But something does happen around the cycle of experience that lends the theme of return its particular danger. Other than cynicism, or beyond it, the return provokes an irretrievable distrust of one's own image thrown back in the mirror of language. This distrust brings us to the fourth order of circularity which introduces the ironic mode.

Invisible Man's persistent anonymity against the specifics of biographical detail is the crucial ingredient of ironic disclosure. He calls himself simply "I," and none of the other characters ever addresses him because he is, he insists, emphatically invisible—people refuse to see him. This no-name seems a contradiction at first, but since he acknowledges invisibility—veritable disembodiment—why should he have a name that could confine him to orders of affection and kinship, therefore, limitation? The novel almost threatens to become an enormous hoax:

> "Ah," you say, "so it was all a build-up to bore us with his buggy jiving. He only wanted us to listen to him rave!" But only partially true: Being invisible and without substance, a disembodied voice, as it were, what else could I do? What else but try to tell you what was really happening when your eyes were looking through? And it is this which frightens me. Who knows but that, on the lower frequencies, I speak for you? (*IM*, 439)

I think that there is a precedent for Invisible Man's disembodiment from another cultural scene, and it is called the "subjectivity of freedom":

> The subject stands freely above that which must be regarded as determining him; he stands freely above it not merely at the instant of choice but at every moment, for the arbitrary will constitutes no law, no constancy, no content.[12]

Since Invisible Man's task of confession has mobilized a plenitude of historical moments, laden with personal significance, we can only view his invisibility as a blazing contradiction that must stand as it is. It becomes the "modified noun," so to speak, in naming the persistently refined features of modern consciousness: We can lay hold of such consciousness both in its abstract form—the "subjectivity of freedom"—and in its concrete manifestation in the living person. "Lower frequencies" belongs to the same order of cases as invisibility. The very possibilities of the terms, their near-endless procession of implicit modification, make it virtually certain that Invisible Man's new position locates an unalterable disenchantment with words and their capacity to mean simply what they say. This sense of the overlapping contexts of meaning defies the "one-for-another" mode of expression and goes along with Invisible Man's shifting sense of identity, at least an identity that remains complicated by experience. The phases of rhetoric that he overthrows point, essentially, to fixed destiny, a notion of permanence that asserts itself against the current of experience, its enemy, but disembodiment as a way of being enters the doors of permanence by another route, backs into it, in the achieving a central allegiance to the priorities of the imagination, in directing its attention toward the theme of potentiality. In this way, lived experience is always an embarkation, returning to the point of departure. The metaphorical order has folded into something else—the double intention, spying its shadows of meaning.

The ironic twist of ending is that Invisible Man discourses on invisibility as a passionately visible vocation, but more than that, he criticizes his effort as a gesture of "destructing" and remaking. He poses an ethical paradox: What is the good of talk if it finds no audience? But an audience is not better than its speaker, and the other way around. In fact, the speaker creates his audience in the remaking of their own tale, and without their consent, the speaker would have no task. This gets fairly tedious as Invisible Man knows, with his new-found sense of humor, and in irony, it appears that nobody wins. There is a nastiness in irony, an eloquent hateful passion that makes us prefer the disposition of metaphor. Ellison, however, chooses for Invisible Man an assault on metaphor in the very guise of its own terms, turning the underground and the theme of blackness into genuinely philosophical propositions. For Invisible Man, the achievement of an ironic voice—perhaps we could substitute inner for ironic—that is seen through the density of struggle and error, proffers a countermyth against the founders of "Sambo," the damaged humanity of an acquisitive culture, its wealth transformed into the visible evidence of status. In the realm of letters this century, *Invisible Man* insists upon the superior function of the daimon—the instrumentality of conscience—in grasping the persistently ethical idea.

At one time, the giving up of oneself to the sway of intellectual power led men to very dangerous acts; we call one of its symptoms "civil disobedience" and the victimage that flowed from it led, in all the cases we know, to the doors of the prisonhouse. In the popular examples, the man who heeds the dictates of conscience opposes to the known order a decisive threat which he asserts as his own countermyth, and it usually takes the form of a language that nobody recognizes at first, or at least doesn't admit recognition: "The individual must no longer act out of respect for the law, but must consciously know why he acts" (*CI*, 249). Invisible Man, seeking the why of his acts, cuts loose from prevailing myth in a sequence of subversive moves that conjoin him with other myths of conscience—the countermythologies. What other way is open to the one who is not seen? In his acceptance of invisibility, he can only choose to undermine, systematically, all vestiges of the established order that has driven him underground. In its articulation of a figure of subversion, *Invisible Man* glitters with a notion of black disobedience. In this case, the qualifier is no necessary illumination since all disobedience, in the very force of the language, is black. The book has never called itself "revolutionary," but it begins and ends with a revolutionist determination: If "I" am to be victimized, why not let it be for good reason?

2

Formalism Comes to Harlem

In attempting to describe the issue through two mutually alien points—
Harlem and Formalism—I think we capture something of the drama that
informs the work of Afro-American critics, for it is in the center of antagonisms that they stand, trying to transform an opposition into a dialectical
encounter. DuBois used other words for it—the warring doubles—two
striving souls held together by an act of will, one black and African, the
other white and European.[1] Fanon saw the same entanglement of opposites, the same endlessly repeating symmetries,[2] which constitute the fabric
of images and practice transmitted by mimetic gesture as well as written
and oral tradition. One aspect of this perilous adventure, as uncomical now
as it was for DuBois a century ago, is conceivable in the symbolisms of
Harlem and Langston Hughes's Simple.[3] This hypothetical confrontation
between Simple and a structure of ideas, which, by implication and design,
relegates the former and his issue to the backwaters of discourse, is not a
well-guarded secret; nor, probably, is Simple himself the modern personality which elitist DuBois imaginatively embodied in his "talented tenth," so
my appropriation of Hughes's character for the purposes of this essay deliberately intrudes an element of radical waywardness on a discussion otherwise engaged by polite combatants.

Simple in his wisdom of the streets of Harlem, or at least the Harlem that
Hughes projected, is not only a contrast to formalism, or the study of art according to its formal properties, but also, we imagine, a detraction from its
most eloquent formulations. In his role as debunker, Simple expresses an
attitude which Afro-American critics might as well elaborate, but precisely
what terms are both available and apposite to them in doing so is not a
question we have settled overnight; nor are we always sure that the question itself is important. For sure, it recurs, by the decades, and I would pose
it again: How does the Afro-American critic preserve the unalterable au-

thenticity of Simple's wisdom, sparing the references to ritual and kinship which Harlem implies, in a conversation which requires the mastery of a technic of ideas and their certain configurations?

In its apparent inclusiveness, in its fertility of vision, the wisdom of Simple never learned to be stunned, or embarrassed, or enraged by the alien or borrowed notation, because it is eventually restored to the most intimate self-reference. The world is judged by *it* and is, therefore, disabled of its own capacity to judge. Since this mode of self-knowing expresses the subversive, or counter-intention, I have no desire to cut it loose. The black critic, then, wants to lose nothing at all, but instead to *attach* the most serviceable of the alien figure-of-thought to his or her efforts to reformulate the propositions that govern the study of literature and critical theory concerning it.

Harlem, to complete the equation, stands here as a common ground of reference for an Afro-American cultural protocol and, further, we could make it synonymous with "jazz," which even musicians make no effort to define forever; it is something one makes, against the force of his or her own intuitions, or whatever arises freely, spontaneously in the human being's address to his or her environment. There really is no evidence for assuming, however, that Harlem as a universally distributed reference engenders no idioms other than jazz, or that jazz itself is simply generated. Anyone who thought so in the golden age of black American music likely learned very quickly what the true story was. Simple, who embodies the place called Harlem, is systematic in his allegiance to folk utterance, close to jazz idiom in its supreme confidence, and the subtle ways of folk utterance, despite mutations of character which he undergoes over thirty years. But what evades Hughes's straight man is Simple's simple conviction that the most abiding truth is democratic, impressionistic; anybody knows it and can say it in short order. Whatever response Simple might give to Derrida's "Diff/e/rence," for instance, is anybody's guess, but we can rest assured that it would remain loyal to the idiom of comic sabotage. We can already anticipate Simple's overall disposition toward an argument that relies so heavily on the malice of alphabets, on their peculiar adultery. If formalism is to Harlem what cotton is to Harlem, then the realignment of purposes which my title intends is instructive: For Simple and those of a given audience who share his views, the vocation of words talking about other words would very likely take on the status of Broadway entertainment.

But much closer to home (and more troubling) than the intellectual showdown of a hip Frenchman, or even the inflated price of a Broadway show, is this rift of opinion between at least two schools of black critics, both of them straighter, perhaps, than the complicated humor of Simple anticipates. There are those who think that Afro-American literature is the narrative of mute social categories, content determined before particular acts of writing. Then there are those who think this view is one-eyed. On two fairly recent occasions panels of Afro-American critics and scholars called for an end to the study of Afro-American literature as an occasion for high political polemic, an extension of theories of sociology, or a projection of the audience's response to the personality of the writer.[4] At both the 1977 annual meetings of the Midwest Modern Language Association and the parent body, panelists proposed that the methods of formalism be generally applied to the assumptions that cluster around the study of Afro-American literature. Within this inclusive fraternity there are certain decisive emphases—mythic, structuralist, phenomenological, etc.—but the common concern of both panels was *differentiation,* the wish to distinguish the logics or systems peculiar to literality in the repertory of cultural modes. One of the terms common to both panels was "criteria": Can anybody judge the literature? Is *any* argument concerning it crucial, or even acceptable? Does the writing itself (critical and creative) mobilize sufficiently certain ideas and displacements so that it gives us the proper response, or a *response,* to our situation in culture at the moment, to this period of consciousness?

It was obvious to me as a panelist on one occasion and a member of the audience on another that there is some impatience about the issue of terms on both sides (subject to change in a sequence of gestures which often resembles "musical chairs"). Some participants thought, apparently, that *formalism,* by name, by implication, embodies yet another instance of Anglo-American adventurism whose dress conceals at least exclusive aims, at most, "genocidal" cultural ones, infinitely more subtle than the arms race because it decides, through intellectual and symbolic sovereignty, precisely what categorical imperatives we will obey. If language is the perfect instrument of empire, then the naming of its formal properties comes to stand for its most privileged manifestation. One part of the audience, for these reasons, which are rarely expressed directly, would, perhaps, prefer to maintain Afro-American literature and theory as a self-generating activity, pure in its aims and directions. On the other side there are those who understand quite well (at least they think they do) how the division came about in the first place, how false it is, and have no interest in choosing between camps of "masters" in the protracted battery of other subjects. As far as I can tell, all the principals agree on the essentials: Both the literature and criticism must finally be expressed as counter-assumptions, not as moments of negation or absence. In order to enforce the point, are we doomed

to repeat and keep on repeating the very clear dilemma of DuBois's generation of the twenties and Chicago's Obassi Movement of the sixties? From
what point can we *move* the discussion ahead? If our brilliant political theorists have taught us anything from the decade of the sixties, it is certainly
a corrected sense of "heightened contradictions." The cycle of cultural
events does repeat, but it also spirals.

There is no more powerful statement of the bases on which the black
critic and writer, among others at work, must build than Ellison's germinal
essay "Little Man at Chehaw Station."[5] Exploding once again the essentially Manichean view of American culture, Ellison calibrates his argument
along several lines of stress, too numerous and involuted to unravel here,
but in readjusting its emphases, I have acquired from his insights another
constellation of terms and images which elaborate "the confounding of hi-
erarchal expectations" as the magical truth of American culture in general
and black American culture in particular. With reference to the scheme I am
working out here, such confounding has special meaning for the critic, for
he or she must await from the writer a content and strategy for its achievement and, in the process, check his or her own presumptions.

My own belief about the relationship between the critical work and that
which it contemplates is this: The literary work describes, or carves out, an
arena of choices, and in doing so, the writer suspends definitive judgment.
I think such modification is crucial to our getting in right perspective the
relationship between dynamic social movement and the narratives which
locate it. I am not prepared to argue—primarily because I don't believe it—
that the art work is autonomously derived, that it is isolated in the laws of
its being from the whole circumstances that engender it; but I am fairly certain that the rather arbitrary moment at which we capture the work (and
vice versa) in its apparent detachment from the historical and most intimate wishes must be both anticipated and sustained as a necessary act in
discrimination. My point is quite simple: The narrative which the writer offers for consideration operates according to the logic of literary form. Just as
we could not have imagined Martin Luther King or Malcolm X contraven-
ing the logic or system of oratory in making a point, we need not insist that
the writer, in turn, preach to us, or make the very same point in the same
way. Certain gestures go along with the "territory," and the critic helps to
map it. Just as the preacher does not say all, even if all his experience is
brought to bear on a performance, the writer also holds something in
abeyance; in other words, the art work for its audience, for the writer, is an
exercise in one system of logic or perception at a time. Whatever else we
bring to it, by grace, by inference, might be considered a bonus. Probably

the critic's task, as Northrop Frye observes, is to *speak* or *explain* where the work does not, to supply the right questions for a proffered riddle, but in any case, I think that it is necessary for both writer and audience to agree that the process of writing is a distinctive act of consciousness. It teaches us something about being alive and asks riddles in a way that is peculiar to itself, and perhaps that really is enough.

The project of reading work by Afro-American writers in accord with formalist methods is an *approach,* not an allegiance. (Black critics are not on the prowl for new religions.) Ultimately, the criticism seeks to restore a particular point of view to its perspective against the whole presence of African-American life in American culture, or what DuBois called the drama of a "tremendous striving." Any suggestion that that presence has been delivered into the American kingdom of God is still a futuristic metaphor. In his four-point program for a Black Aesthetic criticism, Houston Baker makes several useful suggestions:

> First, [the critics] must steep themselves in manifold historical evidence that has been too long ignored. The literary text is most revealing to the critic who possesses a high degree of historical knowledge. Second, those who contribute to a just view of Black American literature must be able to move from the broad historical plane to the distinctive Black word.[6]

There is little evidence to suggest to me that the methodology of formalism contravenes historical perspective or deep political commitment when it is clear that formalism itself arises at a particular moment, or series of moments, in the development and advancement of the idea of linguistics and literary study. In short, a method is not inherently ahistorical, or endemic to a fixed, or divine, order. Formalism is, I believe, preeminently useful. The attempt, then, to treat a literary text by a black writer as *a text* (a spate of written discourse operating according to certain formal principles) need not exclude the critic's whole consciousness, but, of necessity, draws its plenitude into specific concentration. If there were a better word for saying what I mean, one less riddled by tribalistic implications, I'd say it. *Epistemology* is likely not ideal either, but probably subsumes all other formalist acts—exegesis, hermeneutics, historical method; the near-endless array of etymological activity, which Kenneth Burke summed up under the heading of "logology"—under the broadest of intentions: a method of knowledge, of inquiry, capable of supplying Simple and the straight man (for I'd wish to get them together and keep them together) with certain enabling postulates. I would agree with Geoffrey Hartman's point: "To redeem the word from the superstition of the word is to humanize it, to make it participate once more in a living concert of voices, and to raise exegesis to its former state by confronting art with experience as searchingly as if art were scripture."[7]

In order to nail down my theoretical point and to try to silence the loud, who think that a Daniel Moynihan of Afro-American criticism and letters is a mere figment of a too rich imagination, I would like to offer something of a critical parable. Toni Morrison's *Song of Solomon* was greeted in 1977 with immense critical acclaim, but in several instances, what was said of the novel—its authentic testimony to "Black Experience"—could be applied to a repertoire of black events from Gustavus Vassa's *Narrative* to John Coltrane's "Ascension"; from a night at the concert hall with the Alvin Ailey Dancers to Richard Pryor's short-lived and brilliant career on NBC-TV. To identify the novel in no more differentiated terms than that is to accommodate oneself to the least tense assumptions which suggest that "Black Experience," a permanently monolithic form, has been exhausted. It is a museum piece, an artifact, something you visit or slum in, and, above all, it has no integrity of its own, no integrity to be regarded against revised patterns of living relationships. Colette Dowling, for example, two years after the publication of *Song of Solomon,* points out that Morrison gives us "exotic stuff" in the novel, from which basis she goes on the atomize exactly what kind of stuff she means: "voodoo dolls, greenish-gray love potions, a sack of daddy's bones hanging from the ceiling." While I concede that the reader of magazines exercises a poetic faith much less compelling than what he or she requires of him- or herself when reading a novel, or the, "heavies," what does this same reader think when he or she confronts a similar configuration of intentions from, we suppose, more intellectually responsible sources? Dowling goes on to quote Diane Johnson's *New York Review of Books* assessment of Morrison's and Gayl Jones's novels: "They *entirely* concern black people who violate, victimize, and kill each other. . . . *No* relationships endure, and *all* are founded on exploitation. Are *blacks* really like *this?*" (my emphases).[8]

I will not pause (as Dowling's editors clearly did not) to question certain semantically suspect categories from these observations—i.e., "entirely concern," "all are founded," "are blacks" (every one of the thirty or so million souls of them in the continental U.S.A., the question asks!) "like this?"—since I believe that the writer had to have an ending, and these leaping indices give one the sense that *everything* has been accomplished in one bound. Nor will I stop to replay, even if I could and there were time, the level of deception and contempt which guards these precisely segmented portions of American cultural content from profounder inquiry. But I will briefly essay a single symptom of the inevitable: With its intricate network of symbolic supports, the American event of race so thoroughly describes a grammar of negation that those who are subdued by its magic imagine that its traditional sign-vehicles and immanent referential content are not violently arbitrary at all. In short, in some places, there is commentary blissfully unmoved by the course of general linguistics and its aftermath *even* this late in the twentieth century, *even* in the discourse of criticism.

There is, quite legitimately, a category of writing which we designate "black American," but its distinctive traits are not, after all, exhausted by a catalogue of the "exotic," or public memory of Bigger Thomas. I would prefer to begin to talk about Afro-American literature in the following terms: Intent on producing works of filiation, advocacy, preservation, convocation (a literature whose principal movement is informed by an external narrative), black American writers tend to rehearse a metaphorical valuation of human apprenticeship. Inspired by an African myth of flying, *Song of Solomon* attempts to elaborate the myth within the local context of a black American family over three generations.[9] That members of the second generation of the Deads appropriate certain attitudes toward ancestry—Dowling's bones hanging from the ceiling—is Morrison's strategy, I believe, for contrasting structures of feeling and belief between old and young. Morrison applies the flying metaphor and its complementary ideas to a problem: What gestures would make possible the total freedom of movement? The meeting place of opposites—control and surrender—identifies the figurative space which the novel would make manifest. When Milkman discovers that he gains control over his life by surrendering it, Morrison has him fly into the arms of his friend-turned-pursuer, Guitar: "Without wiping away the tears, taking a deep breath, or even bending his knees—he leaped. As fleet and bright as a lodestar he wheeled toward Guitar and it did not matter which one of them would give up his ghost in the killing arms of his brother, for now he knew what Shalimar knew: If you surrendered to the air, you could *ride* it."[10] The transformation of the myth to an alien place and its reidentification as a fictional motif form an economy of analogues which render the first, second, and third generations of the Deads synonymous in their American destiny. There is essentially no discontinuity now between fathers and sons.

The moral universe from which the work is addressed is based in a perception of restored sympathetic identities. By analogy, juxtaposition, imitation, or a grid of correspondences imposed on disparate conditions, Morrison reconsiders the "impulse of pity," as Wright's protagonist calls such perception in "The Man Who Lived Underground," as a legitimate human response. Through the elaboration of a metaphorical device, Morrison resolves Milkman's state of alienation in relationship to a series of human and social issues—for instance, the outraged fraternity between Guitar and himself is driven to extreme conclusions, but the terms of it appear in a terrible act of irony which releases both from the anguish of their ignorance. At the same time its consequences are both illuminated and borne in a startling moment of mutual revelation—Guitar, the revolutionary of perverted aims, can no more liberate his brother as he can take life with impunity, while Milkman himself earns the grace of struggle as he has tried to circumvent it in its familial and broader social meanings. That both are brought together in this scene—poised at last against the background of an initial outcome—extends the auspices of the African myth over the tyranny of the particular, of the momentous. In other words, Milkman, in his newfound knowledge, is standing on the Virginia hillside for more than himself. "Leaping" and "wheeling" in the air, actions which replicate the motor behavior of his African ancestor, escaping captivity, and imitating an airborne movement not conventional to subjects, Milkman probably doesn't "fly," but the censure from empirical fact does not interfere with the dream, while the metaphor connotes a heroic act through what is essentially a marvelous, time-honored "lie." In this case, we embrace untruth gladly.

In its passion to resolve contradiction and impose a harmonious order on combative (or simply different) categories of consciousness, the rhetoric of metaphorical discourse achieves its logic by a sort of elliptical subtlety. To connect one human being with another is a vastly more difficult task than fiction itself (or even the Constitution) allows us to know, but to yoke, by analogy, the human and the universal, the momentary and the infinite, is not so much a merciful stroke of heretical arrogance, as it is the blind excision of distinctive nominative properties. This tension, however, between the unique and its copulative potential not only gives the sentence, and the paragraph, their "delegated efficacy," but also helps us imagine that we are locked, ineffably, in an interminable chain of human kinship and, smaller scaled, of consanguineous alignments. The theme of resemblance, of obviously repeating genetic fortune, is not solely the worry or fascination of fathers, but a principle of inclusion that reappears and disperses among vast orders of cultural events.

I think that we could say with a great deal of justification that the thrust of Afro-American writing this century privileges metaphorical truth, or the transcending human possibility. This mode of work, whose demise Ortega y Gasset predicted nearly a century ago, pursues this community of texts throughout a variety of characters, situations, and closures, but variety complicates a fundamental (and apparently shared) structural motive: An allegiance to the linear progression of time, or an insisting that the time of fiction matches at least an illusion which we honor about objective time, places the accent of the works on visible, explicit motivations. The unbroken progression of mimetic gestures moves toward a point of repose for characters *and* readers. It would be pointless, if not wrong, to argue that other American communities of writers do no such thing, when it seems the trend of American writing up to the mid-twentieth century. I could not claim either that my scheme answers for all black writers in this country for all time; the conclusion is tentative at best. But the suggestion has the virtue of directing one's attention toward *tendencies of form* rather than laws of tribal behavior. Any literature might eventually reembrace its tribe—and how it does so is of no mean interest to me—but not so fast . . .

Under the requirements of an "objective text," the fictive material appears self-generating through disharmonious voices. The accent here, William Gaddis's *The Recognitions,* for instance, falls on the mental or psychic economy of character rather than on what the characters commonly share, witness, or dispute. In other words, the narration as it modulates and ramifies through central intelligences locates no more common ground between them than the unity of the printed page. Gaddis's characters speak to themselves, apparently, or at least toward that silence not interrupted by a reader's presence. We are there, it seems, by the disgrace of certain social violations—i.e., reading another's letters and diaries—and the reward is just as disturbing. *Song of Solomon,* by contrast, deploys a concept of character not only around assumptions accessible *among* characters, but also the latter explicitly reenforced by examples borrowed from a common witness. The reader shares the assumptions, in other words, through this imagined concert of being, and that is possible, in turn, by the reappearance of certain public conventions of figurative speech; for instance, "as fleet and bright as a lodestar" has not only unambiguous suggestion but a comparative reference, which, by precedent, looks beyond the context itself for verification.

At the end of Morrison's novel, we feel that we have come to an end and that there is no very wide disparity between the writer and reader concerning how we got there. The reader feels that various issues of the narrative have been resolved rather than teased or frustrated. The comic closure of *The Recognitions*—with a cathedral destructing in the vibrations of organ music—is, perhaps, a grotesque instance of minor apocalypse or nemesis not unlike Norris's bad guy of *The Octopus,* but, for sure, I am not prepared for it and suspect that the writer and this reader have quite different knowledge concerning the route of escape and how it has been achieved. Gaddis's work appears held together by the logic of association, of obsession; for instance, the recurrence of New England scenery belongs as inescapably to a character as his clothes and indeed constitutes the "tone of voice" by which he is known. Unlike *Song of Solomon*, the characters of *The Recognitions* are not known by name, or more precisely, recognized by name, but, rather, through the repetition of idiomatic gestures and the infinite regression of figurative and scenic details.

It is true that similar structures of imagery, allusion, and syntax are repeated around Morrison's characters, but a crucial difference is that the drama in which they engage is mediated by a narrative intelligence that "explains" the self-sufficient event as it happens. This intercessive token is the voice speaking in the silence which Gaddis's characters, in their respective and separate places, maintain with brilliant, voracious aptitude. With *The Recognitions* one page succeeds another, but the sense that one anticipates of a progressive unfolding, of a character revealed and changing before the eyes, is neither appropriate to this work, nor rewarded. Gaddis's structure is episodic, but just as importantly, his characters seem to exist as an extension of rhetorical choices, or perhaps it could be said that their *narrative* dimension is not preeminently decipherable. In this case, we are confronted with uniqueness—the proliferation of difference—untrammeled by a principle of inclusion. Gaddis's irreducible nominative properties, which appear to cling to Jakobson's metonymic pole, are contiguous in avoidance of any obvious transfer of identities and anxieties. On the other hand, Milkman, under other names, in other contexts, is infinitely repeatable. That he insinuates a drama in addition to whatever linguistic vitality Morrison brings to bear on the novel is as sudden and irretrievable an interruption of his unique status as is his mad leap from the hillside.

The sharp disjunctures in narrative time, the intrusion of rhetorical motives as the primary dictate of character, may not be so keen a deviation from the human problematic as Ortega y Gasset anticipated, but for sure they move us toward a program of action which captures the subject in an autonomous frame of reference. Ortega y Gasset called such a program "alienation"—"an avoidance of living forms."[11]

Thematic variation from the dynamics of connectedness has become the canon of taste rather than an alternative stylistic route. This practice of influence, in short, the abrogation of statements of transcendence, skepticism of the heroical act or intention, the parodic manipulation of feeling, the detachment of speech from an imagined speaker or human center, which returns the implications of words to a dictionary or thesaurus, seem to be the chief literary dictates of the moment, and writers align themselves with their persuasions by degree. Rather than imagine decisive breaks between the modernist/objective text and the text that contrasts with it, I would prefer to imagine a continuum of responses—from the archetypal to the historical, to the individualistic and momentary, each one increasingly subjective in its human emphasis and reception. Against this continuum of creative activity, black writers tend to stay close to the efficacy of words as an act of reciprocity, an address which anticipates reply. In short, it is not the extension of rhetorical energy alone which inspires *Song of Solomon,* or Ellison's *Invisible Man,* to make a different case; but perhaps the power of language to disclose being, rather than conceal it, is neither moot nor disabled from this angle of vision.

Reciprocity as the expected burden of language is not at this moment a popular idea for fiction, and along with its unpopularity, we have probably lost, again by degree, an interest in narrative, having gained a very high tolerance for the contemplation of smaller and smaller units of verbal and symbolic reference. In light of it, the black American writer's decision to be interested in symbolic behavior whose smallest unit is the narrative, the *story,* may strike some readers as a very strange thing, at least, but one might suppose that their decision has a great deal to do with how these writers understand speaking in the first place. Morrison and Ellison, among others, sense too keenly, perhaps, the requirements of their own imposed alienation than to raise it to an act of form. For them, language, withheld for so long, by law, from the African-American as the origin of his human power, does *speak.* The suppressed subject now mobilized toward historical movement particular to itself is not, in this case, an optional principle of composition. It matches, again by analogy and sympathetic agreement, an original scene, primal and sacrificial, when living ancestors lost life, lost language. In either case, the signifier is not meant to be empty. More precisely, it fixes a decisively unambiguous change in the state of nature.

Simple bears the losses from this initial encounter with a kind of terrible finesse and, often enough, in a terrible silence, when in the presence of the many who have forgotten or never knew. And, in effect, his deep knowledge of the implications of unregulated violence against his community becomes the crucial aspect of his own private and corporate identity. He cannot forget it, must not abandon it, and goes about saying it through varying degrees of transmutation. To mistake his purposes, however, would be stupid, perhaps ungrateful. For instance, Simple gives the straight man a history of the origins of "Be-Bop," and the perception is outrageous enough to be true against the four-square fact and at the level of articulation where only the exaggerated word is uncorrupt:

> "Re-Bop certainly sounds like scat to me," [straight man] insisted.
> "No," said Simple, "Daddy-o, you are wrong. Besides it was not *Re-*Bop. It is *Be*-Bop."
> "What's the difference," [straight man] asked, "between *Re* and *Be?*"
>
> "A lot," said Simple, "Re-Bop was an imitation like most of the white boys play. Be-Bop is the real thing like colored boys play . . . From the police beating Negroes' heads . . . Every time a cop hits a Negro with his billy club, that old club says, 'BOP! BOP! . . . BE-BOP! . . . MOP! . . . BOP! . . . That's where Be-Bop came from, beaten right out of some Negro's head into them horns and saxophones and piano keys that plays it. Do you call that nonsense?"[12]

Any questions we might entertain about this mode of saying must make their way through layers of American culture as Simple has witnessed it, then toward the metrical near-unity of *re* and *be.* The French school would have a field day here. As for me, it is one of those projects which is, as Toni Cade says, brewing under the bed.[13] My simpler wish against it is that Simple speak in as many ways as possible—he's certainly earned that right—and that the criticism pay attention to *that.* In the critical act, there is a man or woman revealed, seeking, like Jesse B. Semple, to retrieve the legitimate name of things lost to the violence, forgetfulness, and contradiction which surround the surrogate name. If I, the black person, can speak freely in my choice of critical and creative forms, then my private and collective suffering is not only mobilized on my own behalf, but also preserves me against the "homicidal" tendencies of strangers.

3

A Hateful Passion, A Lost Love: Three Women's Fiction

When I think of how essentially alone black women have been—alone because of our bodies, over which we have had so little control; alone because the damage done to our men has prevented their closeness and protection; and alone because we have had no one to tell us stories about ourselves; I realize that black women writers are an important and comforting presence in my life. Only they know my story. It is absolutely necessary that they be permitted to discover and interpret the entire range and spectrum of the experience of black women and not be stymied by preconceived conclusions. Because of these writers, there are more models of how it is possible for us to live, there are more choices for black women to make, and there is a larger space in the universe for us.[1]

Toni Morrison's *Sula* is a rebel idea, both for her creator[2] and for Morrison's audience. To read *Sula* is to encounter a sentimental education so sharply discontinuous with the dominant traditions of Afro-American literature in the way that it compels and/or deadlocks the responses that the novel, for all its brevity and quiet intrusion on the landscape of American fiction, is, to my mind, the single most important irruption of black women's writing in our era. I am not claiming for this novel any more than its due; *Sula* (1973) is not a stylistic innovation. But in bringing to light dark impulses no longer contraband in black American women's cultural address, the novel inscribes a new dimension of being, moving at last in contradistinction to the tide of virtue and pathos that tends to overwhelm black female characterization in a monolith of terms and possibilities. I regard Sula the character as a literal and figurative *breakthrough* toward the assertion of what we may call, in relation to her literary "relatives," new female being.

Without predecessors in the recent past of Afro-American literature, Sula is anticipated by a figure four decades removed from Morrison's symbol smasher: Janie Starks in Zora Neale Hurston's *Their Eyes Were Watching God* (1937). By intruding still a third figure—Vyry Ware of Margaret Walker's *Jubilee* (1966)—we lay hold of a pattern of contrast among three

African-American female writers, who pose not only differences of character in their perception of female possibilities, but also a widely divergent vocabulary of feeling. This essay traces the changes in black female characterization from *Sula* back toward the literary past, beginning with Margaret Walker's Vyry and Zora Neale Hurston's Janie, forward again to *Sula* and Morrison. It argues that the agents which these novels project are strikingly different, and that the differences take shape primarily around questions of moral and social value. And it explores the mediations through which all three writers translate sociomoral constructs into literary modes of discourse.

Margaret Walker's Vyry Ware belongs to, embodies, a corporate ideal. The female figure in her characterization exists for the race, in its behalf, and in maternal relationship to its profoundest needs and wishes. Sula, on the other hand, lives for Sula and has no wish to "mother" anyone, let alone the black race in some symbolic concession to a collective need. If Vyry is woman-for-the-other, then Sula is woman-for-self. Janie Starks represents a dialectical point between the antitheses, and the primary puzzle of *Their Eyes Were Watching God* is the contradiction of motives through which the character of Janie Starks takes on meaning; in other words, Janie might have been Sula, but the latter only through a resolution of negative impulses. These three characters, then, describe peak points in a cultural and historical configuration of literary inquiry. In Sula's case, the old love of the collective, for the collective, is lost, and passions are turned antagonistic, since, as the myth of the black woman goes, she is honorable only insofar as she protects her children and forgives her man. The title of this writing is a kind of shorthand for these longhanded notations.

The scheme of these observations, as I have already implied, is not strictly chronological. Hurston's affinities are much closer to Morrison's than Walker's, even though Hurston's *Their Eyes Were Watching God* was written over fifty years ago. The critical scheme I offer here is not precisely linear, because the literary movement I perceive, which theoretically might take in more women writers than my representative selections, does not progress neatly from year to year in an orderly advance of literary issues and strategies. My method aims at a dialectics of process, with these affinities and emphases tending to move in cycles rather than straight lines. I see no myth of descent operating here as in Harold Bloom's "anxiety of influence," exerted, in an oedipal-like formation, by great writers on their successors.[3] The idea-form which I trace here, articulated in three individual writers' figurations and structural/thematic patterns, does not emerge within this community of writers in strict sequential order. Ironically, it is exactly the right *not* to accede to the simplifications and mystifications of a strictly historiographical time line that now promises the greatest freedom of discourse to black people, to black women, as critics, teachers, writers, and thinkers.

As the opening exercise in the cultural and literary perspective that this writing wishes to consider, then, we turn immediately to Morrison's *Sula*, the "youngest" of three heroines. Few of the time-honored motifs of female behavioral description will suit her: not "seduction and betrayal," applied to a network of English and American fictions; not the category of "holy fool," as exemplified in various Baldwinian configurations of female character; not the patient long-suffering female, nor the female authenticated by male imagination. Compared with past heroines of black American fiction, Sula exists foremost in her own consciousness. To that extent, *Sula* and *Their Eyes Were Watching God* are studies in contrast to Walker and share the same fabric of values. The problem that Morrison poses in *Sula* is the degree to which her heroine (or antiheroine, depending on one's reading of the character) is self-betrayed. The audience does not have an easy time in responding to the agent, because the usual sentiments about black women have been excised, and what we confront instead is the entanglement of our own conflicting desires, our own contradictory motivations concerning questions of individual woman-freedom. Sula is both loved and hated by the reader, embraced and rejected simultaneously because her audience is forced to accept the corruption of absolutes and what has been left in their place—the complex, alienated, transitory gestures of a personality who has no framework of moral reference beyond or other than herself.

Insofar as Sula is not a loving human being, extending few of the traditional loyalties to those around her, she reverses the customary trend of "moral growth" and embodies, contrarily, a figure of genuine moral ambiguity about whom few comforting conclusions may be drawn. Through Sula's unalterable "badness," black and female are now made to appear as a *single* subject in its own right, fully aware of a plentitude of predicative possibilities, for good and ill.

In Sula's case, virtue is not the sole alternative to powerlessness, or even the primary one, or perhaps even an alternative at all. In the interest of complexity, Sula is Morrison's deliberate hypothesis. A conditional subjunctive replaces an indicative certainty: "In a way her strangeness, her naiveté, her craving for the other half of her equation was the consequence of an idle imagination. Had she paints, or clay, or knew the discipline of the dance, or strings; had she anything to engage her tremendous curiosity and her gift for metaphor, she might have exchanged the restlessness and preoccupation with whim for an activity that provided her with all she yearned for. And like any *artist with no art form* she became dangerous."[4]

In careful, exquisite terms Sula has been endowed with dimensions of other possibility. How they are frustrated occupies us for most of the novel, but what strikes me keenly about the passage is that Morrison imagines a character whose destiny is not coterminous with naturalistic or mystical boundaries. Indeed the possibility of art, of intellectual vocation for black female character, has been offered as a style of defense against the naked brutality of conditions. The efficacy of art cannot be isolated from its social and political means, but Sula is specifically circumscribed by the lack of an explicit tradition of imagination or aesthetic work, and not by the evil force of "white" society, or the absence of a man, or even the presence of a mean one.

Morrison, then, imagines a character whose failings are directly trace- able to the absence of a discursive/imaginative project—some *thing* to do, some object-subject relationship which establishes the identity in time and space. We do not see Sula in relationship to an "oppressor," a "whitey," a male, a dominant and dominating being outside the self. No Manichean analysis demanding a polarity of interest—black/white, male/female, good/ bad—will work here. Instead, Sula emerges as an embodiment of a meta- physical chaos in pursuit of an activity both proper and sufficient to herself. Whatever Sula has become, whatever she is, is a matter of her own choices, often ill formed and ill informed. Even her loneliness, she says to her best friend Nel, is her own—"My own lonely," she claims in typical Sula- bravado, as she lies dying. Despite our misgivings at Sula's insistence and at the very degree of alienation Morrison accords her, we are prepared to ac- cept her negative, naysaying freedom as a necessary declaration of inde- pendence by the black female writer in her pursuit of a vocabulary of gesture—both verbal and motor—that leads us as well as the author away from the limited repertoire of powerless virtue and sentimental pathos. Sula is neither tragic nor pathetic; she does not amuse or accommodate. For black audiences, she is not consciousness of the black race personified, nor "tragic mulatta," nor, for white ones, is she "mammie," "Negress," "coon," or "maid." She is herself, and Morrison, quite rightly, seems little concerned if any of us, at this late date of Sula's appearance in the "house of fiction," minds her heroine or not.

We view Morrison's decision with interest because it departs dramati- cally from both the iconography of virtue and endurance and from the ide- ology of the infamous ogre/bitch complex, alternately poised as the dominant traits of black female personality when the black female personality exists at all in the vocabulary of public symbols.[5] Sula demands, I believe, that we not only see anew, but also *speak* anew in laying to rest the several manifestations of apartheid in its actual practice and in the formulation of the critical postulates that govern our various epistemologies.

That writers like Morrison, Toni Cade Bambara, and Paule Marshall, among them, participate in a tradition of black women writing in their own behalf, close to its moment of inception, lends their work thorough complexity. With the exception of a handful of autobiographical narratives from the nineteenth century, the black woman's realities, *in writing,* are virtually suppressed until the period of the Harlem Renaissance and later.[6] Essentially, the black woman as artist, as intellectual spokesperson for her own cultural apprenticeship, has barely existed before, for anyone. At the source of her own symbol-making task, this community of writers confronts, therefore, a tradition of work that is fairly recent, its continuities broken and sporadic.

It is not at all an exaggeration to say that the black woman's presence as character and movement in the American public world has been *ascribed* a status of impoverishment or pathology, or, at best, an essence that droops down in the midst of things, as Simone de Beauvoir describes female mystery in *The Second Sex.* Against this social knowledge, black women writers likely agree on a single point: whatever the portrayal of female character yields, it will be rendered from the point of view of one whose eyes are not alien to the humanity in front of them. What we can safely assume, then, is that black women write as partisans to a particular historical order—their own, the black and female one, with its hideous strictures against literacy and its subtle activities of censorship even now against words and deeds that would deny or defy the black woman myth. What we can assume with less confidence is that their partisanship, as in the rebellion of Sula, will yield a synonymity of conclusions.

The contrast between Sula and Margaret Walker's Vyry Ware is the difference between captive woman and free woman, but the distinction between them has as much to do with aspects of agency and characterization as it does with the kind of sensibility or sympathy that a writer requires in building one kind of character and not another. In other words, *what* we think of Sula and Vyry, for instance, has something to do with *how* we are taught to *see* and *value* them. In the terms of fiction that they each propose, *Jubilee, Their Eyes Were Watching God,* and *Sula* all represent varying degrees of plausibility, but the critical question is not whether the events they portray are plausible, or whether they confirm what we already believe, or think we do, but, rather, how each writer deploys a concept of character. Of the three, Toni Morrison looks forward to an era of dissensions: Sula's passions are hateful, as we have observed, and though we are not certain that the loss of conventional love brings her down, we are sure that she overthrows received moralities in a heedless quest for her own irreducible self. This radical intrusion of waywardness lends a different thematic emphasis to the woman's tale of generation, receding in Sula's awareness, and the result is a novel whose formal strategies are ambiguous and even discomforting in their uncertainties. Once we have examined an analogy of the archetype from which Sula deviates by turning to Margaret Walker's *Jubilee* and have explored Hurston's novel as a structural advance of the literary problematic, we will return to Sula in a consideration of myth/countermyth as a discourse ordained by history.

In radical opposition to notions of discontinuity, confronting us as a fictional world of consecrated time and space, *Jubilee* worries one of the traditional notions of realism—the stirring to life of the common people[7]—to a modified definition. Walker completed her big novel in the mid-sixties at the University of Iowa Creative Writers' Workshop. She tells the story of the novel, twenty years in the making, in *How I Wrote Jubilee*.[8] This novel of historical content has no immediate precedence in Afro-American literary tradition. To that extent, it bears little structural resemblance to Hurston's work before it, although both Hurston and Walker implement a search for roots, or to Morrison's work after it. *Jubilee*, therefore, assumes a special place in the canon.

From Walker's own point of view, the novel is historical, taking its models from the Russian writers of historical fiction, particularly Tolstoy. In its panoramic display, its massive configurations of characters and implied presences, its movement from a dense point of American history—the era of the Civil War—toward an inevitable, irreversible outcome, the emancipation of ten million African-Americans—*Jubilee* is certainly historical. Even though it is a tale whose end is written on the brain, in the heart, so that there is not even a chance that we will be mistaken about closure, the novel unfolds as if the issues were new. We are sufficiently excited to keep turning the page of a twice-told tale accurately reiterating what we have come to believe is the truth about the "Peculiar Institution." But the high credibility of the text in this case leads us to wonder, eventually, what else is embedded in it that compels us to read our fate by its lights. My own interpretation of the novel is that it is not only historical, but also, and primarily, Historical. In other words, "Historical," in this sense, is a metaphor for the unfolding of the Divine Will. This angle on reality is defined by Paul Tillich as a *theonomy*. Human history is shot through with Divine Presence so that its being and time are consistent with a plan that elaborates and completes the will of God.[9] In this view of things, human doings are only illusions of a counterfeit autonomy; in Walker's novel agents (or characters) are moving and are moved under the aegis of a Higher and Hidden Authority.

For Vyry Ware, the heroine of *Jubilee,* and her family, honor, courage, endurance—in short, the heroic as transparent prophetic utterance—become the privileged center of human response. If Walker's characters are ultimately seen as one-dimensional, either good or bad, speaking in a public rhetoric that assumes the heroic or its opposite, then such portrayal is apt to a fiction whose value is subsumed by a theonomous frame of moral reference. From this angle of advocacy and preservation the writer does not penetrate the core of experience, but encircles it. The heroic intention has no interest in fluctuations or transformations or palpitations of conscience—these will pass away—but monumentality, or fixedness, becomes its striving. Destiny is disclosed to the hero or the heroine as an already-fixed and named event, and this steady reference point is the secret of permanence.

Set on a Georgia plantation before the Civil War, the novel is divided into three parts. The first recalls the infancy and youth of Vyry Ware, the central figure of the novel, and rehearses various modes of the domestic South in slavery. The second part recapitulates the war and its impact on the intimate life of families and individuals. One of the significant threads of the Peculiar Institution in objective time is closely imitated here—how the exigencies of war lead to the destruction of plantation hierarchy. In this vacuum of order a landscape of deracinated women and men dominates the countryside, and Walker's intensity of detail involves the reader in a scene of universal mobility—everything is moving, animate and inanimate, away from the centers of war toward peace, always imminent, in the shadows of Sherman's torch. Vyry and her first love Randall Ware are numbered among the casualties. They are separated as the years of war unhinge all former reality.

The third and final segment of the novel marks Vyry's maturity and the rebirth of a semblance of order in the South. The future is promising for the emancipated, and Vyry takes a new lover, Innis Brown, before the return of Randall Ware. This tying up the various threads of the narrative is undercut by a bitterly ironical perspective. The former enslaved will struggle as she or he has before now, with this difference: free by law, each remains a victim of arbitrary force, but such recognition is the reader's alone. This edge of perception reads into the novel an element of pathos so keenly defined that Vyry's fate verges on the tragic.

Variously encoded by signs associated with a magical/superstitious world order, echoes of maxims and common speech, *Jubilee* is immersed in the material. We are made to feel, in other words, the brutal pull of necessity—the captive's harsh relationship to this earth and its unrelenting requirements of labor—as it impels the captive consciousness toward a terrible knowledge of the tenuousness of life and the certainty of death. The novel conjoins natural setting and social necessity in a dance of temporal unfolding; in fact, the institution of slavery described here is an elaboration of immanence so decisive in its hold on the human scene imposed upon it that Walker's humanity is actually "ventriloquized" through the medium of a third-person narrator. The narrative technique (with its overlay of mystical piety) is negotiated between omniscient and concealed narrators. Whatever the characters think, however they move and feel about their experience, are all rendered through the eyes of another consciousness, not their own. We might say that the characters embody, then, historical symbols—a captive class and their captors—which have been encoded or transliterated as actors in a fiction. Walker's agents are types or valences, and the masks through which they speak might be assumed as well by any other name.

In attributing to Walker a theonomous view of the socius, I am also saying that her characters are larger than life; that they are overdrawn, that, in fact, their compelling agency and motivation are ahistorical, despite the novel's solid historical grounding. Walker's *lexis* operates under quite complicated laws, complicated because such vocabulary is no longer accessible, or even acceptable, to various mythoi of contemporary fiction. Walker is posing a subterranean structure of God terms, articulated in the novel through what we can identify as the *peripeteia*—that point of radical change in the direction toward which the forces of the novel are moving; in historical and secular terms this change is called emancipation. Historiographic method in accounting for the "long-range" and "immediate" causes of the Civil War and its aftermath does not name "God" as a factor in the liberation of black Americans,[10] and neither does Walker in any explicit way. But it seems clear to me that "God" is precisely what she means in all the grandeur and challenge of the Nominative, clear that the agency of Omnipresence—even more reverberative in its imprecise and ubiquitous *thereness*—is for Walker the source of one of the most decisive abruptions in our history.

Walker adopts a syntax and semantics whose meanings are recognizable in an explanation of affairs in human time. But these delegated efficacies register at a deeper level of import so that "nature," for instance, is nature and something more, and character itself acts in accordance with the same kind of mystical or "unrealistic" tendencies.

Walker's backdrop of natural representation has such forcefulness in the work that dialogue itself is undercut by its dominance, but her still life is counterposed by human doings that elaborate the malignancies of nature, that is, torture, beatings, mental cruelty, the ugly effects of nature embodied in the formal and institutional. The slaveholder and his class, in the abrogation of sympathy, lose their human form. The captors' descent into nature is seen as pernicious self-indulgence, ratified by institutional sanction, but it also violates a deeper structural motive, which Walker manipulates in the development of character. Though natural and social events run parallel, they are conjoined by special arrangement, and then there is a name for it—the act of magic or invocation that the enslaved opposes to the arbitrary willfulness of authority.

The evocation of a magical program defines the preeminent formalistic features of the opening segments of the novel. Prayers for the sick and dying and the special atmosphere that surrounds the deathwatch are treated from the outset with particular thematic prominence. In several instances mood is conveyed more by conventional notation—the number thirteen, boiling black pot, full moon, squinch owl, black crone—than any decisive nuance of thought or detail; or more precisely, fear is disembodied from internal agitations of feeling and becomes an attribute of things. "Midnight came and thirteen people waited for death. The black pot boiled, and the full moon rode the clouds high in the heavens and straight up over their heads. . . . It was not a night for people to sleep easy. Every now and then the squinch owl hollered and the crackling fire would glare and the black pot boil."[11]

The suspense that gathers about this scene is brought on by the active interaction of forces that move beyond and above the characters. An outburst would surprise. Sis. Hetta's death is expected here, and nothing more. The odd and insistent contiguity that Walker establishes among a variety of natural and cultural-material signs—"black pot boiled"; "full moon rode"—identifies the kind of magical/mystical grammar of terms to which I have referred.

"Black pot" and "full moon" may be recognized as elements that properly belong to the terrain of witchcraft, but we must understand that magic and witchcraft—two semiological "stops" usually associated with African-American rebellion and revolutionary fervor throughout the New World under the whip of slavery—are ritual terms of a shorthand which authors adopt to describe a system of beliefs and practices not entirely accessible to

us now. In other words, Walker is pointing toward a larger spiritual and religious context through these notations, so that ordinary diurnal events in
the novel are invested with extraordinary meaning. My own terms—
theonomous meaning—would relate this extraordinary attribution to the
Unseen, for which Protestant theology offers other clusters of anomalous
phenomena, including "enthusiasm," "ecstasy," or the equivalent of Emile
Durkheim's "demon of oratorical power."[12] In specific instances of the
novel, we see only pointers toward, or markers of, an entirely compelling
structure of feelings and beliefs, of which "black pot," for instance, is a single sign. The risk I am taking here is to urge a synonymity between "God"
and, for want of a better term, "magic." At least I am suggesting that
Walker's vocabulary of God terms includes magic and the magical and the
enslaved person's special relationship to natural forces.

Walker achieves this "extra" reading by creating a parallelism between
natural and social/domestic issues that dominates the form of the novel. In
its reinforcements, there is an absence of differentiation, or of the interplay
between dominant and subdominant motifs. A nocturnal order pervades
Jubilee—life under the confines of the slave community, where movement
is constantly under surveillance; secret meetings; flights from the overseer's
awful authority; illegal and informal pacts and alliances between slaves;
and above all, the slave's terrible vulnerability to fluctuations of fate.

The scene of Vyry's capture after an attempted escape on the eve of the
Civil War will provide a final example. After their union Vyry and Randall
Ware, the free black man, have two children, Jim and Minna, and Ware
makes plans for their liberation. His idea is that he or Vyry will return for
the children later, but Vyry refuses to desert them. Her negotiation of a
painful passage across the countryside toward the point of rendezvous
groans with material burden. It has rained the day of their attempted escape, and mud is dense around the slave quarters by nightfall. Vyry travels
with the two children—Jim toddling and the younger child Minna in her
arms. The notion of struggle, both against the elements and the powerful
other is so forceful an aspect of tone that the passage itself painfully anticipates the fatefulness of Vyry's move; here are the nodal points:

> Every step Vyry and Jim took, they could feel the mud sucking their
> feet down and fighting them as they withdrew their feet from its elas-
> tic hold. . . . The baby still slept fitfully while Vyry pressed her way
> doggedly to the swamps. . . . At last they were in sight of the swamps.
> Feeling sorry for little Jim she decided to rest a few minutes before try-
> ing to wade the creek. . . . She sat down on an old log, meaning to rest
> only a few minutes. . . . A bad spasm clutched her stomach instinc-

tively. She tensed her body with the sure intuition that she was not only being watched but that the watchful figures would soon surround her. Impassively she saw the patteroller and guards, together with Grimes [the overseer] emerge from the shadows and walk toward her. (169–70)

This grim detail concludes with Vyry's capture and brutal punishment—"seventy-five lashes on her naked back." That Vyry has been robbed of self-hood on its most fundamental level is clear enough, but the passage further suggests that her movements replicate the paralysis of nightmare. One would move, but cannot, and awakens in spasms of terror. This direct articulation of nightmare content—puzzles and haltings, impediments and frights—dictates the crucial psychological boundaries of *Jubilee* and decides, accordingly, the aesthetic rule.

The idea that emerges here is that Vyry's condition is the equivalent of nightmare, a nocturnal order of things that works its way into the resonances of the novel's structure. Her paralysis is symptomatic of a complex of fear and repression in the service of death. We could argue that the culture of slavery projected in the novel—its modalities of work and celebration, its civic functions and legal codes, its elaborate orders of brutality and mutilation—presents a spectacle of a *culture* in the service of death. Given this reality, the slave subject has no life, but only the stirrings of it. Vyry, trapped in a bad dream, cannot shake loose, and this terrible imposed impotence foreshadows the theme of liberation and a higher liberation as well, in which case the stalled movement is overcome in a gesture of revolutionary consciousness. For Vyry the freeing act is sparked by war whose intricate, formal causes are remote to her, though its mandates will require the reorganization of her human resources along new lines of stress. Above all, Vyry must move now without hesitation as the old order collapses around her.

For Vyry's class the postwar years stand as the revelation of the emotional stirrings they have felt all along. "Mine Eyes Have Seen the Glory of the Coming of the Lord" (the title of one of Walker's chapters) is as much a promise as it is an exercise in common meter, but the terms of the promise that Walker imitates are neither modern nor secular. They are eternal and self-generating, authored elsewhere, beyond the reach of human inquiry. Along this axis of time, with its accent on the eternal order of things, women and men in destiny move consistent with the stars of heaven.

This blending of a material culture located in the nineteenth century with a theme which appears timeless and is decisively embedded in a Christian metaphysic reveals the biographical inspiration behind Walker's work.

Jubilee is, in effect, the tale translated of the author's female ancestors. This is a story of the foremothers, a celebration of their stunning faith and intractable powers of endurance. In that sense, it is not so much a study of characters as it is an interrogation into African-American character in its poignant national destiny and through its female line of spiritual descent. A long and protracted praise piece, a transformed and elaborated prayer, *Jubilee* is Walker's invocation of the guiding spirit and genius of her people. Such a novel is not "experimental." In short, it does not introduce ambiguity or irony or uncertainty or perhaps even "individualism" as potentially thematic material because it is a detailed sketch of a *collective* survival. The waywardness of a Sula Peace, or even a Janie Starks's movement toward an individualistic liberation—a separate peace—is a trait of character development engendered by a radically different *Weltanschauung*.

Their Eyes Were Watching God enforces a similar notion of eternal order in the organic, metaphorical structure through which Hurston manipulates her characters, but the complexities of motivation in the novel move the reader some distance from the limited range of responses evoked by *Jubilee*. Janie Starks, the heroine of the novel, defines a conglomerate of human and social interests so contradictory in its emphasis that a study of structural ambiguity in fiction might well include Janie Starks *and* her author. Perhaps "uncertainty" is a more useful word in this case than "ambiguity," since Hurston avoids the full elaboration or display of tensions that Janie herself appears to anticipate. In short, Janie Starks is a bundle of contradictions: raised by women, chiefly her grandmother, to seek security in a male and his properties, Janie, quite early in her career rejects Nanny's wisdom. In love with adventure, in love with the very idea of adventure, Janie is determined to know exactly what independence for the female means for her. This includes the critical quest of sexual self-determination. Janie's quite moving sense of integrity, however, is undercut in puzzling and peculiar ways.

Janie marries her first husband Logan Killicks because her grandmother wants her to do so, but Janie has little interest in a man who is not only not glamorous (as Joe Starks and Vergible "Teacake" Woods will be), but also not enlightened in his outlook on the world and the specifically amorous requirements of female/male relationship. Killicks gets the brunt of a kind of social criticism in *Their Eyes Were Watching God* which mocks rural personality—hardworking, unsophisticated, "straight-arrow," earnest—and Hurston makes her point by having Killicks violate essentially Janie's "dream of the horizon." Janie will shortly desert Killicks for a man far more in keeping with her ideas concerning the romantic, concerning male gracefulness. Jody Starks, up from Georgia and headed for an adventure in real estate and town government, takes the place of Logan Killicks with an immediacy, which, in "real" life, would be somewhat disturbing, a bit indecent; but here the "interruption" is altogether lyrical, appropriate, and unmourned. Starks's appearance and intention are even "cinematic" in their decidedly cryptic and romantic tenor—Janie literally goes off "down the road" with the man.

Their destination is Eatonville, Florida, a town which Joe Starks will bring to life with his own lovely ego, shortly to turn arrogant and insulting as he attempts to impose on Janie his old-fashioned ideas about woman's place and possibilities. The closure on this marriage is not a happy one either, troubled by Starks's chauvinistic recriminations and Janie's own disenchantment. Starks dies of a kidney ailment, leaving Janie "Mrs. Mayor" of Eatonville and not particularly concerned, we are led to believe, to be attached again.

Janie's new love affair with Teacake is untrammeled by incompatibility between the pair, though her friends express great concern that Teacake's social and financial status is not what it ought to be, let alone comparable to Jody Starks's. Janie is, however, at once traditionally romantic in her apparently male-centered yearnings and independent in her own imagination and the readiness to make her own choices. The convergence of these two emotional components is, in fact, not the diametrical opposition that contemporary feminists sometimes suppose; heterosexual love is neither inherently perverse nor necessarily dependence-engendering, except that the power equation between female and male tends to corrupt intimacies.[13] The trouble, then, with the relationship between Janie and Teacake is not its heterosexual ambience, but a curiously exaggerated submissiveness on Janie's part that certain other elements of the heroine's character contradict.

When, for instance, Janie follows Teacake to the Florida Everglades to become a migrant farm worker for several seasons, their love is solid and reliable, but the male in this instance is also perfectly capable, under Hurston's gaze, of exhibiting qualities of jealousy and possession so decisive that his occasional physical abuse of the female and his not-so-subtle manipulation of other females' sexual attraction to him seem condoned in the name of love. Hurston's pursuit of an alleged folk philosophy in this case—as in, all women enjoy an occasional violent outburst from their men because they know then that they are loved—is a concession to an obscene idea. One example will suffice. "Before the week was over he had whipped Janie. Not because her behavior justified his jealousy, but it relieved that awful fear inside him. Being able to whip her reassured him in possession. No brutal beating at all. He just slapped her around a bit to show he was boss. . . . It aroused a sort of envy in both men and women. The way he petted and pampered her as if those two or three slaps had nearly killed her made the women see visions and the helpless way she hung on him made men dream dreams."[14]

One might well wonder, and with a great deal of moral, if not poetic, justification if the scene above describes a *working posture* that Hurston herself might have adopted with various lovers. This scene is paradigmatic of the very quality of ambiguity/ambivalence that I earlier identified for this novel. The piece threatens to abandon primitive modes of consciousness and response from the beginning, but Hurston seems thwarted in bringing this incipience to fruition for reasons which might have to do with the way that the author understood certain popular demands brought to bear on her art. Hurston has detailed some of her notions of what Anglo-American audiences expected of the black writer in general and the black female writer in particular of her time,[15] but it is not clear to me what *African-American* audiences expected of their chroniclers. The more difficult question, however, is what Hurston demanded of herself in imagining what was possible for the female, and it appears that beyond a certain point she could not, or would not, plunge. *Their Eyes Were Watching* God, for all its quite impressive feminist possibilities, is an instance of "double consciousness," to employ W. E. B. DuBois's conceptualization in quite another sense and intention.[16] Looking two ways at once, the novel captivates Janie Starks in an entanglement of conflicting desires.

More concentrated in dramatic focus than *Jubilee,* Hurston's novel was written during the mid-thirties; finished in seven weeks during the author's visit to Haiti, the novel is not simply compact. It is hurried, intense, and above all, haunted by an uneasy measure of control. One suspects that Hurston has not said everything she means, but means everything she says. Within a persistent scheme of metaphor, she seems held back from the awful scream that she has forced Janie to repress through unrelieved tides of change. We mistrust Janie's serenity, spoken to her friend Pheoby Watson in the close of the novel; complementarily, the reconciliation is barely acceptable in either structural or dramatic terms. Janie Starks, not unlike her creator, is gifted with a dimension of worldliness and ambition that puts her in touch with broader experience. This daughter of sharecroppers is not content to be heroic under submissive conditions (except with Teacake?); for her, then, nothing in the manners of small-town Florida bears repeating. Its hateful, antisocial inclinations are symbolized by Janie's grandmother, whom she hates "and [has] hidden from herself all these years under the cloak of pity." "Here Nanny had taken the biggest thing God ever made, the horizon . . . and pinched it into such a little bit of a thing that she could tie it about her granddaughter's neck tight enough to choke her. She hated the old woman who had twisted her so in the name of love" (76–77).

The grandmother not only represents a personal trauma for Janie (as the grandmother does in the author's autobiography),[17] but also terror and repression, intruding a vision of impoverishment on the race. Clustered around the symbolic and living grandmother are the anonymous detractors of experience who assume no dominating feature or motivation beyond the level of the mass. Hurston's rage is directed against this faceless brood with a moral ferociousness that verges on misogyny. This profound undercurrent is relieved, however, by a drift toward caricature. Exaggerating the fat of misshapen men and calling attention in public to their sexual impotence, gaining dimensions of comic monologue, and leaving no genuine clue for those who gaze at her, Janie has elements of a secret life which sustains her through the misadventures of three husbands, a flood, justifiable homicide, trial, and vindication.

This psychological bent informing Janie's character is deflected by an anthropological emphasis that all but ruins this study of a female soul. The pseudodialect of southern patois gives Janie back to the folk ultimately, but this "return" contradicts other syntactical choices which Hurston superimposes on the structure through visions of Janie's interior life and Hurston's own narrative style. Janie implies new moral persuasions, while Hurston has her looking back, even returning, to the small town she desperately wishes to be free of. This dilemma of choices haunts the book from the very beginning and may, indeed, shed light on the "ancestral imperative."[18] That Janie does not break from her southern past, symbolized in the "old talk," but grasps how she might do so is the central problematic feature of the novel, previously alluded to as an undercurrent of doubt running through Hurston's strategies.

Written long before *Jubilee, Their Eyes Were Watching God* anticipates the thematic emphases prominent in *Sula* to the extent that in both the latter novels only the adventurous, deracinated personality is heroic, and that in both, the roots of experience are poisonous. One would do well to avoid the plunge down to the roots, seeking, rather, to lose oneself in a larger world of chance and danger. That woman must break loose from the hold of biography as older generations impose it, even the broader movements of tribe, constitutes a controlling theme of Hurston's work.

Images of space and time, inaugurated in the opening pages of the novel, are sounded across it with oracular intensity, defining the dream of Janie Starks as a cosmic disembodiment that renders her experience unitary with the great fantastic ages. "Ships at a distance have every man's wish on board. For some they come in with the tide" (5). Consonant with this history of fantasy life, Janie is something of a solitary reaper, disillusioned, stoical, in her perception of fate and death. "So the beginning of this was a woman and she had come back from burying the dead. . . . The people all saw her because it was sundown. The sun was gone, but he had left his footprints in the sky. It was time to hear things and talk" (5).

The novel is essentially informed by these ahistorical, specifically rustic, image clusters, giving the whole a topological consistency. Hurston, however, attempts to counterpoise this timeless current with elements of psychic specificity—Janie's growth toward an understanding of mutability and change and other aspects of internal movement. The novel's power of revelation, nonetheless, is rather persistently sabotaged at those times when Hurston intrudes metaphorical symbolism as a substitute for the hard precision of thought. Janie actually promises more than the author delivers. As a result, the novel is facile at times when it ought to be moving, captivated in stereotype when it should be dynamic.

The flood that devastates the Florida Everglades and the homes of the migrant farm workers of which Janie and Teacake are a part provides an example. The storm sequence is the novel's high point, its chief dramatic fulcrum, on which rests the motivation that will spur both Janie's self-defense against a rabid Teacake and her return to Eatonville and the Starks' house. Waiting in their cabins for the storm to recede, Janie, Teacake, and their fellow laborers are senseless with wonder at its power, "They seemed to be staring at the dark, but their eyes were watching God" (131). What one wants in this sequence is a crack in the mental surface of character so acute that the flood cleaves the narrative precisely in half, pre- and postdiluvial responses so distinctly contrasting that the opening lines—"their souls asking if He meant to measure their puny might against His"—mature into the ineluctable event. The reader expects a convergence of outer scene and its inner correspondence, but Hurston appears to forego the fruition of this parallel rhythm, content on delineating the external behavior of the agents.

Nothing specific to the inner life of Janie appears again for several pages; the awe that greets the display of the force of natural phenomena is replayed through the imagination of a third-person observer, dry feet and all, well above the action of furious winds. We miss the concentration on Janie's internal life which saves the entire first half of the narrative from the pathos of character buffeted by external circumstances. Janie never quite regains her former brilliance, and when we meet her considered judgments again, she has fled the 'Glades, after having had to shoot Teacake in self-defense (as a result of his violence, rabies-induced) and is seeking peace in the town where she has been "first lady." "Here was peace. She pulled in her horizon like a great fish-net. Pulled it from around the waist of the world and draped it over her shoulder. So much of life in its meshes! She called in her soul to come and see" (159).

One is not certain how these images of loss and labor should be read, nor why they strike with such finality, except that the lines make a good ending, this rolling in of fish nets and cleaning of meshes, but if we take Janie as a kind of adventurer, as a woman well familiar with the rites of burial and grief, then we read this closure as a eulogy for the living; Janie has been "buried" along with Teacake.

The fault with this scene is not that Janie has loved Teacake, but, rather, that the author has broken the potential pattern of revolt by having her resigned, as if she were ready for a geriatric retirement, to the town of frustrated love. We know that all novels do end, even if they end with "the," and so it is probably fitting for Janie to have a rest after the tragic events unleashed by the flood. But her decision to go back to Eatonville—after the trial—strikes me as a naive fictional pose. Or, more precisely, what she thinks about her life at that point seems inappropriate to the courageous defiance that she has often embodied all along. The logic of the novel tends to abrogate neat conclusions, and their indulgence in the end essentially mitigates the complex painful knowledge that Janie has gained about herself and the other.

The promise to seize upon the central dramatic moment of a woman's self-realization fizzles out in a litany of poetic platitudes about as apposite to Janie's dream of the horizon as the grandmother's obsessive fear of experience has been. We miss the knowledge or wisdom of revelation in the perfectly resolved ending—what is it that Janie knows now that she has come back from burying the dead of the sodden and bloated? Are the words merely decorative, or do they mobilize us toward a deeper mysterious sense? In a mode of fictive assumptions similar to Margaret Walker's, Zora Neale Hurston inherits a fabric of mystery without rethreading it. That is one kind of strategic decision. There are others.

Sula, by contrast, closes with less assurance. "'All that time, all that time, I thought I was missing Jude.' And the loss pressed down on her chest and came up into her throat. 'We was girls together,' she said as though explaining something. 'O Lord, Sula,' she cried, 'girl, girl, girlgirlgirl'" (149).

Nel's lament not only closes *Sula* but also reinforces the crucial dramatic questions which the novel has introduced—the very mystery of a Sula Peace and the extent to which the town of Medallion, Ohio, has been compelled by her, how they yearn for her, even to the point, oddly enough, of a collective rejection. Nel and Sula are more than girls together. They sustain the loss of innocence and its subsequent responsibilities with a degree of tormented passion seldom allowed even to lovers. More than anyone else in Medallion, they have been intimate witnesses of their mutual coming of age in a sequence of gestures that anticipates an ultimate disaffection between them, but the rhythm of its disclosure, determined early on by the reader as inexorable, is sporadic and intermittent enough in the sight of the two women that its fulfillment comes to both as a trauma of recognition. Nel Wright's "girl," repeated five times and run together in an explosion not only of the syntactical integrity of the line, but also of Nel's very heartbeat, is piercing and sudden remorse—remorse so long suspended, so elaborate in its deceptions and evasions that it could very well intimate the onset of a sickness—unto-death.

When Sula comes of age, she leaves Medallion for a decade in the wake, significantly, of Nel's marriage to Jude and her resignation to staid domestic life. Sula's return to Medallion, in a plague of robins, no less, would mark the restoration of an old friendship; Sula, instead, becomes Jude's lover for a brief time before abandoning him as she does other husbands of the town. Nel and Sula's "confrontation," on the deathbed of the latter, tells the reader and the best friend very little about what it is that makes Sula run. All that she admits is that she has "lived" and that if she and Nel had been such good friends, in fact, then her momentary "theft" of Jude might not have made any difference. Nel does not forgive Sula, but experiences, instead, a sense of emptiness and despair grounded, she later discovers after it doesn't matter anymore, in her own personal loss of Sula. She has not missed Jude, she finds out that afternoon, but her alter-ego passionately embodied in the other woman. It turns out that the same degree of emotional ambivalence that haunts Nel plagues the female reader of this novel. What is it about this woman Sula that triggers such attraction and repulsion at once? We have no certain answers, just as Nel does not, but, rather, resign ourselves to a complex resonance of feeling, which suggests that Sula is both necessary and frightening as a character realization.

In the relationship between Nel and Sula, Morrison demonstrates the female's rites-of-passage in their peculiar richness and impoverishment; the fabric of paradoxes—betrayals and sympathies, silences and aggressions, advances and sudden retreats—transmitted from mother to daughter, female to female, by mimetic gesture. That women learn primarily from other women strategies of survival and "homicide" is not news to anyone; indeed, this vocabulary of reference constitutes the chief revisionist, albeit implicit, feature of women's liberation effort. Because Morrison has no political axe to grind in this novel—in other words, she is not writing according to a formula that demands that her female agents demonstrate a simple, transparent love between women—she is free, therefore, to pursue the delicate tissue of intimate patterns of response between women. In doing so, she identifies those meanings of womanhood which statements of public policy are rhetorically bound to suppress.

One of the structural marvels of *Sula* is its capacity to telescope the process of generation and its consequent network of convoluted relationships. *Sula* is a woman's text par excellence, even subscribing in its behavior to Woolf's intimations that the woman's book, given the severe demands on her time, is spare.[19] The novel is less than two hundred pages of prose, but within its imaginative economy various equations of domestic power are explored. For instance, Sula's relationships to her mother Hannah and grandmother Eva Peace are portrayed in selective moments. In other words, Sula's destiny is located only in part by Nel, while the older Peace women in their indifference to decorous social behavior provide the soil in which her moral isolation is seeded and nurtured. Hannah and Eva have quite another story to tell apart from Sula's, much of it induced by Eva's abandonment by her husband BoyBoy and her awful defiance in response. The reader is not privy to various tales of transmission between Eva and Hannah, but we decide by inference that their collective wisdom leads Hannah herself to an authenticity of person not alterable by the iron-clad duties of motherhood, nor the sweet, submissive obligations of female love. In short, Hannah Peace is self-indulgent, full of disregard for the traditional repertoire of women's vanity-related gestures, and the reader tends to love her for it—the "sweet, low and guileless" flirting, no patting of the hair, or rushing to change clothes, or quickly applying makeup, but barefoot in summer, "in the winter her feet in a man's leather slippers with the backs flattened under her heels. . . . Her voice trailed, dipped and bowed; she gave a chord to the simplest words. Nobody, but nobody, could say 'hey sugar' like Hannah" (36).

Just as Hannah's temperament is "light and playful," Morrison's prose glides over the surface of events with a careful allegiance to the riffs of folk utterance—deliberate, inclusive, very often on the verge of laughter—but the profound deception of this kind of plain talk, allegedly "unsophisticated," is the vigil it keeps in killing silence about what it suspects, even knows, but never expresses. This hidden agenda has a malicious side, which Sula inherits without moral revision and correction. Morrison's stylistic choice in this passage is a significant clue to a reading of Hannah's character, a freedom of movement, a liberty of responses, worked out in a local school of realism. Hannah Peace is certainly not a philosopher, not even in secret, but that she rationalizes her address to the other in an unfailing economy of nuances implies a potential for philosophical grace. Among the women of *Sula,* the light rhythms usually conceal a deeper problem.

One of the more perplexing characters of recent American fiction, Eva Peace embodies a figure of both insatiable generosity and insatiable demanding. Like Hannah, Eva is seldom frustrated by the trammels of self-criticism, the terrible indecisiveness and scrupulosity released by doubt. Because Eva goes ahead without halting, ever, we could call her fault nothing less than innocence, and its imponderable cruelty informs her character with a kind of Old Testament logic. Eva behaves as though she were herself the sole instrument of divine inscrutable will. We are not exactly certain what oracular fever decides that she must immolate her son Plum.[20] Perhaps even his heroin addiction does not entirely explain it, but she literally rises to the task in moments of decision, orchestrated in pity and judgment. Like an avenging deity who must sacrifice its creation in order to purify it, Eva swings and swoops on her terrible crutches from her son's room, about to prepare his fire. She holds him in her arms, recalling moments from his childhood before dousing him with kerosene:

> He opened his eyes and saw what he imagined was the great wing of an eagle pouring a wet lightness over him. Some kind of baptism, some kind of blessing, he thought. Everything is going to be all right, it said. Knowing that it was so he closed his eyes and sank back into the bright hole of sleep.
> Eva stepped back from the bed and let the crutches rest under her arms. She rolled a bit of newspaper into a tight stick about six inches long, lit it and threw it onto the bed where the kerosene-soaked Plum lay in smug delight. Quickly, as the *whoosh of* flames engulfed him, she shut the door and made her slow and painful journey back to the top of the house. (40–41)

Not on any level is the reader offered easy access to this scene. Its enumerated, overworked pathos, weighed against the victim's painful ignorance not only of his imminent death but also of the requirements of his manhood generates contradictory feelings between shock and relief. The reader resents the authorial manipulation that engenders such feelings. The act itself, so violently divergent from the normal course of maternal actions and expectations, marks a subclimax. Further, it foreshadows the network of destruction, both willful and fortuitous, that ensnares Sula and Nel in an entanglement of predecided motivations. Eva, in effect, determines her own judgment, which Sula will seal without a hint of recourse to the deceptions or allegiances of kinship. Sula, who puts Eva in old age in an asylum, does not mistake her decision as a stroke of love or duty, nor does it echo any of the ambiguities of mercy.

Like Eva's, Sula's program of action as an adult woman is spontaneous and direct, but the reader in Sula's case does not temper her angle on Sula's behavior with compassion or second thought, as she tends to do in Eva's case. It could be argued, for instance, that Eva sacrifices Plum in order to save him, and however grotesque we probably adjudge her act, inspired by a moral order excluding contingency and doubt, no such excuse can be offered in Sula's behalf. We must also remember that Sula's nubile *singleness* and refusal of the acts and rites of maternity have implicitly corrupted her in our unconscious judgment and at a level of duplicity which our present "sexual arrangements"[21] protect and mandate. We encounter the raw details of her individualism, not engaged by naturalistic piety or existential rage, as a paradigm of wanton vanity. Her moral shape, however, does not come unprecedented or autonomously derived. Merging Eva's arrogance on the one hand and Hannah's self-indulgence on the other, "with a twist that was all her own imagination, she lived out her days exploring her own thoughts and emotions, giving them full reign, feeling no obligation to please anybody unless their pleasure pleased her" (102).

Just as Hannah and Eva have been Sula's principal models, they have also determined certain issues which she will live out in her own career. It is probably not accidental that the question which haunts Hannah—have I been loved?—devolves on Sula with redoubtable fury. If it is true that love does not exist until it is named, then the answer to the enigma of Sula Peace is not any more forthcoming than if it were not so. Yet, certainly the enormous consequences of being loved or not are relevant by implication to the agents of the novel. Morrison does not elaborate, but the instances of the question's appearance—halting, uncertain, embarrassed, or inappropriate words on a character's tongue—conceal the single most important missing element in the women's encounter with each other. A revealing conversation between Eva and Hannah suggests that even for the adult female the intricacies and entanglement of mother love (or perhaps woman love without distinction) is a dangerous inquiry to engage. Hannah cannot even formulate the sentences that would say the magic words, but angles in on the problem with a childlike timidity, which she can neither fake nor conceal.

"I know you fed us and all. I was talking 'bout something else. Like. Like. Playin' with us. Did you ever, you know, play with us?" (59).

This conversation may be compared with one that Sula overhears the summer of her twelfth year, between Hannah and a couple of friends. The three women confirm for each other the agonies of childrearing, but can never quite bring themselves around to admitting that love is contingent and human and all too often connected with notions of duty. Hannah tells one of the friends that her quality of love is sufficient. "You love [your child], like I love Sula. I just don't like her. That's the difference." And that's the "difference" that sends Sula "flying up the stairs," blankly "aware of a sting in her eye," until recalled by Nel's voice.

To pin the entire revelation of the source of Sula's later character development on this single episode would be a fallacy of overdetermination, but its strategic location in the text suggests that its function is crucial to the unfolding of events to come, to the way that Sula responds to them, and to the manner in which we interpret her responses. At least two other events unmistakably hark back to it. Chicken Little joins Sula and Nel later on the same afternoon in their play by the river. In the course of things Sula picked him up and "swung him outward and then around and around. His knickers ballooned and his shrieks of frightened joy startled the birds and the fat grasshoppers. When he slipped from her hands and sailed out over the water they could still hear his bubbly laughter" (52).

Frozen in a moment of terror, neither girl can do more than stare at the "closed place in the water." Morrison aptly recreates the stark helplessness of two trapped people, gaining a dimension of horror because the people are children, drawn up short in a world of chance and danger. That they do nothing in particular, except recognize that Shadrack, the town's crack-brained veteran of World War 1, has seen them and will not tell, consigns them both to a territory of their own most terrible judgment and isolation. In this case the adult conscience of each springs forth in the eyes of the other, leaving childhood abruptly in its wake. The killing edge is that the act itself must remain a secret. Unlike other acts of rites-of-passage, this one must not be communicated. At Chicken Little's funeral, Sula "simply cried" (55), and from his grave site she and Nell, fingers laced, trot up the road "on a summer day wondering what happened to butterflies in the winter" (57).

The interweave of lyricism and dramatic event is consistent with Morrison's strategies. Their juxtaposition does not appear to function ironically, but to present dual motifs in a progressive revelation that allows the reader to "swallow" dramatic occurrences whose rhetoric, on the face of it, is unacceptable. At the same time we get in right perspective Sula's lack of ten-

sion—a tension that distinguishes the character stunned by her own ignorance, or by malice in the order of things. Sula, by contrast, just goes along,
"completely free of ambition, with no affection for money, property, or
things, no greed, no desire to command attention or compliments—no
ego. For that reason she felt no compulsion to verify herself—be consistent
with herself" (103). That Sula apparently wants nothing, is curiously free of
mimetic desire and its consequent pull toward willfulness, keeps pity in
check and releases unease in its absence.

Sula's lack of egoism—which appears an incorrect assessment on the
narrator's part—renders her an antipassionate spectator of the human
scene, even beholding her mother's death by fire in calculated coolness.
Weeks after Chicken's burial Hannah is in the backyard of the Peace household, lighting a fire in which she accidentally catches herself and burns to
death. Eva recalls afterward that "she had seen Sula standing on the back
porch just looking." When her friends insist that she is more than likely
mistaken since Sula was "probably struck dumb" by the awful spectacle, Eva
remains quietly convinced "that Sula had watched Hannah burn not because she was paralyzed, but because she was interested" (67).

This moment of Sula's interestedness, and we tend to give Eva the benefit of the doubt in this case, must be contrasted to her response to Chicken's
drowning, precluding us from remaining impartial judges of her behavior,
even as we understand its sources in the earlier event. Drawn into a cycle of
negation, Sula at twelve is Sula at twenty, and the instruments of perception
which the reader uses to decipher her character do not alter over the whole
terrain of the work. From this point on, any course of action that she takes
is already presumed by negating choices. Whether she steals Nel's husband
or a million dollars matters less to the reader than to the other characters,
since we clearly grasp the structure of her function as that of a radical
amorality and consequently of a radical freedom. We would like to love
Sula, or damn her, inasmuch as the myth of the black American woman allows only Manichean responses, but it is impossible to do either. We can
only behold in an absolute suspension of final judgment.

Morrison induces this ambiguous reading through an economy of
means, none of which relate to the classic *bête noire* of black experience—
the powerful predominance of white and the endless litany of hateful responses associated with it. That Sula is not bound by the customary alliances to naturalism or historical determinism at least tells us what
imperatives she does not pursue. Still, deciding what traditions do inspire
her character is not made easier.

I would suggest that Hurston's Janie Starks presents a clear precedent.

Though not conforming at every point, I think the two characters lend themselves to a comparative formula. In both cases, the writer wishes to examine the particular details and propositions of liberty under constricted conditions in a low mimetic mode of realism, that is, an instance of realism in which the characters are not decisively superior in moral or social condition to the reader.[22] Both Janie and Sula are provided an arena of action within certain limits. In the former case, the character's dreams are usually too encompassing to be accommodated within the space that circumscribes her. The stuff of her dreams, then, remains disembodied, ethereal, out of time, nor are her dreams fully differentiated, inasmuch as all we know about them is their metaphorical conformity to certain natural or romantic configurations. It is probably accurate to say that the crucial absence for Janie has been an intellectual chance, or the absence of a syntax distinctive enough in its analytical requirements to realign a particular order of events to its own demands. In other words, Janie is stuck in the limitations of dialect, while her creator is free to make use of a range of linguistic resources to achieve her vision.

The principle of absence that remains inchoate for Janie is articulate for Sula in terms whose intellectual implications are unmistakable—Sula lacks the shaping vision of art, and the absence is as telling in the formation of her character as the lack of money or an appropriately ordered space might be for the heroines, for example, of Henry James's *Portrait of a Lady* or *Wings of the Dove;* in both of James's works the heroines are provided with *money,* a term that James's narrator assigns great weight in deciding what strategies enable women to do battle with the world, though the equation between gold and freedom is ironically burdened here. In Woolf's conception of personal and creative freedom for the woman, *money, space,* and *time* figure prominently.

It is notable that Janie and Sula, within the social modalities that determine them, are actually quite well off. Their suffering, therefore, transcends the visceral and concrete, moving progressively toward the domain of symbols. In sharp contrast to Walker's Vyry, the latter-day heroines approach the threshold of speaking and acting *for self,* or the organization of one's resources with preeminent reference to the highest form of self-regard, the urge to speak one's own words urgently. Hurston and Morrison after her are both in the process of abandoning the vision of the corporate good as a mode of heroic suffering. Precisely what will take its place defines the dilemma of *Sula* and its protagonist. The dilemma itself highlights problems of figuration for black female character whose future, whose terms of existence, are not entirely known at the moment.

The character of Sula impresses the reader as a problem in interpretation because, for one thing, the objective myth of the black American woman, at least from the black woman's point of view, is drawn in valorized images that intrude against the text, or compete with it like a jealous goddess. That this privileged other narrative is counterbalanced by its opposite, equally exaggerated and distorted, simply reinforces the heroics to the extent that the black woman herself imagines only one heroic possibility—and that is herself. *Sula* attempts a correction of this uninterrupted superiority on the one hand and unrelieved pathology on the other; the reader's dilemma arises in having to choose. The duplicitous reader embraces the heroics with no intent of disproof or unbelief, while the brave one recognizes that the negating countermyth would try to establish a dialectical movement between the subperspectives, gaining a totally altered perspective in the process.[23] In other words, Sula, Vyry, and Janie need not be seen as the terms of an either/or proposition. The three characters here may be identified as subperspectives, or *angles onto* a larger seeing. The struggle that we bring with us to *Sula,* indeed, the implicit proposition upon which the text is based, is the imperative that requires our coming to terms with the very complexities that a juggling of perspectives demands.

Sula is not the "other" as one kind of reading would suggest, or perhaps as we might wish, but a figure of the rejected and vain part of the self—ourselves—who in its thorough corruption and selfishness cannot utter, believe in, nor prepare for, love. I am not entirely sure that Sula speaks for us on the lower frequencies—though she could very well. The importance of this text is that she speaks at all.

In a conversation with Robert Stepto, Toni Morrison confirms certain critical conjectures that are made here concerning the character of Sula. "[She] was hard, for me; very difficult to make up that kind of character. Not difficult to think it up, but difficult to describe a woman who could be used as a classic type of evil force. Other people could use her that way. And at the same time, I didn't want to make her freakish or repulsive or unattractive. I was interested at that time in a very old, worn-out idea, which was to do something with good and evil, but putting it in different terms."[24]

As Morrison goes on to discuss the idea, Sula and Nel are to her mind an alterity of agents—"two sides of the same person, or two sides of one extraordinary character" (216). Morrison does not attribute the birth of her idea to any particular cultural or historical event and certainly not to the most recent wave of American feminism, but it does seem fairly clear that a Sula Peace is *for black American literature,* if not for the incredibly rich potential of black American female personality, a radical alternative to Vyry

Ware and less so, to placid Janie Crawford Starks. "This was really part of the difficulty—I didn't know anyone like her. I never knew a woman like that at any rate. But I knew women who looked like that, who looked like they could be like that. And then you remember women who were a little bit different in [one's] town, you know" (217).

If we identify Sula as a kind of countermythology, we are saying that she is no longer bound by a rigid pattern of predictions, predilections, and anticipations. Even though she is a character in a novel, her strategic place as *potential being* might argue that *subversion* itself—law breaking—is an aspect of liberation that women must confront from its various angles, in its different guises. Sula's outlawry may not be the best kind, but that she has the will toward rebellion itself *is* the stunning idea. This project in liberation, paradoxically, has no particular dimension in time, yet it is for all time.

4

Gwendolyn the Terrible:
Propositions on Eleven Poems

For over four decades, Gwendolyn Brooks[1] wrote poetry which reflected a particular historical order, often close to the heart of the public event, but the dialectic that is engendered between the event and her reception of it remains, perhaps, one of the more subtle confrontations of criticism. We cannot always say with grace or ease that there is a direct correspondence between the issues of her poetry and her race and sex, nor did Brooks make the assertion necessary at every step of our reading. Black and female are basic and inherent in her poetry. The critical question is *how* they are said. Here is what the poet related about her own work:

> My aim, in my next future, is to write poems that will somehow successfully "call" all black people: black people in taverns, black people in alleys, black people in gutters, schools, offices, factories, prisons, the consulate; I wish to reach black people in mines, on farms, on thrones; *not* always to "teach"—I shall wish often to entertain, to illumine. My newish voice will not be an imitation of the contemporary young black voice, which I so admire, but an extending adaptation of today's G.B. voice.[2]

The seventies' G.B. voice was one of the most complex on the American scene precisely because Brooks refused to make easy judgments. In fact, her disposition to preserve judgment is directly mirrored in a poetry of cunning, laconic surprise. Any descriptive catalog can be stretched and strained in her case: I have tried "uncluttered," "clean," "robust," "ingenious," "unorthodox," and in each case a handful of poems will fit. This method of grading and cataloguing, however, is essentially busywork, and we are still left with the main business: What in this poetry is stunning and evasive?

To begin with, one of Brooks's most faithfully anthologized poems, "We

Real Cool," illustrates the wealth of implication that the poet can achieve in a very spare poem:

> We real cool. We
> Left school. We
> Lurk late. We
> Strike straight. We
> Sing sin. We
> Thin gin. We
> Jazz June. We
> Die soon.[3]

The simplicity of the poem is stark to the point of elaborateness. Less than lean, it is virtually coded. Made up entirely of monosyllables and end-stops, the poem is no nonsense at all. Gathered in eight units of three-beat lines, it does not necessarily invite inflection, but its persistent bump on "we" suggests waltz time to my ear. If the reader chooses to render the poem that way, she runs out of breath, or trips her tongue, but it seems that such "breathlessness" is exactly required of dudes hastening toward their death. Deliberately subverting the romance of sociological pathos, Brooks presents the pool players—"seven in the golden shovel"—in their own words and time. They make no excuse for themselves and apparently invite no one else to do so. The poem is their situation as *they* see it. In eight (could be nonstop) lines, here is their total destiny. Perhaps comic geniuses, they could well drink to this poem, making it a drinking/revelry song.[4]

Brooks's poetry, then, is not weighed down by egoistic debris, nor is her world one of private symbolisms alone, or even foremost; rather, she presents a range of temperaments and situations articulated by three narrative voices: a first-person focalization, as in "gay chaps at the bar":

> We knew how to order. Just the dash
> Necessary. The length of gaiety in good taste.
> Whether the raillery should be slightly iced
> And given green, or served up hot and lush.
> And we knew beautifully how to give to women
> The summer spread, the tropics of our love.
> When to persist, or hold a hunger off.
> Knew white speech. How to make a look an omen.   (*WGB*, 48)

An omniscient narrator for the ballads:

> It was Mabbie without the grammar school gates
> And Mabbie was all of seven.

And Mabbie was cut from a chocolate bar.
And Mabbie thought life was heaven.   (*WGB*, 14)

And then a concealed narrator, looking at the situation through a double focus. In other words, the narrator ironically translates her subject's ingenuousness. To this last group of poems belongs "The Anniad," perhaps one of the liveliest demonstrations of the uses to which irony can be put.

A pun on *The Aeneid* or *The Iliad*, the title of this piece prepares us for a mock heroic journey of a particular female soul as she attempts to gain self-knowledge against an unresponsive social backdrop. At the same time, the poem's ironic point of view is a weapon wielded by a concealed narrator who mocks the ritualistic attitudes of love's ceremony. The poem is initially interesting for its wit and ingenuity, but eventually G.B.'s dazzling acrobatics force a "shock of recognition." Annie, in her lofty naïveté, has been her own undoing, transforming mundane love into mystical love, insisting on knights when there are, truly, only men in this world. Annie obviously misses the point, and what we confront in her tale is a riot of humor—her dreams working against reality as it is. We protest in Annie's behalf. We want the dream to come true, but Brooks does not concede, and that she does not confirms the intent of the poem: a parodic portrayal of sexual pursuit and disaster.

Shaped by various elements of surprise, "The Anniad" is a funny poem, but its comedy proceeds from self-recognition. Brooks gives this explanation:

> Well, the girl's name was Annie, and it was my pompous pleasure to raise her to a height that she probably did not have. I thought of *The Iliad* and said: 'I'll call this "The Anniad." At first, interestingly enough, I called her Hester Allen, and I wanted then to say "The Hesteriad," but I forgot why I changed it to Annie. . . . I was fascinated by what words might do there in the poem. You can tell that it's labored, a poem that's very interested in the mysteries and magic of technique.[5]

From the 1949 Pulitzer Prize winning volume, *Annie Allen*, "The Anniad" may be read as a workshop in G.B.'s poetry. Its strategies are echoed in certain shorter poems from *A Street in Bronzeville* and *The Bean Eaters*, particularly the effective use of slurred rime and jarring locution in "Patent Leather" and "The Sundays of Satin-Legs Smith." In narrative scope and dramatic ambition, "The Anniad" anticipates *In the Mecca*, written some twenty years later.

Forty-three stanzas long, "The Anniad" is built on contradictions. Locating their "answer" or meaning constitutes the poem's puzzle and reward. Here are the two opening stanzas:

Think of sweet and chocolate,
Left to folly or to fate,
Whom the higher gods forgot
Whom the lower gods berate;
Physical and underfed
Fancying on the featherbed
What was never and is not.

What is ever and is not.
Pretty tatters blue and red,
Buxom berries beyond rot,
Western clouds and quarter stars,
Fairy sweet of old guitars
Littering the little head
Light upon the featherbed.   (*WGB*, 83)

After saying all we can about the formal qualities of these stanzas, we are still not certain about the subject of the poem. By means of slurs and puzzles of language, the action is hustled on, and circumlocution—"tell all the truth, but tell it slant"—becomes a decisive aspect of the work's style. This Song of Ann is a puzzle to be unraveled, and the catalogue of physical and mental traits deployed in the first fifteen stanzas becomes a set of clues. Not unlike games or riddles played by children, the poem gathers its clues in stanzas, and just as the questioner in the child's game withholds the solution, the speaker here does the same thing, often to the reader's dismay. However, once we know the answer, the game becomes a ritual where feigned puzzlement is part of the ceremony. In a discussion of Emily Dickinson's poetry, Northrop Frye points out that the "riddle or oblique description of some object" is one of the oldest and most primitive forms of poetry.[6] In "The Anniad" the form gains a level of sophistication that is altogether stunning.

The dilemma of Annie is also that of "Chocolate Mabbie": the black-skinned female's rejection by black males. The lesson begins early for the black woman, as it does for young Mabbie. A too well-known theme of black life, this idea is the subject of several G.B. poems, but usually disguised to blunt its edge of madness and pain. With Mabbie's experience in mind, then, we are prepared for the opening lines of "The Anniad" and their peculiar mode of indirection.

The color theme is a crucial aspect of the poem's proposition and procedure, posing light skin and dark skin as antagonists. The question is not merely cosmetic, since hot combs and bleaching creams were once thought to be wonder-workers, but it penetrates far and sharp into the psychic and spiritual reaches of the black woman's soul. I know of no modern poet before Brooks to address this subject, and as she does so, she offers the female a way out not only by awaking the phobia, but also by regarding it as yet another style of absurdity. The point is to bury inverted racism in ridicule and obscure reference, but not before contemplating its effects.

In "the ballad of chocolate Mabbie," the situation goes this way:

> Out came the saucily bold Willie Boone.
> It was woe for our Mabbie now.
> He wore like a jewel a lemon-hued lynx
> With sandwaves loving her brow.
>
> It was Mabbie alone by the grammar school gates.
> Yet chocolate companions had she:
> Mabbie on Mabbie with hush in the heart.
> Mabbie on Mabbie to be.   (*WGB*, 14)

An interesting contrast to Mabbie's ballad is "Stand off, daughter of the dusk":

> And do not wince when the bronzy lads
> Hurry to cream-yellow shining.
> It is plausible. The sun is a lode.
>
> True, there is silver under
> The veils of the darkness
> But few care to dig in the night
> For the possible treasure of stars.   (*WGB*, 121)

If metaphor is a way to utter the unutterable, then "cream-yellow shining" and "veils of darkness" hint at It, but both are needlessly quaint, drawing attention away from the subject. Not one of her best or most interesting poems, it does articulate the notion of rejection without preaching a sermon about it. In "The Anniad," by contrast, the mood is sardonic and words are ablaze with a passion to kill, both the situation and one's tendency to be undone by it.

The male lover's ultimate choice to betray "sweet and chocolate" leads Annie's "tan man" to what he would consider the better stuff:

> Gets a maple banshee. Gets
> A sleek-eyed gypsy moan.
> Oh those violent vinaigrettes!
> Oh bad honey that can hone
> Oilily the bluntest stone!
> Oh mad bacchanalian lass
> That his random passion has!   (*WGB*, 88)

Clever synecdoche works here for the poet rather than against her, as it does in "Stand off," and its comic distortions are reinforced by slant rhyme in the last two lines of the stanza. "Bad" honey is the best kind in colloquial parlance, "bad" having appropriated its antonym, and in the midst of "vinaigrettes" and "bacchanalian lasses," it is a sharp surprise.

"Tan man" himself gets similar treatment:

> And a "man of tan" engages
> For the springtime of her pride,
> Eats the green by easy stages,
> Nibbles at the root beneath
> With intimidating teeth
> But no ravishment enrages.
> No dominion is defied.
>
> Narrow master master-calls;
> And the godhead glitters now
> Cavalierly on his brow.
> What a hot theopathy
> Roisters through her, gnaws her walls,
> And consumes her where she falls
> In her gilt humility.
>
> How he postures at his height;
> Unfamiliar, to be sure,
> With celestial furniture.
> Contemplating by cloud-light
> His bejewelled diadem;
> As for jewels, counting them,
> Trying if the pomp be pure.   (WGB, 84–85)

Rodent, knight, god, by turn, "Tan man" is seen from a triple exposure: his own exaggerated sense of self-worth, the woman's complicity with it, and the poet's assessment, elaborated in the imaginative terms implied by the woman's behavior. Given the poem's logic, the woman and the man are deluded on opposing ends of the axis of self-delusion. As it turns out, he is not the hot lover "theopathy" would make him out to be, but Annie denies it, fearing that to say so would be to evoke an already imminent betrayal:

> Doomer, though, crescendo-comes
> Prophesying hecatombs.
> Surrealist and cynical.
> Garrulous and guttural.

Spits upon the silver leaves.
Denigrates the dainty eves
Dear dexterity achieves.

Vaunting hands are now devoid.
Hieroglyphics of her eyes
Blink upon a paradise
Paralyzed and paranoid.
But idea and body too
Clamor "Skirmishes can do.
Then he will come back to you."   (*WGB*, 85–86)

This scene of "ruin," brought on by sexual impotence, gains a dimension of pathos because it anticipates the woman's ultimate loneliness, but this judgment is undercut by the caricature of the male.

In order to fully appreciate the very pronounced contrast between other G.B. poems and this one, we should note the quality of images in "The Anniad." The dominant function of imagery here is auditory rather than visual, because Brooks, as well as the reader, is so thoroughly fascinated with the sound of words: for example, "Doomer, though, crescendo-comes / Prophesying hecatombs." This heavy word-motion is sustained by the most unlikely combinations—"surrealist and cynical," "garrulous and guttural," etc. The combinations are designed to strike with such forceful contrariness that trying to visualize them would propel us into astigmatism. We confront a situation where the simple image has been replaced by its terministic equivalent, or by words which describe other words in the poem.[7]

Brooks's intensely cultivated language in "The Anniad" appears to rely heavily on the cross-reference of dictionaries and thesauri. *Lexis* here is dazzling to the point of distraction, but it is probably a feature of the poem's moral ferocity. It is clear that the poet, like others, has her eye on the peculiar neurosis that often prevails in sexual relationships. Rather than dignify it, she mocks its vaunted importance, exaggerating its claims nearly beyond endurance. In effect, exaggeration destroys its force, desanctifying hyperbolean phallic status. At the same time, it appears that a secondary motivation shadows the primary one—the poet's desire to suggest a strategy for destroying motives of inferiority in the self. This psychological motif in Brooks's early poetry is disturbing. At times it appears to verge on self-hatred, but style conceals it. "Men of careful turns" (XV, from "The Womanhood," *WGB*, 123) offers an example, I think, by depicting an interracial love affair corrupted by racism and certain intervening class loyalties. To conceal her disappointment, the black female narrator claims moral superiority over the white male, but in this case, as in "The Anniad," the literal situation is carefully disguised.

In the hands of a lesser poet Brooks's pyrotechnics would likely have been disastrous, but G.B. achieved her aim by calibrating the narrative situation of the poem to its counterpart in the "real" world. Grounded in solidly social and human content, the poem is saved from sliding off into mere strangeness. The mischievous, brilliantly ridiculous juxtapositions achieve a perspective in relationship to an imagined context, and we gain thereby a taste for, rather than a surfeit of, exaggeration toward a specific end: to expose the sadness and comedy of self-delusion in an equally deluded world.

By contrast, a poem whose principle of composition is based on continuity of diction is another of the sonnets, "still do I keep my look, my identity." A model of precision, the poem reworks a single sentence to elaborate its message:

> Each body has its art, its precious prescribed
> Pose, that even in passion's droll contortions, waltzes,
> Or push of pain—or when a grief has stabbed,
> Or hatred hacked—is its, and nothing else's.
> Each body has its pose. No other stock
> That is irrevocable, perpetual
> And its to keep. In castle, or in shack.
> With rags or robes. Through good, nothing, or ill.
> And even in death a body, like no other
> On any hill or plain or crawling cot
> Or gentle for the lilyless hasty pall
> (Having twisted, gagged, and then sweet-ceased to
>   bother),
> Shows the old personal art, the look. Shows what
> It showed at baseball. What it showed in school.   (*WGB*, 49)

This concentration on a single notion is essential to the working out of the poem, and the qualifying phrases, which establish momentum, create the effect of the poem's being made in front of us. The careful structuring of the body's lines, imitated in time and space, is inherently strategic.

In its directness of presentation, "still do I keep my look" (like "gay chaps at the bar") may be relegated to the category of what might be called G.B.'s "pretty" poems: the sword has been blunted by a closer concession to the expected. An excerpt from "the old marrieds" provides another example:

But in the crowding darkness not a word did they say.

Though the pretty-coated birds had piped so lightly all
the day.

And he had seen the lovers in the little side streets.
And she had heard the morning stories clogged with
sweets.   (*WGB*, 3)

The opening poem of *A Street in Bronzeville*, "the old marrieds" belongs to
G.B.'s early career. Its tender insistence is matched elsewhere: for instance,
"In Honor of David Anderson Brooks, My Father" and "The Bean Eaters,"
both from the volume *The Bean Eaters*. An aspect of the poet's reality, this
compassionate response to the lives of old people has its complement in
her version of the heroic. Two poems from *In the Mecca*, "Medgar Evers" and
"Malcolm X," are celebratory:

The man whose height his fear improved he
arranged to fear no further. The raw
intoxicated time was time for better birth
or a final death.

Old styles, old tempos, all the engagement of
the day—the sedate, the regulated fray—
the antique light, the Moral Rose, old gusts,
tight whistlings from the past, the mothballs
in the love at last our man forswore.

Medgar Evers annoyed confetti and assorted
brands of businessmen's eyes.

The shows came down: to maxims and surprise.
And palsy.

Roaring no rapt arise-ye to the dead, he
leaned across tomorrow. People said that
he was holding clean globes in his hands.   (*WGB*, 410)

A poem for the slain civil-rights leader of Mississippi, "Medgar Evers" rec-
onciles celebration and surprise. G.B. has not exaggerated a feature of
reality—Evers's heroism—but has invested that reality with unique significance. A similar notion works for "Malcolm X," with a touch of the whimsical added:

Original
Ragged-round.
Rich-robust.

He had the hawk-man's eyes.
We gasped. We saw the maleness.
The maleness raking out and making guttural the air
And pushing us to walls.

And in a soft and fundamental hour
A sorcery devout and vertical
beguiled the world.

He opened us—
who was a key,

who was a man.   (*WGB*, 411)

In these two poems, as well as others from the later volumes, Brooks explores various kinds of heroism by means of a shrewd opposition of understatement and hyperbole. From *The Bean Eaters*, "Strong Men, Riding Horses" provides a final example:

Strong Men, riding horses. In the West
On a range five hundred miles. A thousand. Reaching
From dawn to sunset. Rested blue to orange.
From hope to crying. Except that Strong Men are
Desert-eyed. Except that Strong Men are
Pasted to stars already. Have their cars
Beneath them. Rentless too. Too broad of chest
To shrink when the Rough Man hails. Too flailing
To redirect the Challenger, when the Challenge
Nicks; slams; buttonholes. Too saddled.

I am not like that. I pay rent, am addled
By illegible landlords, run, if robbers call.
What mannerisms I present, employ,
Are camouflage, and what my mouths remark
To word-wall off that broadness of the dark
Is pitiful.

I am not brave at all.   (*WGB*, 313)

This brilliant use of familiar symbols recalls the staccato message of movie advertisements. It conjures up heroes of the Western courtly love tradition from Charlemagne to Gawain to John Wayne and Superman. Counterposed against this implied pantheon of superstars is a simple shrunken confessional, the only complete declaratives in the poem. That the speaker pits herself against the contrived heroes of a public imagination suggests that the comparison is not to be taken seriously. It is sham exactly because of the disparity between public idealism and the private condition, but the comic play-off between the poet's open, self-mocking language (a pose of humility) and the glittering, delirious "dig-me-brag" of the "strong men" is the demonstration, more precisely, of opposing poles of reality—exaggeration and understatement. In the world of Gwendolyn Brooks, the sword is double-edged, constantly turning.

Only a fraction of the canon, the poems discussed in this essay represent the poet's range of strategies and demonstrate her linguistic vitality and her ability to allow language to penetrate to the core of neutral events. The titles of Brooks's volumes, from *A Street in Bronzeville* to *In the Mecca,* suggest her commitment to life in its unextraordinary aspects. Reworking items of common life, Brooks reminded us that creative experience can be mined from this vast store of unshaped material. To see reality through the eyes of the clichéd or the expected, however, is not to revisit it but to hasten the advance of snobbery and exclusion. In her poetry's insistence that common life is not as common as we sometimes suspect, G.B. remains the democratic poet of the late twentieth century. That she neither condescended nor insisted on preciousness is rewarding, but, above all, her detachment from poetry as cult and cant gave her access to lived experience, which always invigorates her lines. By displacing the familiar with the unfamiliar word, Brooks employed a vocabulary that redefines what we know already in a way we have not known it before. The heightened awareness that results brings to our consciousness an interpenetration of events which lends them a new significance.

Some of Brooks's poems speak directly to situations for which black women need names, but this specificity may be broadened to define situations that speak for other women as well. The magic of irony and humor can be brought to bear by any female in her most dangerous life-encounter—the sexual/emotional entanglement. Against that entanglement, her rage and disappointment are poised, but often impotently, unless channeled by positive force. For women writers, decorum, irony, and style itself are often mobilized against chaos. Thus, women don't cry in Brooks's poetry, nor did the poet cry over them, but she was remarkably alive and questioning in the dialectical relationship she posed between feeling and thinking. Hers is a tough choice of weapons because it has little use for the traditional status of woman—connubial, man-obsessed. The style of Brooks's poetry, then, gives us by implication and example a model of power, control, and subtlety. No idealogue, Brooks did not have to be. Enough woman and poet, she merged both realities into a single

achievement. Comedy and pathos, compassion and criticism are not estranged integers in this poetry, but a tangled skein of feeling, both vital and
abstract, imposed on a particular historical order. With a taste for the city
and an ear for change, Gwendolyn Brooks restored the tradition of citizen-
poet.

5

"An Order of Constancy":
Notes on Brooks and the Feminine

The adopted procedure for this essay is neither fish nor fowl and, as such, breathes in the impure air of literary interpretation, verging on social theory. It assumes for the moment a sort of critically illegitimate stance—the literary text *does* point outside itself—in the primary interest of leading the reader back inside the universe of the apparently self-contained artifact. With some luck, we hope to negotiate between two different kinds of related critical inquiry: What does the writer teach us, or illuminate in us, concerning situations for which we need a name,[1] in this case, the "feminine," whose very conjuring broaches more confusion than we can comfortably settle in the course of a workday? What does the writer take with her from "experience" to the transmuting work itself?

I

The stage of interaction that arises between an audience and the visible aspects of a public performance sketches a paradigm for understanding the social dimensions of an aesthetic act, but it also brings into focus the most acute aspects of consciousness—to perceive, to be perceived. On the one hand, the subject is acting; on the other, acted upon. The distance between these related grammatical properties, mobilized by a single term, is precisely the difference and overlap between subjects and objects of interrogation, neither of which can be split off from the other with impunity. To the extent that the writer and the artistic process that she or he engages are neither wholly autonomous nor dependent, but rather, interdependent, suspended between opposing yet mutually coexistent means, both writer and process approach the "feminine," whose elusive claims escape not only precise definition but also decided terrain. Gwendolyn Brooks's "feminine" across the poet's writing career is a nominative of many facets. About this still center, modifiers shift, lose and gain emphases alternately, but there is an "order of constancy" here whose active paradoxes throw light on the paradox of the "feminine."

There are few things riskier at the moment than defining the "feminine" in a way that does not offend what, until yesterday, we thought of as its primary subject—"woman herself." Is this complex of traits gender-related and, therefore, a locus of attributions culturally conferred, biologically sustained? Can we count on its disappearance when the "revolution" comes? Is the "feminine" yet one other heterosexist hoax whose genuinely fraudulent character will be revealed as such in the figurative "new world" of widened sexualities presently upon us?[2] According to the editors of a work on feminist theory,[3] feminine consciousness is only a single aspect of woman-consciousness (whatever we decide that is), but it seems difficult to specify the boundaries of either, except insofar as "woman-consciousness" and "feminine" inscribe the absence of "male" and "masculine." *Feminist Theory: A Critique of Ideology* attempted to correct and revise our negative perspective on ideas regarding the "feminine." For feminist theoreticians, the "feminine" is often, ironically enough, an "object of analysis rather than a source of insight" (ix). Insofar as the subject is the "object of attention of another," we might have anticipated that the "feminine" arises "from the sensation of being looked at" (ix), and involves, relatedly, the dialectical tensions at work in "double consciousness."[4] Simone de Beauvoir in *The Second Sex* describes an existential correspondence between "feminine" and "other" so that both might be seen as a negation of ego (read "male"). We would intrude on this accumulated calculus of power a point of view too often short-shrifted: I would say that the "feminine" and "other" are subjectivities who experience their being from a posture of affirmation. We would regard the exception as aberrance. A theory that maintains the aberrant at the center of its interests might answer the needs of public policy, or unwittingly serve the requirements of the dominant myth, but its responsive capacity to the living situations of the social subject is, at times, embarrassingly limited.

Trapped between the Scylla of feminist mandates on the one hand and the Charybdis of dominative and patriarchal modes of power on the other, the subject of "feminine attributes" is apparently abandoned to a useless set of traits, not unlike a sixth toe or finger in some phase of human evolution. Exactly what it is that women in history are asked to abdicate in order to achieve authentic consciousness has the elusive subtleties of Steuben glass or a cymbidium orchid and is invested with about as much actively negotiable and comparative power, except we know when we have seen either and that it is difficult for us to say now *why* we'd *prefer* not to be without access, real or imagined, to either. The "feminine" evades definition, perhaps, because it is both ubiquitous and shadowy on the world's body:

> The nuances of sensitivity to appearances, the fine distinctions in the observance of one's behavior and that of others, the silent exploration of the consciousness in which one functions as an "other" deserve our attention as means toward understanding human motivation and psychology as well as our condemnations as the product of asymmetrical power.[5]

For Keohane and the other editors of *Feminist Theory*, the "feminine" locates a disposition in the eyes of a gazer, female and male, but if the angle of seeing is obverted, how does the gazed upon see itself, see out?

For Julia Kristeva, the female body, specifically, the "maternal body," takes us to the limen of "nature/culture": The "not-sayable," the body of the mother escapes signification, meaning, sense because the "mother-woman"

> is rather a strange "fold" *(pli)* which turns nature into culture, and the "speaking subject" *(le parlant)* into biology. Although it affects each woman's body, this heterogeneity, which cannot be subsumed by the signifier, literally explodes with pregnancy—the dividing line between nature and culture—and with the arrival of the child—which frees a woman from uniqueness and gives her a chance, albeit not a certainty, of access to the other, to the ethical. These peculiarities of the maternal body make a woman a creature of folds, a catastrophe of being that cannot be subsumed by the dialectic of the trinity or its supplements.[6]

I am not entirely certain that the "feminine" and "female body" may be taken as synonymous constructs, but it does appear that the space of overlap between them is so broad that we cannot imagine one without deploying the other. For theorists of an "écriture feminine," of which Kristeva is said to be one, the "feminine" has little to do with women in history. In fact Alice Jardine's *Gynesis* ("woman-process")[7] concentrates on male writers in modernity and their reinstitution of the female body at a fundamental level of writing: (1) the subversion of the idea of a unified speaking subject; (2) the undermining of all authority; and (3) the figurative use of the female genitalia as a mode of decentering and deconstructing the text. The "fold," or "pli," the "hole," the "gap," or "interstice" become items of a revised critical lexis that is designed—we are led to believe—to engender a radically different ideology and practice of writing, focusing "feminine" and "female body" at the center of altered positions and dispositions.

In Jardine's view, these changes on the textual surface of male-writing

(Derrida, Lacan, Deleuze, Guattari, of *Anti-Oedipus,* specifically) invite a direct response from feminist investigation/theory, lest the latter find itself isolated on the contemporary intellectual scene. What seems to me a fairly complete breach between matters of feminist social theory and feminist metatheory appears beyond repair. If Susan Suleiman is correct, then "the cultural significance of the female body is not only (not even first and foremost) that of a flesh-and-blood entity, but that of a *symbolic* con*struct.*"[8] To see the issue otherwise, Suleiman thinks, is to pursue the archaic. The "programmatic and polemical aspect" of *The Female Body in Western Culture* is to claim for the "feminine," more pointedly, the "female body," a status of contemporaneity: "Not everything we see and hear today deserves to be called contemporary . . . it is not enough to be *of* our time in order to be *with* our time" (2).

Risking the anachronism that Suleiman encourages us to avoid, with no hope at all of doing "my bit" here to rejoin "theory and practice," I would say that the "flesh-and-blood entity" of the female body lends itself to historical enactment—I cannot imagine a more forceful example than the "mother-woman," whose dimensions are *symbolic* at those points of contact where communities of women *live out* symbolicities. If we concede that the discursive manifests a worrisome element of translation, then I see no reason why we might feel compelled to jettison the terrible flesh and blood. Though I am primarily concerned here with the specific uses of a cultural construct that we would designate "feminine" in the case of a particular writer/poet, it is not beyond me to imagine what practical turn a theory *might* take.

The stipulative definition that I would offer for the "feminine" trait of human personality takes us back to Keohane's "Introduction" and an inquiry into the connotations of "everywhereness" and of the shadowy. To the degree that "body" in reference to the "feminine" might be analogously read with an ancient poetic theme, that of William Blake's Tharmas,[9] the principle that contains the rational will, the creative powers, the affective dispositions, the erotic centers, I mean "body" alongside the preceding terms—ubiquity and shadowiness. We might think of all three terms under the head of "surface" and "extensivity," meaning by both the definition that Schiller offers in *Letters on the Aesthetic Education of Man.*[10] If "maximum changeability" and "maximum extensivity" stand here for the "feminine," then we would urge a sense of its application along more than a single line of stress, since neither the "feminine" nor receptivity to phenomena is alien to the masculine. Though Gwendolyn Brooks's "feminine" refers primarily to the female, the resonance of the former is not at all unlike Woolf's "incandescence,"[11] which is not gender-rigid in its artistic practice and inspiration. My aim in trying to free up the "feminine" from its wonted vocation is not to generate an hermaphroditic wonder and lose women/woman in a figurative replication of naive liberalist gestures, but to suggest that we replace our weapon in our holsters until an enemy has clearly shown itself: The idea (if it ever was) is not to be rid of the "feminine," whose details have yet to be fully elaborated, say nothing of exhausted, but, rather, to purge the world for a wider display of its powers. According to Jardine, at least *some* "men" might agree. More precisely, we wish to know what the "feminine" can do from its own vantage point, and such inquiry is "gynocritical" in its profoundest impulses.[12]

II

Gwendolyn Brooks's feminine landscape is clearly demarcated as a heterosexual territory. Males are never far away from its female centers of attention, even when the male presence is overwhelmingly implicit and memorial, as it is in "The Anniad" and various other poems in the volume, *Annie Allen*.[13] The poet's particular address to communities of women in her audience is persistent in the canon across four decades of work, reflecting the storm and stress of the contemporary period of African-American women's political consciousness with the 1981 publication, *Primer for Blacks: Three Preachments*, "To those of My Sisters Who Kept Their Naturals."[14] Brooks's work interweaves the female and her distinctive feelings into a delicate tissue of poetic response to the human situation, defined by a particular historical order—the African-American personality among the urban poor in the city of Chicago between World War II and the present of *Maud Martha*. Within this body of work, the female voice, for all its poignant insistence, is a modified noun of vocality, danced through a range of appetite and desire that does not stand isolated from a masculine complement. If poetry is our teacher in this instance, not entirely estranged from theory, but subsuming it, then the "feminine" is manifest as an emphasis, neither hostile to "masculine" nor silenced by it. We are rather reminded now of an image of Jungian resolution with the circumferences of double circles overlapping to form an altered distance through the diameters of both.[15] It is only by virtue of a perversion in the seeing that the overlapping circles can declare any independence whatsoever. They relinquish their imagined uniqueness to an enlarged order of circularity, as the peripheries of both now involve us at the center of each. Getting the point does not necessarily require that we embrace the idea, or the "man," but that we acknowledge it as a viable figure in the universe of female and "feminine" representability. This involved image of circularity yields a geometry for poets, and those are the depths and surfaces that claim our attention at the moment.

In Brooks's poetic order of things, the "feminine" is neither cause for particular celebration nor certain despair, but near to the "incandescent," it is analogous to that "wedged-shaped core of darkness"[16] through which vision we see things in their fluid passage between dream and waking reality, as multiple meanings impinge on a central event. The poet's novelette *Maud Martha* does not exhaust Brooks's contemplation of the "feminine," but provides a point of illumination and departure concerning an important phase of her long and distinguished career as an American poet. If not chronologically central to the canon, *Maud Martha,* beside "The Anniad," is experienced by the reader as an "impression point."[17] In the Harper and Row edition of her poetry, *Maud Martha* brings to closure the poems in *A Street in Bronzeville* and *Annie Allen,* while it prepares the way for *The Bean Eaters* and, from the sixties, the stunning poetry of *In the Mecca.*

Maud Martha was published in 1953.[18] The leading subject and sole consciousness of the narrative, Maud Martha Brown comes of age during the Depression era. As the work is broadly reflective of the social issues of two American decades, it might be read as the poet's version of a cultural synthesis. By the end of World War II, Maud Martha is expecting her second child; her brother Harry returns home in one piece from combat, and her first child Paulette grows up. Paulette is old enough to recognize that the white "Santa Claus" of a large department store in the city of Chicago does not like little black girls. Somehow, the jolly creature cannot even bring himself to *look* at the child, having hugged all the blond ones, Paulette observes, to her mother's chagrin. The instances that disclose racist sentiment in the text are so muted and understated that they are rendered elements of background in which ambiance the primary issues of the narrative unfold: the extent to which the female can articulate her own values of sanctity and ritual, of aspiration and desire, of order and beauty in a hierarchically male-centered world, limited by the idioms of the literal.

Insofar as Maud Martha sustains heterosexual mating, she is "male-identified," but such identification is much less compelling than the imaginative integrity that keeps her alive and well. The woman reader of this text might well wonder how successfully Maud Martha would negotiate a sphere of influence broader than the domestic and the connubial. It is true that her talents are constrained by what we would now consider four narrow walls that provide her with neither a room of her own nor the time to miss it.[19] She is not a culture heroine, is not a woman warrior, and the big bumbling immensities of the rómantic and epic imagination—Rebellion, Bravery, Courage, Triumph, among them, those capitalized terms that Northrop Frye describes as "aureate"[20] and which Brooks's own "Strong Men, Riding Horses" humorously debunks[21]—do not touch her identity in any remote way. And so we wind down into an arena of choices that take us to the heart of dailiness, of the mundane and the unglamorous, or the carefully circumscribed ambition. We protest—but isn't *this* the customary woman's place?

That the distaff is, from the point of view of the narrative and the world surrounding it, the peculiar custodial property of the female is not a conclusion. It is a beginning. *Maud Martha* commences with the raw elaborations of realism (read also "reality") and transforms them into a habitable space. This talent for the clean and well-lighted, however, is not only the central and embattled miracle of Maud Martha's world, but also a preeminent social value because it represents an actual living of what has been imagined, imagining what is known. We might think of Maud Martha's "miracle" as a gifted kind of "making" that turns the inner to the outer and redeems the room as an elaboration of the human and social body.[22]

If we look at the structurations of Maud Martha's character from her own place in the order of things, then we accord her special attention because of her highly developed powers to *play* and to play well within the framework of possibilities to which she has access. We can very well wish for her, imagine empathetically, a richer field of play; but the limitations imposed on her in no way mitigate her own considerable abilities to shape and define the world as she encounters it. In contrast to her husband, Paul Phillips, who occupies and rents space in his world, without an angle on it, or a critique of it, Maud Martha engages their common circumstance with an eye for the occasion. This looking through, for want of a better term, might be called a kind of displaced fable-making so that Maud Martha might be seen as the "true poet" of the narrative and the writer herself the "imitator" of it. These functions come together under the guise of a central narrator, who speaks Maud Martha's script through a ventriloquized medium—the poet, assigning to the leading agent the primary powers of ordering.

The central thematics of the work are made explicit in the twenty-first and twenty-second episodes:

> Could be nature, which had a seed, or root, or an element (what do you call it) of constancy, under all that system of change. Of course, to say "system" at all implied arrangement, and therefore some order of constancy. (227)

What she had wanted was a solid. She had wanted shimmering form; warm, but hard as a stone and as difficult to break. She wanted to found—tradition. She had wanted to shape, for their use, for hers, for his, for little Paulette's, a set of falterless customs. She had wanted stone. (228)

A "stone," a "solid," as isolated lexical features, convey notions of the concrete and abstract at once. We can contemplate them on their own terms, apart from context to modify their function, but in relationship to "shimmering form," to "tradition," their meaning enriches to insinuate an indefinite specificity—a community of notions that range in weight and appeal from the architectural to the ingeniously diminutive object of decoration; from issues concerning values and aspirations to the specific questions and longings of desire. That the terms overlap on "falterless customs" and, by inference, the whole enterprise of shaping and preserving, foreshortened in the enumerated signs, renders Maud Martha a social "conservative," as "order of constancy" implies. But the wealth of connotative markers that the narrator achieves by mixing the metaphorical referents would suggest that Maud Martha's "conservatism" located not only the preeminent force of intelligence at work in the narrative, but also the intelligence that tries things. I am assuming that Brooks's narrator does not intend irony or mockery when Maud Martha's consciousness speaks a desire for "stone," for "solid," or that she intends to say that Maud Martha is naive in wishing to establish "falterless customs." I would want to see the central figure's essentially experiential character and lust for form as a necessary fable of paradox for living a life—in "literature," or on "the streets"—that is sane and rewarding. For Maud Martha, "tradition" is not a dead letter, or a reliquary of ancestral ghosts. "Tradition" here would be "founded" the hard way, on the living, on a sort of frontier of immediacy, whose ready-to-hand objects might be invested with the only force for magic that there is—that which the imagination attributes to the event of neutral or indifferent meaning.

None of the items in Maud Martha's catalog of transmuted domestic objects can be regarded as esoteric: coffees, fruitcakes, plain shortbread, black walnut candy in "little flat white sheets," a dinner table spread with "white, white cloth . . . china . . . in cheerful dignity, firmly arranged, upon it" (233). Despite the availability of the scene at hand, we are compelled to consider it in a new light, seeing the details as "the plenitude of plan."[23] Maud Martha's "plan," however, is not so much a reflection of the arbitrary as it is a retrieving from chaos or oblivion the ordinary domestic object, much like poems cut "Out of air, / Night color, wind soprano, and such stuff."[24] If we perceive that the narrator is involving us in a romance of the diurnal, there is much to support the conclusion—the central artistic purpose of *Maud Martha* expresses the essentially "heroic" character of the "unheroic" by altering our opinion of "heroism" in the first place. Furthermore, "art" loses its remoteness and its claim to exclusion as Brooks imposes upon it a radically democratic context and purpose.

This capacity to draw the outer into oneself, retranslating it into an altered exterior, as though fields of force magnetized by an abiding centrality, locates the process that I would stipulate as the "feminine," finding in it the maximum exposure of surface to change. We will see shortly how the particular "epistemic habit of meaning"[25] in this narrative reinforces both the artistic energies of the piece and the function of the narrative itself as suggestive "equipment for living."[26]

In steady contrast to Maud Martha, there is a "husband," both a "real" one and the idea of "husband" in its limited masculine composition: "This man was not a lover of tablecloths, he could eat from a splintery board, he could eat from the earth" (232–33). The often sardonic quality of the writing and its persistently ironical force save the narrative from pathos as it challenges our sympathies to focus on specific detail in whimsical combinations. "Tablecloths" acquires metonymic value, as it defines the whole of Paul Phillips's inadequacies of imagination by humorously remarking a partial instance of it. Laughter here is usually ironically pointed so that antagonism to laughter falls into perspective with it rather than exaggeration or prominence. In that sense, the work evinces a tough-minded balance of tensions between the impinging extremes of Maud and Paul's "reality."

Maud Martha is herself as much an observer of her own scene as she is a participant in it, a maker of it. Alongside her dreamwork, she maintains the prerogatives of detachment so that at no point in the narrative—even when Maud Martha thinks the most harshly truthful things about herself and those around her—does the reader "feel sorry" for her. She will thrive not simply because she can bear to suffer—as traditional African-American female iconography valorizes beyond any practical use, beyond any probable endurance in the life of female progeny. Maud Martha thrives because she wills it through diverse acts of form, woven from the stuff of everyday life. Quite simply, she is smarter than Paul, who is not without desire but rather oppressed by the wrong ones.

Paul is not an adequate husband and lover precisely because he is lacking in "capable imagination." To use Alice Walker's terms for the particular etiology that blocks imaginative expansiveness in the man, Paul is a "colorist," with an overwhelming wish to have a liaison with a "light-skinned" female; the prize of "light-skin" would release in him the fruition of a range of fantasies so elusive to his grasp that they would thrill the analyst's heart and pocketbook. It is not an exaggeration to say that even now, at some years' remove from the passions, intensities, and commitments of the six- ties' Black Nationalist movement in the United States, African-American men's community has yet, it seems, to come to terms with its profoundest impulses concerning African-American women and their "Africanity." The failure would appear ongoing, disquieting, repetitive, and disappointing. So close to the new century, this failure to grasp seems threatening in its po- litical, cultural, and possibly genetic implications for an entire American community. From the vantage of the fifties—since the tangle of issues to which I allude is not dated—the poet is not unaware of these charged and searching questions in their immediate impact on the ontological dimen- sions of her characters. Maud Martha is black skinned and, there but by the grace of a keen intelligence and generous affection, might have been un- done by her world's sporadically obscene response to the color of her skin.

Paul's limitations are not solely determined by his interest in the "light- skinned" female. We can grant him whatever wishing his heart can stand, but that he sees no farther than the pointed recurrence of an imagistic symptom makes him ripe for a class of psychological subjects that we rec- ognize in the obsessive-neurotic. That this heterosexual male would poten- tially love many women is not a serious crime, we finally decide, but Paul wants a figure of adoration to fill up his mind; he wants to fall into gyneo- latrous[27] madness at the foot of a marvelous deception, male-engendered. There is more: Having no direct route of access to the originating inspira- tion of the European tradition of courtly love, embodied in "the female body in the West" (and "they" never mean "us"), Paul substitutes the fan- tasy's *next* best thing—the "high yaller" female hybrid of his community's peculiar American nightmare.

Two observations: First, Paul's low-order, low-key madness is decided not by the fictional context of his dreams, but rather by their particular histori- cal context. We are reminded that traditionally a lynching rope awaited the neck of the African-American male so bold as to approach his "it"—"the fe- male body in the West." But we remember not by dint of the local narrative before us, but by the one that *haunts* it—his fate in approaching the woman/ woman-body that is not "black."[28] This terroristic imagery is muted in the contemporary period, but not at all forgotten. Therefore, the "white" female acquires in Paul's eyes an altogether exaggerated status as object of mimetic desire. Second, the amorous figures that surround the characterizations of "black" are *historically* determined as ideas and icons of "not freedom," of bindings and couplings, of bondage and manipulation so complete that we can barely imagine, for example, just what Paul and Maud Martha would look like in a different universe of figuration. The liberation project would release the character from the diseased "fix" of static iconography just as surely as it would the African-American community from the planned obsolescence of national policy and economic practice. While we must ultimately encounter Maud and Paul on the terms that the story offers and *for themselves,* we understand, unmistakably, that an aspect of "extra-territorial" narrative so decisively shadows their tale that the genuinely agonized pairing here is not simply "male and "female," "feminine" and "masculine" (as though they were simple), but these binary oppositions as they have been orchestrated by the loudest and most persistent teleology, "good" and "bad," and finally mediated, through the very force of the language, by the most fateful of culturally ascribed antinomies—"black" and "white." To that extent, Paul is victim. We dislike him because, contrary to Maud Martha, he doesn't *resist;* obeys no individual imperatives or tested arrogance that would push through the accumulated slime of a national history.

III

Chapter 19 of the narrative, "if you're light and have long hair," brings home the particular social dynamics to which I refer. Married for a time, Paul gets his first invitation to the Foxy Cats' Annual Foxy Cats Dawn Ball. Though we recognize a persistent element of parody in the descriptive apparatus adapted to these scenes, we also acknowledge their quite accurate conformity to a certain configuration of African-American middle-class upward mobility. Foxy Cats (who resemble the undergraduate fraternity in its earnest and ingenuous allegiance to fixed notions of proper behavior, sartorial style, and the brainless imitation of what its members *think* "class" is) bears the brunt of a well-deserved satirical commentary. The wording of the invitation to the "Dawn Ball" is humorously, nervously redundant:

> He was to be present, in formal dress. . . . No chances were taken. 'Top hat, white tie and tails,' hastily followed the 'Formal Dress,' and that elucidation was in bold type. (205)

For Paul, the invitation represents "an honor of the first water, and . . . sufficient indication that he was, at last, a social somebody." This ironical vein is underscored and nourished in Maud Martha's thoughts by a brazen stroke of self-admission:

> My type is not a Foxy Cat favorite. But he can't avoid taking me—since he hasn't yet thought of words or ways strong enough, and at the same time soft enough—for he's kind; he doesn't like to injure—to carry

across to me the news that he is not to be held permanently by my type, and that he can go on with this marriage only if I put no ropes or questions around him. Also, he'll want to humor me, now that I'm pregnant. (207)

Days later, in the "main room of the 'Club 99'" Maud and Paul join the other Foxy Cats and their "foxes" at the "Dawn Ball" itself. Paul, in effect, abandons Maud Martha shortly after their arrival, having escorted her to a bench by the wall, leaving her (211). Who he's left her for—"Maella"—is "red-haired and curved," of the "gold-spangled" bosomness. Rhetorically kin to a "sleek slit-eyed gypsy moan" of "The Anniad" and a "lemon-hued lynx / with sandwaves loving her brow" of the "ballad of chocolate Mabbie,"[29] "Maella" is not so much an embodied representation as she is a structure of emblematic traits that we recognize from other textual sources. The narrator needn't "explain." "Maella" need not speak, does not, nor can, since an entire secondary text speaks around her. In the maelstrom of emotions released by the appearance of this Idea to whose bosom Paul salutes, we think of "gold-spangled" as a resonance of "star-spangled" and of Paul as locked in a veritable state of adoration. Maud Martha watches, thinking:

> . . . not that they love each other. It oughta be that simple. Then I could lick it. It oughta be that easy. But it's my color that makes him mad. I try to shut my eyes to that, but it's no good. What I am inside, what is really me, he likes okay. But he keeps looking at my color, which is like a wall. He has to jump over it in order to meet and touch what I've got for him. He has to jump away up high in order to see it. He gets awful tired of all that jumping. (214)

The narrator does not dwell on this aspect of the scene, as we will see, in time, a cluster of intricately differentiated motives involved in it, nor is the painful resonance elaborated here repeated. We understand its perspective against the whole. My isolating it is intended to point an emphasis in suggesting the nature of schismatic tendencies that divide Paul from himself and from those around him and to convey a sense of what it is that Maud Martha strives to overcome as her own imagination projects it, as others impose it.

In psychological terms, we might say that Maud Martha symbolizes a far more successfully "integrated" character than Paul, and this fluency of response is primarily captivated by narrative strategies that blend the advantages and benefits of stream-of-consciousness and concealed narration in bringing to light a character whom we know in the interstices of her thought. The stage of action in *Maud Martha* is embedded in none other than the landscape of its central consciousness, and from this focal point—replete with particular biases and allegiances—we come to know the "world" of the narrative.

What we discover through Maud Martha's perceptions unfolds in a rolling chronology. In other words, the narrator is so selective in the detailing "spots of time" in reference to the character that the work may be described as episodic, paratactic, and notational, or structured from peak points, of which the Foxy Cats Dawn Ball is a single example. This imitative "autobiography" starts almost in the beginning, as we find out that the subject liked "candy buttons, and books, and painted music (deep blue, or delicate silver) and the west sky, so altering, viewed from the steps of the back porch, and dandelions" (127). The sentences are simple, tending toward the fragmentary, and swift on the surface of the visual, tactile world. We imagine not so much a structure of physical and physiological traits called "Maud Martha" as we do a profoundly active poetic sensibility, happily unbound in a world of marvelous color, of infinite allure.

Metaphors of painting seem especially apposite to narrative strategies here since the content of the opening episodes, in particular, is composed primarily of sensual imagery perceived through the brilliant color and texture often associated with impressionism.[30] To say that the "brush strokes" are light and decidedly whimsical is to suggest the paratactic character of the writing: episodes, if not individual sentences, are self-contained units of perceptual activity. To speak of writing as painting (and somehow, the figure never goes the other way) metaphorizes either activity, but the narrator appears deliberately involved in the apparent crossing of arbitrary artistic boundaries in order to delineate character and movement in their initial urgency. To do so, the narrator adopts loose connections between things and weak or fairly discontinuous transitions from point to point. The agent is not a studied, or deliberative, body, and the narrative, consequently, inscribes a deft movement of "symbol-making," as it starts up, we imagine, from the threshold of immediate feeling, of unchecked sensual response.

The painting metaphor further intimates the poet's attempt to invest the diurnal with vibrant color. Even the "grays" of this "universe" invite lyrical play, as Maud Martha roams her kitchenette for our benefit, with a passionate eye for the unique angle on human and object relations. As a result of these self-conscious stylistic moves, the narrator achieves a confluence of thematic and strategic modes so thoroughgoing that Maud Martha stands in synecdochic relationship to the surround. Merging into an untrammeled equality of means, agent and scenic devices are reversible.

Though the episodes are arbitrarily connected, they are logically sequential: Narrative traces lead from childhood and early years at school through adolescence to young womanhood and the adult years that follow. Maud Martha's first beaux, the death of her paternal grandmother, the quality of her dream life, the special nature of her relationship to her father and brother, the affective ambivalence that prevails among the women of the immediate family, for instance, become discrete moments of perception that take on even weight and intensity. Significant elements of the tale are, therefore, dispersed and accumulative, rather than dense and elaborated. In fact, the weakened copulatives create an aesthetic surface without "bulges"—the "peaks" and "valleys" of a schematic plot structure—or syntactic elements that do not adhere in a relationship of subordination and coordination. To that extent, the narrative voice speaks in the concisive rhythms of the contemporary poem. I have in mind symptoms of alignment rather than particular instances.

It doesn't matter, for instance, that the seeds of Maud Martha's troubled "femininity" are planted early on in her own awareness and, consequently, the reader's, because such information assumes no unusual or immediate focus: Two years older than Maud, sister Helen is "almost her own height and weight and thickness. But oh, the long lashes, the grace, the little ways with the hands and feet" (128–29). We will know more in time about Helen, the beautiful sister, but this clue, closing the inaugural scene, so casually intrudes itself that we register it only later as crucial. Even though the bulk of the narrative concerns Maud Martha's marriage and maternal career, these emphases fall into solid perspective with the whole. Relatedly, the narrative is unplotted (or not obviously plotted), pursues no climactic surprises, and resolves in syntactic and dramatic rhythms that evade rigid closure: "And in the meantime, she was going to have another baby. The weather was bidding her bon voyage" (306). The agreeable sense of an ending here could just as easily mark the beginnings of the next excursive phase of "autobiography," since pregnancy announces new life as well as the anticipation of one kind of finish; "bon voyage," analogously, situates a valedictory and salutatory marker. This strategic ambiguity, with its teasing abeyance of resolution, brings us back to questions concerning the "feminine."

IV

Virginia Woolf conjectured that the woman-text adapted to the rules of interruption—by the female writer's children, lovers, and the general imperatives of care taking; it was, then, of necessity, *short*. An "écriture feminine," apparently hinting the functions of the female body—with its fluidities, secret passageways and escape routes, or the convoluted folds along the uterus and vaginal vault—releases the "feminine," as a corporeality turned trope, onto a wider human path, not blocked by the specificities of female reproductive process. Once upon a time, in a cackle of rage, a Boston-not-so-lady declared to me what might well serve as a point of overlap between Woolf and latter-day theoreticians on the body writing: "Anything that takes more than nine months to bear is a joke!" She was talking about *novels.* But is it true that the vital, concentrated intensities of the pregnant body place on urgent notice the artist everywhere—"study long study wrong"?

I would exercise the greatest caution in supporting a "feminine writing" as *practice,* if not as *theory,* however, since we presently have no acceptable name for the same individual writer—female or male—when she or he does *not* write in the suspension of authority, in the subversion of the hierarchical, in the shameless assertion of the vibrant mood. Is "Gwendolyn Brooks," for example, of *In the Mecca,* the same body that produced *Maud Martha?* No outer markings or facings of the surface suggest it. And it is precisely this protocol of radically divergent aims that comes home in the singularity of an artist's career (or even *a* writing) that would challenge a rigorous notion of trophic determinism. There is in my reading of this novelette, however, symptoms of a program that I would designate "feminine," and it is embedded in the work's insistence on *self-involvement;* if this constant reference and return to the "inner" surrenders to figurative movement, then we might say that female person's having to "listen" to her body and its cyclical rhythms dictates "stillness" as a redoubtable human and cultural value. This "serenity," replete with its own active turbulences through the whole being, recovers "invisibility," or the mental "calibrations," as a supremely *active* domain of the human. "Mrs. Ramsey" provides an insight:

> To be silent; to be alone. All the being and the doing, expansive, glittering, vocal, evaporated; and one shrunk, with a sense of solemnity, to being oneself, a *wedge-shaped core of darkness, something invisible to others.* (My emphasis)[31]

I emphasize the latter half of the sentence in order to suggest that the "active"/"passive" split is as culpable in any discussion of the "feminine" as the other patriarchal/patriarchist oppositions that we already know too well to repeat. In a remarkable episode from *Maud Martha,* the narrator provides another example of what I would call a paradoxical nesting of being-impulses—the personality drawn into the pluralities of a self, "shrunk," as it were, opens, capably, outward: As a young woman, Maud Martha essentially preserves her sense of childhood wonder. Walking down a Chicago street, taking in the rich scenes of store windows, she experiences so palpably the objects that she confronts that the reader is not completely sure (and no longer cares to be) if her body remains in Chicago or actually goes off to New York:

> When she was out walking, and with grated iron swish a train whipped by, off, above, its passengers were always, for her comfort, New York-bound. She sat inside with them. She leaned back in the plush. She sped, past farms, through tiny towns, where people slept, kissed, quarreled, ate midnight snacks; unfortunate folk who were not New York-bound and never would be. (174)

This complex of desire, through which the encounters of the subject are refracted, measured, considered, consumed, is poised in brazen contrast to the "actual" world of Maud Martha; that the "imagined" and the "real" abrade unrelentingly is intended, because we gauge Maud Martha's internal resources in even bolder relief against the brute "facts." We could go so far as to say that the poet's insistence on the narrative strategies of the piece and its rhetorical energies that plumb the interior world of the character spares Maud Martha the peculiar burdens of the naturalistic agent. In other words, if *Maud Martha* were read through eyes not the character's own, as would an omniscient voice, bent on imposing a content from the "outside," already made to order, then we would not only lose Maud Martha's complexity, but would also conclude that victimage alone determines her. By forcing the reader, or inducing her, to confront Maud Martha as the primary and central consciousness of the work, its subject *and* object of gazing, speaking through the redoubled enunciations of her own stream-of-thought and a translation of it, the poet reclaims the territorial rights of an internal self and strikes for our mutual benefit a figure of autonomy. Despite her "blackness," her "femaleness," her poverty-line income, and perhaps *because* of these unalterable "facts" of mensuration, Maud Martha is allowed access to her own "moment of being," and the narrative articulates its record.

It is beside the point that Maud Martha speaks few quoted or dramatic lines in the narrative, or that her private ways are quiet and unspectacular, or that she tolerates more of Paul than we think she ought; she is not a feminist, fifties' style. The demonstration, I believe, of woman-freedom is the text itself that has no force, no sticking point other than the imaginative nuances of the subject's consciousness. Maud Martha's drama remains internal, and that interiority engenders the crucial aesthetic address of the work. We might want to alter drastically her "environment," change her clothes, where she lives, grant her a broader sphere of contact, but such is *our* fiction. In spite of it, we suspect that the character already has the capacity to disclose larger and even more refined versions of a fictional self *on her own terms*. Perhaps we could argue that the most impassioned attention to the drama of the interior self exposes the "feminine."

When young Maud Martha looks at magazines that say "New York," describing "good objects there, wonderful people, recalled fine talk, the bristling or the creamy or the tactfully shimmering . . . her whole body become a hunger, she would pore over its pages" (174). That "looking" is governed here by "hunger" in the young Maud Martha reinforces the severe privacy of the perceptual act and provides a remarkable stroke of synaesthesia in the conflating tactile and visual sensation. The subject is not a mere looker, but looks with the entire ingestive range. Maud Martha's "good objects" are placed alongside objects of melancholy or objects of the nakedly furnished within a range of semantic valences that gain distinction solely by her capacity to imbue them with polyvalent meaning. We gather this stylistic trait on the basis of lexical items apparently chosen from two widely divergent arrays of things that operate in a kind of binary adhesion—those "good objects" of the above-quoted passage and those that belong with her kitchen sink, or the radiators in her parents' house, "high and hideous. And underneath the low sink-coiled unlovely pipes, that Helen said made her think of a careless woman's underwear, peeping out" (164). But then there are also natural objects that show the humble in special atmosphere and that persist as the contrapuntal assertion against the ravages of time. From two excerpts of the narrative: The house the Browns fear they might lose to the Home Owners' Loan Association, the one in which Maud Martha and her siblings have grown up, materializes an enamored object of the entire family, but for Maud Martha, "house" abstracts into an object of lyricism—of "writing":

> . . . with the snake plant in the jardiniere in the southwest corner, and the obstinate slip from Aunt Eppie's magnificent Michigan fern at the left side of the friendly door . . . and at the emphatic iron of the fence and . . . the poplar tree. . . . Those shafts and pools of light, the tree, the graceful iron, might soon be viewed possessively by different eyes. (154–55)

From the ending:

> But the sun was shining, and some of the people in the world had been left alive, and it was doubtful whether the ridiculousness of man would

ever completely succeed in destroying the world—or, in fact, the basic equanimity of the least and commonest flower: for would its kind not come up again in the spring? come up, if necessary, among, between, or out of—beastly inconvenient!—the smashed corpses lying in strict composure, in that hush infallible and sincere. (305)

In the first instance, the vocabulary of natural objects so overwhelms the house of the living that the latter takes on a spirit of timelessness, enters a domain of the immutable. It is noteworthy that Maud Martha believes that the western sky acquires a certain unique aspect only from the back of this house: "the little line of white, somewhat ridged with smoked purple, and all that cream-shot saffron" (156). In the second instance, the natural objects—sun and earth—submerge the human deed in a grandly absurd and irresistible carnival of folly. In its concise reverberations of the strangely ridiculous and rhetorical questions of the disembodied voice from *The Waste Land*,[32] Brooks joins Eliot in adopting closural images from the iconic grotesquery of war—World War I for Eliot, World War II for Brooks. For both poets, the corpse loses its gothic and horrible magnificence as it is brought low, so to speak, into the stream of diachronous, even vegetal, being. This collapse of hierarchy in the poetic status of objects is entirely consonant with the principles of writing that order the whole of *Maud Martha*.

Whether or not the objects in Brooks's binary array are human contrivances or aspects of the natural order, both articulate and embody an impression of eternal forms. Their varied aspects and illuminations of the immanent would suggest not only the indeterminacy of their occurrence but also the fluent nature of Maud Martha's stunning perceptual powers in the combinations, recombinations, and juxtapositions that the objects achieve in her sight. A suggestion from the linguists as an insight into "making": If the objects that claim our attention are to the senses what words are to the vertical columns of the dictionary, then the stuff of seeing is the *lexis* of "experience"; their various combinations and laws of revision and recombination, its "syntax"; and the meanings and their arrangements, its "semantics." By calling the "feminine" a power that operates under concealment, I mean primarily the ability it grants us to stand still and see, or in one's perceptual place, await a content, arrange a consequence.

V

Returning momentarily to the scene of the Foxy Cats Ball will provide us, in a final example, with several crucial and interlocking points concerning the subject's consciousness and the study in subtleties that the "feminine" reveals as a theme of convergence between the beholder and the beheld. The rapidly alternating currents through which the reader watches the simultaneity of opposing rhetorical, aesthetic, and dramatic functions in this scene are translatable into the "feminine" beyond this text inasmuch as they express the intricacies of the "double consciousness." If Maud Martha cannot escape the implications of her mirror, or the pretexts that impinge on her, then she is fully capable of exploiting such captivity to the degree that the scene itself, the other agents on it, its purposes and motivations are reflected in her looking glass, whose thaumaturgic properties can bless or damn the occasion as the subject sees fit. Intent on neither, the voice of the interior monologue mobilizes a plenitude of terms that evoke the fundamental ambivalence at the core of consciousness itself.

We have already examined one of the decisive psychological components of this scene as Maud Martha, suddenly not unaware of her dark skin and its dubious social uses, fixes herself as subject and object of deeply embedded public and private motives. In other words, the extra-text that speaks loudly, even when none of the agents "mouth" it dramatically, and the text of Maud Martha's consciousness are interlarded threads cut across the same bias. The "extra-text" to which I refer, examined at greater length in an ongoing work, traces the historical implications of African-American women's community as a special instance of the "ungendered" female, as a vestibular subject of culture, and as an instance of the "flesh" as a primary or first-level "body."[33] Because African-American women in their historic status represent the *only* community of American women *legally* denied the mother's access to her child, their relationship to the prerogatives of "gender" must be reexamined as the select stratagem of an ethnic solidarity; of the dominant community's strict exploitation of the gender rule as an instrument of a supremacist program. This systematic unfolding of iconic and epistemic violence embattles Maud Martha, *without naming itself,* and discloses the central impoverishment of a public naming and imagining that have not yet discovered appropriate terms for this community of social subjects. In that sense, the "mulatta"—and we might assume that "Maella" is either proximate to, or appropriates, such status—figures into this calculus as the historic "alibi" that "shields" the African-American female from sight. The weight of *this* textuality, or a "symbolic construct" that *lives* itself out, or of a corporeality-turned-trope-returned-"corporeality," *falls* on the historical and fictive subject with the convictions of steel. But the interconnections between "given" and "discovered" become the inseparable discretions of the tailor's herringbone. Or, to shift metaphors, an entire central nervous system is at work so that consciousness is perceived as the stunning poise in a dual and complicated awareness.

The paragraphs that inform us that Maud Martha is escorted to a bench and left—"she sat, trying not to show the inferiority she did not feel"—descry a single pattern in the fabric, intersecting others in an arrangement that the eye takes in at once. We are aware of an emphasis of weight, color, texture, mode of design. Just so, Maud Martha wholly experiences the rich implications of her "objectivity" in their yoked occurrence. If she is seen, she also sees, as the scene before us is rendered precisely demonstrative of perceptual activity as an occasion of mutually indulged gazing.

Despite the sharp satirical underpinnings of the scene, Maud Martha acknowledges that the "ball stirred her . . . made toys of her emotions." "The beautiful women in gorgeous attire, bustling and supercilious"; the over gallant young men; the drowsy lights and smell of food and flowers; the body perfumes and "sensuous heaviness of the wine-colored draperies at the many windows" conjure up notions of the sybaritic. The draped gorgeous flesh, divided between female and male, suggests the tease of sexuality: We call it "glamour" and recognize in the scene the ritual of mating behind whose masks the actualities of lust are arrested. The scene's drama relies on the tensions set in motion between the arrested and the enacted. We are drawn to the moment (and moments like it in "real life") because it configures the vertical suspension of love-making as it leads, eventually, toward the bedroom, either *actively* or *fantastically.* But if "to die," to play a moment on the range of conventional literary meanings released in the infinitive, marks the final move of the love game as well, then the narrator cunningly exploits the ambiguities of intention by bringing together objects of decoration and gaiety that evoke shades of the mortal flesh, of death.

"Wine-colored drapery" also belongs to the funeral procession, as does the terrible satiety of flowers. Even the music of the ball runs a chordal progression that describes over the course of the evening the convoluted objectives of the moment: "now steamy and slow, now as clear and fragile as glass, now raging, passionate now moaning and thickly gray" (210). The gallant young men, "who at other times unpleasantly blew their noses," master the required social proprieties of the occasion, but they are also the imagined subjects of promising toilet humor, darting "surreptitiously into alleys to relieve themselves" and the comedy of the private, unguarded self that sweats at work and scratches its "more intimate parts." Maud Martha's dancing partner, another male, dispatched to entertain her while Paul celebrates the red arms of Maella, "*reeked* excitedly of tobacco, liquor, pinesoap, toilet water, and Sen Sen" (my emphasis). This aggregation of disparate olfactory sensations reinforces disparity in the mild tongue-twisting

assonance of the first five-syllable grouping of the line—"tobacco"/liquor."
A deeper structural point obtains. The body, disguising from itself the deep
knowledge of its own mortality, claims this scene for the grave as well as the
bed. We could say that a careful consideration of the weave of the passage
might suggest that their shared imagery of the horizontal posture collapses
distinction. Just as the flesh is seen here in its various lights, *Maud Martha*
dances the range of feeling in its complicated twists and turns.

VI

That the fictional subject disperses across an "inner" and "outer"—differing angles on a mutually concurrent process—fits well with coeval theories
of reading that posit "division" at the center of knowing; *je est un autre*—
there is no subject, only a "barred subject," in a constant oscillation of de-
ferments. But reading counter to the current, we would claim for Maud
Martha a subject's singularity that *contains* "division," in fact, generates it,
through a female body, who, among social bodies, is the only one who can
reproduce sameness and difference at once: The child resembles the begetters, "borrows" their tendencies, yet describes its own features of uniqueness. If we regard the "feminine," in the artistic instance, as a trope of the
reproductive process, we might argue that it, like the female body, locates
the convergence of antithetically destined properties—"female," "male,"
"mind," "body," "same," "other," "past," "future," "gazer," "gazed upon."
Inscribing a notion of containment—in rooms, in the serene and vibrant
spaces of the interior, in the intimacies that pass from lovers to enemies and
back—the narrator suggests that the "feminine" constitutes the particular
gifts of a *materialized* interior. Treating the text as "the strategic naming of a
situation,"[34] we think of it—in its brevity, in its fluent movement among
textures of feeling—as a figure of the "feminine," writing itself into articulate motion.

6

Interstices:
A Small Drama of Words

Who Said It Was Simple?

There are so many roots to the tree of anger
that sometimes the branches shatter
before they bear.

Sitting in Nedicks
the women rally before they march
discussing the problematic girls
they hire to make them free.
An almost white counterman passes
a waiting brother to serve them first
and the ladies neither notice nor reject
the slighter pleasures of their slavery.
But I who am bound by my mirror
as well as my bed
see causes in color
as well as sex

and sit here wondering
which me will survive
all these liberations.[1]

When I told a friend of mine that I was going to address the issue of sexuality as discourse during a spring conference at Barnard College, she laughed: "Is that what you talk about when you make love?" Silence. "Well?" Well, I hadn't thought of that, but now that she had raised the question, what about it? There probably is at least one book to be written on erotic exclamations that would likely enrich our understanding of cultural forms in their sexual dress, but this meeting of terms is both my point and beside it. I am interested here primarily in what we might call discursive and iconic fortunes and misfortunes, facilities, abuses, or plain absences that tend to travel from one generation of kinswomen to another, not unlike love and luck, or money and real estate. Just so, the elders pass on their voice, their tongue, their language, and it might even surprise us that they said the same words, or none at all, in the vaunted coital embrace, or the celebrated post-orgasmic fall-out. Every child in us dreams, we might suppose, of knowing just what "they" said and did in "there" and do they still?

At any rate, sexuality is the locus of great drama—perhaps the fundamental one—and, as we know, wherever there are actors, there are scripts, scenes, gestures, and reenactments, both enunciated and tacit. Across the terrain of feminist thought, the drama of sexuality is a dialectic with at least one missing configuration of terms. Whatever my mother, niece, and I might say and do about our sexuality (the terms of kinship are also meant collectively) remains an unarticulated nuance in various forms of public discourse as though we were figments of the great invisible empire of womankind. In a very real sense, black American women remain invisible to various public discourse, and the state of invisibility for them has its precedent in an analogy on any patriarchal symbolic mode that we might wish to name. However we try not to call up men in this discussion, we know full well, whether we like it or not, that these "they" do constitute an element of woman-scenery. For instance, in my attempt to lay hold of nonfictional texts—of any discursively rendered experience concerning the sexuality of black women in the United States, authored by themselves, for themselves—I encountered a disturbing silence that acquires, paradoxically, the status of contradiction. With the virtually sole exception of Calvin Hernton's *Sex and Racism in America* and less than a handful of very recent texts by black feminist and lesbian writers,[2] black women are the beached whales of the sexual universe, unvoiced, misseen, not doing, awaiting *their* verb. Their sexual experiences are depicted, but not often by them, and if and when by the subject herself, often in the guise of vocal music, often in the self-contained accent and sheer romance of the blues.

My survey, however, is mostly limited to some of the nonfictional texts on sexuality because I wish to examine those rhetorical features of an intellectual/symbolic structure of ideas that purport to describe, illuminate, reveal, and valorize the *truth* about its subject. Fictional texts, which transport us to another world of symbols altogether, are much beyond the scope of this essay and the central tenets of its argument. The nonfictional feminist work along a range of issues is the privileged mode of feminist expression at the moment, and its chief practitioners and revisionists are Anglo-American women/feminists in the academy. The relative absence of African-American women/feminists, in and out of the academic community, from this visionary company, is itself an example of the radically divergent historical situations that intersect with feminism. Such absence quite deliberately constitutes the hidden and implicit critique of this essay. The nonfictional feminist text is, to my mind, the empowered text—not fiction—and I would know how power works in the guise of feminist exposition when "sexuality" is its theme. If African-American women's community is relatively "word-poor" in the critical/argumentative displays of symbolic power, then the silence surrounding their sexuality is most evident in the structure of values I am tracing. It is, then, ironical that some of the words that tend to break silence here are, for whatever their purpose, male-authored.

Hernton's *Sex and Racism in America* proposes to examine the psychological make-up of America's great sexual quartet—the black female, the black male, the white female, the white male—and the historical contexts in which these overlapping complexities work. Each of his chapters provides a study of collective aspects of psyche as Hernton seeks insight into the deep structure of sexual fantasies that operate at the subterranean level of reception. The chapter on the black female interlards anonymous personal witness with the author's historical survey of the black female's social and political situation in the United States. We might call Hernton's text a dialectical/discursive analysis of the question and compare it with words from aspects of oral tradition.

As an example of a spate of discourse that portrays black women as sexual agents, we turn to the world of "toasts," or the extended and elaborate male oratorical display under the ruse of ballad verse. This form of oral narrative projects a female figure most usually poised in an antipathetic, customarily unflattering, sexual relationship to the male.[3] These long oral narratives, which black men often learn in their youth and commit to memory, vary from place to place and time to time, describing contests of male sexual performance. Several versions of "The Titanic,"[4] for instance, project a leading character named "Shine" as the great race/sex man, who not only escapes from the ill-fated maiden voyage of the celebrated ship, but also ends up in a Harlem nightclub, after the disaster, drinking Seagram's Seven and boasting his exploits. Within this community of male-authored texts, the female is appropriately grotesque, tendentiously heterosexual, and comparable in verbal prowess to the male, whom she must sexually best in the paradigmatic battle of the ages—that between the sexes. Relevant to the hyperbolic tall tale, comedian Rudy Moore's version of the battle of the sexes depicts evenly matched opponents, with the world "making book" on one side of the contest or the other. The agents literally "screw" for days in language far bolder than mine. But we already know beforehand, according to the wisdom of Chaucer's Wife of Bath, the outcome of the tale that the lion did not write. The woman in the "toasts" is properly subdued, or, more exactly in the latter-day versions of phallic dominance, "tooled" into oblivion.

So, here are two textual instances—Hernton's sympathetic account of the black female and the subject from the point of view of the people's oral poetry. Both instances insinuate quite different, though gratuitously related, versions of female sexuality. The correspondences are crucial. In the world of "toasts," "roasts," and "boasts," in the universe of unreality and exaggeration, the black female is, if anything, a creature of sex, but *sexuality* touches her nowhere. In the universe of "clean" discourse and muted analysis, to which we relegate Hernton's book, the black woman is reified into a status of non-being. In any comparison with white women in the sexual fantasies of black men, black women flunk—in truth, they barely register as fantastic representability—because of the ravages of the "Peculiar Institution." The latter was not the ideal workshop for refining the feminine sensibilities, Hernton argued. We infer from his reading that the black woman disappears as a legitimate subject of female sexuality. In all fairness to Hernton, however, we are obligated to point out his own acknowledgment of the silence that has been imposed on black American women: "Out of the dark annals of man's inhumanity to woman, the epic of the black woman's ordeal in America is yet to be written. . . . But the change is just beginning, and the beginning is fraught with hazards."[5]

My own interpretation of the historical narrative concerning the lives of black American women accords with Hernton's: Their enslavement relegated them to the marketplace of the flesh, an act of commodification so thoroughgoing that the daughters labor even now under the outcome.[6] Slavery did not transform the black female into an embodiment of carnality at all, as the myth of the black woman would tend to convince us, nor, alone, the primary receptacle of a highly profitable generative act. She became instead the principal point of passage between the human and the non-human world. Her issue became the focus of a cunning difference—visually, psychologically, ontologically—as the route by which the dominant modes decided the distinction between humanity and "other." At this level of radical discontinuity in the "great chain of being," black is vestibular to culture. In other words, the black person mirrored for the society around her what a human being was *not*. Through this stage of the bestial, the act of copulating travels eons before culture incorporates it, before the concept of sexuality can reclaim and "humanize" it.[7] Neither the picture I am drawing here, nor its symbolic interpretation, is unheard of to our understanding of American and New World history. If, however, it is a stunning idea in its ritual repetition, nonetheless, then that is because the black female remains exotic, her history transformed into a pathology turned back on the subject in tenacious blindness.

That this unthinkably vast and criminal fraud created its own contradictions and evasions within the creating brain ultimately does not concern us. The point is that neither we, nor Hernton, can easily approach the subtleties of a descriptive apparatus that would adequately account for the nexus *dis-effected* in this case between female gender and color. The rift translates into unthinkable acts, unspeakable practices. I am not identifying here the black female as the focal point of cultural and political inferiority. I do not mean to pose the black female as an object of the primitive, uxoricidal nightmares, or interrupted nocturnal emissions (elevated to the status of form) as in a Henry Miller or Norman Mailer. The structure of unreality that the black woman must confront originates in the historical moment when language ceases to speak, the historical moment at which hierarchies of power (even the ones to which *some* women belong) simply run out of terms because the empowered meets in the black female the veritable nemesis of degree and difference. Having encountered what they understand as chaos, the empowered need not name further, since chaos is sufficient naming within itself. I am not addressing the black female in her historical apprenticeship as an inferior social subject, but, rather, the paradox of non-being. Under the sign of this particular historical order, black female and black male are absolutely equal. We note with quiet dismay, for instance, the descriptive language of affirmative-action advertisements, or even certain feminist analyses, and sense once again the historical evocation of chaos: The collective and individual "I" lapses into a cul-de-sac, falls into the great black hole of meaning, wherein there are only "women," and "minorities," "blacks" and "other."

I wish to suggest that the lexical gaps I am describing here are manifest along a range of symbolic behavior in reference to black women and that the absence of sexuality as a structure of distinguishing terms is solidly grounded in the negative aspects of symbol-making. The latter, in turn, are wed to the abuses and uses of history, and how it is perceived. The missing word—the interstice—both as that which allows us to speak about and that which enables us to speak at all—shares, in this case, a common border with another country of symbols—the iconographic. Judy Chicago's *Dinner Party,* for example, in the artist's tribute to women, had a place set at table for the black female. Sojourner Truth is their representative symbol, and as the female figures around Truth are imagined through ingenious variations on the vagina, Truth's representation is inscribed by three faces. As Alice Walker comments: "There is of course a case to be made for being 'personified' by a face rather than by a vagina, but that is not what this show [was] about."[8]

The point of the example is self-evident. The excision of the female genitalia here is a symbolic castration. By effacing the genitals, Chicago not only abrogates the disturbing sexuality of her subject, but might well suggest that her sexual being did not exist to be denied in the first place. Truth's "femaleness," then, sustains an element of drag. In fact, she is merged here with a notion of sexual neutrality whose features, because they have not been defined, yet could assume any form, or none at all—in either case, the absence of articulation. Ironically, Sojourner Truth's piercing, rhetorical, now-reputed question on the floor of the second annual Convention of Women's Rights in Akron, 1852—"Ain't I a woman?"—anticipates the "atmosphere" of the artist's deepest assumptions.[9] The displacement of a vagina by a face invites protracted psychological inquiry,[10] but it is enough to guess, almost too much to bear guessing, that if Sojourner, in the female artist's mind, does not have the necessary female equipment, then its absence might be expressed in a face whose orifices are still searching for a *proper* role in relationship to the female body.

While there are numerous references to the black woman in the universe of signs, many of them perverted, the prerogatives of sexuality are refused her because the concept of sexuality originates in, stays with, the dominative mode of culture and its elaborate strategies of thought and expression. As a substitute term for "race" and "racism," I would borrow Edward Said's "dominative mode"[11] because the latter, not unlike "patriarchy," moves us closer to the heart of the matter. We would discover the ways and means of power in its intellectual and contemplative fulfillment—those places where most of us do not think to look because the intellectual enterprise, the lie goes, is so "objective" and so "disinterested" that it has little to do with what impresses the brain and the heart, to say nothing of what the legs straddle. If we are "intellectualizing" the issue away, which feminists used to say we ought not do, yet, interestingly enough, have done most of the time, then we mean to "intellectualize" exactly, since questions about woman-sex and the practices of exclusion that demarcate it are among the more impressive intellectual stunts of our time.

We would argue that sexuality as a term of power belongs to the empowered. Feminist thinking often appropriates the term in its own will to discursive power in a sweeping, patriarchist, symbolic gesture that reduces the human universe of women to its own image. The process might be understood as a kind of deadly metonymic playfulness—a part of the universe of women speaks for the whole of it. The structure of values, the spectacle of symbols under which we presently live and have our being—in short, the theme of domination and subordination—is practiced, even pursued, in many of the leading feminist documents of scholarship this past decade or so. We may affiliate sexuality, then—that term that flirts with the concealment of the activity of sex by way of an exquisite dance of textual priorities and successions, revisions and corrections—with the very project and destiny of power.

Through the institutionalization of sexual reference in the academy, in certain public forums; in the extensive responses to Freud and Lacan; in the eloquent textual discontinuities with the Marquis de Sade and D. H. Lawrence, sexual meaning in the feminist universe of academic discourse threatens to lose its living and palpable connection to training in the feelings and to become, rather, a mode of theater for the dominating mythologies. The discourse of sexuality seems another way, in its present practices, that the world divides decisively between the haves/have-nots, those who may speak and those who may not, those who, by choice or the accident of birth, benefit from the dominative mode, and those who do not. Sexuality describes another type of discourse that splits the world between the "West and the Rest of Us."

Black American women in the public/critical discourse of feminist thought have no acknowledged sexuality because they enter the historical stage from quite another angle of entrance from that of Anglo-American women. Even though my remarks are addressed specifically to feminists, I do not doubt that the different historical occasions implicated here have dictated sharp patterns of divergence not only in living styles but also in ways of speaking between black and white American women, without modification. We must have refinement in the picture at the same time that we recognize that *history* has divided the empire of women against itself. As a result, black American women project in their thinking about the female circumstance and their own discourse concerning it an apparently divergent view from feminist thinking on the issues. I am not comfortable with the "black-woman/feminist" opposition that this argument apparently cannot avoid. I am also not cheered by what seems a little noticed elision of meaning—when we say "feminist" without an adjective in front of it, we mean, of course, white women, who, as a category of social and cultural agents, fully occupy the territory of feminism. Other communities of women, overlapping feminist aims, are noted, therefore, by some qualifying term. Alice Walker's "Coming Apart" addresses this linguistic and cultural issue forthrightly and proposes the term "womanist" for black women and as a way to dissolve these apparently unavoidable locutions.[12] The disparities that we observe in this case are *symptomatic* of the problem and are a *part* of the problem. Because black American women do not participate, as a category of social and cultural agents, in the legacies of symbolic power, they maintain no allegiances to a strategic formation of texts, or ways of talking about sexual experience, that even remotely resemble the paradigm of symbolic domination, except that such paradigm has been their concrete disaster.

We hope to show in time how African-American women's peculiar American encounter, in the specific symbolic formation we mean, differs in both degree and kind from Anglo-American women's. We should not be at all surprised that difference among women is the case, but I am suggesting that in order to anticipate a more definitive social criticism, feminist thinkers, whom African-American women must confront in greater number on the issues, must begin to take on the dialectical challenge of determining *in the discourse* the actual realities of American women in their pluralistic ways of being. By "actual," I do not intend to mean, or even deny, some superior truth about life outside books, but, rather, to say that feminist discourse can risk greater truth by examining its profoundest symbolic assumptions, by inquiring into the herstory of American women with a sharpened integrity of thought and feeling. We are, after all, talking about words, as we realize that by their efficacy we are damned or saved. Furthermore, by talking about words as we have seen them marshaled in the discussion, we hope to provide more clues to the duplicitous involvement of much of feminist thinking in the mythological fortunes (words and images) of patriarchal power. By doing so, I believe that we understand more completely the seductive means of power at whatever point it involves women.

While my analysis here is focused primarily on Shulamith Firestone's *Dialectic of Sex*,[13] one of the earlier documents of the contemporary women's movement, I should point out that the kind of silence and exclusion I am describing is by no means limited to any one particular text. Firestone's work serves a vivid analytical purpose because its "narrative voice," to my mind, replicates the basic flaws of the patriarchal word-game in its unrelenting "objectification" of women and men of color. Firestone addresses black women's issues in a single chapter, and everywhere else in the book, "woman"—a universal and unmodified noun—does not mean *them*. "Woman/women" belong to that cluster of nominatives that includes "feminist," "lesbian," even "man," that purport to define the essence of what they name, and such essence is inherently paradigmatic, or the standard from which deviation and variation are measured. As simple and familiar as the point is, the symbolic behavior is not often checked in our various discourses. An anthropology of women's language would perhaps reveal the conditions in time and space that generate the colonization of words. I do not think that I exaggerate when claiming that there are few exceptions to this general linguistic rule. The exceptions are, of course, dramatic in their isolation: two examples—Adrienne Rich's "Disloyal to Civilization," with its solid reliance on an enlightened feminist critique, and Catharine A. MacKinnon's "Feminism, Marxism, Method and the State."[14] MacKinnon's attempt to understand her own appropriation of "woman" in her essay invites pause:

> Throughout this essay, I have tried to see if women's condition is shared, even when contexts and magnitudes differ. . . . I aspire to include all women in the term "women" in some way, without violating the particularity of any woman's experience. Whenever this fails, the statement is simply wrong and will have to be qualified or the aspiration (or the theory) abandoned. (6, n. 7)

Neither of these essays focuses on the theme of sexuality, but I make use of them in order to point, by inference, to a particular terministic program whose doggedness is symptomatic of the very problems of power and its arrangements that feminists of all descriptions say they would correct.

Besides Firestone's, many of the other premier texts on the entangling issues of female sexuality argue the black woman's case by negation; looking at some examples, we see the following: Kate Millett's early classic, *Sexual Politics,* conflates the black woman under the heading of "blacks," and Susan Brownmiller's *Against Our Will* is so intent on pursuing the black-man-as-rapist theme that her notes on black women's sexual experience, static and reified in "Two Studies in American History: Slavery," strike the reader as a rather perverse and exotic exercise.[15] Stimpson and Person's *Women: Sex and Sexuality* is an elegant metonymic elaboration in its range of inquiry that converges on the theme of sexuality and without any particular nuance or articulation that sounds black female sexual experience.[16] The works of Dorothy Dinnerstein, Nancy Chodorow, and Mary Daly[17] overlap questions of sexuality in drawing out other feminist interrogation, but that we read these texts—and might include along with them an impressive number of gynocritical[18] works in women's literature—as though their emblems, their figures of thought, the purposes and motivations that precede and accompany their execution, the living conditions out of which their search comes and the shape it takes all speak monolithically of women—reminds me of the period of symbolic oppression we believe we're leaving. The assumptions of epistemic power (or gestures toward it) and the ways in which we are governed by them occur in such rapid sequence that we observe no apparent break or disjuncture in the patterns of succession; in short, this *undifferentiated* spatial progression of texts is experienced as an "environment" whose air we quite "naturally" breathe. I make no attempt here to be definitive in these bibliographical notes and queries, since the library of books on women concerning various aspects of experience proliferates with nearly incalculable rapidity, it seems. But the texts I have read point to a center of gravity, a tendency of the field toward a certain word-behavior. It is that apparent centrality that I address here.

A *Dialectic of Sex* has a noble purpose—to propose a program for the liberation of women from the tyranny of reproductive biology. The "master" and precursor texts to which Firestone directly speaks include Marx's. In fact, we could say that A *Dialectic* is a postmodernist and feminist invocation to the Marxian canon in its pursuit of a solidly materialist theme—the site of the child and who will tend it and what caretaking might mean to woman-freedom. To my mind, however, Firestone's chapter on the black female in this projected configuration of social change is not only stridently critical of the Black Nationalist Movement (the only place the book situates black women), but also incredibly ominous in its pronouncements on black women's past and future. A patriarch is not speaking, we have every reason to suppose, but there It is, hustled in under the skirts of Mama in the chapter, "Racism: The Sexism of the Family of Man." In this account, black and white American women are locked in a deadly familial struggle in the House of the White Father. With fathers and sons, they engage in a ferocious Oedipal/Electra contest to the death. Is this writer doing comedy here, or have we misread her text? The object of All-love is of course the white mom-dad duo, and the children—black female and black male—share their first "sympathetic identification" with the white mother.

This titillating riff on Freud calibrates through more thematic layers of American myth-making sleight-of-hand than one has the goodwill to endure, but what strikes this reader most forcefully about Firestone's overlapping typologies is the narcissistic arrogance of the creating feminist narrator so persistently and ingenuously deployed that the parental *possibility* does not even exist for her black characters, is not even *imaginable*. These children—black female and male—spring into being, into time, the spontaneous gagline of an obscene national joke, at best its ambiguous byblow, spawned in some Harlem *estaminet*.[19] Since the line of legitimate descent that Firestone is sketching here can be generated only by virtue of a *real* domestic pair (which black mothers and fathers most certainly are not), then these children are dirty little bastards, who manage, somehow, to grow up. When we finally discover a black female character on the ruins of this cultural debris, she is nothing other than bastard daughter, turned "whore," who belongs to a "pimp," the black bastard's only possible legacy. By 1970, however, Firestone's black whore is on her way to another and more creditable transformation—"Reverend-Black-Queen-Mother-of-my-Children"—in one of the most disdainfully sustained readings of the U.S. Black Nationalist Movement that I've seen.

To Firestone, the Movement was not only the last picture show of phallic domination, but also an ineffective imitation of it. In short, black Americans in this chapter have no human right to aspire to the nuclear family, political and economic freedom, or any of the affective postures since they can only ape WASPs in doing so. Firestone goes on to tell us that the Movement's attempted revision and correction of the historic identity of the black woman that she is imagining is not really possible since its success is based on fantasy:

> For as long as the white man is still in power, he has the privilege to define the black community as he chooses—they are dependent on him for their very survival—and the psychosexual consequences of this inferior definition must continue to operate. Thus the concept of the Dignified Black Family rarely penetrates beyond the circles of the copycat Bourgeoisie or the True Believer Revolutionaries.[20]

Of course the Black Revolutionary in this book—female and male—is not a serious person, but only a parody.

Backing up a moment, we see that the black family in the United States is a recent invention of the late twentieth century: "Attempts are now being made to institute the family in the black community from Whorehouse for the White Family to Black Family."[21] For those of us across the country who grew up in black families, observations like Firestone's are simply astonishing. Some of the readers with whom I have shared this paper have complained that my remarks are based on a book that is by now "old" and that the women's movement has gone well beyond Firestone's opinions. But is that true? The criticism is to say, of course, that there is Progress and that feminists have "gotten their act together" on the question of race, but the complaint about the lament is itself negligible because it would suggest that we are not always properly attuned to the deep chords of deception that sound through the language and the structures of thought in which it fixes us. The version of anomie that Firestone is fabricating in this chapter stretches back through the last five hundred years of human history, and it is hardly my fault that the jaundice is still with us.

Perhaps the genuine culprit here is the "Family," and Firestone is warning her reader against its entrapments, but it is difficult to tell whether we are in the midst of an ironical display, or being forced to reengage an all-too-familiar configuration of violently imposed meanings. At any rate, Firestone manages, by a complicated series of grammatical maneuvers and with enviable journalistic verve, to convoke the entire structure of dominating symbolic moves as it operates against the minority others. The values, the emblems, the modes of perception, their patterns of discourse, and quasi-religious feelings that choreograph male and female, black and white not only into a Manichean frieze, but also, consequently, out of history, are so brazenly deployed in Firestone's drama that with feminist interpretations like this, who in the world needs patriarchs? It is clear: If the Anglo-American father (and by genetic association his woman) is God, then he is also the Devil, which status would assign his household the customary omnipotence that must be a lie. If Firestone is urging us in this discussion to introduce God-terms in their hint of first and last things, of the elected and the damned, then we are no longer in *this* world. We have slipped and slid, shuffled, bucked and winged into Paradise. I would go so far as to say that Firestone reconstitutes the white female as the "gyneolatrous"[22] object of desire, who willingly trades her body for a little piece of the patriarchal soul. In short, Firestone's "Family of Man" is a mysterious essence, drooping down from an ahistorical source, and I am not at all so sure that the reading is ambiguously intended.

A displacement of this psychosexual drama into history would attempt, first of all, a dismantling of the God-terms. For example, "as long as the white man [read white person] is still in power, he has the privilege to define the black community as he chooses" proffers a dose of "necessity" that we might as well refuse, since it gives the white male unlimited power. The fact of domination *is* alterable only to the extent that the dominated subject recognizes the potential power of its own "double-consciousness."[23] The subject is certainly seen, but she also *sees*. It is this return of the gaze that negotiates at every point a space for living, and it is the latter that we must willingly name the counter-power, the counter-mythology.

Firestone, however, is so busy making a case against the patriarchal bogey-man, so passionate in gathering allies against him, and so intent on throwing out the bath water of the nuclear family, babies and all, that she actually reinforces the very notions of victimization that she claims she would undo, and in overstating, misstating the black female "condition," assumes herself the negating posture that will liberate neither black nor white female into the possibilities of her own history. Once the agents are replaced onto a material/historical scene, wherein they recover their collective and individual and differentiated human status, then we can initiate discourse about power in its human and negotiable limit. We do not recognize human agency in Firestone's farce. In fact, one entire group of characters drops out of sight. Dangled by her "pimp," handled by White Daddy, who gets to fondle everybody, held in contempt by White Mother, and uncreated, unimagined, in an existential reality by a biological mother and father, whom she in turn cannot now recreate, Firestone's black woman can only throw the reflections of an imposed pathology.

We know how myths work—through the impoverishment of history—and Firestone's chapter is, for the black woman, an exemplary killing myth. In this account, she is not touched by sexuality either, as we have seen in the toasts, in Calvin Hernton's text, in Judy Chicago's imagistic absences, and in the endless and other-named litanies of epistemic violence on which bases Firestone's work is erected.

The black-female-as-whore forms an iconographic equation with black-female-vagina-less, but in different clothes, we might say. From the point of view of the dominant mythology, it seems that sexual experience among black people (or sex between black and any other) is so boundlessly imagined that it loses meaning and becomes, quite simply, a medium in which the individual is suspended. From this angle, the act of sex has no occasional moments of inauguration, transition, and termination; it does not belong to human and social process, embedded in time, pledged to time and to notions of mortality. It is, on the contrary, a state, of vicious, routinized entanglement, whose passions are pure, direct, and untrammeled by consciousness. Under these conditions of seeing, we lose all nuance, subjects are divested of their names, and, oddly enough, the female has so much sexual potential that she has none at all that anybody is ready and able to recognize at the *level of culture*. Thus, the unsexed black female and the supersexed black female embody the very same vice, cast the very same shadow, since both are an exaggeration of the uses to which sex might be put.

Michel Foucault argues that the whore in European history was a marker of banishment, that point at which institutional Europe in the eighteenth century fixed its sundry perversions, as the latter will reenter the mainstream culture under the rule of psychiatric medicine.[24] According to him, European bourgeois culture and the career of sexuality are linked by the newly empowered as a way to assure their dominance. Those outside the circle of culture, i.e., the whore, the pimp, were robbed of legitimate sexual being and, to that degree, defined the point of passage between inner and outer; the brothel, for instance, became an "insularized form of reality," a place where sex reigned uninterrupted. Consequently, the banished place and the banished person acquire an element of secrecy, and discourse about them is circumscribed and coded.[25] The black American female, whether whore or asexed, serves an analogous function for the symbolically empowered on the American scene in fixing the frontier of "woman" with her own being. If life as the black person—female or male—leads it is the imagined site of an illegitimate sexuality, then it is also, paradoxically enough, the affirmation of asexuality. ("Sidney Poitier," an idea that might be appropriated by female gender in this case, never gets to kiss the bride, we remember, in "Guess Who's Coming to Dinner?") The fiction of this symbolic act does not impress us with its awful tenacity nearly so much as when we witness its repetitions under feminist auspices.

To find another and truer sexual self-image the black woman must turn to the domain of music and America's black female vocalists, who suggest a composite figure of ironical grace. The singer is likely closer to the poetry of black female sexual experience than we might think, not so much, interestingly enough, in the words of her music, but in the sense of dramatic confrontation between ego and world that the vocalist herself embodies. We must be careful here not to romanticize the singer, with her sometimes unlovely self-destructive life, as a lame reading of the content of Sojourner's life turns it into an idea that Truth herself would probably not recognize. I do not intend to take the vocalist out of history, but to try and see her firmly within it.

The Burkean pentad of fiction[26]—agent, agency, act, scene, and purpose as the principal elements involved in the human drama—is compressed in the singer into a living body, insinuating itself through a material scene, and in that dance of motives, in which the motor behavior, the changes of countenance, the vocal dynamics, the calibration of gesture and nuance in relationship to a formal object—the song itself—is a precise demonstration of the subject turning in fully conscious knowledge of her own resources toward her object. In this instance of being-for-self, it does not matter that the vocalist is "entertaining" under American skies because the woman, in her particular and vivid thereness, is an unalterable and discrete moment of self-knowledge. The singer is a good example of "double consciousness" in action. We lay hold of a metaphor of commanding female sexuality with the singer who celebrates, chides, embraces, inquires into, controls her womanhood through the eloquence of form that she both makes use of and brings into being. Black women have learned as much (probably more) that is positive about their sexuality through the *practicing* singer as they have from the polemicist; Bessie Smith, for instance,

> in a deliberate inversion of the Puritanism of the Protestant ethic . . . articulated, as clearly as anyone before or since, how fundamental sexuality was to survival. Where work was often death to us, sex brought us back to life. It was better than food, and sometimes a necessary substitute.
>
> With her, Black women in American culture could no longer just be regarded as sexual objects. She made us sexual subjects, the first step in taking control. She transformed our collective shame at being rape victims, treated like dogs, or worse, the meat dogs eat, by emphasizing the value of our allure. In so doing, she humanized sexuality for black women.[27]

My aim in quoting Michele Russell's valorization of the singer is to trace her proposal that the dancing voice embodied is the chief teaching model for black women of what *their* feminity might consist in and to highlight Russell's discussion of the project implied in some of the Smith discography. The attention that the vocalist pays to building a relationship of equality in the woman's own house with her male lovers is quite explicit in "Get It, Bring It, and Put It Right Here":

> He's got to get it, bring it, and put it right here
> Or else he's gonna keep it out there.
> He can steal it, beg it, borrow it somewhere,
> Long as he gets it, chile, I don't care.[28]

We can perform various exegeses on this text, for example, the modulations through which the singer runs "it" so that the ambiguity of phrasing becomes a point of humor. To that extent, hyperbolean phallic status is restored to quite normal size, and the man himself inverted in the display as the dispenser of gifts. Whatever we might ultimately think of the message of Smith's inversions and its quite explicit heterosexual leanings, as in most of the discography of black female vocalists, we are interested in the singer's *attitude* toward her material, her audience, and, ultimately, her own ego-standing in the world as it is interpreted through form. If we can draw out the emphasis on the female vocalist's art, rather than her biographies, then we gather from the singer that power and control maintain an ontological edge. Whatever luck or misfortune the Player has dealt to her, she is, in the moment of performance, the primary subject of her own invention. Her sexuality is precisely the physical expression of the highest self-regard and, often, the sheer pleasure she takes in her own powers.

The difference and distance between the way black women are seen in their sexual experience and the way that they see themselves are considerable, as Russell's notes on blues tradition attest. We would argue that the black female's sexuality in feminist and patriarchist discourse is paradigmatic of her status in the universe of symbol-making so that our grasp of one complements clarity in the other: The words that would make her the subject of sexual inquiry are analogous to the enabling postulates that would give her the right action in history. To state the problem metaphorically, the black woman must translate the female vocalist's gestures into an apposite structure of terms that will articulate both her kinship to other women and the particular nuances of her own experience.

It is perhaps not useless to repeat an observation that we made earlier in different terms: feminist discourse over the last decade or so has obtained a logological disposition, or words that talk about other words,[29] in a response to prior texts—male- and female-authored. *A Dialectic of Sex* and Dorothy Dinnerstein's *Mermaid and Minotaur,* for instance, are as much a reading on Freud and/or Marx as they are an attempt to establish women at the center of the theoretical enterprise. Firestone's text is in fact enabled by the predecessor texts so that her book and Engels's *Origins of the Family, Private Property and the State,* as a specific precedent, share a category of alignment that establishes a perspective between prior statements and counter- and successive statements.[30] That the feminist writer challenges certain symbolic formations of the past in correcting and revising them does not destroy the previous authority, but extends its possibilities. By reopening the lines of a prior closure, feminist writers at once define a new position of attack and lay claim to a site of ancestral imperative. Do feminist revisionary acts, as a result, become futile? This question that a reader put to me about the last few sentences could not possibly have "yes" for an answer. My point is that the analytical discourse that feminists engage in different ways and for different reasons must not only keep vigil over its procedures, but must also know its hidden and impermissible origins. I am remembering a folk-say from my childhood, and to introduce it seems relevant to what I am driving at: "Mama's baby, papa's maybe." In other words, to know the seductions of the father and *who,* in fact, the father is might also help the subject to know wherein she occasionally speaks when she is least suspecting.

Whether we are talking about sexuality, or some other theme, we would identify this process of categorical aligning with prior acts of the text as the subtle component of power that bars black women, indeed, women of color, as a proper subject of inquiry from the various topics of contemporary feminist discourse. Such exclusion is neither deliberate, perhaps, nor inevitable, for sure, but moves through phases of symbolic *value* that conform precisely to equations of political power: the first order of symbolic "business" within a community is the articulation of what we would call a first-order naming, words that express the experience of a community in diachronic time, in daily social relationships, in economic well-being, in subject identity. A second order of naming, or words about the first order, would articulate another level of symbolic responses. I would be careful not to say a "higher," but "another" in order to get at differences of function. The literature (and the range of the arts) of African-Americans and the criticism of it, for example, constitute a second and third order of naming, with the potential power to become a first order, to the extent that the community and the artist sustain a mutual engagement that might lead to seeing anew in both. Since the content concerning the actual life experiences of black women is barely articulated, to say nothing of exhausted,[31] we are in the incredible position of having either to create a first-order discourse on black women's community and/or speak immediately into the void left by its absence and the next phase of meaning, that stage at which contemporary feminist discourse is situated. The relationship in orders of naming that I suggest here is not as static as the explanation sounds since orders and degrees of naming are simultaneously active and dynamic and can travel among each other with great ease in the life of a community. I do insist, however, on identifying careers of words that do different things with regard to a common point of reference. Essentially, the distinction that I mean here is quite similar to the one that the editors of *New French Feminisms* imply about analyses that "relate discourse to discourse and divorce it from experience."[32] The discourse of sexuality elaborates a logological status, on the pre-eminence of Freud, wherein the writer produces discourse in response to other discourse. In the case of French feminists, the father-text is Lacan. (We note with great interest, by the way, that the term "sexuality" did not enter the English lexis until c. 1800, according to the OED.) It is no use trying to decide whether or not discourse about discourse, or the impure good of theory, is "good" or "bad." The apparent reality is that it is, as the prose disciplines seem fated, for good or ill, to reflect the paucity or sufficiency of a cultural GNP. Symbolic power, like the genetic parent, begets symbolic power, takes pleasure in proliferation. Feminist discourse, to extend the figure, keeps talking, or reproducing itself, tending to do so in its own image, on the bases of initiating symbolic gestures, against which it might struggle, or with which it tacitly seeks alignment by way of various conceptual regimes.

The "Sex and Work" chapter of John Gwaltney's *Drylongso* is an anthropologist's account of a contemporary cross-sectional view of black Americans addressing their life experiences in the post-Black Nationalist era.[33] Gwaltney's procedure is the interview, here a seamlessly woven fabric of conversations, about a wealth of subjects, whose interlocutors appear to speak effortlessly and gracefully into the void. Gwaltney is so skilled an interviewer/worker that the questions that precede the responses, and in fact orchestrate them with masterful direction, are never explicit. We leave the text having heard a concert of voices—male, female, the elderly, the young, with varying grades of education and involvement in dominant American culture—with no sense that Gwaltney himself has been an intrusive presence. The interviews took place during the mid-seventies and in an unidentified urban community of the northeastern United States. Some of the models for the work might have been reminiscence narratives of the progeny of the formerly enslaved and Studs Terkel's *Working*.[34] Gwaltney's text, however, is an attempt to represent the coeval patterns of thinking among African-Americans—those without particular intellectual bias, specified allegiance, or academic and institutional connection of any sort. In other words, Gwaltney's interviewees are just "drylongso," the ordinary people of the family and what they think about money, love, sex, white folk, war, the presidency, pollution, the economy, the future of human society.

The women that Gwaltney interviewed in the "Sex and Work" chapter express what I would call a first-order naming concerning their sexual reality. I would call their words first-order because they speak "naturally," in which case words seem to come off the human tongue and need not be referred back to a dictionary in order to be understood. The impression that Gwaltney manages to convey is that he has entered these lives noiselessly and the lives have gone on, as if he were not there, and with the conversation that the actors were having when he arrived. To say that the book makes us comfortable, gives us feelings of coziness and charm is not to speak pejoratively, but to describe what we mean by first-order naming here; that the speaking is written makes the conversations a naming since we talk all the time, and most of it is not naming, has no significance or record beyond the transitory business of our daily lives. The trick, though, to reading these intriguing witnesses is that, first of all, they are a translation through the medium of a male voice. I personally trust Gwaltney's project and its outcome since I think I know what some black Americans think sometimes about some things. At the same time, I realize that the reader has no way of knowing under what constraints and mandates the women felt compelled to speak, nor whether they reported the truth of their feelings to the interviewer. Second, the women interviewed are not academically affiliated, and while their status does not disqualify them from having an opinion about anything, the cast of their views is not consonant with the arguments I am pursuing here, nor to the discourse of sexuality as we engage it in and out of books; I must observe, then, a disparity of interests which this essay has already anticipated, and I do not quite know where to fit these women's words about their bodies, or the status of their report. We proceed, nevertheless, on a sort of poetic faith that Gwaltney's partially fictionalized women provide clues to the kind of discursive differences that prevail among American women in their sounding the depths of individual and collective sexual differences. Gwaltney's interviewees are also heterosexual women, as far as I can see, and I am not prepared to call them heterosexist or homophobic because of it. The experiences of lesbians of color is as recent a chapter of public discourse (if not the actual experience itself) as are the experiences of lesbians of non-color. At any rate, we believe that the sexual realities of black American women across the spectrum of sexual preference and widened sexual styles tend to be a missing dialectical feature of the entire discussion. In any event, Gwaltney's interlocutors take us to another universe of symbol-making, intimate different ways of saying sexuality, and express *one* of the vocabularies of feeling available to black American women on the meeting between sexuality and survival.

For them sexual experience is overwhelmingly related to the thematics of work. Among the older women, the loss of jobs, because the subject often defended herself against the sexual aggressions of another, is a major focus for feminist inquiry: "Sexual harassment of working women has been one of the most pervasive but carefully ignored features of our national life."[35] The kind of sexual harassment that Gwaltney's interlocutors describe, however, is occasionally lost to feminist discussion because it is often tied up with notions of domestic work and intimacy and, as a result, inhabits a vast domain of silence. That the care of Anglo-American families in certain communities has been entrusted over time to black women remains largely unspoken in feminist discourse. Its articulation would alter considerably feminist thinking about women's social history and the problems evoked by economic and social inequities. But the writing of a new feminist project will require the critic's commitment to a thorough exploration of patterns of domination in its racist, as well as gender and sexual-preferential, manifestations.

Seventy-three years old, Mrs Nancy White, one of the fictitiously named women of Gwaltney's work, talks about her own sexual menace this way:

> I've had to ask some hands off me and I've had to give up some jobs if they got too hot behind me. Now, I have lost some money that way, but that's all right. When you lose control of your body, you have just about lost all you have in this world.[36]

Nancy White's metaphors of the body are scarcely negotiable through layers of abstraction. In this case, tenor and vehicle are virtually useless distinctions, as in the following point: "My mother used to say that the black woman is the white man's mule and the white woman is his dog" (148). According to her conclusions,

> white women are not free either, but most of them think they are and that is because that white man pats them wherever he feels like patting them and throws all that moonlight boogie-joogie on them and they eat it up! It's killing them, but they eat it up and beg the doctor for a prescription so they can get more. (143)

At seventy-three years, which would date her birth near the turn of the country, Mrs White expresses a culture of feeling different from our own, but she touches, nonetheless, the origins of a central vein of disaffection in African-American women not only from the major tenets of the historic feminist movement, but also from the community of Anglo-American women in general. bell hooks's *Ain't I A Woman* rehearses the corruptive tendencies of racist ideology to filter through the cracks of America's earlier women's movement of the late nineteenth and early twentieth centuries. Mrs. White registers an attitude that black women have difficulty overcoming for good reason, and that is their sense of being embattled at once by patriarchal culture and white women complicitous with it. This perceived connection, whether real or imagined, is the "covering cherub" that feminist criticism must reveal.

That no love was lost in Mrs. White's career between herself and white women will not surprise and is complemented by her classic understanding of "male nature." Twice-married, she knows quite well that "boogie-joogie," her play-word that shimmers across the borders of magic, is just so much garbage. Gwaltney's glossary of terms defines the word as "nonsense, trickery." The truth for Mrs. White is that

> men don't need women and women don't need men for nothing but getting children. Now, most of these men out here are not on strike. They will be evermore glad to give you just as much nature as you

need. . . . I listened to all the moonlight boogie-joogie [from black men] and before a hoecake could make a crust, there I was with two children. Well, I promised God that if he would help me through that little tight, that I was going to think about what I did a long time before I done it. Now, that's what I did. (149)

Not only does Mrs. White think "a long time" before trusting the premises of romantic love again, but she also achieves a perspective on the matter that does not allow any confusion in her own mind between sexual indulgence and the mandates of survival: "Hard work don't have a thing between its legs. I know there ain't nothing I don't know about real hard work" (150).

The leisure that Mrs. White does not perceive that she has had to contemplate her sexuality as an isolated ontological detail marks a classically schismatic feature between African-American and Anglo-American historical passage. I observe a tendency, if not a law. A mediation in this case between a first-order expression of sexual practice and the discourse of sexuality would try to elicit the hierarchies of value that the respective terms stand for. "Body," for example, is not a polyvalent or ambiguous referent for a Mrs. White. At the level of analysis and experience, we witness no arbitrary bonding between a signifier and a signified so that for Mrs. White the word, the gesture that fulfills it, and the actual consequences of both converge on a literal moment of time. To lose control of the body is to be hostage to insufferable circumstances; the lack of control is also in the historical outline of black American women often enough the loss of life. In either case, we are exposed immediately to fatal implications of change in the state of nature. The threatened return of the metaphors of experience to their original ground of tangible and material meaning demonstrates the distance we must travel between the status of the protected and that of the unprotected, or the difference between *sex* and *sexuality*.

Gwaltney's May Anna Madison is nearly a generation younger than Nancy White, but the complicated equation that she draws between her own life in relationship to white women, the tenets of feminist social analysis, and sexual experience is comparable:

The t.v. is full of people talking about women's lib. Well, I can handle black men; what I can't handle is this prejudice. White women have done more bad things to me than black men ever thought of doing. . . . It was a female chauvinist sow that worked me a full day for seventy-five cents. When I was nothing but a child myself, white women looked the other way when their fresh little male chauvinist pigs were trying to make a fool out of me! That's why I don't pay any attention to all that stuff! A black man can't do any more to me than I will let him do because I can and have taken care of myself. But I do have to work to be able to do that and that means that I have to be able to deal with white people. (171)

Madison's solution to inequities is radically democratic:

These white people are not really running things right, and that's the fault of the white men mostly and the white women go along with that. I would get color out of it altogether. I just wouldn't let nobody get but so rich and I wouldn't let nobody get but so poor. (175)

In these instances that the text brings to light, Gwaltney's interlocutors perceive their sexual being in so poignant a connection with the requirements of survival that we lose the theme of relationship in its isolated emphasis. The fusion, however, might be useful to feminist critics in suggesting that a contrastive historical order engenders a different slope of consciousness and at least one structure of first-order terms *to be interpreted.* Gwaltney has already provided one interpretive instrument—transcribed interviews edited into a text with the voices speaking to us as in an imagined spontaneity of responses. A third order of naming would attempt to discover, layer by layer, the symptoms of culture that engender this order of things. From whatever angle of history and temperament feminists address cultural issues, they ignore historical particularities as symbol-making refracts them at peril to the program of action that would liberate women from the seductions and betrayals of patriarchal dominance.

To return in conclusion to Kenneth Burke's grammar of motives and the pentad of terms on which it is built refocuses quite deliberately the dramatic character of sexuality as human potential and discursive possibility. In order to supply the missing words in the discourse of sexuality, we would try to encounter agent, agency, act, scene, and purpose in ways that the dominative mode certainly forbids. Its division of women's community along various fault lines is the superior talisman that has worked across the centuries. To dissipate its energies requires that the feminist investigator actively imagine women in their living and pluralistic conformation with experience (at least, the way they report it), and perhaps the best guarantee of such a commitment is the investigator's heightened self-consciousness with regard to the operative conceptual tools.

The dominative symbolic mode proceeds through a sequence of violent acts to attenuate historical particularities, whereas the agents in question become items in the store of mythical signifiers. The image of the "whore" and the "female eunuch," for example, has been invested with semiological and ideological values whose origins are concealed by the image itself. The image/icon acquires mystical attribution doing overtime, divested of specific reference and dispersed over time and space in blind disregard for the particular agents and scenes on which it lands. The reified image can be imposed at any moment on any individual "I." This sort of symbol-making is analogous to an act of mugging that catches the agent not only off guard, but also, most effectively, in the dark. A feminist critique in the specific instance of sexuality would encourage a counter-narrative in pursuit of the provenance and career of word- and image-structures in order that agent, agency, act, scene, and purpose regain their differentiated responsiveness. The aim, though obvious, might be restated: to restore to women's historical movement its complexity of issues and supply the right verb to the subject searching for it, feminists are called upon to initiate a corrected and revised view of women of color on the frontiers of symbolic action.

Because black women have had long experience with the brutalizations of male power, are subject to rape, know their womanhood and sexual being as crucially related and decisively timed moments in the creation and nurture of human life; because they experience their biological and human destiny by way of women and must sooner or later face their mirror and catch their own reflection of imagination in it, they do not live out their destiny on the periphery of American race and gender magic, but in the center of its Manichean darkness. But the forgoing configuration is only part of the picture. There is at least one other. Because they love their fathers, sons, and brothers, yet must be free of them as a willed act of the mind and the heart; because they witness no lapse in this narrative because they have seen their fathers, sons, and brothers cut down in war and even in peace for the very same reasons that they have been, their daughters debased and humiliated and invisible often enough in the company of other women; because other women have helped to foster the myth of their "superotherness" on either end of the scale of being; and after two closely contiguous women's movements in this country, parallel and related to the historical movements of black people, have yet to come to grips with the irremediable rendezvous of race and gender in the subject, black women do not live out their destiny on the borders of femaleness, but in the heart of it. We are urged, then, to raise this energetic scheme of conflicting tensions, allegiances, affirmations, and denials to an act of discursive form that confronts the image of the woman of color with other world women, with other dominated communities. We would try to do so in order that this generation of women ("this" as ongoing) may lay hold at last of a comparative human order, whose primary noun Person has been modified to points of a detailed refinement.

In putting afoot a new woman, we delight in remembering that half the world is female. We are challenged, however, when we recall that more than half the globe's female half is yellow, brown, black, and red. I do not mean to suggest that "white" in this ethnic and political calculus is an addendum, but, rather, only an angle on a thematic vision whose agents in gaining authenticity have the radical chance now, which patriarchy passed up, to help orchestrate the dialectics of a global new woman. As I see it, the goal is not an articulating of sexuality so much as it is a global restoration and dispersal of power. In such an act of restoration, sexuality becomes one of several active predicates. So much depends on it.

7

Changing the Letter:
The Yokes, The Jokes of Discourse,
or, Mrs. Stowe, Mr. Reed

The nineteenth-century phrase "peculiar institution" is richly suggestive in more than one way. If we think of "institution" as a specific sum of practices that so configure our sense of "public" and "private" that the rift between them is not as substantial as we might flatter ourselves to think, then antebellum slavery in the United States offers a preeminent paradigm of conflated motives. Its practices, upheld by an elaborate system of codes, subject to conditions of market, sanctioned by the church (in the American plurality), and generating one of the nation's first communities of fugitives, actually sustained no private realm, even though such practices were central to the "home," to the very stuff of domesticity as planter-aristocrats envisioned it. There is no more ironic, pathetic, or is it cynical, juxtaposition of gazes that capture the attention than this scene from *Uncle Tom's Cabin*: Tom and Master, Inc., including Augustine St. Clare, Vermont cousin Ophelia, and Evangeline St. Clare, have all just arrived at New Orleans after a trek down the Mississippi on the *Belle Rivière*. The carriage in which the party has been delivered to the "many mansions" of St. Clare, so to speak, stops in front of an ancient house,

> built in the odd mixture of Spanish and French style of which there are specimens in some parts of New Orleans. It was built in the Moorish fashion,—a square building inclosing a courtyard, into which the carriage drove through an arched gateway. The court, in the inside, had evidently been arranged to gratify a picturesque and voluptuous ideality. Wide galleries ran all around the four sides, whose Moorish arches, slender pillars, and arabesque ornaments carried the mind back, as in a dream, to the reign of oriental romance in Spain. In the middle of the court, a fountain threw high its silvery water, falling in a never-ceasing

spray into a marble basin, fringed with a deep border of fragrant violets. The water in the fountain, pellucid as crystal, was alive with myriads of gold and silver fishes, twinkling and darting through it like so many living jewels. Around the fountain ran a walk, paved with a mosaic of pebbles, laid in various fanciful patterns; and this again, was surrounded by turf, smooth as green velvet, while a carriage-drive inclosed the whole. Two large orange-trees, now fragrant with blossoms, threw a delicious shade; and, ranged in a circle round upon the turf, were marble vases of arabesque sculpture, containing the choicest flowering plants of the tropics. Huge pomegranate trees, with their glossy leaves and flame-colored flowers, dark-leaved Arabian jessamines, with their silvery stars, geraniums, luxuriant roses bending beneath their heavy abundance of flowers, golden jessamines, lemon-scented verbenas, all united their bloom and fragrance, while here and there a mystic old aloe, with its strange, massive leaves, sat looking like some hoary old enchanter, sitting in weird grandeur among the more perishable bloom and fragrance around it.[1]

In Puritan terms, we might imagine, the landscape of this scene is "heathen" in its excess, openly engaging the senses, and, in case we miss the point the first time, the narrator reinforces a semantics of "oriental romance" and splendor in the "dark-leaved *Arabian* jessamines" (my emphasis). As though Tom "grows" out of the fictive landscape, deeply akin "by nature" to its specular vitality, we are told that he gets down from the carriage and looks around him with an "air of calm, still enjoyment." Tom is the scene's Negro, and the Negro in his fully imagined Africanity: "The Negro, it must be remembered, is an exotic of the most gorgeous and superb countries of the world, and he has, deep in his heart, a passion for all that is splendid, rich, and fanciful; a passion which, rudely indulged by an untrained taste, draws on them the ridicule of the colder and more correct white race" (180).

In explaining the central nervous system of the African in her *Key to Uncle Tom's Cabin,* Stowe expatiates on those symptoms of living being which are proximate to and expressive of this seductive nature; of peculiar susceptibility, the African personality's

sensations and impressions are very vivid, and their fancy and imagination lively. In this respect, the race has an oriental character, and betrays its tropical origin. Like the Hebrews of old and Oriental nations of the present, they give vent to their emotions with the utmost vivacity of expression, and their whole bodily system sympathizes with the movement of their minds. . . . Like Oriental nations, they incline much to outward expression, violent gesticulations, and agitating movements of the body. . . . They will laugh, weep, and embrace each other convulsively, and sometimes become entirely paralyzed and cataleptic.[2]

Exactly *what* the "orient" is has no precision, of course, in Stowe's account, lacking specificity as a potential repertoire of geopolitical traits that flow together toward a cultural synthesis. It is simply *there,* in an unimpeachable unity of essential impression and in fatal binarity with the other great mythical valence of Stowe's discourse—the "Anglo-Saxon-race—cool, logical, and practical." The members of Tom's "African race," of "oriental character," are "in their own climate . . . believers in spells, in 'fetish and obi,' in the 'evil eye,' and other singular influences, for which probably there is an origin in this peculiarity of constitution." We are called upon to imagine that competence and success of magical skill may be "accounted for by supposing peculiarities of nervous constitution quite different from those of the whites" (46).

Even though Augustine St. Clare is, as far as his status goes, a "white" man—and we are also explicitly told this by the narrator—the descriptive apparatus that surrounds him in the New Orleans scene is loaded with intimations of "gorgeousness." St. Clare is, after all, "in his heart a poetical voluptuary" (180). The narrative energies of this scene, in its intense physicality, are decidedly marked for the realm of the natural—forces whose symbolic resonance is "deeply connected with fertility, sexuality, and reproduction,"[3] or what Kenneth Burke identifies as the "realm of ubertas": "the realm of the appetites generally."[4] If the markings of landscape all signify the "exotic," the strange, the foreign, then what better gaze to preside over it than Tom's?—that of the gagged, bewildered, "unreading," but "read," object who representatively and representationally embodies, historically, North America's most *coveted* body, that is, the *captivated* man/woman-child who fulfills a variety of functions at the master's behest?

The horror of slavery was its absolute domesticity that configured the "peculiar institution" into the architectonics of the southern household. So complete was its articulation with domestic economy that from one angle it loses visibility and becomes as "natural" to the dynamics of culture as "luxurious" roses "bending beneath their heavy abundance of flowers" (179). Gillian Brown expresses that "peculiar" relationship in this way:

> Slavery disregards [the] opposition between the family at home and the exterior workplace. The distinction between work and family is eradicated in the slave for whom there is no separation between eco-

nomic and private status. When people themselves are 'articles' subject to 'mercantile dealings,' when 'the souls and bodies of men' are
'equivalent to money,' women can no longer keep houses that provide
refuge from marketplace activites.[5]

Deeply embedded, then, in the heart of American social order, the "peculiar
institution" elaborated "home" and "marketplace" as a useless distinction,
since, at any given moment, and certainly by 1850—the year of the Fugitive—the slave was as much the "property" of the collusive state as he or
she was the personal property of the slaveholder. We could say that slavery
was, at once, the most public private institution *and* the gound of the institutions's most terrifying intimacies, because fathers *could* and *did* sell their
sons and daughters, under the allowance of *law* and the flag of a new nation, "conceived in liberty," and all the rest of it.

It seems to me that every generation of systematic readers is compelled
not only to reinvent "slavery" in its elaborate and peculiar institutional
ways and means but also, in such play of replication, its prominent discursive features as

> a group of objects that can be talked about (or what is forbidden to talk
> about), a field of possible enunciations (whether in lyrical or legal lan-
> guage), a group of concepts (which can no doubt be presented in the
> elementary form of notions and themes), a set of choices (which may
> appear in the coherence of behavior or in systems of prescription).[6]

This field of enunciative elements—its horizon, its limits, its enabling postulates, and its placement in perspective with other fields of signification—
constitutes the discourse of slavery, and, as concretely material as the "institution" was, as a natural historical sequence and as a scene of pulverization
and murder, "slavery," for all that, remains one of the most textualized and
discursive fields of practice that we could posit as a structure for attention.
In a very real sense, a full century and a half "after the fact," "slavery" is
primarily discursive, as we search vainly for a point of absolute and indisputable origin, for a moment of plenitude that would restore us to the real,
rich "thing" itself before discourse touched it. In that regard, "slavery"
becomes the great "test case" around which, for its Afro-American readers,
the circle of mystery is recircumscribed time and again. This realization is
stunning: as many times as we reopen slavery's closure, we are hurtled
rapidly forward into the dizzying motions of a symbolic enterprise, and it
becomes increasingly clear that the cultural synthesis we call "slavery" was
never homogeneous in its practices and conception, nor unitary in the
faces it has yielded. But to behave as if it were so matches precisely the telos

of African personality in the United States—as Tom becomes in Stowe's text *the negro*—this existence of a him/her in a subject-position that unfolds according to a transparent, self-evidentiary motif. In other words, to rob the subject of its dynamic character, to capture it in a fictionalized scheme whose outcome is already inscribed by a higher, different, *other*, power, freezes it in the ahistorical.

The collective and individual reinvention of the discourse of "slavery" is, therefore, nothing other than an attempt to restore to a spatiotemporal object its eminent historicity, to evoke *person/persona* in the place of a "shady" ideal.

My notion of Harriet Beecher Stowe and Ishmael Reed as two impression-points in the articulation of the institution of "slavery" with a national identity has several parts to it: First, I intend no precise analogy on an intertextual juncture by juxtaposing these radically disparate figures of practice. In other words, I am not suggesting any explicit relationship of priority and indebtedness between textual performances in a selected spatiotemporal sequence by invoking these disjunctive literary instances. By bringing them into a posture of alignment, however, I do wish to concede textuality itself as a self-conscious systematicity that never closes, or that distributes itself in a more or less concentrated "mask of repetition." Reed is not so much "rewriting" Stowe as he is elaborating a repertory of strategies that denote, that circumlocute, a particular cluster of discursive acts. In Reed's system, Stowe generates, in that regard, one set of traffic signals, we might say. Further, we are pursuing as systematically as we can what the blurbs for and the critics of *Flight to Canada* have already told us: Afro-American writers, in Richard Yarborough's words, are still striving to "distance themselves from all that *Uncle Tom's Cabin* represents."[7]

In that sense, Stowe, the writer, casts a long shadow, becomes an implacable act of precursor poetics that the latter-day black writer would both outdistance *and* "forget." The 1852 work, in its startling history of publication and, in the view of George Eliot, its "founding" of the "Negro Novel,"[8] apparently has no national precedent in its endless powers of proliferation: If we could recuperate the material and symbolic wealth that has accrued to the gross national product and somebodies' "stash" from the purported repetitions of this work's narrative and iconic treasures, we would have considerable wealth ourselves and, with it, a fairly precise equivalent to the *exchange* and *use* value of the *captured* African body. Yarborough notes that "Stowe's best-seller inspired a veritable flood of Uncle Tom poems, songs, dioramas, plates, busts, embossed spoons, painted scarves, engravings, and other miscellaneous memorabilia, leading one wry commentator to observe '[Uncle Tom] became, in his various forms, the most frequently sold slave in American history.' "[9] And in 1853, a children's version of the novel was offered under the title of *A Peep into Uncle Tom's Cabin*. The prurient, voyeuristic suggestion of "peep" is quite appropriate to a national mentality that wants to "steal" a *look* at the genitals in vague consciousness that they are covered by an interdiction.

For all its undeniable, even seductive, narrative powers, *Uncle Tom's Cabin*—both in itself and in the "fallout" it induced—might be regarded as a lethal weapon, or *because* of such powers, and for at least once in the history of literary production, we can say that we have found in this work a "poem" that *can* "kill."

Second, then, we regard *Flight to Canada*—in its absurdist, dystopian, mocking impulse—as a revisionary, corrective move that wants to speak both *for itself* and *against* something else; it seems to me that we have hold here of *forms of coexistence* in a potential configuration of slavery's discursive field: "statements [for Reed] that are no longer accepted or discussed, and which consequently no longer define either a body of truth or a domain of validity, but in relation to which relations of filiation, genesis, transformation, continuity, and historical discontinuity can be established."[10] Foucault calls this instance of *form of coexistence* a "field of memory" that might obtain between texts and their propositions. When, for example, Reed's invention "Mammy Barracuda" is said to have worn a "diamond crucifix on her bosom" so heavy that it forced her to stoop, and that, further, when she went into the fields once "and the sun reflected on her cross so, two slaves were blinded,"[11] we think instantly and all at once in a sort of static of "confused" imagery. At once, the dazzling cross mocks its founding icon-text in specious display and plays to a notion of *specie* translated into an equivalent materiality. "Mammy Barracuda," in her brilliant captivity, embodies an oxymoronic motion—at the crossroads of wealth and exchange, she is a major player, though not a beneficiary. Wearing wealth's symptoms on her magnanimous bosom and around her neck, she throws a reflection that *shatters* the sight, instead of *healing* it. This Christian "practice," in its complicated maneuvers of displacement, is refracted back on Stowe's Tom, who, according to the way the reader remembers the scene, dies in a gesture of crucifixion in the midst of "two slaves"—Sambo and Quimbo's—act of repentance (441). Although Tom's eyes are closed in the death scene by young George Shelby, a few pages after the flogging scene, we realize essentially that Tom has been murdered by hanging, which thematic recurs with the regularity of clockwork in the annals and narratives of North American enslavement. Stowe's subsequent narrative on prior texts of Scripture and the historical is absorbed and displaced in Reed's contemporary structure through his translation of syntactic elements into an iconic sign, whose "verbal equivalent . . . is not a word but a phrase or indeed a whole story."[12]

Third, if these textualities in a "field of memory" demonstrate historical and literary repetition as the radical disjuncture between "history" on the one hand and "farce" on the other, then we can say that "slavery" as a potential topic of enunciative and discursive practices, is, first and foremost, textual, or eminently constituted *in discourse*, since not only are its objects of selectability neutral, so to speak, or subject to refashioning, but the same terms can entertain different relationships provided they are inserted into different cultural axes.[13] We observe, then, certain structural homologies, or dishomologies, that adhere between *Flight to Canada* and *Uncle Tom's Cabin*, or, more precisely, structural dishomologies that are revealed *only* in the former instance of Reed as dissimilarity of *structure*, and not transparent prophetic utterance.

In other words, with *Flight to Canada*, we are aware that "slavery," in at least one of its dimensions, is claimed by the "lumberroom" of "literature" and that just as Reed invades Stowe's invasion of those symptoms and appurtenances of Gothic convention, which, in Stowe, become the mythical landscape of a principle of inversion ("Simon Legree" is "really" "Augustine St. Clare" with his drawers down), "slavery" inscribes an alignment of relationships between texts and among texts that are purely open to modes of improvisation and rearrangement.[14] These precisely segmented portions of cultural content might be defined as "cultural units," or clusters and systems of interconnected cultural units, in a system of positions and oppositions.[15]

It will be clear, then, that in reading Reed against and with Stowe, I am suggesting *Flight to Canada* as both a systematic protocol and a rereading and redoing of "slavery" and as a moment of "Quickskill," to appropriate the name of one of Reed's chief figures, which would undo the triangle of metaphysical desire[16] that has killed the "slave" in Tom endlessly. What are in Stowe the yokes and the crucifixion of discourse undergo transformation in Reed into the jokes and the liberation of discourse from systems of cultural content that, once upon a time, enslaved "9 million and more," Paule Marshall observes, in their African diaspora.

But, somehow, this is too easy; I am expected to come down on the argument in this way. I must admit that for me, an individual reader/researcher/teacher/writer, not at all entirely disparate from my identity as one of those latter-day survivors of history's nightmare, I am rather predictably selfish in my own desires—I want to eat the cake *and* have it. I *want* a *discursive* "slavery," in part, in order to "explain" what appears to be very rich and recurrent manifestations of neo-enslavement in the very symptoms of discursive production and sociopolitical features that govern our current fictions in the United States. At the same time, I suspect that I occasionally resent the spread-eagle tyranny of discursivity across the terrain of what we used to call, with no self-consciousness, "experience." But I further suspect that this crucial dilemma is rather common among Afro-American scholars, who are pledged to the critical work of the *inventory* and its relationship to a community's survival. Even though we are urged to think that there is no necessary equivalence between the major prongs of the foregoing sentence, I invoke a correspondence between them because I sense a deep and genuine connection between knowledge and its maps of distribution and the economies of dominance and subordination.

In other words, I am conscious that in attempting to "read" "slavery" as it provides the thematic ground that situates these radically disparate acts, I am also critiquing my membership in at least two continuous *and* discontinuous communities of ideological interest. There is a hint of quite similar hermeneutic tensions at play in *Flight to Canada,* whose sustained chuckle over "slavery" seems to me almost always contrived and self-consciously cautious. But I am sure of one thing: Mrs. Stowe's "slavery" gives way to an inexorable grimness, which I really did not want to experience again as a reader, while Reed's work is sufficiently interstitial that "flight to Canada," indeed, "flight," remains entirely possible. After *Uncle Tom's Cabin,* one needs a drink. Reed provides it. If these "sets of choices," translatable into the efficacies and "benign" neglects of public policy, are *virtually* a matter of words, then I see no reason *not* to choose an "out" and the best available one. In short, can Stowe be laughed to death, and is Reed the man for the job?

After contemporary feminist theory has patiently and often impressively "recovered" Harriet Beecher Stowe for a quite visible place in the canon of literary procedure that we study as the "American Renaissance," the posture of the foregoing interrogation will probably strike the mind as adversarial. Even Ann Douglass's negative assessment of Stowe's work,[17] in Jane Tompkins's estimation, is significant as a countercritical move to the inherited opinions of *Uncle Tom's Cabin,* in particular. Tompkins argues in *Sensational Designs* that the effectiveness of Stowe's novel is directly measurable by its "popularity." "Written by, for, and about women,"[18] *Uncle Tom's Cabin,* as sentimental fiction, Tompkins continues, enjoins the reader to different critical assumptions about the nature and function of literature:

In modernist thinking, literature is by definition a form of discourse that has no designs on the world. It does not attempt to change things, but merely to represent them, and it does so in a specifically literary language whose claim to value lies in its uniqueness. Consequently, works whose stated purpose is to influence the course of history, and which therefore employ a language that is not only unique but common and accessible to everyone, do not qualify as works of art. (125)

Rather than aiming, then, to dethrone Melville and Hawthorne, Tompkins would prefer to "argue that the work of the sentimental writers is complex and significant in ways *other than* those that characterize the established masterpieces" (126). The reader is asked to set aside certain

familiar categories for evaluating fiction—stylistic intricacy, psychological subtlety, epistemological complexity—and to see the sentimental novel not as an artifice of eternity answerable to certain formal criteria and to certain psychological and philosophic concerns, but as a *political* enterprise, halfway between sermon and social theory, that both codifies and attempts to mold the values of its time. (126, my emphasis)

While I am wholly sympathetic to Tompkins's project and to that of other corrective feminist readings of *Uncle Tom's Cabin*, like Elizabeth Ammons's[19] and Gillian Brown's, I must say that in my own reading of the statements insinuated in the discourse of this novel, a feminist social paradigm is not only problematized, but made problematic in ways I had not quite expected. Because there is "noise" in the discursive field of this novel, and a path to radical social revision has not been properly cleared, the work *metaphorizes* the very dilemma of *reading* and *living* that Afro-American readers, at least—who, by the way, also come with at least *two* kinds of sexual markings, described as "female" and "male"—have palpably *felt* for over a century about *Uncle Tom's Cabin*.

One of the best readings of this novel remains, to my mind, James Baldwin's "Everybody's Protest Novel,"[20] which posits a "theological terror" at the heart of the work. It is this cultural crux that most worries my own encounter with Stowe's novel—how, for instance, a unitary reading of "slavery," "according to the Gospel," springs the trap of Tom's dismemberment. Even though I would falsify myself and my argument here if I did not admit right away that Baldwin's "reading woman" is, in my opinion, woefully reactionary and static, I think that he nevertheless taps a central vein of inquiry, in particular reference to black readers of Stowe. I am little concerned that *Uncle Tom's Cabin*, written as it was "by, for, and about women"—and that when we say as much, we do not, in our public and critical discourses, at least, *mean* to tell anything at all about the Chloes and the Topsies—represents anti-energy for the captive woman. In the symptoms of anomie and facelessness that constitute them, these fictional cyphers are granted *no* vocality, even in this *fictive* work of a woman's. Enclosed and fashioned by an essential silence, Chloe and Topsy, for all their sporadic "talking," remain the carnivalesque propositions of female character who inscribe "growths" and "bumps" on the surface of Stowe's fiction. "Woman," here and elsewhere, then and now, so elides with a *revoked* adjectival marker named "white" that we barely notice. But this complex of a problematic does not concern me as much here as do the fate and career of discursive bodies, as they are buttressed to death, as it were, by what seems to me an opportunistic deployment of the ideologies of a kerygmatic Gospel.

It is entirely possible to read the texts of a demotic (or preaching) Gospel in a subversive way, that is, in a way that does *not mandate* the sacrifice of children, or the crucifixion of black bodies, male or female. We know this, because the annals of Afro-American narratives in sermons demonstrate quite effectively, in certain notable examples,[21] how the assertions and declaratives of speech acts about words "about God"[22] conduce to a radically different social choreography. That Stowe orchestrates a thematics of sacrifice as a moment of a *posited* "necessity"; that this segment of the eschatological attaches itself to the history, or to the narratives about the history, of children and "The Negro," reinforces the phallogocentric motives of slaveheld "private property" in a woman's hands, since it insists that somebody *else* pay the *price* of its own unmitigated desire. This is exactly what Reed's narrator, Quickskill, means when, outright, he accuses the historical, herefictionalized, Stowe of "stealing" Josiah Henson's story. Can we say that an invented Tom, in fact, *pays* the lady's way?

Gillian Brown introduces the lexicon of "desire" to the criticism I read on *Uncle Tom's Cabin*, but Brown claims that Stowe renounces "desire" *for* and *in* woman, as episodes of the novel reflect the "imagined state of possession, that is, the condition of satiety and fulfillment, the goal of the pursuit of happiness. The nondesiring woman is therefore the embodiment of perfect ownership."[23] Because "private property," we are told, is already compromised and sullied by the alienable, by inequality, by the violence of accumulation, is there possibly "perfection" in it? And what is the status of "perfection?" Unless by it we mean owning "well" and "lots." Even Simon Legree does *that*.

This work, then, poses no pluralism of reference in its reading and interpretation of "Gospel" relating to the work's duo of major figures. If the blueprint for colonizing the world in the name of the "family state," under the leadership of Christian women,[24] is prefigured in this novel, then I know precisely where I belong in its domestic economies, and I want no parts of it. Stowe's view, then, is not *the* "Gospel," already an Ur-text of polyvalence, but it is just *that,* a *view,* which, in its systematic assertions— and ironically enough, this is the foundation of its powers—*rivals,* even *analogizes,* in every sense, the omnipresent and univocal narrative structures in which "slavery" continues to arise in the fiction. In short, Stowe poses a purely local and particularistic notion *as* the place of an imagined and fictitious "universality." But there seems deep division here, and I want to test my reading of a few of its implications. When I say "division," I mean that Stowe and some of her commentators might have been and may be, still, satisfied that a monolithic Calvinist god "dictated" this work, but other readings may detect at least moments of it that reveal themselves as the slippery, unintended messengers of a different and explosive dictation.

I want to return momentarily to the scene whose rhetorical features I highlighted at the beginning of this essay as the ground of concatenation upon which my reading of Stowe's work might be tried. The architecture of the courtyard and the mansion of St. Clare's New Orleans estate is clearly intended as an emblematic gesture. I regard it as a central excerpt of narrative and conceptual features that might well discover their inspiration in Catherine Beecher's *Treatise on Domestic Economy* (1842).[25] But Stowe's sister makes it clear that as the author of the *Treatise,* she is addressing her remarks to nuclear-family heads of *moderate* means. Nonetheless, there is about this "oriental" locus of splendor and hidden cargo a didactic content that conceals a heteroclitic sexual motivation. Even if Augustine St. Clare persists in error as a disbelieving slaveholder, there is no reason why the fleshly beauties of Pontchartrain and the New Orleans place would not captivate and express the most cultivated appetites. But is its appeal to the appetitive also its mischief—the mark of a decided prohibitive context in the system of the work?

A partial answer to this interrogation lies in the fascinating commentary on *Uncle Tom's Cabin* provided by Karen Halttunen, who tracks the Gothic undergirdings of Legree's Red River domain. But inasmuch as Legree and St. Clare might be accorded the same value as the twin and primary moments of the very same "domestic economy," I accede to Halttunen's apt decipherment of the close relationship between "good" and "bad" slaveholders. These figures of inversion both stand on Gothic ground, which becomes, for Ishmael Reed, late in the twentieth century, a profound metaphor of explicit sadomasochistic performance.

Halttunen shows that the appropriation of the discourse of Gothic in the hands of Harriet Beecher Stowe was preceded in the Beecher family by both her father's and brother's use of its strategies in their respective sermonic work. The Gothic literary tradition that underscored Lyman Beecher's 1825 sermon series, entitled "Six Sermons on the Nature, Occasions, Signs, Evils, and Remedy of Intemperance," goes back, Halttunen points out, fifty years to Horace Walpole's *Castle of Otranto* (1764), among other sources. "The haunted house of the 'School of Walpole,' with its standard appointments, including heavy iron doors, trapdoors with metal rings, secret doors hidden behind tapestries, long galleries, winding staircases, underground vaults, labyrinthine passages, neighboring convents, monasteries, and charnel houses,"[26] provided similar impetus for Henry Ward Beecher's 1844 lecture series, "Lectures to Young Men, on Various Important Subjects," preached in Indianapolis. The central sermon of this series, "The Strange Woman," offers a philippic against prostitution and comprises, in Halttunen's view, a narrative of "sexual nausea" (114). A remarkable structural similarity obtains between Stowe's paradisiacal landscape of lush gardens and her brother's sermonic narrative of the garden of seduction: "Stowe's description of St. Clare's exotic house, like her brother Henry's treatment of the Ward of Pleasure, reflected the debt of the Gothic genre to the eighteenth-century oriental tale" (119). But as the ascribed oriental sensuousness of Henry Ward Beecher's "'Ward of Pleasure' points to [*his* narrative's] Ward of Death, St. Clare's gorgeous home serves in Stowe's narrative *as a kind of way station to the ruined mansion of Simon Legree*" (119, my emphasis).

As though we might interpolate the sentences that attach to St. Clare's narrative into the ones that describe Legree's, we could say that St. Clare's discursive career is not finished until we gain the radical shift of geographical and ontological ground provided by the severe isolation of Legree's estate. These sentences are strangely retroversive: "What was once a smooth-shaven lawn before the house, dotted here and there with ornamental shrubs, was now covered with frowsy tangled grass, with horseposts set up, here and there, in it, where the turf was stamped away, and the ground littered with broken pails, cobs of corn, and other slovenly remains" (369). The "dark-leaved Arabian jessamines" of St. Clare's gardens reappear as Legree's ruin—as "mildewed jessamine," a "ragged-hanging honeysuckle," and "what once was a large garden . . . now all grown over with weeds . . . through which . . . some solitary exotic reared its foresaken head" (369). We are teased with intimations of St. Clare, who is, indeed, "former," both as regards the *sold* mansions of New Orleans and Lake

Pontchartrain and the text, with reference to so-called enlightened slave-holding: "[Legree's estate] had formerly belonged to a gentleman of opulence and taste, who had bestowed some considerable attention to the adornment of his grounds" (369). It is as though we have penetrated our own dreams to their foundation in a neurotic context, wherein dream-maker and -work are engendered in the same, continuous moments of an alienated self-identity.

When Stowe places "Little Eva" and "Uncle Tom" in a new and revised "Garden of Eden," she might have aimed for a type of Eva as the mother of resurrected, reconstructed humankind, but there is nothing "pious" or "holy" about the altogether shocking outcome: The sacrificial lamb of *Uncle Tom's Cabin*—in the dual person of Eva the temptress and Tom the castrated—must be expended as *punishment* for crimes against the culture, rather than as *salvation* for the culture. Elizabeth Ammons argues that Stowe proposed

> as the foundation for a new democratic era, in place of masculine authority, feminine nurture: a type of love epitomized in the Christlike girl-child, Eva, whose name calls to mind the Edenic mother of the race. Figuring as Eva's adult counterparts are several mothers and one man: sweet-tempered black Tom, meek like Christ, yet fiercely loyal to a democratic set of values. The author's obvious contradiction of gender in the Eva/Christ and Tom/heroine associations, both of which serve as savior analogues in the novel, animates her conviction, as she later stated it plainly, that "there was in Jesus more of the pure feminine element than in any other man."[27]

As I see this, Stowe herself, "more manly," we might say, than "Christlike," *did* know the *Father,* as it seems to me that the vaunted feminist gaze of this work remains deformed. I do not mean to say that "feminism," as an ideology of discourse, critique, and practice, yields a unitary response, or that it ought to, although it would be easier if there were a single and orthodox critical function that we could all appropriate as "feminism" and leave it at that. I also do not intend our current repertoire of intellectual practices and historical specificity called "feminist" to assume more import than it actually bears. In other words, Stowe's "feminism" and her critics' "feminism" need not duplicate mine in order to command their own considerable weight. But I am saying that the *requirements of sacrifice,* which Stowe's critics inevitably point out as death's raison d'être in the novel and which Stowe herself reinforces in the narrative's habits of pathos, seem to galvanize the murderous instincts of patriarchal and phallogocentric modes of address rather than effectively challenge them. Though much of the way one decides the issue depends on the angle from which she is seeing, I tend to agree with Eric Sundquist, who argues that Stowe "returned . . . to a paternal revolutionary tradition bound up in the wrath of God the father, to the suppressed Calvinistic vengeance of Lyman Beecher's religion to which the novel's immense moral work of mothers may finally give way."[28]

If Stowe's colonizationist vision of the millennium is embedded in a "messianic view of history," then I am not sure that the "good news" of the New Dispensation offers compatibility with an order of things " 'in which all persons tend to lose their individual reality in the great cosmic drama of God's plan.' "[29] For certain, the "theological terror" of a Calvinistic, patriarchal God, the Father, the Name, the Law, is not *commensurate* with a soteriological scheme that watches the sparrow's fall and has already counted the numbers of hairs on one's head. In what does this "terror" consist, this "terror" that has dictated the theft of the Negro's body, in God's name, excised his genitals in print and in fact, and hailed it under the sign of "meekness"; that abdicates from "desire" in its feminine manifestations, but recuperates it in the female child-body; and that so devalues the issue from the black female's body that we have ascribed to it *only* the potential of a wild proliferation—a "jes grew"? Who, in short, is Stowe's "Father-God," who has visited us in so much splendor of dread that even today the book generates a shudder of revulsion?

Even though we assign to the intricate involutions of St. Clare's courtyard the status of high culture by virtue of a literal and exquisitely modulated "cultivation," the New Orleans scene does not escape the markings of a "nature/culture" split. "Everywhere" an invaginated surface—"a deeply fringed border of violets," for example, and enclosures that open into other recesses—threatens to overcome the planned and precise geometries of landscape gardening. The scene, loaded with suggestions of a *tamed* wildness, is repeated in reference to St. Clare's summer house on Pontchartrain:

> St. Clare's villa was an East-Indian cottage, surrounded by light verandas of bamboo-work and opening on all sides into gardens and pleasure-grounds. The common sitting room opened onto a large garden, fragrant with every picturesque plant and flower of the tropics, where winding paths ran down to the very shores of the lake, whose silvery sheet of water lay there, rising and falling in the sunbeams. (281)

One of the *as if* secret places of the Lake Pontchartrain estate belongs, specifically, to Eva and Tom, "a little mossy seat, in an arbor, at the foot of the garden" (281). Tompkins reads the putative visionary import of this scene as typologically paradigmatic, remarking that its "iterative nature . . .

presents in miniature the structure of the whole novel."[30] This assertion is plausible, I think, but I would grant its feasibility for reasons rather to the side of Tompkins's. If, as the female of both scenes, which collide and slip into an imploded unity, Eva (alongside Tom) comes to be associated with "nature," then an explanation is not too far to seek.

Halttunen points out that at least in the Midwest during the nineteenth century "fruits and fountains, most significant, flowers," a euphemism for the female genitals, are situated in a grid of "enchanted objects."[31] Although Halttunen is referring here specifically to William Beckford's *Vathek* (1786) and Edgar Allan Poe's "Masque of the Red Death" (1842), I think we can explore flowers in Stowe's landscape toward similar ends.

In fact, I would go so far as to say that Eva is fatally marked by a lush sensuality in three distinct instances: (1) At the end of the arbor scene, the narrator, discoursing on certain symptoms of immortality in the spiritually precocious child, claims that the "seal of heaven" (283) is upon her. This apparently unmotivated charge is here contextualized by Eva's intimate contact with Tom, whose "blackness" traditionally configures the site of pollution. (2) Pages earlier, Tom, on a typical day of St. Clare's lightly sarcastic banter-at-home, sits on "a little mossy seat in the court, every one of his button-holes stuck full of cape jessamines, and Eva, gayly laughing, was hanging a wreath of roses around his neck; and then she sat down on his knee, like a chip-sparrow, still laughing" (195). (3) In another scene that rehearses this same complex of discursive and kinetic gestures, Eva has just been told the story of Scipio by St. Clare: "A few moments, and merry laughs were heard through the silken curtains, as Eva and St. Clare were pelting each other with roses and chasing each other among the alleys of the court" (255). Drawn together by certain symptoms of domestic intimacy, wherein "mother" has not entirely disappeared, but expresses adequation in the "male" figure of Tom, Eva, St. Clare, and Uncle Tom are snared by the treacheries of an unspoken and deflected seduction.

We might say that the "seal of heaven" *is* upon Little Eva, if we read it as the "mark and the knowledge." But beneath "heaven," the "sacred" intrudes the "seal," or the "mark" of the "sacred," as the latter itself denotes a conjunction of ambivalence—a culture content at once "maleficent and beneficent."[32] When, on two distinct occasions, Ophelia is repelled at the sight of Eva's embracing two "black" figures, we recognize that her behavior accords perfectly well with a culturally dictated fear of *contamination*. We need not seek reasons for Ophelia's scorn in anything that we would remotely call "reasonable," explicit, or immediately open to the understanding, even if the behavior does strike us as systematic and obsessional beyond the idiosyncratic markings of character. But it seems certain that the semantic traces into which "Uncle Tom" is structured—"that far off mystic land of gold, and gems, and spices, and waving palms, and wondrous flowers, and miraculous fertility" (197)—equate "The Negro" not only with "otherness," but with the *matrix* of difference and contradiction that enables this writing. Stowe *needs* "Uncle Tom," along with the novel's considerable display of massive *inarticulation* (the Topsies; the black young, piled in a corner of Uncle Tom's Cabin in a confused heap of noise and motion) in order to *signify* at all, in order, perhaps, to achieve the division in which meaning arises. But distancing herself from her object, the author invests "Little Eva" with the desire to touch, to embrace, the forbidden, concealed like a serpent beneath a bank of flowers.

The renunciation of desire that Gillian Brown argues as the central dynamic of Stowe's "feminine nurture" occurs here under the sign of an indirection as subtle in its appearance as the displaced sexual economies that demarcate Little Eva's connection with both St. Clare and Uncle Tom—and even subtler *because* the line that I am forecasting is *written?* In fact, there is no other sentence like this one in this entire novel of so impressive a scope, and, in a female mouth, perhaps no other like it anywhere in American fiction. Because the sentence belongs to a child actant and is contrived in "innocence" and seeming ingenuousness, we are meant to glide right past it with the same kind of tenderhearted admiration that we bring to the sight of a child dangled on its parent's knee, or embracing a pet larger than itself, but we look again. Haley, in the act of expatiating on Tom's virtures to potential buyers aboard the *Belle Rivière,* senses that St. Clare's pretended indifference is just that—pretending—and, indeed, St. Clare, in his fully urbane sophistication and decided amusement at Haley's relative clownishness, goes along with the show. Misreading St. Clare's gestures, however, Eva softly implores her father to buy Uncle Tom, "putting her arm around [St. Clare's] neck" (166). And then, to my mind, that astonishing sequence of lines is spoken in the aftermath:

"You have money enough, I know. *I want him.*" (166, my emphasis)

The striking simplicity of "I want him," so unlike the complicated and elaborate speech of Eva on other occasions, does not invite gloss, except, what does it mean, and in particular nearness to money? Are we to suppose that out of the mouth of this babe tumble the words that have not only been denied other females in this text, but, even when hinted, very often accomplish very little? Tom and Eliza, for different reasons, are sent away, in spite of what Emily Shelby and Aunt Chloe *want*. Across the writing, black female figures are bereft of their children, regardless of their tearful and profound *wanting* to keep them; Cassy and Emmeline do not *want* the hideously contrived sexual attentions of Simon Legree foisted on them, but none of that matters. Are such words threatening in an adult female's discourse, but palatable in the speech of the prepubescent female child?

It seems to me that Stowe dispatches the child to do a woman's job and that by doing so, she not only spares the female for polite readers, who wanted women but not sex, a "vexing genteel dilemma" in Leslie Fiedler's view.[33] But we also have hold, it seems, of what becomes, in the course of things in the United States, so scandalous an admission for Anglo-American women to make that it describes a site of marginality. "Desire" in *any form* for the female must be silenced, cut out, banished, "killed" off, and in particular reference to African male sexuality, here rendered "harmless" under the auspices of a Christian and "civilizing" "mission." I am not content to believe that we must read this novel *just* "sentimentally," and not try it "analytically," as we infer from, say, Fiedler's earlier reading of *Uncle Tom's Cabin;*[34] I would say that "sentimental fiction," a term like "slavery," represents partial shorthand and mystification so that we have only *commenced* a reading by invoking it, with much work lying ahead.

Given, then, the complicated discursive and descriptive apparatus from which Stowe's *"Little* Eva" arises, soars, disappears, I would not hesitate to propose that the female child figure—in her daring and impermissible *desire*—stands in here for the symptoms of a disturbed female sexuality that American women of Stowe's era could neither articulate nor cancel, only loudly proclaim in the ornamental language, which counterfeits the sacrificial in disguise and substitution. Eva could well embody the "Christ-like," but the "Christ-like" in its overlap with the sacrificial figure that René Girard describes—the *expendable* item of culture whose dying will not release the dynamics of a violent reprisal.[35] That Stowe literally "uses" the female child offers no reason at all for a valorization of the gesture as the leading term of a new and different cultural synthesis. We have seen this before— the *sacrificed* girl-child—and in its wake, all heaven and hell break loose, as well they might, if we learn anything from the mythical figures of Iphigenia and Clytemnestra. But Stowe's culture—its hateful fathers—has dictated an *obedient* maternity, alongside the outraged maternity of Afro-American mothers, which punishes its daughters—as the fathers will do—for the embodiment of its own forbidden desire.

Exactly how "desire"—in whatever way we finally decide to read Little Eva's *wanting*—comes to rest on Tom is not at all clear. Once we can posit a plausibility, which will reside in society's relationships of power, we can determine more precisely what forces have converged in the making of a dyadic taboo—what the shorthand of myth popularly calls, apparently all over "the West" or wherever contact between Africans and their descendants and Europeans and their descendants has been sustained—the "black man" and the "white woman." Because this prohibition was already vividly in place for Stowe's generation of readers, the relationship between the prepubescent white female and the adult black male is shrouded from the start by a past history. In any case, it seems that Little Eva, in her manifest adumbration of female sexuality and its overlap with the realm of "ubertas," matches the "nature" that attached to Tom so precisely that the impuberty implied between the two figures becomes the sole factor in impeding an explosion of culture's "order" and "degree."

To regard Uncle Tom, therefore, with the innocuousness that the avuncular is meant to suggest would again ignore, or slide over, certain signals that are sporadically thrown in Tom's discursive path. He is not only semi-literate, "having learned late in life" (160), and showing symptoms of dyslexia that Reed will advantageously subvert, but he is all the more ripe, consequently, for the signs of a sly watchfulness that would harass any unitary response to this configuration of character. Having been captivated by the stunning "golden head and deep blue eyes [that] peered out upon him from behind some cotton-bale" (162), Tom, in his attraction to Eva, reminds us of the story that is legendarily reported of Pope Gregory's response to the "fair-headed boys" about to be sold into Roman slavery: *non Angli sed Angeli, si forent Christiani.*[36] By virtue of a metathetic error, "Angle" and "Angel" are the same word, as Tom "half believed that he saw one of the angels stepped out of his New Testament" (162). Since Tom cannot quite read or "see" the New, or Old, Testament on his own terms, we know that the tracks through which he is reading the "golden" girl as angelic have been planted in him by other eyes. At any rate, Tom is *not* himself an *angel,* and the reasons for this incapacity do not rely on his "darkness" alone.

Actually too shrewd for "innocence," we are coached into believing, Tom, the artful, like a man bent on courtship, has watched

> the little lady a great deal. He knew an abundance of simple acts to propitiate and invite the approaches of the little people, and he resolved to play his part right skillfully. He could cut cunning little baskets out of cherry-stone, could make grotesque faces on hickory-nuts, or odd-jumping figures out of elder-pith, and he was a very Pan in the manufacture of whistles of all sizes and sorts. His pockets were full of miscellaneous articles of attraction, which he hoarded in days of old for his master's children, and which he now produced, with commendable prudence and economy, one by one, as overtures for acquaintances and friendship. (162–63)

A captive figure with his pockets full of toys strikes a perfectly ludicrous image to my mind, as it constitutes the sort of inadvertence that a satirist like Reed is bound to exploit, but if the seductive resonance of "Pan," "cunning," the "pockets," is allowed to do its work, then we come to regard apects of this persona—"sweet-tempered," Bible-toting, *Uncle* Tom—as a potentially "dirty old man," "under wraps."

In fact, Tom must remain under cover, in the dark. Doing so, he not only satisfies his culture's, this fiction's, need to estrange his sexuality by rendering it "exotic" and unspeakable, but he rewards his observer's fear that he has "one." Negation becomes here an alternative route to confirmation.

Exactly what Stowe had in mind when she canceled the original subtitle of her novel—"the man that was a thing"—is not immediately clear, or, rather, does not offer a clear singularity of impression. Is "thing" in Tom his situation as "an object of desire" for an "essential consciousness"? Is "thinghood" the interpolation of African personality on a horizontal grid that transects a vertical—the "Great Chain of Being"? In other words, is it that juncture at which "mules and men"[37] are situated in a concatenation of differing and contiguous arrangements, as items in Borges's "Chinese Encyclopedia"?[38] At that astonishing juncture of living beings in general, "human" obtains to a status that is both extraordinary, or *more* than human, and under par, *less* than human. But one of the strategies that *Flight to Canada* assumes in the subversion of ontological categories becomes the holding in abeyance of the distance that falls between the writer and his or her "object of desire"—the writing.

The story that is told in Reed's 1976 work is filtered through the fictive consciousness of Reed's poet—Raven Quickskill[39]—who has been commissioned to create the narrative of Uncle Robin. Quickskill's poem, "Flight to Canada," which also provides the novel's epigram, brings celebrity to the poet in a double sense: he is not only a noted author now, anthologized in *The Anthology of Ten Slaves,* but he has been placed on fugitive notice by his master, Arthur Swille III, of the ancestral home at Swine'rd, Virginia, from which place Quickskill has successfully escaped to a Great Lakes neighborhood in the vicinity of Buffalo, New York, and William Wells Brown. Confronted with an "order of repossession" brought to him by the "Nebraska Tracers" (72–73), Quickskill escapes again, together with a former lover, Princess Quaw Quaw Tralaralara, in eventual "flight to Canada." Finding the new place a disappointment to his deepest expectations, Quickskill returns to the Swille Castle after discovering that his former master has been consumed in fire, literally *pushed* into it by the "Etheric Double" of his dead sister Vivian.

But to rehearse the plot of *Flight to Canada* is ultimately dissatisfying it-self because the novel does not actually "concern" the plot very much at all. A clever juxtaposition of prior texts, plots, landscapes, icons, historical and other invented identities, poems, songs, puns, and sight gags, in a dizzying shift of time and textual perspective, Reed's work is closer in spirit and tech-nique to an evening of American television. In actuality, it is a *media* event. As one of Reed's critics, Jerry H. Bryant, observes, Reed's "context is the American pop culture"—the political cartoon, the routine of a stand-up co-median, the high jinks of Mad Comics. "His vocabulary and allusions come from the clichés of t.v., best-selling books, newspaper and magazine com-mercials, and movies."[40] In fact, James R. Lindroth draws a direct connec-tion between *Yellow Back Radio Broke-Down,* one of Reed's first novels, and George Herriman's celebrated cartoon series *Krazy Kat.*[41] Unlike traditional writing, *Flight to Canada* so intrudes on the *linearity* of syntagmatic move-ment that Reed and Stowe cannot be said to share any of the same subject/ aesthetic objects, to say nothing of the same language. It is doubtful, too, that *Flight to Canada* "is about" "discourse," but it most certainly invades the discursive and its properties in order to blast our own habits of language and the configurations of value and belief that arise in them.

The black reader's long-standing quarrel with *Uncle Tom's Cabin* has to do precisely with Stowe's *arrangement* of lexical items. One might use the same "props," or sequence of "props," and derive an altogether different protocol of reading. *Flight to Canada* demonstrates a writing of insurgence as a matter of systematic interest, but no necessary chumminess obtains be-tween Reed and a putative community of Afro-American readers because of it. In fact, I would go so far as to say that *this* interpretive community be-comes one of the *targets* and *topics* of reading, as the overthrow of "slavery" as *the* privileged text of Afro-American historical movement is tried. There are more examples of iconoclastic reinvention in Reed's work than there is space to explore, but one of the most brilliantly concentrated articulations of it occurs when Quickskill, in escape from his button-down pursuers, who are students at a "progressive" school in Nebraska, seeks refuge in the "Slave Hole Café" of "Emancipation City" (77–81). The entire opening paragraph of the passage should be quoted:

> The Slave Hole Café is where the "community" in Emancipation City hangs out. The wallpaper shows a map of the heavens. Prominent is the North Star. A slave with a rucksack is pointing it out to his dog. The Café is furnished with tables, chairs, sofas, from different periods. There are quite a few captain's chairs, deacon's benches. There are posters and paintings and framed programs: *Our American Cousin,* a

play by Tom Tyler; a photo of Lincoln boarding a train on the way back to Washington from a trip to Emancipation. Sawdust on the floor. A barrel of dill pickles. Above the long bar is a sign PABST BLUE RIBBON. Corn-row and nappy-haired field slaves are here as well as a quadroon or two. Carpetbaggers, Abolitionists. Secessionists, or "Seceshes," as they are called, even some copperheads. The secret society known as the "Rattlesnake" order meets here. They advertise their meetings in the Emancipation newspaper: Attention, Rattlesnakes, come out of your holes . . . by order of President Grand Rattle. Poison Fang, Secretary. (77)

The entire passage works as a self-consciously stylistic manipulation of signs that re-encodes particular graphic units to yield a radically different reading from a more conventional one. On the pronunciation of "café," which, in certain speaking communities, is "unFrenchified," partially depends the meaning of the passage. Both "café" and "cáf-e" are simultaneously possible in the hearing since what "happens," graphically, in the passage could occur in both—the "captain's chairs" and the "deacon's benches"—but the narrator does not only mean to signal kinds of period pieces of English and American furniture, but to echo in the repertory of possibilities what a "deacon's bench," or a "captain's chair," might have been in the first place. In black Baptist churches, in parts of the southern United States, at least, there actually is a pew, or set of them, reserved for the clerical functions of "deacons" and "mothers." The referent also sustains this particular resonance. But I am especially interested in the way Reed exploits what seems a lost, or muted, "original" sense that reduces or raises the material object to a commercial status. When I buy, say, a "parson's table," or an art deco replication of the lamps that grace the coaches of the Orient Express, the ritual of exchange so covers these duplicated, mass-produced items that their possible historical context, or ritual/aesthetic function, loses any direct significance for me. They exist as "beautiful" objects that are buyable. In the passage, these items constitute units of information that share the same grid of textures and surfaces with signs as disparately tactile and optical as "sawdust" and theater posters. In fact, this democracy of sign-vehicles is stunning for what adheres and converges—the variety of disjunctive properties "reduced" on a single ground—but also more importantly for their self-referentiality *as* sign.

The "Slave Hole Café" and the figurae of its wallpaper perform a demonstrative reading on "iconism and convention,"[42] as Eco outlines this process of relations in *A Theory of Semiotics*. It seems to me that a great deal of our current anxiety concerning the projection of a "positive black image," for example, stems in part from the knotty problems that converge on the relationship between an actual experience, or sequences of experiential actualities, and perceptual and graphic content that would translate them. Further, it appears that one's "membership" in the "community" and "loyalty" to it become impugnable, certainly questionable, on the basis of some distant, putative radiance that the black person is imagined to revivify.[43] I recognize, too, that much of the internal debate concerning the status of works like *Uncle Tom's Cabin,* for instance, and, closer to mind, Alice Walker's novel-become-film, *The Color Purple,* might be related to this general program of crises. While this is not the occasion to try to unravel the threads of this massive entanglement, I do think that a studied application of semiological strategies would help reveal the "image crisis" as fundamentally fictive. By that I do not mean to suggest that these "fictions" are insignificant; as we know, they are *deadly* and *deadening,* having, quite often, the severest political import. I mean, rather, that the ground upon which we invent and reinvent those yoked repetitions that land on the enterprise of human culture enables the play between "convention" and its possible *translations.*

The "slave hole" was real enough, given everything we already know (or think we do) about the Atlantic slave trade. A male captive with a rucksack on his back, pointing out the North Star to his dog, acquires less certain historical status, although the *conditions* that would constitute such an image are as real as the conditions in which the infamous slave galley appears. We have seen visual representations of both instances, and both tend toward an abstraction of a natural historical/experiential sequence. But there is a difference: whereas "Slave Hole Café" has behind it the numerous descriptions and depictions of "The Brooke Plan," for example, with its representational figurae etched into the drawing, which has behind it, in turn, the plangent "facts of life" that comprise the New World drama of African bodies in passage—their theft and confusion; the actual alteration of human tissue and the blood—the fugitive with a rucksack "imitates" a *possibility,* since no one was there to imagine the runaway gesture, although the icon of the fugitive is a very popular graphic item of the historiographies of the period. But I was led to question my own certainty about the status of the image from quite similar passages in Reed and Stowe. In fact, Reed's translation of the fugitive icon strikes an analogy with a scene from *Uncle Tom's Cabin.* Mary Byrd, in trying to arouse the senator's doubts about his own political position on the Fugitive Slave Law, appears to speak in this passage through the narrative device: "He was as bold as a lion about it, and 'mightily convinced' not only himself, but everybody that heard him;—but then his idea of a fugitive was only an idea of the letters that spell the word,—or, at most, the image of a little newspaper picture of a man with a stick and a bundle, with 'Ran away from the subscriber' under it." The senator has missed "the real presence of distress" (102).

In one instance, it seems that we can track the image back to a *point of density*—the hole of the slave galley—and in the other, a *potentiality* induced from a *dispersion* of gestures; the image in the writing seems to resolve exactly that way—a rucksack, the heavens, the North Star, a dog. "That a certain image," Eco contends, "is similar to something else does not eliminate the fact that similarity is also a matter of cultural convention."[44] The fugitive icon in Reed's work seems adopted to the end of exposing "convention" as it is deployed through various "masks of repetition." This is indeed the subject of the passage. From newsprint to wallpaper shifts the materiality of the scene, thus, its message, or more precisely, the way the receiver feels about the message. An "iconic solution" may not be inaugurated as a convention, "but it becomes so, step by step, the more its addressee becomes acquainted with it."[45] When an "iconic solution" "fixes" on an object, or subject-position, as it were, it engenders what Eco calls a "perceptual cramp," in which case, as Oscar Wilde reminds us in "The Decay of Lying," the representation "comes to be more true than the real experience."[46] A writer's choice of epistemic weapons, of a "poetics," is as dependent on categories of conventional alignment as the graphic artist's. In both cases, and in specific reference to Stowe and Reed, the semantic and iconic folds in which a discourse on "slavery" is embedded situate in "unconventionalized properties," which Eco defines as those that depend "on iconographic [and semantic] convention which has catachresized the previous creative rendering of an actual perceptual experience" (207).

The passage proceeds, then, through a series of "iconic codes" that, according to Eco, "establish either a correlation between a graphic sign-vehicle and already coded perceptual unit [as in the instance of the fugitive icon], or between a pertinent unit of the graphic sign-system and a pertinent unit of a semantic system depending on a previous codification of perceptual experience" (208), as the image of the "hole" in "Slave Hole Café." But in the final instance, the appropriation of semantic and iconic convention, as common and expected a procedure as it is, compels the attention less for itself than for the outcome it might achieve. Unless fiction can generate, analogous to fields of culture theory, new propositions, or *movement* out of the "perceptual cramp," then we would have neither the possibility of convention, nor *arrest* from it. Reed wants to *change the topic* and the strategies that determine it: We can, in fact, construct and reconstruct repertoires of usage out of the most painful human/historical experience. So far as I am concerned, the move is a radical one because it insists that (1) "experience" opens itself to the interpretive and narrative act, and (2), more importantly, the initiative to *enunciate,* to attempt a reconstruction of the politics of enunciation—who may speak, under what conditions, and how such speaking has been enabled—determines the fundamental stakes, sometimes euphemized as "culture." With *Flight to Canada,* a fictionalized "slavery" is conduced to a different *authoring/authority* and a radically determined set of conditions.

Reed's ambitious program might be emblematized in aspects of the name of one of his leading figures—the "Loop Garoo Kid" of *Yellow Back Radio Broke-Down.* Peter Nazareth provides a fascinating gloss on "loop":

> [It] is a sharp bend in a mountain road which almost comes back on itself like a snake. . . . In physics, a loop is an antinode, the node being the point, the line, or surface of a vibrating object free from vibration. To knock for a loop is to throw into confusion. And a loop antenna is used in direction finding equipment and in radio receivers. Once you get to the multiple meanings, you, the reader, begin to "loop."[47]

In all these suggestions, coiling, recoiling, and rotation upon rotation are implied, as even the radio receiver must be open to impressions, all around, in order to do its work. To say that "Reed wants us to short-circuit the whole mess, to break it down,"[48] and I would add, rope it in and tie it up, gives a fairly precise notion of reading Reed as process.

Even though *Flight to Canada feels* like a huge, occasionally striking mural that one might *visit,* compared to Stowe's encyclopedic elaborations that hold us—for days—to the reader's "hot seat," Reed's work actually takes as much "real" reading time as Stowe's precisely because a century and a half have gone by in the American aftermath of *Uncle Tom's Cabin.* The narrative device of *Flight to Canada* traverses a complicated repertoire of textual reference that "loops" in sources as disparate in context as Tennyson's *Idylls of the King,* Poe's *Fall of the House of Usher,* histories of American Reconstruction, and apocrypha and gossip concerning Abraham and Mrs. Lincoln, as well as Jefferson and Mrs. Davis. But Reed also pays a great deal of attention to the "fine print," or the kind of detail that we associate with footnotes and passages in asterisks; for instance, the "copperheads" of the passage I cited denote historical content as well as an associative device. In nearness to the secret society of the "Order of the Rattlesnakes," a "copperhead" is related to the rattlesnake, but does not rattle. The notion of a perniciousness that does not announce itself accords well with the "Copperhead" in culture—the proslavery labor movement, focused in the North, that was enabled, according to DuBois, "to turn the just indignation of the workers against the Negro laborers, rather than against the capitalists."[49] In other words, there are snakes hanging out at the "Slave Hole" in "secret" meeting and "liberal" clothing. The sweep of syncretisms provides here one kind of content; the exploitation of the frozen, reified signification—which we immediately recognize as such—presents another, for example, the "military man," Lincoln's "aide," the "Mammy" of the Swille estate, "Ms. Swille," the "quadroon," and the like. For every single page of the 192 printed pages I am using, there could be as many source pages to read as the novel is long. This multiplying of textual allusiveness and the freedom of movement that is granted the spatiotemporal economies of the work would suggest that "narrative time" for Reed is not imagined as a linear progression alone. It "imitates" the tricks and intricacies of the loop.

Flight to Canada relatedly manipulates narrative time as an "eternal present." In that regard, the past is subject to change,[50] as certain well-known historical episodes are reinvented here from a contemporary angle: The assassination of the novel's "Abe Lincoln" is televised, just as Arthur Swille III is translated into a slaveholding multi-national corporate head, or, in the words of the character of Lincoln, "a swell titanic titan of ten continents" (38). Swille's estate, called "Camelot," is equipped with telephones and sophisticated electronic devices; Stray Leechfield's carriage [features] "factory climate-control air conditioning, vinyl top, AM/FM stereo radio, full leather interior, power lock doors, six-way power seat, power windows, white-wall wheels, door-edge guards, bumper impact strips, rear defroster and soft-ray glass" (46). Reed's stunning anachronisms resituate variously precise portions of cultural content so that we gain a different cartography of historicized fiction. These radical displacements sever *event* from a desiccated spatial focus so that it comes to belong once again to the realm of *possibility*, the possibility of *movement*. The interlardings of reference do not only yield what we currently call a "writerly text," or a *plural* text, but a plurality bent on showing its seams. In other words, artifice, "show," ingenuity, announce themselves as such.

The outcome does not engender a particularly "beautiful" work, nor a work that enamors us to, or engages us with, this writing as process entirely. We are also coerced to change our mind about *who* and *what* "character" is. The discussion that Todorov engages seems to capture *Flight to Canada* as an exemplary case:

The character is the subject of the narrative proposition. As such he is reduced to a pure syntactic function, without any semantic content. The attributes, as well as the actions, play the role of predicate in a proposition and are only provisionally linked to a subject. It will be convenient to identify this subject by a proper name that incarnates him in most cases, insofar as the name identifies a spatio-temporal unity without describing its properties.[51]

Even though we can say, I think, with a great deal of justification that Reed's characters fit, more or less, this discomforting, unromanticized, demystified subject, we must also hold open the possibility that both the reader's and writer's *investment* in these modes of proposition keeps the character alive in the old way.

Because our energies are *always* engaged by the ontological dimension of "character," although we are urged, these days, to "bracket" such concern, or suspend it, or cut it out altogether, we infuse "character" with subjective properties nevertheless. Reed's "Uncle Robin," for example, may be considered a revisionary proposition, since he names a character that appears in the catalog of proslavery fictional responses to *Uncle Tom's Cabin*. According to Richard Yarborough, a novel by John H. Page was published in 1853, the year following *Uncle Tom's Cabin*, in which Page supposedly intended to present the *southern* view of the "peculiar institution." Page entitled his work *Uncle Robin in His Cabin in Virginia and Tom without One in Boston*.[52] A semantic marker called "Uncle Robin" appears in *Flight to Canada*, and "he" lives in the "Frederick Douglass Houses" of Swille's "Virginia." But *this* Uncle Robin proposes so significant a blow to the power relations of dominance and enslavement that we lose entirely any allegiance to a strictly semiologic configuration of "character." In fact, we could say that Uncle Robin, in the manipulation of signs, changes the letter, which insurgency makes a world of difference.

When the relatives and the "property" of Arthur Swille III gather for a reading of his will, following his bizarre death, nothing is revealed by its provisions that we have not expected, given what we know already about "Mammy Barracuda," "Cato, the Graffado," and the rest. But we suspect that a loop in the action—a curve turning back on itself in the road—has been prepared when the officiating magistrate's mouth opens wide and he begins to "stutter and rattle the paper in his trembling hands" as he reads, " 'And to Uncle Robin, I leave this Castle, these hills and everything behind the gates of the Swille Virginia estate.' Much commotion" (180). We miss the isochrony in "gates" and "estate," even though syllabic symmetry elsewhere in the novel has served a parodic function, because the joke is Uncle

Robin's. We concentrate on what becomes as incredible a stroke of the accidental for the reader as it is for the judge. Swille's guilt, however, has not compelled him, we later learn, to an act of unimpeachable magnanimity; rather, Uncle Robin has "dabbled with the will" (183). "I prayed to one of our gods, and he came to me in a dream. He was wearing a top hat, raggedy britches and an old black opera waistcoat. He had on alligator shoes. He was wearing the top hat, too, and was puffing on a cigar. Look like Lincoln's hat. That Stovepipe. He said it was okay to do it. The 'others' had approved" (183). Even if a visual pun on "Lincoln" appears in Uncle Robin's dream, overlapping, unmistakably, with "one of our gods," we recognize the auspiciousness of Uncle Robin's plan. It turns out that "Swille had something called *dyslexia*. Words came to him scrambled and jumbled. I became his reading and writing. Like a computer, only this computer left itself Swille's whole estate. Property joining forces with property. I left me his whole estate. I'm it, too. Me and it got more it" (184; my emphasis).

The reader will recall that Uncle Tom is Stowe's dyslexic man, revealed in young George Shelby's instructing him in the mysteries of "g" and "q," as "Uncle Tom laboriously brought up the tail of his 'g' the wrong side out" (32). Given the propositions that Todorov contends make up "character," *this* "character" capitulates to the closure of mystery. "G" and "q" are easily confused in the abecedarian stages of our apprenticeship in language learning and, beyond that, in the routine play of letters that "confuse" the adult reading, or refuse to stay put, to mean *how* we want. Typewriters and computers have been known to make very similar errors of transposition. But it seems to me that Uncle Robin, in celebrating the sheer malice of an arbitrary materiality, succeeds in cracking the code of meaning, which, for Reed, relies on a riddle: if you change the joke, you slip the yoke.[53]

8

Mama's Baby, Papa's Maybe:
An American Grammar Book

I

Let's face it. I am a marked woman, but not everybody knows my name. "Peaches" and "Brown Sugar," "Sapphire" and "Earth Mother," "Aunty," "Granny," God's "Holy Fool," a "Miss Ebony First," or "Black Woman at the Podium": I describe a locus of confounded identities, a meeting ground of investments and privations in the national treasury of rhetorical wealth. My country needs me, and if I were not here, I would have to be invented.

W. E. B. DuBois predicted earlier than 1903 that the twentieth century would be the century of the "color line." We could add to this spatiotemporal configuration another thematic of analogously terrible weight: if the "black woman" can be seen as a particular figuration of the split subject that psychoanalytic theory posits, then DuBois's century marks the site of "its" profoundest revelation. The problem before us is deceptively simple: the terms enclosed in quotation marks in the preceding paragraph isolate overdetermined nominative properties. Embedded in bizarre axiological ground, they demonstrate a sort of telegraphic coding; they are markers so loaded with mythical prepossession that there is no easy way for the agents buried beneath them to come clean. In that regard, the names by which I am called in the public place render an example of signifying property *plus*. In order for me to speak a truer word concerning myself, I must strip down through layers of attenuated meanings, made an excess in time; over time, assigned by a particular historical order, and there await whatever marvels of my own inventiveness. The personal pronouns are offered in the service of a collective function.

In certain human societies, a child's identity is determined through the line of the Mother, but the United States, from at least one author's point of view, is not one of them: "In essence, the Negro community has been forced into a matriarchal structure which, because it is so far out of line with the *rest of American society,* seriously retards the progress of the group as a whole, and imposes a crushing burden on the Negro male and, in consequence, on a great many Negro women as well."[1]

The notorious bastard, from Vico's dispatched children, to Caliban, to Heathcliff, and Joe Christmas, has no official female equivalent.[2] Because the traditional rites and laws of inheritance rarely pertain to the female child, bastard status signals to those who need to know which son of the Father's is the legitimate heir and which one the impostor. For that reason, property seems wholly the business of the male. A "she" cannot, therefore, qualify for bastard, or "natural son" status, and that she cannot provides further insight into the coils and recoils of patriarchal wealth and fortune. According to Daniel Patrick Moynihan's celebrated "Report" of the late sixties, the "Negro Family" has no father to speak of—his name, his law, his symbolic function mark the impressive missing agencies in the essential life of the black community, the Report maintains, and it is, surprisingly, the fault of the daughter, or the female line. This stunning reversal of the castration thematic, displacing the name and the law of the father to the territory of the mother and daughter, becomes an aspect of the African-American female's misnaming. We attempt to undo this misnaming in order to reclaim the relationship between fathers and daughters within this social matrix for a quite different structure of cultural fictions. For daughters and fathers manifest here the very same *rhetorical* symptoms of absence and denial, to embody the double and contrastive agencies of a *prescribed* internecine degradation. "Sapphire" enacts her "Old Man" in drag, just as her "Old Man" becomes "Sapphire" in outrageous caricature.

In other words, in the historic outline of dominance, the respective subject-positions of "female" and "male" adhere to no symbolic integrity. At a time when current critical discourses appear to compel us more and more decidedly toward gender "undecidability," it would appear reactionary, if not dumb, to insist on the integrity of female/male gender. But undressing these conflations of meaning, as they appear under the rule of dominance, would restore, as figurative possibility, not only power to the female (for maternity), but also power to the male (for paternity). We would gain, in short, the *potential* for gender differentiation as it might express itself along a range of stress points, including human biology in its intersection with the project of culture.

Though among the most readily available "whipping boys" of contemporary public discourse concerning African-Americans and national policy, the Moynihan Report is by no means unprecedented in its conclusions; it belongs, rather, to a class of symbolic paradigms that (1) inscribe "ethnicity" as a scene of negation and (2) confirm the human body as a metonymic figure for an entire repertoire of human and social arrangements. In that regard, the Report pursues a behavioral rule of public documentary. Under the Moynihan rule, "ethnicity" itself identifies a total objectification of human and cultural motives—the "white" family, by implication, and the "Negro Family," by outright assertion, in a constant opposition of binary meanings. Apparently spontaneous, these "actants" are *wholly* generated, with neither past nor future, as tribal currents moving out of time. Moynihan's "families" are pure present and always tense. "Ethnicity" in this case freezes in meaning, takes on constancy, assumes the look and the affects of the eternal. We could say, then, that in its powerful stillness, "ethnicity," from the point of view of the Report, embodies nothing more than a mode of memorial time, as Roland Barthes outlines the dynamics of myth.[3] As a signifier that shows no movement in the field of signification, the use of "ethnicity" for the living becomes purely appreciative, although one would be unwise not to concede its dangerous and fatal effects.

"Ethnicity" perceived as mythical time enables a writer to perform a variety of conceptual moves all at once. Under its hegemony, the human body becomes a defenseless target for rape and veneration, and the body, in its material and abstract phase, a resource for metaphor. For example, Moynihan's "tangle of pathology" provides the descriptive strategy for the work's fourth chapter, which contends that "underachievement" in black males of the lower classes is primarily the fault of black females, who achieve out of all proportion, both to their numbers in the community and to the paradigmatic example before the nation: "Ours is a society which presumes male leadership in private and public affairs. . . . A subculture, such as that of the Negro American, in which this is not the pattern, is placed at a distinct disadvantage" (75). Between charts and diagrams, we are asked to consider the impact of qualitative measure on the black male's performance on standardized examinations and matriculation in schools of higher and professional training, etc. Even though Moynihan sounds a critique on his own argument here, he quickly withdraws from its possibilities, arguing that black males should dominate because that is the way the majority culture carries things out: "it is clearly a disadvantage for a minority group to be operating under one principle, while the great majority of the population . . . is operating on another" (75). Those persons living according to the perceived "matriarchal" pattern are, therefore, caught in a state of social "pathology."

Even though daughters have their own agenda with reference to this order of fathers (imagining for the moment that Moynihan's fiction—and others like it—does not represent an adequate one and that there *is*, once we dis-cover him, a father here), my contention that these social and cultural subjects make doubles, unstable in their respective identities, in effect transports us to a common historical ground, the sociopolitical order of the New World. That order, with its human sequence written in blood, *represents* for its African and indigenous peoples a scene of *actual* mutilation, dismemberment, and exile. First of all, their New World, diasporic plight marked a *theft* of the *body*—a *willful* and violent (and unimaginable from this distance) severing of the captive body from its motive will, its active desire. Under these conditions, we lose at least *gender* difference *in the outcome*, and the female body and the male body become a territory of cultural and political maneuver, not at all gender-related, gender-specific. But this body, at least from the point of view of the captive community, focuses a private and particular space, at which point biological, sexual, social, cultural, linguistic, ritualistic, and psychological fortunes converge. This profound intimacy of interlocking detail is disrupted, however, by externally imposed meanings and uses: (1) the captive body as the source of an irresistible, destructive sensuality; (2) at the same time—in stunning contradiction—it is reduced to a thing, to *being* for the captor; (3) in this distance *from* a subject position, the captured sexualities provide a physical and biological expression of "otherness"; (4) as a category of "otherness," the captive body translates into a potential for pornotroping and embodies sheer physical powerlessness that slides into a more general "powerlessness," resonating through various centers of human and social meaning.

But I would make a distinction in this case between "body" and "flesh" and impose that distinction as the central one between captive and liberated subject-positions. In that sense, before the "body" there is the "flesh," that zero degree of social conceptualization that does not escape concealment under the brush of discourse or the reflexes of iconography. Even though the European hegemonies stole bodies—some of them female—out of West African communities in concert with the African "middleman," we regard this human and social irreparability as high crimes against the *flesh*, as the person of African females and males registered the wounding. If we think of the "flesh" as a primary narrative, then we mean its seared, divided, ripped-apartness, riveted to the ship's hole, fallen, or "escaped" overboard.

One of the most poignant aspects of William Goodell's contemporaneous study of the North American slave codes gives definitive expression to the tortures and instruments of captivity. Reporting an instance of

Jonathan Edwards's observations on the tortures of enslavement, Goodell narrates: "The smack of the whip is all day long in the ears of those who are on the plantation, or in the vicinity; and it is used with such dexterity and severity as not only to lacerate the skin, but to tear out small portions of the flesh at almost every stake."[4] The anatomical specifications of rupture, of altered human tissue, take on the objective description of laboratory prose—eyes beaten out, arms, backs, skulls branded, a left jaw, a right ankle, punctured; teeth missing, as the calculated work of iron, whips, chains, knives, the canine patrol, the bullet.

These undecipherable markings on the captive body render a kind of hieroglyphics of the flesh whose severe disjunctures come to be hidden to the cultural seeing by skin color. We might well ask if this phenomenon of marking and branding actually "transfers" from one generation to another, finding its various *symbolic substitutions* in an efficacy of meanings that repeat the initiating moments? As Elaine Scarry describes the mechanisms of torture,[5] these lacerations, woundings, fissures, tears, scars, openings, ruptures, lesions, rendings, and punctures of the flesh create the distance between what I would designate a cultural *vestibularity* and *culture,* whose state apparatus, including judges, attorneys, "owners," "souldrivers," "overseers," and "men of God," apparently colludes with a protocol of "search and destroy." This body whose flesh carries the female and the male to the frontiers of survival bears in person the marks of a cultural text whose inside has been turned outside.

The flesh is the concentration of "ethnicity" that contemporary critical discourses neither acknowledge nor discourse away. It is this "flesh and blood" entity, in the vestibule (or "pre-view") of a colonized North America, that is essentially ejected from "The Female Body in Western Culture,"[6] but it makes good theory, or commemorative "herstory" to want to "forget," or to have failed to realize, that the African female subject, under these historic conditions, is not only the target of rape—in one sense, an interiorized violation of body and mind—but also the topic of specifically *externalized* acts of torture and prostration that we imagine as the peculiar province of *male* brutality and torture inflicted by other males. A female body strung from a tree limb, or bleeding from the breast on any given day of field work because the "overseer," standing the length of a whip, has popped her flesh open, adds a lexical and living dimension to the narratives of women in culture and society.[7] This materialized scene of unprotected female flesh—of female flesh "ungendered"—offers a praxis and a theory, a text for living and for dying, and a method for reading both through their diverse mediations.

Among the myriad uses to which the enslaved community was put, Goodell identifies its value for medical research: "Assortments of diseased, *damaged*, and disabled Negroes, deemed incurable and otherwise worthless are *bought up*, it seems . . . by medical institutions, to be experimented and operated upon, for purposes of 'medical education' and the interest of medical science" (86–87). From the *Charleston Mercury* for October 12, 1838, Goodell notes this advertisement:

> To planters and others.—Wanted, fifty Negroes, any person, having sick Negroes, considered incurable by their respective physicians, and wishing to dispose of them, Dr. S. will pay cash for Negroes affected with scrofula, or king's evil, confirmed hypochondriasm, apoplexy, diseases of the liver, kidneys, spleen, stomach and intestines, bladder and its appendages, diarrhea, dysentery, etc. The highest cash price will be paid, on application as above, at No. 110 Church Street, Charleston. (87)

This profitable "atomizing" of the captive body provides another angle on the divided flesh: we lose any hint or suggestion of a dimension of ethics, of relatedness between human personality and its anatomical features, between one human personality and another, between human personality and cultural institutions. To that extent, the procedures adopted for the captive flesh demarcate a total objectification, as the entire captive community becomes a living laboratory.

The captive body, then, brings into focus a gathering of social realities as well as a metaphor for *value* so thoroughly interwoven in their literal and figurative emphases that distinctions between them are virtually useless. Even though the captive flesh/body has been "liberated," and no one need pretend that even the quotation marks do not *matter*, dominant symbolic activity, the ruling episteme that releases the dynamics of naming and valuation, remains grounded in the originating metaphors of captivity and mutilation so that it is as if neither time nor history, nor historiography and its topics, show movement, as the human subject is "murdered" over and over again by the passions of a bloodless and anonymous archaism, showing itself in endless disguise. Faulkner's young Chick Mallison in *The Mansion* calls "it" by other names—"the ancient subterrene atavistic fear."[8] And I would call it the Great Long National Shame. But people do not talk like that anymore—it is "embarrassing," just as the retrieval of mutilated female bodies will likely be "backward" for some people. Neither the shameface of the embarrassed, nor the not-looking-back of the self-assured is of much interest to us, and will not help at all if rigor is our dream. We might concede, at the very least, that sticks and bricks *might* break our bones, but words will most certainly *kill* us.

The symbolic order that I wish to trace in this writing, calling it an "American grammar," begins at the "beginning," which is really a rupture and a radically different kind of cultural continuation. The massive demographic shifts, the violent formation of a modern African consciousness, that take place on the sub-Saharan Continent during the initiative strikes which open the Atlantic slave trade in the fifteenth century of our Christ, interrupted hundreds of years of black African culture. We write and think, then, about an outcome of aspects of African-American life in the United States under the pressure of those events. I might as well add that the familiarity of this narrative does nothing to appease the hunger of recorded memory, nor does the persistence of the repeated rob these well-known, oft-told events of their power, even now, to startle. In a very real sense, every writing as revision makes the discovery all over again.

II

The narratives by African peoples and their descendants, though not as numerous from those early centuries of the "execrable trade" as the researcher would wish, indicate, in their rare occurrence, that the visual shock waves touched off when African and European met reverberated on both sides of the encounter. The narrative of the *Life of Olaudah Equiano, or Gustavus Vassa, the African. Written by Himself,*[9] first published in London in 1789, makes it quite clear that the first Europeans Equiano observed on what is now Nigerian soil were as unreal for him as he and others must have been for the European captors. The cruelty of "these white men with horrible looks, red faces, and long hair," of these "spirits," as the narrator would have it, occupies several pages of Equiano's attention, alongside a firsthand account of Nigerian interior life (27ff.). We are justified in regarding the outcome of Equiano's experience in the same light as he himself might have—as a "fall," as a veritable descent into the loss of communicative force.

If, as Todorov points out, the Mayan and Aztec peoples "lost control of communication"[10] in light of Spanish intervention, we could observe, similarly, that Vassa falls among men whose language is not only strange to him, but whose habits and practices strike him as "astonishing":

> [The sea, the slave ship] filled me with astonishment, which was soon converted into terror, when I was carried on board. I was immediately handled, and tossed up to see if I were sound, by some of the crew; and I was now persuaded that I had gotten into a world of bad spirits, and

that they were going to kill me. Their complexions, too, differing so much from ours, their long hair, and the language they spoke (which was different from any I had ever heard), united to confirm me in this belief. (27)

The captivating party does not only earn the right to dispose of the captive body as it sees fit, but gains, consequently, the right to name and "name" it: Equiano, for instance, identifies at least three different names that he is given in numerous passages between his Benin homeland and the Virginia colony, the latter and England—"Michael," "Jacob," "Gustavus Vassa" (35, 36).

The nicknames by which African-American women have been called, or regarded, or imagined on the New World scene—the opening lines of this essay provide examples—demonstrate the powers of distortion that the dominant community seizes as its unlawful prerogative. Moynihan's *Negro Family,* then, borrows its narrative energies from the grid of associations, from the semantic and iconic folds buried deep in the collective past, that come to surround and signify the captive. Though there is no absolute point of chronological initiation, we might repeat certain familiar impression points that lend shape to the business of dehumanized naming. Expecting to find direct and amplified reference to African women during the opening years of the Trade, the observer is disappointed time and again that this cultural subject is concealed beneath the overwhelming debris of the itemized account, between the lines of the massive logs of commercial enterprise that overrun the sense of clarity we believed we had gained concerning this collective humiliation. Elizabeth Donnan's enormous, four-volume documentation becomes a case in point.[11]

Turning directly to this source, we discover what we had not expected to find—that this aspect of the search is rendered problematic and that observations of a field of manners and its related sociometries are an outgrowth of the industry of the "exterior other,"[12] called "anthropology" later on. The European males who laded and captained these galleys and who policed and corralled these human beings, in hundreds of vessels from Liverpool to Elmina, to Jamaica; from the Cayenne Islands, to the ports at Charleston and Salem, and for three centuries of human life, were not curious about this "cargo" that bled, packed like so many live sardines among the immovable objects. Such inveterate obscene blindness might be denied, point blank, as a possibility for *anyone,* except that we know it happened.

Donnan's first volume covers three centuries of European "discovery" and "conquest," beginning fifty years before pious Cristobal, Christum Ferens, the bearer of Christ, laid claim to what he thought was the "Indies."

From Gomes Eannes de Azurara's *Chronicle of the Discovery and Conquest of Guinea, 1441–1448,*[13] we learn that the Portuguese probably gain the dubious distinction of having introduced black Africans to the European market of servitude. We are also reminded that "Geography" is not a divine gift. Quite to the contrary, its boundaries were shifted during the European "Age of Conquest" in giddy desperation, according to the dictates of conquering armies, the edicts of prelates, the peculiar myopia of the medieval Christian mind. Looking for the Nile River, for example, according to the fifteenth-century Portuguese notion, is someone's joke. For all that the pre-Columbian explorers knew about the sciences of navigation and geography, we are surprised that more parties of them did not end up "discovering" Europe. Perhaps, from a certain angle, that is precisely all that they found—an alternative reading of ego. The Portuguese, having little idea where the Nile ran, at least understood right away that there were men and women darker-skinned than themselves, but they were not specifically knowledgeable, or ingenious, about the various families and groupings represented by them. Azurara records encounters with "Moors," "Mooresses," "Mulattoes," and people "black as Ethiops" (1:28), but it seems that the "Land of Guinea," or of "Black Men," or of "The Negroes" (1:35) was located anywhere southeast of Cape Verde, the Canaries, and the River Senegal, looking at an eighteenth-century European version of the sub-Saharan Continent along the West African coast (1: frontispiece).

Three genetic distinctions are available to the Portuguese eye, all along the riffs of melanin in the skin: in a field of captives, some of the observed are "white enough, fair to look upon, and well-proportioned." Others are less "white like mulattoes," and still others "black as Ethiops, and so ugly, both in features and in body, as almost to appear (to those who saw them) the images of a lower hemisphere" (1:28). By implication, this "third man," standing for the most aberrant phenotype to the observing eye, embodies the linguistic community most unknown to the European. Arabic translators among the Europeans could at least "talk" to the "Moors" and instruct them to ransom themselves, or else . . .

Typically, there is in this grammar of description the perspective of declension, not of simultaneity, and its point of initiation is solipsistic—it begins with a narrative self, in an apparent unity of feeling, and unlike Equiano, who also saw "ugly" when he looked out, this collective self uncovers the means by which to subjugate the "foreign code of conscience," whose most easily remarkable and irremediable difference is perceived in skin color. By the time of Azurara's mid-fifteenth-century narrative and a century and a half before Shakespeare's "old black ram" of an Othello "tups" that "white ewe" of a Desdemona, the magic of skin color is already installed as a decisive factor in human dealings.

In Azurara's narrative, we observe males looking at other males, as "female" is subsumed here under the general category of estrangement. Few places in these excerpts carve out a distinctive female space, though there are moments of portrayal that perceive female captives in the implications of sociocultural function. When the field of captives (referred to above) is divided among the spoilers, no heed is paid to relations, as fathers are separated from sons, husbands from wives, brothers from sisters and brothers, mothers from children—male and female. It seems clear that the political program of European Christianity promotes this hierarchical view among *males*, although it remains puzzling to us exactly how this version of Christianity transforms the "pagan" also into the "ugly." It appears that human beings came up with degrees of "fair" and then the "hideous," in its overtones of bestiality, as the opposite of "fair," all by themselves, without stage direction, even though there is the curious and blazing exception of Nietzsche's Socrates, who was Athens' ugliest and wisest and best citizen. The intimate choreography that the Portuguese narrator sets going between the "faithless" and the "ugly" transforms a partnership of dancers into a single figure. Once the "faithless," indiscriminate of the three stops of Portuguese skin color, are transported to Europe, they become an altered human factor:

> And so their lot was now quite contrary to what it had been, since before they had lived in perdition of soul and body; of their souls, in that they were yet pagans, without the clearness and the light of the Holy Faith; and of their bodies, in that they lived like beasts, without any custom of reasonable beings—for they had no knowledge of bread and wine, and they were without covering of clothes, or the lodgment of houses; and worse than all, through the great ignorance that was in them, in that they had no understanding of good, but only knew how to live in bestial sloth. (1:30)

The altered human factor renders an alterity to European ego, an invention, or "discovery" as decisive in the full range of its social implications as the birth of a newborn. According to the semantic alignments of the excerpted passage, personhood, for this European observer, locates an immediately outward and superficial determination, gauged by quite arbitrarily opposed and *specular* categories: that these "pagans" did not have "bread" and "wine" did not mean that they were feastless, as Equiano observes about the Benin diet, c. 1745, in the province of Essaka:

Our manner of living is entirely plain; for as yet the natives are unac-
quainted with those refinements in cookery which debauch the taste;
bullocks, goats, and poultry supply the greatest part of their food.
(These constitute likewise the principal wealth of the country, and the
chief articles of its commerce.) The flesh is usually stewed in a pan; to
make it savory we sometimes use pepper, and other spices, and we
have salt made of wood ashes. Our vegetables are mostly plaintains,
eadas, yams, beans and Indian corn. The head of the family usually
eats alone, his wives and slaves have also their separate tables. (8)

Just as fufu serves the Ghanaian diet today as a starch-and-bread substitute,
palm wine (an item by the same name in the eighteenth-century palate of
the Benin community) need not be Heitz Cellars Martha's Vineyard and
vice-versa in order for a guest, say, to imagine that she has enjoyed. That
African housing arrangements of the fifteenth century did not resemble
those familiar to Azurara need not have meant that the African communities he encountered were without dwellings. Again, Equiano's narrative suggests that by the middle of the eighteenth century, at least, African living
patterns were not only quite distinct in their sociometrical arrangements,
but that their design accurately reflected the climate and availability of resources in the locale: "These houses never exceed one story in height; they
are always built of wood, or stakes driven into the ground, crossed with wat-
tles, and neatly plastered within and without" (9). Hierarchical impulses in
both Azurara's and Equiano's narratives translate all *perceived* difference as a
fundamental degradation or transcendence, but at least in Equiano's case,
cultural practices are not observed in any intimate connection with skin
color. For all intents and purposes, the politics of melanin, not isolated in its
strange powers from the imperatives of a mercantile economy and competitive European nation-states, will make of "transcendence" and "degradation" the basis of a historic violence that will rewrite the histories of modern
Europe and black Africa. These mutually exclusive nominative elements
come to rest on the same governing semantics—the ahistorical, or symptoms of the sacred.

By August 1518, the Spanish king, Francisco de Los Covos, under the
aegis of a powerful negation, could order "4,000 negro slaves both male and
female, provided they be Christians" to be taken to the Caribbean, "the islands and the mainland of the ocean sea already discovered or to be discovered."[14] Though the notorious "Middle Passage" appears to the investigator
as a vast background without boundaries in time and space, we see it related
in Donnan's accounts to the opening up of the entire Western hemisphere

for the specific purposes of enslavement and colonization. Azurara's narrative belongs, then, to a discourse of appropriation whose strategies will prove fatal to communities along the coastline of West Africa, stretching, according to Olaudah Equiano, "3,400 miles, from Senegal to Angola, and [will include] a variety of kingdoms" (5).

The conditions of "Middle Passage" are among the most incredible narratives available to the investigator, as it remains not easily imaginable. Late in the chronicles of the Atlantic slave trade, Britain's Parliament entertained discussions concerning possible regulations for slave vessels. A Captain Perry visited the Liverpool port, and among the ships that he inspected was the *Brookes,* probably the most well-known image of the slave galley with its representative *personae* etched into the drawing like so many cartoon figures. Elizabeth Donnan's second volume carries a drawing of the "Brookes Plan," along with an elaborate delineation of its dimensions from the investigative reporting of Perry himself: "Let it now be supposed . . . further, that every man slave is to be allowed six feet by one foot four inches for room, every woman five feet ten by one foot four, every boy five feet by one foot two, and every girl four feet six by one foot."[15] The owner of the *Brookes,* James Jones, had recommended that "five females be reckoned as four males, and three boys or girls as equal to two grown persons" (2:592).

These scaled inequalities complement the commanding terms of the dehumanizing, ungendering, and defacing project of Africans that Azurara might have recognized. It has been pointed out to me that these measurements do reveal the application of the gender rule to the material conditions of passage, but I would suggest that "gendering" takes place within the confines of the domestic, an essential metaphor that then spreads its tentacles for male and female subjects over a wider ground of human and social purposes. Domesticity appears to gain its power by way of a common origin of cultural fictions that are grounded in the specificity of proper names, more exactly, a patronymic, which, in turn, situates those subjects that it covers in a particular place. Contrarily, the cargo of a ship might not be regarded as elements of the domestic, even though the vessel that carries the cargo is sometimes romantically personified as "she." The human cargo of a slave vessel—in the effacement and remission of African family and proper names—contravenes notions of the domestic.

Those African persons in "Middle Passage" were literally suspended in the oceanic, if we think of the latter in its Freudian orientation as an analogy on undifferentiated identity: removed from the indigenous land and culture, and not-yet "American" either, these captives, without names that their captors would recognize, were in movement across the Atlantic, but they were also *nowhere* at all. Because, on any given day, we might imagine, the captive personality did not know where s/he was, we could say that they were the culturally "unmade," thrown in the midst of a figurative darkness that exposed their destinies to an unknown course. Often enough for the captains of these galleys, navigational science of the day was not sufficient to guarantee the intended destination. We might say that the slave ship, its crew, and its human-as-cargo stand for a wild and unclaimed richness of *possibility* that is not interrupted, not counted/accounted, or differentiated, until its movement gains the land thousands of miles away from the point of departure. Under these conditions, one is neither female, nor male, as both subjects are taken into account as *quantities*. The female in "Middle Passage," as the apparently smaller physical mass, occupies "less room" in a directly translatable money economy. But she is, nevertheless, quantifiable by the same rules of accounting as her male counterpart.

It is not only difficult for the investigator to find females in "Middle Passage," but also, as Herbert S. Klein observes, "African women did not enter the Atlantic slave trade in anything like the numbers of African men. At all ages, men outnumbered women on the slave ships bound for America from Africa."[16] Though this observation does not change the reality of African women's captivity and servitude in New World communities, it does provide a perspective from which to contemplate the *internal* African slave trade, which, according to Africanists, remained a predominantly *female* market. Klein nevertheless affirms that those females forced into the trade were segregated "from men for policing purposes" (35). He claims that both "were allotted the same space between decks . . . and both were fed the same food" (35). It is not altogether clear from Klein's observations *for whom* the "police" kept vigil. It is certainly known from evidence presented in Donnan's third volume *(New England and the Middle Colonies)* that insurrection was both frequent and feared in passage, and we have not yet found a great deal of evidence to support a thesis that female captives participated in insurrectionary activity.[17] Because it was the rule, however—not the exception—that the African female, in both indigenous African cultures and in what becomes her "home," performed tasks of hard physical labor—so much so that the quintessential "slave" is *not* a male, but a female—we wonder at the seeming docility of the subject, granting her a "feminization" that enslavement kept at bay. Indeed, across the spate of discourse examined in this writing, I found that the acts of enslavement and responses to it comprise a more or less agonistic engagement of confrontational hostilities among males. The visual and historical evidence betrays the dominant discourse on the matter as incomplete, but *counter*-evidence is inadequate as well: the sexual violation of captive females and their own express rage against their oppressors did not constitute events that captains and their crews rushed to record in letters to their sponsoring companies, or sons on board in letters home to their New England mamas.

I suspect that there are several ways to snare a mockingbird, so that insurrection might have involved, from time to time, rather more subtle means than mutiny on the *Felicity*, for instance. At any rate, we get very little notion in the written record of the life of women, children, and infants in "Middle Passage," and no idea of the fate of the pregnant female captive and the unborn, which startling thematic bell hooks addresses in the opening chapter of her pathfinding work.[18] From hooks's lead, however, we might guess that the "reproduction of mothering" in this historic instance carries few of the benefits of a *patriarchilized* female gender, which, from one point of view, is the only female gender there is.

The relative silence of the record on this point makes up some of the disquieting lacunae that feminist investigation seeks to fill. Such silence is the nickname of distortion, of the unknown human factor that a revised public discourse would both undo *and* reveal. This cultural subject is inscribed historically as anonymity/anomie in various public documents of European-American mal(e)venture, from Portuguese Azurara in the middle of the fifteenth century, to South Carolina's Henry Laurens in the eighteenth.

What confuses and enriches the picture is precisely the sameness of anonymous portrayal that adheres tenaciously across the division of gender. In the vertical columns of accounts and ledgers that comprise Donnan's work, the terms "Negroes" and "Slaves" denote a common status. For instance, entries in one account, from September 1700 through September 1702, specifically list the names of ships and the private traders in Barbados who will receive the stipulated goods, but "No. Negroes" and "Sum sold for per head" are so arithmetical that it is as if these additions and multiplications belong to the other side of an equation (2:25). One is struck by the detail and precision that characterize these accounts, as a narrative, or story, is always implied by a man or woman's name: "Wm. Webster," "John Dunn," "Thos. Brownbill," "Robt. Knowles." But the other side of the page, as it were, equally precise, throws no face in view. It seems that nothing breaks the uniformity in this guise. If in no other way, the destruction of the African name, of kin, of linguistic, and ritual connections is so obvious in the vital stats sheet that we tend to overlook it. Quite naturally, the trader is not interested, in any *semantic* sense, in this "baggage" that he must deliver, but that he is not is all the more reason to search out the metaphorical implications of *naming* as one of the key sources of a bitter Americanizing for Africans.

The loss of the indigenous name/land marks a metaphor of displacement for other human and cultural features and relations, including the displacement of the genitalia, the female's and the male's desire that engenders future. The fact that the enslaved person's access to the issue of his/her own body is not entirely clear in this historic period throws in crisis all aspects of the blood relations, as captors apparently felt no obligation to acknowledge them. Actually trying to understand how the confusions of consanguinity worked is part of the project, because the outcome goes far to explain the rule of gender and its application to African females in captivity.

III

Even though the essays in Claire C. Robertson and Martin A. Klein's *Women and Slavery in Africa* have specifically to do with aspects of the internal African slave trade, some of their observations shed light on the captivities of the Diaspora. At least these observations have the benefit of altering the kind of questions we might ask of these incomplete chapters. For example, Claire Robertson and Martin Klein's essay,[19] which opens the volume, discusses the term "slavery" in a wide variety of relationships. The enslaved as *property* identifies the most familiar element of a startling proposition. But to overlap *kinlessness* on the requirements of property might enlarge our view of the conditions of enslavement. Looking specifically at documents from the West African societies of Songhay and Dahomey, Claude Meillassoux elaborates several features of the property/ kinless constellation that are highly suggestive for our own quite different purposes.[20]

Meillassoux argues that "slavery creates an economic and social agent whose virtue lies in being outside the kinship system" (50). Because the Atlantic trade involved heterogeneous social and ethnic formations in an explicit power relationship, we certainly cannot mean "kinship system" in precisely the same way that Meillassoux observes at work within the intricate calculus of descent among West African societies. However, the idea becomes useful as a point of contemplation when we try to sharpen our own sense of the African female's reproductive uses within the diasporic enterprise of enslavement and the genetic reproduction of the enslaved. In effect, under conditions of captivity, the offspring of the female does not "belong" to the mother, nor is s/he "related" to the "owner," though the owner "possesses" it, and in the African-American instance, often fathered it, *and, as often,* without whatever benefit of patrimony. In the social outline that Meillassoux is pursuing, the offspring of the enslaved, "being unrelated both to their begetters and to their owners find themselves in the situation of being orphans" (50).

In the context of the United States, we could not say that the enslaved offspring was "orphaned," but the child does become, under the press of a patronymic, patrifocal, patrilineal, and patriarchal order, the man/woman on the boundary, whose human and familial status, by the very nature of the case, had yet to be defined. I would call this enforced state of breach another instance of vestibular cultural formation where "kinship" loses meaning, *since it can be invaded at any given and arbitrary moment by the property relations.* I certainly do not mean to say that African peoples in the New World did not maintain powerful ties of sympathy that bind blood-relations in a network of feeling, of continuity. It is precisely that relationship—not customarily recognized by the codes of slavery—that historians have long identified as the inviolable "Black Family" and further suggest that this structure remains one of the supreme social achievements of African-Americans under conditions of enslavement.[21]

Indeed, *the revised* "Black Family" of enslavement has engendered an older tradition of historiographical and sociological writings than we usually think. Ironically enough, E. Franklin Frazier's *Negro Family in the United States* likely provides the closest contemporary narrative of conceptualization that precedes the Moynihan Report.[22] Originally published in 1939, Frazier's work underwent two redactions in 1948 and 1966. Even though Frazier's outlook on this familial configuration remains basically sanguine, I would support Angela Davis's skeptical reading of Frazier's "Black Matriarchate."[23] *"Except where the master's will* was concerned," Frazier contends, this matriarchal figure "developed a spirit of independence and a keen sense of her personal rights" (47, my emphasis). The "exception" in this instance tends to be overwhelming, as the African-American female's "dominance" and "strength" come to be interpreted by later generations—both white and black, oddly enough—as a pathology, as an instrument of castration. Frazier's larger point, we might suppose, is that African-Americans developed such resourcefulness under conditions of captivity that "family" must be conceded as one of their redoubtable social attainments. This line of interpretation is pursued by Blassingame and Eugene Genovese,[24] among other U.S. historians, and indeed assumes a centrality of focus in our own thinking about the impact and outcome of captivity.

It seems clear, however, that "family," as we practice and understand it "in the West"—the vertical transfer of a bloodline, of a patronymic, of titles and entitlements, of real estate and the prerogatives of "cold cash," from fathers to sons and in the supposedly free exchange of affectional ties between a male and a female of his choice—becomes the mythically revered privilege of a free and freed community. In that sense, African peoples in the historic Diaspora had nothing to prove, if the point had been that they were not capable of "family" (read "civilization"), since it is evident, in Equiano's narrative, for instance, that Africans were not only capable of the concept and the practice of "family," including "slaves," but in modes of elaboration and naming that were at least as complex as those of the "nuclear family" "in the West."

Whether or not we decide that the support systems that African-Americans derived under conditions of captivity *should be* called "family," or something else, strikes me as supremely impertinent. The point remains that captives were forced into patterns of dispersal, beginning with the Trade itself, into *the horizontal* relatedness of language groups, discourse formations, bloodlines, names, *and* properties by the legal arrangements of enslavement. It is true that the most *"well-meaning"* of "masters" (and there must have been *some) could not, did* not alter the *ideological* and hegemonic cadences of dominance. It must be conceded that African-Americans, under the press of a hostile and compulsory patriarchal order, bound and determined to destroy them, or to preserve them only in the service and at the behest of the master class, exercised a degree of courage and will to survive that startles the imagination even now. Although it makes good revisionist history to read this tale *liberally,* it is probably truer than we know at this distance (and truer than contemporary social practice in the community would suggest on occasion) that the captive developed, time and again, certain ethical and sentimental features that tied her and him across the landscape to others, often sold from hand to hand, of the same and different blood in a common fabric of memory and inspiration.

We might choose to call this connectedness "family," or "support structure," but that is a rather different case from the moves of a dominant symbolic order, pledged to maintain the supremacy of race. It is that order that forces "family" to modify itself when it does not mean family of the master, or dominant enclave. It is this rhetorical and symbolic move that declares primacy over any other *human and social claim,* and in that political order of things, kin, just as gender formation, has no decisive legal or social efficacy.

We return frequently to Frederick Douglass's careful elaborations of the arrangements of captivity, and we are struck each reading by two dispersed, yet poignantly related, familial enactments that indicate a connection between kinship and property. Douglass tells us early in the opening chapter of the 1845 *Narrative* that he was separated in infancy from his mother: "For what this separation is done, I do not know, unless it be to hinder the development of the child's affection toward its mother, and to blunt and destroy the natural affection of the mother for the child. This is the inevitable result."[25]

Perhaps one of the assertions that Meillassoux advances concerning indigenous African formations of enslavement might be turned as a question, against the perspective of Douglass's witness: is the genetic reproduction of the slave and the recognition of the rights of the slave to his or her offspring a check on the *profitability* of slavery? And how so, if so? We see vaguely the route to framing a response, especially to the question's second half and perhaps to the first: the enslaved must not be permitted to perceive that he or she has any human rights that matter. Certainly if kinship were possible, the property relations would be undermined, since the offspring would then "belong" *to* a mother and a father. In the system that Douglass is explaining, genetic reproduction is not the elaboration of the life-principle in its cultural overlap, but an extension of the boundaries of proliferating properties. Meillassoux goes so far as to argue that "slavery exists where the slave class is reproduced through *institutional* apparatus: war and market" (50). Since, in the United States, the *market* of slavery identified the chief institutional means for maintaining a class of enforced servile labor, it seems that the biological reproduction of the enslaved was not alone sufficient to reenforce the estate of slavery. If, as Meillassoux contends, "femininity loses its sacredness in slavery" (64), then so does "motherhood" as female blood-rite/right. To that extent, the captive female body locates precisely a moment of converging political and social vectors that mark the flesh as a prime commodity of exchange. While this proposition is open to further exploration, suffice it to say now that this open exchange *of female* bodies in the raw offers a kind of Ur-text to the dynamics of signification and representation that the gendered female would unravel.

For Douglass, the loss of his mother eventuates in alienation from his brother and sisters, who live in the same house with him: "The early separation of us from our mother had well nigh blotted the fact of our relationship from our memories" (45). What could this mean? The *physical* proximity of the siblings survives the mother's death. They grasp their connection in the physical sense, but Douglass appears to mean a *psychological* bonding whose successful execution mandates the *mother's presence*. Could we say, then, that the *feeling of* kinship is *not* inevitable? That it describes a relationship that appears natural, but that must be cultivated under actual material conditions? If the child's humanity is mirrored initially in the eyes of its mother, or the maternal function, then we might be able to guess that the social subject grasps the whole dynamic of resemblance and kinship by way of the same source.

There is an amazing thematic synonymity on this point between aspects of Douglass's *Narrative* and Malcolm El-Hajj Malik El-Shabazz's *Autobiography of Malcolm X*.[26] Through the loss of the mother, in the latter instance, to the institution of insanity and the state—a full century after Douglass's writing and under social conditions that might be designated a post-emancipation neo-enslavement—Malcolm and his siblings, robbed of their activist father in a KKK-like ambush, are not only widely dispersed across a makeshift social terrain, but also show symptoms of estrangement and disremembering that require many years to heal, and even then, only by way of Malcolm's prison ordeal turned, eventually, into a redemptive occurrence.

The destructive loss of the natural mother, whose biological/genetic relationship to the child remains unique and unambiguous, opens the enslaved young to social ambiguity and chaos: the ambiguity of his/her fatherhood and to a structure of other relational elements, now threatened, that would declare the young's connection to a genetic and historic future by way of their own siblings. That the father in Douglass's case was most likely the "master," not by any means unique to Douglass, involves a hideous paradox. Fatherhood, at best a supreme cultural courtesy, attenuates here on the one hand into a monstrous accumulation of power on the other. One has been "made" and "bought" by disparate currencies, linking back to a common origin of exchange and domination. The denied genetic link becomes the chief strategy of an undenied ownership, as if the interrogation into the father's identity—the blank space where his proper name would fit—were answered by the fact, de jure, of a material possession. "And this is done," Douglass asserts, "too obviously to administer to the [masters'] own lusts, and make a gratification of their wicked desires profitable as well as pleasurable" (23).

Whether or not the captive female and/or her sexual oppressor derived "pleasure" from their seductions and couplings is not a question we can politely ask. Whether or not "pleasure" is possible at all under conditions that I would aver as non-freedom for both or either of the parties has not been settled. Indeed, we could go so far as to entertain the very real possibility that sexuality, as a term of implied relatedness, is dubiously appropriate, manageable, or accurate to *any* of the familial arrangements under a system of enslavement, from the master's family to the captive enclave. Under these circumstances, the customary aspects of sexuality, including "reproduction," "motherhood," "pleasure," and "desire," are all thrown in crisis.

If the testimony of Linda Brent/Harriet Jacobs is to be believed, the official mistresses of slavery's masters make up a privileged class of the tormented, if such a contradiction can be entertained.[27] Linda Brent/Harriet Jacobs recounts in the course of her narrative scenes from a psychodrama, opposing herself and "Mrs. Flint," in what we have come to consider the classic alignment between captive woman and free. Suspecting that her husband, Dr. Flint, has sexual designs on the young Linda (and the doctor is nearly humorously incompetent at it, according to the story line), Mrs. Flint assumes the role of a perambulatory nightmare who visits the captive in the spirit of a veiled seduction. Mrs. Flint imitates the incubus who "rides" its victim in order to exact confession, expiation, and anything else that the immaterial power might want. (Gayle Jones's *Corregidora* [1975] weaves a contemporary fictional situation around the historic motif of entangled female sexualities.) This narrative scene from Brent's work, dictated to Lydia Maria Child, instantiates a repeated sequence, purportedly based on "real" life. But the scene in question appears to so commingle its signals with the fictitious, with casebook narratives from psychoanalysis, that we are certain that the narrator has her hands on an explosive moment of New World/U.S. history that feminist investigation is beginning to examine. The narrator recalls:

> Sometimes I woke up, and found her bending over me. At other times she whispered in my ear, as though it were her husband who was speaking to me, and listened to hear what I would answer. If she startled me, on such occasion, she would glide stealthily away; and the next morning she would tell me I had been talking in my sleep, and ask who I was talking to. At last, I began to be fearful for my life. (33)

The "jealous mistress" here (but "jealous" for whom?) is analogous to the master to the extent that male domination gives the male the material means to fully act out what the female might only *wish*. The mistress in the case of Brent's narrative *embodies his* madness that arises in the ecstasy of unchecked power. Mrs. Flint enacts a male alibi and prosthetic motion that is mobilized at *night,* at the material place of the dream work. In both male and female instances, the subject attempts to *insinuate* his or her will into the vulnerable, supine body. Though this is barely hinted on the surface of the text, we might say that Brent, between the lines of her narrative, demarcates a sexuality that is neuterbound, because it represents an open vulnerability to a gigantic sexualized repertoire that may be alternately expressed as male and/or female. Since the gendered female *exists* for the male, we might say that the ungendered female—in an amazing stroke of pansexual potential—might be invaded/raided by another woman or man.

If *Incidents in the Life of a Slave Girl* were a novel, and not the memoir of an escaped female captive, then we might say that Mrs. Flint is also the narrator's projection, her creation, so that for all her pious and correct umbrage toward the outrage of her captivity, some aspect of Linda Brent is released in a manifold repetition crisis that the doctor's wife comes to stand in for. In the case of both an imagined fiction and the narrative we have from Brent/Jacobs/Child, published only four years before the official proclamations of Freedom, we could say that African-American women's community and Anglo-American women's community, under certain shared cultural conditions, were the twin actants on a common psychic landscape, were subject to the same fabric of dread and humiliation. Neither could claim *her* body and its various productions—for quite different reasons, albeit—as her own, and in the case of the doctor's wife, *she* appears not to have wanted her body at all, but to desire to enter someone else's, specifically, Linda Brent's, in an apparently classic instance of sexual "jealousy" and appropriation. In fact, from one point of view, we cannot unravel one female's narrative from the other's, cannot decipher one without tripping over the other. In that sense, these "threads cable-strong" of an incestuous, interracial genealogy uncover slavery in the United States as one of the richest displays of the psychoanalytic dimensions of culture before the science of European psychoanalysis takes hold.

IV

But just as we duly note similarities between life conditions of American women—captive and free—we must observe those undeniable contrasts and differences so decisive that the African-American female's historic claim to the territory of womanhood and femininity still tends to rest too solidly on the subtle and shifting calibrations of a liberal ideology. Valerie Smith's reading of the tale of Linda Brent as a tale of "garreting" enables our notion that female gender for captive women's community is the tale writ between the lines and in the not-quite spaces of an American domesticity.[28] It is this tale that we try to make clearer, or, keeping with the metaphor, "bring on line."

If the point is that the historic conditions of African-American women might be read as an unprecedented occasion in the national context, then gender and the arrangements of gender are both crucial and evasive. Holding, however, to a specialized reading of female gender as an *outcome* of a certain political, sociocultural empowerment within the context of the United States, we would regard dispossession as the *loss* of gender, or one of the chief elements in an altered reading of gender: "Women are considered of no value, *unless* they continually increase their owner's stock. They were put on par with animals" (Brent, 49, my emphasis). Linda Brent's witness appears to contradict the point I would make, but I am suggesting that even though the enslaved female reproduced other enslaved subjects, we do not read "birth" in this instance as a reproduction of mothering precisely because the female, like the male, has been robbed of the parental right, the parental function. One treads dangerous ground in suggesting an equation between female gender and mothering; in fact, feminist inquiry/praxis and the actual day-to-day living of numberless American women—black and white—have gone far to break the enthrallment of a female subject-position to the theoretical and actual situation of maternity. Our task here would be lightened considerably if we could simply slide over the powerful "no," the significant *exception*. In the historic formation to which I point, however, motherhood and female gendering/ungendering appear so intimately aligned that they seem to speak the same language. At least it is plausible to say that motherhood, while it does not exhaust the problematics of female gender, offers one prominent line of approach to it. I would go farther: Because African-American women experienced uncertainty regarding their infants' lives in the historic situation, gendering, in its coeval reference to African-American women, *insinuates* an implicit and unresolved puzzle both within current feminist discourse *and* within those discursive communities that investigate the entire problematics of culture. Are we mistaken to suspect that history—at least in this instance—repeats itself yet again?

Every feature of social and human differentiation disappears in public discourses regarding African-Americans, as we encounter, in the juridical codes of slavery, personality reified. William Goodell's study not only demonstrates the rhetorical and moral passions of the abolitionist project, but also lends insight into the corpus of law that underwrites enslavement. If "slave" is perceived as the essence of stillness (an early version of "ethnicity"), or of an undynamic human state, fixed in time and space, then the law articulates this impossibility as its inherent feature: "Slaves shall be deemed, sold, taken, reputed and adjudged in law to be *chattels personal*, in the hands of their owners and possessors, and their executors, administrators, and assigns, to all intents, constructions, and purposes whatsoever" (23).

Even though we tend to parody and simplify matters to behave as if the various civil codes of the slave-holding United States were monolithically informed, unified, and executed in their application, or that the code itself is spontaneously generated in an undivided historic moment, we read it nevertheless as exactly this—the *peak* points, the salient and characteristic

features of a human and social procedure that evolves over a natural historical sequence and represents, consequently, the narrative *shorthand of* a
transaction that is riddled, *in practice,* with contradictions, accident, and
surprise. We could suppose that the legal encodations of enslavement stand
for the statistically average case, that the legal code provides the *topics* of a
project increasingly threatened and self-conscious. It is, perhaps, not by
chance that the laws regarding slavery appear to crystallize in the precise
moment when agitation against the arrangement becomes articulate in certain European and New World communities. In that regard, the slave codes
that Goodell describes are themselves an instance of the counter and isolated text that seeks to silence the contradictions and antitheses engendered by it. For example, aspects of Article 461 of the South Carolina Civil
Code call attention to just the sort of uneasy oxymoronic character that the
"peculiar institution" attempts to sustain in transforming *personality* into
property.

(1) The "slave" is movable by nature, but "immovable by the operation
of law" (24). As I read this, the law itself is compelled to a point of saturation, or a reverse zero degree, beyond which it cannot move in the behalf of
the enslaved *or* the free. We recall, too, that the "master," under these perversions of judicial power, is impelled to *treat* the enslaved as property, and
not as personality. These laws stand for the kind of social formulation that
armed forces will help excise from a living context in the campaigns of civil
war. They also embody the untenable human relationship that Henry
David Thoreau believed occasioned "acts of civil disobedience," the moral
philosophy to which Martin Luther King Jr. would subscribe in the latter
half of the twentieth century.

(2) Slaves shall be *reputed* and *considered* real estate, "subject to be mort-
gaged, according to the rules prescribed by law" (24). I emphasize "reputed"
and "considered" as predicate adjectives that invite attention because they
denote a *contrivance,* not an intransitive "is," or the transfer of nominative
property from one syntactic point to another by way of a weakened copulative. The status of the "reputed" can change, as it will significantly before
the nineteenth century closes. The mood here—the "shall be"—is pointedly subjunctive, or the situation devoutly to be wished. That the slave-
holding class is forced, in time, to think and do something else is the narrative of violence that enslavement itself has been preparing for a couple of
centuries.

Louisiana's and South Carolina's written codes are paradigmatic for
praxis in those instances where a *written* text is missing. In that case, the
"chattel principle has . . . been affirmed and maintained by the courts, and

involved in legislative acts" (25). In Maryland, a legislative enactment of 1798 shows so forceful a synonymity of motives between branches of comparable governance that a line between "judicial" and "legislative" functions is useless to draw: "In case the personal property of a ward shall consist of specific articles, such as slaves, working beasts, animals of any kind, stock, furniture, plates, books, and so forth, the Court if it shall deem it advantageous to the ward, may at any time, pass an order for the sale thereof" (56). This inanimate and corporate ownership—the voting district of a ward—is here spoken for, or might be, as a single slave-holding male in determinations concerning property. (If, as one reader argues, "ward" in this provision means a *person*—a minor or incapacitated adult, for example—and not a voting district as I understand it, then the point still holds that the "logic" of property in the eyes of the magistrates and lawmakers would prevail. As Leon Higginbotham observes about the example of Virginia, "court and legislature alike" had, by 1700, "boxed in the colony's black population." But the general assembly of the state definitively moved in 1705 to effectually remove "blacks from the family of man, reassigning them to the classification of real property.")[29]

The eye pauses, however, not so much at the provisions of this enactment as at the details of its delineation. Everywhere in the descriptive document, we are stunned by the simultaneity of disparate items in a grammatical series: "Slave" appears in the same context with beasts of burden, *all* and *any* animal(s), various livestock, and a virtually endless profusion of domestic content from the culinary item to the book. Unlike the taxonomy of Borges's "Certain Chinese encyclopedia," whose contemplation opens Foucault's *Order of Things*, these items from a certain American encyclopedia do not sustain discrete and localized "powers of contagion," nor has the ground of their concatenation been desiccated beneath them. That imposed uniformity comprises the shock, that somehow this mix of named things, live and inanimate, collapsed by contiguity to the same text of realism, carries a disturbingly prominent item of misplacement. To that extent, the project of liberation for African-Americans has found urgency in two passionate motivations that are twinned—(1) to break apart, to rupture violently the laws of American behavior that make such syntax possible; (2) to introduce a new *semantic* field/fold more appropriate to his/her own historic movement. I regard this twin compulsion as distinct, though related, moments of the very same narrative process that might appear as a concentration or a dispersal. The narratives of Linda Brent, Frederick Douglass, and Malcolm El-Hajj Malik El-Shabazz (aspects of which are examined in this essay) each represent both narrative ambitions as they occur under the auspices of "author."

Relatedly, we might interpret the whole career of African-Americans, a decisive factor in national political life since the mid-seventeenth century, in light of the *intervening*, intruding tale, or the tale—like Brent's "garret" space—"between the lines," which are already inscribed, as a *metaphor* of social and cultural management. According to this reading, gender, or sex-role assignation, or the clear differentiation of sexual stuff, sustained elsewhere in the culture, does not emerge for the African-American female in this historic instance, except indirectly, except as a way to reenforce through the process of birthing, "the reproduction of the relations of pro-duction" that, according to Margaret Strobel, involves "the reproduction of the values and behavior patterns necessary to maintain the system of hier-archy in its various aspects of gender, class, and race or ethnicity."[30] Fol-lowing Strobel's lead, I would argue that the foregoing identifies one of the three categories of reproductive labor that African-American females carry out under the regime of captivity. But this replication of ideology is never simple in the case of female subject-positions, and it appears to acquire a thickened layer of motives in the case of African-American females.

If we can account for an originary narrative and judicial principle that might have engendered a Moynihan Report many years into the twentieth century, we cannot do much better than look at Goodell's reading of the *partus sequitur ventrem*: the condition of the slave mother is "forever en-tailed on all her remotest posterity." This maxim of civil law, in Goodell's view, the "genuine and degrading principle of slavery, inasmuch as it places the slave upon a level with brute animals, prevails universally in the slave-holding states" (27). But what is the "condition" of the mother? Is it the "condition" of enslavement the writer means, or does he mean the "mark" and the "knowledge" of the mother upon the child that here trans-lates into the culturally forbidden and impure? In an elision of terms, "mother" and "enslavement" are indistinct categories of the illegitimate inasmuch as these synonymous elements define, in effect, a cultural situa-tion that is *father-lacking*. Goodell, who does not only report this maxim of law as an aspect of his own contemporaneity, but also regards it, as does Douglass, as a fundamental degradation, supposing descent and identity through the female line as comparable to a brute animality. Knowing al-ready that there are human communities that align social reproductive procedure according to the line of the mother, and Goodell himself might have known it some years later, we can only conclude that the provisions of patriarchy, here exacerbated by the preponderant powers of an enslav-ing class, declare mother right, by definition, a negating feature of human community.

Even though we are not even talking about *any* of the matriarchal features of social production/reproduction—matrifocality, matrilinearity, matriarchy—when we speak of the enslaved person, we perceive that the dominant culture, in a fatal misunderstanding, assigns a matriarchist value where it does not belong; actually *misnames* the power of the female regarding the enslaved community. Such naming is false because the female could not, in fact, claim her child, and false, once again, because motherhood is not perceived in the prevailing social climate as a legitimate procedure of cultural inheritance.

The African-American male has been touched, therefore, by the mother, *handed by* her in ways that he cannot escape, and in ways that the white American male is allowed to temporize by a fatherly reprieve. This human and historic development—the text that has been inscribed on the benighted heart of the continent—takes us to the center of an inexorable difference in the depths of American women's community: the African-American woman, the mother, the daughter, becomes historically the powerful and shadowy evocation of a cultural synthesis long evaporated—the law of the mother—only and precisely because legal enslavement removed the African-American male not so much from sight as from *mimetic* view as a partner in the prevailing social fiction of the father's name, the father's law.

Therefore, the female, in this order of things, breaks in upon the imagination with a forcefulness that marks both a denial and an "illegitimacy." Because of this peculiar American denial, the black American male embodies the *only* American community of males handed the specific occasion to learn *who* the female is within itself, the infant child who bears life against the could-be fateful gamble, against the odds of pulverization and murder, including her own. It is the heritage of the mother that the African-American male must regain as an aspect of his own personhood—the power of "yes" to the "female" within.

This different cultural text actually reconfigures, in historically ordained discourse, certain *representational* potentialities for African-Americans: (1) motherhood as female bloodrite is outraged, is denied, at the *very same time* that it becomes the founding term of a human and social enactment; (2) a dual fatherhood is set in motion, comprised of the African father's *banished* name and body and the captor father's mocking presence. In this play of paradox, only the female stands *in the flesh,* both mother and mother-dispossessed. This problematizing of gender places her, in my view, out of the traditional symbolics of female gender, and it is our task to make a place for this different social subject. In doing so, we are less interested in joining the ranks of gendered femaleness than gaining the *insurgent* ground as female social subject. Actually *claiming* the monstrosity (of a female with the potential to "name"), which her culture imposes in blindness, "Sapphire" might rewrite after all a radically different text for female empowerment.

9

"The Permanent Obliquity of an In(pha)llibly Straight": In the Time of the Daughters and the Fathers

The title's reference to a passage from *Moby-Dick* is itself an obliquity in relationship to the theme of this essay. But I adopt it here as a kind of lookout on the subject as it concerns kinship and filiation among African-Americans cast as daughters and fathers. In short, the line of inheritance from a male parent to a female child is not straight. It is "oblique," since she, if everybody looks handsome, will one day shed his name, his law, and the effects of his household for another male's. In that regard, the patriarchal daughter remains suspended as a social positionality between already established territories. Bearing a name that she carries by courtesy of legal fiction and bound toward one that she must acquire in order "to have" her own children, "daughter" maintains status only insofar as she succeeds in disappearing, in deconstructing into "wife" and "mother" of *his* children. This is the familiar law of high patriarchist culture in a heterosexual synthesis as the little girl imbibes it, and from then on she is a more or less willing agent in the text of a cultural conspiracy. Among African-Americans in the midst of violent historic intervention that, for all intents and purposes, has banished the father, if not in fact murdered him, the father's law embodies still the guilt that hovers: one feels called on to explain, make excuses, for his "absence." But the African-American-Father-Gone is the partial invention of sociologists, as the African-American female-as-daughter is consumed in their tale of the "Black Matriarchate."[1]

This lopsided textual sociometry that eats up female difference and identity in notions of the ahistoric "Familius Aeternus" essentially reconfigures in fiction by black American writers as a puzzle, not a closure. This articulated problematic comes nearer the truth because it plants ambiguity at the heart of an interpretation of the father's law. What secrets do these texts cover up? Maya Angelou's *I Know Why the Caged Bird Sings* (putative autobiography), Gayl Jones's *Corregidora,* James Baldwin's *Just Above My Head,* Ralph Ellison's *Invisible Man,* and Alice Walker's "The Child Who Favored Daughter" (from *In Love and Trouble*), and Walker's *Color Purple,* as well as Toni Morrison's *Bluest Eye,* all embody fictions concerned in part with fathers and daughters, and all of these works posit an incestuous link between them.[2] But of these selected texts, only Ellison's *Invisible Man* and Walker's "Child Who Favored Daughter" project, to my mind, a sufficient symbolic apparatus that renders bearable a sustained contemplation of the theme of father-daughter incest. Indeed, it seems that certain ideas, like the face of the Divine, can only be approached with a very wide-angle lens; intimations of incest are among them.

It seems that parent-child incest, in its various ramifications, remains the preeminent dream-thought that not only evades interpretation (or dreaming), but is so layered itself in avoidance and censorship that an interpretive project regarding it appears ludicrous. On one level of imagination incest simply cannot occur and never does.[3] Under the auspices of denial, incest becomes the measure of an absolute negativity, the paradigm of an outright assertion *against*—the resounding no! But on the level of the symbolic, at which point the "metaevent" is sovereign, incest translates into the unsayable which is all the more sayable by very virtue of one's muteness before it. The fictions of incest therefore repose in the involuted interfaces between ephemeral event and interpretive context, but more than that, these fictions materialize that other and alien life that we cannot recognize or acknowledge (and it's probable a good thing!) as being for consciousness. In that regard, fictions about incest provide an enclosure, a sort of confessional space between postures of the absolute, and in a very real sense it is only in fiction—and perhaps the psychoanalytic session—that incest as dramatic enactment and sexual economy can take place at all. Whether or not father-daughter incest actually happens and with what frequency is not a problem for literary interpretation. For good or ill, it belongs to the precincts of the local police department.

But before we attempt a reading of portions of Walker's and Ellison's work, we should make a handful of admissions that are permissible. I attempt this writing, in fact, as the trial of an interlocking interrogation that I am persuaded in by only fifty percent: Is the Freudian landscape an applicable text (to say nothing of appropriate) to social and historic situations that do not replicate moments of its own origins and involvements? The prestigious Oedipal dis-ease/complex, which apparently subsumes the Electra myth, embeds in the heterosexual "nuclear family" that disperses its

fruits in vertical array. The father's law, the father's name pass down in concentrated linearity and exclusion. Not only "one man, one woman," but
these two—this law—in a specific locus of economic and cultural means.
But how does this model, or does this model, suffice for occupied or captive
persons and communities in which the rites and rights of gender function
have been exploded, historically, into sexual neutralities?

The original captive status of African females and males in the context
of American enslavement permitted none of the traditional rights of consanguinity. The laws of the North American Slave Code stipulated that the
newborn would follow the status of its mother—the *partus sequitur ventrem*—but that stroke of legal genius, while assuring hegemony of the
dominant class, did nothing to establish maternal prerogative for the
African female.[4] The child,though flesh of her flesh, did not "belong" to
her, as the separation of mothers and children becomes a primary social
motif of the "peculiar institution." Exceptions to the gender rule intrude
a note of the arbitrary, but this very arbitrariness, depending on individual instances of human kindness in slaveholders, throws in even bolder
relief the subjugative arrangements of the "institution." For the African
female, then, the various inflections of patriarchilized female gender—
"mother," "daughter," "sister," "wife"—are not available in the historical
instance.

If North American slavery in its laws outraged the classic status of motherhood in the African case, then it asymmetrically complicated notions of
fatherhood. In effect, the African person was twice-fathered, but could not
be claimed by the one and would not be claimed by the other. The person,
following the "condition" of the mother, very often bore only a first
name—Niger I, Niger II, Phoeby, Cassius, Jane, Sue, and so forth.[5] While
the suppression of the patronymic engenders a radically different social
and political economy for African-Americans, it involves us, relatedly, in
nested semiotic readings: the African name is not only "lost" to cultural
memory, but on that single ground the captive African is symbolically broken in two—ruptured along the fault of a "double consciousness"[6] in
which case the break with an indigenous African situation is complete, but
one's cultural membership in the American one remains inchoate. A social
subject in abeyance, in an absolute deferral that becomes itself a new synthesis, is born—the African-American, whose last name, for all intents and
purposes, becomes historically X, the mark of his/her borrowed culture's
profound illiteracy.

In this fatal play of literally misplaced/displaced names, the African father is figuratively banished; fatherhood, at best, a cultural courtesy, since

only mother knows for sure, is not a social fiction into which he enters. Participation in the life of his children, indeed the rights of patriarchal privilege, are extended to him at someone else's behest. In this historical instance, the *unnatural* character of the reproductive process is rendered startlingly clear—reproduction is covered by culture, in culture, at every stage so that "free" sexuality remains the scandalous secret in the father's house. Only by executive order and legislative edict does the reproductive process gain cultural legitimacy for African-Americans as freed persons, which suggests the origins of the myth of parenting in sociopolitical consensus. In this calculus of motives, the master and his class—those subjects of an alternative fatherhood—cannot be said to be "fathers" of African-American children at all (without the benefit of quotation marks) since, by their own law, the newborn follows the "condition" of the mother. But in those instances where they were begetters of children, the puzzle of the father is fully elaborated. As "owners" of human "property," they impede the operations of kinship; by denial of kinship, they act out symbolically the ambiguous character of fatherhood itself, perpetuating it in this case as blank parody. In that regard, the notorious X, adopted by the illiterate as the signatory mark and by literate Black Muslims in the United States of the twentieth century as the slash mark against a first offensive, comes to stand for the blank drawn by father's "gun."

We situate ourselves, then, at the center of a mess, convoluted in its crosshatch of historical purposes. There is no simple way to state the case, but crudely put, we might ask: to what extent do the texts of a psychoanalytic ahistoricism, out of which the report, the transactions of incest arise, abrade against or clarify scenes of the past and their subsequent drama? Does the Freudian text translate, in short (and here we would include the Freudian progeny, Lévi-Strauss and Lacan among them)? This question in its various guises provides the background against which the hermeneutical enterprise unfolds to the black scholar-critic. We are a long way from specific acts of texts, but Every [Black] Reader shall be discomfited. Let that be a law, since the critic is attempting to read not only a given text—Foucault's "parallelepiped"-and the vortices of subtexts spinning around it, but also this against and/or despite those pretexts that neither go away nor yield the secret.

The preeminent rule of incest and the incest taboo is that Everybody has one.[7] This universal prohibition involves us in a democracy of ancient scandal that must be related in some sense to the architectonics of domesticity. If possible, children have their own bed in their own room, as do adults, or the circumstance (at least in the United States) is identified as poverty. By six years old, the child, mysteriously, has already acquired a sexual consciousness and loses her place in the parental bed, between the lovers. The Lacanian "imaginary" has long ago dissipated into the "symbolic"—the realm of division, of father-sovereignty.[8] But how many layers of flesh, like so many blankets, are required to cover household carnality? The violation of this fundamental layering generates the drama of Ellison's Trueblood clan, and Houston Baker's interpretation of the incest scene in *Invisible Man* (1952) is solidly grounded in an economically determined reading.[9] The latter, however, is put in perspective with Baker's model of the black artist, grounded, in turn, in American culture. "Daughter," however, drops out of Baker's critical protocol of the family. But in the sexual confusion engendered by incest, family loses the delicate balance of sexual economy and hierarchization that makes "father" father, "daughter" daughter, and the entire household gender-distinctive. It would appear that the incest prohibition obtains to a symbolic function as well as an actual and historical function: to fix the male and female in specific cultural work, it is male sexuality that must be sealed off, impeded, by implication, in order to found female sexuality and its limits. It is not surprising, then, that the legends of incest tend to be male-identified and phallogocentrically determined.

But the excess implied in the prohibitive status of incest also leads us to suspect that it engages us (under wraps) with its opposite—the failure of potence as human possibility, which is the only way we could explain the unwritten law that surrounds and covers the nubile young female in the father's household. Alice Walker inscribes her story "The Child Who Favored Daughter" with this epigram: "that my daughter should / fancy herself in love / with *any* man! / How can this be?" (emphasis added). Why does father need to pose to himself such an inquiry unless there is an element of too much protest buried in it? In other words, the drama of incest as it plays in fiction expresses the fatherly fear—on the level of the symbolic—that his "cargo" is hardly sufficient to bring under permanent rein the sexual impulses represented (in his own febrile imagination) by the silent and powerful sexualities of the females within his purview. Why else would the father want to appropriate a lover's status (since, theoretically, all other women outside his sphere of influence are available to him) unless the very ground on which his sexuality is founded (the household) threatens to slide beneath him in the prohibitive mark itself? These counters of interdiction, then, do not ease the way to a phallic sovereignty, but open to even greater exposure the principle upon which a threatened male sexuality is said to turn.

The entire tale of incest in *Invisible Man* is told by Trueblood, who is also a singer of the blues, "a good tenor." For all intents and purposes, the wife/mother Kate and the daughter/surrogate lover Matty Lou are deprived of speech, since what they said and did and when are reported/translated though the medium of Trueblood. These silent figures, like materialized vectors in a field of force, are curiously silent in the sense that incest fiction, even written by women, never, as far as I know, establishes the agency of the incestuous act inside female character. This fiction in a fiction, central to the kind of symbolic content that the "I" must absorb here in order to achieve the biographical uses of history, is articulated on the margins of the novel's society: In the approach to the Trueblood cabin, the driver of the car that bears Mr. Norton must turn off the highway "down a road that seemed unfamiliar. There were no trees and the air was brilliant. Far down the road the sun glared cruelly against a tin sign nailed to a barn. A lone figure bending over a hoe on the hillside raised up wearily and waved, more a shadow against the skyline than a man" (31). Farther on we are told that, taking a hill, the occupants of the chauffeured car are "swept by a wave of scorching air and it was as though we were approaching a desert" (36). This abrupt fall into an alternative topographical center catches invisible man and his charge out on a radically different plain of human and symbolic activity wherein the play of signs between interlocutors focuses a mismatch of meanings and intentions. Because the road is "unfamiliar" to invisible man, he both knows it and he doesn't, which suggests that he has no exact idea where he is and every right to dread the undifferentiated and impulsive intimations hinted in the "crude, high, plaintively animal sounds Jim Trueblood made as he led [his] quartet" in song. (36–37). "Out here," where time has ceased, attested in the parallelism and contrast between an ox team, sunlight on a tin sign, a lone figure bending over a hoe, and "a powerful motor purring" in the precise articulations of a measurable and oscillating mph, we are prepared, without even knowing it, for a venture into the marginal state; the suspension of rules; the cultural vestibularity that transports us to the regions of "danger and purity."[10] But danger and purity for whom? In a traditional reading of this forcefully intruded narrative, Jim Trueblood emerges wealthier, healthier (because of new wealth, we are led to suppose), and wise. But is it true?

In his marginality, Trueblood becomes a twice-marked figure: (1) by his literally peripheral status to the novel's college community from which he is set apart, as though criminal and contaminated (as he is, in fact, according to the rules of "civilization"), and (2) by the hideous, fly-swarmed ax mark that he will carry for an eternity, inflicted by his wife Kate, who sides with civilization and determines, according to Trueblood's imitation of her, that he "done fouled." This terrible scar that designates him (until his "change comes") a mesmerized, agonized precultural inscription suggests that no man crosses the boundary of undifferentiated sexuality, even in a dream, unless he is prepared to pay the cost of a crucifixion/castration. Even though the evidence tells us no such thing about Trueblood, since wife and daughter are simultaneously pregnant, as though the promise of a twin birth, we might imagine that Ellison's narrator is telling us—between the lines, where the actual sex act has indeed occurred—that Trueblood has not only copulated his last "blow," but will live to tell his privation (equal to the silence of the pregnant females) over and over again in a stunning repetition crisis and narrative obsession that resembles in every way the awful perambulatory nightmare of Coleridge's ancient mariner. Trueblood tells his story because he cannot help himself, and he has no idea why white men, in their exhibitionist urge, need to pay him (somebody-anybody) to hear what they would love to perform. Trueblood becomes their whore/gal of dangerous, powerful entertainment, appointed to maintain their notions of the "civilized" (by refocusing marginality as a living space) as well as provide them the kicks they need—substituting his flesh for their distanced and protected bodies—that orality renders. This oral tale is articulated in a novel, a writing, as Trueblood enters the chain of signifiers as an item of syntax, albeit a wild one. But the tale is essentially absorbed by invisible man as an aspect of elixir with which he returns to the world as a *novelist,* as one who has discarded rather more simplified narrative urges. Trueblood is the man whom invisible man must slay then reencounter and make articulate, if he will comprehend the coeval period of African-American consciousness. Trueblood is, as Baker contends, the "true Blood," and that is precisely the problem.

The violation of the incest taboo entangles Trueblood, it seems, in his own blood lines which merge inner and outer at the source of difference—the ahistoric, reified female. So trammeled, father/man, as such, disappears into an endless progression of enclosures that replicate the vaginal/uterine structure in which he has every right to fear that he will get lost and, quite correctly, fall bereft of his penal powers. I am not certain that this reading is right, but Ellison's narrator has so loaded the dream sequence—the major portion of the tale—with an invaginated symbolic plan that we seem justified in reading the breach of the incest taboo, as it is elaborated in this scene, as a symptom of an inverted castration complex. We could say, if this notion holds water, that the implanted fetus *is* the male-loss, as the vaginal vault swallows the thrust toward it. Taking the relevant text apart at this point would test the assertion.

As Trueblood explains to an anxious, greedy-for-adventure Norton, the family, on the particular night of cold, huddles together for warmth—"me on one side and the old lady on the other and the gal in the middle" (42). The daughter's intermediary position here is highly suggestive. Since Matty Lou is pubescent, we might say she is made to effect a sexually competitive posture between husband and wife. In that sense, we are close to a marriage of three. From another point of view, the intervening child-body poses as a "cock-blocker," a strategy of contraception that is not necessarily recognized as such. In that sense the male must penetrate layers of mediation in order to reach the target, and as unhappy fathers, unbedded by the presence of infant sons and daughters grudgingly admit, no man can get through all that. But the narrator plants a female body in this space for quite obviously practical narrative reasons. We might wonder to what extent, under the circumstances, "daughter" forms a collusive bond with "mother" in opposition to the vaunted powers of the male organ. From this angle, the doubled female body becomes a frontier that resists assault: in order to "enter," Trueblood must first climb Brodnax Hill, as it were, and run the gauntlet of a scalding landscape before the awful climax of this tale can be reached.

Falling off to sleep in this "dark, plum black" atmosphere, Trueblood thinks his way back to Mobile and a particular young woman he knew then. Living in a two-story house on the river, Trueblood and his lover would listen to the sounds of the Mississippi and of boats moving along it. But sound modulates into visual synesthesia, translating into "young juicy melons split wide open a-layin all spread out and cool and sweet on top of all the striped green ones like it's waitin just for you, so you can see how red and ripe and juicy it is and all the shiny black seeds it's got and all." (43). These contiguous rhetorical properties that make sound visible not only suggest the loosening of coherence, as the liminal state between waking and dreaming induces, but also the lapse of distinctions that sustain boundaries between parts of the family. Trueblood, at this point, transforms into the mercurial "boundary crosser," no longer conscious that it is his daughter sleeping beside him. But this loss of customary place that installs us on a frontier of danger has already been prepared for by the sort of sleeping arrangements that adhere and according to the absence of even a hint of light. As Trueblood tells it, the room is as "black as the middle of a bucket of tar" (42). Things turn elemental—"me, the old lady and the gal"—even though Trueblood discovers a plenitude of narrative turns to elaborate the event.

If the preceding sequence might be termed a narrative preplay, then what follows equals a full-dress opening night. Trueblood recalls, in the inauguration of the dream proper, that he is looking for "fat meat," but appropriate to the charged insinuations of nearly every line of his narrative, fat meat is exactly what we think it is—a full-grown watermelon. (One thinks also of the strickoline, or "fatback" of a southern diet that garnishes a vegetable platter, or serves as a bacon substitute with a cerealized rice dish, buttermilk biscuits, and sweetened coffee spiked with Old Grand Dad. Many a southern child remembers that bourbon in certain southern households is refrigerated.) Trueblood, aptly, then, is looking for the grail of his environment, as it runs parallel to the symbolically inscribed female flesh. Because it is basic for him, it is holy, as one must risk his life, his sex, in order to have it. Yes, the "watermelons" are lying in wait for Jim Trueblood, but he mistakes the reasons why.

Because, we are told, we are not responsible in any ethical sense for what we dream, nor can we be held accountable for what we desire, Trueblood is, technically speaking, not guilty. In fact, he was not "there" when it happened, so he has made no mistake, even though his "innocence" (de facto, or is his guilt de jure?) provokes in him the sense of unconscionable error and the terrible consequence of guilty ignorance. Trueblood has prestigious predecessors in this regard, as invisible man recalls a fictitious English professor named Woodridge, who assigned his class readings from Greek plays (31). But the single impenetrable element of the puzzle of fatherhood as Trueblood enacts it has to do with the manifestations of the feminine that appear across the dreamscape. It is as though another layer of intrusion is intercalated between Trueblood and his woman/women, which introduces an Ellisonian boomerang into this otherwise straight Freudian family drama with an Electra twist. Brodnax holds the key to "fat meat," as Trueblood climbs to his place, but not finding the "master" at home, Trueblood enters anyway, and we appear to mix signals, momentarily, with Richard Wright's Bigger Thomas and the pervasive "whiteness" that surrounds Mary Dalton. Trueblood enters a door into a "big white bedroom"; as on an occasion with his Ma, Trueblood has gone to the "big house."

But is Ma in this instance a function of the gigolo between her boy and "Miss Thang," so that, for him, carnality comes to rest in a surrogate female, an other woman, who initiates the young male into the ceremonies of the throbbing flesh? (In Faulkner's *Absalom, Absalom!* we are led to surmise that sexual license arises always *in* the "other" woman). In Ellison's case, it is a white woman who engenders Trueblood's entry onto the terrain of interdiction. A "white lady" steps out of a grandfather's clock, and she is robed in "white milky stuff and nothin else" (45). Clearly we are meant to understand a doubling of the prohibitive effect in this scene, as we already know, without Trueblood having to tell us, that she is "holding" him and he is "scared to touch her cause she's white" (45). But this she is holding his fantasies as much as anything else his dream-body brings to bear on the scene; we could even say that Trueblood's body "perambulates" and materializes his fantasies so that the real world of scarcity, to which Trueblood is fixed like an object in protective coloration, has always historically translated him into a potentially mutilated body. In that regard, this transactional scene ejects a body turned inside out, in which case the symbolic thrust of the passage does nothing to disguise or ameliorate the real situation of the dreaming body. The power and the danger that this moment projects apparently claim it under the auspices of pleasure, but the end of the dream and of the tale brings on Trueblood the truth of a severe disjuncture: the torn flesh of his face—the branding that establishes his deep knowledge of the forbidden female.

Frantz Fanon projects a white woman in the big house at the center of the displaced African male's prerevolutionary consciousness, but in the Fanonian scheme, the woman appears to be a familiar appurtenance of a politicocultural empowerment.[11] We expect from her (at this angle) an implacable muteness just as Ellison's female bodies speak only through the embodied vocality of Jim Trueblood. But is it possible to retrieve from this representational cul de sac a different reading? How did this woman get in Trueblood's dream, and/or the other way around? In other words, what does this scene suggest about the daughter of this incestuous coupling, and does she, on the "lower frequencies"—which is exactly where *this* daughter occurs spatially in the dream, beneath the blond—speak also for the white woman?

Because Matty Lou, the ole lady, Ma, and the white woman—essentially appropriating the same function of the feminine, melding into a gigantic sexualized repertoire—all occupy the same semantic/symbolic fold, we have no business telling them apart, except that the intrusive markers of whiteness (and they fix this scene in obsessive repetition) signal the difference that we cannot overlook. But we assume that we know already what the *not overlooking* means. This shrouding detail not only obstructs and evades what might have occurred—"that woman just seemed to sink outta sight, that there bed was so soft"—but also covers the identity of the daughter so completely that she is configured as an obscured aspect of landscape—a "dark tunnel . . . like the power plant they got up to the school":

> It's burnin' hot as iffen the house was caught on fire, and I starts to run-nin', tryin' to get out. I runs and runs til I should be tired but ain't tired but feelin' more rested as I runs, and runnin' so good it's like flying' and I'm flyin' and sailin' and floatin' right up over the town. Only I'm still in the *tunnel*. Then way up ahead I sees a bright light like a jack-o-lantern over a graveyard. It gets brighter and brighter and I know I got to catch up with it or else. Then all at once I was right up with it and it burst like a great big electric light in my eyes and scalded me all over. Only it wasn't a scald, but like I was drownin' in a lake where the water was hot on the top and had cold numbin' currents down under it. Then all at once I'm through it and I'm relieved to be out and in the cool daylight agin. (45–46)

Since Trueblood's dream is literary, we have nothing, we assume, to dis-cover that the narrator does not deliberately mean. The symbol system of the dream apparatus appears to work, then, both transparently and sym-bolically as the consciously manipulated stuff of a waking intelligence, at work through Trueblood as a mimetic device. We rightly assume that Matty Lou and Trueblood are already sexually entangled at this point and that the "scalding" stands for an ejaculation. When Trueblood wakes, he will try "to move without movin'," or having "flown" in must now "walk out" (46). But these contradictory signals point, in a deeper sense, to an even greater para-dox, which I think the narrator does not foresee: The white woman be-comes the symptom of a sexual desire that finds expression in the daughter so that the former is the *term* that drops out of sight, as the latter loses both human and social identity. We could say by way of these subtlelized dis-placements that sexuality, domesticated as a sacralized body and firmly in-scribed within an enclosure that hides its "true" purposes in objects of evasion, escape, decor, can only be executed in the "underground" of sex—the actual confrontation between the genitalia. This basic situation, wherein subjectivity "thingifies," transposes into an unlocalized space that is nei-ther here nor there. This "u-topic" suspension, brought on by a burning house, which mobilizes the droll and the dreadful (a "jack-o-lantern over a graveyard"), is appropriately undifferentiated, as the "dark tunnel" and the pit-black dark in which the dreaming bodies sleep have already signaled. In this order of things, father runs, sails, floats as though rescued from the im-mediate situation that moors him even to a dream context, and daughter becomes the instrument of his release. In this dark of the oceanic, there are no fathers and daughters, but only children, whose being finds the perfectly magical formula that abandons them to the situation of a not-human other.

The scene splits wide open not only between a pair of female legs, but at the moment of conjuncture between houses—civilization, sexuality, and a feminine body identified as such—and the "lay of the land"—tunnels, graveyards, and the open air.[12] But each of these externalized interiorities that suggest freedom within a uterine enclosure translates as marginality—the tunnel is nowhere yet, and the graveyard describes the largest future. We are here in passage, at the entrance to the forbidden currents of a civilized sexuality, under the auspices of a white man-not-at-home. That a woman guards the inner sanctum of Brodnax's big house poses blond and daughter in the way of a furious combat that neither can win, as such. But even before these faces of the feminine can be brought into contact, the intervened masculine must be moved aside as the teller of the tale. There is no simple leaping of the breach, and moreover, this sexual drama essentially poses a male and only one of the two females; if that is so, then sexuality also eludes the house of the father (or the circumstance of the true blood) as that boundary across which subject/subjectivity cannot go. The white woman in that regard is fixed as the "female body in the West"[13] in the first and last frontier of a "barred subject."[14] "Daughter," the *stuff* of which "she," the white woman of the dream, is made, is established, relatedly, as a "barred subject," both plus and minus. That "she" bears the pregnant body shadows forth a fundamental economy of female signification: a body integrates and hides those layers of the flesh that give it identity and differentiation. There is at work in the black woman of the dream a different and informing femininity for which we yet have no name, except to call it "not woman." In this place of incestuous linkage, there is also "not man." In the fictional enactment of incest, then, black is not a color; it is a circumstance, wherein human becomes "thing" and thing turns "human" in an absolute lapse of a hierarchical movement.

We would go further: Wherever incest occurs as a fictional/symbolic motion, it takes place in the "dark, plum black . . . as the middle of a bucket of tar." The shape, the outline, melt down in an inexorable play of sameness, of identities misplaced and exchanged. One can no more find a "father" here as she can a "daughter," and the one thing we cannot account for is Trueblood's presence in the big house in the first place, except that his fantasies must have put him there. The male body between female stuff, the forbidden presence on the run from the burning dream house, becomes a fugitive and an outlaw; this father, in the twice-theft of the prohibited gift, is analogous to the band of the banished brothers. But it is not Trueblood's place to kill the fathers who have run him off, but the task of invisible man in the making of a fictionalized social order that resurrects history and steps into culture/differentiation. Here the theme of a fictional incest allows us to see closer up the failure of phallic signification, not its fulfillment.

Even though Alice Walker's father by implication, in "The Child Who Favored Daughter," executes "the judge, the giver of life" (35), his doing so impels him to madness. In fact, the closural passage of the narrative, in its fierce immobilization of human and natural subjects, poses a sculptural stasis as (and in the place of a) dramatic immediacy: "Today" hardly registers a near-presence of chronology, but all the "nows" that possibly roll in upon the standing mastectomy inflicted on the "child, who favored Daughter," who is *his* daughter. These embodied surrogate motions, in which this father replays *his* father and this daughter replays his sister called "Daughter," touch neither time nor realism, but intrude themselves as an awful lyrical moment of eleven published pages between a birth (the tale's inauguration) and a death (its closure) in the subjunctive passivity of an aftermath, stylized by anaphora and the hint of the paradox of motion:

> Today he is slumped in the same chair facing the road. The yellow school bus sends up clouds of red dust on its way. If he stirs it may be to Daughter shuffling lightly along the red dirt road, her dark hair down her back and her eyes looking intently at buttercups, and stray black-eyed Susans along the way. If he stirs it may be he will see his own child, a black-eyed Susan from the soil on which she walks. A slight, pretty flower that grows on any ground; and flowers pledge no allegiance to banners of any man. If he stirs he might see the *perfection of an ancient dream still whispered about, undefined*. If he stirs he might feel the energetic whirling of wasps about his head and think of ripe late summer days and time when scent makes a garden of the air. If he stirs he might wipe dust from the dirt daubers out of his jellied eyes. If he stirs he might take up the heavy empty shotgun and rock it back and forth on his knees, like a baby. (45–46, my emphasis)

It is as though the narrator has not told us a tale at all, but a short-hand of one, an idea that lights across the mind and is gone. In that regard, "The Child Who Favored Daughter" renders a dream that actualizes a nightmare that reflects a "might have happened." But does this dreamer awake to discover that it is not so? Trueblood lives to talk; the father of daughter never did, except that in an unguarded moment of self-reflection the deepest layers of his psyche find a ventriloquist. This story does not read like a case history, but it seems to embody one.

The story has two beginnings, one of them seen through the lens of the character called "child" (35–36) and the other, over the same objective terrain of a given nature, filtered through the eyes of the character called "he" (37ff). In the second segment, the narrator sketches in relevant psychological detail concerning his past—a beautiful and beloved sister, "impaled on one of the steel-spike fences near the house" (39). "Cut down" by a father dishonored and shamed by her liaison with "the lord of his own bondage," she has already come again in the atavistic nightmare alluded to in the opening line: "She knows he has read the letter," whose contents will crucify the child. In this deadlock grid of original sin (and incest is certainly a candidate for "it"), and on the terrain of the intramural and the internecine that stages the family as a network of shared neuroses, fathers and sons link back to a common ancestry of "unnamable desire" that threatens every female alike—in these lines of poetry from the tale, sisters and spouses enjamb across run-on lines that do not stop:

Memories of Years
Unknowable women-
sisters
spouses
illusions of soul   (repeated twice on 38; emphasis is Walker's)

Because "he" has lost "daughter" and is never the same, "the women in his life faced a sullen barrier of distrust and hateful mockery. . . . His own wife, beaten into a cripple to prevent her from returning the imaginary overtures of the white landlord, killed herself while she was still young enough and strong enough to escape him" (40). But she leaves "a child, a girl, a daughter." Seizing on a striking narrative/descriptive detail that becomes a powerful lacuna in the Walker text, Harryette Mullen points out that Walker's female characters are often in search of mothers. Specifically addressing *The Color Purple* as a critique of patriarchy in the West, Mullen argues: "The story presupposes two things: a powerful black husband/father with the financial means to dominate his family; and a weak, dead, or otherwise absent or estranged mother who is unable to protect herself or her children from this man."[15] I would not necessarily agree with Mullen that Walker's man is powerful, but in the case of *The Color Purple*, he is certainly powerful enough, and enough is as much as a feast. But the critical thematic of the missing/absent mother (who is always assumed) throws a different light on fictionalized father-daughter incest: we recall that in James Baldwin's *Just Above My Head*, the mother of Julia Miller is deceased when Joel turns his daughter into more than his sporadic lover; the mother figure of Maya Angelou's *I know Why the Caged Bird Sings* has either just abandoned her bed, with her daughter in it, beside Freeman, or just left the house, permitting him the space of isolation he needs to ostracize himself and the twice-abandoned girl-child still farther. In the tale of Trueblood, Kate, who will raise very hell when the "dead" awakens, is asleep when her mate commits the mistake of his life. In Walker's *Color Purple*, Celie apparently takes on the function of a surrogate wife; as in "The Child Who Favored Daughter," "daughter" becomes proto-, or Ur-lover, who makes the wife a superfluity, if not an outright impossibility. In effect, there can be no daughter without wife/mother, as this story lives and breathes the consequences of such absence. Appropriately, a girl-child springs up over a female's dead body, having none of the prerogatives extended to a daughter in the hierarchic, father-centered household. Exposed, therefore, to a child-man who is locked in powerful infantile memory that lives on into the moment, Walker's child reinscribes the surrogate subject of a man who wishes to sleep with his sister. Failing that, he invents a female body, in his imagination, who essentially reinstitutes the sister's erotic reign that leads instead to daughter-murder.

There is an immediate cause of war in this male character's soul that offers an element of intrusion comparable to Trueblood's white woman of his dream. Daughter of the story, like the real daughter, loves a white man and has apparently written him a love letter, which becomes, in proximity to the gun across his knees, a major dramatic prop of the tale. Armed with his evidence—"white man's slut!"—(Would it have made a difference had the white man married her? one doubts it)—he is determined to beat this hell out of her and to force her to deny that she wrote the letter, in short, to deny the erotic signature behind which she stands firmly ensconced, that fills him with a desire that agonizes. And kills. We could say that this occasion marks one of those rare fictional instances in which a woman's scribbling will bring on her literal castration. These marks on the page precisely time and measure the short distance between her life and death, and we nearly wish that she had not written it, or had not been discovered or betrayed until we realize that this is not an avoidable tale of detection. It is Walker's version of an allegory in which race becomes the most pellucid, loud alibi for the male to act out a fundamental psychodrama: having had a sister whom he could not love in an open consummated way, this father never finds love at all. Carnality knocks him down, and his response to it is typically penal: he flails and beats; his medium and his memory are guns, "steel-spiked fences," and great big butcher knives. In short, he is a perfect Sadeian sadist with none of the ostensible pleasures, so far as we can tell. I doubt that the sniff of white man's flesh makes a great deal of difference here, except that it breaks the law, and this male character knows only that—the heat, the rush, the dread, the domination of his enforced, ball-busting, back-breaking labor. He will not use his "gun" where it counts, but only against one who will whimper and drag her hair in the dirt before him. Because he will toss her castrated breasts to the dogs, yelping at his feet, we are led to suppose, he joins them, and no man can or should live as a dog. (Even though some of them have done remarkably well as cockroaches.) The ambiguous closure in which the male figure is either dead or as dead as we need him reminds us, however, that imputing blame and coming up with a moral would make the story realistic. The narrator, I think, means anything but that, as we are called upon to observe, to inquire into, a configuration of psychic forces, of imaginative possibilities that might/not be enacted, as fictionalized incest remains a negative drive in a field of force.

Inasmuch as incest in Walker's tale must be described between quotation marks twice (in fiction, and then not "really"), it probably goes even farther than Trueblood's narrative to alert us to the familial economies of symbolic father-daughter incest. All the instruments of torture in this feminized space of the shed are an unmistakable weaponry: a "harness from the stable" whose buckles draw blood, "curling into the dust of the floor" (42). They are wielded, unmistakably, in an attitude of maiming, but in the allegory it is either never clear or conflatedly transparent exactly what the father wants to murder. Clearly, ambiguously, he loves her, as the lines from the letter, in his night-long vigil (it seems), refer to both her own writing and what runs through his mind in a wounding flash: "It is rain soaked, but he can make out 'I love you' written in a firm hand across the blue face of the letter" (42). This is fairly remarkable because we are almost persuaded to say that the one thing that rushes him out of his father's closet, so to speak, is this female's writing—even rain-soaked, it is a firm hand "across the blue." Would she still have been a girl-child alive, riding on a yellow school bus, except for that act of inscription that affirms beyond conjecture her powers of desire? To choose, to say who and when she wants? Her crime has been her desire. The daughter cannot want, and so far as this one is concerned, "no amount of churchgoing changed her ways" (43). It is a patent contradiction to the father's law that the young nubile female in his midst should desire. (The wishes of a wife, even an adulterous one, do not matter, since she has already been had.) He is flummoxed, however, in the face of the daughter's vast and untried sexual possibilities, and we suspect why: he, essentially, drew his woman out of another man's familial/sexual integrity, which move kills the father, if the law works, throughout all the generations; I suppose we could say that not until a man marries—which, humorously, depends on a woman's consent—does he complete his Oedipal mission and gain, thusly, brotherhood in the status of a patrimonial destiny.

Does the incestuous instinct become, then, in the fictional text the fatherly plea that the young woman not "disgrace" her father, not "cut him loose" in the transfer of unspoken sexual allegiance? We are accustomed to think that men exchange women, as the fundamental reason of property behind the prohibition, but is it possible that the female figure, the woman, simply by looking at what she wants, fixing it at eye level, effects the point of transfer and transit that must be blocked off at all costs? Does this vast and fundamental negation, then, cover this muted place at which the father gains insight into his own limitations of body and flesh? Perhaps it is not by accident that the unwed daughter, especially in the house of a dead father, is viciously referred to in heterosexist language and tradition as the old maid, the aged female "stuff" whom father needn't marry?

Because this daughter writes her wish, she assumes the proportions of a monstrosity (the narrator has also given her school books off whose sight the father's eyes glide down to the point of promise), as she becomes, exactly, "in the shed"—rain-soaked, hair-draggled, immured in the blood of her flesh. He sees her blouse, "wet and slippery from the rain," sliding off her shoulders, "and her high young breasts are bare":

> He gathers their fullness in his fingers and begins a slow twisting. The barking of the dogs create a frenzy in his ears and he is suddenly burning with unnameable desire. In his agony he draws the girl away from him as one pulling off his own arm and with quick slashes of his knife leaves two bleeding craters the size of grapefruits on her bare bronze breast and flings what he finds in his hands to the yelping dogs. (45)

Any woman reader of this paragraph is convinced by now, if not by anything that precedes it, that this swift, matter-of-fact, verbal gesture does not qualify as the imitation of any conceivable action. We must be somewhere else in a region of imagined revenge. There is no apparent and immediate aftermath that the text records: No noise? No hysterical motion? No drowning? And no Divinity comes down here now? And how could a woman write this, without self- (or other?) intervention? We read it again and decide that it is comparable to a female body "impaled on a steel-spiked fence *near the house*" (my emphasis). And it remains unbearable. No act of criticism that I could perform on the text at this point would retry the passage for me as a usable text, since it transgresses every sexual/sexually discursive aspect of a cultural code that I have received from father/mother (the most immediate and evident sexual origin) as a plausible carnality and therefore a potential mimesis/representation of a sort. But that point at which my own readerly sensibilities switch off, at which my own aesthetic rules go in revolt, at which, in this case, I, in an empathetic gesture that has no business intruding itself between the clean text and me, may well mark precisely that moment at which I should hang on. It possibly signalizes the "quick slash marks" that divide the subject—violently—from the peace and "piece" of self-imputed w(hole)ness. "This sex which is not one"[16] not only inscribes the symbolic outcome of the female's divided labial economy, but offers this configuration as the groundwork of a different system of signification altogether. If this is so, then the daughter in Walker's text not only escapes the patriarchal household of this tale (by death) but also, consequently, the unitary implications of the phallic by which she is adjudged an other.

If the daughter escapes patriarchy by mutilation and effacement only, then the victory is hardly worth the father's cost, since this fictionalized circuit of desire has shorted out, as it were. If the incestuous impulse leads, by a detour, to a "more or less manifest endogamy," then the "realization of incest is not only possible, it is necessary albeit through a third party, lest any form of relationship between human beings become exhausted."[17] According to this theory, father-daughter incest must occur on the symbolic level and therefore in its manifestations as the incest taboo, in order to bring about "differences in cases where identity threatens to block the functioning of some fixed culture." Roustang goes so far as to contend that

> Incestuous desire is operative for the individual only if it actually remains a possibility, but that possibility, to remain valid, must be the effective deviation, the actual derivation of incest. If incest is unrecognized, rejected, repressed, the individual will be left with nothing but the arid, closed field of some abandonment or deadly depression. If incest is overtly practiced and the individual has eyes, ears, and sex only for those closest to him or their surrogates, then he will always be on the verge of fragmentation and breakdown.[18]

The father of Walker's text cannot recognize the ground of his own "unnameable desire," or else he recognizes it all too well. Having "eyes, ears, and sex only for those closest to him"—in this instance, a ruse or surrogate for "Daughter"—he actually carries out, on the level of an inverted dream, the motions of breakdown and falling apart that the text displaces through the daughter's dismemberment. We are left, I believe, with a stunning excision, pointing in two directions at once. The text both engenders and conceals these oppositional vectors by circumvention. The slumping figure that we encounter in the closural scene of the tale cradles a "heavy empty shotgun" that might be read as a deflated tumescence. But the essential stillness of the passage, as though time will not cease in an eternity of undifferentiated movement, also claims it for death at the level of vegetal growth: the dirt daubers have seized this body, jellied its eyes, as the choreographed effects of the natural overwhelm names, identities, and genders in a democratic rage for sameness. This reduction to the fundamental, brought on by an oversupply of the domestic phallus (the one "near the house"), not only parodies a "return of the repressed," but also mocks the father's law as a basic castration fear.

But what might it mean for this daughter to "underwrite" this father? In other words, how is it that we know daughter only through father? Indeed, it seems that he marks the founding auspices of a female representation and that we have no way out. I maintain, however, that the loss of difference—which occurs in an actualized fictitious outcome of incest, as in the tale of Trueblood, or in a surrogate fictitious outcome, as in "The Child Who Favored Daughter"—abolishes those very sexual distinctions that hold the father-daughter relationship in a delicate balance. Its violation, in at least two contemporary fictional instances, brings about castration, or its equivalent: in the case of Trueblood, the daughter's pregnancy and a sexual future from which Trueblood has been barred; in Walker's father's case, a future rolling backward and ahead toward unlocalized human origins. In either instance, sexual life or human-as-sexed-subject stalls at the moment of penetration so that the penis, in this speaking, actually lops itself off. If this is so, then the suspension of the taboo generates the deepest division, if to signify here is to break up into layers of fragmentation. A sort of magic pervades this economy: fathers and daughters are called upon to divide without division, to acquire that difference that no one ever thought was other than difference in the first place; since this is true, father can save himself only in bypassing the daughter's sex, which is also anatomically inscribed, but it is the "difference within" that he must only guess. Have we, then, done nothing more than point out that even in fiction, especially in fiction, the incest taboo prevails and prevails for very good reason?

It seems that we have arrived at the household of the African-American daughter and father by a kind of detour of our own. This arriving possibly demarcates a text running parallel to that of a Eurocentric psychomythology, and I would concede that by way of it we land also on the ground of pure (fictional?) speculation: the Freudian/Lacanian text of incest and phallic signification might apply to this community of texts—both fictional and historic—by analogy, which the writers sense more palpably, it seems, than the sociologists. The father *and* the daughter of this social configuration are missing historically because the laws and practices of enslavement did not recognize, as a rule, the vertical arrangements of their family. From this angle, fathers, daughters, mothers, sons, sisters, brothers spread across the social terrain in horizontal display, which exactly occurred in the dispersal of the historic African-American domestic unit. In this movement outward from a nuclear centrality, the family becomes an extension and inclusion—anyone who preserves life and its callings becomes a member of the family, whose patterns of kinship and resemblance fall into broader meaning. In other words, the "romance" of African-American fiction is a tale of origins that brings together once again children lost, stolen, or strayed from their mothers. We pursue these thematics in works by Frances E. W. Harper, Pauline Hopkins, and Charles W. Chesnutt, among others, who wrote in the late nineteenth century and early into the twentieth century.[19] We also encounter the changeling, the orphaned or lost child in other fictions, but I am not acquainted with any other cluster of fictional texts based in historical experience that seems *designed* to sever the maternal bond, shuttering the paternal connection in redoubled uncertainty. On this basis, it is fair to say that one aspect of the liberational urge for freed persons is not so much the right to achieve the nuclear family as it is the wish to rescue African-Americans from flight, to arrest their wandering away from . . . toward—essentially, to bring the *present* into view rather than the past. We could go so far as to say that African-Americans in historic flight perfectly inscribe the "body in pain,"[20] on a contracted world ground, whose sole concern becomes the protection of the corporeal body, and it is the corporeal, carnal body that incest brings brazenly into relief precisely because it is prohibited.

If the family, on this historic occasion, describes, for all intents and purposes, a site of interdiction and denial, we could go so far as to say that the mark of incestuous desire and enactment—a concentrated carnality—speaks for its losses, confusions, and, above all else, its imposed abeyance of order and degree. We might tentatively look at the situation this way: moments of African-American fiction show father-daughter incest or its surrogate motions as an absence, not an overdetermination. Something is wrong, precisely because fathers and daughters, in a cultural marginality, fictively inscribed, are impeded in their movement toward culture/difference/division. The urge here compels characters to get out of incest, out of the carnal body, whose only means of expression remains the flesh, as Trueblood's branding makes evident, into the "clean" blood. If this is true, then the prohibition must be embraced (in order to cancel out the other inter-diction) not only in father's interest, but that the daughters might know the appropriate lover and the future. In this case, the origins of the incest taboo are not at all shrouded in mystery, insofar as the taboo is reenacted over and over again: Wherever human society wishes to move into an articulation, or clearly differentiated familial roles, the father must discover and humbly observe his limit. In that regard, and at least from the viewpoint of a couple of writers, father-daughter incestuous desire and taboo possesses no origi-nary moment, but arises each day, as a precise diachronic unfolding, in a situation of blindness and overcoming.

10

Moving On Down the Line: Variations on the African-American Sermon

Let us stand with both feet upon the shoulders of the past and gather before us the events of today as an horoscope of time; and we will be able to detect and depict, in the gray dawn of the new morning, the events that will transpire and to read between the lines *the story of the age.*

From "What Shall the Harvest Be?" preached by the Rev. J. W. E. Bowen, 1892 (my emphasis)

I

On a late July Sunday a few years ago, following an observance of the midday office, I stood shyly spectating beneath the dome of Milan's Cathedral of San Carlo. But at least twelve months would pass before I understood why the moment might have provided me a useful hesitation. Remembering from childhood how Southerners—en route to New York especially—were warned not to betray their comical foreignness, I almost laughed out loud that I was not only about to look, but look *way* up, toward a distance farther—it felt—from the earth plane than the most brazen astronaut travels. The ceiling of Il Duomo de San Carlo requires that the observer virtually assume a supine posture in order to see it properly. One is inclined to topple over backward in a dizzying effort to grasp that incredible distance between self and topmost, floor and apex. The neck strains, the whole torso falls back, and even now, I recall not seeing entirely that single clear path of zooming light that hooks two distant points in a geometry of sudden recognition. This momentary parallelism, which almost flattens out the perpendicular human plane, seems adapted to the functions of humility: the "I" repeats the gestures of a crucifixion as the eye travels—startled—upward, in a sudden nausea of helplessness.

But I didn't know any of that until, months later, reading through some of the sermons on which this essay is based, I concocted this analogy: what the feast of the gaze is to the great churches of Europe,[1] built in early Christian centuries with the money of the prince, the feast of hearing is to the church of the insurgent and the dispossessed, whose "prince" is surrounded by "clouds and darkness . . . his pavilion . . . dark waters and thick clouds." In the church of the prince, ecclesiastical architecture accomplishes the project of awe through the play of light, the immediated spaces along the line of horizontal vision, the sweep, the curve of the soaring angle.[2] The *eye* initiates a vault, a leap of faith. In the church of the insurgent, the hierarchy of the ecclesia, of the political body, is razed, as nuance is stripped down to its bare, necessary minimum. In this church of democratic forms, attested to by a far humbler architectural display, the listening *ear* becomes the privileged sensual organ, as the sermon attempts to embody the Word. Between eye and ear, there is not much to choose regarding human status in the places of the Holy. We are small there. But through the Protestant sermon's rhetoric of admonition, through the African-American's sermon of exhortation, "I" improve; "I" "hear"/"have" the Word, at last, in a gesture of intervention that the physical and psychic violence of the North American slave trade neither anticipated, nor could ward off. The African-American church, therefore, sustains a special relationship of *attentiveness* to the literal Word that liberates.

In this case, the churchgoer hears double, or in excess, because it is between the lines of Scripture that the narratives of insurgence are delivered. We address here the requirements of literacy as the ear takes on the functions of "reading."

II

This essay pursues, then, a fundamental assumption; the religious sentiment and the documents of homiletics that inscribe it bring into play the preeminent mode of discourse by which African-Americans envisioned a transcendent human possibility under captive conditions. It is no accident, either of language or intent, that African-American preachers in the twentieth century have variously chosen the "Eagle" as the figurative embodiment of a thematics of liberation.[3] But just as the Eagle in its emblematic history conflates notions of freedom under military might, just as it elides in a distinct visual field a protocol of the imperialistic and the free, the African-American's relationship to Christianity and the state is marked completely by ambivalence; we could even say that at moments such a relationship gropes toward a radically alternative program. For instance, on November 2, 1845, J. W. C. Pennington—whose powerful narrative of captivity instantly yokes the contents of literacy and conversion to the very same epiphanic instance—preaches a farewell sermon on the occasion of his imminent two-year departure from the pulpit of the Fifth Congregational Church of Hartford, Connecticut.[4] Developing the rhetorical pivot of the sermon around a central dramatic question—"Does the Bible condemn slavery without any regard to circumstances, or not?"—Pennington *thunders:*

> If you stand commended to the guidance of the Word of God, you are bound to know its position in reference to certain overt acts that crowd the land with curses. Take the last and greatest of the curses that I named above. Is the word of God silent on this subject? I, for one, desire to know. My repentance, my faith, my hope, my love, and my perseverance all, all, I conceal it not, I repeat it, all turn upon this point. If I am deceived here—if the word of God does sanction slavery, I want another book, another repentance, another faith, and another hope![5]

Pennington's urgent address, just as that of many of the documents of printed religious narratives and sermons from this community of texts, marks the central paradox of an American identity that seeks transformation, has so far evaded resolution, and stays urged toward a dialectical movement.[6] These documents provide systematic access to a spate of discourse that intersects at least two culture maps at an overwhelming problematic: the African-American, long before the barred subject of Lacanian discourse brought it to our attention, becomes the hyphenated proper noun that belongs neither "here," nor "there." This deferment of place provides the background thematic of this essay, which tracks, more precisely, some of the narrative implications of the stories that certain African-American preachers tell and have told through their sermons and how their parishioners "read" and hear them.

The issues that Pennington raises in his address relate specifically to his own fugitive status, narrated in his autobiography. Pennington's story of escape, conversion, and literacy links contrastive narrative energies to a single line of inquiry: for the captive personality to learn to read is not only mastery of the inherited texts of his or her culture, but also its *subversion,* or a seeking after those moments that enable a different, or "thickened" reading. The auditors of Pennington's sermon(s) are called upon to perform essentially the same task as Pennington, and that is to read/hear a Gospel message that would now incorporate the "stolen" man or woman. This "drama of a tremendous striving," to borrow W. E. B. DuBois's more urgent formulation, everywhere insinuates itself into the project of literacy for African-Americans, inasmuch as it defines their fundamental relationship to dominant culture. In that regard, African-American sermons offer a paradigmatic instance of reading as process, encounter, and potential transformation.

Fleeing the scene of captivity and dismemberment is not only Penning-ton's story and not just the actual move that has brought on the heat of the farewell sermon. It is the thematic implied across the discourse of these ser-mons. It further suggests the hoped-for definitive motion, I believe, of African peoples in the New World, less "new" now and still delinquent in the fleshing out the vision of a Christian "City on a Hill."[7] The sermon doc-uments addressed here provide an imaginative field of inquiry into the strategies of African survival, evinced on a hostile landscape of social and political praxis. We would not exaggerate the case to assert that the sermon, as the African-American's prototypical public speaking, locates the primary instrument of moral and political change within the community. But at crucial times, the sermon not only catalyzes movement, but *embodies* it, *is movement*. We vividly observed such examples in the public career of at least two contemporary figures, in the persons of Martin Luther King Jr., and Malcolm El-Hajj Malik El-Shabazz.[8] Whether or not we encounter the sermon in its customary social context, as the driving words of inspiration and devotion, or in its variously secular transformations and revisions as urgent political address, we perceive it fundamentally as a symbolic form that not only lends shape to the contours and outcome of African-Ameri-cans' verbal fortunes under American skies, but also plays a key role in the psychic configuring of their community.

How this is so is not entirely clear to me, but figuring it out is the crucial reading and execution of my own involvement in the collective. Because the captive's exposure to American Protestantism was more or less immedi-ate, and because he came to the New World with, already, a profound reli-gious capacity from the Old World, religion for black Americans has never been anything *but* complicated. The sermon, I believe, not only gestures to-ward these forces, but in a sense, *knots* them up, proffers a syntactic possi-bility for reading them. The program of reading, hearing, and listening to the sermons yields no metaphor that applies, at once, to all three. But one might say that unknotting this fabric of a complicated national identity brings all three into related play.

III

I regard African-American sermons as a paradigm of the structure of am-bivalence that constitutes the black person's relationship to American cul-ture and apprenticeship in it. These documents provide a means for examining the broad and unspoken tensions of that relationship. But what is the risk, though we have considerable precedent here, for removing the sermon from its accustomed setting—an architecture that marks it in a more or less isolated spatial economy; a social relationship among discrete subject-positions in a lapse of difference; a participatory configuration not entirely unlike that between "audience" and "stage," and above all else, out of the eye of the storm, so to speak?[9] If James Cone is right, then the best way to study a sermon is to hear one and to hear it in the customary context of ritual and consecration.[10] In short, I am as aware as Cone that an analysis of sermons not only scandalizes people who grew up "in church," but that an analysis also renders sermons, perhaps, *anti*-sermons, for an exhortation *not* heard becomes something else entirely—maybe. Though we reenact it and though it participates in a material and commercial dimension when subjected to print and the bookseller, how might we now describe its new status? To try and answer those questions, we cannot ask the sermon itself, since its mission has little to do with the mundane. Yet in trying to respond to its contents, both on its own ground and against one's own immediate situation, we are trapped somewhere between the church doors and the library.

We tread a discursive boundary, then, that must be reached by certain elaborately observed mediations, hardly exhausted in this writing: the sermons that I address here are all *written* and preserved in that manner and all of them were preached before the twentieth century. Because the oral/spoken sermon is granted, at the moment, privileged status in African-American life and thought, we must seek a place for the written/spoken documents.[11] An American community that reads itself primarily as "oral" and "musical" and remains in its critical/theoretical disposition divided between "folklore"/"vernacular" on the one hand, and the "literary"/theoretical" on the other is presently called upon to rethink itself. We have yet to examine fully the dramatic encounters of New World Africans as *texts* and the impact of the latter on the cultural development of strangers in a strange land. Ages ago, in this land, the book for the black person was a mysterious (and therefore) precious formula to be known, precisely because his or her captors did not want them to know, and the captors actually enacted anti-literacy laws. In that regard, the "folk" are simply the *thousands* who would immerse themselves in the knowledge of the world, and that would include, we suppose, even those illiterate preachers who learned the Gospel by heart.

The occasion, then, to look at some of the written documents, now transformed from an immediate vocality into a delayed, or muted one, long removed from the literal day and the immediate history of their writing and publication, offers certain advantages. Black American apprentice-culture and its aftermath problematize along different lines of stress, as we must now consider possibilities of the Book—some of the leaves torn out, albeit—as one other shaping (and powerful) metaphor in a situation that has been too long narrated as basically *text-deprived*. The written sermons draw another line of inquiry, intrude another dimension of discursive possibility into our thinking.

Because these sermons were preserved as a writing, they were intended not only for particular congregations, but to be disseminated to a larger audience of readers and students of the sermon. We currently have no information regarding the intellectual habits of consumption for a national black readership, but taking two of the sermons of the Rev. J. W. E. Bowen, for example, we might say that his series of "plain Talks" were meant for the "colored people of America." It is doubtful that these particular documents reached their putative target, or that their influence stretched much wider than the congregation to which they were preached. But certainly for *that* audience, they served an inspirational function as published material. Historiographically, the sermon documents in their preserved state are useful for rather different reasons: they not only shed light on the habits of public discourse evolved by particular communities, but also assert an element of self-consciousness intruded on a form popularly thought of as "spontaneous." The written sermon suggests that *no* sermon is without contrivance, or a considerable degree of forethought. If that is so, then the "folk" sermon is actually misnamed, if by "folk" we mean devised on the spot, or plucked from thin air. Not that a written sermon might not sustain an important element of the extemporaneous, but that the sermon itself, written down, or "remembered" from other sermonic practice, inscribes the self-conscious pursuit of form. The written documents imply a certain class of *readers* who might have been, for the most part, the sermons' hearers. In their overlap, these functions induced, we might imagine, the rise of a religious readership that consumed the popular religious journals of the late nineteenth century and the literature produced by the Sunday School movement of the same era.

IV

In offering the student a community of texts and propositions, the sermons help to sketch a concept of "community" in its various and dynamic transmutations. On closer reading, one perceives that the initial "community" of this paragraph seems settled, while the subsequent one stays open to a kind of crisis. But in truth, all "community" in this writing falls into suspension, and we might inquire if either version does not, in fact, assume its density, in part, by an element of the arbitrary. A "community of texts and propositions" offers one way of avoiding "tradition," which appears to gain dominant ground through notions of the dynastic, the hierarchical, and the prior. But "community" seems to hold out the possibility of intervention, of inclusion. For example, the sermons about which I write here are drawn from a "community" at the fundamental level of data—the material belongs to an alphabetical file, photocopied for scholarly use, and comes from two separate archives, both of them located on the East Coast of the United States. Most of them conform to this geographical region, delivered in eastern cities and towns from North Carolina to Vermont. I would not claim here any master code sermon, though there are masterful documents/performances among them. A different pair of archives, from another part of the country, would soundly intrude upon any conceptual narrative that valorized notions of the "traditional." Though one inevitably privileges one sermon by talking about it and not another, I would much prefer to leave this survey exposed to trends and forces that I have not yet considered, or about which I have no information.

If the possibilities of the survey are virtually endless, we might say that any assertion concerning pieces of it is compromised. The student, however, must be willing to settle for an aspect of an imagined totality, just as one particular thematizing might speak metonymically for the whole that never appears. But is the whole as much a fiction as the part-for-whole in this case? As a totality, or part-for-whole, a "community" of subject-positions is always a partial effect of some putative plenitude. Yet we *need* the fiction of "community" in order to speak at all. I must say that a few of the familiar terms and assumptions of a currently discredited Western metaphysic—primarily, the stability and primacy of a subject-position and the capacity of a text to *mean*—are reclaimed in this writing as (1) an "imitation" of the material that I address; (2) in order to set this configuration of discourse in place for other and different readings; (3) to suggest that in certain places, at this table, for instance, the subject suspects that it lives on. But just as the concept of "community" takes on complications for this writer, it offers different occasions for analytical discourse within the sermons and for those who preach them.

If we think of "community" as the elaboration of a "critical mass" differentiated from others that surround it, then the African-American community in the United Stated becomes at once distinct within the larger field of American culture and distinct from that series of geopolitical moments that constitute its racial, or African, origins. This precisely segmented portion of American cultural content designates what I have identified before as a *hyphenated* national identity divided in the first instance both from its new situation and severed from the old one. We can either read "community" as homogeneous memory and experience, laying claim to a collective voice and rendering an apparently unified and uniform narrative, or we might think of it as a content whose time and meaning are "discovered," but a meaning, in any case, that has not already been decided. In other words, "community," in the latter instance, becomes *potentiality*; an unfolding to be attended. One might go on to say, then, that African-American community articulated in these documents becomes, at times, a systematic elaboration of a particular historical order that one makes up as she or he goes along, with whatever comes to hand and is already at hand; at other times, an invention of the dominant culture (to the extent that the violence of captivity has been imposed on the subject). Needless to say, these processes and positionalities are simultaneous and progressive, inasmuch as "inner" and "outer" converge in this case on the subject. By way of this inquiry, we see more clearly that human culture is both a groping and a given. It is precisely in this paradoxical sense that "community" for African-Americans has been an enablement *and* an accommodation.

As an enabling postulate, the sermons provide a strategy of identity for persons forced to operate under a foreign code of culture; they offer an equipment not only for literacy, but a ground for hermeneutical play in which the subject gains competence in the interpretation and manipulation of systems of signs and their ground of interrelatedness. The "reader" of the culture is involved in the interpretation of both texts and "texts"— those actual densities of social meaning that converge on the terrain of power relations. This latter "reading" takes place "within" and "outside" texts, while it mandates a wider grasp of relationships than a specific reading might call for. In other words, reader-as-captive is confronted with what is spoken and written as well as the immeasurable repertoire of implications and responses ("nowhere" necessarily inscribed, or materialized) out of which the situation of dominance and subordination arises. This reader, then, in participatory readership, is *given* a history at the same time that she or he seeks to fabricate one. (In one notable instance, for example, the domestication of Scripture is achieved as a series of nationalist narratives in which the personae of Genesis "speak" in the "voices" of the preacher.)[12]

The sermons, preached across denominational and doctrinal differences, actually help create the sense of "a people" forged from a background of divergent and originating African families. Against a pattern of radical discontinuity—in every sense, a *rupture* among African languages and "natal communities"[13]—the sermons assert the same story with significant variation: the liberating word that Pennington wishes *his* Bible to speak is none other than the "Good News" of divine force working in the captive situation to free it. Acting coterminously with this program of cultural development, however, is the subversive motion of a narrative "underdevelopment": Christianity, in its ability to stand in for "civilization," "patriarchy," "hierarchy," "enlightenment," "progress, "culture"—a series of lexical items that inaugurate one of the grammars of otherness—renders a text for dominant culture. Since we will spend the better portion of this essay looking at sermons that offer a narrative of "development," we might examine now a couple of instances that intrude on this description.

V

On July 17, 1794, Samuel Magaw delivered the inaugural sermon of the African Church of Philadelphia. In Richard Allen's "Life Experiences," which sketches the early history of what becomes the African Methodist Episcopal Church in the United States, there is no record of this sermon event, nor does Bishop Daniel A. Payne's *History of the African Methodist Episcopal Church* carry a reference to it in Payne's opening chapter.[14] "A Brief History of St. Thomas's Church," appended to Allen's short "Life," does note this sermon in a calendar of church events.[15] Remarkable for its structure of assumptions that both incorporate and eject African personality from the body of Christianity, Magaw's sermon is brilliantly developed around the topos of light and its generative schema. Magaw prays that this congregation will keep a lively remembrance of the mercy that has been proffered to them, for they have been called "out of the darkness of paganism, and the bondage of ignorance and error into the clear light of Gospel Revelation."[16] The sermon offers an exemplary exposition in the use of binary modes. We see in operation not only the play of contrarieties, but a contradiction that takes on teleological status: the fixed otherness, for which the "world" of "pagan" stands and for which African personality and its progeny materialize, situated in natural opposition to Judeo-Christian culture.

These hallowed and hollowed signifieds, or subjects without verbs, so to speak, show essentially no historical movement (just as Hegel, in the nineteenth century, declared for all of the African continent south of Egypt, and for the whole of the Americas with its indigenous populations). Magaw's sermon invites attention to those structures of belief that make it possible to install the African/African-American person on the landscape of social praxis as the very embodiment of anomie, as that almost-human principle that occupies the vestibule of culture—"The people that walked in darkness have seen a great light" (Isaiah 9:2). From one point of view, seeing is not believing, or *seeing* alone falls short of the Promised Land. Yet St. Thomas's congregants, according to Magaw, have been prepared for a total benefi-cence under the rule of Christianity, despite their dark-skinned selves.

To take a different case, we situate Magaw's words in perspective with those of William Miller, from a sermon delivered on the occasion of the abolition of the African slave trade, January 1, 1810, to the African Church of New York:

> I cannot forego the satisfaction of expressing my acknowledgment to my brethren, for having conferred on me the honor of addressing them from the pulpit, on an occasion so auspicious to Africans as the celebration of a day, the contemplation of which is sufficient to inspire the heart of every African with fervent gratitude to the throne of grace, for having directed the councils of our legislature and the parliament of Great Britain, to the consideration of the deplorable and ignomin-ious condition of Africans and their descendants; and in opening a way for their relief, by prohibiting that abominable traffic, the Slave Trade.[17]

Miller goes on to evoke the litany of a great African past, pointing out that the decline and abasement of African peoples were largely initiated by the Moors and exploited by the Europeans. As Miller approaches the closure of the sermon, we encounter those features of semantic attention that would claim this document as an able candidate for a confounded or complicated reading. In other words, "Africa" in this sermon marks a site of degradation at the same time that Miller embraces it as a point of cultural origin. In fact, Miller appears to approach the sociopolitical sensibilities of the Black Na-tionalist movement of the 1960s in imagining "Africa" in continuity with African-Americans in the Diaspora. "Our *improved* state in the arts" implies a "before" and "after" that link continental African culture and the current situation of African-Americans to the same spatiotemporal modality.

As a step toward "raising" the Africans, he would have it, Sierra Leone was carved out of the West Africa Coast by Great Britain in 1789, and num-bers of missionaries sent there "for the identical purposes of civilizing and improving the continent." Then, says Miller, "although we cannot, consis-tent with our feelings, thank the oppressors of our forefathers for bringing them to the civilized world, yet when we compare our improved state in the arts to the state of improvement and civilization in Africa, we are ready to cry to God, individually, like David, 'It is good for me that I have been af-flicted, that I may learn thy statutes, the law of thy mouth is better unto me than thousands of pure gold and silver.'"[18]

Showing no equivalence to a contemporary sensibility and self-conscious-ness that delight in the "undecidability" of the current order of things, from literary historiography, to gender and sexual positionalities, Miller's address poses its own embarrassment of riches. Situated in an abeyance of closure, Miller appears to speak out of both sides of his mouth, and it seems that this double-speaking precisely characterizes African-American appren-tice-culture and its latter-day manifestations. Miller is not alone in the use of certain major figures of thought available to him regarding continental Africans in their autochthonous cultural enterprise. Alongside Miller's ser-mon, we could place Jupiter Hammon's *Winter Piece* and some of Phillis Wheatley's shorter poems from the same era of writing and history in the mid-to-late eighteenth century.[19]

Yet to dismiss these writings as inadequate political response would generate, in turn, its own critical inadequacy. We are called upon instead to try to grasp more completely the "Rule of Gospel Order" in the life of an un-folding national purpose, whose religious impulse tends toward the enthu-siastic. "The intense emphasis upon conversion," Albert Raboteau argues,

> the primary characteristic of evangelical, revivalistic Protestantism,
> tended to level all men before God as sinners in need of salvation. This
> tendency opened the way for black converts to participate actively in
> the religious culture of the new nation as exhorters, preachers, and
> even founders of churches, and created occasions of mutual religious
> influence across racial boundaries whereby blacks converted whites
> and whites converted blacks in the heat of revival fervor.[20]

The charismatic itinerancy of England's Methodist preachers—among them, George Whitefield, the subject of address of one of Phillis Wheatley's eulogies—provides an impetus to revivalistic religion in the pre-Revolu-tionary colonies of North America.[21] But as vulnerable as the captive com-munity was to the will of its captors, there was no sparing its members from the influences—for good or ill—of a democratic religious force. Historians point out that the Great Awakening of the mid-eighteenth century demar-cates one of four crucial stages in the Christianizing of Africans.[22]

We observe that the period engendered its own paradoxes: as the free community contemplated its own liberational project, the captive com-munity became immured in its condition, as the slave codes of various southern states assured that conversion and manumission were not syn-onymous. It must be true, however, that the "Rule of Gospel Order" became the flaming sword that cut two ways. If the captive could make the Gospel "speak" his or her own state, then the subversion of dominance was entirely possible. So powerful a force must therefore reduce the world to a single human order. Read from this perspective, an "unchristian" Africa lost its use for the captive person, now freed by the Single and Singular Truth. Even though the erasure of ethnicity from its capital place in social configuration strikes the contemporary mind as a blunder, we recognize that the impact of race conceals the profound question of culture. By 1794, the year of Magaw's address to the Philadelphia church; by 1810, the year of William Miller's schizophrenic embrace and denial of Africa, the black person in the United States is already adrift between two vast continents, both in his body and brain.

Because a contemporary audience has no ready analogy with which to gauge the impact of kerygmatic religion, the worldview purported by certain of these sermons appears alien, and perhaps "ambivalence," as the controlling metaphor of my own conceptual narrative, is nothing more than a different term for emotional distance. But if by ambivalence we might mean that abeyance of closure, or *break* in the passage of syntagmatic movement from one more or less stable property to another, as in the radical disjuncture between "African" and "American," then ambivalence remains not only the privileged and arbitrary judgment of a postmodernist imperative, but also a strategy that names the new cultural situation as a *wounding*. We recall the undeniable catachresis buried in "African Methodist Episcopal Church" itself, for example, as historic and narrative cross-purposes elide into an imagined unity of religious organization and praxis.

VI

Because Christianity identifies the cultural ground upon which one stands and for that reason, precisely, is not always immediately visible, we might assume that the crisis of faith has no particular efficacy in this analysis, but how it is possible, or is it possible, to bracket belief in reference to a structure of human attention that looks back, ultimately, to the primary text of Judeo-Christian synthesis? To questions that might best be negotiated by sacred theology and the vastly empowered patriarchal traditions of hermeneutics and interpretation, reverting, in turn, to the first post-Christian centuries and the canonical urgencies to establish the right texts and ground for legitimation?[23] The response that I would sketch to this self-inquiry scatters in different directions. (1) If one accepts the posture of critical insurgency, then the contradictions of *speaking through* the alien and foreign notation are visibly raised; (2) but the posture of a critical insurgency must be achieved. It cannot be assumed. Essentially, the test of belief that is crucial to our purposes here has less to do with the Word of God, or words pertaining to God, than with the words and texts of human community in their liberational and enslaving power, refracted in the Gospel. We stand here. Without doubt, the Good News that the New World African understood and preached, in its radical *this-worldliness,* speaks to us in ways that we had not anticipated, and that is to say, that the words and texts of human encounter, of which the Gospel provides an Ur-text, render the most powerful and dangerous "making" that we can imagine. The insurgent critical activity acting upon that encounter becomes the very Gospel reenacted both in its transformative potential and as it actually arises in the inclusionary praxis of an altered social scene. Is it too much to say that the African could not *but* have become Christian in the sociopolitical context of the United States, as a *strategy* for gaining her historical ground and humanation here? And is the preacher and the sermon the first-run event of an African *critical* subject-position in such a context? These questions loom before us in an investigation that straddles this (our current situation in the world) and that (the ever-deferred perfections of a becoming). Between worlds stands the sermon. With both feet planted in the actual mess of human being, the sermon would convince the chicken that it is an eagle.

In trying to find a way, over time, to address this often familiar material now made alien by our own habits of language and current critical practices, one decides that the sermon reenacts a ritual and necessary fable, a fable whose actants and end are already known. An aspect of the sermon's miracle is that its audience already knows that there are no suspended or ironic conclusions to the tales that sermons project. In fact, there is only *one* sermonic conclusion, and that is the ultimate triumph over defeat and death that the Resurrection promises. In this case, the processes of hearing/reading lose their character of uncertainty in the Single Surprise that matters. I would go so far as to say that this rewarded anticipation of an outcome is the most prominent feature of temperament in a reading/auditory variable that distinguishes an African-American readership from other constituent reading communities trained in and on the economies of irony. It is important to add that these communities of readers are often interchangeable; they do not stay fixed. The sermon itself has formal success only to the extent that the preacher knows that his or her "readers" *choose* to agree with the sermon "contract"—to obey the rules of listenership that obtain in the situation.

One of those "rules" of behavior would suggest to the reader/hearer that the sermon's repetitive character does nothing to mitigate the suspenseful eschatology that the Gospels inscribe concerning the life, career, and death of Jesus Christ. The annual Protestant sermons of the Christmas and Easter rituals, for example, in their insistence on mercy and forgiveness, do not suffer because the hearer knows the story both "by heart" and by the Book, but appear to gain prestige for the narratives they tell by way of this process. To say the same thing over and over again not only induces a headache of conviction, but creates a *fellowship* of belief. The ritual narrative in this way bears an element of infection; everyone is compelled toward the same story.

Roland Barthes called the revelation of an already anticipated subject and outcome the "hermeneutic narrative." He wrote: "Just as any grammar, however new, once it is based on the dyad of subject and predicate, noun and verb, can only be a historical grammar, linked to classical metaphysics, so the hermeneutic narrative, in which truth predicates an incomplete subject, based on expectation of and desire for its imminent closure, *is dated*, linked to the kerygmatic civilization of meaning and truth, appeal and fulfillment."[24] The sermons addressed here inscribe an incomparable "hermeneutic narrative," and it would appear that they succeed precisely because they project an incomplete subject, engendered in the expectation of and desire for the imaginably blissful end of truth. But as *dated* as the narrative process is, and moreover, as "unprogressive" as the relevant reading sensibilities are, the "hermeneutic narrative" for the sermon's "readers" matches—perfectly—the "end" of the world; in the black community, this is Freedom, and the beginning.

To say that these sermons exert a pull on the hearer is to reassert what we already know, but the dynamics of this exertion remain somewhat unclear. No narrative genre appears to depend so solidly upon the cooperative agency at work in others. The sermon seeks to *inculcate* its words; to make them enter the hearer, and this would account for the rhetorical tenacity of the form, as we will see shortly in two of J. W. E. Bowen's performances. The sermon's rhetoric of admonition appears to behave on a contrastive analogy with dramatic form. Whereas the latter marks a verbalization through a material scene, a sermon inscribes a verbalization that substitutes "hearer" for "stage." To that extent the "scene" of the sermon opens onto an interior space, and here it seeks to enact and reenact its narrative urgencies against an invisible scenic apparatus. In the interior of the listener, doubt is subjected to severe criticism, as the sermon is grounded, without apology, in the conviction of human error. In the interior space, a repertoire of feeling is aroused to heightened consciousness. Though the sermon embodies a particular form, its primary function may well be transcultural, subject to a number of narrative and thematic variations, for it is public discourse, ideologically sanitized, it would seem, that cannot execute its program without a hearer, in this case, a "reader."

Even though the confrontation with the small, helpless self is accomplished in the Protestant sermon of the insurgent through the rhetoric of admonition, the confrontation itself becomes enabling, because the relationship between pulpit and parishioner has shifted: *both* subject-positions now occupy a common ground of inquiry, a common ground of suffering.

In order to demonstrate how certain black sermons call forth the interpretive project as it points both toward this world and the transcendent human possibility, I would like to look closely at two sermons from the Reverend J. W. E. Bowen's "What Shall the Harvest Be?" Even though I have examined these texts as if they were literary documents, I have also attempted to situate my own hearing, first of all, within the imagined context of the particular setting of the church and, second, within the immediate history of the climate in which these sermons were rendered. What one loses as a participant on the spot one gains after the fact. As a writing, Bowen's sermons offer a remarkable analogy and reading of *history as process,* in specific reference to African-Americans. As spoken address, they are not recoverable to a listening ear, except that I have "repeated" them according to the dictates of my own readerly responses. In other words, Bowen's "voice" and "personality" are none other than a current articulation for the strategies of a specific cultural management. On balance, the net result for different audiences, far removed in time and circumstance, might be amazingly similar; a certain reading/hearing of history ordains *struggle,* or *movement* as the key text of human community in general and African-American community in particular.

These sermons provide a demonstration of the rhetoric of admonition; but they also suggest, as a result, how the symptoms of "hermeneutic narrative" bring its lost, wounded subject into view. Moving on down the line, Bowen anticipates the future as he comprehends past and present in a narrative sweep that explains the inexplicable. Is it not at least ironic, if not altogether devastating, that the Christian witness, insinuating itself throughout the colonial experience and parallel to the captivity and enslavement of millions of Africans in the New World, not only attracted the religious loyalties of much of that captive population, but also described the primary discourse of its radically altered historic situation? Operating under a vivid fiction of the "powers of presence," these sermons *make it all right.*[25] But isn't *that* the trouble, that we must become reconciled to death? In the closing sections of this essay, I will attempt to provide a systematic reading of Bowen's response.

VII

William J. Simmons's *Men of Mark: Eminent, Progressive, and Rising* was published in 1887 and carried some 1,300 biographical entries, which provided, in Ernest Kaiser's words, "a much needed dictionary of Negro biography . . . of nearly all of the great and near great Negro men of history."[26] This work was published in Bowen's thirty-second year, at which time he was preaching in Newark, New Jersey, but *Men of Mark* makes no note of him. We can only guess, then, how Bowen might have been characterized in the hortatory rhetoric of Simmons's late-century prose. It is important to observe that even though death interrupted the biographer's plan to make a comparable volume of black American women, both Simmons and Bowen conceive of history as a grand affair of men. From this point of view, a race, a people must think its way back through the *fathers*, if they will claim their rightful human place. This version of history becomes less odd, once we contemplate it in the light of the African-American male's peculiar status in a decidedly phallocentric, slave-holding America: for all intents and purposes, *banished* (not absent) from their issue, African-American males were moved to make themselves twice over—once, with regard to female and family, whom they are theoretically obligated to protect, and again, in light of the phallic economies of naming and empowerment by which standard they are measured, *qua* male. It is probably no simple sexist maneuver (if any such gesture can ever be called merely simple) that drives a William Simmons to collect information *first* on black American men, which would exhaust volumes on today's market,[27] or a J. W. E. Bowen to found his narratives of history on a reconstituted, reconstructed male subject. We might say that men of their class, of their generation, did the right thing for the wrong reasons, or the wrong thing for reasons that seemed right to them, given the cultural imperatives of high heterosexism under which they operated.[28] In other words, I am prepared for Bowen's "problem" with the pronouns and the man-noun and would consider this problematic fit for another study.

Cornel West's impressive work on the points of intersection between aspects of revolutionary Christianity and Marxist thought would help us place Bowen's ministry. West identifies four distinct phases of "black prophetic theology" in the United States. His second stage, designated the "Black Theology of Liberation as Critique of Institutional Racism," covers the period 1864–1969, which embraces Bowen's years. Occupying a little over a century, West's second movement comprehends the careers, also, of Francis L. Grimké, Howard Thurman, and Martin Luther King Jr., among others. Because Martin Luther King won renewed respect for the national black clerical community, these years are among the most crucial of West's outline. The period "found black prophetic Christians principally focusing attention on the racist institutional structures in the United States which rendered the majority of black people politically powerless (deprived of the right to vote or participate in governmental affairs), economically exploited (in dependent positions as sharecroppers or in unskilled jobs), and socially degraded (separate, segregated and unequal eating and recreational facilities, housing, education, transportation, and police protection)."[29] It is against this background of social and political deprivation that the African-American pulpit of these years becomes, in certain notable instances, a different version of the church militant.

We recall that 1892, for example, the year that Bowen preached these sermons to the members of his congregation at Washington, D.C.'s Asbury Methodist Episcopal Church, is not very far removed from 1878 and the congressional compromise that brought to closure the Union's military occupation of the Old Confederacy and generated the entire configuration of backlash that would essentially revoke Fifteenth Amendment rights and other constitutional guarantees granted to the newly emancipated. Out of this violent turnaround which modulated into the southern "Reign of Terror," in the awful, new specter of the Klansman's robe and lynching rope, much of contemporary United States history is engendered. It is safe to say that the pulpit of the 1890s and the turn of the century—whose merciful God was evoked to bear witness against the invidious protocol of racist doctrine, pursued by the national press and excoriated in the sermons of D.C.'s Francis Grimké—was embattled in every sense by the social and political ecologies in which the Church Insurgent is situated.[30]

The 1928–29 edition of *Who's Who in Colored America* records Bowen's December 1855 birth in New Orleans.[31] Some five degrees were conferred on him, including the Doctors of Philosophy and Divinity, both from the Gammon Theological Seminary (now absorbed into Atlanta's Interdenominational Theological Center). A teacher of remarkable versatility, the Rev. Bowen also served Gammon in top administrative posts between the late 1890s and the late 1920s. Writer and editor, Bowen became a prominent figure of the official establishment of the Methodist Episcopal Church. According to Carter G. Woodson, Bowen missed election to the regular bishopric of the church by a hair.[32] Into this recorded eminence, John Hope Franklin intrudes a note of terror: during the month of September 1906, one of the most sensational race riots in the country occurred in Atlanta. On the riot's second day, "Dr. J. W. E. Bowen, the president of Gammon, was beaten over the head with a rifle butt by a police official."[33]

Years earlier, Bowen was ministering to the congregants of Asbury Methodist Episcopal Church, and during the months of January and February 1892 he delivered the series of sermons that his Official Board would request him to disseminate: "Resolved: That the Official Board heartily endorse and unanimously approve of the ideas expressed by our pastor . . . in the series of sermons entitled 'What Shall the Harvest Be?' delivered in our Church during the past four weeks; and we unite in requesting him to publish the same pamphlet form for distribution with the conviction that a general reading of the same will produce a healthful moral effect upon us as a people."[34]

Sermonic form in general is not shy, nor does it believe that ego-particularity matters very much. In the case of the African-American pulpit, the Gospel remains the greatest glory of a democratic governance, and vice versa. The sermon invests in the fundamental belief that the Gospel and democracy are complementary forces and that a message emphatically delivered actually generates conviction. In the case of Bowen's sermons, his parishioners, at least, equate "healthful moral effect," assertive speaking, and the unitarian appeal of a free peoplehood. The notion that once "the people" read these sermons they will be changed reinforces the sense of urgency out of which the texts come.

Many of the written sermons of African-American preachers found their way to print and a wider public because their audience first made the request.[35] We might assume, however, that the minister spoke, in the initial instance, from a text already prepared, as Coretta Scott King observed about her husband's celebrated address, "I Have a Dream," delivered at Lincoln's Memorial in 1963.[36] Because the sermon appears to "think" itself as "message," its seams cannot show. In other words, the sermon is successful to the extent that it conceals its efforts to *be* a text. This is appropriate behavior for words that proffer themselves as a divine prosthesis and as the crucial strong words in the formal history of a people. Because we now have the capacity, as in King's case, to compare a written text with the electronically recorded one, we can better conjecture the play of mediation between the premeditated word and the extemporaneous tongue that literally "arises," unexpectedly, on the cutting edge of the hot, crowded, public event. In Bowen's case, the stutters, the halting, the play and plasticity of the human face "in motion" with its speaking, the peculiar dynamics of the voice in occasional "forgetfulness" of the paragraph in front of it, have been excised from the page; no meddling and meticulous editorial hand, of either the preacher, or any of the auditory, has left its mark.

In response to his board's request, Bowen assumes a typical pose of theatrical modesty, publicly witnessed, as the "disclaimer" marks out its own discursive ground: "The writer of these sermons makes no such pretentious claim as to have sounded the depths or to have given the final word upon the vital questions herein touched upon. All that can be claimed is that they are the honest convictions of an honest student of history and of the affairs of men, delivered for the good of the race" (12). As we have observed before, this modulation of a theological praxis into a key of social and political militance effects common ground between the ministries of such figures as J. W. E. Bowen and Martin Luther King more than fifty years later. More precisely, we might argue that the already political and historic matrix of theological discourse and practice is clearly revealed at certain points of spatiotemporal impression. Bowen makes his own intentions quite clear: "I call particular attention to the 'Manhood Problem' as the one that takes priority in importance and consideration. I also refer to what is popularly known as the 'Negro Problem,' and to its all-comprehending feature. 'Political Equality,' as secondary and as existing only because the first and great problem remains unsolved. I believe that the solution of the first will dissipate the second as the sun scatters the morning dew" (12–13).[37]

Clearly, Bowen alludes in the "Preface" to the necessity for a systematic ontological dimension concerning the life and thought of African-Americans, but it is not until W. E. B. DuBois writes his *Souls of Black Folk* (1903) that the question of manhood acquires a radically different formulation. The DuBoisian "double-consciousness," with its Hegelian overtones, proposes at once a paradigm shift and a different discursive code through which "colored," "Negro," "black" might be restated. With DuBois, "black," as a preeminent situation of culture, gains contemplative status that will be elaborated some decades later in the stunning fictional project of Ralph Ellison's *Invisible Man*. In the absence of an epistemic formula that might have provided a more adequate reading of the problematics of culture and society, Bowen, near the turn of the century, dramatically offers, nonetheless, the critical content of an agonistic and "hermeneutic" narrative that re-visions human society by way of African-American personality. We might restate Bowen's interrogation along the lines of analogy: if Hegel wished to make philosophy "speak German," then Bowen, in these sermons, projects the processes of humanization as they "speak" and iconize as "black." He narrates the fundamental human rhythm, as we have already observed, as a movement of the spirit through history, metaphorically configured as a progression from "darkness" to "light." Inasmuch as every human community must negotiate this motion, African-Americans are enjoined to confront their future as an inevitable overcoming. But in the structure of "What Shall the Harvest Be?" this motion *toward* . . . is dramatically focused as "struggle."

Bowen's idea of historic movement in struggle is explored systematically in the second sermon of the series, "The Disciplinary Character of Affliction," wherein he asserts for "discipline" and "punishment" the "iron hand of law" that brings a nation or race to maturity. Passing through successive periods of growth, a nation or race, like man, like *a* man, "must subject itself to the discipline peculiar to the periods, each in its order, that it may become a fit heir to the blessings and fruits of the following, and in order that it may realize the possibilities of each to its fullest extent" (33). The law must be "engraved" upon the conscience, just as "violence, unrestraint, sensuality, and disrespect for law must be beaten out of the racial system with the iron hand of law" (34). A race, in order to reach this high conception of law, "requires many years of discipline and years of affliction." This disciplinary regime prepared the Puritan nation for July 4, 1776, and January 1, 1863, "the mightiest days in the Christian calendar since the birth of Christ." Without its "afflictions, trials, wars, defeats, deaths, and successes, and withal its juridical morality," the "full realization of its majority among the nations of the world" could not have been accomplished (35–36).

Bowen not only has before him the rise of the United States and the ancient history of Israel, attested by Scripture, but also intimations of a great African past, whose legendary script is invoked in the opening sermon of this four-part series. Both the "Negro Problem" and the "Manhood Problem" are linked, through a series of mediating questions, to a narrative of the "fallen" continent/man. Against this interrogation, interlocking several parts—"whether the Negro will vindicate for himself a right to stand among the thinking nations of the world, and to claim citizenship by contributing to the thoughtful and material products of civilization in the republic of thought" (23)—Bowen infers a *counternarrative* that leans on the American Negro's regaining his "pristine position in arts and sciences, in literature and history, in architecture and philosophy; the position that he held in his original home: whether he will come back to the heights from which he had fallen; to a civilization second only to this Christian civilization in that it lacked the touch of a divine afflatus" (23–24).

This swerve off the trajectory of culture development, which, for Bowen, culminates in the plight of the American Negro, makes for no simple rupture. It has exploded, in fact, an originating continuity:

> For, be it remembered, that in his original home there reigned once "all the pomp and magnificence of oriental splendor; that the grandest

ruins of antiquity are here; that architecture has here been carried to a perfection which baffled the skill of modern artisans; that here flourished large and beautiful cities filled with literary, military and commercial men; that Europe is indebted to Africa for letters and arts; that Greece even traces her civilization to Egypt; and that while all Europe was covered with gross darkness, Africa was radiant with science and literature. Astronomy was taught in African schools before Germany had heard of a schoolhouse. Africans were clothed in purple and dwelt in palaces when Englishmen covered themselves with skins of wild beasts and crawled into low mud huts nothing superior to those now occupied by the Kaffirs and Hottentots." This is the second or manhood problem, and I ask what people under the sun has its equal? (23–24)

This text of history, covered over now by the radically altered situation of the African in the New World, belongs, astonishingly, to the past and the future. It is past-oriented in the procession of past/past-progressive tense verbs that crowd the quoted passage of the citation; the adverbial marker, "once," the distinguishing "not now" of the fairy tale, clearly evinces a reversal of script in the current one out of which Bowen's address gains efficacy. But this spectacular narrative orients also toward the future, belonging to the "golden age . . . before us, somewhere in the dim tracery of the future" (18). "Upon the shoulders of [this] past," Bowen and congregants stand to gain the capacity to "detect and depict, in the gray dawn of the new morning," events to come (but now *repeated*) and "to read between the lines the story of the age" (22).

To "augur" is "reading" deeply, as Bowen, in the hortative mood—"let us stand"—mandates the visionary and the literate response. In this moving overlap of a double-seeing, the American Negro, the African-American "reads" what his or her culture has made "dim" and what they can barely detect between the lines of script that "come up" into view. It is this making the text plain in this series of "plain talks" that Bowen addresses in these sermons.

Bowen's found *and* made text participates in opposing realities, but those realities are antipathetic, in his view, because human society remains intransigent to providential will, made plain in the Scripture. Though divine order has already written the answer to the "Manhood Problem" and the "Negro Problem," by implication, the race itself must bring it to bear. Two propositions obtain here. On the one hand, Bowen asserts that "God has hidden somewhere in the unrevealed future the solution of all these problems which so vex and disturb us today" (26). On the other hand, a people "that would be free must strike the first blow: and this race, if it is to be counted, must resolutely set itself to the answering of the question, What shall *we* do for ourselves? It must give up the unreasonable and unhistorical basis of expecting to have its future made for it, and begin with might and main to write its own history and make its own future" (27–28, Bowen's emphasis).

"Writing" and "Making," as different aspects of the same visionary moment, are literally and figuratively determined. But these processes of making are not at all polite activity, nor must we assume that the rule of kindness oversees their production. Writing the collective self into history belongs to the offices of affliction, as Bowen would see it, and even though we might use a different vocabulary for the agonistic now, we understand the same thing in reference to it that Bowen understood—no human community is admitted to fellowship, or the essential right to self-determination, without undergoing the ways and means of confrontational violence.

If African-Americans have been taught anything under the regimes of New World domination, it adheres in the very close analogy between dominant behavior and the shape of the information in which it is conveyed.[38] If I am captive and under dominance, there can be no doubt of this reading in the woundings and rendings of my flesh. As African-Americans read their own history in the United States, the *wounded, divided* flesh opens itself to a metaphorical rendering both for the principle of self-determination and as a figurative economy for its peculiar national encounter. In other words, one seeks an adequate expression of equivalence, in "reading" the culture, between the situation of captivity and its violent markings. The *imprint* of words articulates with "inscriptions" made on the material body, so that an actual "reading" of captivity brings us to consider those changes in the very tissue-life of the organism; to consider those differences of nuance inflicted on individual and collective identities, which help create the American regime of difference that only the Gospel, from a certain perspective, can reconcile or satisfy. We do not wonder, then, that the narratives of ancient Israel shadow Bowen's sermons, nor are we surprised that the narratives, specifically, of the wonderful deliverance of the Jews from their Egyptian overlords, yield a central metaphor of African-American religious expression. Though "Old Pharaoh" is situated in a specific historical sequence, "Old Pharaoh"—metaphorically—has the power to come again. This repetitive potential underscores Bowen's vision of history and the figures of an instrumental, cleansing violence that bolster it.

The procession of suffering configured in Bowen's narrative marks the human scene as fateful movement. At the same time, we are bound to an outcome that is both known and delayed: "The sorrowful chapter of our afflictions, when held up before the light of Revelation, reveals between the lines the grand story of the divine purpose" (23). This intersticial narrative—read in an interface between the given text of the apocalyptic vision and the unwritten texts of future, ordained by it—becomes precisely the "invisible" line that the collective must make manifest; must "practice," must "write" into history as its own powerful tale of human freedom. *This* speaker and his hearers/readers now embody the content of a different narrative that would make positively distinct the *African* element of an American identity. At the same time "human"/"humanity" is now read in the light of "African-American." As an unexplored narrative resource, black personality elaborates human freedom as a single chapter of transition between the beginning and the end.

"The Disciplinary Character of Affliction," the second sermon in the series, not only provides the high point, but also distinguishes itself as a testing ground for Bowen's gifts. Energized by the tensions of this particular moment in the cultural career of black Americans and called upon to display the full range of sermonic mastery for which his own career has prepared him, Bowen reaches towards the forceful culmination that will urgently declare the meaning and import of his ministry. He pleads, he prays, he urges, he hopes, he knows, in a supreme agitation of feeling that conveys its message the long distance between an immediate history and the present. We read this climactic movement in three parts:

(1) It seems to be in the very constitution of affairs that affliction is necessary to bring out our virtues. All races before us that have made a history worth reading, have had to suffer and to write it with the crimson ink that came from their veins. The Asiatic nations of ancient history and the European nations, likewise, all have been obligated to pass through the fires of affliction, discipline and punishment to purify their gold. (39)

(2) I am a strong believer in the future destiny of greatness for my people, I believe that God has kept hid from us all, what he has in store for us; and that in the future, when the race shall have been purged in the furnace of afflictions, and its virtues shall sparkle like burnished silver; when it shall reveal the elements of character that God can trust; and when it shall have divested itself of the filthy rags of that black civilization, whose noxious stench is an offense in the nostrils of God and of good men; yea, a thousand times, when the carcasses of those who have come up from the land of slavery, and upon which may be found the marks of the curse, and even when this present generation, so

worthless, helpless, and godless in so many cases, have all rotted in the wilderness of forgetfulness, and a new generation shall spring forth whose feet shall catch the first rays of yon rising sun, and whose God shall be the "Lord of Lords and King of Kings"; then, and not till then, will the crown of honor, glory, power, and victory adorn his sable brow. (43–44)

(3) I repeat, my hope is fixed. And standing upon the top of this present Mt. Nebo, and letting my eyes sweep through the dark past up along the shores of the river we have crossed, and now into the wilderness with our churches, school-houses, trade schools, and various Christian and civilizing agencies; with faith in God, I am certain that I see, through the thick darkness that envelops us, the gray rays of a new morn, and I hear the tramp of a new civilization and the music of its *avant-courier* joyfully shouting; "There's a good time coming, boys, a good time coming."

And rising in my meditations upon the afflictions of my fathers that made them groan, I hear the united voice of all nations that have preceded us as the voice of many waters, saying: "For our light affliction, which is but for a moment, worketh out for us a far more exceeding and eternal weight of glory." And rising still higher, I listen again, and the voice of prophecy rings with the distinctness of a clarion note and with the sweetness of an angelic harp and the melody of a heavenly lyre; "Though thou hast lain among the pots, yet shall ye be as the wings of a dove covered with silver and her feathers with yellow gold." (46–47)

The power of delay, achieved in the second passage by impacted modification and the parallelism of noun and number, is appropriate to the conflated sense of time that the speaking assumes. "When . . . Then," in rapid movement through violent change in the corporate body, is nearly subjunctive, except that the insistence of the future/future-progressive tense slides it into decree. It is the language of the public document (the courts of civil and criminal law); the oracular pronouncement (Lincoln at Gettysburg); the reverberative prohibition, spoken (the fiery speech of the Ten Commandments), not mindful of locale or weather, and above all else, it is the discourse of primary certainty that banishes all doubt to the realm of the inconsequential: "But they that wait upon the Lord shall renew their strength; they shall mount up with wings as eagles; they shall run, and not be weary; and they shall walk, and not faint." The Baptist songbook, in a clerical organization even less hieratic than Bowen's Methodist Episcopal Church, extends Isaiah to read, therefore, "teach us, Lord, teach us, Lord, how to wait." Hearing through a kind of palimpsest of voices, the female hearer/reader, in a turmoil of alternatives, eventually recognizes that the tongue, in the general, in this specific, instance, "belongs" to Father.[39] The power of enunciation and decree assimilates to the phallic mightiness. But Bowen is also black; knows that the "carcasses . . . from the land of slavery" and the "marks of the curse" are not only metaphorical, but a corporeality turned back upon its tropic possibilities with a vengeance. Brought to a common coronation—"the crown of honor, glory, power and victory [upon] his sable brow"—what is the common ground of the discretely embodied sexualities between speaker and hearer/reader within a shared historic destiny that has stripped gender distinctions just about down to nil?

In this third passage, "I see . . . I hear" invite momentary confusion, compete for equal time in a strained figurative move that would comprehend—as in an Adamic vision—what is past and what is to come. But the power of the gaze relinquishes to the ear, and could it be said in this case that "we encounter in awe the transcendent attentive breath moving upon the surface of the waters"?[40] The posture of *waiting*—profoundly associated with the female—that the sixties generation of political activists and scholars generally regarded as inappropriate passiveness in the face of danger assumes here an entirely different thrust. The listening, the waiting to which Bowen refers are *meditative,* a term that shows root kinship with *medicine*—having to do with notions of thinking about, caring for, curing. From this angle, hearing, listening, waiting, meditating give way to a deep height, if we could say so, of activity omnipresent in its "everywhereness." But it becomes the empowered seeing of the blind one, or more precisely, the Pauline situation of "faith"—the "substance of things *hoped for,* the evidence of things *not* seen." Even though from our current point of view the sciences of medicine designate a more or less apodictic certainty, the profession seems to adhere—in its deepest motivations—to the optimism of the cure, the stochastic game of healing. The "Doctor of Philosophy" *waits* as long as the "Doctor of Medicine," but Bowen occupies the midst of an overlapping ground that conflates these social tasks. "Rising in [his] meditations upon the afflictions of his fathers that made them groan," he is quickened by the mother's powerful hearing, the philosopher's "concernful care" that opens him, in effect, to a *pregnancy of attentiveness.* We are signaled, in turn: *this man,* in *caring for* his kin, the literally wounded ones, takes upon himself the "letterings," the "writings" of the dismembered.

In the context of domination, African-Americans, in the split between "homes," inhabit the subject-position whose corporate body is shattered between worlds. In the first excerpt from Bowen's ending, these rifts on the surface of the body situate in general and specific figurative reference: "All races before us" in the making of a "history worth *reading*" have had to write it "with the crimson ink that came from their veins." But this "writing of the flesh" is inscribed—"engraved" is Bowen's word—on a physical/material actuality that throws meditation on the image into confusion, even resistance, as the metaphor dissolves on the very ground of its concatenation. About fifty years before Bowen's address, Frederick Douglass laid hold of a terrible juncture—elements in a syncretic fusion *meet* with the body's wreck and the autobiographical topic that has enabled its saying. Douglass wrote, "My feet have been so cracked with the frost that the pen with which I am writing might be laid in the gashes."[41]

If we think of the cultural situation of African-Americans as a wounding, or a writing in [the] blood, the ground of such conjecture traces back to those branded and marked bodies that Bowen "remembers." In meditating on the breaking point, Bowen, as well as other preachers and caretakers, whose address, in various forms, compels attention, arrives at the place where others have stood. At this place of fracture, we listen attentively for the moving line that is made articulate to living. In this case, the sermonic word does not soar; it does not leap, it never leaves the ground. It *scatters* instead through the cultural situation and, like the force of gravity, holds us fast to the mortal means. Bound to this earth by the historical particularity of the body's wounding, the community comes face to face with the very limit of identity—the indomitable, irremediable otherness of death, metaphorized, in this instance, by the institution of slavery. But this apparent fatality, in binding speakers and hearers/readers to the material situation, quickens us all the more to the radicalizing move. It seems to me that it is the role of the sermon to replay not only *this* narrative, but its *outcome* on the other side of disaster, as Bowen's "good time coming" would have us believe. Against this single passion—to repeat, to remember—the narratives of African-American history and becoming are read and interpreted.

Black, White, and in Color, or Learning How to Paint: Toward an Intramural Protocol of Reading

I

In a footnote in response to highly contested passages from Paule Marshall's *Chosen Place, Timeless People*,[1] I discuss "an epistemological ground for locating centers of interpretation." The central query here is not only if Marshall's work might be read in some of its lights as "homophobic," but also how the latter criticism is muted, or assumes a different perspective, if the ideology and practice of race are thrown into the mix. From the vantage of power relations, wherein race admittedly situates, the claims of "homophobia" on this novel are both misleading and inadequate. If we are right to look for the "science of a general economy of practices,"[2] then no single aspect/event of the socionom (the web of identity) can be perfectly isolated, nor can it occupy, from its local and particular site, the sovereign position. The ground for locating competing interpretive interests—Barbara Herrnstein Smith calls them "communities"[3]—for placing them in relation to one another is made up of one's leanings and inclinations toward one system, or logics of representation, and not another. This much must be admitted. It seems to me that the repertoire of isolated strands of subject-effect, which characterize our current critical inquiries, are interpenetrating and incontrovertible and that they are at play, first and last, in the realm of history and its key moments of power relations. One might attempt to forge, realizing this, a "critical pertinence" that would mobilize, at least implicitly, its own ideological biases, perhaps even *use* them, that would recognize the play of contradiction and difference as an aspect of her own critical project. What we posit as a "thereness" in any given surface of a text is as much one's conjuring with her own social positionality, as it is with a repertory of practices designated "author." The rupture of certainty, of the "colonization" of discourses by a mighty and irrevocable gesture of appropriation, is the promise of a fairly new reader's tale, the outcome of which cannot be anticipated. But this jamming of the expectations, we grow accustomed to think, constitutes an intervention that could render the new attitude *serviceable,* I would dare say, to what we might think of as an "intramural protocol of reading," how to see, really, when what you're looking at is perceived to be some of your own stuff—a subject history, a historical subjectivity. Or, to put the matter somewhat differently, how do "look alikes" behave toward one another?

Marshall's *Chosen Place, Timeless People* systematized a response, and how I think it is done lends focus to this essay. The conflated allusion of my title to film[4] and to painting offers a visual metaphor: one would try to negotiate, across a plurality of seeing, numerous, and subtle coordinations, as if pieces of identity as different from each other as the nerve endings of the fingers and the sense of aspiration and desire were all groping toward an exercise of attention and memory as precise as the mathematical. Heaven forbid that the reader/critic must now learn to paint and do numbers, but the protocol of reading that I would imagine is now called upon to disabuse us of the unacknowledged tyrannies of our own involvement in dominative forms. "Black," "white," and "in color" are precisely the figurative stops that I would engage in arriving at an adequate examination of a different interpretive practice for an African-American readership in particular.

In preparing to reread moments of Marshall's novel[5] and attempt another writing concerning it, I was especially interested in Roland Barthes's *S/Z* and its five codes of reading: the hermeneutic, semic, symbolic, proairetic, and cultural codes (and we should add a sixth here, the "translative," since the "Barthes" I mean is "in English") inscribe a work of severe fragmentation—93 sections, 561 items, to be exact, in which the most brilliantly bizarre textual calculus is hurtled against Balzac's *Sarrasine*—to cite, for instance, given its "tauromachian" emphasis, implies the *citar:* "the stamp of the heel, the torero's arched stance which summons the bull to the banderilleros,"[6] or the career of the signifier as a *citing* or *siting*. Items of textuality treated as lexical instances, followed by a running, seamless commentary that make up Barthes's own metacritical gesture, *S/Z* demonstrates the critical project as a subversion of the proper name, just as it celebrates the proper name to be undetermined in the first place—"BARTHES" as a gathering of decided critical and cultural forces and as a dispersion of energies that replicate themselves pitilessly, as though to say that the transparent utterance of the bourgeois text must be laboriously revealed as the distance between itself and the opaque lie that transforms "culture" into "nature." The Barthesian performance meets our own purposes here in the most general sense: looking at a carnival scene from Marshall's work, I will attempt to recover whatever pluralities of meaning the text might lead us to consider. Barthes's work filters through my own understanding of reading as an elaboration and complication of competing, overlapping, and complementary discourses.

II

I will forgo the usual courtesy of providing, here and now and all at once, a plot summary of the novel, though doing so is barely avoidable. Instead, my observations start in the middle, where the carnival scenes fall in the midst of an orientation and a conclusion. We are concerned with a character named Vere and a female figure, who, for all intents and purposes, remains anonymous, except for a tribal marker in a last name called "MacFarland." Though the events to which I refer are traversed and cross-hatched several times, they come to focus in Book III, "Carnival," chapter 1, 267–77.

I have isolated this ten-page sequence because its riddle stands out from the surrounding narratives at the same time that it serves to reinforce the latter by (a) specifying carnival in the fictitious community as a hyperbolic function, (b) articulating "namelessness" as the central dread of an impoverished culture, whose fictional limits are traced in the novel, and (c) metaphorizing the uncanny at the crossroads of cultural exchange, or the excessively unfamiliar as a quite familiar aspect of all social choreographies. In other words, this chapter, in its terrible centrality, situates the problematic that the novel retraces as an interrogation into the *interior* dynamics of otheredness: If "I" is another, then "I" will never know other than this otherness, even if the texts of my history call upon me to think and act as if it were not so. This ambivalence in both the fictional and historical text is neither permissible, nor near the surface, but it might explain, at heart, the peculiar texture of hostilities that prevail, both openly and covertly, over the social economies of Bourne Island. But that is a tentative conclusion. What steps have induced it?

By these signs you shall know them . . .

1. Through a principle of convergence and enumeration, Marshall's narrators range between and within scenes as the subtle admixture of omniscient and local narrative properties. Four of the actors of the plot converge on Book I, chapter 1: Vere, Allen Fuso, and Saul and Harriet Amron, each, in turn, observing the other and self in an inward narrative movement, confer

on the plot the gifts of their sharply divergent points of view. In more than one instance, we see aspects of Bourne Island from an aerial vantage through their eyes. But the magic of seeing here is that one is also observed in a ruthless democracy of the specular: even before Allen Fuso knows Vere, the motherless, he recognized, on board the small twin-engine plane, "Farm Labor Scheme" in Vere's "high-crowned, wide-brimmed sharpie's hat of blue velour, the same light powder-blue as his suit"—the passenger and stranger a few seats ahead of him (14–15).

Vere comes to be associated, then, with vivid color, a wild, delightful impertinence of taste (which signal his youth and lack of exposure to a broader world), and an excess of the dramatic, which aggressive indulgence leads to a spectacular moment of carnival on the one hand and his death on the other. In the first instance, only the reader oversees the event, in the second, the "world" looks on. But in any case, we experience this character in sharp alignment with the breathtaking and the rending, the decorative and the exaggerated.

The inference of associations that we make belies the real Vere, who maintains, outwardly, a virtual silence of manner and the unobtrusive arrogance of an "essential immunity" (30). If the ironical is the chief trick of a reversal of intention, then Vere, under its sign, is not so much a bad guy as hardly the good one that everybody loves—toward whom Allen Fuso entertains homoerotic ambitions, for whom Merle Kinbona weeps interminably, and over whom great-aunt Leesy Walkes suffers soundlessly.

2. This character, who draws the reflexes of pathos to his *persona* like a moth to flames—the death of his mother in birthing him, his disappointment and betrayal in America, the loss of his child at the hands of the anonymous woman—is paired with an agent observed through the filter of scattered and ephemeral impressions. Her "crime" is never clarified in the course of things, except that it appears that various narrators indict what we take to be her incestuous origins and nasty skin color. But more than that this character without name comes from "up Canterbury" that remains somewhere beyond and peripheral to the primary demographic centers of the fiction—New Bristol, Bournehills, and Spiretown. She is estranged and without defenders, or a legitimate "citizenship" in a novel of impeccable ceremony and belonging. Her membership, however, in a clan of "Backra," or "red people" flings the possibilities of kinship and filiation outward, in the direction of the chaotic and uncontainable.

That the Canterbury woman is indigenous to this fictitious Caribbean island sounds the thematic of estrangement all the more intently because it would suggest that the metaphysics of the social and political body has little to do with "color," but everything concerning any arbitrary basis for determining "near" and "far," "inner" and "outer," "licit," and "illicit," whose bondings and manipulations hold in place the cultural necessity of order and degree. The breach of it, embodied in the female figure's irrupture on the textual surface, creates the crisis that is punishable by whipping and banishment. The tall, red-boned female instantiates the novel's puzzle and nightmare because she is not only unoriginated, but also, like the classically marked figure, the bearer of a secret contamination, on par with the "sins" of Merle Kinbona in her London years, or the "touch" by black Lyle Hutson that would turn the inward dread of white Harriet Amron outward.

"Those red people from up Canterbury are all cross-bred and worthless," Leesy speaks in despair to Vere (upon his return to Bourne Island from Florida) (31). And several pages later, in Sugar's Nightclub at the tip of New Bristol, Merle introduces Saul to aspects of local society by dramatic enumeration—the finger point—Bourne Island is a nation of diabetics, to a man and woman: "'Take for example that young miss yonder . . . ' a tall, thin, indifferently pretty girl in a colorful skirt puffed up by a score of can-can petticoats":

> "Everyone up there has the *same name* and looks the same. We call them Backras, meaning more white than black and poor as the devil. This one had a nice boy liking her, but when he went to America on the labor scheme she turned wild. She wouldn't even take care of the child she had for him and it died." (85; my emphasis)

A third narrator traverses the same semantic field, as though these characters were, pointedly, the repetition of certain rhetorical symptoms: working behind the counter of the store at Delbert's Rumshop in Spiretown, there is this woman, who duplicates the figure of female anonymity:

> The woman, a large, raw-boned Backra, was from Canterbury, a hill southeast of Westminster where everyone in the small settlement there was related and shared the same crinkled, snuff-colored hair, rough reddish near-white skin and the same name MacFarland. (157)

The very notion of duplication, of the human look-alike, is striking, because it suggests the absence of discriminating genetic features at the level of the eyesight. The manipulations of sameness, or twinness open the door to the potential for comic error and confusion and posit an excess in the already powerful stuff of the life principle. But sameness here, raised to the level of the clan and the pervasive last name that does not conjugate in difference through the vertical and spatial timeline of generations, evokes a fable of inheritance that is not permissible. We would also assume that this shadow of illegitimate endogamous mating implicates the fathers, since other last names of the novel, "Vaughn," "Walkes," "Pollard," "Kingsley," "Bryam," all capable of endless modification by a Christian name and the prerogatives of patriarchal marriage, are the marks of a proper cultural function.

But two dramatic features here seem overwhelming: (1) that the Backra "tribe" of Bourne Island, peripheral to the fiction's central culture, is already fabled, or "written" as an exotic history, in which case nobody knows their name, but only their sign and (2) the sign "MacFarland," contiguous with other traits, that is, skin color, body type, loses its efficacy to name precisely because it becomes preponderant indiscriminate naming; in that regard, "MacFarland" imitates the status of a geographical site. It *is* a place, of taboo, to be avoided.

In Harlem Heights, the figure of anonymity makes a new home for herself neighboring the city of New Bristol, with its shops, hotels, and nightclubs; of her "ramshackle house," in the hills above New Bristol's wealthy, Vere will track her down and inflict on her the terrible whipping with his *family's* Malacca cane.

We observe as an aspect of her estrangement that she is seldom cast with other characters, except for cameo figures—young officers from a tracking station near Sugar's, who appear to have a purely commercial relationship with her, buying her body for the course of a night. But we only guess as much, since the activities that define her *persona* remain shrouded in mystery. This enigmatic figure, difficult to envision, with her "can-can petticoats" and a physiognomy fractured by descriptive details, assumes a centrality to the novel by virtue of her marginal status. The narrator can only point to her, can only suggest an iconographic value, whose integrity is impure. We are offered a cluster of traits whose aspects of identity split up in contiguous elements. To my mind, this is not an enigmatic property known only to the text, or to the author, but invokes a repertoire of unresolved, ambiguous issues that cannot be "answered," even said with ease. Perhaps the Canterbury woman is meant to "say" that Bourne Island, in its tenacious clinging to the very elements of human oppression that it would undo, reinforces its own appropriative violence. "MacFarland" is no longer a "person" or a "character," but in this instance, the emptiness and abstraction of a "thing."

A Mirror Stage

John T. Irwin in his study of William Faulkner's *Absalom, Absalom!* and *The Sound and the Fury*,[7] points out, after Otto Rank, that "the brother and the shadow are two of the most common forms that the figure of the double assumes." We might conclude, after Irwin, that the sister and the double, or the woman in the mirror, are not as well known; in this case, the subject identifies with the object thrown before her, at the same time that she recognizes that she is not one with it. Nevertheless, no amount of recognition forestalls the peculiar and unique pleasure that the looker derives from seeing *in,* if not *through,* the glass. That Marshall's narrator introduces a mirror to the scene of Vere's and the female figure's encounter claims its entire dramatic import for difference, *as* difference.[8]

We are amazed that the communicative exchange between the pair has been conducted up to the moment of their would-be face to face meeting in an exquisitely terrifying silence. It is as though the two figures have agreed beforehand to "act" themselves, to mime this pre- text through dramatic gestures that keep strictly to an already assumed outcome. Though one might explain these scenes to herself as if they were a rational whole of fiction—and that they are rational is the trouble—there is no explaining what we sense, what is insinuated, in the self-contained dreadfulness that is trapped in the rationally ordered syntax of these paragraphs of narrative. There *are* other things, and this extra, immured in the folds of the rational and erupting as an unspecified irrational content that can only be *signaled,* is the secret of Bournehills, looking in the direction of first traumas. If psychoanalytic theory offers the analysand a narrative, a text in the "place" of a dropped-out content, or a content that was never there, then what is the relationship between a fictional text and the historical, or the community in history, both *inventing* and *invented* by its texts?

Imagine this: Vere soundlessly tracks the woman (again, "a tall, thin, sharp-boned girl of perhaps twenty with snuff-colored hair and the eyes and the coarse mottled skin typical of those from up Canterbury" [190]), several times before he enters the house in Harlem Heights. "Her petticoats pushing around her knees," she leads him nightly, "down Whitehall Lane past the bawdy sailor clubs and rumshops lining the street to Sugar's at the tip of the long finger of land that marked the extremity of the deep bay upon which New Bristol stood" (119). He never announces himself, but simply falls in behind her as she "moves up the narrow cobblestone street." Eventually, she sees him, as he exerts no effort to hide. Head suddenly snapping around, she looks "over her shoulder to where he had come to a halt under a street lamp some yards behind to wait for her to continue on." Knowing all along that he has been there, she simply stares at him, "one bony arm akimbo," determined to brazen it out, if need be, but does not speak.

Replete with bodily tensions and haltings, this scene could be scored as a hunter stalking his quarry, an appropriate figure for city streets, but Vere also stages the "haunter," a sort of poltergeist that neither reveals itself, nor goes away. In effect, the narrator implies that he is the female agent's "shadow"—"She had known all along, it was clear, that he had been shadowing her, but for reasons of her own had waited until this moment to acknowledge it" (191). Terror and dread do not here consist in the lack of knowledge that would make surprise inevitable, but in the acquaintance that boomerangs, when one's own projected shadow falls down, abruptly, in her path, between herself and the light. Though the Freudian view of the "uncanny" does not indicate this version of the dramatic as a case in point, we could very well place these haunting scenes under its auspices and say that the shadow—a "not-me" as the mirror image is not—is so apt an analogy on the living body, so remarkable a trace of its occurrence, that the shadow's sudden projection can take a body out, so to speak, destroy it. It would appear, then, that the male agent, in the outward overlap between the city's terrors and the psyche's dread, entertains just such ambitions regarding this fictive female body.

Thus, the scene is set, precisely staged, for even greater and more matured agitations of the spirit. The preceding scenes concerning Vere and his prey, dispersed along the line of intervening fictions, have opened the door to the funhouse that is ironically misnamed. Carnival itself, though a celebration, marks the social body turned inside out; the preserved, secreted fantasies, from which the ego shrinks, or about which it quietly boasts, erupt into play. That the scene to come takes place without witness, except that of the readers', heightens its bizarre import, lends it a purity of narrative and dramatic function that parodies the solitude of lone readers and narrators.

When Vere enters the woman's place unannounced, the streets of Harlem Heights and New Bristol are virtually deserted. Everyone has gone, or will go shortly, to Carnival Monday Night dance at the Sports Oval outside New Bristol. This is the interrupted destination of the lone female figure in the mirror when Vere bears down upon her with his streamlined black self and his family's Malacca cane, snugly secured to his spine: "She was busy applying the make-up to her neck and throat, having finished her face, when the door behind her opened, and as she saw Vere suddenly well up in the mirror to the makeshift vanity table at which she was sitting, her hand paused half-way to her raised chin, but she did not start. She made no outcry. Nothing crossed her eyes as they encountered his in the glass" (272).

This tight space brims over with her bed, her clothing, and most astonishingly, her dolls,

> to be seen everywhere in the packed untidy room—large, expensive boudoir dolls with deeply lashed, painted blue eyes and painted smiles and pink brushed lightly over their white cheeks. . . . They lazed amid the tumbled sheet on the unmade bed, where they obviously served as the girl's sleeping companions. . . . And they were all dressed, even the ones lounging in bed, in an exact copy of her lavish gown; and their spun-gold hair, piled in the same elaborate tower of curls as her wig, was studded with fake jewels also. (272, 273)

Vere watches the reflection in the glass, and the image trapped there watches him watching her. In this tenacious play of replication, we suddenly enter a factitious world of invariably contrived and counterfeit identities. One might say that we are aware of our self-conscious involvement in a fictional moment that bares its props, that names its game as the falsehood; "a heavy stark-white pancake make-up that looked like grease paint," or "her white mime's face, [that] of a sullen, intractable child" (272). The duplicitous mirror participates in the transaction as a source of enrichment, making, in effect, *two* of everything that catches in the frame. But in this simple scheme of multiplied images, the dolls and the woman increase multifold in a hideously curious spectacle of undifferentiated objects on a scale of impressions. The dolls are grand, but a miniature version of the woman, and the woman an outsized instance of the dolls. If we imagine that at any quirky moment in the "life" of objects, the doll might move—there is that astonishing moment for the spectator looking through the glass of the wax museum at figures that seem just on the verge of movement, or to have completed a nuance that the eye just missed—then we recognize the cunning of dolls and manikins (should we add the corpse?), or even the Buckingham Palace guard, and the scary street mime, from New Orleans to Berlin, as the threat of life in still things, or the menace of death in the living. The tension that shudders across the moment between properties and their energies in a potential exchange and transfer of stuff reveals a suppressed contradiction—we have just missed the passing of a distinction between things and human that *almost* collapses into a single identity. The "almost" equals the Freudian "uncanny."

We must concede to the Canterbury woman a superior imagination; she knows that in her selection of a carnival costume in tulle, which copies the boudoir dolls exactly, she has not achieved "beauté," nor is that her purpose. She appears to aim, instead, at the reconstitution of a protocol whose iconographic significance/signal has already been established. (And what else is "beauty" or "unbeauty" "in the West," if not an *unspontaneous* perception of a spontaneously emergent female body?) Even if we decide that "stark-white pancake make-up" (even difficult to get off the tongue) and the look of greasepaint are displeasing to the eye, we must admit that the special occasion of ritual, or of a designated event of the hyperbolic, lends costuming/signifying a certain immunity. We suspend judgment on the clown, for instance, or the character of the masque, deciding that the grotesque—a human deficiency on the one hand and an excess on the other—holds a crucial place in the order of things. Our acceptance of the extraordinary look comes to rely on the tease. The audience suspects that, beyond the mask, the actor looks different, or "all too human." But the embodied lie, which the costume and makeup achieve, creates the illusion that outruns the truth. It is appropriate, then, that the Canterbury woman never turns her face, in effect, to Vere, or to the audience of this scene and that we see her as Vere does (and as we see him as well), through the mediations of the looking glass.

Seeing thus, we decide that the woman in the mirror is not what she appears to be, though we could say that "what you see is what you get." And what of the male figure conjured up in *her* mirror? The figure "wells up," we are told, *gushes* to the surface, as if by magic. The fluid verbal metaphor that takes its cue from dream work tempts us to read Vere as a superimposed image on an image that, in the revisionary ratio of dreams, produces multiple characters who collapse into one. Does Vere become, in effect, the woman's own dream stuff—induced by guilt—that spontaneously appears in her own looking glass? How else might we explain: (1) Vere's obsessive potential for her mind (as he has literally put himself there in order to mature at some later moment); (2) her incapacity to shake him, or even turn around from the mirror to confront the interrogation; (3) the failed magic of her words to dispel the intruder?

The dreamer is trammeled upon "being shot," pulls a "gun" that doesn't fire, or that miraculously transforms itself into an umbrella; locks do not secure doors and electrical switches click on blown-out lights; hurled insults do not send the pursuer flying—but waking, in anguished astonishment, the dreamer discovers that it wasn't so. But somehow, it is the recall of disempowerment that provides waking with its own brand of trouble in mind. Even if the agent who inflicts the "blow" is only a proxy, an alibi for Vere, the dream and the waking for the Canterbury woman are charged with the same unrelieved tensions of lack, of insufficiency, so that truth and illusion come to share the same place. This entire scene is truly illusory for actors and spectators, occurring as it does in the radical alterity of makeup and mirrors. In the intersection of *personae*, both characters, having become the centrally embodied deferment and evasion that neither can any longer forestall, discover each other as the realized aspect of a self-alienation.

But is such an explanation sufficient for the man who "wells" up in the woman's mirror? In more than one way, Vere has no business there, even though, in his "essential immunity" (and *what*, or *who* has immunized him?), he takes it as his right. We could say that the woman who stays in man's company keeps alive the possibility of one day having an unwanted guest, the one who decides to "hump the hostess." It is surely more than co-incidental that her involvement with the dolls, of her carrying out a program of the dolls, is essentially contextualized in a male eyeball. (We cannot imagine, for instance, that these scenes could ever reverse locations.) It is *she* who presents to *him* a passive, inert female back, in the fetal curve, as he flails away. How far removed are we from a notion of sexual use/abuse, recalling the telling symbolism, caught by the Malacca cane? And it is only *he* whose realizations are both *writ* and *written:*

> And then suddenly he was angry. Perhaps it was the sight of that hardened back which sent the blows rebounding his way so that he almost felt he was whipping himself. Or the realization that no matter how long he flailed away at her he would never be able to convey to her what it was he had been seeking in having her as his woman and giving her the child, and how deeply she had wronged him by denying them both. (275)

And so, we discover that the male agent here has gained entry into the female house and the female mirror by *breaking* in, by intruding himself in the split between the woman and her other, content not yet specified. It is precisely this *process of obtrusion* that stands between Bournehills and the *texts* of its own re-invention. Never mind what the texts are, never mind that they might, in fact, tell a "lie." But the freeing gesture would be that they ARE. In other words, the island's coming into possession of its own material resources—its sugarcane crop, for instance—and the modes of production sufficient to transform them would undo Bournehills' bondage to its absentee landlords. This strategic rewriting of the practices of political economy in the local instance would yield revised social relations: not only would the cane farmers, for example, have the assurance of benefiting, *themselves,* from the annual harvest, but also the conditions of work would be so restructured that Gwen, in another instance, could feed her children and no longer have to perform labor's tediums under conditions of pregnancy.

The economic oppression of Bournehills is, at once, the novel's most implicit and obvious feature of travail. Its effects must be reckoned with at all times, beginning with the hierarchy of social being and value that situates the Canterbury woman on the bottom. It is certainly not "written" that the Bournehills collective, freed from its neocolonial trap, would uplift the woman's status by much. But the point is that the well-rehearsed *excuse* could be jettisoned, as the "authors" of modes of reconfigured social relations are now none other than the local citizenry itself. Fallen between the gaps of her culture, the Canterbury woman, whom the text refuses anything beyond a vain and parodic movement, remains the unspoken. But *that* is also a text.

The Paradox of the "Non-Dit"

In order to say the "not-sayable," I must say—must enter the chain of significant differences inscribed by the sentence. One almost "gets" what theorists of female representation mean in their insistence that "the woman," "the female" escape representability, or what I mean when I claim that the Canterbury woman remains "unspoken." Not absolutely certain what the theorists have in mind, since, by their own various witness, key historical moments "in the West" are *based* on "the female" and its ascribed symptoms of lack, we might conclude that "unrepresentability" and "un-sayableness" are the preeminent features of a paradox. For Julia Kristeva, the "maternal body," specifically, locates the meeting place of "nature" and "culture." This point of intersection, to which Lévi-Strauss tracked the incest taboo, also marks the explosion of grammatical and logical purities. In this atmosphere, we cannot think of things as simply differentiated. Each haunts and shadows the other as meaning moves into radical abeyance.

For Kristeva, the "non-dit" and the maternal body are twinned:

> The weight of the "non-said" *(non-dit)* no doubt affects the mother's body first of all: no signifier can cover it completely, for the signifier is always meaning *(sens)*, communication or structure, whereas a mother-woman is rather a strange "fold" *(pli)* which turns nature into culture, and the "speaking subject" *(le parlant)* into biology. Although it affects each woman's body, this heterogeneity, which cannot be subsumed by the signifier, literally explodes with pregnancy—the dividing line between nature and culture—and with the arrival of the child—which frees a woman from uniqueness and gives her a chance, albeit not a certainty, of access to the other, to the ethical. These peculiarities of the maternal body make a woman a creature of folds, a dialectic of the trinity or its supplements.[9]

That the Canterbury woman has had a child, according to Kristeva's theory, would heighten the contradictions surrounding her. Having undergone pregnancy, or straddled the line, she now has nothing the show for her pain. From this angle, she has been restored, theoretically, to the unique, to the "heterogeneity" of the female body. But this outcome is hardly felicitous, since both mothers and not-mothers on Bourne Island can neither forge their access to others—the ethical vocation that Kristeva suggests belongs to maternity—nor rehearse their uniqueness, dependent as it is on a degree of freedom. In the situation of neocolonialism, which the novel stages, motherhood is really *not* available as a *choice*. The *fruits* of mother-labor set the children's teeth on edge.

Under these conditions of work and living, we would not be shocked to have forgotten that Vere's mother died in childbirth and that the infant of the Canterbury woman did not live for very long. According to her own angered outburst, thrown in the direction of Vere's feet, the dead child was already fated:

> "But I bet none of them told you that from the day that child was born you could tell it wasn't going to live any time. It was a sickly something!" she shouted at the floor. "And t'besides," she cried at the same defiant pitch, all the silver dust and sequins on her dress shimmering amber in the dull amber light as she stuck her arms akimbo, "who told you the child was even yours? Who said you was man enough then to be giving anybody a baby . . . ?" She sucked her teeth in scorn. (274)

It is, of course, harmful to the female—she will be beaten with many "stripes"—to laugh at, to traduce paternity, both in the specific occurrence of fatherhood (as with Vere) and in the mythical notion of the father who bestows culture on the child. Is it that a woman who "does away" with her child (abortions here included)—unlike a father who abandons them—not only meets with particular violence, but also encounters the generalized opprobrium of the community-at-large?

That the Canterbury woman is *just* a woman would make her *the* woman of this fiction. "Arms akimbo," a repeated gesture, modified by "skinny," isolates her within a special category of contempt and apartness. It seems that the narrator(s) chooses sides here and speaks for Bournehills society. In doing so, the implied narrative judgments contradict Canterbury and its tribe of women who *look* different, *do* different. These females live alone, prostitute their bodies, and do not (cannot?) maintain their children at all cost. I am not suggesting that we make a heroine of the woman from "up Canterbury," but that we recognize in her antiheroic stress provocation to the hierarchical arrangements of patriarchy. The latter, as we know, is difficult, if not impossible, to escape. We may even wonder if such arrangements are as desirable to release as we might publicly assert and privately imagine. For instance, the lesson for me is that aspects of my own readerly, sentimental, and ideological biases *agree* with Vere's. Because she has been disobedient to the female's vocation, she *should* be dishonored and unveiled. But on second thought that conclusion does not quite add up, inasmuch as the "Rat" in Bournehills is only *partially* "Western man" in so simplistic a guise.

If, as in Kristeva's view, the maternal body straddles the "nature/culture" split, then what might be said of the Canterbury woman, who is situated on the line, but retreats from it with a different story?

Made to approach the gateway to madness, the Canterbury woman turns her own body into a symptom of fetish-adoration. The dolls serve in complementary ways, insofar as they restore her body to her, by reflecting it, amended and corrected. When Vere, in ecstatic rage, looking for something to destroy, turns on the dolls, the woman, for the first time, "veers" toward him with the ferocity of the mother protecting her child. In what seems a hideous caricature of the protecting mother, the woman, suddenly mobilized and animated beyond recognition, releases the mask, figuratively speaking, in order to play out quite a different role:

> She looked up then, her face emerging from the safe hollow between her shoulders like a bird's head from under its wing, and seeing the doll swinging by a leg from his hand, its gown already torn and hair in disarray, its blue painted eyes terrified, a look of horror came over her face, and she leaped from her stool, screaming "Leave that! Put it down! God blind you in hell, leave my doll baby." (276)

Anticipating the reader, the narrator even describes her movements in the ensuing tussle as that of someone struggling "with the strength of a mother who sees her child murdered before her eyes" (276). In this "furious pantomime dance," the body of the doll is "ripped wide, and all its sawdust and cotton innards" explode in her face. The rhetorical thrust of the passage slides toward human description; the cry of the woman,"give it to me, I beg you, don't you see you're hurting it" and the finishing gestures of Vere, "[He] flung the remains of the mangled doll at her and strode from the room."

I think we would do well to recognize in this furious dance a not-very-amusing parody of a killed infant and all the stirrings of emotions that might accompany such an event. If the pantomime acts the unspoken, then the scene before us goes far to explore the dynamics of maternal help-lessness. But here such outcome is *staged;* the props are dolls, after all. In the historical outline that subsumes Bournehills culture, however, mangled bodies describe the irrevocable circumstance from which little distance can be struck. It is plausible, then, that the Canterbury woman, in her ceremo-nial and dramatic features, "makes meaning," but in a way that riddles sense.

If we think of the mangled doll and her companions as an *investment* and as the objects in which the woman is *invested,* then we bring together two related components of desire. As items of investment, the dolls not only close the distance successfully overcome between the desiring subject and the something desired,[10] but also reconfigure and analogize the woman's location *as* exchange in the sexual economies of Bournehills. That the dolls are "bought," just as the woman is, replicates the mirror's imaging on yet another level, while it is clear that the circulation of desire in this case involves very different stakes for desiring subjects. On the other end of the sailors' casual, body-for-money transaction, a woman eats, adorns her-self, and brazenly indulges her fantasies. That there are several such "in-vestments" in the crowded room might argue that the Canterbury woman experiences at least a certain amount of success at her "trade," though it is likely not enough, since her house is "ramshackle." Unlike Enid, the barris-ter's wife, the Canterbury woman has not yet breached that class of male clients whose cash and cachet might improve her status of prostitution. But in any event, the prostitute and the sailors demonstrate, in their economic relatedness, the primacy of cold hard cash in the island's human and social nexus.

As invested objects, the dolls are laden with an emotional weight that focuses their subjective value. "The girl's sleeping companions," they might well embody and express "all the things she had ever wanted and been de-nied." Empty themselves of value, the dolls are assigned it by the desiring subject, whose disrupted unity[11] reveals nothing less than the deepest hunger. In that case, the equation between money and dolls concretizes an-guish beyond its theoretical and psychoanalytic import. Anguish now courses the blood vessels, just as surely as money is "eaten."

We might assume as well that desire subtended by a foreign code of con-science marks the needs of strangers in pathetically memorable ways. Thinking about the locus of these particular objects on the grid of Bourne-hills society invites decided pause, inasmuch as they "look like" none of the characters who may so invest them. The "white mime's face" interjects a startling note of physiognomy onto a fictional site whose critical populace is black, but it is carnival in Bournehills, when the extraordinary is normal, and the normal disappears. That the Canterbury woman apes a *boudoir* doll brings several things to mind, but preeminent among them is that she embraces the "import" as *masked* desire. (The traveler in erstwhile colonized societies recognizes right away that the former are glutted markets for the discarded, expensive junk of the metropolitan cultures. These protuberances on the landscape of the new capitals stand out like a bulging eyeball. In the case of the Canterbury woman, the foreign products are taken to bed and strike as discordant a note in the brimming-over room as old abandoned Chevrolets in the midst of kiosks and houses of slatted windows.) We might say that the "domestication" of the "foreign," its *inculcation* where we live, offers the subtle complexity that stalls most radical change. In other words, revolutions are not very well equipped to recognize, or even acknowledge, the "unscientific" errancy of *want,* or the stringent demands of the unconscious.

Desiring, therefore, runs along the strangest channels, the farther away the point of origin, the more powerfully seductive the pull. Europe's and North America's goods provide a table of contents not-at-home with the island's material culture, from Merle's beat-up Bentley, to Vere's raggedy Opel; from Lyle Hutson's costly Savile Row suits, to the Canterbury woman's expensive boudoir dolls. Subsequently, Bournehills is bereft of a correct history of its material layers, inasmuch as the latter are buried in the earth. In other words, the dolls, for instance, do not "grow" out of an embedded memory of evolved or related forms. For example, changing moments of a body-politic might be mirrored in altered stages of diminutive objects. In considering how so, we gain a different angle on the historical sequence: perhaps in recognition of the rising human rights movement of African-Americans, my best doll "Patti Jo" was special-delivered "black and beautiful" from Lincoln, Nebraska sometime during the 1950s. "Walking" on cue from the constant up and down motion of either arm, Patti Jo was adorned in pink silk-taffeta. U.S. involvement in Vietnam evoked a great deal of national ambivalence, perhaps reflected in one of my nephews' "G.I. Joe," the dismembering, falling apart male doll. Then, in anticipation of the strict sexual neutralities of the contemporary period, the interchangeable female/male "cabbage patch" doll was neither here nor there. With a touch of realism, dolls are made even larger now, nicely modeled after one's relatives and friends.

If we studied this cross section of time, technique, and material we might be able to write a piece of U.S. history in its interstate trade relations, small industry factors and output, the concatenation between "homegrown" and "made in Taiwan," the glamour of the toy, and the desiring games that adults hint to their children.[12] In other words, we could discover and make sense of certain continuities in changes of national taste. What I am suggesting about boudoir dolls in Bournehills is that they are quite literally plucked from a divergent cultural semantics. As a result of transactions like this one across the society and without the benefit of a "favorable balance of trade," either real or symbolic, the local culture swims the broken currents of its own time's flow.

In an uneven cross-cultural exchange, the Canterbury woman desires what comes to hand. Reinventing self-image in play, she reverts to the emotional doll-stage of the child. For her, the dolls not only symptomatize the "return" of the baby (as the latter is the child's anticipation), but also mark a "return" with perfection, minus the contingencies of the material world. Whatever the sickly, living infant might have lacked, the dolls provide. At the same time, the objects of play repeat none of the mistakes of "his/her majesty, the baby," or what some observers speak of as the nursery's messiness. We might say that the boudoir dolls are the surrogate baby body. At the site of a fantastic displacement, whose living subject has dropped out, so to speak, the dolls are both "themselves" and repression's symptoms. In manipulating this double inscription, the narrator shows both the lapsed maternal body and its outright reversion into the fantastic realm of childhood. In that sense, the Canterbury woman contains and contained not only the baby, but also the embedded child, whose traces stay. The maternal body here is dramatically configured as the sign of the female child-become-adult and child-at-play in the fantasies that "answer."

That the woman can "have her cake and eat it too," in playing out the real and symbolic capabilities of the female body, places her at odds with some of the novel's other female figures. Pregnancy for them is the mortal debt that must be paid in eternal and endless child care. As I observed before, the fatality of multiple births, under conditions of impoverishment, bears down on Gwen, Stinger's woman, with unrelieved harshness. It would be absurd, consequently, to compare these social positionalities in the fiction against some putative ideal of maternal behavior, but it does appear that the Canterbury woman is being punished for "playing" in all the nuances of the term: "playing" her sex for monetary gain; "playing" mother against the real thing; "playing" at a kind of self-indulgence that partially determines its own movement; "playing" out the assumptions of carnival in taking on the mask, albeit a "borrowed" one. Though we view her behavior through the distortions of the *reflected*, we do not have much choice but to conclude that the fictional world we are in is twisted entirely by the political logics of foreign occupation.

III

Once the doll loses its innards, exploding in the woman's face, the character is permitted a prolonged cry that the ear cannot quite register. It is a "sudden shrill atonal scream . . . with the regularity of a siren," and it calls to mind "in its almost ritualistic fluting, the high-pitched, tremolant keening of Arab women mourning their dead" (276). Well beyond the point of contact, it travels the "length and depth of the Heights," continues long after Vere has departed, and signals the reader that perhaps we have touched an edge of mimetic behavior. The "loud ululation" in italics runs approximately: "oh God oh God Oh God oh god Oh God" for thirty-seven such intervals, in what seems to be the rising and falling motion of the voice and arms. Trying to accurately record the recurrence for citation obliges the reader to *count*, but it does little good to do so, since, it seems, enumeration is not the point, though *repetition* is. The decisive punctualities of the lines, determined by their spacing and the simple manipulation of small and capital letters, suggest a ritualized dance, so that the passage might also be read as a version of labanotation, or notes for a dance score.

The lines cannot be spoken, or "naturally" spoken, but only read and gazed at. Perhaps they might satisfy what Robert Scholes describes as "phatic," or that utterance whose primary urge is contact itself.[13] Could we also include in the phatic dimension processes of learning a language? It is striking that the Canterbury woman, in the synthesis of displacements "spoken" by her body, "answers" effectively both programs of action.

IV
After Westminster: Coming to Conclusions

Marshall's exquisite lyrical talent evinces mastery of multiple discursive orders. A cultural code, for example, specific to a fictionalized Caribbean instance, draws on a repertoire of linguistic, historical, ethical, geophysical, geopolitical, ritualistic, decorative, sartorial, gustatory, amorous, and celebrative elements. Even the Canterbury woman's "Oh God," in the general category of imprecation, seemingly based in the removal of the Christ-Body from the eye of the human, bears the distinctive inflections of Caribbean English. Or so it seems to my ear. But the dispersed commingling of an ecclesiastical density with specific elements of a contrasting cultural landscape creates a rhetoric of dissonance. From one point of view, this disjuncture serves the narrative purposes of the novel quite well since it situates the economies of conflict and ambivalence inside decided dramatic goals. From another angle, however, this clash of regimes, so effectively mediated that we catch the binarity only on studied reflection, would appear to make peace with traces of a dominant order precisely *because* this rapprochement is rendered perfectly natural. The symbolic density that I specify as "ecclesiastical" is embedded in imagery adopted from the hierarchical church. Its subtle weave of textures accounts for one of the most skillfully handled elements of narrative that the work affords.

Merle Kinbona, for instance, wears a pair of "pendant silver earrings carved in the form of those saints to be found on certain European churches." The earrings, fixed as a continuous dramatic prop on Merle's person, sustain an impressively rich history and destination: copied for Merle from "the saints on the outside of Westminster Abbey," which also lends its name to an overwhelming hill that bears down on Bourne Island, the earrings are a gift from the wealthy and mysterious Englishwoman, whose relationship to Merle remains ambiguous (4, 327). That an object the dimensions of an earring carries its weight in gold, both literally and figuratively, embodies a synecdochic echo that reverberates through various nerve centers of the novel. The saints on "certain European churches," now reduced on a pinpoint in the ear lobe, are no longer just "gaunt with piety." In the symbolic power that they have come to assert over European imagination, the saints suggest that indeed a world of cultural exchanges, which includes unsaintly lives, unseemly tales, is immured within their intricate handiwork. That the Atlantic slave trade originated in and proceeded with the blessings of the hierarchical church of Europe never leaves the reader's mind. The idea lends a subtext to every reference that slips and slides between a symbolic modulation and its outright pointing back toward the past. In that sense, the saints' past, here standing in for the European cultural complexity, reconfigures the future of what is already known.

The ironizing possibilities of agreement between African-Caribbean things and European things are not at all lost to the novel's narrative strategies. But while irony apparently offers a superior interpretive model, it can also accommodate to a "domestication of dissent": Merle, for instance, wears not only the earrings of the saints, but also the bracelets of the enslaved. Heavy, clangorous, crudely made, the bracelets create an ambiance of sound in which she moves and "like a monk's beads or a captive's chains," the sound "announced her" (5). The symbolic equivalent of another kind of silver-working, these "numerous bracelets," similar to the monk's prayer beads, present a choice between items no longer sharply antithetical by virtue of their adherence to the coordinate conjunction. Read another way, "or" outlines two radically divergent crossways, as in "life" or "death." In either case a conflicted movement runs through the semantic chain, which marks uncertainty for character in the narrative's psychological work.

This symbolic structure, working its way through the gaps of the novel, meets on every hand the semantics of a particular historical order. These texts-before-hand, subtly encoded as the novel's given, rapidly oscillate between two unspecified political ends, except that we know them both all too well. The narrators brilliantly proceed to frustrate any program of Manichean investment, nevertheless. By endowing each situation and character who responds in its context with sufficiently sullied, corrupt, unclear, naive, and self-interested motives, the narrative strategies force the reader to rethink whatever certainties of outcome she had wagered. To put it crudely, we cannot choose "Africa" over "Europe," or "Europe" over "Africa," inasmuch as we recognize that not a little of our own emotional/cultural capital is tied up in an international currency whose profoundest grammars are "pidgin," the impurities that fall between the cracks of "STANDARD." Yet, in this high and impressive adventure in irony, everybody has a place, not always certain, but nonetheless the symptoms of a place, with the vexing exception of the Canterbury woman. Apparently a sign of Bournehills' other, she marks, in effect, a tribal limit, and all her kin follows her status. Neither absorbed, nor absolved by the structure of irony, this character without a *first* name, or a *last* one that would claim precise differentiation, enters the fiction and leaves it—is *abandoned* by it, more appropriately—as the single figure who is not exhausted by the work's rhetorical resources.

First names in the novel are the origin of a narrative repletion or saturation: Merle, Vere, Saul, Harriet, Leesy, Gwen, Stinger, Ferguson, Lyle, Enid are not only the names of characters, but the characters' naming suggests a site of traits founded on the *assumption* of completeness; the characters' movement between "inner" and "outer," or the tension that arises between an interior and exterior function. What we recognize as "act" consists in the cross-traversing of these rhetorical lines that conventionally gesture when we have moved into a character's "brain" and when the character has moved, so to speak, "out" of it into the broader circumstances of the narrative. Without an "inner," the Canterbury woman discovers no fictional "autonomy" that would explain the mode of narrative chosen for her.

However, the clues to the Canterbury woman's identity converge on a lucidly specified place: "MacFarland" equals "Backra" (play on "Buckra," a West African term for the "white man"), which equals Merle's "more white than black." The Canterbury woman stands for a local version of "mulatta," who, from the standpoint of a humiliating past, may be described as a "black" masquerading as a "white." There is never a political need for the proposition or practice to reverse itself; reversal occurs as a ruse of entertainment; the minstrel's blackened face not only parodies the African person, but actually erases him or her as a human possibility. From the angle of stratagem and disguise, the Canterbury woman cannot turn round from the mirror to either the audience of the fiction, or the one outside it, since *to turn* would bring this figure into the one symbolic confrontation that all the parties have not engaged systematically, cannot engage at all, except in the most violent manner as the scene depicts: *Who* is the "European" in me that the "African" in me need fear?

At this point, the strangeness of the stranger is far clearer: it is the stranger in the house, reading that formulation in its figurative emphasis as fictional Bournehills society. The woman at the threshold of meaning has no name, and how could she, if the conditions that engendered her cannot be spoken, say nothing of bragged about, if such conditions inscribe the impermissible—the "white man" in a black woman's house, in her mirror, in her "boudoir," *in* her? And whose *fault?* For that reason, the Canterbury woman involves us in the *intramural dynamics of alterity,* and it is, doubtlessly, the interior, in this historical instance, that counts far more than we credit or acknowledge; that would account for the "secret" text of the African-American fictional text in a world of keen ears, of decisively configured discursive interests. By interior, we mean, of course, that chain of *intracommunal* enactments, reenactments, and engagements yoking members of the same "natal community." Even though the Canterbury woman "belongs" to Bournehills, she is situated decisively at its borders, at the limit.

In this fictional instance, we are compelled to read "race" as an outcome rather than an originary source of power relations. It seems quite clear that this figure of anonymity carries about her all the traits of "race," but does not embody one. "Otherness," therefore, cannot be asserted simply as the condition in *others* from the vantage of a dominant community. "Otherness" declares itself instead as the infectious cultural property that bears a secret contamination, an impurity showing itself "in the blood."

The Canterbury woman, however, is not the sole "mulatta" figure of the novel: Enid Hutson, of the Vaughn paternity, shares membership in a similar category of kinship alignment, but with a crucial difference, as we have observed before. The wife of a charming, corrupt, successful man, Enid lives on her own private hill *looking down on* New Bristol. The demographic and figurative distance places her in proximity to a symbolic order that takes in Lyle's Oxonian accent and manners appropriate to the Inns of Court. To the contamination of the blood, we might add the privations of the flesh in order to understand more precisely the dreadful exposure of the Canterbury woman to the wolves of namelessness.

Under the influence of Old Testament scripture, we are accustomed to think "chosen people" in specific reference to the historic Jewish community and to confront "timelessness" with an idea of spatial dispersion. In fact, saying the title, the reader often gets it wrong, transposing "timeless" with "place," "chosen" with "people." This inversion and reversal of semantic destinies invite the reader to splice disparate cultural expectations as we bend the attention away from certain inherited cultural properties. Opening the way to contrastive and antithetical possibilities, the epigraph that inscribes *The Chosen Place, the Timeless People* is "copied" from another book (not of Christian origin) attributed to the Tiv people of West Africa:[14] "Once a great wrong has been done, it never dies. People speak the words of peace, but their hearts do not forgive. Generations perform ceremonies of reconciliation but there is no end." Right away, we perceive a combat of culture codes in the making, without announcing itself as such. This opposition between cultures of the fiction and the operations of antithesis within the mimetic frame that grounds it offer but a single route of critical maneuver. Within the intricacies of the structure, however, this clear route to combat is continuously demolished in the interest of greater ironic subtlety.

The force of anonymity in the Tiv epigraph, its ahistorical drive and appeal, as if words spoken from an undated past are being spoken still, in a contemporary fictional mode, represents unimpeachable authority, on par with biblical scripture in its annulment of local contexts. "An epistemological ground for locating centers of interpretation" would attempt to move among the novel's various centers of authorities that manipulate quite successfully the reader's own divided allegiance among diverse processes of appeal. To read "race" alone, or "sexual preference" by itself, bogs down in one of several possibilities. "Namelessness," for instance, is configured in the novel along various lines of stress: (1) Caribbean/ritual versus U.S. and European capitalist machinery; (2) agents as bearers of these moments of cultural production; (3) an interiorized apparatus that throws "male" against "female," blood" against "blood," a heterosexual synthesis of sexuality and desire against unspecified, barely hinted different possibilities of sexual congress; (4) a "natural" landscape that performs its own semiotics in relationship to the semantic chains of character. At no point does any single cluster of these modalities *exhaust* the fiction, though any one might metaphorize it, may substitute for the whole in its partialness. In fact, I have privileged a single one of these, aspects of interiority, that gathers up "critical pertinences" that move off in different directions.

In positing a "ground" of any sort, one is not only attempting to clear floor space, but also to ascertain that there *is* a floor, or some basic point of structure that would grant the free flow of movement among various appointments. I am suggesting that an interpretive ground for this novel, perhaps *any* text of fiction, rests on a thematics that falls completely outside its express boundaries. The historical basis is not totally exhausted by "race," "class," gender" "previous state of servitude," "sexual preference," "last name," "region of birth," "religious faith," etc. These elements of social modality come to bear on the historical situation of the text, the writer, and various constituent reader-groups that "choose" the text, but I mean *historical situatedness* primarily as the *enunciative conditions* that surround a particular act of speaking/writing and the textual densities ("writings" that precede) flowing back against it. In that regard, African-American fictional texts declare, by definition, a subversive move; not empowered to speak in the historical instance by any act of morality, legislation, or rule of cultural precedence; by tradition, the subject of speaking in others, but not a speaking subject itself, the "largest poet" (who has far less to do with particular writers' identities than I personally like) of writings by black writers inscribes a fugitive condition. She or he is history's "runaway" person, the missing commodity of the gross national product, whose whereabouts were once top secret (from about A.D. 1619, Jamestown, the colonial South, to the present).

The fugitive poet bears a fundamental obsession, and that is *to speak* even though the "law" at one time did not allow it, and to break the equation between her/his flesh and any nation's 30 pounds sterling. It is axiomatic that the fugitive poet takes up the vocation of the enunciative/enunciating in certain danger by "revealing" her or his whereabouts and that of significant others, *the interior landscape*. It seems to me that any critical act of reading and interpretation, with reference to this community of texts and whatever *conclusions* it reaches, must begin with *that* story, as assumptive ground, in the fundamental ambience of the fugitive man and woman *against the law*.

Because particular poets must pit themselves against texts written long before, we engage in their works the peculiar tensions established between a priority and a succession. In fact, we observe Marshall's writing against this current of the inexorable as she mobilizes the offices of irony. But can the particular poet set in motion a new structure of enunciative rules? *The*

Chosen Place, The Timeless People offers just such possibilities by insisting that the politics of culture are not solely made by the logics of domination; the dominated have some say, especially "where we live." This perspective forecasts essentially a critical ways and means that must situate itself not only in opposition to the expectations of critical behavior, but also in self-service to one's own ideological investments. "Black, white, and in color" promises one thing for certain: that the reader shall be discomfited.

12

Notes on an Alternative Model—
Neither/Nor

Language has always been the companion of empire.

Antonio de Nebrija, 1492—"The Year of the Other"

In an inventory of American ideas, the thematic of the "tragic mulatto/a" seems to disappear at the end of the nineteenth century.[1] Even though certain writers in the United States have pursued this configuration of character well into the twentieth, with varying and divergent purposes in mind,[2] it is as though both the dominant and dominated national interests eventually abandoned the vocation of naming, perceiving, and explaining to themselves the identity of this peculiar New World invention. A retrieval of this topic will, therefore, appear anachronistic and irrelevant to African-American critical projects at the moment. Furthermore, the term itself and the issues that it raises are so thoroughly circumscribed by historical closure and apparently bankrupt in the situation of their origin that my attempt to revivify them is burdened, already, in the beginning, with doubt, with the necessity to prove their revised critical point. But it seems to me that the mulatto figure, stranded in cultural ambiguity, conceals the very strategies of feministic violence and displacement that have enabled a problematics of alterity regarding the African-American community in the United States. Created to provide a middle ground of latitude between "black" and "white," the customary and permissible binary agencies of the national adventure, mulatto being, as a neither/nor proposition, inscribed no historic locus, or materiality, that was other than evasive and shadowy on the national landscape. To that extent, the mulatto/a embodied an alibi, an excuse for "other/otherness" that the dominant culture could not (cannot now either) appropriate, or wish away. An accretion of signs that embody the "unspeakable," of the very thing that the dominant culture would forget, the mulatto/a, as term, designates a disguise, a cover up, in the century of Emancipation and beyond, of the social and political reality of the dreaded African presence. Behind the African-become-American stands the shadow, the unsubstantial "double" that the culture dreamed *in the place of* that humanity transformed into its profoundest challenge and by the impositions of policy, its deepest "un-American" activity.

To understand, then, the American invention of the mulatto, a term imported from the European lexis,[3] is to understand more completely, I feel, the false opposition of cultural traits that converge on the binary distribution of "black" and "white." My further aim in exploring this topic, however, is to try to discover how "mulatto-ness," the covering term, explains the workings of gender as a category of social production that has not yet assimilated to women of color. Rather than proof of the point, I see these notes as a trial of it.

Before pursuing these observations further, I should point out certain difficulties of this analysis. Those historical subjects subsumed under "mulatto/a" cannot be so easily banished to the realm of the mythical, nor is it my wish to do so. I should make it clear that I am drawing a distinction throughout between historical figures like Frederick Douglass, or Lemuel Haynes, Vermont preacher of the early nineteenth century, and the *appropriation* of the interracial child by the genocidal forces of dominance. The latter concerns a violence, or fatal ignorance, of naming and placing that is itself paradigmatic of the model of alterity, and to discover its ways and means is our persistent and urgent aim.

To compare, then, historical subjects with idea-forms, or iconographic content, or characters from novels might suggest an incommensurability, or even inaptitude of critical method, but the comparison could be instructive, since it alerts us to the subtleties that threaten to transform the living subject into an inert mass and suggests the reincarnations of human violence in their intellectual and symbolic array. The "mulatto/a," just as the "nigger," tells us little or nothing about the subject buried beneath the epithets, but quite a great deal more concerning the psychic and cultural reflexes that invent and invoke them. I am suggesting that in the *stillness* of time and space eventuated by the "mulatto/a"—its apparent sameness of fictional, historical, and auto/biographical content—we gain insight into the *theft of* the dynamic principle of the living that distinguishes the subject from his/her objectification. Such difference remains evident in the institution of New World enslavement and the captivity and production of, for example, William Faulkner's narrator's "wise supine" female of *Absalom, Absalom!*

The questionable paternity of the mulatto character in fiction, just as its parallel in the historical sequence, marks the beginning and end of cultural and symbolic illegitimacy. We shall try to see more fully how and why that is the case. In a very real sense, America's historic mulatto subject plays out his/her character on the ground of a fiction made public and decisive by dimensions of the spectacular and the specular. In his/her face, the deceits of a culture are mirrored; the deeds of a secret and unnamed fatherhood made known: "My father was a white man. He was admitted to be such by all I ever heard speak of my parentage. The opinion was also whispered that my master was my father, but of the correctness of this opinion, I know nothing."[4]

Frederick Douglass by any other name would tell the same tale over and over again with frightening consistency. But mulatto-ness is not, fortunately, a figure of self-referentiality.[5] Neither the enslaved man/woman, nor the fugitive-in-freedom would call *himself/herself* "mulatto/a," a special category of thingness that isolates and overdetermines the human charac-
. ter to which it points. A semantic marker, already fully inhabited by a content and an expectation, America's "tragic mulatto" exists for others—and a particular male other—in an attribution of the illicit that designates the violent mingling and commingling of bloodlines that a simplified cultural patrimony wishes to deny. But in that very denial, the most dramatic and visible of admissions is evident.

The site of a contamination, this marked figure has no name that is not parodic. In Faulkner's *Light in August,* Joe Christmas, for example, connected with the realm of pure nature makes no claim to rational force in the eyes of his maker. Standing outside the ruined house of Joanna Burden, at the broken gate, in thigh tall weeds, Christmas, in an erection scene, engages gestures of alienation that overlap the erotic: "watching his body, seeming to watch it turning slow and lascivious in a whispering of gutter filth like a drowned corpse in a thick still black pool of more than water."[6] Shortly following this bizarre moment, a car emerges in Christmas's hearing, as he observes his body "grow white out of the darkness like a kodak print emerging from the liquid." Just as the photograph releases an inherent biochemical response, Christmas materializes the unarticulated, unaccommodated American identity—raw and fundamental in a portrayal of basic, unmitigated urge. We cannot even call Christmas's compulsion desire yet, since it is untouched by the mediations and remediations of culture. Transformed into naked, grotesque, hungry man at the world's margin, Christmas speaks the radical disjuncture of human experience as his own private chaos. Christmas's narrative takes hold of a conscious infinity of pain as we see him refracted through an endless regression of events in the re-encounter of former selves. We observe a figure drowning in a sea of phenomena, enacting and re-enacting a purposeful purposelessness of movement that is bizarre, madly pointed. Animated by forces beyond his knowing, Christmas provides an analogy on the deracinated person, fixed in cultural vestibularity. Time passes for him, over and around him, but it has no subjective properties that he might call his own.

A "unanimity-minus-one,"[7] who assumes the terror and crucifixion of his natal community's "expendable figure," Christmas is Faulkner's powerful effort to give a grammar to American race magic. But "race" itself is already a mystification by 1929, which year witnesses the publication of Nella Larsen's *Passing,* another sortie into the intrigues of genetic determinism. "Race" becomes for Faulkner, as for Larsen and Jessie Fauset, a metaphor through which the chaotic and primitive urges of human community find systematic expression. In that sense, "community" comes weighted with the burden of history, since, in Faulkner's case, its ultimate embodiment is one Percy Grimm, one's perfect kamikazi. It is, therefore, both stunning and to be expected that, for Grimm and his kind, Christmas's jugular relocates in his genitals: the flight of Joe Christmas, arrested in the kitchen of the outraged Reverend Gail Hightower, ends in a bloodbath. Grimm pursues him through the mob that wants his flesh for the death of Joanna Burden, but more precisely, his killing is a castration, as Grimm hacks away at the forbidden "cargo" in the name of white women's honor.

It would seem, then, that the mulatto *in the text of fiction* provides a strategy for naming and celebrating the phallus. In other words, the play and interplay of an open and undisguised sexuality are mapped on the body of the mulatto character, who allows the dominant culture to say without parting its lips that "we have willed to sin," the puritan recoil at the sight and the site of the genitals. In that regard, Percy Grimm is his culture's good little factotum, who understands on some dark level of unknowing that the culture, more pointedly, the culture of the fathers, can never admit, as Joe Christmas's wildness reminds them, that the law is based on phallic violence in an array of other names and symbols. The term "mulatto/a," then, becomes a displacement for a proper name, an instance of the "paradox of the negative" that signifies what it does not mean. In Faulkner's work, at least, sexuality is literally monumental, with none of the antiseptic saving grace that psychoanalysis lends it. The unavoidable bedrock of human and fictional complication, sexuality is here restored to nearness to the terrible.

If, as old mad Doc Hines, in enraged and consistent babble contends, Joe Christmas—his probable grandson—describes "the mark and the knowledge," then Christmas is the first and last victim on his way out, given the peculiar occasion to understand history and culture, or those economies of violence that carefully differentiate "inner" and "outer," "order" and "degree."

In his *Conquest of America*,[8] Tzvetan Todorov distinguishes three dimensions of the problematics of alterity: (1) the *axiological* level—"the other is good or bad, I love or do not love him, or . . . he is my equal or my inferior (for there is usually no question that I am good and that I esteem myself"); (2) the *praxeological* level—the placing of distance or proximity between oneself and an imagined other—"I embrace the other's values, I identify myself with him; or else I identify the other with myself, I impose my own image upon him; between submission to the other and the other's submission, there is also a third term, which is neutrality, or indifference"; (3) the *epistemic* level—"I know or am ignorant of the other's identity . . . of course, there is no absolute here, but an endless gradation between the lower or higher states of knowledge."

As an instance of the exterior other in *negative* identity, Christmas, on Todorov's levels of analysis, is made the absolute equivalent of anomie. At no time in his fictional development do we not see him in clear association with wild, untamed plenitude, from Faulkner's version of terrifying female sexuality in the figures of Joanna Burden and Burden's good double in the pregnant Lena Grove, to the unspeaking, unspeakable neologism of filth—the "womanshenegro" of a particular Christmas nightmare—to the moonscape of urns, associated with the menses and Christmas's initiation into the rites of the sexual and sacrificial, to the cosmic infinity of days and space that swallow him up in a hideous repetition crisis that precedes his end. But if it is possible to say so, we observe in Faulkner instances of the exterior other in positive identity whose laws of behavior are much harder and more challenging to detect.

The exterior other in positive identity is, for Faulkner, a female, and in the Faulknerian situation of the female, we gain good insight into the processes of gender-making as a special outcome of modes of dominance. But even more importantly, we observe gender as a special feature of a racialistic ideology. In other words, the African-American female, in her historic identity, robbed of the benefits of the "reproduction of mothering," is, consequently, the very negation of femaleness that accrues as the peculiar cultural property of Anglo-American women, in the national instance, and more generally, of the female of not-color: Faulkner's *Absalom, Absalom!* might be considered a case in point.[9]

This novel renders a fiction of misplaced incestuous longings and the play of homoerotic motives by way of a Freudian family drama.[10] It is key that the children of unreconstructed Thomas Sutpen, the great obsession of Rosa Coldfield's furious speaking, are actually and symbolically "white" and "colored." In effect, this character out of the Virginia wilds, with a crucial *stop* in Haiti (or a Francophone location in the Caribbean), lends an analogy on a fatherhood that founds a "civilization" and a continuity that terminates in a version of return of the repressed—French *Bon*-become-black *Bond*, that Faulkner's Luster says the law puts on you when it catches up with you. The route from Haiti, say, to New Orleans, to Sutpen's Hundred, Yoknapatawpha County, is purposefully and gravidly suggestive, as it involves the worlds of sub-Saharan Africa, the Caribbean, and the United States in the replay of an economic triangulation whose wealth is built solidly on the backs and with the blood of captive human cargo. It is, then, not at all accidental, or academic, to the scheme of history implied by Faulkner's fiction that the savage and dangerous denial of Charles Bon's paternity has precedent in the cultural institution of New World enslavement, as attested by Frederick Douglass, and that this enslavement has a special place, meaning, and economics for the female, as witnessed in the narrative of Linda Brent.[11]

Vagaries of Faulkner's trammeled semantics aside for the moment, this novel quite simply concerns a man who had two sons, one of them the would-be morganatic byblow of an obscure white male on the run, except that Sutpen did marry the mother of Charles Bon to discover, after the fact, that he had been betrayed by the makers of this contrived connubial arrangement. The overseer of a sugar plantation on an island like Santo Domingo—scored into historical memory by the successful revolt of Touissant L'Ouverture—Sutpen tells his version of his story to his contemporary, the grandfather of Quentin, and that, heroically, singlehandedly, he quelled a siege of insurgent African captives on the island. The reward for his bravery, the dowry of the marriage bed, so to speak, is the hand of the master's daughter, whose mother, in turn, is Spanish, the dark suggestion, not French. When Sutpen discovers that the woman to whom he is married has "Negro blood" in her veins, that single most powerful drop of dexyribose nucleic acid, he decides simultaneously that she cannot, for that reason, contribute to the increment of his "design." He then abandons her and her son, or repudiates them in the name of a higher social and moral purity, but compensates, he imagines, by relinquishing his legal right to various island properties accruing to him as marital lagniappe. Said properties revert back to the plantation owner's daughter.

Leaving the West Indies for other New World territory, Sutpen arrives in

Mississippi to take up land and build his "empire." With white Ellen Coldfield, of the indubitable blood, Sutpen has a daughter and son, Henry and
Judith. But in the Caribbean a full decade before, Charles, the Good—
forced into the estate of the prodigal—has been denied the name, if not the
connubial inheritance, of the father. At "Ole Miss" on the eve of civil war,
brother and brother meet—the marked and the untainted—their consanguinity not known to either. This disastrous encounter that possibly ends in
fratricide bears the earmarks of sexual attraction, incestuously linked. But
parallel to it is the complementing sybaritic tale, staked out in massive
erotic display, of Charles Bon, installed with his mother in New Orleans under conditions of a severe and privileged privacy. In the narrative of Quentin Compson's father, not definitively informed by the apposite "facts" of
the case, a probable fiction is hatched—or a fiction true enough—concerning Bon's octoroon mistress and the intricately manufactured arts of pleasure that distinguish the fictive New Orleans whorehouse.

Compson's social and political sense makes a few things evident at
once: he imagines himself the embodiment of that "heritage peculiarly Anglo-Saxon—of fierce proud mysticism" (108). The world that he narrates
through his son Quentin is permeated by notions of caste and hierarchy.
This order of things, eminently linear, is identified by its interdictive color-
ing, whose primary object of desire and placement is the female. But in this
instance, femaleness is abstracted by legal practice and social custom into
an idea that may be sealed off at any concrete point as forbidden territory.
In other words, female, in the brain of the creating male narrator, allows access only insofar as she approximates physical/sexual function. A curious
split of motives takes place here so that on the one hand the last woman in
this hierarchical scale of values—the "slave girls," for instance—are both
more and less female, while, on the other, the same may be said for the first
"lady," albeit for radically different reasons. Compson's "ladies, women, females" specify an increasingly visual and dramatic enactment of male heterosexuality along three dimensions of female being—"the virgins whom
gentlemen someday married, the courtesans to whom they went while on
sabbaticals to the cities, the slave girls and women upon whom the first
caste rested and to whom in certain cases it doubtless owed the very fact of
its virginity" (109).

In this economy of delegated sexual efficacies, the castes of women enter into a drama of exchange value, predicated on the dominant male's self-
deceit. The third caste robs the first of a putative clitoral and vaginal
pleasure, as the first purloins from the third a uterine functionality.[12] Only
the first caste gains here the right to the rites and claims of motherhood,

blind to its potential female pleasure and reduced, paradoxically, in the scale of things to a transcendent and opaque Womanhood. In fact, we could say that whatever "essence," or "stuff" of the female genitalia that is lost in Compson's first estate of females is more than compensated by the third estate, inexorably fixed in the condition of a mindless fertility, just as bereft as the first of the possibilities of its own potential female pleasure.[13] But quite obviously the ways and means of domination are not adopted with cultural/historical subjects-become-objects in mind, nor is "gender" here any more than, or other than, an apt articulation of a divided male heteroticism.

Inside the split ego of the dominant male falls the "mulatta," or the "octoroon," or the "quadroon"—those disturbing vectors of social and political identity—who heals the rupture at points of wounding. Allowing the male to have his cake and eat it too, or to rejoin the "female" with the "woman," the mulatta has no name because there is not a locus, or a strategy, for this unitarian principle of the erotic in the nineteenth-century mentality of Faulkner's male character. Bon's female forebear and his octoroon mistress, the unvoiced shadowy creatures who inhabit the content of the narratives of three male figures in the novel, suggest both the vaginal and the prohibitive pleasure.

The patriarchal prerogatives outlined by Compson are centered in notions that concern the domestication of female sexuality—how it is thwarted, contained, circumscribed, and above all, *narrated,* and not a single female character here escapes the outcome, from the infantilized, doll-like figures of the master class, to the brutalized who serve them. Under these conditions, sexuality is permissible, but silenced, only within the precincts of the father's house. We should say in the place of the *permissible* that sexuality is *clean* only in the father's house. Beyond the sphere of domesticity, the sexual—tenaciously named—effects synonymity with the illicit, the wild, the mysterious; without permutation.[14] And one of its signs is the "mulatta," who has no personhood, but locates in the flesh a site of cultural and political maneuver. Unlike African female personality, implied in her presence, the "mulatta" designates those notions of femaleness that would re-enforce the latter as an object of gazing—the dimensions of the spectacular that we addressed before as the virtually unique social property of the "mulatto/a."

Noted for his/her "beauty," the "mulatta/o" in fiction bears a secret, the taint of evil in the blood, but paradoxically, the secret is vividly worn, made clear. Unlike Joe Christmas, whom we pointed as an example of the exterior other in negative identity, the mulatta, in positive identity, has value for the dominant other only insofar as she becomes the inaccessible female property that can be rendered, at his behest, instantly accessible. Teasing himself with her presence, the dominant other re-intersects the lines of sexuality and "civilization" forced to diverge by the requirements of the family, the private property, and the state. "Virility" reveals itself in the whorehouse as the scandal that is not only *sufferable,* but also primarily *applauded* as the singular fact and privilege of the phallus.

It doesn't matter if the principle of virility is, among living historic male subjects, an engagement fraught with *chance,* or the erection that occasionally fails, or the sporadic impotence about which living historic female subjects remain loyally silent. We are talking about myth here, or those boundaries of discourse that fix and determine belief, practice, and desire. To that extent, all "gendering" activity—"male," "female," and its manifold ramifications—constitutes the Grand Lie about which novels are written and for which cause history hurts.[15]

Even though Compson the narrator does not entirely grasp the political and ironic trenchancies of his own conjecture (as *reported* to Shreve by Quentin at Harvard), nor know in those recalled narrative moments that Charles Bon is not an Anglo-Saxon male, he adequately identifies the complementary strands of relationship between chattel slavery and a eugenics of pleasure. Imagining what young Henry Sutpen, the Mississippi provincial, might have observed in his exposure to certain peculiarities of New Orleans life, Compson draws out the hidden exchange value of female use here as a commodification of the flesh that takes place according to intricate rules of gallantry. The caste/cast of octoroon females (in which Bon's mistress with child is installed) literally belongs to a class of masters, who protect their property by way of various devices that cluster in notions of "honor." It would not do, for instance, for Henry Sutpen to call Bon's mistress a "whore," since he, or any other male committing the *faux pas,* would be "forced to purchase that privilege with some of [his] blood from probably a thousand men" (115) The protection of chattel property in this instance occasions the ethics of the duel as the vertical version of the tumescent male. In other words, maleness is centered here almost entirely in sexual activity covered over by acts of courtesy and carefully choreographed through an entire field of manners from a certain architectural structure and accoutrements of the interior, to modes of dress and address.

This relocated mimesis of European courtly love traditions places "gender" squarely within the perspective of cultural invention whose primary aim is the gratifying appetites of the flesh. This materialist philosophy, modulated through various points of human valuation, would suggest that culture itself elaborates a structure of production and reproduction that posits, quite arbitrarily, "higher" and "lower" reaches of human society, immersed in the principle of desire in the Dominant Other. But it seems that powers of domination succeed only to the extent that their permeation remains silent and concealed to those very historical subjects—"higher" and "lower"—upon whom the entire structure rests, upon whom it depends. In other words, the fictions and realities of domination are not only opaque (not everywhere and at once visible) to the subject (and *narrated*) community, but also remain evasive, in their authentic character as raw and violent assertion, to the dominant (and *narrating*) community. Compson, for example, as a materialized fictive presence, assumes a piacular, or religious, function of female use. His hyperbolic sense of "Anglo Saxon" male mission is grammatically similar to Perry Miller's classic analysis of the puritan colonial's "errand in the wilderness."[16] That Compson's grammar crosses its wires with the "religious impulse" suggests not only the vanities of self-deceit, but also the implicit obscenities of an unironized view of any human and social scheme. Further, his shortsightedness problematizes the religious itself as a special means of domination; as a dominant discourse hiding its hand, veiling its baser motivations.

But Compson initiates the first half of his analysis in correct assessment: the invention of the octoroon mistress rests on the "supreme apotheosis of chattelry . . . human flesh bred of the two races for that sale" (112). That the sentence does not finish itself, overwhelmed by intervening and obstructing periods, ambiguates meaning: "that sale" *of?* "*that* sale," period? And no presumption of ignorance on the hearer's part—we all know, I think, *which sale that is.* "Apotheosis" proximate to "chattelry," however, gives rise to an untenable—one might even say godless—oxymoron. It is also a filthy joke. But none need call it "sacrilege," though, since, in Compson's view at least, this very discourse of contiguity has been ordained by God Himself.

A divine prosthesis, the narrator's "thousand, the white men—made [the octoroon mistress], created and produced them; we even made the laws which declare that one eighth of a specified kind of blood shall outweigh seven eighths of another kind" (115). This refined prattle of a pseudo human science is not entirely misleading since it designates the bestial character of human breeding. If "mulatto" originates etymologically in notions of "sterile mule," then mulatto-ness is not a genetically transferable trait. It must be calculated and preserved as a particularistic project in "race." The southern personality's historic fear that the binary "races" might come together in the spawn of the "miscegenous" is absolutely assured and pursued in the presence of the "mulatto." In fact, it would seem that this presence describes that point of intersection between the *fulfill-ment* of the prohibitive wish and the *prohibition* itself,[17] so that the narra-tive energies of the narrator's recalled text are part and parcel of an enor-mous struggle to ward off a successfully *willed* and *willful* compulsion:

> the white blood to give the shape and pigment of what the white man calls female beauty, to a female principle which existed, queenly and complete, in the hot equatorial groin of the world long before that white one of ours came down from trees and lost its hair and bleached out—a principle apt docile and instinct with strange and curious plea-sures of the flesh (which is all: there is nothing else) which her white sisters of a mushroom yesterday fled from in moral and outraged hor-ror—a principle which, where her white sister must needs try to make an economic matter of it like someone who insists upon installing a counter or a scales or a safe in a store or business for a certain percent-age of the profits, reigns, wise supine and all-powerful, from the sun-less and silken bed which is her throne. (116–17)

What Compson imagines concerning "the hot equatorial groin of the world" can be guessed only too well and has, embarrassingly, no historic basis and needn't, for the narrator, since the subject, one narrator remove, is addressing its own overdetermined sexuality. In the process, "black" re-mains unnamed except by implication in an imagined metonymic substi-tution. To return a moment to Todorov's dynamics of alterity, we observe that the narrator has (1) *epistemically* no valuable, or enviable knowledge of the female subjects in question; (2) distances himself *praxeologically* from the subjects so that they reveal to him no dynamic historical movement, remaining for the reader the fictional counters that they are; (3) accommo-dates *axiologically* those subjects in a stunning act of obverted condescen-sion that objectifies the other at the same time that the other is isolated as a potentially sacred feature.

What has been created here is not so much a fiction of the octoroon heroine as a text of an evoked "Anglo-Saxon" male presence *having*, essen-tially, a creation myth, not unlike one's giving birth or begetting. But this behaving as *though* the fictive text were "real," that it ought to give the reader valuable information about the historical sequence, contravenes the assumptions of our present critical practices, but the misstep is useful, nev-ertheless, in what might be abstracted from it. "White" women and those historical subjects trapped in the figuration of "hot equatorial groin of the world" modulate into the very same economic, if not cultural, principle by sheer semantic proximity. The distinction that I wish to make here between "economic" and "cultural" is meant to identify in the economic instance those social and political uses to which the subject is put, while the cultural is intended to define the translation of such uses—in actual cash value, but more ordinarily, in the symbolic and figurative currencies entailed by such translation. The processes that I would keep discrete here so overlap in actual social practice that a distinction seems wrong. But the narrator's insistence on the "economic matter" of, by implication, a hired vaginal substance makes clear that dollars and ledgers are what *he* means as the materialized figurative value of the "white sister." It is less clear, from his point of view, though doubtless true, that the reign of the "wise supine" is just as costly and dear for the very same commodity, even if a "sunless and silken bed" carries a richer poetic and visual echo than counters and scales and stores and business.

Thrown down into the narrator's sentences as extended parentheses, these abrupt elaborations yoke "white" and "not-white" female in figurative alliance and likely, historic alignment that only the ahistoricity of "color," or the "proud fierce mysticism" of "Anglo-Saxon" race ideology, has excised. If the Compsons of the world enforce order and degree in their "casting" of women, then at least they suspect that fundamentally, the female substance—everywhere the same—acquires *different* value according to the very same standard of measure—its *imagined* and *posited* worth to a client, made supreme by his ability to command desire.

The missing *persona* from Compson's scheme is already there in what the metonymic figure keeps concealed. But "equator," in its cotermity with portions of the sub-Saharan African continent, proclaims the narrator's suggested meaning. But indirection in this case, which is itself a mode of figurative elaboration, brings us to a crucial point. In attempting to articulate a theory of difference regarding African-American women, we have begun the effort by looking at semantic processes of appeal that occur in certain textual evidence, including fiction. The Faulknerian excerpt, though isolatable in its persistent, stylistic mannerisms, provides, in that regard, points of concentration in what we might call the historical narratives that refer to this community of women. I have in mind here not primarily, if at all, those written texts of history, or those texts based in self-conscious historiographical pursuit. I mean, rather, those configurations of discursive experience *about* ... that appear dispersed across a range of public address and that may or may not find their way to topics of the historical discipline. These configurations, embedded in public consciousness, enact a symbolic behavior that is actually metatextual in its political efficacy, in its impact on the individual life-narratives of historical subjects.

Though "African-American women's community" and "mulatto/a" may appear to be widely divergent structures of appeal, the one claimed by the historical dimension, the other stalled on the terrain of the reified object, they share common ground in two crucial ways: (1) The proximity effected between *real* and *imagined* properties. The "mulatto/a" appears, historically, when African female and male personality become hyphenated American political entities, at that moment when they enter public and political discourse in the codes of slavery, the rise of the fugitive, the advertisement of the run-away man/woman.[18] (2) Both effecting a radical alterity with the dominant one, they demonstrate the extent to which modes of substitution can be adopted as strategies of containment. In other words, if African-American women's community can be silenced in its historic movement, then it will happen because the narratives concerning them have managed successfully to capture the subject in time's vacuum. By denying the presence of the black female, or assimilating her historic identity, more precisely, to a false body, ventriloquized through a factitious public discourse concerning the "blood" and "breeding," the dominant mode succeeds in transposing the real into the mythical/magical.

The situation of the "mulatta" in the same field of signification with the black female juxtaposes contrastive social and political uses, but their simultaneous appearance at the time of the national consolidation of slaveholding power is, on the one hand, no longer a secret—if it ever were—and a problem of meaning on the other. That class of historical subjects fathered by captive owners and following the condition of the mother were never, color of skin aside, surrogate Anglo-American, though they did stand in for black, for African. I am less interested in the class implications of this cultural phenomenon than its symbolic processes and their outcome. Subsequent to the intrusion of a middle term, or middle ground—figuratively—between the subjugated and dominant interests, public discourse gains, essentially, the advantages of a lie by orchestrating otherness through degrees of difference. The philosopher's "great chain of being" ramifies now to disclose within American Africanity itself literal shades of human value so that the subject community refracts the oppressive mechanism just as certainly as the authoring forms put them in place. This fatalistic motion that turns the potentially insurgent community furiously back on itself proceeds by way of processes we might call "archaizing." Faulkner's narrative voices provide examples of this trait when Quentin as Compson posits in the "hot equatorial groin of the world" and "those white ones of ours [come] down from trees and . . . bleached out" aspects of the magical, or the ahistorical, not at all responsive to context, or contingency. The "mulatta," in prominent isolation from the living subject, just as, by suggestion, "black" and "white" women are, shows this process in concision. "Power" in this instance consists in the prerogative to name human value, to distribute and arrogate it.

The world according to captives and their captors strikes the imagination as a grid of identities running at perpendicular angles to each other: *things* in serial and lateral array; beings in hierarchical and vertical array. On the serial grid, the captive—the chattel property—is the equivalent of inanimate and other living things:

Transactions at: Anamaboe 1736[19]
Nov. 24th Sold Capt. Hammond 4 women for Recd. the following goods

		OZ.	A.
Viz.	16 perpets	5	
	7 half Says	3	8
	3 half Ells	1	8
	1 ps. Niconee		5
	4 qr bb powder	2	
	14 sheets		14
	2 paper Sleties		5
	112 galls rum	7	

This itemized excerpt from the accounts from an African Trade-Book for the colony of Rhode Island vividly illustrates the dehumanization of African personality. Frederick Douglass, however, provides a narrative a full century later for such a scenario, remembering the division of property upon the death of one of his former masters. Having to return from Baltimore to the site of Captain Anthony's estate, he writes of the occasion: "We were all ranked together at the valuation. Men and women, old and young, married and single, were ranked with horses, sheep, and swine. There were horses and men, cattle and women, pigs and children, all holding the same rank in the scale of being, and were all subjected to the same narrow examination."[20]

From Donnan's accounts of the slave galley's logs and bills of lading and of sales, to Douglass's *Narrative*, we discover time and again the collapse of human identity adopted to the needs of commerce and economic profit. But even more startling than this nominal "crisis of degree" (which renders an equality of substances not unlike the figurative collapse of disparities in metaphorical display) is the *recovery* of difference in a hierarchical and vertical distribution of being, as though this cultural disarray stood corrected, or compensated. In the intersection of these axes, at the point of "mules and men"—the human ownership and possession of other human beings—the notion of property so penetrates the order of things that the entire structure is undermined by a simple change and overwhelming paradox: those sub-jects located at this juncture of saturated elements are both more and less human, the former because they enter into a wider ecumenicalism with named and claimed things, or vocabularies of experience; the latter because it is their destiny by virtue of Christ's church, by whom the country swears, and the spirit of national insurgence and constitutionality to be human first and only. That we find no comparable "list" of being, as we do the care-fully accounted for commercial item, simply suggests to me that "laterality" had done its job, and no more needed to be said, if it were possible to rank human with animal. In effect, the humanity of African personality is placed in quotation marks under these signs and problematized as a leading ques-tion for public policy and a philosophical inquiry of the nicest sort.

Alterity, therefore, describes not only an inauthentic human status, but also the locus of a relationship between non-historical elements that come to rest beyond the pale of human and its discourses; this lack of movement in the field of signification seems to me the origin of "mulatto/a-ness"—the *inherent* name and naming—the *wedge* between the world of light and the step beyond—into the undifferentiated, unarticulated mass of moving and movable *things*.

Between these dualities, the "shadow" of the "mulatto/a" is interposed. It is a matter of surprise to me that there is in William Faulkner, writing in the twentieth century, and Frances E. W. Harper, writing in the nineteenth, a certain lexical recurrence that initiated my observations in the opening pages of this essay: Quentin/Compson the narrator describes Charles Bon in terms of an appropriation that are just as apposite to his octoroon inven-tion. In fact, Charles Bon is thrice made—once by the attenuated concepts of history that haunt the characterization; once by the structure of mimesis that the character is purported to display; and yet again by the appropriat-ing speaker as a "shadowy" presence: "A myth, a phantom: something which [Ellen and Judith Sutpen] engendered and created whole themselves; some effluvium of Sutpen blood and character, as though as a man he did not exist at all" (104). Frances Harper entitled her 1893 novel *Iola Leroy, or Shadows Uplifted*. Though it is appropriately not clear what dramatic and rhetorical function the topos of "shadow" serves in the novel, it is at least probable that its ambiguity complements its topic—the fate of Iola Leroy, mulatta girl remanded back into slavery and overcoming, at last, the pain and confusion of her biography. But the novel just as certainly concerns the reunion of mothers and children—the blood line of slavery—divided across the cleavage of "race."

In each instance of re-encounter, the pilgrimage that precedes it seems compelled by the mulatto status of the character, as though, as in comic resolution, the peace and order of the world were restored in *their* happiness. For Harper's narrator, at least, only the mulatto characters enter an ascension, as Iola Leroy, in the closure of the novel, is not only a character, but also Character Extraordinaire. These agents "too white to be black, too black to be white" share with Bon and Christmas the magical status of liminality (as it is not clear, recent criticism argues, just what "color" Joe Christmas is),[21] but in the case of Harper's eponymous heroine, the piously sacred overtakes her. Just so, she assumes the equally ambiguous estate of the blessed: "The shadows have been lifted from all their lives; and peace, like bright dew, has descended upon their paths. Blessed themselves, their lives are a blessing to others."[22]

In effect, the law and the order of this world have not simply been fully regained. This world has ended as the character slips away from earth into the non-historical eternity of the unchanging. This false movement takes us back to the notion of the intruded wedge between opposed dualities. In this instance, the mulatta mediates between dualities, which would suggest that at least mimetic movement, imitating *successful* historical movement, is *upward,* along the vertical scale of being. The only "black" in this case who can move is not quite "black" enough, or certainly not enough that the people who need to know can tell. We observe in the female a similar complex of assumptions at work in the Faulknerian case.

The "shadow" as a center of ambiguity in Faulkner's and Harper's work might disclose the dramatic surprise that lends these divergent writings a stunning mutuality. As a way of concluding these notes, I want to point out three moments of crux: the lifting of the shadows from the one-dimensionality of Harper's characters' lives; the phantom-like, shadowy aspects that cluster in Compson's version of Charles Bon; the terrible, ascensive epiphany of Joe Christmas's slaughter: "Then his face, body, all seemed to collapse, to fall in upon itself, and from out the slashed garments about his hips and loins the pent black blood seemed to rush like a released breath. It seemed to rush out of his pale body like a rush of sparks from a rising rocket; upon the black blast the man seemed to rise soaring into their memories forever and ever."[23]

In all three moments, the character achieves, at last, the superior talismanic force, a preponderance, or a preponderant lack, of humanity. This attribution of extraordinary humanity obviously works in contrastive ways: as we have seen in the case of *Iola Leroy,* the closural device points toward a divine and beneficent ground of potentialities; in the case of *Light in August,* toward a sacrificial torture. In *Absalom, Absalom!* Charles Bon, immersed in the secrecies of origin, is invested by effects of adoration, as he becomes the veritable love object of brother and sister Sutpen. But these opposing indices—pointing upward and downward—mobilize character toward the very same region of finality. "Hell" is "heaven" turned upside down, as "heaven" comprehends "hell" in the classic scheme of cosmogony.

That the semantic field here clings tenaciously to notions of the transcendent without openly declaring them as such provides what seems an apt demonstration of Foucault's "enunciative field" by way of concomitance.[24] In this instance of discursive relations between what I would call a founding concept and "forms of succession," "quite different domains of objects" are involved that "belong to quite different types of discourse." Concomitance is generated "either because they serve as analogical confirmation [of the founding concept] or because they serve as a general principle and as premises accepted by a reasoning, or because they serve as models that can be transferred to other contents." The founding concept here may be generally regarded as a religiously discursive pointer, as we observed in Compson's blank parody of the creation process. But the analogues on a religious discursivity in these works fracture in contradiction: the "sacred" mulatto figure simultaneously repels and attracts because of his/her blood-crossed career. Faulkner's narrators attribute to Joe Christmas the "pent black blood" and to the octoroon female "seven-eighths" of the *right* blood type. It is not until Bon's blood connection is revealed that Henry Sutpen most probably commits fratricide of the "blood" brother whom he has loved.

Throughout Harper's work the narrator refers to blood along various lines of stress: the "tainted blood" of "white Negroes"; the "trick of the blood"; "outcast blood in the veins"; "traditions of blood" and the human estate; "the imperceptible infusion of Negro blood," etc. As the life essence, the human blood, for all that scientific knowledge teaches concerning it, persists in notions of the mysterious. At least one tends to regard it mysteriously, as if the scientific topicality of it were insufficient to exhaust its range of figurative notions.

The blood to which these fictive narrators speak has little to do with the scientific, even when they suggest, and perhaps all the more so, mensural dimensions of the substance, as in one-half, one-fourth, one-eighth "black." It appears that medical and scientific knowledges are not, after all, the arbiters of the blood *where we live,* nor yet the origin of recourse when genealogies, or the "transfer" of time through children and properties, are concerned. The blood remains impervious, at the level of folklore and myth, to incursions of the "reasonable" and inscribes the unique barrier beyond which human community has not yet passed into the "brotherhood of man" and the "Fatherhood of God." But this very difficulty of the blood is the hinge upon which the concept of community, as we now understand it, appears to turn; extends itself.

Like the *pharmikon,* the blood is both the antidote and the poison,[25] as the intrusion of mystery in its place segregated the menstruating female, banished the "ugly and deformed" infants of the unhusbanded woman,[26] and rendered "femaleness" itself the site of absence. On its basis, American Africanity was assigned to the axis of "thingness" in a vision of human community that replicates time and again notions of hierarchical order. If there is mystery or spirit drooping down in the midst of things, then someone must safeguard its secrets; traditionally, the offices of the priestly function (and here I mean any structure of the esoteric), of the recondite in general, of the Dominant One, of a hyperbolean phallic status have fallen to the lot of the male. It is this inner and licit circle of a coveted and mystified knower and knowledge that determines the configurations of the law and the order. But the mystery apparently yields its secret, despite the covering names, as the glorification of a male heteronormativity, which designates the only "maleness" that can lay claim to the phallic principle. Under these conditions of culture and acculturation, we regard the "mulatta" as the recovery of female gender beyond the father's house, beyond the lights of the female who falls *legitimately* within its precincts. The borders of the endogamous arrangement are extended without guilt. But the "master," not always sufficiently protected against the burden of incest, might well have discovered his daughter (by African female personality) in the bed of his wife. The invention of the American "mulatta" virtually assured his success.

13

Who Cuts the Border? Some Readings on America

For Roberto and Maddie Marquez

The January 10, 1891 edition of *La Revista Illustrada* carried the initial publication of José Martí's celebrated essay, "Our America."[1] Later, almost exactly a year to the day, "El Partido Revolucionario Cubano"—the Cuban Revolutionary Party—was created, with Martí acknowledged as "its leading spirit, inspirer, and organizer."[2] The compressed background of historical events that Philip Foner provides in the Introduction to the second of four English-language editions of Martí's writings[3] reacquaints readers in the United States with a larger-than-life romantic instance, whose initiating moments date back to one's childhood and its ephemeral encounters with symptoms of the heroic: Simón Bolivar, Father Hidalgo, and "the cry of Dolores," alongside Martí, are entailed with the same fabric of cultural memory and a curiously elided time-space continuum that threads the name of A. Philip Randolph with the successes of the Brotherhood of Sleeping Car Porters and the heady political maneuvers of Adam Clayton Powell Jr. It remains, then, a matter of surprise that, even as one eventually grasps the reasons why, Martí's "our" and "America" do not usually embrace US at all—except by the logic of a clearly defined dualism of antagonists, who, in the febrile imagination of his writings, must contend, in effect, for the right to name and claim "America." As Foner observes, that vast stretch of formidably organized political power, ninety miles north of the island and nation of Cuba, demarcates, for Martí that "other America," neither "*his* America," nor "Mother America" of Martí's dream of wholeness.[4] About seventy years following the writing of the lectures that comprise *The Philosophy of History*,[5] G. W. F. Hegel himself might have been offered occasion for surprise at the exemplary boldness of one José Martí:

The European university must bow to the American university. The history of America, from the Incas to the present must be taught in clear detail and to the letter, even if the archons of Greece are overlooked. Our Greece must take priority over the Greece which is not ours. We need it more. Nationalist statesmen must replace foreign statesmen. Let the world be grafted onto our republics, but the trunk must be our own. And let the vanquished pedant hold his tongue, for there are not lands in which a man may take greater pride than in our long-suffering American republics. (88)

Interestingly enough, Martí and Hegel, inhabiting either end of the nineteenth century, posited, for radically different reasons and toward radically different and reversed ends, two contrastive "Americas." For Martí, as the excerpted passage suggests, "Our America," of indigenous historical currents, fires, on the one hand, the profoundly figurative polemic of his revolutionary moment and impulse, those "long suffering American republics, raised up from among the silent Indian masses by the bleeding arms of a hundred apostles, to the sounds of battle between the book and the processional candle" (86). On the other hand, the "other America," the United States, "this avaricious neighbor who admittedly has designs on us,"⁶ arouses Martí to the visionary urgencies of an Armageddon. Perhaps the longest syntactic chain in "Our America" throws forth immitigable linking between "since/then," *post hoc, ergo propter hoc*, embedded in oppositional ground:

And since strong nations, self-made by law and shotgun, love strong nations, and them alone; since the time of madness and ambition— from which North America may be freed by the predominance of the purest elements in its blood, or on which it may be launched by its vindictive and sordid masses, its tradition of expansion, or the ambitions of some powerful leader . . . since its good name as a republic in the eyes of the world's perceptive nations puts upon North America a restraint that cannot be taken away by childish provocations or pompous arrogance or parricidal discords among our American nations—the pressing need of Our America is to show itself as it is, one in spirit and intent. (93)

Though far too schematic, one learns, to exhaust, or even adequately account for, the range of Martí's thought,⁷ his rhetorical binary, nonetheless, subtends one of the chief critical functions of his solidary political and intellectual engagement.

Martí's expressly dramatic protocol of pronouns is neither more nor less presumptuous than Hegel's implied one, which also distinguishes

"America," New World, from the "United States of North America, but an emanation from Europe" (82). Hegel's "other America" "has always shown itself physically and psychically powerless, and still shows itself so" (81). These aboriginal societies "gradually vanished at the breath of European activity" (81); we needn't add that such "breath" ferociously animated the winds of multiple violence—epistemic, linguistic, iconographic, genocidal. Hegel's European-emanated United States, with its "republican constitution," its Christian sects of Protestant enthusiasm, its "universal protection for property" belongs, finally and dismissively, for Hegel, to an American "future," "where, in the ages that lie before us, the burden of the World's History shall reveal itself—perhaps in a contest between North and South America" (86).

The Hegelian "perhaps" is borne out, amazingly so, in hemispheric wars of national liberation, so far, including Cuba (in its First and Second Wars of Independence) and Cuba again, under the successful insurgency of Fidel Castro, shortly past the mid-point of the twentieth century. No one can fail to read current affairs in Ibero-Hispanic America and the Caribbean—from Sandinista Nicaragua, to post-Noriega Panama—outside an ironized perspective on this "future" and the culture texts inscribed and unfolding about it.

Ensnared, then, between Old World and New, past and future, the contrary ideas of "America" instantiate the text and the materiality on a historico-cultural ground long fabled and discursive in acts of European invention and intervention. It is as if the Word, for Europe, engenders Flesh. Peter Hulme argues, for example, that the discourse of English colonialism arises fundamentally on the career of two key terms—"hurricanes" and "Caribbees"—that mark relatively new lexemes in the English language. "Not found before the middle of the sixteenth century," these terms do not settle into "their present forms before the latter half of the seventeenth."[8] Both originate in Native American languages, and "both were quickly adopted into all the major European languages" (58). Raymond Williams's *Keywords* does not carry entries on either term, but it is rather startling that as innocuous as they might appear in the lexicon, "hurricanes" and "Caribbees/Caribbean," especially the latter, have achieved keyword status over a significant spate of modern intellectual history. Any subsequent addenda that we might devise on Williams's project concerning the evolution of terministic cruxes "in the West" might well inaugurate around "Caribbean" and its own emanations.

Contemporary Cuban intellectual, Roberto Fernández Retamar—poet, essayist, and distinguished editor of *Casa de las Americas*—offers, in his clas-

sic essay, a highly informative synthesis[9] of the history of related terms—
"Caribbean/Caribbees/Caliban." As background and framework that situate Retamar's reading of culture in "Our America," this rich congruence of
terms is biographically reinscribed in the exemplary instance of Martí's
public life and career. Retamar tracks "Caribbean" from its eponymous
Carib community of Native Americans, who, we are told, valiantly resisted
European incursion in the sixteenth century, to its philosophical and terministic transformations, by way of "Caliban," in the contemporary period, with specific reference to the works of Aimé Césaire, Frantz Fanon,
and O. Mannoni.[10] As if a moment of phantasmagoria that perfectly mirrors the Freudian formula of media cross-dressing—the dream as *visual*
transliteration of the day's *grammar* events—"Carib" is translated as a "de-
formation" and "defamation" into "cannibal." The latter generates an ana-
gram in "Caliban," as Shakespeare had already made use of "cannibal" to
mean anthropophagus "in the third part of *Henry IV* and *Othello*" (11).

This nested semiotic filiation, inaugurated by a reputed "look," retailed
as truth to Christopher Columbus, will stage a paradigm of discursive and
scopophilic behavior for colonizing and enslaving powers toward "peoples
of color," and most dramatically in its duration, for Hegel's "Negro" of sub-
Saharan "Africa," which demonstrates "no historical part of the world," it
was said; " . . . has no movement or development to exhibit," it was concluded (99). For Columbus's reporters (and Hegel), anthropophagi reside on
that border between nature and culture, inhabited by "men with one eye
and others with dog's muzzles, who ate human beings."[11]

Would we dare, then, risk a simplistic and essentialist reduction? "Someone," perhaps, saw "something" or "someone" in a stage of cultural production long before Columbus came,[12] and even now with pure revisionary
heart-work and devotion to the politics of the plural, we cannot decipher
exactly what it was. Having few corrective narratives to counterpoise, the
future-laden actor reenacts an analogy on a child's game: a sentence is
passed along a spatial sequence, person to person, and at the end of it the
garbled "message" makes only comic sense. Just so (or almost), we will not
know now, since the first speakers, either way, are not available. By the time
Shakespeare sifts "cannibal" through the sieve of his imagination, it is an
already inspissated narrative of plenitude, crystallized in the sixteenth century by, among other sources, Thomas More's *Utopia* (1580) and Michel de
Montaigne's "De los Caníbales" (1580); the translation of Montaigne's
work by way of Giovanni Floro's *Essays* was available to Shakespeare, Retamar observes (14).

The construction and invention of "America," then—a dizzying concoction of writing and reportage, lying and "signifying," jokes, "tall tales," and transgenerational nightmare, all conflated under the banner of Our Lord—exemplify, for all intents and purposes, the oldest game of trompe de l'oeil, the perhaps-mistaken-glance-of-the-eye, that certain European powers carried out regarding indigenous Americans. *Misprision,* therefore, constitutes law and rule of "Our America" in its "beginnings" for Europe. Made up in the gaze of Europe, "America" was as much a "discovery" on the retinal surface as it was the appropriation of land and historical subjects.

From what angle does one insert the "United States but-an-emanation from Europe" into this picture, or perhaps, more ambitiously, a series of perpendicular pronouns—the "I's"/"eyes" of writings on the New World?

At least one thing is doubtless: At whatever point one cuts into this early modern discourse on what will become, quite by accident, by arbitrary design, by the most complicated means of economic (and otherwise) exchange, and the entire repertoire of genetic play and chance, her space, his space, of central habitation in the unimagined "future" of World History, the initial news is hardly good for anyone. "Physically and psychically powerless" and overcome by men who *eat* (the) other(s), this orientalized, Europe-fabled "America" could not be salvaged by even the hippest stunts of the televisual medium, except that a Martí, for one, will reclaim it as a necessary project of historical demolition and reconstruction. But the United States, carved out of this New World ground, must be read, just as it is intimately connected, with this unfolding historical text of unpromise. The seams will show now, but that is also part of the picture. This ground is broken—by culture and "race," language and ethnicity, weather and land formation, in generative and historical time, as more or less gendered "situation-specificities,"[13] in various postures of loves and hungers, cohabit it—even though, given any point at which the multiple "I"/"We" are positioned on its axes, it appears to be monolithic ground. Retamar, pursuing the implications of Martí's "mestizo America," identifies as *the* "distinctive sign of our culture," those "descendants both ethnically and culturally speaking, of aborigines, Africans, and Europeans" (9). He goes on to interrogate, in rhetorical accents sometime reminiscent of Martí's own writings: "From Túpac Amaru . . . to Nicolás Guillén, to Aimé Césaire, to Violeta Parra, to Frantz Fanon—what is our history, what is our culture, if not the history and culture of Caliban?" (24).

It seems clear that at great expense to the national "pursuit of happiness," a United States culture text/praxis, in the dreamful flattening out of textures of the historical, would repress its calibanesque potential, just as we would amend Retamar's strategy of evocation to account for at least one other strand of the "sixties without apology."[14] If, for instance, Bartolomeo Las Casas and José Martí touch my life-line at some distant point of reverberation, then certainly Isabella Baumfree, become "Sojourner Truth," and Rosa Parks, Malcolm El-Hajj Malik, and Martin Luther King Jr., among others, must sound through Retamar's at no greater distance. The problem of the pronouns—and *we* mustn't mistake this, as the late sixties taught—cannot, will not resolve itself in a too-easy "hands around the world" embrace among hemispheric cross-cultural communities. But if one concedes "Caliban" as a joining figure, then by virtue of what set of moves is the notion applicable along a range of culture practices in light of the hegemonic entailment of operations out of which certain US communities express relations to "Our America"? In other words, in order to disrupt the homogeneous narrative that the United States, as an idea-form, or that "other America" provokes in Martí's, or Retamar's view, or even George Bush Sr.'s view, the contradictions of proximity must be brought further out: Some of US render unto Caesar, more or less, is not simply locutional.

Apparently everywhere one might look on this massive scene of heterogeneous historical attitudes, it seems that "Caliban" designates a copulative potential by way of the Atlantic system of slavery—the ownership of man by man (Virginia's "chattels personal," say), man's ownership of "private property" (Cuba's seigneurial ownership of the sugar product, say), and the captive communities' occasional revolt in the teeth of it (Canada's Caribbean marronage, for example). In the sociopolitical arrangements here stipulated, "man," wherever he appears in the bargain, articulates with juridical, axiomatic, historical, ontological, and local *specificity*. "America," with its US, locates a prime time of "the fruits of merchant capital"[15] as a stunning chapter in the modern history of patriarchal law and will. In other words, America/US shows itself as a "scene of instruction" in the objectifying human possibility across an incredibly various real estate and human being. This vulgar oxymoron of purposes and motivations insists on the combo—human-as-property—and there, in all the astonishing foreclosures of certainty, "English," among other Indo-European languages, enters its currency in the "execrable trade."

It would seem highhanded, then, to read this Real as *a discourse,* but certainly the conceptual narratives around "cannibal"/"Caliban"—a colonial topos, common to the seventeenth century, Hulme argues—projects slavery "as the necessary stage between savagery and civilization" (62). "Caliban" designates itself a moment of convergence between Old World and New, inasmuch as the idea-formation demonstrates "features of both the Mediterranean wild man, or classical monster . . . with an African mother, whose pedigree leads back to Book X of *The Odyssey*" (70). Further, Caliban, as the issue of Sycorax,[16] entertains "particular connection with the moon . . . whose signs the Caribs could read" (70). Need we be reminded here of the "intersections of blood and the moon, the mother and home: towards that terrain which traditionally has been given and denied the name of 'woman'"?[17]

When Martí invokes "Mother America," one imagines that he means the formulation of "mother" in relation to nurture and security, but the term might also mark, under the precise historical circumstance upon which his vision of "America" is raised, the *silence* bred by defeat. If Columbus's *Diaries*, compounded of report, offered the explorer a useful fiction for entering New World communities, then that available discourse evinces a remarkable instance of "rhetorical enargeia," which Patricia Parker describes as "convincing description or vivid report, [containing] within it the same visual root as the name of 'Argus,' sent with his many eyes to spy."[18] The Columbian reporters, for example, were not only providing "promotional narratives," but "a 'blazing,' or publishing of the glories of this *feminized* New World, of the possibilities of commercial abundance and 'return'" (141, my emphasis). Perceiving a link here between language and spectacle, Parker speaks of discursive inventiveness as a "transgressive uncovering, or opening up of a secret place, of exposing what was hidden in the womb of a feminized Nature" (142). These "ocular proofs," giving rise to discursive elaboration, as we have observed in the Caliban/Caribbean/cannibal semiosis, yoke the gaze and the profit in a rhetorics of property (147).

The inventory of both the American land and the figure of Caliban—"ugly, hostile, ignorant, devilish"—inscribes a "rhetorical and an economic instrument, one way of controlling the territory in question" (150). Even though Sycorax is given no script in *The Tempest,* as we recall, her "absence," except in comminatory provocation, confirms the "unrepresentability" of Caliban, the mothered-womaned, to a spectator-audience.[19] A not-sayable offers a strategy for describing the "future," which is always a pregnant possibility in the now.

Hulme describes the locus of *The Tempest* as an "extraordinary topographical dualism" because of its "double series of connotations"—the Mediterranean and the Caribbean. This scene of double inscription is borne out further in "tempest" itself, from the Mediterranean repertoire, and Gonzolo's "plantation," from the Atlantic repertoire (71). But practically speaking, beyond the "rarified latitudes" of Shakespeare's art, the "discovery of America" may be read as "a magnetic pole compelling a reorientation of traditional axes." Superimposing two planes—a palimpsest, "on which there are two texts" (72), "America" juxtaposes "two referential systems" that inhabit "different spaces except for that area which is the island [neither here nor there] and its first native Caliban" (72). As a "geometrical metaphor," Caliban intermediates a "central axis about which both planes swivel free of one another." As a "textual metaphor," Caliban inscribes an "overdetermination," "peculiarly at odds with his place of habitation which is described as an 'uninhabitable island'" (72). Caliban translates the "monstrous" in his mediating posture "between two sets of connotations" and a "compromise formation . . . achieved . . . only at the expense of distortion elsewhere" (72). Precisely metaphorical in the collapse of distinctive features of contrast, Caliban can "exist only within discourse . . . fundamentally and essentially beyond the bounds of representation" (72).

Or is it the *bonds*, the *bonds* of representation? William Faulkner's Luster, the grandson of his "enduring" Dilsey,[20] tries to recall to young Quentin Compson, his proximate age-mate, the name of the wild male child now installed in the shadows of "Sutpen's Hundred"[21] and decides that his not-so-ready-to-hand last name exemplifies a "lawyer's word": "what they puts you under when the Law catches you" (215). Inflected from "Bon," by way of his paternity in Charles Etienne de Saint Valery Bon and a maternity situated by Faulkner's narrator as a "gorilla" of a woman, "Jim Bond" stands free, if not emancipated, in his US/African/European/Americanity as an embodied instance of the "ferocious play of alphabets,"[22] but not unlike Caliban, "he" also marks a would-be place, or a "geometrical metaphor" on the verge of being in an American wilderness—fictitious Jefferson, Mississippi (trapped in a once dark pastoral frame) after the "fall" of the South. Verging on past and future, Jim Bond, a live-wire instance of the law's most persistent social invention, assumes the status of deictic, of nonverbal marker, *here* and *there* , *this* and *that,* as the conventions of discourse out of which he arises proffer him no claim to a "present/presence," except as the unkinned "monster," feared and despised, from Caliban, to Bigger Thomas. Though I am suggesting here a narrative of filiations across a broad swatch of Western discourse, there are, admittedly, considerable differences between these "impression-points": If we accept the argument of Hulme and others that Caliban describes sheer and fateful discursivity that evades the trammels of representation, then what must we make of a figure like Jim Bond whose representability prescribes and provokes *all* that he is?

Both cultural vestibularity and an after-word, "America/US," from Caliban's perspective and that of his diverse relations, must come upon Language and the Law (and in a sense, they overlap the same item from the store of Europe's hardy beneficence) as the inimical "property" of "civilized man." ("You taught me language, and my profit on't / Is, I know how to curse. The red plague rid you / For learning me your language.") This place, this text, as Jim Bond embodies it, as the European interventionist/invader might have imagined, orchestrates representation as the already coded "future." Some of US know this process—in discourse and discourse/politics— as history as *mugging*.

This overdetermined representability, or texts overwritten, locates authority on an exterior, as the seizing of discursive initiative seems to define a first order of insurgency wherever it appears in the New World. Colonial North America as the final port-of-call on a trajectory that starts up the triangular trade all over again would mute its involvement in the narratives of Caliban, as we have observed before, by the fateful creation of "minority" communities in the United States, but it is the ascribed task of such communities to keep the story of difference under wraps through the enactments and reenactments of difference in the flesh. The single basis for a myth of national unity is predicated, therefore, on negation and denial that would bring a Jim Bond to stand in the first place. In that space—like the return to the scene of a crime—we can recite the triangulation of a particular mapping that might demonstrate new ground for the workings of Hulme's "geometrical metaphor."

The historic triangular trade interlarded a third of the known world in a fabric of commercial intimacy so tightly interwoven that the politics of the New World cannot always be so easily disentangled as locally discrete moments. Nowhere is this narrative of involvement more pointedly essayed than in Faulkner's *Absalom, Absalom!* that choreographs Canada, the Caribbean, Africa, Europe, and the United States as geographical and/or figurative points of contact in this fictive discourse. If Caliban as a narrative paradigm links American communities in a repertoire of sporadic historico-cultural reference, then we might traverse its play in *Absalom, Absalom!*

In this layer upon layer of "graphireading,"[23] Faulkner never quite comes to the point, but puts it off again and again in the successful evasion of closure. The tales that converge on "Thomas Sutpen," both the narrated and the sign-vehicle that starts up the narrative and sustains it, are related by speakers who recall the character from some vantage of time long past (as Rosa Coldfield), or, at even greater narrative remove, the recollections of others' *inherited* recollection of Sutpen (as Quentin Compson). At the intersection of a plurality of texts, Sutpen aptly demonstrates the notion of character as a structure of assumptions that reading embodies and, not altogether unlike the orientalized Carib/cannibal formation, is concocted in the imaginings of each speaker from a repertory of rancor, grudging admiration, gossip, rumor, hearsay, and more or less stabilized impression. The work plunders and reworks itself as narrators not only elaborate what they cannot have known, but also correct passed-down information, fill in gaps, piece together disparities, disprove or improve inherited conclusions, assume identities, even invent new ones, that the novel has not embedded. For instance, Quentin Compson's Canadian roommate Shreve McCannon/McKenzie (also "transported" from *The Sound and the Fury* to *Absalom, Absalom!*) posits a quite likely character of a lawyer to the mother of Charles Bon and offers an intercessory gift that the author, we're led to imagine, had not thought of. We also learn from McKenzie that Thomas Sutpen could not have been born in *West* Virginia, if he were 25 years old in Mississippi in 1833, which would establish his birth year as 1808 (220). Having acquired his "American history" in a western Canadian classroom, Shreve, after all, a Harvard man, knows very well that West Virginia was not admitted to the Union until 1863. But the traditional reading on Sutpen, as Quentin receives it down the paternal line, requires him to have been born "in West Virginia, in the mountains." Reading in the interstices, we surmise that Sutpen "comes from" nowhere that an early US map would have articulated.

Essentially originless, if the continuities of kinship and place of birth, relatedly, mean anything, Thomas Sutpen, reminiscent of the colonized European subject before him, "arises" in "Old Bailey" and a criminality inscribed in notary's ink. But achieving the means to efface these corrupt beginnings founds both the desire of Sutpen's own fictional biotext and "Sutpen's Hundred," the one hundred miles of virgin land carved out of north Mississippi. The shadow of Sutpen's imputed desire falls between two poignant moments, collapsed into a single, dreaded economy of recall and forgetfulness. The homeless prepubescent boy, wandering the surrounding country with an unspecified number of siblings, and a drunken father, learns very slowly (in the tempo of the Faulknerian sentence) what hierarchy and difference are and how they work: "He had learned the difference between white men and black ones, but he was learning that there was a difference between white men and white men, not to be measured by lifting anvils or gouging eyes or how much whiskey you could drink then get up and walk out of the room" (226).

As the story is interpreted by Quentin and Shreve, somewhere in Harvard Yard, Sutpen's memory so freezes on these scenes that it would be plausible to think of them as analogous to birth trauma. But if one's "second birth" marks the coming to "consciousness," then the second time around for Sutpen is doubly painful, engendered by the outraged shame of *being-*

looked-at. The drunken father has somehow landed work on a plantation whose owner lives in the "biggest house [Sutpen] had ever seen" (227). This man who owns things—"all the land and the niggers"—spends "most of the afternoon . . . in a barrel stave hammock between two trees, with his shoes ['that he didn't even need to wear'] off" (227–28). When young Sutpen, bearing an unread message from his father to the man in the Big House, arrives at the front door, something quite astonishing takes place: "the monkey-dressed nigger butler kept the door barred with his body while he spoke" (231), and "even before [Sutpen] had had time to say what he came for," the butler tells him "never to come to that front door again but to go around to the back" (232).

Sutpen's "birth" in the moment strikes with such force that the narrator insinuates it as *rupture:* Even before the butler completes the message, Sutpen "seemed to kind of dissolve and a part of him turn and rush back through the two years they had lived there" (229–30). The rip in the fabric of memory occurs, so to speak , over the bar of the black body, standing in the doorway so that the enormous privation in young Sutpen is abruptly named, materialized, and objectified in the butler's own impeding presence. Suddenly, the boy gets an inkling of what he looks like to a momentarily superior other, denied by the statistical recurrence of the lexemes "nigger," "monkey-nigger," "niggers," that overtakes the passage, but be that as it may, Sutpen gets the point and it sticks: This *face,* and "he was unable to close the *eyes* of it—was looking out from *within* . . . just as the man who did not even have to wear the shoes he owned . . . looked out from whatever *invisible place* he (the man) happened to be at the moment, at the boy *outside* the barred door in his patched garments and *splayed bare feet*" (234–35, my emphasis).

"Outside" the bar defines precisely that moment of negation from which meaning can work, since, in the positing of a not-"inside" and a not-"within," Sutpen brutally discovers who is/not. Not only is he "born" to himself then, but commences to read his history as it is rendered through the borrowed gaze of his profoundest beholders: "he himself seeing his own father and sisters and brothers as the owner . . . must have been seeing them all the time"—

> as cattle, creatures heavy and without grace, brutally evacuated into a world without hope or purpose for them, who would in turn spawn with brutish and vicious prolixity, populate, double treble compound, fill space and earth with a *race* whose future would be a succession of cut-down and patched and made-over garments bought on exorbitant credit because they were white people. (235, my emphasis)

It is fair to say that the young Thomas Sutpen "gets" his culture's sociotext violently and all at once through the ventriloquized medium of others' seeing, as "race"—now objectified *for* him by way of a barred doorway—and the threat of castration—in the hint of male bonding and hierarchy—become the power drive of his fundamental hunger. "Splayed bare feet" and "shoes," projecting a theory here from off the ground, let's say, not only address the downcast, cut-down detail, but also flirt with the missing phallus. "Niggers" will take on a certain usefulness of social economy for Sutpen, as it is surprising to him and the reader that "they" are not "inside" the bar so much as its moment of substantiation to be transcended. Sutpen is marked, then, by the "discovery" of "race," or more pointedly, by the striking news that he "has" "race," as the message is hammered home by the crucial marker of difference in a US Real—the vital sign of Africanity itself. In a very real sense, this coming to manhood, in all the brutality of ungentle revelation, fixes Thomas Sutpen in the inescapable madness of his own veritably now-felt difference. Mattering even less in the relay of gazes than that "monkey-dressed nigger," who is "given . . . garments free" (235), Sutpen instantiates the barefoot, bareass white boy who will spend his fictional career overcoming.

Since human valuation is posited in this narrative as the distance between privation and gratification, we observe that the young Sutpen also comes upon the efficacies of "class" in this episode, but features of the sociotext are so carefully intertwined here that "race," "class," and masculine (hetero) "sexuality" are represented as a single bundle of nerves. For sure, the character, as imputed to him, grasps a human psychology and sociometry under the auspices of *lack,* as the latter offers its unsaid name to a far more sophisticated, covering notion—*desire* writ large and, in this particular instance, inscribed in the balloon face of the Negro butler. To say that Sutpen imposes, in time, the weight of his rage on "peoples of color" will not surprise; indeed, we can anticipate it with a good degree of certainty, but *how* it is so (inasmuch as the African-American has very little to do with him in the historical situations that we come to accept as true) focuses the puzzle of US "race" magic itself: We might suggest now that the ideology of "race" in the New World text is founded on the fundamental suspicion that one is *not* a "man," if, as in Sutpen's case, castration fear and the mark and knowledge of "race" can be said to belong to the same stuff of cognition/recognition. The utter ruthlessness of "class," then, with its relegation of women, period, though for radically different reasons, to the circuit of exchange, not only describes the violence that is interrupted by nothing at all, but does not bear distinction as a discrete feature of the socionom[24] from "race" and "sexuality." Thomas Sutpen, in the course of things, will efface his "race" (as the myth of the "land of opportunity" requires the ascendant "race" to do) and take on a new "class" (the displacement of "race" onto "property"), but in order to do so, he must not only run away from those viciously spawned siblings, but must split the unmapped countryside and the unfinished cartographies of the new nation.

To make an interminable story quite a bit shorter (Faulkner, after all, was trying to capture the whole world between "a cap and a period"):[25] Sutpen, and *how* he does so is about as clear as the involuted syntax of the narrative can be, lands on a "little island set in a smiling and fury-lurked and incredible indigo sea, which was the halfway point between what we call the jungle and what we call civilization, halfway between the dark inscrutable continent . . . and the cold known land to which it was doomed" (250). The narrative remains ignorant of the proper name of this "little island," but plants symptoms of it, as if the name itself were a postponed expectation, just as that mountainous region of Virginia, where Sutpen was born, will come to be called *West* Virginia. In effect, this generalized nominative order—"in a latitude which would require ten thousand years of equatorial heritage to bear its climate" (251)—cannot be named in its global dispersion insofar as it revolves in a "heart of darkness" that cannot read itself. (This conjecture is aided by our knowledge that Sutpen is semiliterate at best.) To that extent, Conrad's Marlowe/Kurtz and Faulkner's Sutpen/Quentin/Shreve—variously positioned in the scale of literate-being—encounter the same massive display of a self-generated phantasm that bites back. Sutpen nonetheless falls in the binary between that "dark inscrutable continent" on the one hand and, on the other, that "cold known land . . . the civilized land and people which had expelled some of its own blood and thinking and desires that had become too crass to be faced and borne longer" (250–51). In this romance of the "bloods," the narrator does not actually approach a geopolitical order that could be thought of as a mimesis of some "real" place, but Sutpen's role in the scheme as an overseer and "the incredible paradox of peaceful greenery and crimson flowers and sugar cane sapling size and three times the height of a man" gesture symptomatically toward the notion of the colonial/plantation system of the Hispanic and Francophone Caribbean; that "cold known land" seems to look toward Europe, as ambiguity of reference delineates the entire passage in paroxysms of modification.

In this fret and fever of telling, layers of other narratives "migrate" to the different context and signify on Faulkner's semantic surface, but at least one of the convergent texts (or shades of it) is rewritten here to establish

Sutpen as an apprentice-factotum of Law and Order: The revolt of the little island's by-now indigenous black population is put down, *singlehandedly,* in John Wayne style, by Sutpen, who "[walks] out into the darkness and [subdues] them, maybe by yelling louder, maybe by standing, bearing more than they believed any bones and flesh could or should" (254). The most celebrated revolution in the colonial African Diaspora, or, perhaps, within this complex at *any* time, records quite a different outcome: "The slaves defeated . . . the local whites and the soldiers of the French monarchy, a Spanish invasion, a British expedition of some 60,000 men, and a French expedition of similar size under Bonaparte's brother-in-law."[26] Historian C. L. R. James is referring here, of course, to the San Domingo struggle (1791–1803), which established Haiti as the modern world's first black nation-state. Sutpen's "creators," however, are not only constructing/reconstructing Sutpen's biotext through willful and wishful distortions that posit the deeds of an "identity," but even at the risk of parody, insinuating an exalted and aggrandized figure. This economy of narrative means dwarfs the background and its particularities, as the "hero" is dramatically foregrounded at all costs.

But there is still something on Thomas Sutpen's mind. That face with eyes that "he was unable to close" acquires obsessive force, *is* the all-over memory that repeats like a rhetorical tic. Here, in an ambiguous space, Sutpen, searching for one of the missing house servants, "the half breeds," "hunts" for two days, "without even knowing that what he was meeting was a blank wall of black secret faces, a wall behind which almost anything could be preparing to happen and, as he later learned, almost anything was" (252). This "text," which Sutpen can neither read, nor erase, overlaps the tale of the butler, as both episodes share their common source in a weave of related textures—from some secret and invisible posture, a putative subject of an interior generates unspecified, unspecifiable power that Sutpen can only guess. In both instances, he, we might say, intimates his own production *as* knowledge-for-another, so that in his own eyes, he has taken on objectness, "double-consciousness," or the seeing himself as an interiorized other (to his "outsiderliness") might see him. The founding of "Sutpen's Hundred," with its handcrafted, baronial mimicries, is vexed by a habit and poetics of pathos that now seem clearer to the grasp—"Home" breaches the blank wall; the barred doorway. Gaining "Home" offers him the key and extraordinary imperative.

One final piece: Sutpen's first-born son, Charles Bon, who is the father, in turn, of Charles Etienne de St. Valery Bon, is given birth to in the ambiguously fictionalized space—the son of Eulalia Bon, the daughter of the

Haitian sugar plantation's owner.[27] When Sutpen, discovering his new wife's suspect racial origins, descends, finally, on Mississippi, Eulalia and the child have been installed in New Orleans, perhaps, and in a more or less morganatic arrangement—at least this is the plausible text that Quentin and Shreve co-hatch. The meeting of Henry Sutpen, the "true" son and legitimate heir of Thomas by Ellen Coldfield, and Charles Bon (whom—like Sutpen—we never actually "see," except as the splendidly regressive, sartorial, and eroticized narrative object of desire in others) provides the vertiginous motions that take the reader toward the storm center of the US culture text—"race" as that awful moment of incestuous possibility *and* praxis, yearning *and* denial, refusal *and* accomplishment, wild desire *and* repression, that cannot be uttered and that cannot *but* be uttered: Jim Bond, the grandson of Charles, outside the burning ruins of an impossible and impassable history, with "Africa," "Europe," and "African-America" coursing his veins, abrupts the "return" that Sutpen wished to repress altogether. At the embodied intersection of heteronymous elements—and they are just about all there in the play of demography, geography, history, ethnicity, sexuality, the declensions of "class," and the signs of repression and difference in "race"—Jim Bond, in the flesh, installs a reading on the paralogisms[28] of US in "Our America."

It seems that Sutpen has been perfectly poised for this tale of contingency by way of a great-grandson whom he could not/would not have *recognized,* starting in the son. Going back to keywords in his early fictive biotext, we would try to tease out a meaning as to *how* in recourse to three scattered resonances: (1) ambiguity; (2) evacuate/evacuations; (3) blank wall/barred entry. It will not be surprising that "blankness" does not describe a not-written upon so much as it locates a site for new, or over-inscriptions—Lillian Hellman's "pentimento,"[29] Hulme's "palimpsest." The screen, or canvas, or framed circumstance carries traces of preceding moments that alter the contemporaneous rendition, making the latter both an "originality" and an "affiliated," or the initiation of a new chain of signifying as well as an instance of significations already in intervened motion. The descriptive discourse attributed to Sutpen's dream of the "nigger" (which arises *persistently* after the fact of his coming into knowledge of self-division and "race") is laden with notions of surface and masking. It could be said that Sutpen's first and most significant hodological instruments[30] are "flashed" by the "monkey-dressed nigger," who sends him spinning in negative self-reflection. But I think that in this particular instance, it would be too easy to dismiss the occurrence of the butler as simple mirroring, or the surface upon which young Sutpen is played back to himself. (The latter case would identify more precisely the cultural production of minstrelsy, wherein the "blank wall" of faces is "made up" in hideous, even pornotropic, caricature. The segregation of lips, teeth, eyes, and hair, for instance, in the facial contour would fit any number of artistic programs, but wed to a scheme of [over] representation—both "over and over again," and "written" on top of, designed to reinforce instances of sociopolitical dominance—the surreal strategies of minstrelsy exact a fatal mockery of art and entertainment.) In Sutpen's case, contrastingly, the commotions stirred up on the interior *posit* an "inward." I actually mean to say that the commotions *are* the coming about of, the markings of, an interior space. (A wedge that is driven between a Real and an Imaginary, even though the verb here is perhaps too volitional?) Sutpen's "blank" describes, then, the moment of tension between a "self-created" and a "self-alienated," or the moment when he "realizes" that he is not who he thought he was; *as* he thought he was. This enabling occurs under the auspices of ignorance (a conundrum that he cannot read) and hindrance (his stalled movement forward). *Blocking* and *puzzlement* compel him—literally—to *flight* and the alienated "inwardness."

This thematic might be positioned to gather up "ambiguity" and "evacuate/evacuation" as contrastive movements of a local narrative etiology. Since "evacuate" is itself a figure of ambiguity in juxtaposing double meaning, it works well to describe Sutpen's new moment of being (an emptying out of contents) and the "his-story" that he wears on his feet (those "cattle, creatures heavy . . . without grace . . . brutely *evacuated* . . . "). Trapped always between pre- and co-eval texts, Sutpen himself is nowhere to be found, "in person," in Faulkner's work, but those symptoms of him, dreadfully, densely read through the various narrative devices of *Absalom, Absalom!* suggest that such as "he" still haunts the memory of a nation that commits the Sutpen error: Bearing the weight of knowledge, one cannot act *otherwise,* or *simply.* (Can he?) Sometimes, one's cultural project mandates the tracking down his own contingent ambiguous that was "written" long before.

So, who cuts the border? This question is not as mysterious as it might sound. It arose from a real circumstance around my house one summer when we wondered out loud who was responsible for cutting the border of grass on the edge of our property, contiguous with the church's, south of the house. For several days the grass grew there, making neat quarantine in the midst of mowed lawn all around it. Small, local wars must start that way and massive, international ones, too, concerning the touchy question of borders. An instantaneous household narrative lays hold here of a broader purpose: We might ask not only where the Sutpens belong in an America/US order of things, but by what finalities of various historico-cultural situations are we frozen forever in precisely defined portions of culture content?

The ways and means of negotiating borders and centers virtually constitute a new area studies in the liberal arts curriculum in the US today. (Professor Valerie Smith calls this ascendant discipline "doing" "otherness.")[31] This different economy of emphasis seems to offer an important critical tool for the chase of contradictions: Surmising from Foner's edition of Martí's writings, we guess that *La Revista Illustrada* might have been published in New York, as Martí spent several crucial years in the city and wrote many of his essays, including "Our America," on that site of contingencies. Even in the discursive play of the binary, Martí reflects in his biography certain elements of the ambiguous—at "home" in "exile," forging a revolutionary praxis in the very heartland of the "enemy" and its various culture-stuff. It would seem, then, that no "real" biotext (and/or culture text, for that matter) ever achieves much more than an unstable relationship to some abidingly imagined, or putative, centrality, even though one is surely loathe to admit *that* possibility. By the same token, America/US[32] presents various faces to the world concerning, precisely, a contents in flux (and often enough, indeterminate). Landing on the smallest point, one might say, then, regarding the shifting position of the socionom, that there are days when her household cuts the border, then there are days when someone else's does.

14

Faulkner Adds Up: Reading *Absalom, Absalom!* and *The Sound and the Fury*

I

In the midst of the 1998 Faulkner Conference, to which I had been invited as a guest speaker, it occurred to me—rather stunningly, I should add, because it was too late to alter course—that I had actually misconstrued my assignment: my remarks should have been based on the thematics of Faulkner's writings and the implications for conceptualizing "America." But I had been captivated by something else altogether different, it seemed—quite simply, the awesome repetitive schemes inherent in Faulknerian address and how the former help shape and sustain the readerly response. After years of teaching Faulkner to undergraduate constituencies, literally up and down the length of the country, I am still amazed (a good Faulkner word) that this work remains news and provocation for me and as importantly, that out of this ever-newness some aspect of reading emerges to draw the attention that had missed it before. I should acknowledge, however, that it was the work of Gertrude Stein, especially *The Autobiography of Alice B. Toklas* and *The Making of Americans*,[1] that raised the problematics of repetition to the forefront of my interest, and while I have not even come close to solving, or dissipating, the puzzle that this epiphenomenon of writing occupies in my imagination, I must express profound thanks to my host and convenor of the Faulkner Conference, Professor Donald Kartiganer, for providing me the occasion to have a few first thoughts on the subject in a "rich and strange" (and welcoming) public forum. (What a sense of humor he and that Tuesday night audience must have had to pretend not to notice that the name "America" did not escape my lips more than once that evening!)

II

In the fourth chapter of *Absalom, Absalom!* Jason Compson III is speaking to his Harvard-bound, much-put-upon son, Quentin III, when he expresses what I would regard as one of the driving metacritical motions that subtend the work.[2] Quentin, tapped by Rosa Coldfield to be the chosen auditory in the next generation of her forty-three years' worth of impressive outrage, might be thought of as a kind of punctuality—an omniscient narrator calls him a "commonwealth": "his very body was an empty hall echoing with sonorous defeated names; he was not a being, an entity, he was a commonwealth" (6). The moment of convergence of numerous vectors, Quentin is not entirely unlike an epical proper name or instrumentality, insofar as the space of a proper name conforms to a geopolitical and generational denomination; nearly all of the *personae* of *The Odyssey,* for instance, are identified as the "son/or daughter of," the ineluctable apposition and repetition in which case the law of the phallus is not only "photographed," as it were, but assumes an obligatory appeal in the poetics. (Could it be said that the Appendix of *The Sound and the Fury* and the Chronology of *Absalom, Absalom!,* both added after the respective facts of publication, parody epical, even biblical, design by staging the ambition of the genome?) Quentin, of course, comes to us far removed from the mandates and practices of epic genre in any sense, even as it is fairly clear that he has no text, no *word/verbe*[3] that he could call his ownmost. Along the course of the narrative, Quentin keeps thinking that he will never hear anything else his whole life, will never have to hear anything else, cannot but hear and have heard through his sinews, his muscle-build, on the pulse of the nerve, what his elders obsessively repeat about the South. Perhaps that intense concentration of narrative energy, even an investment of it, finds an analogy in Benjy's howling that lines *The Sound and the Fury*[4] with its feel of irresistible madness and in its disembodied match that presides over the conflagration of Sutpen's Hundred and its aftermath in *Absalom, Absalom!* In any case Quentin, ringing like a commonwealth, is loaded with discursive and narrative registers, foisted on him by his elders, which Rosa Coldfield believes might well have a market equivalent, and which his father explains this way:

> We have a few old mouth-to-mouth tales; we exhume from old trunks and boxes and drawers letters without salutation or signature, in which men and women who once lived and breathed are now merely initials or nicknames out of some now incomprehensible affection which sound to us like Sanskrit or Chocktaw. (102–3)

These tales of mouth-to-mouth resuscitation, as it were, are nevertheless stripped by Compson of their mystical valence—another way to put it would be to say that "being" has been subtracted from the objects—as they translate into sign-vehicles, whose messages are no longer transparent, if they ever were, or any more meaningful than marks on a page of foreign language; in this case, the foreignness skips several beats, leaps over the modern, and looks toward some passage or doorway even more inaccessible, even though we imagine that Compson, one of Faulkner's most cynical and voluble speakers, is here "putting on the dog" of impressing the troubled young man poised before him by signaling what would be, to his mind, the outlandish and the romantic—*Sanskrit,* the mother-tongue of the Indo-European families of language, and *Chocktaw,* the language of the Chocktaw and Chicasaw peoples,[5] once installed, ages ago, in what is now Mississippi, Alabama, and Louisiana of the American New World. (And for all that, perhaps no strangeness to "Ikemotubbe," which invocation inaugurates the Compson line of the "sons and daughters of.") What these buried, now exhumed, objects-monuments, proffered like so many tokens of historical and semantic trust and brought to the half-light of Faulknerian narrative, require, then, is a speculative instrument, an interpretive and heuristic device of which the novel itself, in its unrelenting narrative pressures, is prime suspect and motive. I would go farther: Faulknerian narratologies appear to have sprung into this world for the express purpose of breaking the reader's heart (say nothing of Quentin's in the particular case in question), to make her lose sleep, and to doubt the intuitive "logic" of reading as a forward and progressive momentum in time which takes us steadily along a trajectory initiated in ignorance and brought to closure on knowledge and certainty. But in reading Faulkner, one cancels all the bets, holds all torn tickets, as we enter the realm of the stochastic; as we learn, in fact, to shake loose the time-honored faith of the "English major" that reading, if you just stick to it long enough, will bring you to a successful end. On this ground of interrogation, reading becomes the quintessential human stake, if not folly: "You re-read," Compson muses, "tedious and intent, poring, making sure that you have forgotten nothing, made no miscalculation; you bring them together again and again nothing happens: just the words, the symbols, the shapes themselves, shadowy, inscrutable and serene" (103).

These signatures of a dead past, which claims and marks the body of Quentin Compson in *symtomaticity,* account for one kind of repetitive enterprise at work in *Absalom, Absalom!* At the level of the line (in the semantic and lexical folds of the novel), as well as in the larger temporal units that we would demarcate as "narrative" (in the *diegesis,*[6] the would-be trajectory of plot, here stalled and subverted and we could even say "bereaved" by Faulknerian recurrence and delay, and in the narrative duration of the plot device), we are confronted with the truth of sheer accumulation as a "return" with a difference, sometimes marked, and an "addition," which compounds the puzzle rather than dissolves it. The problem that I am attempting to track, then, is twofold, separated by neighboring territories of discursive organization: (1) those of prose stylistics, on the one hand, and that of the (2) "function and field of speech in psychoanalysis," on the other; it seems that in both *The Sound and the Fury* and *Absalom, Absalom!* these "neighbors," we might call them, experience *detente* on a new frontier of fictive persuasions, wherein stylistic repetition, to put the matter another way, sounds the depths of an itinerary of the "one," whose conceptual career is mapped in the Lacanian project.[7] In neither field is the matter of repetition new and therefore, a cause for anxiety—at least in *theory*—but to speak them together, as I believe Faulkner's writings urge, is not automatic: whereas repetition—the same word for orders of the socius that differ in both degree and kind—is regarded in the poetics sphere as a positive trait and may be said to conduce to pleasurable feeling,[8] the appearance of the phenomenon in everyday life, or in the experiential sphere (routine, boring activity that *must* be repeated) generates ambiguous value; the latter, when taken over by the discourses of psychoanalysis, becomes the high-water mark of a special category of "psychic material," if not that of a symptom of trauma and neurosis.[9] What Faulkner's writings manage to achieve—with quite stunning success—is an economy of praxis that relies on both attitudes or postures and postulates to engender *style*. In what ways might we think of *style*, however, as a *symptom?*

What I hope to do here, then, is to gain a bit of ground on understanding a deepened dialogism between these discursive terrains, straddled by an American writer, who, for the longest time, I suspect, was quite probably thought of as "quaint" and merely "southern," as though the latter were a flat surface, by portions of an American readership. As one blurber puts it, regarding a Faulkner reading from his own work, "he conjures up many vivid, picturesque images for his listening audience."[10] In my view, never "quaint," Faulkner, the southerner, "told" us a great deal about the workings of language and discursive regimes long before the protocols of structuralism and post-structuralism had given us names for them. In fact, I think of this canon, especially the two novels examined here, in addition to *Light in August, As I Lay Dying*, part 4 of "The Bear," spates of *The Mansion*, and *A Fable*, through and through, as the site of a radical discursivity and in that regard well ahead of the modernist language game, which Faulkner himself was likely *not* very interested in playing, per se. Of course, I am suggesting that whatever Faulkner's project might have been *for him* is not everywhere consonant with what it is for us, the epigone, if related at all. I cannot even remotely imagine what the world of everyday readers, beyond the ken of official notice and review, must have thought in 1929, when *The Sound and the Fury* appeared (along with the Great Depression), and in 1936, when *Absalom, Absalom!* was published (toward the end of FDR's initial term of office). It is also useful to keep in mind that Faulkner did not exactly fit the mythical fashion mode in which lights we read his generation's avant-garde—the sexy, glamorous, "lost," young American male in exile, while hanging about the premises of 27 rue de Fleurus, lamenting the decline and fall of Western Civilization, or acting out the alter-ego of Nick Carraway and Jake Barnes. William Faulkner's consumer packaging, let's call it, was somewhat different, it seems to me, *because* he was southern, at the time he was southern, and as the "South"/"New South" was, until fairly recently, always cast as the nation's backward "other," who, in turn, engendered, in fear and trembling and terror, its own "others." Might it be that this "South," through William Faulkner, is liberating the word of its truth and the truth of its word on the nation-ground?

If Compson's lines might be taken as an apt metaphor for reading *Absalom, Absalom!* (or other Faulkner, for that matter) and as an adequate précis of what its various speakers enact, each with his/her own "hermeneutic demand" concerning the "self-life-writing" of Thomas Sutpen and the mystery of his children, then they point the actual crisis that readers face in the onslaught of a *tsunami* of prose, or perhaps more locally, going through a high- powered car wash *without* your car—that getting the world down between a cap and a period.[11] Our readerly position imitates Quentin and roommate Shreve's, desperate to solve the riddle which the pair, in some sense, have invented. In the iron grip of a New England winter bearing down on Harvard Yard, as the radiators lose heat over the course of the night, that small enclosed space resembles a crypt, if anything at all, which would render the task of creation quite a lot closer to a small death: "Wait," either of them and both of them think(s), "For God's sake wait!" And what is it that they are *waiting* for? It is certainly for no lack of a pregnant narrative generation—it has no rival in U.S. letters this century, to my mind, and to match it, even approach it, we would have to drop back to Melville in the nineteenth—that they are on pins, at pains, no semantic or lexical impoverishment that needs fleshing out, but, rather, a discursive drowning, more precisely, that requires the reading a Faulkner novel as we would a poem, line by line, as Ezra Pound claimed the basic unit of composition should be. In the modernist project, the line would be replicated as signature for Faulkner and his fellow visionaries. But Faulkner seems to achieve striking emotional intensity and affect by accumulation in repetition, analogy, and correspondence or correlation in lines and scenes that do not always "go" somewhere, although they stir up quite a commotion. We should take a minute to try to explain how it happens.

Longer novels than *Absalom, Absalom!* have been written, but it would be difficult to find a *denser* literary texture than this work that cannot be said to have a beginning, a middle, or an end. It is as though the story that the novel tells does not commence at all—even *could not*—as we are dropped into the midst of a "long still hot weary dead September afternoon" (1), blinds closed in Rosa Coldfield's "office," with her speaking a dependent clause into a vacuum, three paragraphs later—"Because you are going away to attend the college at Harvard they tell me" (3). The syntax implies that Rosa has already explained to Quentin why he has been summoned, but her explanations follow, as they are shortly supplemented by Quentin's father, who will clarify for him, later that day, some of which sequence breaks in concurrently with Rosa's narrative, why Quentin is just the man that Rosa wishes to call on. The problems posed to our reading, then, are soon urgent because the novel's orientation is foreshortened by a thickened interrelatedness between what Gérard Genette might have called "narration," as opposed to "description."[12] In other words, the *distance* that an intercessory device would interpose between the textual matter and the reading eye is closed up, as if the narrational order of the story were gasping for breath. The distinction that I am making here may be less definitive than I am asserting, but *proportionality* is the issue—how much space there is for drawing back from what is read in the interest of "seeing" it, or gaining perspective on it, which process traditionally partners a putative author and reader in a kind of conspiratorial play; modernist writing would break the contract, as Faulkner here is one of the field marshals leading the charge. Genette suggests that narration is concerned "with actions or events considered as pure processes, and by that very fact it stresses the temporal, dramatic aspect of the narrative" (136). By contrast, description, or what I would call the more or less comfortable distance exacted between the matter of the reading and its translation into a "cognizable object," "lingers on objects and beings considered in their simultaneity, and because it considers the processes themselves as spectacles, seems to suspend the course of time and to contribute to spreading the narrative in space" (136). Here is an example from the opening passage that problematizes the distinction Genette makes:

> . . . and opposite Quentin, Miss Coldfield in the eternal black which she had worn for forty-three years now, whether for sister, father, or nothusband none knew, sitting so bolt upright in the straight hard

chair that was so tall for her that her legs hung straight and rigid as if she had iron shinbones and ankles, clear of the floor with an air of impotent and static rage like children's feet, and talking in that grim haggard amazed voice until at last listening would renege and hearing-sense self-confound and the long-dead object of her impotent yet indomitable frustration would appear, as though by outraged recapitulation evoked, quiet inattentive and harmless, out of the biding and dreamy and victorious dust. (1–2)

Even if we conceded that lines like these belong to the descriptive order, with its third person referentialities—"Quentin" and "Miss Coldfield," for example—we would have to say that the length of the passage, its insistent modification that forces the attention down, and the ongoingness signaled by the gerunds, "sitting" and "talking," etc. (as opposed to "sat" and "talked," say) embed this stalling or delay in the narrative order. In fact, it appears that the role of the descriptive in *Absalom, Absalom!* is always deployed in the interest of the narrative frame and cannot be easily segregated from it. There are no "pure actions or events" in this novel that are not already engaged with the discursive project that wishes to "linger," or wait, to prod every imaginable nuance to the surface. In that regard, reading here is something of a dare, insofar as there are no rest stops, for all intents and purposes, until the text suspends.

And because we are not released in time to avoid the agony of "intent, poring," the sense of being immersed in Faulknerian text is overwhelming. As Genette put it, criticism had to decide to regard the work initially as a text—"a woven tissue of figures in which time (or, as one says, the life) of the writing writer and the time (life) of the reading reader are tied together and twisted into the paradoxical medium of the page and the volume."[13] This observation seems to say that whatever demons the "writing writer" might have met and wrestled in process pass over to the "reading reader," as I acknowledge, with a bit of chagrin, that reading Faulkner is not entirely unlike placing one's own time on hold in a state of supreme irritability and aggravation.

In addition to trying to penetrate textual density in this case, we must confront a plot structure that can only be described as vertiginous: while plot does not exactly articulate what a work "is about," it at least maps and delimits a reading space as one sort of saturation and not another. In *Absalom, Absalom!,* there are several plot lines, or two central plot lines and strands of others, which is fine, except that the writer's ambition appears to have been to conduct them all at once. But inasmuch as not even William Faulkner could achieve a temporal simultaneity of spatial representation, the text gets as close to such goal as possible by: (1) deploying multiple narrative perspectives, or enunciative "centers," which strategy the writer had already accomplished in a spectacular way in both *The Sound and the Fury* and *As I Lay Dying* (a year apart), (2) juggling the plot sequence so that "now" might be right "now," or whatever we would regard as the "present" of the enunciation, or it might be the "present" of some past event or occurrence in the story; furthermore, *linearity* is absolutely ruined here, insofar as the reasonable expectation that night will follow day, or that characters move off stage at their death, means nothing: chapter 1, Rosa's narrative, for example, is broken into at least twice (as three chapters, presumably spoken at some other time, either that day or some other day over the collective life of the "town," fall between her start and her resuming), and we only discover the key to the mysterious "something hidden" out there in the Big House after Rosa is already dead, posited at chapter 6. We actually do not "know" what the something is, suddenly projected at the end of a long italicized passage, attributed to Rosa, until we come to chapter 9, where it seems that Quentin and Shreve must cease speaking because their dorm room in the Yard "seemed colder than ever" now (376), and finally, (3) rehearsing the same calculus of motives over and over again so that the putative subject of the novel's desire, "Thomas Sutpen," is "everywhere"—the omnipresence, "now" and "then," between 1833, when he abrupts onto the landscape of Yoknapatawpha country, and late fall 1909, we presume, when Rosa returns, in Quentin's absence, to Sutpen's Hundred, determined to bring Henry Sutpen—the hidden something—back to the living, and Clytemnestra, her ageless black step-, or half niece, refuses the offer by burning down the rotting shell of house that has served as the flagship of Sutpen's Hundred.

We might as well call this aspect of the story its pretense, the outer frame of it, which dresses itself up rather like a Gothic mystery, with all the trappings of literary decor on which Edgar Allan Poe might have been right at home. But if Rosa's tale is the outer packaging—like Marlowe's "heart of darkness"—it is just about overrun by what is "in" it, inasmuch as aspects of the Sutpen outline compel the blasts of discourse that constitute the novel: (1) Sutpen's coming into Jefferson, (2) his installation of Sutpen's Hundred, posited as the narrative's creation myth—his taking a wife, having children, repudiating some others from his past, and (3) his Ahabian greed and lust and willfulness and perversity, all played out against the backdrop of a developing geopolitical order called Mississippi, indeed, the United States, with its "high and impossible destiny," and the Civil War, with its stern consequences for a rebellious, slave-holding South. That a

Canadian-soon-to-be-practicing-surgeon, Shrevlin McCannon (the Genealogy), of Edmonton, Alberta, brings the novel to its penultimate enunciative finality convokes Canada and the United States, as well as the Caribbean and the West African Continent, by suggestion, in a nested semiosis of
ineluctable relatedness.[14] Even though we have presumably never left
Rosa's office, Compson's front porch, a slow buggy-ride in the "speaking"
dust, twelve miles from Jefferson, and a dorm room, somewhere off Massachusetts Avenue, Cambridge, U.S.A., we have touched on capital parts of
the New World and some of the Old, during a crisis time in Western culture—"the problem of slavery in the age of revolution."

The novel is, therefore, working like a Blakean beast on multiple and virtually simultaneous levels of narrative production and process—the *micro-*
and the *macro-* and then playing, too, on the *intimate* register. In my latest,
nearly annual reading reincarnation of this novel, I have been close enough
to shock, jolted, for sure, by its powerful and powerfully displaced sexual
currencies: if Gothic forms, in their obsessive and excessive poltergeistian
rocking, freight along a humorous potential—at least for a coeval sensibility—then the laugh that is welling up is suddenly cut short when we remember to ask what the ghosts and the transgenerational haunting all
mean, behind those stage-effects and miracles of cybernoise that the Hollywood industry can evoke at a moment's notice, to the tune of millions of
dollars. The "Young Frankenstein(s)" have all but killed off any serious reading of young Mary Wollstonecraft's creature and the repertoire of exceeded
boundaries—human/social, geopolitical/historical, literary/discursive—to
which it belongs, except that we must decide—it seems to me—*why* "it" is
still there—that "something hidden" in Rosa's knowing is rather like that
creature, huge, fantastic, terrifying, and nameless, even if we call it, after
Rosa, "Henry Sutpen," or even "miscegenation," or "race," or the misguided
fear of "pollution." But that it is "hidden" in the "house" would suggest to
me that Rosa is quite plausibly addressing sexual desire and how terribly and
massively its fulfillment has eluded her grasp, and the biggest surprise of all
the jewels, that *carnal knowledge,* even its privileges, will not stay not the
hand of death—which might, in fact, be the goal, Freud conjectured—but
the ravages of loss and decay. After "all polymath love's androgynous advocacy" (apologies to the "old dame"), we come, with Faulkner, to lights out
and the howling wilderness, even in the voice of the black manchild.

If the novel is mimicking living state (the libidinal urge) versus after-
living state, beyond which Faulkner really couldn't go either, then the former, in its massive invocatory appeal, provides the succulence that makes
this novel go, it is the veritable *frisson* of it: from the repulsive possibility

that Thomas Sutpen sexually abused his children, especially Judith (does anybody know why the girl of six or seven *screams* at the sight of her mother's phaeton, drawn up before the door? [20–22], or why the childhood of both Henry and Judith seems to have been so joyless?), to Rosa's nearly unbearable autoerotic and androgynous yearnings (that fourteenth summer of wistaria and its "friction ravishing of the male-furrowed meat, also weaponed and panoplied as a man instead of a hollow woman" [150]), to Quentin/Henry/Charles/Shreve's homoerotic mimeses and repetitions, to the missed consummation between young adult Judith Sutpen and Charles Bon and what is palpably, achingly breathed of what it promised, once upon a time—"We have waited long enough . . . expect me" (134, 135)—to the cross-racial, cross-cultural sexual congress that *Absalom* gestures toward, but stops short of unveiling all the way; if this novel plays with the world, then the name of the game is desire. Just that and perhaps only that in its omnivorous wanting properties-to-the-death—recognize me, love me, value me, the unanswerable demand that lends mortality its palate: in that sense, how could it miss *repetition,* the encounter with a reality forever missed?

III

> And the king was much moved and went up to the chamber over the gate, and wept: and as he went, thus he said, O my son Absalom, my son, my son Absalom! would God I had died for thee, O Absalom, my son, my son!
>
> (2 Samuel 18:33)

And, perhaps, from the "lumberroom of literature":

> Our revels now are ended. These our actors,
> As I foretold you, were all spirits, and
> Are melted into air, into thin air.
> And, like the baseless fabric of this vision,
> The cloud-capped towers, the gorgeous palaces,
> The solemn temples, the great globe itself—
> Yea, all which it inherit—shall dissolve
> And, like this insubstantial pageant faded,
> Leave not a rack behind. We are such stuff
> As dreams are made on, and our little life
> Is rounded with a sleep.
>
> The Tempest 4.1.148–58

> (. . . the two of them creating between them, out of the rag-tag and bob-ends of old tales and talking, people who perhaps never existed at all anywhere, who, shadows, were shadows not of flesh and blood which had lived and died, but shadows in turn of what were . . . shades too.)
>
> Absalom, Absalom!

The Faulkner reader will recall that discursive/narrative moments like the one cited in the third epigraphic piece of this section not only appear frequently in *Absalom, Absalom!* but appear at random, as they are scattered across the novel in a kind of tantalizing recurrence, meant to remind him, it seems, that he is in the midst of both *invention* and *inventory*. The particular citation falls along the course of chapter 8, which, alongside the preceding chapters, constitutes the vortices of narrative—with their interstitial interstices and doubling back points of reference—that render this novel just short of irreadable: the question is not so much, if at all, the word choice (after all, one can always look it up, Thurber reminded us!), but the flat-out syntactical explosion and momentum that would make the act of reading here an agonistic meeting with the clock—reading it *fast enough* and accurately enough to remember from one end of a period to the next, from one paragraph to another, and page by wearying page, what one is being told. Perhaps *that* one is being told *that* way is much the entire point. It is fair to say that just as Quentin Compson is hearing it all again, we are, in a kind of dizzying kinetic mimesis that affects the rhythm of one's breathing and the responses of her nervous system, hearing it all again, too, as well as having to absorb brand new information: (1) the life of Thomas Sutpen in the West Indies, most probably Haiti, (2) the murder of Sutpen, at the scythe-full hand of Wash Jones (of the scuppernong arbor), whose granddaughter Milly has been unfavorably compared—upon giving birth to Sutpen's last heir(ess)—to a mare, (3) the "facts" concerning the second generation of Bon(d)s, and (4) what may or may not have been a final and momentary encounter between Thomas Sutpen and Charles Bon.

This complex repertoire of stories consumes nine chapters and as we have already remarked, several far-flung changes of scene, between the birth of Thomas Sutpen, posited, somewhat disputatiously by Quentin and Shreve, about 1808, the later childhood of the son of Charles Bon, Charles Etienne Saint-Valery Bon, who dies from yellow fever in 1884, the birth of his son Jim Bond, posited (in the Chronology) at 1882, and the burial of Rosa Coldfield (death by shock, we guess) on 9 January 1910, propinquitous to the conflagration of Sutpen's Hundred, fired by Clytemnestra Sutpen, the patriarch's *other* daughter and/or Jim Bond, now the idiotic ward and keep of the latter; these and other events are actually recounted in the novel, while Rosa's tale/apologia (chapters 1, 5, and 9), Mr. Compson's version of events (part of chapter 2 and all of 3 and 4), and Quentin and Shreve's replay of select peak points of the entire discourse (chapters 6–9, or what we might call the Harvard sequence), intertwined with the reported events, might be thought of as the present tense of the enunciation of the story. There is, of course, the enunciation of the enunciation, or the accu-mulative moments of the "writing writer," from which place, we imagine, those heavy, sententious metacritical, "over time" assertions emerge: those "rag-tag and bob-ends of old tales and talking" (316–17) apparently em-anate from such place.

It is winter in New England, at Harvard, and approximately six months before Quentin Compson will commit suicide by drowning, which event is implicit to Quentin's narrative in *The Sound and the Fury*. But for now, Quentin and his roommate are talking, literally, furiously, as unto death, sometime between eleven o'clock in the evening and one o'clock in the morning, as chronic specificity assumes a distinctively dramatic character: with two or three exceptions, the quad beyond the room is empty, "already dark," as the couple—the Canadian, "huge and shapeless like a disheveled bear" and the Mississippian, of the suppler blood—attempts to get inside the skin and the condition of two young males in "a Mississippi library sixty years ago, with holly and mistletoe in vases on the mantel" (307). Not now two, but four, Quentin and Shreve would be rid of historicity and con-text and the special signatory and singular way in which both mark the body *qua* body and no other, to open themselves to the imaginative range, in order, precisely, to enter a historical moment and metaphysical order not their own. For long stretches of time, we actually do "forget" that we are centered in *performance* and *performativity as narrative* and that, paradoxi-cally, a world is *not* being brought to stand before our very eyes, though there is always the nagging question at the end: Well, what was all this *for*, if not? Intruded in the middle of paragraphs, on either side of dash marks, and, like the passage on the shades, inside the folds of parentheses, these deictic suggestions,[15] planted by concealed narrative devices, seem to re-tract with the left hand what has been proffered with the right: in fact, it would not be entirely wrong to say that the novel finds a thousand ways to induce the crisis of belief about both its rhetorical claims and what might be plausibly understood about their meaning, this apart from the sheer challenge of the linguistic fecundity that comes home to it. We are prepared to endorse the "theory" adduced in the passage before us as true enough—that Quentin and Shreve are addressing shadows of shades and that they are crucially bent on an interpretive reading of fictions, just as they are themselves "people who perhaps had never existed at all anywhere." But if we are invested in fiction as a sort of truth that cannot be reached through empirical utterance, or verified as a discourse ordained by history, then what is the "truth" about the story of *Absalom?*

Not the same thing, apparently, as the "truth" about the novel—You are my brother, so how can I, in all love and honor, or any love and honor at all, kill you? No, I'm the nigger who's going to sleep with your sister, unless you stop me—the truth about the *story* has to do with the reliability of the *props* upon which and against which we realize that *Absalom* comes to rest on the massive national question, staged most dramatically in southern encounter, which is centered in the power and the danger of the sign and material practices of "race." There are other names for it, ugly ones, like "miscegenation," blood pollution, defilement, and the whole shebang of pathetic claptrap, adopted from late-medieval European irrationality, which locates a welcome host to its virus on the other side of the Big Pond. A reader must get used to the discomfiting fact that Faulkner, if not a racist in the classical sense of the term, took his cues about "race" from his environment; if so, then as one of two capital "its" of the Faulknerian canon, it is probably not for nothing that it is there. But this truth about the story, inasmuch as we are circling and encircling it (sets and sets and sets of notes, copious comments in the margins of the pages, falling always into the same traps and minefields each voyage out, but thinking each time—all right, *next* time, I'll remember [for instance] where I saw that thing about the sherbet *before* it is elaborated on by Shreve) and never reaching it, quite, suggests to my mind that perhaps there is something lurking behind the race piece that makes the sign of race both its surrogate name and its primary expressive vehicle. We should keep in mind that the subject of race, as well as that of other economies of victimage, is not really a *pointee* (although she might have to pay for it), but a *pointer,* the one doing the pointing. To that extent, it is an endlessly fascinating phenomenon, but—and let's be clear about this—no less dangerous for all that. It seems to me, then, that *repetition* is the problem that marks the obsession whose "cover story," let's say, is provided by the sign of "race." Because suspension and delay are primarily achieved here in the repetitive, the story of the novel opens widely to puzzle and uncertainty.

Stylistically speaking, the repetitive game is spotted early on, as in, for example, the application of some of the same rhetorical figures or features to diverse characters and positionalities: Rosa Coldfield's "grim haggard amazed voice" (1) shortly runs over in reference to the "stolen" Martinican architect, with "his air grim, haggard, and tatter-ran" (2). Although not serving the same linguistic and performative function that critics observe about the role of the formulaic in poetry,[16] these repeated tags do behave rather like ornamental epithets, though their pattern of recurrence is hardly predictable. In that regard, the opening narrative of *Absalom,* however, demonstrates enough recurrent patterning around key words, phrases, and their variations—"dead," "dry/dried," "dim," "airless," "gloom," etc.—that the droning sense of the incantatory goes far to establish notions of somnolence and decay.

The invocation of ghosts—by definition, a repeating—is not a choice, it seems, that Rosa Coldfield is making, but is rather compelled or induced by a moment of trauma, certainly shock, from which she has not recovered; we learn in due course that Rosa Coldfield, like other members of this tight clique of Jefferson families, with the Coldfields and the Compsons, among them, bears deep malice toward Thomas Sutpen, and it marks a break, in effect, in the wall of her time, the *béance* or torn place that would separate her from the life unfolding around her. If the room, as stifling and close as a tomb, has been shuttered for forty-three years, then the living death (on the vertical) that Rosa signals is the acting out of her own halting in time. That certain words in reference to her character are borrowed, or "transported," with slight differences, across another would lend divergent positions a similar figural identity. But the similarity seems adopted, on the one hand, to sheer linguistic playfulness that is calling attention to itself and, on the other, signaling a certain interchangeability of characterological function and positioning. This economy of rhetorical means might be assigned a thematic dimension as well, insofar as the repetitive earmarks the character not as a unique instance of signatures, but as a narrative punctuality, among others, in a field of signification: if, as Quentin claims, neither a man, nor his roommate, outlives his father, then repetition demarcates a trend toward the inexorable—words, words, words, yes, in their twice-ghastly glitter.

We observe similar patterning in the inflections on "resolve"—"resolving/resolved" (8, 17)—as Quentin "seemed to see them," the Sutpen family group of four—Thomas, Ellen, Henry, and Judith—which vision the "voice," in its unceasing and disembodied continuity, wished to conjure; but the photographic figure, just as "doors" and "blank" walls, faces, and façades, takes on extended life here and recurs in variant form throughout: it is there, for example, in Compson's homoerotic rendering of the Henry Sutpen/Charles Bon connection in chapter 4—the Mississippian, on a visit to New Orleans, confronting the complicated social arrangements of that society's epistemologies of pleasure, let's call them, becomes, in one of Compson's descriptive forays, the "puritan mind," being prepared by Charles Bon as a "cramped and rocky field" might have been and as Bon, in turn, might then plant and raise on it "the crop which he wanted" (111). One of multiple extended conceits, or similes, which add layers of linguistic exuberance and delay to the novel, expand its temporal and spatial reach, and deepen its intertextual involvement—from the exquisite "damask before the Haviland beneath the candelabra" (65, with its hint of American David Haviland's porcelain factory, built at Limoges c. 1839, and quite likely standard import issue to a wealthy slave-holding enclave in the middle of the nineteenth century), to that "constant and perpetual instant when the arras-veil before what-is-to-be hangs docile" (147, evoking shades of Hamlet's play in the play)—the "cramped and rocky field," as an agrarian figure, perfectly orchestrates the figuration with the level of material culture that Henry Sutpen and Charles Bon might have experienced during the fall of 1859, on the eve of war and their meeting. But the photographic image, even in its dimensions of the still frame, seems to anticipate the relatively new cinematic apparatus, which Faulkner would witness, first hand, as a Hollywood screen writer in the 1930s. That the novel juxtaposes widely dispersed image-hordes helps to create here a textual surface that is brilliantly heterogeneous in its discursive and semiotic cross-currencies—if Henry's "puritan mind" is ripe to be plowed like a field, it is also vulnerable to a wordless "writing":

> . . . a dialogue without words, speech, which would fix then remove without obliterating one line the picture, this background, leaving the background, the plate prepared and innocent again: the plate docile, with that puritan's humility toward anything which is a matter of sense rather than logic, fact, the man, the struggling and suffocating heart behind it saying I will believe! I will! I will! (113)

Puns on seeing/vision/perception play at different levels of meaning and emphasis here, regarding, as we have seen, the eye and mechanism of the camera, but also in relationship to the *plausibility* of certain reports: who is "authoring" it and according to what motivation and personal investment. It is fair to say that not a single one of the characters in *Absalom* "saw" anything, except that Quentin does *not* explain to Shreve, even though the passage appears in a suitable context, that he laid eyes on Henry Sutpen (389). Not only that, but in the twinkling of an eye, he conducts a brief interview with him, which establishes his identity and the length of time that he (Henry) has been back at Sutpen's Hundred; this is fine, it solves the mystery, except that Quentin might not have seen what he thinks he did: back on that night with Miss Rosa, Quentin might have been, out of fear and startlement, somewhat beside himself, say nothing of the pitch-black ogre house, like something in a nightmare: "it was all the same, there was no difference: waking or sleeping, he walked down the upper hall." What, then, do we make of the italicized passage that marks

Quentin's exchange with Henry? Rosa Coldfield-wanna-be-Sutpen did see Thomas and other major players in the story (except for Charles Bon), but in a real sense, the character that she remembers imagining, or imagines re-membering might as well have been as "borrowed" a composite as Comp-son's "recall" through the report of his father Brigadier General Compson, who was "there." As for Rosa's knowledge of Thomas Sutpen, Quentin's fa-ther offers this thesis: when Sutpen returns home after the War in 1866, Rosa has not seen him more than "a hundred times in her whole life," al-though he was her brother-in-law:

> And what she saw then was just that ogre-face of her childhood seen once and then repeated at intervals and on occasions which she could neither count nor recall, like the mask in Greek tragedy interchange-able not only from scene to scene but from actor to actor and behind which the events and occasions took place without chronology or se-quence and leaving her actually incapable of saying how many sepa-rate times she had seen him for the reason that, waking or sleeping, the aunt had taught her to see nothing else. (60–61)

If seeing is a matter of being "taught," as though even it cannot be reliably depended on as the first and last instance of the truth, then sight itself is as negotiable a term or tenure of the *existent* as any other claim to "experi-ence."

These elements of a revenge play and domestic mystery, based on inter-racial fratricide—all posited or imputed events—might have added up to a made-for-television miniseries, or a cinematic blockbuster, but any inclina-tion to yield to the popular demand, or to middle-brow taste, is wholly sub-verted by a structure that places profound epistemological questions front and center. In other words, the novel stages the problem of knowledge as a fiction and seems to decide that the former (at least what often passes for it) is riddled with instability; insofar as it is often concatenated from the im-perfections of information, iron-clad conviction (frequently, nothing more than a soup, or pablum of prejudicial feeling), and the built-up authority of the duplicative paradigm, it is a phantasmal tissue of misperception, passed on and embellished from one generation of actors to the next, as though it were gospel, and in fact, in its repetitive engines, it assumes a gravitas virtu-ally as weighty as Scripture. Rosa Coldfield, for example, believes that the language spoken by Sutpen's so-called "wild niggers" is simply gibberish, when it is, rather, a Francophone patois, or creole, developed by certain African captives, in their transactions with their European overlords, under the stern finalities of the Atlantic slave trade—running from the middle of the fifteenth century—opening with the trade to Portugal—to the end of the nineteenth—closing with Emancipation in Brazil. But what Rosa and the Town saw were naked creatures, up from the "absolute mud," moving through the provincial climate of mid-nineteenth century Jefferson like the devil itself, although, in their imputed cannibalism, hardly as glamorous! The novel, of course, is neither passing itself off as, or posing in the place of, the historiographical text, nor is it concerned about the inquiry that the latter conducts per se, but in its rotations about the same key points, it does resemble those structures of knowledge whose vocation is tied to the *precise*.

But over and over, it is put before us that precision has no truck, really, with a religious myth of reading.[17] As Rosa paces along the opening, she insists at crucial points that she was "not there," having been "born too late." At the same time, she invokes nevertheless a quite stunning certainty that we are apt to buy: "That is what Ellen saw . . . " (25). The same locution, regarding Sutpen's advent to Jefferson, appears in the mouth of the Town, so to speak, in its recall of the man the flesh of whose face "had the appearance of pottery . . . of glazed clay"—"That was what they saw" (29).

We might want to call these moments negotiated instances of first sight, but in their obvious partiality and limitation (for who is speaking for the Town?), further obscured by distance, or varying degrees of proximity, they might as well be accompanied by the modification "seemed" to see, which trails Quentin's discourse like a bad penny. In fact, it is as if the successful generation and replication of narrative here is incrementally proportionate to the distance that the subject stands *away* from the object in question so that an event does not assume the status of *eventuality* until one, for whatever reason, is bereft of immediacy, does not obtain to the status of the transmittable until it has been worked and massaged into a position in discourse: for what else might Quentin mean, when, in his stream of thought, he observes (in the sixth chapter) "he could see it; [Thomas Sutpen briefly home from the War for a twenty-four hour period in order to deliver the imported Italian marble headstone for his wife Ellen's grave] he might even have been there. Then he thought *No. If I had been there I could not have seen it so plain*"? (198). If seeing is a matter of distance in this case, or a temporally and spatially mediated vocation, then it must be that sight for the character is coming from somewhere in actual contradistinction to the naked eye, and if there is such a thing as the latter in the story of *Absalom,* then its standing is altogether dubious.

Repetition, then, is adopted in the interest of (1) the social contagion of mimesis and toward (2) the dispersal of doubt, which activity is ceaseless and therefore *as though* mandated by the symbolic law and order that is inescapable; style in *Absalom* advances both motivations as they are drawn together and tightened in an inextricable tweed of figuration. Before moving on to the second proposition, which I should like to turn over in some detail, I want to briefly examine an instance of the first proposition, and two examples that relate most emphatically to Faulkner and humor. Faulkner, the "writing writer," *laughs* on rare enough occasions, and when he does it's a hoot, I would say; two of the moments that I would point to concern levity, pure and simple (for Faulkner), while the third and final example is a bit more involved and elaborates on the first proposition. Starting with the first two examples of levity, we continue with Rosa's narrative.

That at the end of Rosa's resumed narration (chapter 5), Quentin, in his head, has not gotten beyond that door, which Rosa claims she was barred from entering (on the other side of which lay the dead Charles Bon, supposedly murdered by his brother Henry) is simply unthinkable because the door passage (145) is separated from the end of the segment by some thirty pages of print, but moreover, by Rosa Coldfield's tortuous syntax, quite a lot of it exquisitely rendered. That Quentin, allegedly, *missed* much of it is hilariously surprising—we are actually caught off guard, cued by the tone and tenor of Rosa's address, as it seems out of order for the narrator to assert: "But Quentin was not listening, because there was also something which he too could not pass—that door" (179). Flipping right back to the beginning of the segment, the observation is wonderfully light and releasing.

This spate of discourse also carries what I would regard as at least one implanted joke on the narrator's part, not Rosa's: Rosa, who, I would guess, was a student of Shakespeare, especially *Macbeth*, in imagining that she could have given, had the occasion fructified, scope and method to Sutpen's madness, had already completed a folio of odes to the Confederate soldier, which work Brigadier General Compson saw in 1885, according to his son (83). She would have thought of herself, then, as a custodian of informed usage and refined intention. Remembering that an "odist" is speaking to Quentin, one with a respectable claim to rhetorical and linguistic savoir faire, we read the following lines with more than passing interest:

> Oh no, I was not spying [on Judith and Bon, whose togetherness she has capably imagined] while I dreamed in the lurking harborage of my own shrub and vine as I believed she dreamed upon the *nooky* seat which held invisible imprint of his absent thighs (153, my emphasis)

"Nooky," in one way of reading this, mimics the poetic diction that we might associate with the English romantics, or even the earlier school of seventeenth-century secular and devotional lyricists; it means, according to the traditional paradigms, an adjective that is now full of its noun. But in rereading the passage, I recalled that "nooky," on my southern childhood playground, was a nominative in the American 1950s and one of the terms that young boys used as a name for the stuff of female sex. It is nearly too perfect to be an inadvertent paronomastic accident, given what Rosa is describing here—her own sexual longing as the "untried Thisbe," as Shreve would have it—but its split level function in the sentence (and I have no idea what else "nooky" might have meant to William Faulkner in the 1930s) instances exactly the sort of sly humor that the novel sometime deploys.

The third example of humor not only stages a repetitive instance in *Absalom*, but also executes a direct link to the mimetic narrational calling that Quentin and Shreve obey. As one of the names of the object of desire in the story, Thomas Sutpen is constituted as an object of male gaze, the psychic economy usually applied to female characters; in that regard, we might think of him as the "spectatorial" man, or the "spectated" man, who takes provincial Jefferson by storm, "like the forefront of a tornado," Rosa would have it. As Sutpen's Hundred is under construction, it draws to it crowds of Jefferson males, who regard the Haitian blacks and the games of intensive labor and hunting that they engage with Sutpen as a kind of spectator sport. The "legend of the wild men [comes] gradually back to town" by way of those "who would ride out to watch what was going on" (32). The gazeful fascination continues over a two-year period, with Sutpen playing host to his fellows in a carnivalesque atmosphere, when, in the course of things, Sutpen's Hundred, once completed, moves into its second phase—the getting the accoutrements of the property, "the feminized softness of window pane or door or mattress" (36). In the interest of availing himself of the proper things, Sutpen quits Jefferson a second time and returns with "the whole durn steamboat"—kitchen things, crystal chandeliers for the parlors, furniture, curtains, rugs (41). Then "public opinion" reaches "an acute state of indigestion" (43) because the town cannot be satisfied that a criminal imagination is not reposing in their midst and, very shortly, their pots and pans, as it were. Having already decided that Sutpen, *"given the occasion and the need . . . can and will do anything,"* the town spontaneously generates a vigilance committee to do what is hardly clear, inasmuch as Sutpen has not broken any law *on the books,* we imagine. That their boiling civic resentment is exacted toward conduct that falls between the gaps of legality makes the town's behavior that much more irrational, that much more in tune with acts of social contagion and identity, which are all the closer, as a result, to the mechanisms of violence and the sacred.[18]

One day shortly after his return, the county sheriff and eight or ten other Jeffersonians ride out to Sutpen's Hundred, meet Sutpen on his way back to town, and proceed to follow him in the direction from which they've just come. This veritable procession of citizens follows Sutpen, as the numbers swell en route, for several scenes in what must be one of the most rollicking narratives imaginable: (1) no one "speaks" the mission or engages Sutpen; (2) the "look" magnetizes other "looks" so that the men on the gallery at Holston House in town, with their feet propped up on the railing, now look as well. Sutpen enters Holston, "with his portmanteau and the basket" intact, and looks around himself at the men again "where they huddled on their horses, not knowing what to do exactly" (42). When he exits Holston House again, the men are still there on their horses, waiting for him. By now, an entire posse of men on horses occupies the field of vision in a spectacle whose sole content is spectacle: Sutpen stopping (at the Coldfields', for example), the others waiting, until Sutpen is finally arrested and bonded out of jail by his soon-to-be-father-in-law Goodhue Coldfield and his good friend, Jason Compson II.

Now, importing her recall of these scenes to later passages in the novel, the reader becomes aware of their strategically figural, even iconic, status because, with some variation, they are repeated: in chapter 7, Quentin is retailing the narrative of Sutpen's early life and career as a sugar plantation foreman in the Caribbean, but this tale is running concurrently with the story of the captured or cajoled Martinican architect who makes a valiant attempt to escape Sutpen's Hundred and its reported cannibals, is hunted down like a fugitive bondsman, and brought back to the Sutpen enterprise. After the capture, full of fanfare and savoir vivre, the architect raises the bottle of whiskey proffered to him by (grandfather) Jason Compson and bows first to the latter, "then to all the other men sitting their horses in a circle looking at him" (269). Both this speculative event and its earlier match take on prominent notice because they not only repeat an intratextual element, but also imitate the by-now familiar reverse shot sequence of the cinematic repertoire, as this particular choreography of the pose recites what is perhaps one of the best-known signatures of the westerns genre of American film. The point-of-view shot that captures an object at the center of its vision, in the mid-range, perfectly dances the interrogative stance. It wouldn't be wrong to think of it as a masterful synecdoche for the processes of spectatorship and performance. Furthermore, in the case of *Absalom* the crowds signal both pleasure and danger, insofar as the ruling social energy that urges them can turn, on a dime, into the lynch mob, turn it again, the wedding party. If it is so easy to raise a crowd—and in Faulkner, any aberration or anomaly can draw one—then we have the model, the leading heuristic, even motive, device that puts conviction and the social order in place.

If the success of those scenes arises in part from an intertextual citation, specifically, a cinematographic one, there are repetitive moments in Faulkner that directly contrast them, that do not rely on the photographic. I want to use for examples a single scene from *The Sound and the Fury*, at the risk of breaking one stride and entering another. But the move, I hope, will be illustrative and incorporated into my examination of *Absalom, Absalom!*

Because Quentin Compson in both *The Sound and the Fury* and *Absalom, Absalom!* plays out his career in obsession with a kind of strident commitment, objects stick to him like a second skin: meandering toward the bake shop in Italian Boston, where he first "picks up" the "little sister," Quentin remembers, back along a memory trace through centers of attention that always include "Caddy" and other home-related phantastical material, this: "The buggy was drawn by a white horse, his feet clopping in the thin dust; spidery wheels chattering thin and dry, moving uphill beneath a rippling shawl of leaves" (76). In the same stream of thought, lines later: "The wheels were spidery. Beneath the sag of the buggy the hooves neatly rapid like the motions of a lady doing embroidery, diminishing without progress like a figure on a treadmill being drawn rapidly offstage." Then, finally, after he has entered the bake shop and purchased two buns from the "neat grey face lady," who "looked like a librarian," the scene washes back over his thoughts: "A buggy, the one with the white horse it was. Only Doc Peabody is fat. Three hundred pounds" (78). Repetition here is simple recurrence, with grace notes, as we see it choreographed in the three movements, but it also creates a coherence of mental disarray that lifts the mundanity of Quentin's psychic wounding to a level of powerful poetic ritual and achievement. Quentin's madness, in other words, exhibits a perfection and precision of logic that now relentlessly looks ahead to a syntax that not only repeats the textual grooves in which consciousness is stuck (as he also does in *Absalom*), but repeats as if compelled by law, and it is the law of a missed encounter with reality[19] that repetition is said to commemorate.

The character shows fidelity, then, to the poetics of style that circumvents him—a sentence structure with the ellipses and points of transition that ought to draw blanks and spaces soldered to contents broken and parceled out over highly disparate spatio-temporal occurrences—-and this would mean that the character is never other than *beside* himself, is never other than *other than* himself; colloquially speaking, the lights are on, but nobody's home. In strict complementarity with modes of psychic behavior to which Quentin remains captive, his syntax proffers all the earmarks of puzzle and halting that competing claims of attention would reenforce: we are at once both in the moment with him and all the capital elsewheres that overtake him with immeasurable speed on this, his last day's odyssey.

In *Talking Voices*,[20] Deborah Tannen investigates the phenomenon of repetition and image-making in conversational discourse and suggests that it lies at the heart of particular and general discursive production; modalities of "prepatterning" in language—"formulaicity" and "idiomaticity," for example—would support the view that "the actual apriori of any language event—the real deep structure—is an accumulation of remembered prior texts."[21] To that extent, "languaging," the sociolinguists call it, involves a competence that has gained access, by way of memory, to this horde of linguistic treasure—Jakobson speaks of it as "the filing cabinet of *prefabricated* representations"[22]—delimited by a code. Each "message," or new use context, witnesses the efficacy of the code. While Tannen's study has to do primarily with instances of speech, her work on figures of style, examined in the opening chapter of *Talking Voices,* is complementary to studies in rhetoric that have long occupied an honored place in the general fields of literary criticism and stylistics. I find especially suggestive for my purposes here her view on the interactional aspects of "languaging":

> Seeing language as relatively imitative or prepatterned rather than freely generated seems to push us toward automatism rather than autonomy—make each of us more "it" and less "I." But a view of language as relatively prepatterned does not have to be seen this way. Rather, we may see it as making of us more interactional "I's."[23]

It seems that this reading accords well with the notion that I am advancing here of the Faulknerian character as the subject of *other* address. If Quentin, the "commonwealth," bears the symptoms of a cultural and historical wounding, then the repetitive and obsessive onrush that grinds him down offers monumental tribute to that past. What the latter induces as pathological figures of character yields, remarkably, in the hands of the "writing writer" to narrative space as temporal plasticity, in which event a point in time is saturated with entirely disparate elements. Related Quentin passages from *The Sound and the Fury* demonstrate a similar duplicity of motives which seems to make it difficult to determine how to evaluate the auspices of a scene, or where to apportion responsibility for it; recognizing Quentin's obsessive gaze as a mode of signature, would we attribute what I would call the "objective" world of his narrative to his own inventiveness, or is it the work of an objective narrative device, e.g., the types of street cars out of Cambridge and back, the Charles River and landscape on which Gerald Bland's long-handled oars appear? And what about that "gull on an invisible wire attached through space dragged" (64), or variations on it—"a gull motionless in mid-air, like an invisible wire between the masts," or "with three gulls hovering above the stern like toys on invisible wires" (55)? Because the gulls, on the one hand, are juxtaposed here with inanimate or automotive referents, which make them appear to be parodic instances of flight, we may tend to say that they are products of Quentin's perversely keen vision, while, on the other, the excerpts, appropriate to poetic machinery, draw the attention for *that* reason. If that is so, then Quentin Compson, as well as Darl Bundren *(As I Lay Dying)*, plausibly demarcates a common ground between the workings of insanity and the discourses of fictive and poetic invention. The idea is hardly new, but in Faulkner's case, the puzzle is woven into the thematic fabric of the discourse.

Another such moment invites attention: on the way to the bake shop— a serendipitous destination for Quentin—he comes upon three boys, each with a fishing pole, busying themselves in child's play of an early summer afternoon, 1910. Apparently a small foot bridge, suspended over a pond or reservoir, the fishing spot seems to be a favorite rendezvous of the trio, primarily because of the trout, a neighborhood character in its own right, that makes its home there and refuses to be reeled in. Quentin only later notices the boys themselves, but is, at first, hooked—like the three lads—by the elegant geometry unfolding before him: "And then I saw a shadow hanging like a fat arrow stemming into the current. . . . The arrow increased without motion, then in a quick swirl, the trout lipped a fly beneath the surface with that sort of gigantic delicacy of an elephant picking up a peanut" (71).

The humorous simile that draws this nimble filip to a close relies on sharp contrast, distributed over the law of couples ("gigantic . . . elephant"; "delicacy . . . peanut"), to drive the play of oppositions at the lexical and dramatic levels—as severe as Quentin's situation may be, the eruption of wry humor and detachment withdraws it from the wasted energy of the lachrymose and melodramatic. In other words, one must pay attention to Quentin, as Quentin does the trout, than feel pity for him; in fact, the survey of mental activity expressed in Quentin's narrative is so exercised by fastidious detail that we nearly forget the fatalism in which he is suspended and that we are effectually spending the day with an anal, meticulous, drowning man. The seagulls, the trout, and the fishing poles all belong to a carefully crafted repertory of inflections which suggest that "action" in this narrative is not defined by movement through a material scene, but across an intrapsychic space of the most refined neurotic order. *The Sound and the Fury* and *Absalom, Absalom!* may both be regarded as quintessential fictions of the mental theater. In that regard, repetition is experienced as one of the enabling postulates of both novels.

A kind of extended conceit, the fishing poles, borne by the trio, migrate through objects and textures of the near-at-hand, as well as angles of sunlight. Schematizing the instances might be useful. At first, the boys

> leaned on the rail, looking down into the water, the three poles like *three slanting threads of yellow fire in the sun.*

Shortly thereafter, nearly all the elements in this paradigmatic syntactical pattern recur in a dazzling circuitry of transposition and exchange:

> The shadows on the road were still as if they had been put there with a *stencil, with slanting pencils of sunlight.*

> Their voices came over the hill, and *the three slender poles like balanced threads of running fire.*

> The third boy slowed and halted. The first went on, *flecks of sunlight slipping along the pole across his shoulder* and down the back of his shirt.

> *Sunlight slanted into* it [an orchard buzzing with bees], sparse and eager.

> *Yellow butterflies flickered along the shade like flecks of sun.*

> *Sunlight slid patchily across his walking shoulders, glinting along the pole like yellow ants.*

> They turned into the lane and went on, the *yellow butterflies slanting about them along the shade.*

> And the *dappled sun motionless* at last upon his *white shirt.* (73–75, my emphasis)

The intense focus on aspects of landscape may be thought of as instances of the "objective correlative," or a kind of synecdochic close-up, but it would be difficult to imagine how a cinematographer could demonstrate or capture *nuance* in this case; a picture here would *not* be worth a thousand words, as impact is carried by purely textual and linguistic means. Though the latter induces image-making, it seems that its effects are not translatable into a literal economy of signs or messages. These verbal cross-cuttings of angles of light and texture convey, for only an instant, the rare playfulness, even "lightness of being," that works against the mournful quality of Quentin's suicidal day. Perhaps these discrete moments of perception—not "seen" before and not ever again—are the sort of thing, in their perfections of the harmonious, that one carries to the grave.

These photographic elements, paradoxically, not *of* the photograph, render the mental landscape of Quentin Compson of a piece from *The Sound and the Fury* to *Absalom, Absalom!* His very career, mirrored in this grammar of figurative and rhetorical play, becomes the labor of repeating, and having found a complementary auditory—the soulmate—in the third ear of Shrevlin McCannon, his couple is wed to the iron-clad laws of generational order, metaphorized in *Absalom, Absalom!* as the repetitious narrative claim. As grandfather Compson was alleged to have thought about Sutpen's version of his own biography, it may be said of this non-traditional couple in a sexually displaced attitude:

> They . . . drank some of the whiskey and ate and then sat before the fire drinking some more of the whiskey and he telling it all over and still it was not absolutely clear. (257–58)

This rage to get it straight, if not in the name of "logical sequence and continuity," then with "at least some regard for cause and effect," motivates the post-prandial lucubrations unfolding in the room in the Yard, and insofar as no one else the next morning will know that it happened, that Quentin even shuddered at some point and declared that he did not hate the South, the couple—as it is with yokings—will have something between them. No whiskey passes the lips here—in fact, it appears that the enterprise is conducted as spartan and cold and dry as a class in mathematics. But it is signed by no less passion for all that.

It is easy to believe that Quentin's state of annoyance and agitation is keenly felt; since September, when he arrived at Harvard: "*Tell about the South. What's it like there. What do they do there. Why do they live there. Why do they live at all*" (181, emphasis Faulkner). Just queries whose answers are already embedded in them, which might explain why they are not posed in his hearing as interrogatives at all, but emphatically insistent nonetheless. Jason's letter to Quentin, announcing Miss Rosa's death, fires up the next round of expostulations and replies so structured as to appear interlocutive. But the grammatical cues of the entire Harvard sequence (chapters 6–9) make it difficult to decide if the talking is as interactional as it seems, or if, rather, Shreve is "speaking" Quentin's thoughts. I believe that the writing aims to stage the simultaneity of thinking and speaking and the extent to which the personalities of Quentin and Shreve are now compounded in a single overwhelming discursive motion. But inasmuch as the literary surface cannot accomplish the "all at once," the next best thing is the sequential sentence, loaded with sorts of "stage direction," or cues that map onto subtly differentiated textures of address. At one point describing Shreve's appearance, the narrator has him "leaning forward into the lamp . . . the twin moons of his spectacles glinting against his moonlike rubicund face, smelling (Quentin) the cigar and the wisteria, seeing the fireflies" (188–89). These sudden jerks in the momentum that splinter concentration in a split second of reading time signal, in effect, that the talking and the thinking are not only seamlessly jointed, but occurring without break or pause. To convey this idea, whole paragraphs (and there actually aren't any, except for the usual typographical conventions that set off an exchange between characters) run in a single breath until a particular thread of narrative unwinds on a mark of punctuation. (One needs to complete that errand *before* she starts this passage!) In chapter 6, Shreve, for example, takes up the narrative thread from Quentin's and Rosa's buggy ride out to Sutpen's Hundred, gathers up, in the process, Rosa's relationship with her father, her aunt, and Sutpen, and finally, tracks Sutpen's movements in the aftermath of the war. The rest marks are occasionally placed, most of them external to Shreve's speaking—as in Quentin's three "yeses"—while the strongest stop in the interior of his speech is a semicolon and dashes.

As if all I have just described were not enough, the conventional marking of the parenthesis intrudes an interpretive device here that encourages the reader to think that perhaps she has lost her grip: an open-ended parenthesis falls rather unobtrusively, mid-sentence, about three pages into the chapter, and it has no boundary or close, although, if I have not erred somewhere along the way, I have concluded that it incorporates the *entirety* of the chapter, starting at page 183 of my edition, coursing straight to the end of the segment:

"Wait then." Shreve. said. "For God's sake wait.") (225)

Since a candidate for the longest parenthesis in the language is encompassed within Quentin's stream-of-thought, the strategy suggests that he is actually thinking *over* Shreve's speaking, about *that* door, the buggy ride and the night of Rosa—"*Good lord yes, let's don't find him or it, try to find him or it, risk disturbing him or it:* (then Shreve again, 'Wait. Wait.')" (183). The chapter rotates, then, from wheel to wheel and returns to the place of its generation, triggered by Compson's letter. But isn't this announcement— "so that his father's hand could lie on a strange lamplit table in Cambridge" (180)—the "hand," the *mortmain,* both in its proximity to "that dead September twilight," as well as the tyrannical governance of the past over the present, this moment, in which Quentin is not? We are already familiar with this mental trick of his, both from his not really listening to Rosa, as well as his schizophrenic meandering over parts of Boston/Cambridge in his twin story. In the case of *The Sound and the Fury*, Quentin's mental landscape is parceled out over far briefer syntactical units than it is in *Absalom*, where he shares the psychic furniture, as it were, with his roommate.

If there are other methodological surprises in this sequence, then I have missed them and better luck next year, but I think we may tentatively conclude an overview of Faulknerian style in this segment by saying that the "full speech" of it, in filling up every imaginable writing space of an open surface, in the distribution of the stuff of the narrative over every conceivable mode of focalization—omniscient, concealed, or limited omniscience, implied first persons, streams-of-consciousness—with a grammatical structure that valorizes the long period, with heady interstitial manipulations, and a lexical field that draws from a vast repertoire of literary, figurative, and colloquial citations, such speech is bent on the dazzling pyrotechnical display of *linguisticity*, if we may say such a thing, and it seems to me that if there is a "truth" about the *story* of *Absalom, Absalom!*, then we must look for it there.

Perhaps it is charming to think that the story of *Absalom* is still being told somewhere, and knowing it as we do, the behavior would not be the least bit bizarre for this modernist novel. In fact, there may be some support for the idea in the way that the story suspends: "I don't hate it" is not to say "I love it," as the thought resonates in Quentin's mind in absolute ambivalence and irresolution. That the stories are, for all intents and purposes, *bedtime stories* staves off the threat of sleep—the little death that the child in the man or woman still remembers fearing and resisting. If we think of the repetitive strategies and the dazzle of language as a way *to keep it going*, then the dispersal of doubt, which I earlier posited as one of two central functions of the repetitive here, would paradoxically militate against such aims. It is almost as if Quentin, without knowing it, needs someone to watch with him, to invigilate his thinking, his reading, and Shreve is just the man for the job, in his inquisitive, even nosey, urge to fill in all the gaps. When, in chapter 7, Quentin reaches what is for him a narrative oasis, Shreve drives him on: " 'Then he [Sutpen telling grandfather his version of the story] stopped.' . . . 'All right,' Shreve said. 'Go on' " (265). That no punctuation is sufficient to the project of inquiry seems appropriate not only to at least one of these characters, but also to those symbolic constituencies that work the language game—"that meagre and fragile thread"[24] by which the little surface corners and edges of men's secret and solitary lives may be joined for an instant now and then before sinking back into the darkness where the spirit cried for the first time and was not heard and will cry for the last time and will not be heard then either. (262)

It is a hard thing to say and perhaps quite a lot closer to what the "writing writer" might have actually felt than all that brilliant mendacity about "endurance," etc. And from this agnostic, if not atheistic, angle, narrative becomes an article of faith shored against the ruins of the only certainty we can anticipate—which needn't even be said, if we go back through the passage; repetition is keeping these fellows warm, so to speak, in an exquisite talking to the last.

In trying to carve out of this architectonic enormity a single patch of brick that I can follow, I have had to impose a strictly arbitrary order on my reading of the last two chapters of the novel. The repetitive patterns that I will focus on are an attempt to simplify a process that is far more complicated than one can describe in fairly short order. That said, we might concentrate for a moment only on elements of the Sutpen/Henry/Bon nexus that Quentin and Shreve patch together from the rag-tag and bob-ends of old tales.

For one thing, Sutpen, who "speaks" here only under the auspices of the second and third generations (not counting Rosa, perhaps) provides the story's centrality; like the "dirty drawers" in Quentin's twin story of Caddy, "Sutpen" might be thought of as an unnameable principle or object or calculus for more than one reason—his shadowy origins and as we have observed before, the extent to which various passions and investments are located in him, stick to him like the tarbaby. The "Holy Grail," "the Maltese falcon," the Hope diamond—name it—are just so many nominatives for the indeterminate, but the focus nonetheless for the concretely (and contingently) felt greed or hope or love or ambition that spins off the human sport. I would say that "Sutpen" plays a comparable role in *Absalom* as the center that cannot be named, but becomes a designated space chosen rather arbitrarily. Quentin drives home the idea when he guesses that Sutpen, in talking to his grandfather, was "telling a story." Not bragging , "he was just telling a story about something a man named Thomas Sutpen had experienced, which would still have been the same story if the man had had no name at all, if it had been about any man or no man over whiskey at night" (258). If that is the case, then we can speak of Thomas Sutpen only as the fiction of a fiction, which would mark him as the "cognizable object" par excellence.

In Quentin and Shreve's narrative, Sutpen assumes the shape of the prototype of a post-colonial personality and self-fashioning hero, insofar as he and his family/class occupy the lowest rung of the social hierarchy in the aftermath of the American Revolution. With Old Bailey and the colonial prison culture at his back, Sutpen's early years read like the chronicle of a subhuman formation, slouching, in a "sloven and inert coherence," toward a maieutic surgery and the light of birth into human apprenticeship. Their story, then, focuses on Sutpen's "rise," his "progress" and progression, according to the Jacksonian democratic myth, from a cultural zero degree— "he knew neither where he had come from nor where he was nor why" (236)—to a man with a paunch and a grandiloquent tongue. I would even say that their version of Sutpen—in its sympathetic address to the center, unlike Rosa's different narrative investment—is entirely apposite to a *son's* story, the sartorial fit, let's say, with the father and the brothers, or the riddle of origins as Freud examines it in *Moses and Monotheism*. We gain a good deal of information about Sutpen from the couple over and beyond what we have learned from Compson and Rosa. But perhaps the most important insight we carry away from their narrative is Sutpen's initiation into the "double consciousness"[25] by way of the penetrating regard of the other—it is the advent to "self-difference" that appears to mimic self-objectification and entry into what resembles the Lacanian symbolic order. Nowhere is his coming into focus more exactly and brazenly stated than in the observation "Now he was hungry" (245), following on the transformative moment that drives him fleeing the master's door.[26] That *hunger* in the psychoanalytic literature offers an imperfect translation (shall we say "bastard"?) of *libido* is nearly too good to be true, but it takes us a good way nevertheless toward a clearer understanding of Sutpen's flight in the object choice, or what he is imputed to have called his "design."

The son of no one, we might say, becomes the father of three (at the very least), although the first-born Charles Bon is illegitimate, both in the sense that Sutpen does not marry his mother, someone named (only in the Genealogy) "Eulalia Bon," and in the sense that no one, according to Quentin, ever knew whether or not Bon ever knew for sure that Sutpen was his father. These two problems that borrow the depth of their power and signification from the patrimonial provenance—not only whose child are you, but also, consequently, what inheritances you might claim—adhere as well to the first questions one seeks to answer about love and hate, identity and alliance. Inasmuch as Sutpen acknowledges only those children born to his white/legal wife Ellen, his illegitimate issue, including all the ones who are "known" to be "black," inhabit a different place in the scheme of inheritance, and for Bon's part, no place in it at all. Quentin and Shreve *plant* the vengeful mother and the disappointed son as the primary vehicle of their story of Sutpen. Both the incest motive between Judith/Henry/Bon and the fratricidal one between Henry/Bon draw their juice from this initial implantation.

Compson's narrative, by contrast, intriguingly exploits the displacements and surrogations afoot in an erotic economy that demonstrates all the elements of incestual and homoerotic yearning, phantasmatically produced, among *three* figures—Judith/Henry/Bon (79–80, 98). But it is only Henry, in Compson's reading, who is inflected through the entire copulative register— greedy, he would be *both* Judith and Bon. But it is also a matter of interest that what a teller "sees" in his materials tells us more about him/her than a putative object of address; could it be that we are looking on, in Compson's case, an early "epistemology of the closet,"[27] landed in Jefferson and "blinded," or "window-shaded" by the marriage contract and family values?

Quentin and Shreve, in concentrating on the filial link between father and son, posit the figure of the outcast child on three occasions: (1) the young Sutpen made to go to the back door of the Big House (242–45); (2) Sutpen recollecting the "amazed and desperate child" some years later (272); (3) Sutpen's encounter with the "forlorn nameless and homeless lost child" at a still later date, which "child" might now be embodied in the figure of Charles Bon (278). In the first instance, the child driven away will incur the full costs of a self-alienation and division that perfectly repose on a historical materialist analysis: both psychoanalytic and Marxist insights sharpen a vantage on "homo economicus" in his psychic investments and ideological interpellations—before he can explain his mission, the Negro servant has ordered boy Sutpen away from the front, to the back, and right then, "something in him had escaped,"

> and—he unable to close the eyes of it—was looking out from within the balloon face just as the man who did not even have to wear the shoes he owned, whom the laughter which the balloon held barricaded and protected from such as he, looked out from whatever invisible place he . . . happened to be at the moment, at the boy outside the barred door in his patched garments and splayed bare feet. (244)

This escaped "something" now lends Sutpen the ability to see himself as he might appear through another's eyes, which "speculative instruments," in turn, become in him a kind of DuBoisian "second sight." In the second instance, it seems that the "recollecting ego" is rehearsing the "boy-symbol at the door":

the *figment* of the amazed and desperate child . . . now he would take that boy in where he would never again need to stand on the outside of a white door and knock at it: and not at all for mere shelter but so that that boy, that whatever nameless stranger, could shut that door forever behind him on all that he had ever known, and look ahead. (272, emphasis added)

Collapsing the two occasions, we lay hold of an urgently telescoped reading of the fiction of the recalled child, later looked on by a "recollecting subject" "as an observer from outside the scene would see him."[28] When, on the third occasion, two freshmen from "Ole Miss" come riding up that long scenic view of the driveway of Sutpen's Hundred, Christmas 1859, Sutpen, according to father/Quentin, recognizes in the face of the stranger,

just as he had imagined, planned, designed, and sure enough . . . fifty years later [which mathematics, by the way, couldn't be right, if Sutpen were born—he supposedly didn't really know when—c. 1808] the forlorn nameless and homeless lost child [come] to knock . . . and no monkey-dressed nigger anywhere under the sun to come to the door and order the child away. (278–79)

If we link these repeated instances and their enabling figure, which leaves its traces across the final third of the novel, to Shreve's intensely felt, movingly rendered disquisition on love, then we could posit the latter as the capital "grammar of motives" that not only drives Bon to his death— even though no one, as near as the reader can tell, ever *saw* the body of Bon, with the probable exception of Wash Jones and Judith Sutpen—but also figures the diapasonal arrangements of grief and mourning which changes on chordal structure we cannot but hear. In fact, it seems that all the counting of patterns of recurrence and the search for them and, moreover, the entire critical apparatus and imperative, whatever our bent in that direction might be, melt away as futile gestures in the pungent aroma of a palpably imagined agony: over Quentin's protestations that the narrative that Shreve is spinning is "not love," we seem to experience right through those startlingly accurate non-sequiturs of Shreve's that perhaps it is, or love's *lack*. If Sutpen could have shown some sign, an eye contact, a touch of the hand, the shoulders, the least glint of recognition—"*Maybe he will write it then. He would just have to write 'I am your father. Burn this' and I would do it*" (341)—or have embraced his *own* first wounded child, as in Henry, during a private meeting on a night of the war—"Henry . . . my son" (369)—then that might have settled the whole thing. It appears somehow *poetically* unjust, perhaps even laughably weak, and it is certainly no match for the soft

and subdued night light of the bivouac fires right there on the firing line between the Feds and the Rebs, that in the disembodied "mind" narrating the
latter passage, Sutpen, in flat, stale, even lame words, expresses himself: *"He
must not marry her, Henry. His mother's father told me that her mother had been
a Spanish woman. I believed him; it was not until after he was born that I found
out that his mother was part negro"* (371). If through such calamity and a narrative witness to it of such unparalleled force, one can *think* (anyone, who-
ever it is here) so vain a thing, then, yes, indeed, the Civil War ended the
right way.

IV

But I am saying that Freud addresses the subject in order to say to him the following, which is
new—*Here, in the field of the dream, you are at home.*

(Jacques Lacan, *The Four Fundamental Concepts of Psychoanalysis*)

After so long and patient a time, one should be able to say what repetition
is without further ado. But somehow the problem seems harder to solve
than that: is it the exact or approximate replication of lexical, syntactical,
semantic, and scenic elements, as we have seen in numerous examples
from the two Faulkner novels? And is the sign of repeating just the replicative? Is it an interval that works a seed planted at some prior time in the
consciousness of the "reading reader," who then bears out the second and
subsequent instances *as instances,* as the fruit of the first, whether or not the
words are the same? If the latter is so, then what factors must be present in
order for the reader to posit a kind of "pronoun/antecedent" relationship
in the first place? Is "theme," then, the built-up impact of these resem-
blances over narrative intervals so that the whole narrative structure is
nothing but the repetition of itself? Enough questions of the kind I have
just posed would pulverize the problem into a "not there," or a "there
there" by some other name. And certainly the problem appears quite a lot
easier to dispose of when we are dealing with smaller units of measure than
fictive temporality. In short, the problem of repetition leads us into an
examination of the "philosophy of literary form,"[29] the just treatment of
which is a subject for volumes. At the same time, we do not forget, either,
that seismic shifts in the critical topography that reconfigure the very
concept of "literary form"—today, one of several semiotic ranges on the
landscape, ever vulnerable to the wrecking crews of deconstructive acts—
have not only changed the topic and altered the status of the object, but
dissolved object-positionality itself as a *figment,* or *shadow* of subject/sub-
jectivity. From that angle, repetition is only in "me," where it might not
have been in 1941, when Kenneth Burke first published an astonishing

piece called *The Philosophy of Literary Form*. We are dropping back, then, to claim an anachronism in order to hear what it might "say" now.

A gathering of "thirty-minded" essays, *The Philosophy of Literary Form* is both brilliantly speculative and doggedly quirky and peculiar. Not a standard academic work—as the author himself was not standardly academic—this study of "symbolic action" carries only two entries on the subject of "repetition," one of them encompassed within Burke's review of Adolf Hitler's *Mein Kampf,* the other, in a reading of Erskine Caldwell's *Tobacco Road* and *God's Little Acre*. On both counts, repetition for him holds negative value, and in the case of Caldwell, conduces to trivial pursuit: "Sometimes when reading Caldwell, I feel as though I were playing with my toes," because Caldwell "seems as contented as a savage to say the same thing again and again."[30] That is hardly what one expected (even needed) Burke to say! But at least it signals that the quality of repetitiousness has built into it a negative charge, as well as a pleasurable one.

Studies in classical rhetoric often discuss repetition as one of the inherited figures of speech—with neither "good" nor "bad" energy—that takes the form of the foreshortened space, usually at the level of the sentence or the line. Winifred Horner's *Rhetoric in the Classical Tradition,* for example, disposes of the question as one of *utility:* "Repetition of words or patterns of words can be used for good stylistic effect, for reinforcement of meaning, and for emphasis."[31] She then demonstrates examples of it by way of three figures, starting with *anadiplosis* (also the chiasmatic figure)—the "doubling back," wherein "the last word of one clause or phrase is used as the beginning word in the following clause or phrase." The beautiful "twirling" effect of "people are trapped in history, and history is trapped in them" is shared by instances of *polyptoton* and *anaphora:* in the former, "the same root word is used in different parts of speech," as in, "I agree if agreement is required."[32] In the latter, the "carrying back" of *anaphora*—"the regular repetition of the same word or phrase at the beginning of successive phrases or clauses"—behaves rather like *alliteration,* even though it seems that the alliterative explodes the sound *intra*syntactically and over a shorter distance, while the anaphoric is summoned to handle longer units of recurrence. Horner's example of the latter from Martin Luther King's well-known 1963 address at the "March on Washington" rally, "I Have a Dream," perfectly illustrates the idea, with added value—the nervous rush of sound over the same footage, so to speak, builds the climax. The ear can hear it coming on like a jet engine, roaring in the distance, and stronger, unbearably, as it comes in for the landing. But on paper, the effect appears to be quite the same, as in King's "Letter from Birmingham Jail,"[33] which text, as far as I am aware, was never spoken. We could multiply examples of this very effective rhetorical resource, but suffice it to say that *anaphora* seems to have been made for the exhortative/persuasive/comminatory task, as the entire era of the Civil Rights movement in the United States, for instance, became, among other considerations, a prime stage for the use and display of rhetorical power turned toward quintessentially democratic goals.

Richard A. Lanham's *Analyzing Prose* carries a description of a repetitive function in the figure of *ploce:* "repetition of a word with a different meaning after the interval of another word or words." The example that he provides is a delightful one: "On the walls were pictured groups of early Americans signing things and still earlier Americans shooting arrows at things. But all over the immaculate mushroom-coloured carpet . . . stood groups of present-day Americans drinking things."[34]

In both Horner's and Lanham's work, terror has been stricken from the heart of the rhetorical in the sense that what they and other rhetors describe as process has been delivered from the strict uncertainties of the free fall—the encounter with a "wild man," like Faulkner, who apparently suspended all the rules. There is significant repetitiousness in his order of the case, but it seems to defy any attempt at classification and to carry right over, for that precise reason, into the translation of an *affect*. The haunting mournful tenor of Benjy's narrative in *The Sound and the Fury* offers a good example because it asserts the same thing "over and over again," Burke's bane of syntactic existence. But it is the "over again," which totality strikes my ear as a dirge; if this "thing" of Benjy's were ever scored, it would have to be thought of as an American version of the classical mass—a subterranean *hum*—in the mass, the *drone* of the organ—beneath all that howling and yelling. It doesn't even make sense that my ear registers in Benjy's narrative a profound and steady *silence,* when, as one of my fellow Faulkner readers once keenly observed, Benjy must howl throughout the novel. But it is also the unanswering noise of the silence that *isolates* it that I mark as well. If, as critics have argued, *Sound and Fury* offers formal incoherence as "the form that is the consequence of contingent being,"[35] as Donald Kartiganer rightly contends, then the belated reader is still confronted with something of a paradox: how the "remainder" of the novel, the discourses of it that flicker in the mind's awareness as a completely finished, even self-sufficient project, "becomes" the novel.

What remains for me in an aftermath of reading here is an unmistakable sense of loss and mourning, when it is fairly undeniable that such a thematics does not "announce" itself as such. Kartiganer explains that Benjy's narrative, for example, does not yield an interpretation, but that, rather, "his succession of lived images passes over into our interpretation, becomes a temporal fiction of Compson history that is so clear it is unbelievable."[36] The sense of mourning that I am referring to, then, is related both to our understanding of what we posit in the *affectual* dispositions of the characters and also in that "passing over" of its mournful affects into the reading reader, who receives them, in turn, in a mimesis of grief—not *as,* but *in* the reading reader's *felt* grief. It is in this "passing over" into our interpretation and responses that incoherence is undermined, perhaps we could even say *redeemed* and accepted, as a different fictive logic.

As we have pointed out before, Faulknerian narrative space is frequently redefined as temporal porosity—the overlay, the superimposition of "times," whereby a single space is filled up with discontinuous properties, in some cases, triggered by associative devices, in some others, an opening, or cleavage along the seams of memory, in still others, simple juxtaposition. In any case, we are confronting alignments that are both *contiguous* (juxtaposition that would define an interval) and *continuous* (the wreck and ruin of the same). The sign-vehicle "Caddy"/"caddie" appears in all three cases: as a proper name, with its paronomastic figure in the homonym of "caddie," it is both juxtapositional and associational in Benjy's narrative; it performs a juxtapositional, or contiguous, function, as well as an associational one, in Quentin's, albeit for quite different reasons. A visual, or graphic sign, "Caddy" operates like a sight-gag, but on the ear, except that on the page, it also works like an eye rhyme. A brilliant find for the writing writer, "Caddy" is chief among several saturated elements. (Its recurrence in both Benjy's and Quentin's narratives is so frequent that it is no longer even repetition, perhaps, since the latter is recognizable because it is generated around a gap, or an interval, or how else would we perceive it? We need another name, then, for this aural image that appears in so great a quantity of replication that it obtains to a different *quality* and valence of the repeated.)

We should also include "hush" in this repertory, which sound belongs, most often, to Dilsey Gibson, the Compsons' black matriarch *and* mama, who must worry—as was the traditional circumstance—about both her family and her charges. Dilsey's admonitions to the children to keep quiet on crucial occasions seem to accompany nearly every utterance by the powerful fact that Benjy's narrative marks no fewer than three Compson deaths in its duration and because the register of dying does not appear *in seriatum* (as it must have happened over the years), but as a complicated steady state of sonal markers (words and noises): (1) his grandmother's ("Damuddy") death, which occurs when Benjy is approximately three years old and still named "Maury"; (2) Quentin's death by suicide, which we deduce must have taken place when Benjy was about fifteen years old; (3) Jason III's death, which seems to have occurred about three years later, approximate to Benjy's eighteenth birthday. All the deaths, then, are "blocked," or punctuated by Dilsey's "hush," which also plays another important dramatic role, insofar as Caroline Compson, who *ought* to be mama, is dysfunctional—hypochrondriac and infantalized, in short, a veritable mess, "Miss Kahline" might be thought of as the *fifth* Compson child. Any child's play disturbs her already disturbed mind, which renders Dilsey's tasks all the more onerous. But as the only one capable of managing this pathological nucleated family, Dilsey assumes the good offices of an angel of mercy.

Is "hush" a word, or is it a signal? If that is an interesting problem, we add to it its onomatapoetic translation in "shhh," as well as Benjy's materialized howling, which noise we can only imagine. These "agitated layers of air," I think Marx called it, reverberate across the text so that its walking and talking "knock" against the ear like echoes. If grief makes a noise, then I would say that Faulkner not only found it, but discovered a way to represent it by the manipulation of marks on the page. Much of the magic here is conveyed by the labor of repetition.

What I would like to propose, then, is that repetition in Faulkner's work is an act of rhetorical *regression,* demarcated by various periodicities; a breach that is distinct from its environment, it is represented by a clustering or isolating that would identify a common ground between territories of the symbolic: in Kenneth Burke's view, the Freudian theories, while not designed for literary criticism at all, developed a perspective that "was able (by reason of its scope) to migrate into the aesthetic field."[37] For him, the "margin of overlap" is captured in the behavior of a symbolic sphere, broadly defined: "The acts of the neurotic are symbolic acts. Hence in so far as both the neurotic act and the poetic act share this property in common, they may share a terminological chart in common. But in so far as they deviate, terminology likewise must deviate."[38] It seems to me that *regression,* a term borrowed from the nosological chart, may be applied, in a suggestive way, to the literary critico-theoretical one without violating either its psychoanalytical properties or the rhetorical ones that I mean. With the work of structuralists and post-structuralists, however, particularly the Lacanian project, bent on a Freudian revision in a specific historical juncture, the territories are brought into closer alignment by way of the operations of the *linguistic.* The latter provides the hinge that swings between two doors.

It is useful to our purposes here that the classical etymology that names certain figures of speech—the "doubling back" of chiasmus, the "carrying back" of anaphora, for example—are, technically speaking, a kind of regressive move, insofar as they execute the word's doubling back on itself. In the case of Faulknerian repetition, words do "double back" and "come back," which processes may or may not entail replication, since *synonymity* may occur instead. In either case, we lay hold of an analogy on the metaphoric operations as one of "two aspects of language" and language disturbance as Roman Jakobson described them.[39] The play between the "concurrence of simultaneous entities and the concatenation of successive entities" becomes not only "the two ways in which we speakers combine linguistic constituents,"[40] but also the ways by which the literary surface is created and sustained as a *generative* (progression) and *regenerative* (repetition/regression) field of signifying.

This "return," more or less demarcated, to a discursive condition, or circumstance, that Burke referred to as a "causal ancestor" reveals itself in all forms of similarity—doubling[41] and replication, synonymity and reverberation. These phenomena of the same would benefit, however, from a strategy of naming that could distinguish between their role and status in the expression of a truly multiple order of cases. Interestingly, a "first" appearance on a given literary surface cannot be finessed away by scare quotes, but must be naively and "really" registered as the "first" time that a mark or series of them appears on it, which would be, by definition, *a repeat*. Since we have here to do with the business of the "res," some future itinerary of theoretical alignments might pursue repetition on the literary surface against the problems of reproduction in a no-longer mechanical age[42] and the dizzying duplicities of cyberspace.

If we accept the notion that psychoanalytic readings might be analogously applied, only where fitting, to an engagement with literary texts, then we are less inclined to commit the Procrustean error. But the difficulties that the literary critic experiences, even by way of analogy, or even especially by way of it, must be squared with the originations and the destinations of psychoanalytic practices in the first place. The lures are significant and far too attractive: for one thing, psychoanalytic researches were forwarded in the interest of bio-historical subjects, not made-up ones, even though both, given the narrative genre of the case history, are immersed in fictions. One of the important differentials here is outcome and orientation—one repertory of subjects can only go in one direction—straight ahead toward a future—except under very special, strictly limited, and decidedly circumscribed conditions, called "analysis," in the one case, and/or, more commonly, the circumference of the dream; whereas, the other repertory of subjects earns the future only insofar as a community of readers reenacts and reengages the printed page. The "times" of the literary character, then, are not actually its own, but persist in temporalities borrowed from its bio-historical constituents. There is, moreover, an inbuilt salvific dimension to psychoanalytic practices and theories, critiqued from its inception and mockingly disparaged in certain quarters today, that literary ones most usually do not sustain. While they have induced much talk about their ties to the project of upliftment, such talk is sometimes regarded as the equivalent of the sirens' call, some misprision of a public or an institutional nature. The psychoanalytic, on its side, was, on occasion at least, thought to be fitted to the vocation of the *ecclesia super cloacam*. Burke described this "church over a sewer" and the arts of "haruspicy" this way: "over the course of [Freud's] work, it is the matter of human rescue that he is concerned with. . . . The very essence of his studies, even at their most forbidding moments (in fact, precisely at those moments), is its charitableness, its concern with salvation." This "charitableness," he goes on, is approached in terms of "secular hospitalization," as opposed to, "religious hospitality," and it was "the spirit of Freud; it [was] what Freud's courage [was] for."[43]

Translating the verbs of the passage into the past tense robs it of its felt historical immediacy, given that Burke was writing these essays contemporaneously with the nightmare blossoming over Europe and the final days in exile of Sigmund Freud. Was it any wonder, then, that *rhetoric/symbolic action* (as the route to a just "attitude") were felt to be essential instruments in the "battle" against a massive and global psychosis—"let us try to discover what kind of 'medicine' this medicine-man [Hitler] has concocted, that we may know, with greater accuracy, exactly, what to guard against, if we are to forestall the concocting of similar medicine in America"?[44] Few literary texts are accorded such direct efficacy as Burke here attributes to dialectical reading; which leads to the last catch: having in common with the psychoanalytic reading the paying attention to the slope and play of signs, the literary critic/theorist is engaged with the *word* so that his/her work makes a kind of mimesis to the analyst's.

We can only mean the repetition compulsion and the complex of regression, then, in a shadow dance to the psychoanalytic sphere. Faulknerian repetition/regression must be entertained at that level. But insofar as it becomes a mode of *representation* of the speaking subject entangled in the Symbolic order, as one's membership in it remains captive to the Imaginary,[45] it bristles with all the borrowed thrust and vitality of the bio-historical subject. If the unconscious is "*structured like a language,*" as Lacan contended, and if "linguistic structure gives its status to the unconscious,"[46] furthermore, then where are we placing the repetitive/regressive moment? Whose "unconscious" does this fictive speaking subject show? If we locate the compulsion in the character, then how do we explain its appearance otherwise? And is there a way to account for such recurrences "beyond" the *rhetoric* of the structure, without appeal to biographical claims? I cannot answer these questions any more directly now than I have already attempted to suggest in the course of this essay. But it seems to me that we must eventually get there since *that* place constitutes our sole license to "practice."

My own responses to Faulkner are shaped, primarily, by the monumental sense of loss and mourning, scored in these novels, that the encounter with modernity has installed. But we will find such routings only indirectly, or should we say that some ghastly demarcations leave their traces there? I am suggesting that *grief* in Faulkner is not simply limited to an American region—the South of the United States—but that the sketch of a configuration of it in his work, the excruciating care to ferret it out, render it a gift to the national culture. That loss, without content, on the one hand, and full of it, on the other, is as close as I can come to naming "it," which begins to explain, I think, the powerful import of repetition in the canon. It is the repetition of loss, as Jacqueline Rose describes it, that can never be satisfied in a subject with an answer to a demand: "That loss will persist over and above anything which [the mother, say] can possibly give, or say, in reply."[47] A demand, or what cannot be named, actually exceeds what is called for, Rose argues, "and each time the demand of the child is answered by the satisfaction of its needs . . . this 'something other' is relegated to the place of its original possibility."[48] In reference to the Lacanian synthesis, Rose interrogates the protocol of the remainder of the subject, which is called "desire."

It would be incorrect, I think, to try to boil these novels down to a capital promise, but I would read both the scopic and invocatory initiations of the small Compson boys beneath the death tree (at Damuddy's death), an earlier scene that same day, when Caddy falls down in the "branch" and dirties her underwear, and the utter terror that Quentin feels in that dorm room years later, forestalling the lures of death with *stories,* by the lights of desire—its misses and the mourning that ensues.

In closing, I want to try a *glissando:* we are reminded now of the little girl's "dirty drawers," as if a sacred object, but certainly something that looks like, behaves like, the Lacanian "petit objet," which the brothers saw close up and at a distance and probably recognized even then the moment of loss that it portended. Having no idea what it meant, although the moment is forever linked in Benjy's mind with the *smell* of death, and in

Quentin's, with the rage to obsessive focus on anything, and perhaps in Jason, the younger's money-craze, the adult brothers have each "forgotten" where it all started. It reappears for Quentin in *The Sound and the Fury* as the near-at-hand summer wedding—a beautiful young woman, running out of a bank of flowers in a shining veil—and in the fear of carnal knowledge, registered in all those "doors" in *Absalom,* and it will likely repeat in his brother Jason as a tendency to migraine, camphor rags, and a near-scatological vileness of speech. Its substitutions, detours, and reroutings will reappear in Harvard Quentin's stutterings and puzzlements as the anguish to recover the forgotten. But the words are not his; they are someone else's— all the someone elses that fall under the father's law and the generative order, which he wishes to reverse. If Quentin and company have been "mugged by a metaphor," as Wahneema Lubiano puts it,[49] then the language of return that captures them is forever the grand tautology, forever the round and round. As the subject of speech, *as if* they were bio-historical subjects, they would be subject to the processes of symbolization which begin "when the child gets its first sense that something could be missing; words stand for objects, because they have only to be spoken at the moment when the first object is lost."[50] In the child's mind, the words *stand for,* the words *are,* the absent thing: "For Lacan, the subject can only operate within language by constantly repeating that moment of fundamental and irreducible division. The subject is therefore constituted in language as this division or splitting."[51] But in the case of Faulkner's character, this "moment" can only be posited, remains abstract, and must be regarded as the absolute *irrecoverable:* cantilevered over the desiring, the words keep trying to say over and over; the only problem is that what they are saying they don't say!

Mrs. Ramsay reported that Mr. Ramsay had gotten all the way up to "R," I believe it was. We are still abecedarian with this "R," but it is a good place to end by promising to work on it.

15

"All the Things You Could Be by Now, If Sigmund Freud's Wife Was Your Mother": Psychoanalysis and Race

I

The view from here is old fashioned. One might even call it lame, predicated as it is on the proposition that self-knowledge has its uses. From here, we might be invested in a reinvigorated social practice, whose aim is ethical and restorative. To say so, however, is to start at the end of this piece, where and when and if the writing has not only congealed but explained itself. We have now to do with beginnings.

A framework that would properly contextualize a confrontation between "psychoanalysis" and "race" is not imaginable without a handful of prior questions, usually left unarticulated, that set it in motion in the first place. The new social practices toward which I have gestured cannot proceed, however, unless we are willing to pose the not-quite thinkable, on which bases the converging issues have previously rested. In other words, culture theorists on either side of the question would rule out, as tradition has it, any meeting ground between race matters, on the one hand, and psychoanalytic theories, on the other. But I want to shift ground, mindful of this caveat: little or nothing in the intellectual history of African-Americans within the social and political context of the United States would suggest the effectiveness of a psychoanalytic discourse, revised or classical, in illuminating the problematic of "race" on an intersubjective field of play, nor do we yet know how to historicize the psychoanalytic object and objective, invade its hereditary premises and insulations, and open its insights, subsequently, to cultural and social forms that are disjunctive to its originary imperatives. In short, how might psychoanalytic theories speak about "race" as a self-consciously assertive reflexivity, and how might "race" expose the gaps that psychoanalytic theories awaken? Neither from the point of view of African-Americans' relationship to the dominant culture nor, just as important, from that of the community's *intramural* engagements have we been obliged in our analytical/critical writings to consider the place, for example, of fantasy, desire, and the "unconscious," of conflict, envy, aggression, and ambivalence in the repertoire of elements that are perceived to fashion the lifeworld. Some of the writers of fiction, Nella Larsen, Jessie Fauset, Ralph Ellison, Toni Cade Bambara, Alice Walker, David Bradley, Paule Marshall, and Toni Morrison, among them, have posed, at different times across the twentieth century, a staging of the mental theater as an articulate structure of critical inquiries into the "souls of black folk," though my having recourse to W. E. B. DuBois's 1903 work indeed suggests that the black New Englander was on course nearly a century ago. Among DuBois's generation of thinkers, poet Jean Toomer comes as close as anyone within this repertory of writings to the coherent laying out of a paradigm of the imaginary (*Cane,* 1922) even though, in a very real sense, we could say that the artwork, in its intelligent "muteness," is already a "translation" that requires a didactic rereading back into its eventuality from concatenations on the real object—in other words, the "message" of art is hardly transparent, or to be read like the palms of the hands. Paule Marshall's fiction, as another example, plays a similar role in the contemporary period, especially *The Chosen Place, The Timeless People* and *Praisesong for the Widow.* I think it is safe to say, however, that the psychoanalytic object, subject, subjectivity now constitute the missing layer of *hermeneutic/interpretive* projects of an entire generation of black intellectuals now at work. The absence is not only glaring but perhaps most curious in its persistence. There are genuine costs as a result, whose upshot may be observed in what I would consider occasional lapses of ethical practice in social relations among black intellectuals themselves. Such lapses are most painfully obvious and dramatically demonstrable in cross gender exchanges within this social formation, although this outcome is not the only way to read the picture. *Within* genders, the black intellectual class is establishing few models of conduct and social responsibility, but perhaps change is in the making.[1] Relatedly, we appear to be at a crossroads in trying to determine who "owns" African-American cultural production as an "intellectual property," who may "speak" for it, and whether or not "possession" itself is the always-exploitative end of kinds of access, even when the investigator looks like me.

While a sustained reading of this manifestation is beside the point of this essay, it hovers in the background as precisely the sort of problem that a revised and corrected social- political practice might field, if not solve, and might mobilize to pointed attention, if not drive out altogether. As a demo-cratic idealist, even I need not be so naive as to believe that nostrums are available to us and that there are, in fact, a cluster of "god-terms" waiting in the wings if only our collective genius could put them in the right order. We should be so lucky. I do want to contend, nevertheless, that psychoanalytic discourse might offer a supplementary protocol we might consider. And if one is going to posit such a thing, then those prior questions I have alluded to ought to be spelled out. This essay attempts to provide such an opening.

II

By juxtaposing psychoanalysis and "race," is one bringing them into align-ment in the hope that these structures of attention will be mutually illumi-nating and interpenetrative? By contrast, does one mean to suggest the impossibility of the latter, which reinforces the impression that these punc-tualities are so insistently disparate in the cultural and historical claims that they each invoke that the ground of their speaking together would dissolve in conceptual chaos? One pair of well-known critics even ventured that it is the "cure" from which we need curing.[2] And if one is *not* going to speak, eventually, of a cure from whatever perceived ailment, then what exactly is the point? We could spend as much time interrogating both psychoanaly-sis and "race" as more or less fixed conceptual narratives and social praxes that occupy their own definitive moment in a semiotic chain. What those are might be as useful as any "fix." This is what I mean: "race," on the one hand, speaks through multiple discourses that inhabit intersecting axes of relations that banish once and for all the illusion of a split between "public" and "private." The individual in the collective traversed by "race"—and there are no known exceptions, as far as I can tell—is covered by it before language and its differential laws take hold. It is the perfect affliction, if by that we mean an undeniable setup that not only shapes one's view of things but demands an endless response from him. Unscientific in the eyes of "proofs," governed by the inverted comma, unnatural and preponderant in its grotesque mandates on the socius, "race" is destiny in the world we have made. Is it not the unequable dinosaur of postmodernist sensibilities, en-amored of instant addictions and handguns? Seemingly out of place along-side the hipness of DNA research, interplanetary probings, and televised repairs on the Hubble telescope, suspended "nowhere" we know, it is our firm and inexorable link to the logics and appeal of the irrational. From Bosnia-Herzegovina to Los Angeles, from Riyadh to Boston, and back across the spine of Europe and Africa, "race" asserts itself as the contagious magic in substitution for totemic collapse and the gods gone astray. What is this thing called "race"?[3] Our deadliest abstraction? Our most nonmaterial actuality? Not fact, but our deadliest fiction that gives the lie to doubt about ghosts? In a word, "race" haunts the air where women and men in social organization are most reasonable.

"Race," therefore, travels: while we are confronted, from time to time, with almost-evidence that the age of the postrace subject is upon us, we are just as certain that its efficacies can, and do, move from one position to another and back again. It is fair to say that "gays in the military" inscribed a social posture that was race-like in its dramatic concentration of negative semantic energy, in the surfeit of blind panic that underscored it, and in the terrifying certainty by which its target was marked. The generals who opposed the early Clinton administration's proposal to reverse the ban on gay and lesbian military personnel were both right and wrong in their objections to the analogizing of gay sexuality to the situation of black soldiers in the armed forces of the Truman era. They were right to observe that black people cannot conceal the color of their skin, while gay subjects, even when black, can keep "it" from sight. From this angle, to have been a black person in arms during World War II and the Korean War must have been analogous to nothing else. (The phenomenon of racial "passing" is roughly comparable, one might guess, to sexuality under concealment, but Africanity, by definition, describes the essence of *visibility,* which contains its own contradiction, insofar as it not only embodies a marked position but also specifies for the nervous beholder an overinvestment of anxiety because it is so marked. Trouble comes double when "race" determines a marker for the person who "has" it. This is not exactly tautological, or question begging, as the processes—phenotypic assignment/recognition, over and against a spurt of psychic energy—interconnect with the actual presence of the black person, who, gratefully, under "normal" circumstances, remains oblivious to the slight stir that her/his appearance has caused in places. Frantz Fanon spoke of the "Negro of the Antilles" [and by association, any "Negro"] as a "phobogenic object, a stimulus to anxiety."[4] It would be useful to know, however, how bodies in general, respond to bodies not like their own, and what it is that "sees"—in other words, do we look with eyes, or with the psyche? The sight disturbance is activated on the streets of Accra, for example, when a white person erupts from the front door of a Barclay's Bank, say, at high noon in the midst of Ghanaian market women at their work, though I think it would be an error to gauge the latter happening as a simple reversal of this: a black person, with nappy hair, come upon all of a sudden by a band of Russian children outside Moscow, is instantly aware that someone has blundered.) From the point of view of power relations, which remained unstated in their objections, the generals, in the controversy with the White House, knew well that racist practices, as a rule, habitually focus on "black," as racism even sprints across the jazzy frontiers of sexual preference. Practically speaking, then, their nay-saying was accurate.

What the generals got wrong, however, was the following: (1) the arbitrariness of difference can occur along *any* lines of stress and for reasons that are, at once, elaborate and simpleminded; and (2) "race" is both concentrated and dispersed in its locations—in other words, "race" alone bears no inherent meaning, even though it reifies in personality, but gains its power from what it signifies by point, in what it allows to come to meaning (i.e., the synonymity struck between Africanness and enslavement by the close of the seventeenth century in the English colonies marked the boundary of freedom, which decided, in turn, a subject's social and political status). In the context of the United States, "race" clings, primitively, to a Manichean overtness—"black" and "white." But it is evident that "race" by other names may operate within homogeneous social formations that lose their apparent "same" under hierarchical value: from an American point of view, Haitian and Somalian societies, as well as the complex ethnic groupings that constitute the former Yugoslavia, are less racially diverse than the United States, since here, *skin color* is the deciding factor. But in all three instances of community shattered by conflict and killing, "color" was—still is—displaced onto other features of the discriminatory. To that extent, "race" marks both an in-itselfness and a figurative economy that can take on any number of different faces at the drop of a hat. Understanding how this mechanism works is crucial: "race" is not *simply* a metaphor and nothing more; it is the outcome of a politics. For one to mistake it is to be politically stupid and endangered. It is also a *complicated* figure, or metaphoricity, that demonstrates the power and danger of difference, that signs and assigns difference as a way to situate social subjects. If we did not already have "race" and its quite impressive powers of proliferation, we would need to invent them. The social mechanism at work here is *difference in, and as, hierarchy,* although "race" remains one of its most venerable master signs.

Unhooked from land, custom, language, lineage, and clan/tribal arrangements, modern "race" joins the repertoire of fetish names bolstered by legislative strategy, public policy, and the entire apparatus of the courts and police force. It appears to best advantage under the regime of exile, estrangement, and struggle—in brief, where and when heterogeneous social subjects invoke their humanness and its orders under the signs of enmity and alienation. With the new global arrangement portended by European incursions around the Atlantic-Gulf rim of the New World,[5] conquest and warfare seem automatic to cross-racial exchange, and fortune, the crown of the colonizing spirit. Michel de Certeau speaks of the New World as "nuova terra," an "unknown body" then covered over by discourses of power. This "writing that conquers . . . will use the New World as if it were a blank 'savage' page on which Western desire will be written."[6] Under this fairly novel scheme of orientations, "race" will malocclude culture, as the former becomes fatally wed to questions of value. The processes set in motion in de Certeau's conceptual narrative, wherein the new land is allegorized as an unclothed female figure,[7] will come to exact a cultural denuding, an emptying out of culture; this lesion on the world surface, this gap in its "brain," will be filled up, and filled in, by "race." In the long aftermath, however, where we are currently located, we already know that "race," even then, "passed" for the Harvest but was, in fact, the great Big Empty.

Centuries down the line, the problem is how to explain the way by which "race" translates into cultural self-production, at the same time that it is evidently imposed by agencies (agentification) that come to rest in the public/administrative sphere, or what we understand as such. The provocation is to grasp its self-reflexivity, which is presumptively "private" and "mine." The relay between self-fashioning and "out there" is only intricately revealed, however. The three dimensions of subjectivity offered by Lacanian psychoanalysis, the Symbolic, the Imaginary, and the Real,[8] broach an interpretation that could be articulated with racial economy, but in its muddle concerning the Real, which is not *the* real, according to certain theorists,[9] we are left stunned in the breach. J. Laplanche and J.-B. Pontalis's *Language of Psycho-analysis*,[10] for example, carries substantial entries on the Symbolic and the Imaginary, but nothing under the name of the "Real." What one anticipates, then, is that a fourth register[11] will be called for in establishing "reality" (of the dominated political position) as the psychic burden, acquired post-mirror stage, that reads back onto the Lacanian triangulation a distended organizational calculus. In short, the Lacanians do not give us a great deal of help, as far as I can tell, with the "reality" that breaks in on the person.

Before we could even attempt such revisionary reading, we should ask of psychoanalysis generally what objects in its field might come into play in the understanding of "race," as well as what business we have here. As a literary critic/theorist might deploy it, psychoanalytic theory has little or nothing to do with psychoanalysis defined by an object, a field delimited by a practice, or the desire of the analyst, as Lacan elaborated the problematic in *The Four Fundamental Concepts*.[12] Clearly, we are making use of the psychoanalytic echo toward an end that practitioners would neither recognize nor endorse, though aberrant performances to which psychoanalytic theory is occasionally subjected are nothing new or especially daring these days: psychoanalytic insights, transported into the fields of feminist and critical inquiries, for example, are already a well-known quantity. (Perhaps the problem of poaching could be disposed of if we called such forays as this one an exercise in *psychoanalytics,* a project that would think through aspects of a psychoanalytic culture criticism and how one might go about determining its shape and style.)[13] We are thrown here onto some vaguely defined territory between well-established republics. The point, I believe, is to put down tracks for some future investigation/investigator, whose "citizenship" might remain as generously undefined as the space I would claim. Putting the best face we can on such a state of things, we could call this investigator of the future a "cosmopolite." In a very real sense, our corrected relationship to the realities of "race" might induce a "negative capability" in the place of guilt and an openness to a world that now appears final and closed. Stretching the metaphor, we might say that one goes in search of a "homeland" that is as sufficient to the needs of strangers as of kin.

Negotiating the ground between forms of exile and belonging captures precisely the historic vocation of communities of individuals on the periphery of the dominant order, but it is difficult now to focus on and to keep in view a distinct margin and center. So much of the work of domination appears to be aided by an erstwhile "outsider," reproduced within the very precincts of the dominated, that a rigid demarcation of the social order into cultural dominant, and dominated, positions seems ever more inadequate. There is, in fact, an element of antagonistic cooperation involved in sociocultural work, from whatever vantage one is situated. The degree to which cooperation can be distinguished from complicity, or consensus from compromise, calls for discernment of the nicest sort, but the prior problem, as I have observed, is that the inquiry itself has been put only sporadically, if at all. A psychoanalytic culture criticism would not only attempt to name such contradictions but would establish the name of inquiry itself as the goal of an *interior intersubjectivity.* As it seems clear to me at the moment, the African-American collective denotes the quintessential object of the discourses of social science, insofar as the overwhelming number of commentaries concerning it have to do with the "findings" of the sociological and the collective situation within economy. The limitation of this view, if not of particular projects, is that it achieves little perspective with a "general science of the economy of practices."[14] What is more, naming here becomes destiny, to the extent that the social formation, or individual communities within it, more accurately, comprehend themselves, almost entirely, as an innocence or a passivity worked upon, worked over, by others. While it would be much too simplistic and erroneous to say, "all we have to do . . . " we can guess without apology that there is an aspect of human agency that cannot be bestowed or restored by others, even though the philosopher's "recognition," or lack of it, will, in fact, support it, and it is this aspect of the historical and cultural apprenticeship—strategies for gaining agency—that we wish to describe in a systematic way.

I have chosen to call this strategy the *interior intersubjectivity*, which I would, in turn, designate as the locus at which *self-interrogation* takes place. It is not an arrival but a departure, not a goal but a process, and it conduces to neither an answer nor a "cure," because it is not engendered in formulae and prescriptions. More precisely, its operations are torque-like to the extent that they throw certainty and dogma (the static, passive, monumental aim) into doubt. This process situates a content to work on as a discipline, as an askesis, and I would specify it on the interior because it is found in economy but is not exhausted by it. Persistently motivated in inwardness, in-flux, it is the "mine" of social production that arises, in part, from interacting with others, yet it bears the imprint of a particularity. In the rotations of certainty, this "mine" gets away with very little, scot-free, and *that*, I believe, rebounds back upon the ethical wish that commences this writing.

Questions pertaining to the ethical—to the *relational* dimension of the lifeworld—have become urgent over the last thirty years for reasons too complicated to explain quickly here, but we could say, in brief, that the postmodern economy, both in real and symbolic terms, has been devastating for both the concept and practice of "community." My deep worry and surprise is that the African-American community no longer appears to grasp what I am at pains to describe as an intelligent response to a myriad of crises, as it seems that we were able to marshal considerable resources over the long and terrific century after Emancipation. We would have to account for powerful and *systemic* changes in national life following the period of the Vietnam War [1964–1973], but apart from that, one feels something quite private and unofficial about the post–Civil Rights era that no amount of analysis can sufficiently explain: it would appear that certain social capabilities have been dissipated—a certain lightness of being, if we could say so, observable in the community's superior music and in some of its best writings, in its commitment to taste, to style, to the masks of self-humor— just as we note, ironically, unprecedented upward mobility for black Americans at the same time. In the wake of loss, we only have left, it seems, the inexorable grimness of "competition," of "getting over," of "role-model-ing," of "success" for the well-credentialed, and a thorough commodification of black culture. My nostalgia for the lost love-object cannot be entirely laid down, I suspect, to the affects of anxiety's displacements alone, but relates as well to the *dispersal* of community across so wide a social terrain that Robert Stepto's "symbolic geography"[15] takes on added explanatory power. The outcome of the national flight of labor, the demise of Fordist regimes of production and industry, and the radical reorganization of global capital, which fundamentally archaizes the sovereign nation-state, with certain features held over from the nineteenth-century, engender a "community" that is to be understood, desired, reproduced, and consumed in a different way. An apparently homogeneous social form with strictly determined borderlines, within and without, is no longer located in the same place, or, perhaps more accurately, no longer configured in the same way, if by that we mean zones of safety in the familiar. The old community, which presented its aspects to the eyes of the child as the first and monumental stability, is no longer a space I would swear I know.

I would say, then, that from my limited acquaintance with classical psychoanalytic theory, the missing pieces that would help us to articulate a protocol of healing in reference to the African-American lifeworld have to do with the dimensions of the socio-ethical. Even though the Freudian archive offers a rich itinerary of narratives and their context, beginning with Fräulein Anna O's family situation, we cannot trace from there, for example, a systematic trajectory of wider social engagement and implication: we cannot tell where a household is located in political economy or the stresses generated by the positioning, although it is clear from the discourse on the early psychoanalytic movement[16] that its initial subjects were, to a degree, quite comfortably installed in the environment and were even "at home" in it. (But was *that* the problem? That what might have been a rebellion, or the site of an "uncanny," or a "not home," reappeared as a symptom instead?) The relationship, then, between the "nuclear family" and the intervening sociometries of the bourgeois household of Viennese society of that era generated the neurosis and its science out of a social fabric that feminist investigation has been keen to rethread.[17] It seems that Freud wrote as if his man/woman were Everybody's, were constitutive of the social order, and that coeval particularities carried little or no weight. The universal sound of psychoanalysis, in giving short shrift to cultural uniqueness (which it had to circumvent, we suppose, in order to win the day for itself and, furthermore, in order to undermine, to throw off the track, the anti-Semitic impulses of Freud's era), must be invigilated as its limit: in other words, precisely because its theories seduce us to want to concede, to "give in" to its seeming naturalness, to its apparent rightness to the way we live, we must be on guard all the more against assimilating other cultural regimes to its modes of analyses too quickly and without question, if at all.

But for all that, I have no evidence that what are for me, at least, the major topics of its field are not in fact stringently operative in African-American community: (1) self-division; (2) the mimetic and transitive character of desire; (3) the economies of displacement—associative and disjunctive; (4) the paradox of the life-death pull; (5) the tragic elements couched in the transfer of social powers from one generation of historical actors to another; (6) the preeminent distinctions that attach to the "Twin Towers" of human/social being—"Mama" and "Papa" (this item does invite sustained attention, because parenting in black communities is historically fraught with laws that at one time overdetermined the legal status of the child as property; but the question is, to what extent the legal relations of a child who neither "belonged" to the mother nor to an *African* father might have been translated into an affective one); (7) the "paradox of the negative,"[18] or the sign's power to delegate by negation; and (8) the special relationship that adheres between exile and writing (which may be retroactively viewed here through the lens of de Certeau). It seems, then, that the lifeworld offers a quintessential occasion for a psychoanalytic reading, given the losses that converge on its naming, and given the historic cuts that have starcrossed its journey. The situation of African-American community is more precisely *ambivalent* than any American case we can concoct, in light of its incomplete "Americanization" even at this late date. The way it is situated in American culture precisely defines the human-social element trapped between divergent cultural mappings, as well as an oppositional *and* collusive circuit of desire itself. The question, then, for this project is not so much why and how "race" makes the difference—the police will see to it—but how that difference carries over its message onto an interior, how "race," as a poisonous idea, insinuates itself not only across and between ethnicities but within. What I am positing here is the *blankness* of "race" where something else ought to be, that emptying out of which I spoke earlier, the evacuation to be restituted and recalled as the discipline of a self-critical inquiry. In calling this process an *interior intersubjectivity,* I would position it as a sort of power that countervails another by an ethical decision, but would this countervalence belong, by definition, to what Freud called the "secondary processes"[19] of consciousness, and would a radical shift of *consciousness* adequately effect the kind of root change I mean? In my view, classical psychoanalytic theory offers some interesting suggestions along this route by way of (1) the fetish object (if we read Freud with Marx on the fetish); and

(2) certain Lacanian schemes, corrected for what I have called the "so-cionom," or the speaking subject's involvements with ideological appara-tuses, which would embrace, in turn, a theory of domination (to that extent, Lacanian psychoanalytic theory is simply heavenly, insofar as it has no eyes for the grammar and politics of power). The insights of psycho-analysis might be carefully scrutinized for what they might teach, but any investigator must attempt to illuminate the *ground* as the premier state-ment of a theory rather than its "blindness," to state systematically why it is important to do so. Concerning the latter point, Freud could not "see" his own connection to the "race"/culture orbit, or could not theorize it, be-cause the place of their elision marked the vantage point from which he spoke. Because it constituted his enabling postulate, it went "without say-ing." Perhaps we could argue that the "race" matrix was the fundamental *interdiction* within the enabling discourse of founding psychoanalytic the-ory and practice itself. But it is the missing element here that helps to define Freud's significance as one of the preeminent punctualities of Western time in modernity. But how to deal with the resistances—both those necessary caveats and those rather revealing fears?

III

"Man got everything else. Can't have my soul, too," goes the wisdom. Once, in a gathering of colleagues, I even heard a heart-wrenchingly dis-dainful "F—a Freud!" A friend of a friend, upon hearing that some people were going out to Santa Cruz for a symposium entitled "Psychoanalysis in an African-American Context," replied, "That *sounds* just like that place!" Not real promising for those who might want to have a "tetch" of conver-sation? It need not be idol worship that we engage in but a genuine desire to improve on black intramural relations in the here and now. Doing so seems to me fairly imperative to our taking the next step. But how to go?

The way here is basically unmapped, except for a handful of venturers, Frantz Fanon the most eminent among them. Because we have inserted this proper name into the pantheon of revolutionary figures, sixties style, we tend to forget that Fanon converted to political activism by degree and, somewhat unusually, from the field of medicine and psychiatric practice. Not a natural actor on the political stage, Fanon (who almost became a den-tist, we learn!) might be considered a man disillusioned with the science and arts of healing, turning ever more forcefully toward polemical address and lyrical emphasis in order to make his points. While Fanon offers our clearest link to psychoanalysis in the African/Third World field, there is suf-ficient enough doubt concerning the efficacy of psychoanalysis, implied in some of his writings, that he appears to withdraw with the left hand what he proffers with the right. If, as Irene Gendzier suggests,[20] Fanon did not evolve thorough contempt for Western psychoanalytic practice, then his ironic stance toward it increasingly marked his career, most notably, she urges, in the shift of tone from *Black Skin, White Masks* to *Wretched of the Earth*, written as he approached the premature close of his life in his thirty-sixth year. If we can be certain of anything, though, it is that our reading of the Fanon canon will most likely be inadequate, because the writing is shot through with contradiction. Knowing that, a reader tries to isolate the broadest themes in his work and should hope to reach a few tentative conclusions. Even though the translations of *Les Damnés de la terre*,[21] with its introduction provided by Jean-Paul Sartre, became, alongside the sayings of Mao Tse-Tung and Ho Chi Minh and *The Autobiography of Malcolm X*, a sacred work for African-American students in revolt thirty-five years ago, it is in *Black Skin, White Masks* that Fanon draws and quarters a fictive composite called the "Negro of the Antilles" and the complexes that come to infect his mental life in proximity to Western white society. In other words, the very text by which the signature of Fanon is most vividly inscribed in "minority" memory not only deals with Maghreb societies, specifically Algeria, but with cultures whose language—Arabic—he never really mastered, according to one of his biographers, and whose religion—Islam—he cannot really be said to have denied, since the latter stance would have required sufficient knowledge of what exactly one was repudiating in the first place. Further, "Concerning Violence" (the opening chapter of *Wretched*), twisted out of perspective with what surrounds it, apparently tempts one to boil Fanon's activist career down to a Manichean emphasis that is belied by "The Pitfalls of National Consciousness" and "On National Culture" of the same work and by ironic, even comic, turns that crosshatch the fabric of *Black Skin*. In brief, the Frantz Fanon we believe we know brings on a kind of astigmatism, or superimposition of contradictory messages that might have been provocative to a forthright self-analysis. A full decade before *Wretched*, the "apostle" of violence, forced to an extreme view of things by the intransigence of the empowered, we take it, and by the heightened revolutionary tensions that marked the North African field, wrote, "I, the man of color, want only this: That the tool never possess the man. That the enslavement of man by man cease forever. That is, one by another. That it be possible for me to discover and love man, wherever he may be" (*BS*, 231).

Because *Black Skin* and some of the essays that comprise *Toward the African Revolution*[22] fix their laser on the self-deceived "Negro of Antilles," these writings strike closer home to the desired target, even though the population I am alluding to was never strictly colonized (the phenomenon of the absentee landlord and its related parasitic economies, as, for example, one of Ousmane Sembene's early films, *Emitai*, demonstrates)[23] but shares the narratives and emplotment strategies of enslavement and domination with groups across the geopolitical-ethnic spread of the New World. For that reason, Fanon instructs us in the general notion that psychoanalytic discourse, with its originating purposes pointed toward European community, might be understood as the bracketed portions of a sociopolitical analysis in reference to New World Africanity, but to parenthesize is to complicate, to make potholes in the way of an otherwise smooth ride. It annuls nothing, figuring its traces on the dynamic play of signifiers. Precisely because social engagement might be accurately portrayed as a scene of massive contagion *(sensibilisation)*, we are all the more compelled to inquire not only into the psychic character of those cultural and social forms that experience "no disproportion between the life of the family and the life of the nation" (*BS*, 142) but also into those demographic elements cut on the bias of a theoretical symmetry. (It must be said that the clinical case, at least insofar as the lay person might perceive it, already suggests that the synonymity that Fanon posits between European society and European family is as mythic in its texture of reality as its opposite. In other words, it seems to me that "individual," "family," and "society" are, by definition, particles in constant bombardment—across the "race" spectacle, between and within the races, and according to a modern cultural synthesis, brought on by industrialized capital in its precise historic formation and its aftermath that divide and specify "persons" from "land," "family," and "other" in the competitive machineries of living. The individual, in his/her peculiar nervous temperament, emerges not so much as the solution of a willful struggle against the mass but as the name of new relations of labor and sociality. The psychoanalytic subject, then, along related lines of stress, and whether it is Freud/Lacan's or Fanon's, is already incipient in the very forces of the historical labor that will bring the modern world to stand.) How does Fanon see the picture?

In "The Negro and Psychopathology," the sixth chapter of *Black Skin,* Fanon proceeds on the basis of a couple of key assumptions:

1. The "Negro of the Antilles" is, for all intents and purposes, a European, having been placed under the burden of an "unreflected imposition of . . . culture" (*BS*, 191). Denouncing Carl Jung's cerebrally inherited "collective unconscious," Fanon proposes that it is "normal for the Antillean to be anti-Negro," inasmuch as he "partakes of the same collective unconscious as the European." How could it be otherwise, he conjectures, since, for example, "the works of 'our' novelists—Balzac, Bazin, Anatole France,

among them—utter never a word about an ethereal yet ever present black woman or about a dark Apollo with sparkling eyes"? Having "breathed and eaten the myths and prejudices of racist Europe, and assimilated the collective unconscious of that Europe, [the Antillean] will be able, if he stands outside himself, to express only his hatred of the Negro" (BS, 188).

2. The corollary of this disheartening conclusion—even though one would be led to concede that the Antillean is likely a cultural *persona* in the intersection of divergently pointing vectors—bursts upon a twinned contradiction:

(a) There is a "normal" psychic economy that flows from the homogeneous circumstance—"as long as he remains among his own people, the little black follows very nearly the same course as the little white" (BS, 149). In Fanon's apparently closed society, which Martinican society, for instance, most certainly was *not*, as a "département" of France, the child emerges from the parental cocoon to find "himself once more among the same laws, the same principles, the same values. A normal child that has grown up in a normal family will be a normal man" (BS, 142). (And begging the question to beat the band, we might point out!) Even though Fanon sideswipes "normal" by not saying what he intends by it, he does suggest, in a footnote, that in the "psychological sphere," the *"abnormal* man is he who demands, who appeals, who begs" (BS, 142, my emphasis). Taking him where he leaves it, we have already anticipated the obverse of the Manichean allegory he seems to be building.

(b) "A normal Negro child, having grown up within a normal family, will become *abnormal* on the *slightest* contact with the white world" (BS, 143, my emphasis). If colonized societies embed "contact," even in the absence of "The Man," then it is puzzling to me where a "normal" would come from, or even how it is possible to conceive it. Under such circumstances, "same laws, same principles, same values" are the mirage of the homogeneous social forms, insofar as their foundation is already riddled with difference from jump. At the least, we can say that in Fanon's fiction, it is altogether possible to start well. A very curious thing happens, however, if "the little black follows very nearly the same course as the little white" is read in exactly the opposite way from my own interpretation. It was recently pointed out to me that Fanon meant that the "little black" imagines that he is "white," not "black" as I had assumed, and that Fanon is deploying the elements of an *abnormal* scene—that of the colonized. If my colleagues are right, then the following paragraph turns somersault, except that I still want to trouble the "same," and the apparently unruffled surface of affects that the "little black" is believed to traverse.[24]

In either case, the problem with this picture is that it is perfect *as far as it goes,* but it might not take us the distance. Conceded, African-American/ U.S. culture offers a rather different case, although Fanon believes that the black is "black" wherever he might be in the world, whatever the particularities of his condition. In the U.S. field of social relations, African-American culture is open, by definition, if by that we mean a constant commerce in real and symbolic capital among struggling intersubjectivities. Even though the "neighborhood" that we spoke of earlier comes close, on the mythic level, to the cocoon of kin and relatedness that Fanon imagines for the black-before-going-to-Europe, it was always quite literally *crossed* by something else—the General Motors car, for example, the old assembly-line technologies replaced by automation and the service economy, the ubiquitous television and media blitz—those metropolitan/urban byways and by-the-ways along the borders of particular cultural enclosure. If we translate these technological means into a figural and semiotic use, then clearly African-American personality is situated in the crossroads of conflicting motivations so entangled that it is not always easy to designate what is "black" and "white" here. In contradistinction, then, to Fanon, I actually doubt that the black person is, at bottom, the empty vessel that "slightest contact"/"abnormal" would lead us to believe. Does he wither in "white" air? If Fanon is right about this, then the colonized person has every reason to fall into abnormality when he crosses the Atlantic, because it is on the *other* side that he becomes the "phobogenic object" that we met with earlier. In that event, the crisis of collapse passes over the black and is "answered" in the white, whose imaginary is insulted and assaulted by this radically different bodily manifestation. This identifies the terrain of racism and the racist, which remained, for Fanon, the white problem. But inasmuch as the white problem redounds on black personality, its burden is generously shared. For Fanon, the activist, a commitment to revolutionary struggle would change the entire relation between black and white, colonized and colonizer, the European and the Negro.

Fanon seems caught, however, in a wholly binary disposition, which pins him everywhere: not only does he deeply engage the ideology of "black"/"white" but also of "man"/"woman" in the classic heterosexual arrangement. He readily acknowledges, for instance, that so far as the "woman of color" is concerned, he "know[s] nothing about her" (*BS,* 180). This familiar repudiation (and in Fanon, it seems rather playful), with its riff on Freud and "female sexuality,"[25] not only limits his view of the "woman of color," all tricked out in the melodrama of one Mayotte Capécia, but also, for that very reason, the conclusions that he draws about the "man of color," for it is against the sexualized bodies of "male"/"female," installed in the local effects of political economy and the life of the culture, that the black and human child—our charming "little" fellow—will realize his ethical vocation.

It seems to me that the Fanonian approach to the psychoanalytic object spins its wheels because it cannot discover a practice of "disalienation" (Fanon's word for it) within the resources of black culture, or an ethical position that is worth delineating according to the *future* of those cultures— how, for example, the "Negro of the Antilles," and I should like to add, for all that, the "Negro of Memphis" (Tennessee, where I grew up), sustained human and social activity, *despite* the awful press of racist sickness *not her own* that bore down on her. If colonized society, as the colonized experienced it, is entirely predicated on negativity, or I would dare say, on negativity at all, then we should not be surprised that the way out of its quite terrible aftermath is shot through with unbearable travail, that the way out appears to be entirely impossible. I would go so far as to contend that the limitations of a nationalist or ethnic analysis will not be surmounted unless and until the culture worker breaks through the "perceptual cramp" that focuses his/her eyeball on "The Man" rather than the *dynamics of structure* that would articulate psychic order and its massive displacements *with the realm of social-political-administrative institutions.* To that extent, the culture worker's object of investigation begins where the epistelist said charity started—"at home." The Fanonian narrative of the Antillean supposes that this "he" spends every waking moment (and otherwise) in the "presence" of "whites," and while, to a certain extent, this must be so, insofar as the cultural apparatus is commandeered beyond his control, if not his sights, he nevertheless executes an entire human being whose nuanced particularities escape calculation beforehand.

Though such propositions fly in the face of accounts offered by historical materialism, as early as the *German Ideology,* my view does not so much oppose a materialist reading of "concrete oppression" as it seeks to gain perspective with it. (One contemporary theoretician attributes materialist objection "to a certain type of Marxism," which, in his view, misreads portions of *Capital*.)[26] In the place of the Fanonian narrative, I should like to intrude a slightly different one: if psychic economy "grows," as it were, with the historical subject, doesn't she have one long before she "knows" that there is a "white man" and certainly well in advance of her caring about him at all? If black is "normal," so long as . . . , then mustn't this normalcy persist in an economized relationship to the shock/trauma of white encounter? In other words, this "I," it seems, operates as the embodiment of a dialectical plot, or sufficiency, in the midst of normal/abnormal oscillations. In this case, being will stutter—yes—but this can be helped, and the aid, we can very well imagine, will not come from any of the sources of friction, even though the latter specifies the moment of "cure," to the extent that the stutterer is embroiled in it. In the brilliantly moving closure of *Black Skin*, beginning with "The body of history does not determine a single one of my actions" through the disarmingly simple "The Negro is not. Any more than the white man" (*BS*, 231), Fanon appeals to our higher sense of moral and imaginative daring that locates the point at which an enlightened (small *e*) political witness commences its work, from Gandhi to King to Mandela, in the second half of the twentieth century. But I must say that in order for the address to insinuate itself into our deepest determinations, the addresser must effect a cold, calculated wager *against* the official odds: that enough of the consciousness of agency still resides within colonized and enslaved personalities that liberational movement remains a distinct possibility. This "enough" may be good enough, but for sure, it is nearly *all* we have, wherever we may be situated along the spectrum of practice.

We must assume, on the one hand, that the pressures of Fanon's rhetorical choices hustled him on toward teleological closure with his subject, in which case an allegory of black/white confrontational hostility offered the sole alternative to wretched conditions, while, on the other, his sense of poetic intensity, everywhere evident in the declamatory thrusts of his argument and the constancy of reference to Aimé Césaire's lyric voice, running like flame stitch through the texture of his own semantics, urged him toward suspicion of a programmatic appeal. There is, however, a rather sharp contradistinction to that refusal, a dogmatic peevishness that occasionally erupts across the discourse, sometimes in humor: "It is too often forgotten that neurosis is not a basic element of human reality. Like it or not, the Oedipus complex is far from coming into being among Negroes," for example (*BS*, 151–52). The question, in that case, might well be, What is a "Negro"?—insofar as at least one itinerary of psychoanalytic researches[27] would suggest that Fanon's sentiment here might mark a leap of faith more than a good guess. Marie-Cécile and Edmond Ortigues's *Oedipe Africain* argues, on the basis of their clinical observations in Dakar, Senegal, West Africa, that the question of the father presented itself in the African milieu with the same constancy as in the European setting, and according to varied familial configurations—with the matrilineal Serer as well as the patrilineal Wolof ("Les observations cliniques à Dakar nous ont montré que la question du père se présentait en milieu africain avec la même constance qu'en Europe, et chez les Serer matrilinéaires aussi bien que chez les Wolof patrilinéaires. La référence constante au père était un test décisif, un fait undéniable" [*OA*, 9]). Whether or not, then, Fanon's conclusions on this point are tenable is less the issue than the absence in *Black Skin* of a systematic inquiry of differences in the psychoanalytic object that would specify the location of the "Negro of the Antilles," as much a *fictive* invention as an anthropological toponym, or a signifier in a hat. While I can agree that an application of classical psychoanalytic theory or its modifications, as "black psychoanalysis" or "black psychology," or even an "African-Caribbean-American imaginary," would need to examine very carefully the conditions of its discursivity and its relations to the entire repertoire of social productions and reproductions in question, I would still look askance at an unmediated dismissal: "I have preferred to call this chapter 'The Negro and Psychopathology,' well aware that Freud and Adler and even the cosmic Jung did not think of the Negro in all their investigations. And they were right not to have" (*BS*, 151). The dogmatizers of classical psychoanalytic theory and practice "did not think of the Negro" because "the Negro," quite literally, did not come before them, even though Freud himself had absorbed, interestingly enough, a heady figurative concoction called the "dark continent" in his approach to his "querelle de femme."[28] Actually, though he tells us quite a lot about "the Negro," Fanon's "Negro" does not have a name, and as worrisome as it is to behave as if he did, the investigator, from now on, ought to inquire what it is; it seems that everybody wants to tell the black person what he *should* think—at least the "races" agree on that—while wanting too quickly to dismiss his words as unofficial, untraditional, inappropriate, or some such thing as that. As a result, we know "the Negro" rather as an ambulatory instance of what we have assumed, and it is not at all clear to me that Fanon has escaped this general charge of reductive interpretation, despite his riveting commitment to the notion of human freedom. In the play between the discourse of racial orthodoxy and its ironic subversion across the rhetorical surface of Fanon's work, a central problematic emerges, to my mind, and we would call it the *dissolution* of the psychoanalytic object in the hiatus that yawns between his "great black mirage" and "great white error."[29] It seems that the status of the interrogation, indeed its very form, has little altered between his time, over three decades ago, and our own.

In trying, then, to specify the breaks (not to fill them) in a conceptual crux that attempted to site a different psychoanalytic subject, we have recourse to Fanon in a post-Fanonian juncture. (How his theoretical views might have shifted over the intervening decades is anybody's guess, but certainly we tend to conclude that he would have remained a dynamic thinker.) Having recourse is also to inquire: what follows inaugurates nothing more than a sketch of a gambit.

IV

It seems to me that any investigation that would make track on this issue must—ironically enough—"forget" "race," or more precisely, "racism," although such a venture is firmly installed in its awful powers, just long enough to open the question. I would start there. If we could eventually explicate the "interior intersubjectivity" as a useful concept, or one we could improve on, we must, in effect, start from scratch and try to rethink "race" as a piece of political reality, inculcated soon enough, but as something that belongs to an entire ensemble of givens to be managed. Part of the problem is to grasp the whole issue as a feature of the human ecosystem that arises in the historical moment rather than in nature and divine force. What I mean is clear enough, but it would do no harm to repeat it—"race" is not ordained by orders from Providence, even though the politics of race might as well be. Related to the aims of human and historical agency, the following remarks might be read in light of some of the closing articulations of Jürgen Habermas's *Knowledge and Human Interests*. Addressing the project of psychoanalysis related to the critique of ideology, Habermas contends that both take

> into account that information about lawlike connections sets off a process of reflection in the consciousness of those whom the laws are about. Thus the level of unreflected consciousness, which is one of the conditions of such laws, can be transformed. Of course, to this end a critically mediated knowledge of laws cannot through reflection alone render the law itself inoperative, but it can render it inapplicable.[30]

If such applicability is thinkable, then racism and its conceptual minions are consistently revealed as bogus social form. Stopping at such a revelation would not be enough, Marx thought, but trying to see with greater clarity what the problem is might be no mean thing.

What is missing in African-American cultural analysis is a concept of the "one." Though there is a hidden allegiance to the idea of the "superstar"/"hero"—the emplotments of both the autobiography and the form of the slave narrative are firmly grounded in old-fashioned notions of bourgeois "individualism"—it is widely believed that black people cannot afford to be individualistic. I must admit that most of the black people I know who think this are, by the way, the intellectuals who, in practice, not only insist on their own particularity but in some cases even posit a uniqueness.

But if we can, we must maintain a distinction between the "one" and the "individual," even though the positions overlap. The individual of black culture exists strictly by virtue of the "masses," which is the only image of social formation that traditional analysis recognizes. Practically speaking, the "masses" were all there were against the other great totalizing narratives—"white" and "Indian"—in the historical period stretching from colonization to nationhood. The individual of the lifeworld does not stand in opposition to the mass but at any given moment along the continuum might be taken as a supreme instance of its synecdochic representation.[31] In other words, Every Black Man/Woman *is* the "race"—as the logic of slave narratives amply demonstrates—and the elements of the formula are reversible and commensurate. Imagining, then, that African-American culture, under extreme historical conditions, was not simply at odds with the cultural dominant but opposed to it, the intellectual/activist has concluded that his culture inscribes an inherent and coherent difference. African-American culture, then, on the supposed African model, is advanced as a collective enterprise in strict antinomy to the individualistic synthesis of the dominant culture, as well as the summation and reification of the indigenous mass. The individual-in-the-mass and the mass-in-the-individual mark an iconic thickness: a concerted function whose abiding centrality is embodied *in the flesh.* But before the "individual," properly speaking, with its overtones of property ownership and access, more or less complete, stands the "one," who is both a position in discourse—the spoken subject of *énoncé* that figures a grammatical instance[32] and a consciousness of positionality—the speaking subject of the *énonciation,* the one in the act of speaking as consciousness of position. As the former is mapped onto his/her world by social and discursive practices, the latter comes into the realization that he/she is the "one" who "counts." This one is not only a psychic model of layered histories of a multiform past; he/she is the only riskable certainty or grant of a social fiction, insofar as the *point* mimics the place where the speaker/speaking is constituted. In other words, "I" grants its validity in assuming the social for itself, and not unlike the other,[33] whose gaze floods what it grasps and summons the attention at the same time, the "one" is both conceded and not-oneself; it is not to be doubted, as its sureness is tentative. To that degree, the mass is the *posited* belief that empirical data insist on, but where is it? Could we say the "one," by contrast, is always "here," not "there"? That it is concrete and specific, even if anonymous? This is not to choose "one" over the "mass" but to ask a different question, for we know no other gauge of the intersubjective than the one who would assure the more. On this view, the mass is not only putative and abstract but never emerges otherwise. It would be absurd to say that there is no mass but, rather, that its historical and social materiality can be brought to stand, stage by stage, and bit by bit, in a way that begins unimpressively on the smaller scale of something local and at hand. For openers, it is exactly too massive and disappears under the weight of report. The picture will change right away when mass movement is required, but that is something else again, and demands several, shouting.

In the meantime, who is this one? I am referring to a *structure* in this instance: the small integrity of the now that accumulates the tense of the presents as proofs of the past, and as experience that would warrant, might earn, the future. In the classical model, the mental apparatus, Freud argued, can be analogized to a compound microscope or photographic apparatus.[34] Instantly defensive about the "unscientific" status of assertion by analogy, Freud claims that his procedure is permissible so long as the "scaffolding" is not mistaken for the "building." The single lesson that we take away from Freud, in this case, is the split function of subjectivity at the heart of subject formation. The crux of the matter is concentrated in *The Interpretation of Dreams*, which assigns to consciousness itself a relatively minor role in the drama of mind-life. Consequently, Freud apportions a far greater share of mental activity to the functions of the unconscious and the primary processes that suggest their import, he holds, in dreams and the neurosis. Related to the dynamic play of mental forces, *"psychotherapy,"* Freud contends, *"can pursue no other course than to bring the [unconscious] under the domination of the [preconscious]"* (Freud's emphasis).[35] As Lacan will have it decades later, the particular aim of psychoanalysis is "historically defined by the elaboration of the notion of the subject. It poses this question in a new way, by leading the subject back to his signifying dependence."[36]

The Freudian and Lacanian fields of discourse are not only separated from each other by considerable disparity in time, conditions of material culture, and the narrative/conceptual modalities that would situate and explain them; but both, because they reach subject formation by an act of poetic faith that imagines subjectivity hermetically sealed off from other informing discourses and practices, are foreign, if not inimical, to subject formations defined by the suppression of discourse. In other words, the social subject of "race" is not only gaining access to her own garbled, private language, as psychoanalysis would have it, but to language as an aspect of the public trust. (That the language of our contemporaneity is beating a hasty retreat from the tasks of consensus and public address does not alter my thesis here, because we have no difficulty imagining a public sphere, or a beyond-ego position, as a desirable goal for several reasons. For one thing, we would not be able to explain "politics" and "culture" as the ground of contention without acknowledging a public sphere, even though American politics and culture today, dishearteningly, attract often enough the most cynical and unattractive of players.) The one that I am after, then, must be built up from the ground, so to speak, inasmuch as classical psychoanalytic theory and its aftermath contradictorily point toward it—a subject in its "signifying dependence," which means that the subject's profound engagement with, and involvement in, symbolicity is everywhere social—yet such theories cannot exhaust it. As far as I can tell, African-American cultural analysis, as black intellectuals carry it out, has not explained either a subject in discourse crossed by stigmata or the nonfantastical markings of a history whose shorthand is "race." From that angle, the most promising of trails may be false, since it does not necessarily lead to a destination but circles back to the same place. The problem here, which fractures somewhat chaotically in many directions at once, is how to break the circle, how to pursue a theoretical model that might pose the pacing along to the next step, even if such pacing effects a halting progression. The interior intersubjectivity would substitute an *agent* for a spoken-for, a "see-er," as well as a "seen." Habermas's self-reflection, in which case the laws are *operative* but do not apply, appears to be predicated on the agency of self- knowing, but DuBois's figure of the "double consciousness"[37] suggests the complications through which such agency must pass.

When DuBois spoke earlier in the century about the protocol of "double consciousness," he was gesturing toward a duality of cultural fields metaphorized by "African" and "American." Though the former term had been used in self-reference to the American Negro long before DuBois's era and would be again in our own, DuBois was working under the assumption that "Africa" more than vaguely signaled the origins of black culture. It is also noteworthy that his provocative claims, barely elaborated beyond that short paragraph that the student knows virtually by heart,[38] cross their wires with the *specular* and the *spectacular*—the sensation of looking at oneself and of imagining oneself being looked at through the eyes of the other/another is precisely performative in what it demands of a participant on the other end of the gaze. To that extent, the Fanonian "phobogenic" object meets up with the DuBoisian "double consciousness," but it seems that DuBois was trying to discover—indeed, to posit—an *ontological* meaning in the dilemma of blackness, working out its human vocation in the midst of overwhelming social and political power. It was not enough to be seen; one was called upon to decide what it meant. To that degree, Du Bois's idea posed a route to self-reflexivity. Addressing the aims and objectives of consciousness, then, as it negotiated the terrain of a given reality, DuBois, writing contemporaneously with Freud, was interested in providing a new mythography, or a new way of seeing the black problem, for the "souls of black folk," as he called it.

The subject of double consciousness is divided across cultural valences, but DuBois did not exhaust the formulation. For him, nothing was hidden from the *sight* of the man in the mirror, who not only recognized the falseness of his countenance, as in a kind of theatrical mask, but how he had come to wear it. From that angle, the subject already "knows" as much as he knew, for all intents and purposes, on the day he was born. But DuBois's economy of doubleness was adequate insofar as it proffered a name for cultural ambivalence, while seeking a reconciliation of putative opposites; it is clear that the DuBoisian knot cannot be healed or resolved on the level where DuBois was posing the question, because: (1) the act of seeing oneself rested, rests, in the subject's head and is only partially shaped and motivated by the official deed; and (2) the change of seeing mostly depends on a change of mind coming from the direction of a power imagined to be entirely other, but an entirely other from outside. While DuBois understood quite correctly that an effective political solution did remain in the hands of black community—the Niagara Movement, and the NAACP springing from it, constituted his practical response—the latter was conflated in his scheme with an ontology. He was not so much wrong in making this move as too quick to reach a conclusion; but, despite that, the dilemma that DuBois justly posed is the *psychocultural* situation of minorities in the West, even though he specifically targeted the "problem of the color line" as it traversed the body of the seventh son, born with a caul over the face, the American Negro. In working with the DuBoisian double, we recover the sociopolitical dimensions that classical psychoanalysis and its aftermath sutured in a homogeneity of class interests, just as DuBois's scheme must be pressured toward a reopened closure: the subject in the borrowed mirror is essentially mute. DuBois is speaking for him. It is time now, if it were not in 1903, for him to speak for himself, if he dares. That this speaking will not be simple is all the more reason why it must be done.

The interior intersubjectivity is predicated, then, on *speaking*. If we cannot identify a "first" step here in any systematic way, we can put our finger on the point: to overcome the officially imposed silence engendered by exclusive traditions of power—state- and corporate-sponsored—that, in turn, go on to be taken over by "personality," under the influence of those powers that properly belong to the repertories of learning and naming that both "piggyback" on the self-evidentiary wisdom of "received opinion" (i.e., IQ testing, bell curves, the criminality of the poor, etc.) and help to create it; in brief, the weight of the discursive debris that comes to rest on subjects a priori the local and specific fields of cultural play that they are called upon to negotiate. The unavoidable contradiction in what I am proposing, which would historically resemble the Freudian "talking cure,"[39] but which would also share in the dialectics of Toni Morrison's character called Sethe,[40] is that my solution specifically relates to a social positioning vis-à-vis discourse. Perhaps the speaking of intersubjectivity effects a kind of mimicry of the professional wordsmith's relationship to symbolic capital, but how is the speaking I mean here to be differentiated from professional discourse?

There is much insistence, at least in our customary way of viewing things, that the professional has little in common with the majority of the population. True enough as far as it goes, this truism is tinged with animus toward activity perceived to be esoteric, elitist, uncommon. But this simplified reading of the social map, sealing off entire regions and territories of experience from the reciprocal contagion proper to them, offers us a slim opportunity to understand how the social fabric, like an intricate tweed, is sewn across fibers and textures of meaning. There is the discourse in which the professional, as de Certeau observes, dares and labors,[41] the discourse of *travail;* but there is also the mark of the professional's human striving in terms of the everyday world of the citizen-person—coming to grips with the pain of loss and loneliness; getting from point *a* to *b;* the inexorable passing of time, change, and money; the agonies of friendship and love, and so on. *This* speaking, and the one I refer to, is nothing less than the whole measure of the tirelessly mundane element on which ground, we recall, Freud placed the key to the mental theater, the unconscious and the dream life, the apparent junk tossed off by the deepest impulses. In that regard, the professional's relationship to discourse is tiered, but it is also imbricated by forms of dialects through which she lives her human and professional calling, as work is rent through with the trace of the uncommon and the more common. On this level, speaking is democratically impoverished for a range of subjects, insofar as it is not sufficient to the greedy urge to revelation of motives that the social both impedes and permits, nor is it adequate to the gaps in kinetic and emotional continuity that the subject experiences as discomfort. Psychoanalytic literature might suggest the word *desire* here to designate the slit through which consciousness falls according to the laws of unpredictability. In that sense, the subject lives with desire as intrusive, as the estranged, irrational, burdensome illfit that alights between where she "is at" and would/wanna be. On this level of the everyday, the professional discourser, if we could say so, and the women

commandeering the butcher's stand at the A&P have in common a mutually scandalous secret about which they feel they must remain silent, but
which speaking, more emphatically, *talking,* about appeases, compensates,
deflects, disguises, and translates into usable, recognizable social energy. I
mean, then, this speaking as it turns us off the track of isolation into which
the preciosity and lowness of desire, persistent in solid juxtaposition in the
same person, might tend to lead. I believe that this arena of the emotionally
charged and discharged is not only where the subject lives but is the position through which she speaks a particular syntax.

Is it not, then, the task of a psychoanalytic protocol to effect a translation from the muteness of desire/wish—that which shames and baffles the
subject, even if its origins are dim, not especially known—into an *articulated* syntactic particularity? This seems to me a passable psychoanalytic
goal, but perhaps there is more to it than simply a nice thing to happen. At
the very least, I am suggesting that an aspect of the emancipatory project
hinges on what would appear to be simple self-attention, except that reaching the articulation requires a process, that of making one's subjectness the
object of a disciplined and potentially displaceable attentiveness. To the extent that the psychoanalytic provides, at least in theory, a protocol for the
"care of the self" on several planes of intersecting concern, it seems vital to
the *political* interests of the black community, even as we argue (endlessly)
about its generative schools of thought. I should think that the *process* of
self-reflection, of the pressing urgency to make articulate what is left in the
shadows of the unreflected, participates in a sociopolitical engagement of
the utmost importance. If we think of *speaking* along this line of stress, then
we cut right through the elitist connotations of "discourse" to the basic uses
of literacy, whose attainment is currently regarded by the postmodernists as
something of an embarrassment. But if we imagine such achievement as an
emancipatory aim, then the perceived advantages of it lose their sting of
privilege. Relatedly, both speaking and literacy, in the ways I am stipulat-
ing, might be understood as the *right* to use, which certain theoreticians regard as one of the premier destinies of property.[42] This entire discussion is
caught up in questions of power in the last instance, but we are concerned
with only a single one of its multiple and interpenetrative phases, and that
is the power and position of a specific speaking.

To speak is to occupy a place in social economy, and, in the case of the
racialized subject, his history has dictated that this linguistic *right to use* is
never easily granted with his human and social legacy but must be earned,
over and over again, on the level of a personal and collective struggle that
requires in some way a confrontation with the principle of language *as pro-*

hibition, as the withheld. An irony here ensues that the researcher/subject must both surmount and ride: the historic prohibition can only be spoken within language, yes, but also within discourse (the particular dialects of criticism, resistance, testimonial and witness, etc.). What must be emphasized here is the symbolic value of the subject's exchanges with others, and it is within the intersubjective nexus that the inequalities of linguistic use and value are made manifest—what one can do with signs in the presence and perspective of others—and it is only within those circuits that a solution can be worked out. The unalterable difficulty is that such an operation cannot escape the Western context, and this is crucial. As we observed before, the traditional subject of psychoanalytic process was deceptively "at home" in the culture; he seemed to believe that he "belonged," whereas the minority subject does not start there. DuBois clearly understood both the Western context and the cut from it that African personality inscribed. But can we derive a formal coherence, related to the psychoanalytic, from these general ideas, springing up from the historic, whose pitch and thrust are, by definition, public, definitive, consensus-driven?

Though a psychoanalytics related to the lifeworld would implicitly maintain contact with its predecessor texts, with the conceptual horizon that situates it, it is equally true that such a protocol would be guided by a new aim, insofar as the analysis must make a place for it—the speaking that self-reflection begins to demand. The scarcity, the deficit, is located in the occasion for this private discourse that is not satisfied by the public forms and proprieties of narrative, autobiographical and otherwise, that remain substantially malleable to market forces and fickle public opinion. A cultural analysis revised and corrected for this most difficult of tasks is called upon to: (1) substitute the problematics of culture for that of "race," or a determinate group interest whose outcome is always already known; and (2) articulate its investigations along three lines of stress: (a) the diurnal, or the everyday; (b) the dimension of the practical/pragmatic; and (c) the dimension of the contemplative. Of these three registers of analysis, the first and third dimensions are the least developed in the field. Currently, the cultural analysis offers no theory of the "everyday" and appears to have no firm grasp of social subjects in relationship to it. Such an understanding would conduce to a systematic materialist reading, which would establish "race," in turn, in perspective with other strategies of marking and stigmata. Because of its allegiance to ideologies of empiricism, material success, and the transparencies of reading,[43] the analysis provides no clue to the contemplative register of the lifeworld. I am not talking about the recognition of the significance of rumor, gossip, and jaw-wagging, nor about armchair reading and philosophizing, but rather about a *name* for the *sense of time* that we could call *distancing,* standing apart momentarily from the roll and moil of Event and ways to introduce it to the repertoire of human and social relations that traverse communities of interest. Because our analysis of the fields of the everyday and the contemplative are tangled up in the confusions of crisis-response (the threat to "affirmative action" policies, for example), we flounder, therefore, on the pragmatic point, or the realm of direct political action and engagement. But it seems clear that the dimension of the contemplative practice, contextualized in relationship to the "science of a general economy of practices,"[44] must be quite literally pronounced as an aspect of cultural continuity and struggle.

Contrary to the position taken by certain black leadership, we would say that "analysis" is not "paralysis," as it certainly seems that the absence of it is a living social death. Practically speaking, the leadership, wherever it arranges itself along the axes of responses, must update its "message,"[45] send a different one, and, in my view, link its own destiny more fully to the work of scholarship and reading. (DuBois remains our exemplary figure in this.) Exactly how today's leadership—and I do not exempt the intellectuals as a social formation from the general charge—is itself an elaboration of the problem it would solve should be thought about with a careful and, where possible, generous attitude, though such an investigation is not my aim here. If the psychoanalytic hermeneutic has any bearing at all on the lifeworld, and I believe that it does, then it will enter the picture at the third level of stress, even though, dynamically speaking, these layers of human time are interpenetrative. Their articulation, however, very much depends on the extent to which we differentiate pieces of the social content and demand.

The formal coherence that we seek for an apposite psychoanalytic practice, then, does not commence in the psychoanalytic at all but is firmly rooted in habits and levels of communication, reading, and interpretation—in short, how communities are apprenticed and interpellated in culture and the ways in which such lessons are transmitted. Even though we customarily attribute reading and interpretive activity to an advantageous class position, the conclusion is inaccurate—the wide dissemination of literacies, visual and cybernetic, as well as literary, necessitates the negotiation of signs at whatever level, to whatever degree of competence. Sign reading, or the field of the semiotic, is democratically executed, as the culture worker can do nothing more or less than point this out as a strategy for opening the way to the third dimension of social engagement. (To nail down the point, I will run the risk of redundance: the Rodney King event, for example, to say nothing of the reaction to the jury's verdict in the O. J.

Simpson trial, the end of which was oddly linked by an accident of timing to the Farrakhan-convoked "Million Man March," all occurred on two levels of stress. In the Rodney King case, the event itself and what it told us yet once more about the potential for the abuse of police power and its impact on black communities across the United States were a terrible shock that even exceeded, perhaps, the strange, chilling, nightmarish experience of listening to the Fuhrman tapes, introduced by the Simpson defense toward the end of this interminable trial for double murder. I personally gauged my own shock reaction to the King occurrence and the "revelation" of former L.A.P.D. detective Mark Fuhrman [the man who spoke out of his unconscious] by a penetrating sensitivity to *exactly* what my *location* was during those days—in the latter case, in an apartment complex in a university town with the nearest black person I knew at all a car-ride away. With no immediate or visible signs of threat on the horizon, I remained, nevertheless, *all* ears and eyes to the least alteration of nuance in the surround. This response was dictated by my cultural apprenticeship as a black American woman of a certain generation in U.S. history "talkin'" to me with the acuteness of the Richter scale measure. It was also, quite specifically, the immediate reaction to shock that brings one to her feet in nearly unspeakable anxiety. At some point, however, one steps back from the horror that recedes as a blow and consumes it in a different way. I am suggesting that all *eventuality* comes vested with a timing mechanism that releases one from the shock, that grants us time to *think* the event; if that were not so, then memory would be neither possible nor even thinkable.)

If we cut through this human section in order to retrieve schematically the contemplative practice as a point of entry to the entire ensemble, then we mean no less than the capacity to detach oneself from the requirements of self-attention long enough to concentrate on something else; transformative labor marks a distinctive activity, then, from that of the everyday and that of the practical/pragmatic, but such labor is contextualized and shaped by both, and translates its living in both by other means. In other words, there is a dimension of activity in the lifeworld that lays claim not only to the materiality and immediacy of labor but also to its *difference* of perspective. Distancing here might be regarded as the mark of self-displacement in the social given: if the aim of a radical democratization is to free up more and more subjects to their transformative potential—is this not the point of a "pedagogy of the oppressed"?[46]—wresting their time farther and farther away from the necessity to concentrate on the needs of the biological creature and whether or not it is safe and secure, then such an aim will be carried out in the sphere of political practice and engagement. This is not to suggest that the range of cultural expression is apolitical, or above the ground, nor is it to contend that access to work is unrelated to the economy and public policy, but it is to insist that each of these temporal emphases of the speaking/historical subject bears significance in relation to the human project. Such an insistence will operate as if we mean, in fact, a social division of labor, and so be it, but I mean division as the scissiparous effect *within* subjects rather than *between* them. Just as the culture worker maintains for himself/herself, so he/she must ever more forcefully hold out for others the subject's right of access to his double in the place where it is created.

The double resonates here through intentionalities: it means at once the "add on" that comes to the subject in her access to work and by way of that other scene evoked in the psychoanalytic reading. We must acknowledge what the classical psychoanalytic writers could take for granted, and that is the extent to which information about the other scene was predicated on access to literacy and economic resources; in short, we mean a more or less exact correspondence between the body freed from the harshest, most oppressive labor regime and emancipated to labor abstracted in an intellectual or imaginative/creative quantum. In other words, African-American cultural analysis must actually knot the relations between work increasingly rationalized in a service economy that counts the turning of alphabets on a television game show as a "career" and self-reflection/self-knowledge, or end up being choked by it. But it would seem odd, if not downright perverse, to insist that only bourgeois subjects operate in the way of the double, although, for sure, the *explanatory* discourses and enabling postulates of differentiated speaking and practice are brought about by the same power differential that disperses subjects along the paths of political economy in unequal ways. In that sense, symbolic economies, of which psychoanalytic practice and theories are one, are directly tied to the sociopolitical sphere. The culture worker, because he understands this connection, or will soon, is called upon, therefore, to behave as though his work carried the ultimately *political* meaning that it does.

I believe that the problem here, then, has more to do with evolving a language appropriate to the subjects differently constructed from the classical moment of psychoanalytic theory and its postmodern aftermath than deciding "for" or "against" the psychoanalytic aim. This task will eventually require a lengthy and patient revisiting of the key questions of those theories with a result that I certainly could not predict, except that the main thing appears to be, for the culture critic, the *articulation of a position in discourse and practice along the lines of a more carefully modulated reading of human and social performances in the lifeworld* than an actual psychoanalytic model for it. Pronouncements ex cathedra are, in any event, flat wrong. (I am suggesting that such a model can occur *only* as psychoanalytic practice and in it. The only sources with which I am familiar that offer the reader outlines of practice based on case histories of African subjects and peoples of color are Frantz Fanon's *Wretched of the Earth* and the Ortigueses' *Oedipe Africain*.[47] Dr. Ibrâhîm Sow's *Les Structures anthropologiques de la folie en Afrique noire*,[48] as if in response to *Oedipe Africain*, argues that an efficacious psychoanalytic instrument can be fabricated solely in relation to a global cultural harmony: in his monograph, West African structures of belief are traced back to African systems of cosmology, which irradiate, in turn, the grids of sociology and religious practice.[49] But Sow and the Ortigueses agree that the *age group*, the horizontal relation among confreres of the same bio-logical age, proposes a crucial thematic of African social and psychic orga-nization.) I am suggesting that such a model for diasporic communities might initiate its protocols: (1) with a practice "on the ground"—the case histories of subjects who speak their word to the analyst, not unlike John Gwaltney's quite different venture in *Drylongso;*[50] and (2) on the other side, as it were, of the "white man." It seems to me that such a model cannot be based in, does not commence with, "race" but rather in the intimate spaces where his almighty form is, in fact, "forgotten" and misbegotten in the funny and satirical. It would be neither accurate nor useful to propose an ir-reparable split between the intimate and the public, for doing so would simply reverse and compound the error that I am contending traditional analysis has made all along. Rather, a subtler modulation of the flows from one to the other must be sought. As the critics have correctly maintained, much of the activity of self-defining, which describes the goal of self-reflection, or what I am calling here the "interior intersubjectivity," has occurred in the transgressive unpredictable play of language. For that rea-son, a psychoanalytic model appropriate to the lifeworld and courageous enough to forego the refuges of delusion that wrap around this world like a shroud would risk its occasions in language, not only the locus of the sub-ject's practice of culture—both the natal and the broader one that traverses it—but the single feature of cultural apprenticeship that has been the most *denied*. Above all, we must admit the scandalous: African subjects and sub-jectivity are infinitely more unknown "at home" than anywhere else.

V

When I was young and free and used to wear silks[51] (and sat in the front pew, left of center, I might add), I used to think that my childhood minister occasionally made the oddest announcement. Whenever any one of our three church choirs was invited to perform at another congregation, our minister, suspecting that several of his members would stay home or do something else that afternoon, having already spent some hours at worship, skillfully anticipated them. Those who were not going with the choir were importuned to "send go." The injunction always tickled me, as I took considerable pleasure in conjuring up the image of a snaggle-toothed replica of my seven-year-old self going off in my place. But the minister meant "send money" (i.e., pass the collection plate). Decades later, I decided that the "send go" of my childhood had an equivalent in the semiotic/philosophical discourse as the mark of substitution, the translated inflections of selves beyond the threshold of the fleshed, natural girl. It was not only a delightful but also useful idea to me that one herself need not always turn up. One and one did not always make two but might well yield some indeterminate sum, according to the context in which the arithmetic was carried out, indeed *which* arithmetic was performed. I have been suggesting that we need to work the double in this discussion.

Perhaps this is as factual as I know: in any investigatory procedure concerning African-American culture, a given episteme fractures into negative and positive stresses that could be designated the crisis of inquiry that reveals where a kind of abandonment—we could also call it a gap—has occurred. Rather than running straight ahead toward a goal, the positivity (a given theoretical instrument) loops back and forward at once. For example, the notion of substitutive identity, not named as such in the literature of sociocultural critique, is analogous to the more familiar concept of negation. On the one hand, negation is a time-honored concept of philosophical discourse and is already nuanced and absorbed, if not left behind, by linked discursive moves, from Hegel to Marx, from Kojève to Sartre and Lacan.[52] On the other hand, it is a useful concept to "introduce," alongside the psychoanalytic hermeneutic, to a particular historical order located in the postmodern time frame as a move toward self-empowerment, but in an era of discourse that needn't spell out the efficacy of either. (The same might be said for the concept of the subject.) We are confronted, then, by divergent temporal frames, or beats, that pose the problem of adequacy—how to reclaim an abandoned site of inquiry in the critical discourse when the very question that it articulates is carried along as a part of the methodological structure, as a feature of the paradigm that is itself under suspicion, while the question itself foregrounds a thematic that cannot be approached in any other way. If one needs a subject here, with its repertoire of shifts and transformations, and negation, with its successive generational closures and displacements, though both might be regarded as a disappeared quest-object at best, or a past tense for theory at worst, then we have come to the crisis that I have told, the instrument trapped in a looping movement or behind-time momentousness that need jump ahead. One tries, in this fog of claims, to keep her eyes on the prize; if by substitutive identities—the "send go"—we mean the capacity to represent a self through masks of self-negation, then the dialectics of self-reflection and the strategies of a psychoanalytic hermeneutic come together at the site of a "new woman"/"man." That, I believe, is the aim of the cultural analysis.

A break toward the potentiality of becoming, or the formation of substitutive identities, consists in going beyond what is given; it is also the exceeding of necessity. While this gesture toward a theory of the transcendent is deeply implicated in the passage and itinerary of modern philosophy and the Cartesian subject, it is not so alien to the narratives and teachings of overcoming long associated not only with native traditions of philosophy in the lifeworld (via the teachings of the Christian church) but is entirely consonant with the democratic principles on which the United States was founded (though immensely simplified in the discourses of liberal democracy). But the resonance that I would rely on here is less dependent on a narrative genealogy, whose plotline culminates in an epiphany of triumph, than on a different relation to the "Real," where I would situate the politics and the reality of "race." Even though it is fairly clear that "race" can be inflected (and should be) through the Lacanian dimensions, its face, as an aspect of the "Real," brings to light its most persistent perversity. In Mikkel Borch-Jacobsen's reading of Lacan's "linguisteries," the "Real" is said to be "pure and simple," "undifferentiated, . . . without fissure," and "always in the same place" (*LAM*, 192). As these Lacanian assertions seem to match precisely the mythical behavior of "race," or of any "myth today,"[53] they pointedly refer to the situation of the subject of enunciation—his or her own most "Real," or the status quo. In the classical narratives of psychoanalytic theory, the status quo, the standing pat, does not by error open onto death's corridor inasmuch as it freezes and fixes subjectivity in a status permanently achieved. The outcome breezes by us in the very notion of status, with its play on *statue, sto, stant,* and so on. In this sense, "overcoming" is the cancellation of what is given. Borch-Jacobsen offers this explanation: "Thus language, the manifestation of the negativity of the subject who posits himself by negating (himself as) the Real, works the miracle of manifesting what is not; the tearing apart, the ek-sistence, and the perpetual self-overtaking that 'is' the subject who speaks himself in everything by negating everything" (*LAM*, 193). "Speaking" here is both process and paradigm, to the extent that signifying enables the presence of an absence and registers the absence of a presence, but it is also a superior mark of the trans-formative, insofar as it makes something by cutting through the "pure and simple" of the "undifferentiated" in the gaps and spacings of signifiers. If potentiality, then, can be said to be the site of the human, rather than the nonhuman fixedness—more precisely, if it is the "place" of the subjectivity, the condition of being/becoming subject—then its mission is to unfold, through "words, words, words" (*LAM,* 193), yes, but "words, words, words" as they lead us out to the re-presentational where the subject commences its journey in the looking glass of the symbolic.

Thus, to represent a self through masks of self-negation is to take on the work of discovering where one "is at"—the subject led back to his signify-ing dependence. Freud had thought a different idea—bringing unconscious-ness under the domination of the preconscious—while Lacan, Freud's post-Saussurian poet, revised the idea as the "mapped" "network of signi-fiers" brought into existence at the place where the subject was, has always been: "Wo es war, soll Ich werden."[54] We could speak of this process as the subject making its mark through the transitivity of reobjectivations, the silent traces of desire on which the object of the subject hinges. This move-ment across an interior space demarcates the discipline of self-reflection, or the content of a self-interrogation that "race" always covers over as an al-ready-answered. But for oneself, another question is posed: What might I become, insofar as . . . ? To the extent that "I" "signs" itself "elsewhere," represents itself beyond the given, the onus of becoming boomerangs[55]— Ralph Ellison's word—as it rebounds on the one putting the question. But what *impedes* the function of the question?

Once posed, the interrogative gesture, the interior intersubjectivity, would fill up the Fanonian *abîme,* "the great white error . . . the great black mirage." Might we suggest, however, that a different question could come about with the acquisition of a supplemental literacy, one that could be regarded as *alien* and, for that very reason, to be learned and pressed into service? Frantz Fanon assumed that his great positivities (conceptual narra-tives) were always and constantly equal to themselves, and he was exactly right. But he went farther by saying that both of them were "not" in the sense that they were borne on the wings of an illusion and to the extent that they were both unsatisfactory as self-sufficient points of the stationary, and this seems right, too. He did not, however, ask of himself and his for-mulation, So what? Such a question could not have been posed by him, be-cause his allegory had not only responded to the "so what?" but had preempted, indeed, any other impudent intervention. But if we move back in the direction of a "prior" moment, the seven year old in the front pew, for instance, we can then go forward with another set of competencies that originate, we might say, in the bone ignorance of curiosity, the child's gift for strange dreams of flying and bizarre, yet correct, notions about the adult bodies around her—how, for example, her father and brothers bent forward in a grimace when mischievously struck in a certain place above the knees by a little girl, propelling herself off a rollaway bed into their arms. The foreignness had already begun in the instant grasp of sexual and embodied division. But from that moment on, the imposition of homogeneity and sameness would also be understood as the great text of the "tradition" of "race." The Fanonian abyss requires this Ur-text as the "answer" that fosters a two-way immobility. But before "race," something else has happened, both within the context of "race" and alongside it.

Does tradition, then—depositories of discourse and ways of speaking, kinds of social practice and relations—enable some questions and not others? It seems so, but tradition, which hides its own crevices and interstices, is offered as the suture that takes on all the features of smoothness; in order to present itself as transparent, unruffled surface, it absorbs the rejects according to its most prominent configurations. But it seems that the move toward self-reflexivity demands a test of inherited portions of cultural content in order to discover not only what tradition conceals but, as a result, what one, under its auspices, is forced to blindside. What difference did it make that Fanon was a native speaker of French? That he had earned a significant place in French intellectual circles? His response seems appropriate—the sideways glance, the superbly ironical look, which marked the effect of scission at the heart of the disasporic utterance. What he could not do, however, was read its outcome in reference to the "Negro of the Antilles," as well as "Frantz Fanon." To have admitted that the diasporic African is cut on the bias to the West, and not sharply at odds with it, would have involved him in a contradiction that his polemic against the West could not abide. Nevertheless, the problematic that he carved out remains intact, and that is the extent to which the psychoanalytic hermeneutic has the least relevance to African diasporic lifeworlds.

We already know what Fanon might have thought of this question and the limited usefulness of raising it in reference to psychoanalytic theory as "we know it," at least from the point of view of those portions of *Black Skin, White Masks* that we've examined. With the neurosis and the oedipal complex out the window, the black man does not have time to make racist practice "unconscious."[56] But turning now to another protocol, we have the chance to pose the question again in an altered context. I want to look briefly at aspects of Marie-Cécile and Edmond Ortigues's *Oedipe Africain* as an instance of psychoanalytic reference to a non-European community of subjects and as a systematic examination of symbolic currency *(symbolisation)* as a response to the riddle that Fanon advances concerning the "Negro of the Antilles." Again, it is important, to my mind, to insist that even though diasporic African and continental African communities share "race," they pointedly differ in cultural ways and means; the contrary view, which flattens out black into the same thing despite time, weather, geography, and the entire range of complicating factors that go into the fashioning of persons, is difficult to put to rest, given, especially, what seems to be the unchanging face of racism. But unless we introduce cultural specificity to the picture, we run the risk of reinforcing the very myth that we would subvert. In that regard, the emphasis that *Oedipe Africain* places on the processes of symbolization, not only in the workings of psychoanalytic practice but in the making of human culture, more broadly speaking, offers a powerful antidote to reductive formulations. I have also examined aspects of Sow's *Les Structures anthropologiques de la folie en Afrique noire* as a francophone reading from "inside" African culture. I try to bring the texts here into dialogue.

Oedipe Africain is not available in English translation and was originally published in 1966 by French psychoanalysts who carried out clinical practice and observation in Dakar, Senegal, from 1962 to 1966; a redacted version, which text I use for this essay, came out in 1984. Anthony Wilden comments at length on the Lacanian nuances of this work, especially the Oedipal complex "as a structure of intersecting relationships where the *loci* are 'empty spaces.'" Wilden reads the Ortigueses' "fourth term" in the Oedipal structure as an especially strong Lacanian echo and argues that this mediation among the triadic elements of the familial configuration is synonymous with the "image of the phallus, which founds, structures, and mediates the relationships of the biological family and converts it into a *human* family." In the Senegalese case, the "fourth term" is the maternal uncle.[57] My own interest in the Ortigueses' work comes to focus on the practitioners' emphasis on *language* as a primary tool for understanding moments of black cultural production. While the authors acknowledge that the analyst must attempt to understand the patient in the entire context of his or her lifeworld and that no point of comparison can be sustained between one culture and another along a particular line of stress without an examination of the whole, they do contend that the Oedipal complex pertains to all human societies. Its nuances will differ, however, according to one's standing in the social order and the strategies of acculturation that are available to subjects within a given natal community. The authors suggest here that "a practitioner at work in a society foreign to his own definitively illustrates an essential characteristic of the analytic attitude; that is to say, no proposition can be understood without reference to a familial, social, and cultural context."[58]

If the knowledge that the analyst has about the total context is not exhaustive, "then what counts above all else is the analytical attitude that seeks to understand the place of the subject in what he says."[59] It seems to me that all dogmatic pronouncement, *before* and *despite* "what the subject says," is precisely the way in which traditional analyses, of various schools of thought, have failed, including all brands of nationalist thinking, as well as more informed opinions that have evolved a *template* of values to which "the black man" is supposed to conform, and, moreover, "the black man" as a formulation itself. This whole vital soul, imagined to be snoring beneath the wisdom of the ages, conveniently poised for the exact liberatory moment, or "leader," is actually an unknown quantity in this very "soul" we thought we knew. Because the analyst, from the Ortigueses' point of view, awaits a content, he has, in effect, no program to "sell." But the analyst here does not even do that much; he or she *responds* to a seeker.

Attempting to understand the subject in his or her discourse, the Ortigueses address the specificity of illness by way of a number of case studies (references to aggression, the persecution complex and its intricate functions, and so on). But in each instance, the doctors, in touch with patients who have sought them out or have been referred to them by parents or school administrators, are not treating a single individual alone but an *ensemble*. Even the latter is not limited to the familial nucleus but may include ancestral and religious figures; in some cases, these might be the *rab*—an otherworldly figure—and the *marabout,* both of whom are active cultural agents in the Wolof, Lebou, and Serer communities of Senegal. The unseen seen, the "evidence" of things not seen, the *rab,* who may be either perverse of conduct, "or possessively loving regarding a subject," is often felt to be responsible for certain facets of the subject's behavior. In this cultural setting, "illness is not a clinical entity at all," and certainly not foremost, but is "attributed by subjects to magical causality or the intervention of the divine."[60] The cultures in question are not only not of the West but are situated on the cultural map of Islam. The Western doctors, then, are attempting to work within the limitations posed by linguistic difference as well as differences of religious and ethnic reference.

If "the element of coherence," or consistency, by which illness is represented, is embodied in the *rab,* then this intervention would pose one more reason, among a variety of others, why "the doctors and their consultants might have been derailed in their interrogation."[61] In any case, however, this complicating factor in the relationship between a speaking subject and the grammar of his speaking brings to focus one of the key differences between tools of Western practice and the African context, as Sow will spell out: *who* is the subject of treatment? In the African context, there are no lone subjects of mental illness. A profoundly anthropological reading of subject disorder and its essentially communal and familial character in traditional (and this distinction is crucial for Sow) African societies defines the project of *Les Structures anthropologiques de la folie en Afrique noire.* Sow's work, given the extensive biographical sources that inform *Les Structures anthropologiques,* takes its place within a well-developed field of West African psychiatric practice and theory. The general view that African societies have had no need to generate theories of the mental theater seems as ill informed as a range of mythical beliefs concerning cultures in the sub-Saharan continent.

While the Ortigueses are aware that their project comes freighted with its own peculiar cultural baggage and bias, they nevertheless take their chances within the framework of certain psychoanalytic assumptions, as we have seen. Sow, on the other hand, locates the subject *at last* within a global scheme of reading that examines the basic tenets of West African culture. As informative as this method may be, it is in its own way as general and generalist as he claims that the classical descriptions of mental illnesses are to the African field. Too "superficial and artificial" to account for "psychological, social, human, and clinical realities" encountered in traditional African communities, the nosographical and nosological categories and tables, Sow argues, are themselves less objectionable to him than the inadequate supplement of their means with culture-specific strategies (*SA,* 48; *AS,* 53).[62] In *Les Structures anthropologiques,* he attempts to go beneath the manifestations of Western practice to penetrate its leading premises, to address and correct the problem, except that, in doing so, his chief actors are the macroelements of narrative and belief—the thematics of myth, of ancient tale and report. In that regard, he paints with a broader brush, as it were, and covers a canvas of wider scope, but, ironically, it seems that we lose the import of the psychoanalytic in the process precisely because, to Sow, it is unimpressively grounded in the messiness of the everyday world, in the utter evasion of the neat and rational category.

For example, madness in Sow's critique is similarly configured to the way it is sketched in *Oedipe Africain*—as a mishap in an ensemble of sociocultural relations. Sow calls it a "sign" that indicates straightaway that the subject is expressing conflict between himself and the constitutive authorities of his personality that are external to him (*SA*, 42; *AS*, 44). Sow consistently distinguishes between *personnalité* and *personne*.[63] It is the role of traditional therapy, then, alongside the interactive participation of family and community, to read and interpret the sign, to determine at what point in the constitutive network of the intimate structure of personality there has been breakdown or rupture in an otherwise highly articulated social function (see *SA*, 42; *AS*, 44). While it is fairly clear that Sow's "extérieures" look and behave suspiciously like the Lacanian "supports" through which the subject of enunciation is "spoken," Sow appears to so disjoin particular acts of enunciation from the culturally permissible that the neurosis itself erupts in "oneness." The double dose of narcissistic desire, therefore, follows from "individuality," when the neurotic *personne* behaves as if he were an end within himself:

> In effect, what is signified for the neurotic is buried in his individuality and, in the final analysis, "doubles" or duplicates his narcissistic desire, which functions as if he were his own end in himself. For man confronting the sacred, however, what is signified is the Word, Law, Tradition—in short, man's Origin, in the sacrifice of the founding Ancestor, creator of the Law, guarantor of peace and coexistence among present-day human beings. (*AS*, 207)[64]

But the real question for me, in light of this formulation, is, What is the relationship between the Word and the word in which *personne*, neurotic and otherwise, is orchestrated? It appears that we pass here rather too quickly—dropping the ball is more like it—from a social dysfunction to a coerced repair in the formidable evocation of overwhelming devices, the great *di ex machina* that silence all before them—the Law, the Origin, the Tradition. "Man confronting the sacred" is a mighty idea, but who can stand before it? And isn't it quite possible that such standing would be unique? Would represent an inimitable moment or an originary and irrecoverable act? But another way to interpret this passage from Sow is to read it as the sacred *as* or *become man's signified*. In that case, the sacred object is unavoidably the origin and ground of meaning, which would claim all human order in turn, since one subject would become (if we applied a Lacanian riff here) a *signifier* for another subject.

Nevertheless, Sow's insistence on a *constitutive network* restores the psychoanalytic hermeneutic to its social coherence, to its intersubjective function. As traditional therapy in his account seeks to transform mental illness into an articulated language, it would repair the broken link in which the individual is not located alone: "Reestablishing order in the subject reconstitutes the loose connection and reinserts the subject into the place from which he has been expelled, cut off from his source of nourishment by an 'aggressor'" (AS, 44).[65]

An "affliction" in the structure of communication implies an aversive meeting of paroles, and, to that extent, the anthropological elements of madness in African society do not deny, at the very least, conflict at the heart of human relations. Sow's "answer," however, by deferring or displacing the source of illness onto a global abstracted Outer, envisages an absolute otherness, whereas the struggle for meaning appears to "reduce" the absolute by dispersing its centrality. In other words, the subject, in a different order of things, must discover the degree to which he has engendered his own alienation. Consequently, the Western subject, it seems, sprouts guilt and big shoulders in taking on responsibility for an outcome, whereas his African counterpart, at least if Sow is right, does not acquire a discourse for the *guilty conscience* inasmuch as his ultimate ground of social and moral reference is situated "outside" himself.

In a sense, the universe projected in *Les Structures anthropologiques* is vestibular to both the historical and posthistorical moment insofar as it is finished and elegantly arranged according to an immemorial Law and Order that Sow elaborates at length. We can do no more than sketch some of its prominent features here. In West African cosmography, human and social order is based on an imbricated, yet hierarchical, grid of functions marked according to three levels of stress: (1) the sensible, given world of the *microcosmos*—the world that is immediate and given, the world of the social; (2) "the intermediary world of the genies, the spirits, and a repertoire of malevolent and beneficent forces [of the *mésocosmos*]"; and (3) "the *suprasensible* world [of the Spirits elect, the Ancestors, the Godhead]" (SA, 45; AS, 48). But there are ancestors and *the* Ancestor(s), as it seems apparent that the capitalized *Ancêtre* is the equivalent of the Godhead, if not exactly synonymous with it. Given this elaborate schematization, there is, in effect, "no one"— in a rather different sense from the "nothing" and "no one" of Western philosophical/psychoanalytic discourse—with its eye trained, finally, on an eclipsed God, or the One about whom silence is in order. In African discursive and social practice, as Sow narrates the scene, "one" is nothing more or less than a link through which the three great valences of order reverberate. Therapy thus consists in bringing one back to harmonious relations with a cosmogonic principle whose intent can be teased out in various mythic narratives. There, "the prescriptions, rules, interdictions, and models of conduct" aim toward a definitive suggestion: that "cultural order and coherence repose on a delicate, subtle balance of the *differentiated* identity of each and all" (*SA*, 154; *AS*, 159), primarily the continuity of the generations in the passage of the biological age group, wave on wave of horizontal confraternities in progression toward the status of ancestry. In such a system, the strategies of rapprochement between God and human appear in language—"in speech, prayer, and dream, as the dialogue between distant interlocutors must pass through the privileged intercessory office of the Ancestors" (*AS*, 210 n. 9).[66]

From this perspective, mental illness is read as the interrupted circuitry between carefully delineated parts (see *SA*, 10–11; *AS*, 6). But the texts of role and agency are not discoverable, inasmuch as they are already known from a transmitted structure of articulated cause and effect. Moreover, this symbolic economy, which rests in a transcendent signifier, generates a Story, unlike the discourse that breaks up into the atomized particles of evasive meaning, or a meaning delayed in the "effects" of the signifier. We would regard the latter as a symptom of modern social analysis that follows the trails of fragmented social objects—in short, a world defined by the loss of hierarchy, privileged moments, and ineluctably declarative—ambiguity expelled—utterances. We recognize this world as our own—the scene of scission and displacement.

But where would this buzz of the harmonious leave the culturally "illiterate," the one who misreads the traffic signals? In the opening chapter *of Les Structures anthropologiques,* Sow treats at length the occurrence and frequency of mental illness in West African communities. As he adopts nosographical categories of description familiar to Western psychiatric practice, he is convinced that the categories themselves are often ill equipped to treat key questions, such as "the problem of the stain, of the pure and impure, that dominates Swedish psychopathology, for instance" (*SA*, 31 n. 36; *AS*, 32 n. 10), or the phenomenon of "la bouffée psychotique": the most characteristic *formal* aspect of African psychiatry (*AS*, 31; *SA*, 31). If the "bouffée psychotique" is a characteristic form in African medicine, then *persecution* is the most frequently and meaningfully recurrent thematic of Continental practice (see *SA*, 34; *AS*, 35). Sow claims that the latter not only colors the entire field of practice but also occupies a privileged place in the anthropological system of representations across Black Africa. The ensemble of premises against which Sow leads up to his reading of the African conception of the cosmos and its signifying role in the mental theater might be summarized according to two binarily opposed tables of value: traditional African institutions, in their preventive or prophylactic capacity, effectively maintain personal, interpersonal, and communal equilibrium. The psychological defenses are *cultural* and *collective* and may be compared with what we spoke of earlier as the Western implantation or interiorization of guilt.[67] In other words, the *persecutor* in African culture embodies the externalization of guilt, whereas in Western culture, the guilt function is assumed by the person. Sow evaluates the internalizing of guilt as (1) "the origin of the morbid structure" and (2) "the sociocultural context of sin and blame" (*SA*, 25 n. 20; *AS*, 24 n. 7). But is it possible that the binary disposition is less than dispositive, even in a traditional African setting? Is it possible that traditional structures, precisely because they are time-honored, do not always respond to a particular demand?

Among the case studies presented in *Oedipe Africain,* the Ortigueses' Samba C., a fourteen-year-old Wolof Muslim, might raise interesting problems for Sow's scheme. "According to the psychotherapeutic material presented to them," the authors believe that Samba did reach the internalization of conflict, which process Sow identifies as the origin of morbidity in Western disorders, and that a dream reported to them by the analysand not only signaled such internalization but announced it as the onset of a series of psychotic episodes. The dream, which occurrence led him to the Western doctors, is described this way: "The baobab tree" (the renowned tree of African lore and legend) "of Samba's initial vision, at the time of this dream . . . cried out that the dead must be buried at his feet and not in the cemetery; the terrifying *persona* of Samba's hallucinations was transformed into a man who declared these words: 'It is the father of fathers.'"[68] Samba's confrontation with representative instances of the paternal image—in the baobab tree and the transformations that it induced—suggested to the doctors that Samba's troubles were related to the ancestors. In attempting to retrace the trajectory of the Ortigueses' conclusions, which follow below, we hope to see at least the divergence of interpretation between two styles of analytic practice and assumption. We can only guess how Sow might have read Samba's case.

> Samba C. first encountered trouble, when, passing under a baobab tree on returning to school one day, he heard a voice that called out to him by his family name three times. Samba does not answer, for responding would have been incorrect, but he does not continue on his way, and quite frightened, turns back toward home. He takes to his bed, trembling, vomiting during the night. For the rest of the following day and for some months afterward, Samba keeps his eyes closed, as if he feared a terrifying vision, "like children, something big, a devil." He suffered from migraine headaches in the course of things, refused to eat, and in any case only imbibed small amounts of food and drink. He remained inert, prostrate, arms bent in moaning. His groans

would intensify for hours at a time, in extended and monotonous plaint. The words that escaped from him came torn, babbled, barely audible, and were accompanied by an involuntary shaking of the head.

Samba's parents reported that the outbreak persisted for several months, and he was eventually led to neurological consultation and hospitalized. All the tests administered to him proved negative. During hospitalization, Samba's state was unchanged three weeks later; he left the hospital after insisting upon it, having attempted escapes daily. Shortly thereafter, he was hospitalized in the psychiatric unit. In the course of a year, he was hospitalized three times and during interim periods was treated as an outpatient, subjected, during each term of hospitalization, to a series of electroshocks at the same time as psychotherapy. A neuroleptic treatment was pursued as well.

In Samba's case, it is legitimate to speak of psychoanalytic psychotherapy in the most classic sense of the term. Samba's demand was clear: He came "to talk in order to get well." A rich transferential relation was quickly established, as his treatment lasted a year and included some fifty-one sessions with the doctors. Samba was regarded as intelligent and sought to verbalize everything that he lived.[69]

Summarizing, we would make the following observations:

1. After two months and nine sessions of treatment, Samba barely got beyond the hallucinations that haunted his nights. "The visual representations ranged from children, to snakes, to a very large black man, who frightened him." Samba reported auditory and visual hallucinations that included "snakes invading his body, drinking his blood, and the attacks made him feel that he would die soon."[70] The doctors were caught by the binary equation in Samba's description—"fear"/"bliss-happiness" *("peur"/ "bonheur")* as they came to discover "that the voice of the baobab, which was the voice of the devil, was actually the projected *persona* of an older companion of Samba's, one Malik, who, in Samba's eyes, incorporated at once the manhood virtues of boldness, physical force, and endurance, as well as the temptations to fall that led to Samba's madness" (*OA*, 98).

2. "La folie" was understood by the doctors to have conformed to "désocialisation," into which Malik had led his younger companion over a few years—disobeying and deceiving his parents, showing insolence toward authority, committing thievery, and the violation of a fundamental prohibition, "going out at night." The latter activity was strictly forbidden children, especially treks into the bush or the countryside, those reputedly dangerous places thought to be inhabited by evil figures. This crossing the bar, we might say, manifested in various antisocial behaviors that chal-

lenged authority, was accompanied by gross misconduct toward Malik's and Samba's female peers. The doctors observed that "Malik's 'leadership' was exercised in a decidedly sadistic tonality" and that none of the authority figures, including parents and teachers, were ever able to bring him in line. "Above all, Malik embodied for Samba an element of undeniable fascination" (*OA*, 98).

3. Samba, then, "was frightened by his desire to look like Malik, to *be* Malik [*d'être un Malik*]. The temptation was projected as the 'devil'"—the "saytané." The attending *marabouts*, preceding consultation with the Western doctors, believed that the problem was the "devil," who wanted to harm Samba. But as it turned out, Samba's family, "his entourage," had themselves had similar experiences, "since childhood, with the evidentiary presence of djinns and devils" (*OA*, 98).[71]

4. "Samba finally arrived on the threshold of an interiorization" of guilt. The "devil" was Malik, wanting him to do ill, yet "he realized that he admired the older boy and that the latter was a thug" ("celui-ci était un voyou ignorant") (*OA*, 99). Over time, "his fantasies concerning the *personae* of the devil . . . terrifying and attractive at once, were doubled and divided among three or four persons, as this game of doubling, coupling, and dividing allowed Samba ever greater suppleness in projecting himself into variable positions regarding his desire and its related anxiety."[72]

Even though Samba's condition was ameliorated by treatment, the authors maintain that his state, for all that, proved irreversibly psychotic. To the question, what if the prognosis were inept, or unrelated to the strategies of cure available in Wolof society, the Ortigueses respond with what is, for all intents and purposes, a question of their own: "Did not Samba's culture impose on him, or propose to him in a privileged way the solution to his hallucinatory psychosis, vis-à-vis the theme of persecution?"[73] The doctors believed that Samba had "jumped"—my word—his circumstance by internalizing his dilemma, by seeking to resolve it at the level of personality. In a sense, cutting loose from certain communal beliefs, feeling himself driven to the wall, he had sought other means of address and "become a stranger to himself while doing so, acceding to the level of personal conscience that had situated him 'well ahead of the fathers.'"[74] In the culture in question, one did not reach for advancement beyond or away from the group, as they read the picture. At best, Samba's condition in the end "appeared fragile, as the 'devil' remained discretely present" (*OA*, 100).

What I have interpreted in the foregoing paragraphs as declarative assertions are advanced as inquiries in the text, and this fact is important to note, inasmuch as the doctors are themselves aware that their speculative instruments are adopted from a very different cultural framework. For instance, they question whether or not it is *thinkable* that Samba had arrived at the interiorization of the conflict that he clearly expressed and whose implications he could explain—*"Est-il pensable qu'il parvienne à intérioriser sa culpabilité?"* (*OA,* 99). Furthermore, they handle certain conclusions that they have tentatively reached in a subjunctive appeal: In effect, Samba's assumption of guilt *would suppose* that he had disconnected himself from certain communal values, and is such delinking not only possible but even *desirable?* The Ortigueses go on to say that everything during the course of initial treatment happened "as if" Samba, feeling no way out, had placed all his hope, had articulated all his demand in the opening dialogue of the first interviews and as if "he assumed the risk of an unknown outcome" ("il assumait le risque de l'issue inconnue") (*OA,*100). His parents, "feeling anxious, powerless, and overwhelmed by Samba's auto-aggressive conduct," following the failure of traditional treatment, "sought to turn him over to 'the doctors' and also accepted the risks." During the course of the doctors' treatment, Samba's family consulted "un marabout 'plus fort' que les précédents," as the doctors were in accord with the decision. "This procedure, no more than prior consultations with the marabout, did not interrupt the psychoanalytic course," as the differing strategies were simultaneously pursued (*OA,* 100).

As a reader goes back and forth on this, grappling in another language, about a vastly different culture, not Western, French, English, or diasporic, for that matter, trying to see through other eyes to the truth of the matter or even gain some clarity concerning it, we are confronted with mutually exclusive questions. Perhaps all the doctors and theorists are right, or more precisely, *know how to be,* within the particular parameters of insight and blindness that frame their discourse. But the affecting line, "tout son espoir, toute sa demande" (*OA,* 100), sketches a face before us whose details are unreadable, except that we hear in its trace of the paraphrase the stunning bafflement of one at pains to know why he suffers, and it seems that we are captivated right there—in the inscription of particular address. There is the society, doubtlessly so, but what about *Samba?* Another way to ask this question is the impossible, What does he say he wants? Unless I have misunderstood the matter, the "hermeneutic demand" of the psychoanalytic itinerary unfolds from each of the Sambas' articulated wannas-be, but in *what* world? Is it thinkable that Samba was raising, in the depths of his being, a question that his culture could not answer, even though the latter had opened the place of the question by giving it its props, its materiality? Is the quest conditioned by the epistemic choices available to the want-to-be of the subject? And if the subject "overreaches" the given discursive conditions, does madness attend, no one quite knowing what he is saying, as indeed it was reported to have happened at the onset of Samba's psychotic course? For the Ortigueses, Samba's dilemma raises the question of *recognition by the brothers,* which they contend is routed through "Oedipe Africain." It is at heart an inquiry concerning *status* and the variable positions through which it is expressed.

In Samba's society, "the search for status recognition by the 'brothers' is a dominant mode of manhood affirmation" ("La recherche d'une reconnaissance de mon statut par les 'frères' est un mode dominant de l'affirmation virile") (*OA,* 135). As we observed before, the brothers are the progressive, or processual, confraternity of age-mates precisely linked by the time of birth. "The wish to be a man expresses itself here in a form and content different from the ones that we know in European societies," say the Ortigueses. "In Europe, young Oedipus wishes to be a rival in tasks, actions, and realizations; it is a rivalry that is manifest by objective sanction," or we could say that the objectifiable nature of goals acts to mediate the rivalry—making a better boat, for instance, or hurling a discus farther than another. In brief, it seems that the socius of the objectifiable aim may be called *competitive.* In the Senegalese field, rivalry is accentuated by a

> stress on status, on prestige. It has to do with demonstrating or showing a certain image of the self to the "brothers," or of doing what they believe conforms to the image in the eyes of the brothers. . . . For the young Dakarois whom we saw, plans for the future . . . were hardly based on performance or personalized activity, as it was in small measure a question of inventing something, or exceeding some achievement, but was tied up with the theme of *giving oneself to be looked at.* A subject might have said, for instance, that he wanted to wear beautiful clothes, or have a good position, but the precise activity, the métier, the vocation that supported the good position or the beautiful clothes was not considered in and for itself. The wish, then, had less to do with a more interesting or efficacious performance of some task, but more to do with achieving higher visibility for socially prominent reasons. . . . To improve one's status, one might say "I did this or that," or "Such and such admires me," or "such and such said that I was intelligent" [or] . . . "great." . . . If a subject reported: "I have more success with the females than my buddies," he was appealing less to his relationship with the girls in question than reflecting on the admiration or the jealousy of his comrades.[75]

It is difficult to decide from what the authors report about such assertions whether or not bragging among the young is common across cultures.

I actually think that it might well be, but one is nevertheless struck by the importance of the *specular* and the *spectacular* here, which is precisely where DuBois placed the significance of the look regarding the "seventh son," albeit for radically different historical reasons.[76] Yet, I believe that this stunning thematic running through a milieu of West African society is well worth keeping in mind. Though far too quick, as it were, to be given more than passing thought, the concern about "how's it hanging"—which would mark an especially male anxiety—may actually "translate" into diasporic communities as the analogous stress on looks, prestige, success, and the entire repertoire of tensions that have to do with the outer trapping, that is, one's appearance. The Ortigueses suggest that with all their subjects, "references to fathers and uncles bore the character of spectacle, witness, and display offered to the look of others. The child felt empowered by the father, loved by the father, when he was well dressed by him, when he imagined others looking at him well dressed."[77] Among Europeans, they contend, "a boy of a certain age might think: 'My father is stronger than a lion . . . my father has the biggest car . . . my father is rich and commanding,'" whereas among the young Dakarois, "the boy thinks: 'My father is going to buy me a beautiful shirt, a beautiful suit.'"[78] The instances could be multiplied, they tell us, but they sum up the point: "The desire for better clothes, for more beautiful clothes, was the first desire expressed by the young men, the desire to show their father, and for those who suffered his indifference or estrangement, it was not rare to encounter an obsessive concern about appearance to the extent of seeking homosexual engagement in the search for ostentation."[79]

By "the look . . . the subject decides if he is mocked, held in contempt, thought to be disagreeable," and so on. "The frequency with which distressful sensations were triggered by the look of another, or perceived at the level of the skin or the superficial musculature" because of another's "regard," was considerable in their estimation. Relatedly, the Ortigueses evolved from the cases a veritable "grammar" of the look: "formidable," "contemptuous," "masked," "averted," "eyes turned sideways," "looks and laughs," "looks down (or lowers head)" ("formidable," "méprisant," "est masqué," "détourné," "les yeux de côté," "regard et il rit," "garde la tête baisée").[80] Prominently placed in the discourse of "the first interviews was the subject's concern about the troubling look; from instances of hysteria, having to do with a transient evil eye *(d'un mal aux yeux passager)* . . . to fantasies surging up in the here and now, we were always told: 'Je ne me donne pas le droit de voir.'" Because one's own look is disabled, or because one cannot seize the right to look, as I understand this, which frequently occurs in one's own bad dreams, perhaps we bear this rubric away from the scene: "The sight appears as a privileged place of castration" here (*OA*, 105).

By a detour off the customary path, the Oedipal problematic travels in this instance through the peer group, snared in the coils of looking and being seen. Quoting from the 1966 edition of *Oedipe Africain,* Wilden cites the Ortigueses on the theoretical implications of the confraternal figure: "Instead of being displayed vertically or diachronically as a conflict between successive generations, aggressivity tends to unfold in horizontal lines within the limits of the same generation."[81] This synchronicity apparently prepares the age group to accede, finally, to the ancestral status; but moreover, horizontality appears to organize the social order—in its phallic mediation by way of the maternal uncle—in the marriage arrangement in the same generation and the mediation between parent and child of succeeding generations.[82] It is the gaze here, however, that I want to linger on for a moment. The Ortigueses do not pause to elaborate on what is, to my mind, a point of saturation in their itinerary that could possibly bridge across Old and New World African cultures in a consideration of *unconscious* material, but I am not, for all that, claiming that there would be good reason on that basis to pose or even anticipate moments of a transhistorical (black) collective psyche. Nevertheless it seems to me that any sustained investigation along these lines might usefully isolate the gaze in its discrete cultural property as a route of organization for a comparative reading of intersubjective signals in divergent lifeworlds. But I should try to be clear about this. The inquiry that I am describing would occur under some other auspices than that of the psychoanalytic, even though it might be informed by its protocols. In any case, the *look* and its dynamics would bring to focus several topics that come together in the name of subjectivity, that is, the extent to which self-formation is authored elsewhere, in the split between the wannabe and its objectivations in the place of another. The *eyes* in this case are nothing more or less than the crucial relay of a "message" that either proffers or denies, though denial, as we know, is also a most powerful offer. The tales of the young Dakarois reinforce the unthinkable—it is all too often up to someone else—and for my money, we have little idea what this particular exchange of subtextual motives, "choreographed" in the rise and fall of the eyelid, actually "sounds" like in *cultural theory* concerning black communities. Relatedly, is there not this conundrum: If the young male consultants of the Ortigueses' "récits" are bound to the "look" of others—as feminist film theorists have suggested that the female "star" is[83]—then what revisionary notions might be introduced to the conceptualization of the gaze as *heterosexual,* as well as homosexual, currency? At least to the extent that it induces more questions than it disposes of, the "récit" of the consultation expands the genre of narrative art.

The coil of the looks for the Ortigueses, however, is entirely related to the psychoanalytic aims of *Oedipe Africain,* and that is to explore how the Oedipal crisis—finding one's place in the social order—is resolved in a cultural context where the symbolic function of the father remains tied to the ancestors. We can only sketch out a few more details of this running narrative:

1. In the case where the father mediates between the dead ancestors and the living sons, the sons cannot think of themselves as the equal of the ancestor (and therefore not the father either) and certainly not his superior. What one must confront instead is the right to claim his place within the group, as castration here is based on the collective register of obedience to the law of the dead, the law of the ancestors. To be excluded from the group or abandoned by it is the equivalent of castration (see *OA,* 75). When Samba, in the case that we have examined, was confronted by the baobab tree in his disturbing dream, he was essentially coming face-to-face, as it were, with a representative ancestral figure, as the baobab holds a privileged place in the culture as the site of the wisdom of the dead and of the living fathers. It is, therefore, collectively possessed. The appearance of the tree in the young man's dream apparently signaled his arrival on the threshold of manhood.

In contrasting European Oedipus with its African equivalent, the Ortigueses suggest that the youth in the latter setting does not imagine killing the father but must be referred to the ancestors through him.

2. Because the ancestor is "déjà mort" and "inattaquable" the sons constitute their brothers in rivalry, the group that they must enter. This horizontal social arrangement yields two crucial representations—"the collective phallus and the unbeatable ancestor," which conduces to "the game of rivalry-solidarity between the brothers" (79). In this setup, everything that the brothers do regarding one another acquires profound weight, inasmuch as one's successful achievement of status is predicated on it. *"Rivalry, then, appears to be systematically displaced onto the 'brothers' who polarize the aggressive drives,"* as *"aggression itself is primarily expressed under the form of persecutive reaction-formations"* (92). "The network of intersubjective relations would be strongly colored here by the fact that everyone is easily perceived as both vulnerable to persecution" and capable of serving its ends through the medium of a superior force or talisman (93). "Under all circumstances, it is appropriate to protect oneself against harmful intentions," against apparently aggressive moves in the other, which energy, the authors observe, is deflected away from self-affirmation through action to-

ward self-defense (93). "Blame, then, is barely internalized or constituted as such," since the material cause of the harm "lies outside oneself," where the "badness" reigns: "Everything happens as if the individual cannot bear to be perceived as internally divided and driven by contradictory desires" (94). *Les Structures anthropologiques* and *Oedipe Africain* seem to strike a common chord on this point. We would also read Samba's predicament in this light.[84]

"To the extent that the aggressive drives are not projected onto another, the subject remains conscious of them, but represses them, tries to control them. Aggressive fantasies and emotions might then take the route of the secretive, muted, destructive, unacknowledgeable material about which silence is deemed appropriate," because mouthing it might "discourage my parents," or "they would count against me," or expressing it would expose one's vulnerability, his "location," as it were. "Often, somatizations appeared as a means of inhibiting the instantaneous expression of fantasies and aggressive impulses." What might occur in the event of a repression is the dissimulation of mistrust and suspicion under the guise of an "imperturbable gentillese" that is aimed at warding off a blow. But such a "separate peace" might not yield the expected "detente," but could well result in "immediate depression" or the "emergence of aggressive fantasies":

> Unless a subject sought solitude in order to protect himself against anxiety reactions that had become overwhelming, the young consultants described to us the high degree to which they felt compelled to be with their friends . . . to be part of the group, of the crowd. Even if nothing of particular importance accrued from a sporting event, a dance outing, an interminable round of talk . . . the real thing was the presence of others—necessary and reassuring—in keeping the latent aggressive fantasies in the background.[85]

Could it be that male bonding or confraternity is based on keeping the latent aggressive fantasies at bay? In that sense, perhaps, the solidarity piece of the rivalrous relations would sheathe, at all times, a decidedly violent possibility, all the more so for what it covers over. The "gang" in diasporic communities may well replicate this pattern of repression and closure.

We recall that the social formation of the brothers, banished in the Freudian myth for the crime of patricide and other impressive infamies, is the triggering mechanism of the incest taboo and the cut into human community. But Freud's exiled issue have the opportunity to "return" with the boon of guilt. As we think about the African Oedipus, according to the Ortigueses' sketch of it, several half-formed, obscure questions crowd in: Did

African Oedipus show a break in the fabric of narrative, in the incontestable roll and continuity of generation after generation, reaching the shores of death and the "full fatherhood" ("père à part entière" [*OA*, 110]), by way of the Atlantic slave trade? The question springs to mind from a suggestive passage in Claude Meillassoux's *Maidens, Meal, and Money*, wherein Meillassoux, in elaborating the role of elders and juniors in the African "domestic community," cites other historical research on the matter: populations that had been "brutally subjected to the effects of the European slave trade" often used the juniors not only as producers, "but ultimately commodities as well." Their severity toward them exaggerated by greed, the elders banished the juniors "for real or imagined crimes," as the young "were transformed into goods for the slave trade."[86] The latter, of course, bears none of the advantages of myth but shows some of its earmarks, as the Atlantic trade might be thought of as one of the founding events of modern history and economy. But for our purposes here, the execrable trade, in radically altering the social system in Old and New World "domestic community," is as violent and disruptive as the never-did-happenstance of mythic and oneiric inevitability. In other words, this historical event, like a myth, marks so rigorous a transition in the order of things that it launches a new way of gauging time and human origin: it underwrites, in short, a new genealogy defined by a break with Tradition—with the Law of the Ancestors and the paternal intermediary.

From my perspective, then, *African Oedipus* is the term that mediates a new symbolic order. It allows us to see that "father" designates a *function* rather than, as Meillassoux points out, a "genitor": the father is *"he who nourishes* and protects you, and who claims your produce and labor in return."[87] In that regard, the African Oedipus removes the element of sentimentality from the myth and exposes it as a *structure of relations* instead. The riddle of origin that the Oedipus myth is supposed to constitute, first, as a crisis, then as a resolution of order and degree, was essentially canceled by the Atlantic trade, as the "crisis," for all intents and purposes, has continued on the other side, the vantage from which I am writing. I spoke earlier about a subject in discourse, crossed by stigmata, as the psychoanalytic *difference* that has yet to be articulated. I am defining the stigmatized subject as he or she whose access to discourse must be established as a human right and cannot be assumed. I am specifically referring here to the history of slavery in the Americas and not only its traditions and practices of "chattel property" but, related to it, the strictures against literacy imposed on the bonded. Inasmuch as classical psychoanalytic practice works to transform symptomaticity into a narrative, I take it that discourse constitutes its primary value. The raced subject in an American context must, therefore, work his way through a *layered* imperative and impediment, which deeply implicates History in any autobiographical project. I think that I am prepared to say that those markings on the social body of New World Africanity are the stripes of an Oedipal crisis (for male and female children) that can only be cleared away now by a "confrontation" with the "scene" of its occurrence, but as if in myth. In other words, the *discontinuity* that the abandoned son demarcates here must be carried out as a kind of new article of faith in the non-Traditional, in the discovery of the Law of the living, not the dead, and in the circulation of a new social energy that confronts the future, not the past.

Carrying out that line of thinking, we might be able to see in an apposite psychoanalytic protocol for the subjects of "race," broken away from the point of origin, which rupture has left a hole that speech can only point to and circle around, an entirely new repertoire of inquiry into human relations. Perhaps I come out here where I least expected: Fanon, to that extent—my history must not imprison me, once I *recognize* it for what it is— might well have been right.

VI

Among all the things you could be by now, if Sigmund Freud's wife were your mother, is someone who understands the dozens, the intricate verboseness of America's inner city. The big-mouth brag, as much a sort of art form as a strategy of insult, the dozens takes the assaulted home to the backbone by "talking about" his mama and daddy. It is a choice weapon of defense and *always* changes the topic; bloodless, because it is all wounding words and outrageous combinations of imagery, and democratic, because anyone can play and *be* played, it outsmarts the Uzi—not that it is pleasant for all that—by re-siting (and "reciting"?) the stress. The game of living, after all, is played between the ears, up in the head. Instead of dispatching a body, one straightens its posture; instead of offering up a body, one sends his word. It is the realm of the ludic and the ludicrous that the jazz bassist Charlie Mingus was playing around in when he concocted, as if on the spot, the title of the melody from which the title of this essay is borrowed. Responding to his own question—"What does it mean?"—that he poses to himself on the recording, he follows along the lines of his own cryptic signature, "Nothing. It means nothing." And what he proceeds to perform on the cut is certainly no thing we know. But that really is the point—to extend the realm of possibility for what might be known, and, not unlike the dozens, we will not easily decide if it is fun.

We traditionally understand the psychoanalytic in a pathological register, and there must be a very real question as to whether or not it remains psychoanalysis without its principal features—a "third ear," something like the "fourth wall," or the speech that unfolds in the pristinely silent arena of two star witnesses—a patient and he or she "who is supposed to know." The scene of assumptions is completed in the privileged relations of client and doctor in the atmosphere of the confessional. But my interest in this ethical self-knowing wants to unhook the psychoanalytic hermeneutic from its rigorous curative framework and try to recover it in a free-floating realm of self-didactic possibility that might decentralize and disperse the knowing one. We might need help here, for sure, but the uncertainty of where we'd be headed virtually makes no guarantee of that. Out here, the only music they are playing is Mingus's, or Cecil Taylor's or much like both, and I should think that it would take a good long time to learn to hear it well.

16

The Crisis of the Negro Intellectual:
A Post-Date

I

The silver anniversary of Harold Cruse's *Crisis of the Negro Intellectual*[1] has passed without remark. The occasion of the lapse, as well as a few notes on the situation of the black creative intellectual today, provides the impetus for this writing. From the distance of twenty-seven years, the "crisis" that Cruse explored appeared infinitely more complex than it might have been in 1967, when the work was published to controversial hue and cry. One's impression is that the project did not win the writer very many friends or influence the right people,[2] but that it was as necessary a reading and calling out as we had had in quite a while, and, I would go so far as to say, have not quite matched since that time, even though we have been treated to a few celebrated "licks" on the theme by prominent black intellectuals along the way. I recall with some nostalgic yearning, related both to my youth and to what must have seemed to many of us then a period of great optimism, reading *The Crisis,* a couple of years after its publication, in great excitement and agitation of feeling. First, here was an explicit statement, *at length,* concerning the vocation of the black intellectual for the first time, as far as I could tell, since W. E. B. DuBois's autobiographical projects, beginning with *The Souls of Black Folk* (1903), that blended the strategies of the "self-life-writing" with those of cultural and political critique. In other words, DuBois's autobiographies were themselves a demonstration of the project that the black creative intellectual might engage when he or she defines his/her auto-bios-graphe in the perspective of historical time and agency. Between DuBois and Cruse, with the possible exceptions of Richard Wright and Ralph Ellison, who had both focused on the fictional writer's commitment and vocation, we had to wait awhile, as though poised, it seemed, for an apposite interpretive gesture at the close of an era of cataclysmic events between *Brown v. Board of Education* (Topeka) (1954) and the

1964 Civil Rights legislation—the two punctualities that frame one of the most fateful decades of African-American cultural and historical apprenticeship in the United States. Second, Cruse appears to have been up to the job, not mincing words about the intellectual failures of the dominant culture, not biting his tongue, either, about the abysmal conceptual lapses of the minority one in question, specifically, the ill-preparedness of my generation of political activists to take on the strenuous task of sustained analytical labor. Now it seems that we have not only not yet articulated a systematic response to Cruse's "crisis" but that the problems that he was courageous enough to confront have not been better formulated, despite our improved *access* to certain cultural institutions and conceptual apparati. Taking Cruse, then, as one of our chief cartographers, can we begin to map the terrain anew? Can we say more clearly now, *after his example,* perhaps *because* of it, what the problem is that constitutes a "crisis" for the African-American creative intellectual at the moment?

Our crisis today is confounded not only because so much time has passed between one systematic articulation and the next (still slumbering somewhere) but primarily because the peculiar conjunction of historical forces has brought us to an uncanny site of contradictions: when Cruse wrote his work, the impulse of the revolutionary—at least the spirit of revolt—was everywhere inchoate, although there had not yet been massive public reaction against American involvement in Vietnam. Student rebellion at the time was largely centered in the southern United States, taking its major impetus from Martin Luther King's nonviolent protocols—voter registration campaigning and grass-roots organizing in rural and urban centers across the South, and the whole range of acts of civil disobedience, from sit-ins, pray-ins, and wade-ins at pools, restaurants, movie houses, and other places of public accommodation, to the economic tool of the boycott. But Stokeley Carmichael's (Kwame Toure) cry of "Black Power" on a Mississippi road one day (which event Cruse historicizes in the closing chapter of *The Crisis*), the assassination of Martin Luther King Jr., the inspired witness of Malcolm X, and the dramatic rise of the national Black Panther Party were driven like a wedge through black psyche, an occurrence that had been prepared by the Watts rebellion of 1965 and the assassination of Malcolm El-Hajj Malik El Shabazz that same year. But it seems that something so awful crystallized in 1968, on either side of the Atlantic, that in my own autobiographical sense, at least, the year irrevocably split time around it between a "before" and "after," finding closure *only* during the fall of *1969.* It is as if one day the familiar world spun out of control, as, for instance, two cultural icons fell over within six weeks of each other in the raw display of a national pathology. That incredible year—which marked the assassination of both King and Robert Kennedy, witnessed the most brutal National Democratic Party Convention in living memory, and, by its close, saw the instauration of Republican rule that would run unbroken in the nation from 1968 to 1993, with a four-year respite during the Carter presidential era—would inscribe as well the inauguration of changes that we could absolutely not have foreseen in their broader scope and meaning.

The period 1968–1970 meant, at least, the fruition of a radical and pluralistic democracy, or *so it seemed*, with, for example, comparatively larger numbers of African-American students admitted to the mainstream academy and agitation for the movements in black studies and women's studies, and their far-reaching implications for a radically altered curriculum, especially in the humanities. These initiatives constituted the vanguard of an attitudinal sea change, which, coterminous with the Continental movements in structuralist criticism, linguistics, feminist theory, and philosophy, would so reconfigure the leading assumptions of the traditional humanistic order, that within twenty years of the American withdrawal from Vietnam, the "English department," for example, as an institutional disciplinary site, would be virtually evacuated as a unified course of study, grounded in an indisputable canon of "great" literary work and supplemented by a more or less homogeneous critical establishment.

In brief, as turbulent as the 1960s were for those of us who lived the era, as crisis-ridden as the situation was for the black creative intellectual, as Cruse understood it, nothing within his lights or our own could have sufficiently prepared us for what I would regard as the central paradox of this social formation nearly thirty years later: Although African-American intellectuals as a class have gained great access to organs of public opinion and dissemination, although its critical enterprise has opened communication onto a repertoire of stresses that traverse the newly organized humanistic field, and although we can boast today a considerably larger black middle and upper-middle class, with its avenues into the professions, including elective office, some corporate affiliation, virtually *all* of the NBA, and the NFL, and a fast break into the nation's multimillion dollar "image" industries, the news concerning the African-American life-world generally is quite grim. In fact, it is chilling news, as we learn from certain observers, that the black prison population in the United States, for example, is substantial enough to outfit a good sized city—some six hundred thousand subjects, by the mid-nineties, most of them male. And, indeed there seems very little reason to believe that certain undiminished symptoms of social dysfunction will do anything but exacerbate what is, for all intents and purposes, a genocidal circumstance: the unabated availability not only of drugs but of the social and economic network of relations that have engendered a veritable drug culture; the ravages of poverty and illiteracy; a vital international arms market that directly feeds a nation in love with the idea and practice of violence; and race hatred/"tribalism," restituted by an entrenched and immoral political reactionism, whose targets are the city—its poor, its young mothers and their children.

To call attention to these vital details is to indulge the litany of responses that is by now customary for the black creative intellectual.[3] Though no one ever quite says it this way, it is as if the intellectual himself/herself is culpable, both as a social formation within the larger ensemble and *in person,* for this precise structure of contradictions. Because Cruse is working off the traditional emplotment, *The Crisis,* too, refracts culpability of the black creative intellectual; in fact, we might even say that disparagement of the intellectual in general and of the African-American intellectual in particular constitutes a rhetorical form of utterance. But if the intellectual subject, as I see it, can accept no credit for whatever gains black Americans have made over the past thirty years, except that he/she has been a beneficiary, then one is hard put to impute blame at his doorstep for the failures. It seems to me that a more useful way of analytical and declamatory procedure would be the attempt to establish a *total perspective* against which the work of the intellectual unfolds. In other words, the plight of the American city and its implications for the social landscape must be examined as one of the primary structural givens to which social formations variously respond. I attempt such a sketch below.

While the desegregation of the nation's public school systems was *intended* to address and ameliorate inferior educational facilities provided for America's black population, it appears to have induced, *by the way,* the collapse of a homogeneous structure of feeling and value that had consolidated notions of self-esteem and steeled the soul of the black young against the assaults that awaited it. But the liquidation of a traditional program of values, as it relates to African-Americans, is only a single feature of the radical swerve that worries one's perspective; in fact, we might even go so far as to say that the dispersal of black intellectual talent, and its deflection away from its customary social target, is a *symptom* of certain *global* forces that have had a negative impact on the life of American society in general, rather than the primary *cause* of devastation: the entire array of postmodernist sociality, whose chief engine is fueled by late-capital economies,[4] has homed in on black life with laser-like precision. Very specifically, the condensation and displacement of labor (intruding Freud where one never expected to find him) favor the well-educated social subject who can dance the new technologies of automated work, moving the society toward less and less *physical* labor, altering notions of liberal property in the process, and toward those subjects who can interpret the social organism back to itself as readers, writers, and managers of highly consolidated social properties, both real and symbolic.[5] The actual flight of labor, which one had not quite realized was "flight" until the dramatic closing of the General Motors plant at Willow Run, Michigan, for example, during the national political campaigns of 1992, quite likely originated when one was simply being annoyed rather than watchful—during the era of what we have come to call the oil crisis of 1973, with its attendant manipulation of the global money supply, the increasing political clout of the Organization of Petroleum Exporting Countries (OPEC), and the coming to international dominance of the Asian market, particularly the awesome competitive machinery of Japan's. (Those of us who grew up in strong, black nuclear families quite simply shudder to think what might have happened to ourselves in the absence of, say, a Memphis International Harvester, the company from which my father retired in the early seventies. A manufacturer of farm implements, based in Illinois, Memphis International Harvester moved away from this major southern city shortly thereafter, phasing out several thousand jobs with its departure. One of the city's other major industries—Firestone Tire and Rubber—closed at about the same time, as it, and other post–World War II enterprises, whose workers had educated a good number of the early and late "boomer" crop on workers' salaries, either disappeared altogether or converted to greater automation. It is not by error that a phenomenon named "the consumer," the origin and end of mass distribution and production, was "born" to us with vivid presence at the close of the sixties. Automated machinery, of course, "automatically" consolidates labor's quantity, as it alters work type and content, and as President Clinton alluded to the point by encouraging the national business community to practice and elaborate protocols of job retraining. He predicted during his years in office that America's current college population, for instance, would change job *type* at least a half dozen times before retirement.)

The decline of the American market, then, which Reagan's "Morning in America" low-tax program did not quite forestall, has joined forces with late-capital schemes of global reorganization in a dizzying velocity of change that has shifted the very imaginary object on which the black creative intellectual had worked at one time—a stake in the soil, actually bound by coordinates on the map of the inner city, the old "community" is neither *what* nor *where* it used to be; the tax base could not but have followed the wealth—both in and of itself and of labor's potentials—to the city's rim and well beyond.[6] Even though it seems that this latest version of urban flight might be traced back rather pointedly to a month and a day in 1954 and the famous (or infamous, depending on one's viewpoint) Supreme Court mandate to public school districts to desegregate "with all deliberate speed," such movement, along the rift of America's sharply drawn binary markers—"black" and "white"—was underscored by voting patterns that brought massive gains to a new, post-Goldwater Republican Party. At the very moment, however, that the new studies movements and widespread student protests were making their witness felt on college campuses across the United States, a mature political backlash—which the Clinton "Third Way" interrupted, three decades later, by interpolating a different political strategy between a strictly urban, predominantly minority, and poor electorate, on the one hand, and a basically suburban, predominately white and middle-class electorate, on the other—had been preparing itself for well over a decade.

Within this maelstrom of forces, the black, upwardly mobile, well-educated subject has not only "fled" the old neighborhood (in some cases, the old neighborhood isn't even there anymore!) but, just as importantly, has been *dispersed* across the social terrain to unwonted sites of work and calling. From my point of view, this marks the ace development that today's black creative intellectual neither grasps in its awful sufficiency nor wants to bear up under since she is implicated in its stark ramifications. (We instead chase after fantastic notions, quite an easier pastime than looking at what has happened to community.) It would be an error to assume that he/she has had the *choice* to do other than go out, just as our current social and political analyses are spectacularly hung up on a too literal and simpleminded idea of what community might mean in the first place and in addition to a location called home. I believe that an understanding of this internal diaspora would bring the black creative intellectual to a more satisfactory view of the thematics of flight, a rather contrastive nuance, after all, to that of *dispersal*. A revised view of the matter would certainly redirect our wasted energy, moaning over a monomyth of a version of community that only needs enterprise zones in order to be whole again. This paralysis of understanding, brought on by guilt over one's relative success and profound delusion about one's capacity to lead the masses (of which, one supposes, it is certain that she is not one!) out of their Babylon, disables the intellectual on the very ground where he now stands: on the site of the mainstream academy and its various ideological commitments. The values of the progressive movements that propelled him to such status in the first place are widely threatened now by a well-heeled, highly efficient coordination of right-wing forces,[7] spreading like mycelium through the body politic. The conservative agitation that Cruse must have urgently felt during the writing of *Crisis* is fully unfolded in our midst today, and the picture is not pretty. As I see it, the most assertive domestic enemy since the ravages and excesses of the McCarthy era drove a punishing offensive through the heart of an older cadre of left-wing intellectuals, this new immorality of power, tricked out in the discourses of political and economic rationalism and binding an array of appallingly ignorant media in its thrall (to wit, the canard of "political correctness," virtually unquestioned by nearly *all* print media in the United States), goes basically unchallenged by today's comfortable left-wing intellectual subjects. Of this social formation the black creative intellectual *ought* to be not only a member in good standing, but perhaps among the *first* standing. Distracted, instead, by false or secondary issues, yielding apparently little resistance to the sound intrusions of market imperatives on the entire intellectual object, including that of African-American studies, today's black creative intellectual lends herself/himself—like candy being taken from a child—to the seductions of publicity and the "pinup," rather like what an editor of *Lingua Franca* only half-jokingly called once the "African-American du jour." Might we suggest that *before* the black creative intellectual can "heal" her people, she must consider to what extent she must "heal" herself, and that *before* the intellectual can offer a salvific program against crack and crack-up, she is called upon to consider what immediate conversion she must herself undergo? And is it too much to imagine that what is wrong with "the community" is wrong with oneself? And furthermore, could we say that the black creative intellectual, like the black musician whom she so admires, has an object in fact, but that she is not always interested in what it is?

We should not be at all surprised, then, that the post-Cruse intellectual "throws down," in the midst of coeval pressures and forces, looking and feeling, at least some of the time, like a lost ball in high weeds. In fact, Cruse now appears to have been far better situated than we, in our "lateness," in our rather startling ethical laxity on occasion. In the wake of a powerful spectacle of pain and loss, the old vocabularies of moral suasion and consensual conscience—and we feel it everywhere, from our relations with African-American students and colleagues alike, and theirs with ourselves, to our considerable indifference to anything outside career—seem peculiarly impotent and moribund now. Not only have we lost a considerable percentage of our natal population to the arts and stratagems of destruction—and realize that we will lose quite a few more before this massive hemorrhaging ceases—but also our customary discourses of the moral and ethical quickening, with its evocative lament, its vision of the redemptive possibility, the old faiths that could move a mountain, or so one believed, all mark the lost love-object now.

But certain fatalism need not be the outcome; instead, we are called upon to restitute the centrality of Cruse's interrogation—what is the work of the black creative intellectual?—*for all we know now?*

II

While the fundamental charge that Cruse laid out is not different, *by definition,* in the contemporary period, it seems infinitely harder to grasp because of "conditions on the ground," some of which I have briefly attempted to explore. In short, the apparent homogeneity of the mass, which black life offered to the imagination in the late sixties, is more or less revealed now as the necessary fiction that has come unraveled at the seams. Cruse worked his two major premises against the notion of an ethnic group consciousness *in place;* this economy of motives defined for him the reality of black people, as a *homogeneous social formation,* in America: (1) on the one hand, the impulse to collective self-determination and economic independence, or an African-American cultural and economic nationalism—"Black Power," in short (after Congressman Adam Clayton Powell Jr.), and (2) the impulse to assimilation of the ideals and promises of American democracy, on the other. For Cruse, the nationalist strain was "strikingly cogent" across lines of class and could be thought of as a "residuum of what might be called the Afro-American ethnic group consciousness in a society whose legal Constitution recognizes the rights, privileges, and aspirations of the individual, but whose political institutions recognize the reality of ethnic groups only during election contests" (4, 6). The integrationist strain opposes the nationalist in Cruse's scheme, while both have their roots in the nineteenth century. Even though "integrationism" was not available as a concept to Frederick Douglass, the latter embodies nevertheless Cruse's prototypical representative of the integrationist urge, as Douglass's contemporary, Martin R. Delany, for example, stands for the "rejected strain," or the nationalist impulse. The dilemma for Cruse was the capitulation of black intellectual leadership to integrationist formulas that essentially depleted the energies of the community, as they robbed it of its crucial human and symbolic capital. In DuBois, the two strains "nearly merged into a new synthesis," inasmuch as DuBois was "a leading exponent of the Pan-Africanism that had its origins with Martin R. Delany," as well as one of the key movers of the Niagara Movement (1905) and what Cruse calls the "NAACP [growing out of Niagara] integrationist trend" (6).

The thrust of *The Crisis*, then, is to demonstrate systematically the default of black intellectual leadership in relinquishing its agenda to the mainstream apparatus and personalities, focusing on the fate of the Harlem community as a quintessential instance of the life-world in the post–World War II era. However, Cruse is careful to sketch a backdrop to Harlem in the fifties and sixties by examining the political pressures brought to bear on it during the twenties and the period of the Harlem Renaissance. Pushing the analysis back in the early chapters to the 'teens and to Philip A. Payton's Afro-American Realty Company, a movement in which black economic independence was principally responsible for the black influx into Harlem, Cruse rehearses the impact of the Bolshevik Revolution of 1917 on the conceptual weave of ideas available to black intellectuals along an evolving political spectrum. In fact, Harlem's political landscape was grounded in the antipodal oppositions that reflect Cruse's primary binarism—nationalism versus integration: Garvey's "Back-to-Africa" movement and its attendant black nationalism, on the one hand, and the radical historical materialists, on the other, and their alliance with Marxist thinkers, who refracted the political imperatives of the Communist movement in their theory and practice.

As these considerable antagonistic forces warred over time for the soul of Harlem, as it were, in the pages of *The Messenger, The Masses/The New Masses*, and *The Partisan Review*, among other organs of public opinion, Harlem itself lost its resources in black theater, for example—to wit, the American Negro Theater—and a paradigmatic occasion to hammer out an infrastructure of institutional support that would generate and sustain African-American cultural life. While the powerful declamatory and polemical ambitions of Cruse's work are central to his project, he lays out, early on, a ten-point plan not only to correct the errors of the past (which continue into the present) but also to set the community and its leadership on a different future course. For Cruse, the answer was primarily economic in the pursuit of a cooperative economic idea against the ideology of competitive market economics. Under "basic organizational objectives" spelled out in the third chapter of Part 1, Cruse elaborates the following aims for the Harlem community and, by metonymic substitution, for the entire life-world:

1. The immediate "formation of community-wide citizens' planning groups for a complete overhaul and reorganization of Harlem's political, economic, and cultural life."[8]

2. Black people with business competence should form cooperatives "which will take over completely the buying, distributing, and selling of all basic commodities used and consumed in Harlem, such as food, clothing, luxuries, services, etc."

3. Harlem's proliferation of small, privately owned black businesses should give way to consolidated cooperatives that "would eliminate this overlapping, lower prices, and improve quality. Cooperatives would also create jobs. Many of the excess stores could be transformed into nurseries, medical dispensaries for drug addicts, etc."

4. "Citizens' committees to combat crime and drug peddling. These committees should seek legal permission to be armed to fight the dangerous network of drug-selling."

5. "A new, all-Negro, community-wide political party to add bargaining force to social, cultural and economic reforms."

6. "Extensive federal and state aid . . . to finance complete economic, political and cultural reforms in Harlem. Without political power these social changes cannot be won."

7. Tenants' cooperative ownership of housing, "or at least, municipally controlled housing."

8. "Citizens' planning groups on the reorganization of Harlem's political, economic, and cultural life should aim to establish *direct* lines of communication from the community to appropriate departments and agencies of the federal government. . . . Whenever it is deemed necessary and politically apropos, and in the interest of expediting community decisions, municipal and state echelons should be by-passed."

9. "Citizens' planning groups must devise a new school of economics based on class and community organization. Such a school should be predicated on the need to create a *new black middle class* organized on the principle of cooperative economic ownership and technical administration."

10. "Citizens' planning groups should petition the Federal Communications Commission on the social need to allocate television and radio facilities to community group corporations rather than only to private interests" (88–89).

The Cruse cooperative model, with its egalitarian attitudes and roots in the indigenous locale, would have had to situate itself in perspective with wider national and international interests—in effect, would have had to *compete* against such interest formulas—but Cruse recognized the latent capitalist desire in the African-American middle-class subject, at least, that would challenge his model, if not wreck it, so that a good deal of the urgency of *The Crisis* is directed toward its contradictions. It should be pointed out that the fractured scene of ideological belief has not been healed, inasmuch as the African-American community remains muddled about capitalistic practices, or so it seems, tending to believe that only white racist supremacy has prevented it from sharing in, from, in fact, helping to generate, the fruits of "business," what a Steinbeck narrator once called a "curious ritualized thievery." What this belief means is that black Americans *would be* capitalistic, *except for;* this rather unarticulated wish is quite a different thing from belief in a systemic and radical uprooting of the dominant paradigm of liberal economics. At any rate, Cruse's ten-point plan shares a resonance with classical black models of economic and cultural independence in its appeal to a materialist deep reading, at the same time that it anticipates schemes of collective wealth and accountability.

Cruse develops his interrogation around the Harlem scene because of its critical black mass, its concentration of symbolic capital, and its sensitive location in what was, at the time of the writing, a preeminent world-class city. Harlem, (or more precisely, Manhattan) as the cultural capital of black America, had held this position for at least a century, and probably a bit longer, when we recall the sites of beneficent and cooperative societies, church activities, and women's support networks, lifelines which are detailed in Dorothy Sterling's *We Are Your Sisters.*[9] New York City, if not Harlem per se, along with Philadelphia, offered early black self-help programs through clerical organizations, particularly the African-Methodist Episcopal Church, as early as, in the case of Philadelphia's "Mother Bethel," the late eighteenth century. The reign of New York City as one of two of the urban centers that focused the liberational energies of America's free black population remained unchallenged through the period of post-Reconstruction and gained reenforcement in the post–World War I period as an outcome of massive black flight from the South. The year 1918, with its record number of lynchings across the southern United States, as black soldiers returned home from the killing fields of Europe, effecting common cause with labor recruitment efforts and the trials of the peonage-sharecropping system, delivered unprecedented numbers of black people to the New York scene of Harlem and what Cruse tracks of Phil Payton's Afro-American real-estate ventures. Its culmination is expressed as a cultural/arts movement in the Harlem Renaissance, but Cruse would attribute the failure of this arts movement to sustain itself to that complex of forces that remained knotted and left over from the tensions between Garveyism and black radicalism, à la Marxist thought.

The official home of the NAACP, the National Urban League, and their respective organs of public address, *Crisis* magazine and *Opportunity,* Harlem was poised, at the close of the war, to begin to exploit its proximity to the publishing houses and the major presses, the salon culture of the Big Apple (for example, Mabel Dodge Luhan as chief hostess of the 1912 renaissance), and those agencies of cultural and artistic brokering that would offer critical access to figures like James Weldon Johnson and Claude McKay, who both figure prominently in Cruse's reading of early Harlem culture. Harlem's wealth of symbolic capital, including the Schomburg Collection of the New York Public Library and powerful local organizations such as the Abyssinian Missionary Baptist Church—pastored by the Clayton Powells and Wyatt T. Walker, among others—offers additional reasons why its appeal seemed only natural to Cruse, who had spent a good part of his young manhood in the community. At one time the home of Sugar Hill, with its substantial bourgeois and professional-class black folk, Harlem is today the shattered "dream-deferred" of one of its finest poets—Langston Hughes, who, in the heyday of *his* Harlem, sang its democratic possibilities, its *mezclada* of African-American and African-diasporic elements. Hughes (as did John Coltrane) died the year that Cruse's *Crisis* was published, as though marking the collapse of a particular cultural synthesis.

It seems fair to observe, then, that Harlem's centrality as cultural capital of black America has been effectively eroded by forces too complex to exhaust here;[10] some of them, however, are immediately explicable in Republican political schemes of the early eighties and beyond, if not the late difficult years of the Carter presidency, whose policies of "benign neglect" of America's great cities in the East, and chiefly of New York City, aided in their depopulation trends and the subsequent economic maturity of the country's Sun Belt, certain major southern cities, especially Miami and Atlanta—both capitals now of the *new* New South—and California's fabulous Route 1, the gateway to the Pacific Rim and Central America. When one speaks today about a cultural and intellectual capital of black America, the mind scatters in different directions, as it is at least clear that "it" is no longer a single place. But certainly Atlanta, with its favorable climate, its black critical mass and manageable human scale, its affordable real estate, and its efficient infrastructure and hospitable disposition to high-yield investment capital has become, since the publication of *The Crisis,* a major competitor for such honors. DuBois's "hymn" to "Atlantis"—an imaginative tour de force on the principal stop along the old "Black Belt" nearly a century ago—seems, from our current perspective, appropriately forward-looking. But however one might respond to this question for the pollsters, the contradictory impulses that stamp African-American life and thought as an unmistakable ambivalence is supplemented now by the subject's need to work out a new poetics of travel and exile, a new sort of relation to home that is no longer bound to the specificity of place but that the subject must now learn to *remember*. In other words, because Harlem is no longer quite in vogue, nor yet the City on a Hill in Cruse's central vision, one must decide anew what she now thinks about Memphis and Birmingham.

Though Cruse does not touch on DuBois and travel as a significant theme in the life of black creative intellectuals, it is nonetheless imperative that DuBois's and Cruse's successors do so, because its attendant anxieties bear on a subject that African-American culture criticism *does* make explicit: DuBois had called it the "double consciousness." And while the DuBoisian paradigm is not exactly the same idea as Cruse's nationalism versus "integrationism," both concepts resemble each other in the emphatic split that they each posit at the center of black life.

The distance and the difference between DuBois and Cruse are not contextual alone, but signal an epistemic shift of terms, the differing critical postulates and instruments that bring new objects on the social landscape into view, or ones that show new facets of relationship between one object and another. DuBois was writing in the early decades—he lived so *long*—of the appearance of the disciplines of the social sciences in the United States: sociology, economics, and psychology, in particular. Cruse, by contrast, was at work, having come of age in the 1940s, in the triumphant era of the object of the social science; "man" in his milieu, as the Marxian homo economicus, as the primary target of elements of the socius (work and labor relations, family life, leisure time, sickness, aging and dying), and as the major features of "human" were atomized in the particular protocols of a specific disciplinary object. These rather sharp contextual and epistemic contrasts do not just describe but foreshadow one of the central concerns of this writing—the matter was not entirely lost on Cruse—and that is the extent to which the intellectual is *chosen* and formed for his task by the prevailing critico-theoretical paradigms, rather than simply *choosing* and getting down to work; as I hope to suggest shortly (and in short), following the lead of Thomas Kuhn[11] and Louis Althusser[12] on constituting the cognitive apparatus, the "crisis" of Cruse's "Negro intellectual," and the rather serious mess that today's African-American creative intellectual finds himself situated in, arises partially from the ill-fit between our perception of the "real object" and just how it is "mimicked" by, yet distinct from, what Althusser called the "cognitive object of knowledge." In other words, today's black creative intellectual tends to continue to see the *same old problem* in the *same old way* (an activity that Umberto Eco called a "perceptual cramp")[13] so that solving this problem (and to that extent the *fixed* idea of "community" is a *symptom* of what is to be relieved) will consist not only in reformulating the *object* of the search, but in rethinking, as well, one's own involvement—where he is situated regarding the conceptual apparatus—in identifying just what the object is.

It is precisely that shift in the way that community is formulated as an idea-object, this monolithic sameness that threads through the discourse from Cruse, to now; it is *that* momentous change, in fact, in figurative value, in materialist analysis and implications, that the culture theorist has barely approached. So far as Cruse was concerned, the "Negro intellectual," as *he* was called then, was isolated, in the main, from the prevailing theoretical positions of Cruse's time: his absence, for instance, from the national debate concerning left-wing liberal practices, and the requirements of a responsive political culture that came to focus on two major combatants of the era, C. Wright Mills and Daniel Bell. By Cruse's time, long before the collapse of the Soviet state, communist theoretical positions were notoriously disabled in providing an adequate response both to the problems of a pluralistic democracy and to the exigencies confronting the national black community, as Ralph Ellison—and Cruse bafflingly elides this point—had already captured the moment so well in his novel *Invisible Man* more than a full decade before *The Crisis*. In short, orthodox Marxist positions were insensitive to the nationalist element alive in black culture, were in fact, hostile to it as one intellectual and writer after another ended their careers disillusioned over this peculiar lapse. Others besides Cruse have asked why the radicals could make room for, or accommodate, every other nationalistic interest, *except* the black one. Cruse said as much, offering, as a result, an incisive critique of entrenched Marxist dogma.

Though Cruse might have gone even farther himself toward exposing the fault lines of his own theoretical moment, of his own distinct contribution to precisely the Mills-Bell debate that he valorizes in the final chapter of *The Crisis,* no one, I believe, has spoken more forcefully of what must be done; particular paragraphs from the peroration of *The Crisis* still lacerate:

> The special function of the Negro intellectual is a cultural one. He should take to the rostrum and assail the stultifying blight of the commercially depraved white middle class who has poisoned the structural roots of the American ethos and transformed the American people into a nation of intellectual dolts. He should explain the economic and institutional causes of this American cultural depravity. He should tell black America how and why Negroes are trapped in this cultural degeneracy, and how it has dehumanized their essential identity, squeezed the lifeblood of their inherited cultural ingredients out

of them, and then relegated them to the cultural slums. They should tell this brain-washed white America, this "nation of sheep," this over-fed, overdeveloped, over privileged (but culturally pauperized) federa-tion of unassimilated European remnants that their days of grace are numbered. (455–56)

Cruse goes on, but we see right away in this paragraph's unmitigated commitment to the declamatory word, to the polemical address, marked by anaphora and a virtually visionary appeal, what was driving Cruse and how right he was; the passage rather reminds me of the rhythmical and perfor-mative steam behind particular clusters of sentences by Cornel West, from *Breaking Bread,*[14] in his dialogue with bell hooks. Though I have decided quarrel with aspects of the West/hooks text, I nevertheless recognize the role that rhetorical inspiration is called upon to play in intellectual work. For West, the dilemma of the black intellectual will not be healed until this social formation of thinkers articulates a new, Foucault-inspired "regime of truth" that is "linked to, yet not confined by, indigenous institutional prac-tices permeated by kinetic orality and emotional physicality, the rhythmic syncopation, the protean improvisation, and the religious, rhetorical, and antiphonal elements of Afro-American life."[15] One spies the black preacher in the heart of this model, and while such transformation might help (and I rather doubt that it will), one can guess that it would be as easy to turn the preacher into an intellectual, as it would to turn an intellectual into a preacher. At any rate, both Cruse and West capture *in the writing* the heart-felt passion that I believe has compelled the black creative intellectual all along. For Cruse, the African-American culture worker was a *man* (Lorraine Hansberry is one of the few women whose work makes an appearance in *The Crisis,* and not very flatteringly), a man bent upon a mission, apocalyp-tic in character, upon whose effectiveness the very survival of not only the community but the very nation itself depended. Cruse concludes the para-graph:

The job has hardly begun. America is an unfinished nation—the prod-uct of a badly-bungled process of inter-group cultural fusion. America is a nation that lies to itself about who and what it is. It is a nation of minorities ruled by a majority of one—it thinks and acts as if it were a nation of white Anglo-Saxon Protestants. This white Anglo-Saxon ideal, this lofty dream of a minority at the summit of its economic and political power and the height of its historical self-delusions, has led this nation to the brink of self-destruction. And on its way, it has effec-tively dissuaded, crippled and smothered the cultivation of a demo-cratic cultural pluralism in America. (456)

I think that Cruse here is calling upon his intellectual John the Baptist to step into the fray and lead the charge that Randolph Bourne had dared to imagine in the twenties. Troping on Bourne, Cruse suggests, "For American society, the most crucial requirement at this point is a complete democratization of the national cultural ethos. This requires a thorough, democratic overhauling of the social functions of the entire American cultural apparatus" (457).

For all his prickliness of style and certitude of conviction in his own superiority to the task—and in some ways, that only Cruse appears to understand what is needed offers a needless distraction for the reader—Harold Cruse betrays, in *The Crisis,* his link to the times: He was its child in language, as we recall that the late sixties were one of America's great eras of black preaching, in King, in Malcolm X, in Baldwin's writings, even though we do not customarily think of James Baldwin as *preaching* in his written work, and Cruse was his time's child in the sure beauty of hopefulness, of looking toward higher ground, and he was most certainly its child in the evocation of a scene of confrontational hostility between dual and distinctive agonists, or opponents. While Cruse had quite forcefully and persuasively urged the black creative intellectual of his audience to look toward his numerous affiliations with a critical eye, indeed, to try to forge strategic alliances and politically appropriate friendships, he falls back in the press of closure on the time-honored literary device known as "Black America" and "White Anglo-Saxon Protestant" America. While there is never a doubt that "Black" and "Wasp" are sign-vehicles that signify real political constituencies and concrete cultural allegiances, it is also true that there is enough overlap between these intersubjectivities—for good or ill—on the cultural and social plane that a strict division between them is messed up everywhere *but on paper;* in other words, the black creative intellectual of Cruse's time, with his increasingly "integrated" social status, was being importuned to assail *some* of his friends. And *benefits.*

If living in the time after Cruse has taught us anything, it has been virtually knee-jerk doubt, unease, and suspicion of what we have come to recognize as binary claims. That old American mine field, wired with updated booby traps, staked out the terrain that Cruse had to cross. He negotiated it fairly well, in my view—our age, as I suggested at the beginning of this essay, has not yet produced an even remotely comparable reading in imitation of its patient and skillful exegesis. Nevertheless, that was then, and here we are now, in the aftermath of not only his writing but also a deranged global order and a decentered, if not jettisoned, subject of history. Because Cruse could not have anticipated the massive project of decon-

struction—and here I do not mean specific texts but, rather, an entire repertory of gestures that have dismantled many of the very assumptions of humanistic inquiry—Cruse becomes for us, from this distance, a *closed* mastery, dated by its era, yet useful in its incisive daring. That he spoke to his
time in the name of the black creative intellectual is sufficient.

III. Do You Know What They Call You Behind Your Back?

Even though starting from a different point, the intellectual is situated in
African-American culture in precisely the same manner that Cruse was—
poised toward the history that hurts, to echo Jameson.[16] But the link between this hurting history and the step beyond marks the immeasurable
distance that separates us from Cruse's certainties and those of the late sixties. The intellectual, then, installed in her own autobiographical moment,
is always wrestling with a tale of the same two cities; one of them goes this
way: *The Autobiography of Malcolm X* recounts a tale in which the hero/pro-
tagonist is confronted in an open forum by a Negro who asks a real question. The setting is the university, and the audience, of course, is predominantly white (as it gallingly shows the tendency to be, and as the question
itself implied criticism of Malcolm's position). For all of his significant
beauty, a dogmatist, nevertheless, the public Malcolm assumed that his fellow and brother was "trying to get house," as we used to say in the neighborhood, by posing that kind of query, in *that* kind of space. When one
attempts "to get house," he wishes to make points at his interlocutor's expense, to win the crowd and its approbation. The man may or may not have
been up to this game of signifying,[17] but it felt so to Malcolm, who delivered, in turn, the withering "answer" that stops black blood cold: Do you
know what they call you behind your back? And by the age of six, if not before, every black child knows that the answer is "nigger."

Malcolm, himself signifying, was illegitimately silencing debate, which
marks the difference, at the same time that his interlocutor, in case he'd
"forgotten," was being reminded of his *positionality*, despite. In other words,
the tacit agreement that prevailed between parties—to submit the behavior
and the desire to the *rules of the moment*—was disrupted by its sudden return to the moment's diegesis. (It goes without saying that to do so is
rather like striking a tear through the fabric of film stock at the moment
that a segment is rolling through the projector.) The black creative intellectual, then, is rarely afforded *the occasion of the moment* clean; either he
will remind himself, or someone else will, of the "big picture," let's say, of
the material scene through which he is moving. The very ability to *differentiate* oneself as an *intellectual worker* under the historicizing conditions of

African-American culture, long constituted in and by dominance as a mute *facticity* and *tactility,* has barely been achieved by African-Americans across the life-world. In fact, as one speaks, he does so against the background that Malcolm X (and, I dare say, *any* figure of public standing) exploited with considerable cunning.

So it is that the "homegrown" intellectual is addressing her hermeneutic demand not only to the cultural dominant but to her natal community as well. Furthermore, it is by sectors of both that she is, in effect, interpellated, or summoned, as a responsible subject and subjectivity. And how could it be otherwise? How could it not be double trouble that her very vocation is itself a space not yet entirely cleared out, as it were, by a culture that maintains no obligation at all to believe *her,* especially; to treat her, to imagine her, as a credible discursive subject, working on an intellectually identifiable object, at the same time that she encounters it as contradictory, if not adversarial, that she proceeds in a sort of "negative capability"? The *other* tale, then, that the black creative intellectual confronts marks the weave of contradiction as a fruitful one, but only if . . . It is, perhaps, too soon here to speak of bravery, but I suspect that a bit of it must involve our destination through the reversals of assumption that now make it difficult, if not impossible, to (1) reconstitute a "talented tenth," which is itself the culminative position of the *myth of representation* (as both DuBois and Cruse embraced it from their common historic past); (2) sustain the idea of the intellectual as a leading and heroic *personality* rather than a local point of oscillation among contending conceptual claims; and (3) continue to pursue a theory and practice of intellectual or cultural work that is *performative* rather than, for lack of a better word, unfortunately, "scientific," or responsible to a "cognitive apparatus," or a "thought-idea." These "impossibles," we ought to add, began to take shape long before *The Crisis of the Negro Intellectual* was published, if we push the reel back to the generation of Randolph Bourne, Kenneth Burke, and "The Fugitives," on the one hand and of W. E. B. DuBois, "The Niagara Movement"/NAACP, and early Pan-Africanism, on the other. But if our predication of cataclysmic change on a geopolitical scale has led us to imagine an earthquake in one direction, then we could sketch a dismantling, equally as powerful, from another and overlapping one that bore down more directly on Cruse's era; in short, 1968 was engendered by an additional context that brought movement, indeed, crisis, across fields of signification.[18]

I would track its more or less arbitrary moment of origin to 1966, when a series of seminars and colloquia, convened by the Humanities Center at Johns Hopkins University, resulted in the publication of a gathering of essays entitled *The Structuralist Controversy: The Languages of Criticism and the Sciences of Man*, edited by Richard Macksey and Eugenio Donato.[19] The parent sessions had been convoked during a week in October 1966, at an international symposium called "The Languages of Criticism and the Sciences of Man" ("Les Langages Critiques et Les Sciences de l'Homme"), with support from the Ford Foundation. Humanists and social scientists from across the United States and eight other countries converged on Baltimore at the time. This symposium series led to a two-year protocol, "which sought to explore the impact of contemporary 'structuralist' thought on critical methods in humanistic and social studies" (*SC*, xv). Seminar participants included, among others, René Girard, Lucien Goldmann, Tzvetan Todorov, Roland Barthes, Jacques Lacan, and Jacques Derrida. While the choice of this date may be somewhat questionable, it serves a purpose nevertheless for situating the arguments and propositions of structuralism[20]—the cross-disciplinary and systematic examination of the *conditions of discursivity*—to the fore in relationship to a wider audience of academics in the United States. As the editors of *The Structuralist Controversy* explained the impetus behind both the symposium and the volume, structuralist method itself had come to redefine a plurality of disciplinary procedures:

> As this was the first time in the United States that structuralist thought had been considered as a cross-disciplinary phenomenon, the organizers of the program sought to identify certain basic problems and concerns common to every field of study: the status of the subject, the general theory of signs and language systems, the use and abuse of models, homologies and transformations as analytic techniques, synchronic (vs) diachronic descriptions, the question of "mediations" between objective and subjective judgments, and the possible relationship between microcosmic and macrocosmic social or symbolic dimensions. (*SC*, "Preface to First Edition," xvi)

I did not become familiar with this work, however, until the following decade, when, as a first-appointment assistant professor of English and Black Studies, and an NEH post-doctoral fellow, I attended the opening sessions of the School of Criticism and Theory, convened June/July 1976, on the campus of the University of California, Irvine. Having been captivated a couple of years before by the corpus of Kenneth Burke, which suddenly made clearer to me exactly what I had been attempting to achieve in my doctoral dissertation and the undifferentiated restlessness to change and inform my own conceptual language, I had been prepared, without knowing it, for the tonic instruction of Hayden White, before *The Tropics of Discourse;* of Fredric Jameson, before *The Political Unconscious;* René Girard, just after *Violence and the Sacred;* of Edward Said, shortly before *Orientalism,* a topic that he introduced to the student body that summer in an evening lecture; of Hazard Adams; and of Frank Kermode, the wry, authoritative figure in the mix. When I returned on an occasion of the next generation of the School, as an instructor, during the summer of 1990, at the home of SCT on the campus of Dartmouth College, what had been news to myself nearly fifteen years before had become by then standard (perhaps even glib) operating procedure.[21]

To my mind, at least—and this imagined nexus seems worthy of extended investigation—the new procedural methods of reading "naturally" belonged to their historic moment as the iconoclastic blast from the teachers of students in rebellion. As buildings were being seized and occupied by students on college campuses across the United States, in opposition to the Vietnam War, in support of the Black Studies and women's movements, it seems that certain teachers, on the other side of the Atlantic, were preparing the epistemological foundations of profound change: (1) a rereading of the Marxist theoretical revolution; (2) the unconscious as (if) a linguistic structure; (3) mythic systems as the paradigmatic semiotic; (4) the rupture of the transcendental signifier and the undivided subject of presence; (5) the deployment of a natural historical sequence, reconfigured as a discursive series of relations; (6) the conversion of the women's movement into a theoretical and curricular object—to name a few of the more obvious developments. Looking across the disciplines revised and corrected by radical procedure, Macksey and Donato perceived a "horizon of a conceptual system" that had given way to "philosophical metaphors of defeat–'supplement,' 'trace,' 'simulacrum,' 'series,' 'archive,' 'errancy,' and the like" (*SC,* xii). Such an outcome had indeed induced a "climate" of opinion in which

> today's task for thinkers . . . resides in the possibility of developing a critical discourse without identities to sustain concepts, without privileged origins, or without an ordered temporality to guarantee the mimetic possibilities of representation. The fundamental entities of such systems, adrift in radical discontinuity, are *Events* which cannot be accounted for by transcendental idealities. (*SC,* "The Space Between—1971," xii)

A shaken academy, by 1971, would certainly be able to attest to "Events" no longer explicable, in the main, by the "transcendental idealities" that had subtended a "divided house."

It is precisely the asymmetrical poise of the period—students in rebellion "everywhere," but the most innovative instruction coming, often, from the other side of the Atlantic—that lends the era its haze of conceptual origins, which Paul Bové's work, *Intellectuals in Power,* goes far to clarify in the figure of Erich Auerbach.[22] It should be noted, however, that the "New Criticism" movement that had captured the imagination of America's literary/critical establishment from the twenties on had already succeeded in divorcing an object, the "heterocosm,"[23] from its sociopolitical context. It was not necessarily difficult, then, to transfer a sensibility, trained on the academy's "close reading" and the conventions of irony/ambiguity, to the world of text and discursivity. In fact, it would appear that the New Criticism, in certain of its critical dispositions at least, had anticipated the Continental drift. Moving out of its customary orbit, English and American literary studies came, increasingly, to mark the vanishing center of a centrifugal motion as literary criticism gave way, in time, to literary theory, and as the object of investigation was itself reconfigured: Instead of a hierarchical canon of literature, defined by periods, anxieties of influence, eminent practitioners and their derivatives, the literary object was knocked over and flattened out into a sea of discursive possibilities that swam rather unfamiliar currents—philosophy, linguistics, anthropology, film studies, feminist discourse and theory, Black Studies and African-American expressive culture, and, lately, newer occasions in post-colonial, multicultural, lesbian/bisexual/gay, cultural, popular, studies, "minority discourse(s)," and even stock market narratives. From that point of view, the ensuing fifteen years or so have been heady with a progressive unfolding, instigated by a handful of enabling postulates that we have already identified.

Whenever a thorough intellectual historiography of the period is attempted, we imagine that it will flesh out these impression points that have not only marked their objects but, in a very real sense, constituted them: Sausserian linguistics and its aftermath; Freudian psychoanalytic work, restituted in the writings of Jacques Lacan; Derridan philosophy and its implications for an American school of deconstruction;[24] the strategies of structuralist and post-structuralist cultural practice, the Foucaultian shift of paradigm, from the delineation of objects to their relationship in the ensemble, contextualized by enunciative fields and their inscriptions in the regimes of power and domination; the extensive Marxist critique by Marxists themselves, who sought to reinterpret historical materialism in light of late capital and the pervasive force of market that further disrupts our notions of a sacrosanct privacy. These far-reaching changes, carried through in a number of disciplines, have altered our view of the historical, as well as the literary, object, which now belongs to textual production and discursive positioning as the new rule. With Gayatri Spivak's English translation of *De la Grammatologie*,[25] the project of deconstruction, which dismantled the centrality of a unified subject in logos, gained ground as the new technic of reading. Between 1966 and 1976, then, the outline of the new academy was laid down, or, more precisely, a revised and corrected curriculum of the humanities was inaugurated. Converging on this scene of displaced conceptual objects were numbers of new academic players, from the late sixties on, a consequence that has conduced to a terminal degree, for example, and "full-time equivalents" in the university's departments of literature that bear no exact semblance to degree and curricular protocols as short a time ago as *The Crisis of the Negro Intellectual*.

The implications of the paradigm shift for black creative intellectuals have been fairly massive, or, more exactly, have not been isolated in their impact. For one thing, the black intellectual, firmly installed, during DuBois's era and overlapping onto Cruse's, in indigenous black institutions, or the HBC/U's (historic black colleges/universities), as a rule, have been repositioned in the mainstream academy. It is fair to say that whatever spaces of creative autonomy were yielded by a more homogeneous culture and life-world tended to dissipate by the late sixties. In other words, it is rare today that a black writer or critic finds means of support outside the academy or some other institution situated in the cultural dominant (e.g. ,mainstream publishers, etc.). One could even go so far as to say that mainstream institutions appear to meet the intellectual's *desire*, however he or she might "carry on" about the community. The "organic intellectual" that we have imagined after Antonio Gramsci names a romantic, liberated figure, then, who never really fructified and who remains a symptom of nostalgic yearning, looking back on a childhood perfected through the lens of distance and distortion. The truth, more nearly, is that writers, in particular, and certainly the critics/theorists, have been as compelled as any other subject of economy to follow whatever fortunes, in this case, of the "prose arts," into the contemplative sanctums, in an age dominated by communications technologies. The younger members of Cruse's initial audience, then, either leaving undergraduate schools or entering graduate programs at the time that *The Crisis* was published, were never wholly destined, by very virtue of the aims of the Civil Rights movement itself, for the singularity of motive and address, that Cruse's passionate invocation conjured up. Many of those persons, like Cruse himself at the University of Michigan, would be exactly positioned, in their future, between a putative community on the one hand and the politics and discursivities of the predominantly white academy on the other. We could say with great deal of justification that the black creative intellectual has been more hesitant than not to acknowledge precisely *where* and *how* she "is coming from" and in what ways *location* marks in fact a chunk of the *historical material.* A more efficacious critique, or, I should say, one that is less loaded with pretenses and pretensions, altogether depends on such acknowledgments.

Furthermore, if Steiner and Foucault were right, man is not only no longer the linchpin of historical movement but history itself demonstrates a minimal resiliency of meaning as a self-reflective tool in the current inventory of media-inspired, constructed punctualities. Certain idols of narrative have lost their explanatory power for American culture in general and for African-American culture in particular, if its contemporary music tells us anything, so that the key question for the black creative intellectual now is: How does one grasp her membership in, or relatedness to, a culture that defines itself by the very logics of the historical? Or, as I queried earlier, What is the work of the black creative intellectual, *for all we know now?*

The short answer is that the black creative intellectual must get busy *where he is.* There *is* no other work, if he has defined an essential aspect of his personhood as the commitment to reading, writing, and teaching. From Howard University to Cornell; from Wilberforce to Berkeley; from Tuskegee to Harvard; the relational object does not change, and *that,* it seems to me, decides the main problem to be disposed of—how to take hold, at last, of the intellectual object of work *in language.* The black creative intellectual, from Ralph Ellison, in *Invisible Man,*[26] to Imamu Baraka, in *Home,*[27] to Toni Morrison, in interview,[28] to name some of the most eminent cultural figures, embraces the black musician and his music as the most desirable model/object. While African-American music, across long centuries, offers the single form of cultural production that the life-world can "read" through thick and thin, and while so consistent a genius glimmers through the music that it seems ordained by divine authority its very self, the intellectual rightly grasps the figure of the musician for the *wrong reasons:* not often do we get the impression that the musical performer promotes his own ego over the music, or that he prefers *it* to the requirements, conventions, and history of practices that converge *on the music;* if that were not so, then little in this arena of activity would exhibit the staying power that our arts of performance have shown over the long haul. In other words, though ego-consciousness is necessary, it is the *performance* of the music that counts here, apparently, as we know black musicians and remember them by the instruments of their performance, and performance marks exactly the standard of work and evaluation that has not changed, from the Fisk University Jubilee Singers, Bessie Smith, and Thomas Dorsey on one end of the spectrum, to Charlie Mingus, Phineas Newburn, and Mulgrew Miller on the other, with Willie Mitchell and Booker T. and the MGs in between. Across nearly a century of African-American musical performance, implied in the foregoing figures, a variety of syntheses is at work, so that, for instance, Billie Holiday and Leontyne Price are not judged by the same musical standards, do not perform the same instrumentality, just as Theolonious Monk and Keith Jarrett each demonstrates a respective brilliance. What they have in common in their considerable divergence of time, location, and calling is performative excellence, and it seems to me that *this* is the page of music from which the black creative intellectual must learn to read. (One might also bear in mind that musical excellence *historically* relates to the *entertainment* needs of the dominant culture: at least one captivity narrative by an African-American writer rehearses a horrifying story of the bonded, who were forced to dance.[29] In other words, music in black culture achieved its superior degree of development, in part, because its ancestral forces were *occasioned, allowed.* The culture's relationship to language is the radically different story too familiar to repeat.) The black creative intellectual does not make music, as it were, and should not try, but he *can* "play." What, then, is his "instrument"?

Sharply and flatly: it is the "production process of the object of knowledge" (*RC,* 41). A seminar on Marx's *Capital,* conducted by Louis Althusser and Etienne Balibar at the École Normale Supérieure in early 1965, resulted in a publication that was translated into English in 1970—*Reading Capital (Lire le Capital).* In a complicated reformulation of the Marxist epistemological moment, Althusser, in the opening segment of the text, patiently elaborates the problem that Marx exploited as that of reading itself, but a *reading* no longer "innocent." In the course of that discussion, Althusser retrieves the "object of knowledge," concealed by a "reading at sight" (*RC,* 16) and the "empiricist conception of knowledge" (*RC,* 35), as a distinction to be made from the "real object." It seems to me that it is precisely that confusion in one of its avatars that persistently dogs African-American sociocultural work as the hidden component of analysis. Bringing it out, I think, would set the work and the culture worker on a different course and induce a new set of demands. While we can not exhaustively reread Althusser "reading Marx" here, a few contextualizing observations are in order.

Althusser is poised toward *Capital*—about a century after the first volume was written[30]—as a philosopher might be, and Althusser differentiates such disposition from that of the economist, the historian, and the philologist who not only would have addressed the work in a different way from the philosopher but would have *assumed* the object, comparing it (and here we might conjecture that Althusser means effecting a commensurability) "with an object already defined outside it, without questioning that object itself" (*RC*, 14). But to read *Capital* "as philosophers" would be to interrogate "the specific object of a specific discourse, and the specific relationship between this discourse and its object" (*RC*, 15). One would gauge the place of *Capital* in the history of knowledge by putting to the "discourse object unity" that it presents "the question of the epistemological status which distinguishes this particular unity from other forms of discourse-object unity" (*RC*, 15). *Capital*, as the object of this sort of inquiry, is, within itself, a rather remarkable occurrence, inasmuch as the Marxist canon, in general, is assumed by black creative intellectuals—and this was certainly the rule of the past—to be a quintessential character by virtue of a "privileged model of anchorage," an "expressive reading, the open and bare-faced" witness of the "essence in existence" (*RC*, 35). But it is precisely this "reading at sight," Althusser contends, that the Marxist episteme disrupted. Taking his introduction to the seminar at face value, we can insert his move within the general climate of critical opinion—including a prior moment in French intellectual history by way of a veiled reference to existentialism's "essence/existence" debate—coming to prevail on both sides of the Atlantic. In short, it seems that the blindnesses and insights, the visions and oversights, the "marks of an omission produced by the 'fullness' of the utterance itself" (*RC*, 23) were enabled, as a self-reflexive project, *only* at that moment. "Seeing, listening, speaking, reading," those "simplest acts of existence"—*in light of* Marx, Nietzsche, and Freud—were reopened to unsettling oscillation. "Only since Freud," Althusser claims, "have we begun to suspect what listening and hence what speaking (and keeping silent) *means (veut dire);* that this 'meaning' . . . of speaking and listening reveals beneath the innocence of speech and hearing the culpable depth of a second, *quite different discourse,* the discourse of the unconscious" (*RC*, 16).

Capital is repositioned, then, as the reading target, whose transparency "in the dramas and dreams of our history . . . its disputes and conflicts . . . its defeats and victories of the workers' movement" (*RC*, 13) will be rendered an instance of the very thing that Althusser is calling for in a reading that has lost its "innocence": the "sighting" of an "opacity" that addresses another "thought-object" and that demonstrates the special domain of that object on the historical material ground. Taking the "empiricist concept of knowledge," which defines knowledge as the function of the real object, to be the culminative movement of ideology, Althusser effectively "retroacts" *Capital* as postmodernist critique, insofar as Marx posed the answer to the question that classical political economy hadn't even asked. ("What is the value of labour-*power?*") Asking, instead, "What is the value of labour," classical economists had elided terrains of inquiry, "by substituting for the value of labour . . . *the apparent object of its investigations,* the value of labor power, a power which only exists in the personality of the labourer, and is as different from its function, labour, as a machine is from its performance" (*RC,* 20).[31] Not aware of the substitution, Marx argued, classical political economy was led down the road to "inextricable contradictions" that induced exclusive preoccupation with labor value and its prices, with the relation of this value to the value of commodities, and so forth. By inserting "the personality of the labourer" into the equation, Marx was enabled to see that the "oversight" that classical political economy had made on its own answer "is equal to the value of the subsistence goods necessary for the maintenance and reproduction of labour." The question that Marx restituted, then, had as its answer: "*The value of labour-power is equal to the value of the subsistence goods necessary for the maintenance and reproduction of labour-power*" (*RC,* 23). According to Althusser's reading of this outcome, what the classicists did *not* see is precisely what they *saw* as the "invisibility" of "sight" (*RC,* 21ff). The oversight was not performed on the object but in the sight—"an oversight that concerns *vision;* non-vision is therefore inside vision, it is a form of vision and hence has a necessary relationship with vision" (*RC,* 21). (Perhaps Ralph Ellison's protagonist of *Invisible Man* had already anticipated such a reading as Althusser performs?) Althusser's demonstration of the disruptive syntax, which the unasked question provoked, induces this graphic equivalent: "The value of labour ( ) is equal to the value of the subsistence goods necessary for the maintenance and reproduction of labour ( )" (*RC,* 22). Marx, in effect, he is claiming, indexes the silences, the aporias, in the discourse of classical political economy.

Teasing out Marx's reading farther, Althusser is led to the empiricist critique, which, he believes, will compel us to reorganize our idea of knowledge as the "mirror myths of immediate vision and reading" and to conceive it, instead, "as a production" (*RC,* 24). By "production," Althusser refers to those "structural conditions" that enable knowledge; "sighting," then, is no longer the peculiar perceptual endowment of an individual subject, but is, rather, "the relation of immanent reflection between the field of [a] problematic and *its* objects and *its* problems" (*RC,* 25). Clearing ground for "earthliness," or the Marxian "absolute immanence" (*RC,* 131), Althusser wants to reconfigure the relation between a knowing subject and how he arrives at knowing—in other words, the latter is neither given in the thing itself, nor is it the transparent transcendent:

Vision then loses the religious privileges of divine reading: it is no more than a reflection of the immanent necessity that ties an object or problem to its conditions of existence, which lie in the conditions of its production. It is literally no longer the eye (the mind's eye) of a subject which *sees* what exists in the field defined by a theoretical problematic: it is this field itself which *sees itself* in the objects or problems it defines—sighting being merely the necessary reflection of the field on its objects. (*RC*, 25)

The empiricist concept of knowledge, which implies the transparency of reading, offers the "secular transcription" of a "religious phantasm," grounded in "the Logos and its Scriptures" (*RC*, 35). The empiricist function of knowledge can be said to effect an occlusion, insofar as the knowledge that it derives is revelatory—it is to be supposed—of a real object, or is itself the *space* of such knowledge. Althusser represents this process of derivation as an "abstraction," a separating out of the thing itself from the "dross," or irrelevancy, that conceals it:

> To know is to abstract from the real object its essence, the possession of which by the subject is then called knowledge. . . . Just as gold, before its abstraction, exists as gold unseparated from its dross in the dross itself, so the essence of the real exists as a real essence *in* the real which contains it. (*RC*, 35, 36)

In this case, the special vocation of knowledge is "to separate, in the object, the two parts which exist in it, the essential and the inessential—by the special procedures whose aim is to *eliminate the inessential real*" (*RC*, 36). By way of a series of operations and probings—"sortings, sievings, scrapings, and rubbings"—the subject who knows hits pay dirt, as it were, the "second part of the real which is its essence, itself real" (*RC*, 36). The object then stands revealed before us in all its pristine clarity of origin, purpose, motivation, no trace of hands touching it. Thus, "the relation between the visible and the invisible is therefore identical to the relation between the outside and the inside, between the dross and the kernel" (*RC*, 37). A variant on the conception of epiphanic vision, the empiricist concept would hold that transparency

> is separated from itself precisely by the *veil*, the dross of impurities, of the inessential which steal the essence from us, and which abstraction, by its techniques of separation and scouring, *sets aside*, in order to give us the real presence of the pure naked essence, knowledge of which is then merely sight. (*RC*, 37)

Althusser is then able to poise the empiricist concept against the Marxian episteme, which makes a distinction, say, between "the idea of the circle" (after Spinoza)—which demarcates the space of knowledge of the object—and the circle itself, "which is the real object" (*RC,* 40).

Two final citations of moves in *Reading Capital* should bring us to the desired intersection; this seems to me the principal lesson to be pondered: Althusser spends considerable time attempting to deconcatenate (1) "the real-concrete" from the "thought-object," a distinction, he tells us, that Marx defended. The "real-concrete," or the "real totality," "survives in its independence, after as before, outside the head" (*RC,* 41). The object of knowledge—"a product of the thought which produces it in itself as a thought-concrete . . . as a thought-totality . . . as a *thought-object,* absolutely distinct from the real object, the real-concrete, the real totality, knowledge of which is obtained precisely by the thought-concrete, the thought-totality"—does not simply describe a different object from the real, but a different process of production as well:

> While the production process of a given real object, a given real-concrete totality (e.g., a given historical nation) takes place entirely in the real and is carried out according to the real order of *real* genesis (the order of succession of the moments of *historical* genesis), the production process of the object of knowledge takes place entirely in knowledge and is carried out according to *a different order,* in which the thought categories which "reproduce" the real categories do *not* occupy *the same* place as they do in the order of real historical genesis, but quite different places assigned them by their function in the production process of the object of knowledge. (*RC,* 41)

But this thought-object of knowledge is not an equivalent of what Simone de Beauvoir said that the magical was—"spirit drooping down in the midst of things"—but is, rather,

> the historically constituted system of an *apparatus of thought,* founded on and articulated to natural and social reality. It is defined by the system of real conditions which make it, if I dare use the phrase, a determinate *mode of production* of knowledges. As such, it is constituted by a structure which combines (*Verbindung*) the type of object (raw material) on which it labours, the theoretical means of production available (its theory, its method and its technique, experimental or otherwise) and the historical relations (both theoretical, ideological and social) in which it produces. (*RC,* 41)

This "system of conditions of theoretical practice," then, "is what assigns *any given thinking subject* (individual) its place and function in the production of knowledges." (*RC*, 41–42, my emphasis). I italicize in order to say that *the central positionality* of the black creative intellectual is constituted by systematic *theoretical practice* and that *this* is her "instrument," forever and anon. If, like Duke Ellington, she wants to be famous and celebrated, then, perhaps, she has landed in the wrong orchestra pit. Althusser does not say as much, and needn't have, insofar as the dilemma before me is not the problematic that concerned him in the least, but I emphatically mark the point in order to expose the primary *non-dit—not said*—of African-American intellectual work, ironically, and that is its *right to exist* not only within the "real totality" of its natal life-world but within the "real-concrete" of knowledge production, of which one of its key sites in American society is the academy, mainstream and otherwise. The "real-concrete" question, then, that is posed to black creative intellectuals—What will you do to save your people?—and its thousand and one knee-jerk variations, is, therefore, misplaced. It seems to me that the only question that the intellectual can actually *use* is: To what extent do the "conditions of theoretical practice" pass through him, as the *living site of a significant intervention?* In other words, as it passes through "I," what alterations of its properties does the "I/eye" perform? Quite obviously I mean to say that the shifter in the formulation need not refer, *at all times,* to an autobiographical itinerary but might describe an *ensemble* of efforts—the research center, the think tank, the thematic fellowship, and so forth—defined along particular lines of stress. The journal and the periodical also come to mind as an analogy on a single mode of collective intent, although, locked as we are in our notions of heroic individualism and the allure of romantic aloneness, which the academy fosters daily, we can neither easily imagine it, nor always positively *desire* it. This seems to me the *test* of the theoretical paradigm *at any given moment* and its—*of necessity*—*hegemonic possibilities* in *this here* moment, especially, if we take "hegemonic" in the sense that Ernesto Laclau and Chantal Mouffe redefined it: an open and indeterminate range of elements that "fill a hiatus that ha[s] opened in the chain of necessity."[32] From the beginning of Marxist theoretical practice, they tell us, hegemony and its logics had offered itself "as a *complementary* and *contingent* operation, required for conjunctual imbalances within an evolutionary paradigm whose essential or 'morphological' validity was not for a moment placed in question."[33] If that is so, then Laclau and Mouffe have danced hegemony around to a user-friendly "socialist strategy" that is open to new democratic cunning, and this seems to me *exactly* the meaning of America in the sixties—that American intellectual life, with its rapid incursions and cross-racial fusions since Cruse, has brought us face-to-face with explosive potential *in the theoretical object.* To fritter the time away thumb-sucking would give revitalized meaning to *tragedy* and *farce.*

Now, I do not intend to lightly dismiss the tireless, cross-generational question that is put to black creative intellectuals, but I do mean, and want, to *displace* it—to *interrogate the question,* as Randall Kennedy only barely began to do in a recent public forum on this matter, "The Special Responsibility of the Black Intellectual in the Age of Crack."[34] (Isn't it also the "age" of e-mail and the deadly "virus," disseminated over various fault lines, from the immunodeficiency syndrome to computers? Isn't it also the age of armed kids and the first open and dramatic signs of society's return to the rule and the law of the *patronne,* the pimp, as an intermediary and prophylactic device against rape and hunger, and sewered through the nation's underground of drugs and firearms? The sign of the father that is missing? What does it mean to sum up the age under the rubric of crack? Why not flight, or fantasy and the peculiar turn of the screw that black people bring to it? And who said that the intellectual could even begin to know how to fix it?) One knows what the question *says,* but what does it *mean? As formulated,* it means nothing, yet; in other words, it might mean Everything, in which event it is unanswerable. In a different way, it means something entirely different from the thing it is *asking, demanding.* The black creative intellectual might evolve, instead, a whole catalog of inquiries, deliberately left unstable in order to allow for self-revision—not entirely unlike the Lutheran theses posted on that church door at Wittenberg so long ago— that would move the theoretical, if we could imagine the thought-totality and its discrete moments, moving in a mortal knower, as a kind of *torque.* His is not the salvation "business," though *if* he "saves," *if so,* he will do it in the only way he knows how—as a reader/writer/thinker/teacher.

The "raw material" that the black creative intellectual works on, then, is not the "real-concrete," or "'pure' sensuous intuition or mere representation," but, as Althusser contends about the conceptual apparatus, "an *ever-already* complex raw material, a structure of 'intuition' or 'representation' which combines together in a peculiar '*Verbindung*' sensuous, technical and ideological elements" (*RC,* 43). Against the imperial demands of the empiricist concept, he goes on, knowledge does not confront

> a *pure object* which is then identical to the *real object* of which knowledge aimed to produce precisely . . . the knowledge. . . . For that raw material is ever-already . . . matter already elaborated and transformed,

precisely by the imposition of the complex (sensuous-technical-ideological) structure which constitutes it as an *object of knowledge*. (*RC*, 43)

Perhaps the "purest" object that the black creative intellectual always imagines as the unmediated "thereness" is situated in her concept of natal community. But in my view, the time has come for us to rethink community, if we dare, precisely as an "object of knowledge," beginning with our false relations to it as an "unchanging same."[35] Earlier in this essay, I attempted to demonstrate how the black intellectual's current view of community is not only fictional—such status is *not* the problem—but that it describes an *inadequate* fiction, precisely because it is not rich enough either in content or transitional elements to encompass change, both willed and induced. Attempting, further, to understand how that is so, against some of the ideas deployed here, should bring us to closure.

IV
For L.B.

Is Cruse's community the same as our own, as DuBois's? And what might it have been in the past, which they have consistently represented here? Perhaps one can back into a response: in order to think community, one must be, in some way, separated, or apart, from it, for it marks the complicated viaticum of travel. To that extent, it is the *differentiated* portion of consciousness from which one splits off in the inception of language and division. It is unspeakable that it is so, not easily borne as knowledge about myself and my premiere others: that some time, I will leave this house of my father's support and my mother's pacification in order to take my place, make my way, in the midst of strangers who have unanswered needs. But I am bound for this alienation that demands its reconciliations, bound for the wider village of worldlings, each "overhearing" his own tale of the sorrowful report that cannot be uttered, all at once, and, perhaps, not at all, and to what other end do I acquire and practice the strategy of *memory*, unless it is to allow myself the occasional revisions of my loss? But I only knew this *afterward*. This is the *personal* economy that is not unfamiliar to the black creative intellectual, or, let's say, to the serious sojourner: in fact, community is my primary speech, the genesis of "I," the awful gauge of my time. Is it true, then, that one leaves home to learn to remember? If it is true, then we encounter the truth of paradox, and that is to say, that *because* I remember, I never departed.

But this phenomenon that we grasp as an unbroken fabric of relations is already constituted and handed over to the subject as a kind of layered, invented trust—it is itself an *idea,* materialized in a *location,* but by no means limited to the spaces identified as a topographical specificity. Infinitely representable, community is both a sum total and a not-entirely thinkable, except by way of the metonymic device. As a sum total, it is all affect, too multiple, individualistic, and porous to catalog, but its subjects, by virtue of interpellation, insertion, and agreement to play the game, as it were, find common ground in the *narrative emplotments* that converge on it; thus, community is also a *position in discourse.* For both DuBois and Cruse, community stood in for a preeminent stability, except that both writers left its borders open to expansion: Cruse, for example, selects representative figures of West Indian origin to portray his notion of Harlem as a cosmopolitan city within a city. But precisely because his West Indian characters did not share an indigenous culture with his black American ones, community, in *The Crisis,* is troubled by the assumption of sameness. From that point of view, community hides the suture that stitches together certain discrete elements of identity, especially differences of class. While DuBois's community slightly varies over the course of his considerable project, it overlaps features of Cruse's own: (1) a commonality of "suffering" that overruns difference; (2) an easily isolated social formation within a larger sociopolitical scheme; (3) or, to reverse the foregoing, a marked position that defines itself against an unmarked one. DuBoisian community inscribes not only a sameness but an *allegory* on the same that DuBois called "souls of black folk" and their "drama of a tremendous striving." In both emplotments, one can, in effect, grasp community in the palm of the hand as a smoothed over, globular complex. DuBois and Cruse are not alone in perceiving the problematic in this way, for it marks the leading figurative construct in African-American writing—sermons, poems, fiction, polemic, argument—over two centuries of endeavor. The young sixties intellectuals did not intervene a different idea, except that community became for them an obsessive feature of speech, underscored by certain anxiety. It demarcated the place one had *abandoned,* or had been abandoned by. The cultural analysis has not moved beyond the benchmarks left by DuBois and Cruse, and the problem seems to be how to convert a *negative* affect into *meaning by negation.* A new cultural analysis starts there—surmounting the fear of culture/analysis itself.

Since 1968, virtually all public exchange to which I've been an ear concerning intellectuals and the community has been fraught with anxiety and confusion, and indeed it would appear that the very *public* nature of the address goes far to hamper incisiveness: microphones, which amplify one's words, often spontaneous and improvised on the spot, define the exchange as ritualistic display—an occasion *to posture;* against the background of an auditory, which, in its silence, sends up its own demands, not at all answerable in the moment, the participants have "face" to save, to preserve, and from that point of view, the public forum tends toward the conservative instinct. It was precisely such circumstances, we imagine, that provided the frame through which Malcolm X's "answer" rolled toward his interlocutor. Add to the scene the imperial camera and its magnificent array of lights, and we have pure "theater," by definition fantastic and deceptive. If anything, the participants are transformed, in the flow of nervous energy and expectation, into actors, of a borrowed shape, an amplified identity, whose text is now self-consciously geared toward the repertoire of signals that fix and capture them in a momentary stardom. It would be exact to say that under these conditions, the play *is* the thing, and nothing more. In fact, one might go so far as to say that the participants are using the name of the interrogation as an alibi to *perform personality* rather than using the latter to execute the former. Furthermore, it might not be by accident that, since the late sixties and the explosion of the image industries, our public discourses have been immeasurably impoverished—or so it seems—precisely by way of the theatricalization of culture analysis and the "object of knowledge," from presidential politics to the politics of the black creative intellectuals and the community. *Both* have been redefined by new regimes of domination that do not, in their comprehensive powers of attraction, always allow themselves to be clearly understood in that way. If African-American culture has been transformed by internal divisions of flight and dispersal—and the latter must also mean various *repositionings* in the national culture and not simple, physical movement, or mobility, alone—then the object of analysis must be grasped in light of it.

But the intellectual has imagined flight only in its negative instance as a supposed rejection, when his very status, or standing, *as an intellectual* requires that he take on a language and disposition that are "foreign." In other words, the work of the academy, or more specifically, the "cognitive apparatus," is defined, symbolically speaking, as "not-mother," a "not-my-own." I am referring less to the maternal and paternal objects here as gendered actants of precisely defined sexual role than as the *ground of intimacy* that the subject *assumes:* the more or less harmonious ensemble of impressions that bound me not only to my body, but my body as it is reflected back to me in the eyes of others that I recognize *as like myself.* Whether or not this relation is troubled is less the point than that its complexities convey to one the sense of ease—the relay of constitutive continuities among particular kinetic, linguistic, sensual, and material gestures—through which one comes to experience home. From this point of view, community describes both the extension of home as well as its spatial/temporal genesis. As I understand it, community, however, is already a *cross-weave*—its local economisms linked into a larger network of sociopolitical/cultural relations and the messages that traverse it consequently—that prepares its subjects to receive the supplemental. We cannot imagine learning, acquisition, the *foreign* language, precisely as the various pains of intrusion unless we first understand how community has intimately prepared the ground as the apparent continuing unity against which "unhome" is measured.

While it is clear that I am reading the weave of issues by way of a different narrative emplotment, borrowed, in part, from psychoanalytic theme work, this interpretive device, to my mind, has the advantage of allowing for a conceptualization that is open to contemporaneity and what precedes it—an idea of the past. Because our current state of cultural analysis can only imagine, in large part, the life-world as the motion of *crisis,* as the urgent immediacy, overwhelmed by the "real," it, therefore, has no *theory* of the past, even though it brims over with it as the coercive, unreflected principle, or law, of our present. Because we have only managed to rethread a *politics of representation* and its theoretical paradigms, based on a false idea of the collective, we currently have no theory of a "one" and cannot, consequently, imagine the "many." In other words, liberal, bourgeois "individualism," which the intellectuals only claim to eschew, is a different proposition from the individuated nominative property who locates herself in historical/cultural apprenticeship and is also *located* there. But hauling an uncritical individualism into the backdoor of the analysis (and practicing it quite rawly and openly), the intellectuals can well imagine a *representative hero* whom they, in turn, embody. But it seems to me that if community is embedded in each, so to speak, then its restitution will commence with a theory of "one," in short, the capacity to perceive community as a *layering of negotiable differences.* Doing so would allow us to understand how change, or altered positioning, is itself an elaboration of community, rather than its foundering.

The model that I am proposing would be based on a theorization that melds various aspects of the human sciences and a mode of culture analysis for which we currently have no name, but one might think of it as *a cultural demography;* this new "science" would be alert to the *cultural* implications of movement, which is not only a primary meaning of the life-world, but one of its most significant literary tropes[36]—the "symbolic geography" that would explain (1) diasporic movement, (2) internal migration, and (3) the mechanisms of fantasy and ambition that contextualize African-American struggle. In short, we would seek a theoretical apparatus that could measure deviance, not *as deviance* (or sociopathological dysfunction) but as the "mark off" from legacy, or the making use of what one has been given.

If we attempted to flesh out this model, we might derive the following topics:

1. Marking overlaid by opportunity. If we concede to DuBois and Cruse that there is an African-American culture, distinct within the framework of American culture, then we will also concede that its subjects can *reflect* on its status, as DuBois and Cruse are representative instances of just such reflective powers. This marks the space of the hiatus—the break from dailiness, the distancing time, which I have addressed before.[37] In other words, being a subject of "community" means not only *reacting* but also *reflecting,* and it is within the context of reflection that the work of culture analysis proceeds. Quite obviously, the point is to imagine as many in reflection as possible—is that not one of the *political* aims of "struggle"?—but certainly the culture worker/intellectual cannot be embarrassed out of this advantage, as today's black creative intellectual appears to be too often. Concession to the political implications of "race," of racialistic ideology, is required, but the question for theory is what contribution the thought-object can make to exposing and illuminating it.

2. African-American culture, as a distinctive social formation, disappears into a general economy of practices, but it has been difficult for the intellectuals to follow its trails; in fact, the analysis traditionally frames itself as a neatly rectangular object, whose "geometry" might be read in rather precise dimensions of closure, when it seems, more exactly, that the life-world is not a plane figure at all. In work and labor, property and the judicial system, standard grammars and social behaviors, the school system and taxation, medical practice and health care, buying habits and consumerism, susceptibility to certain common national narratives (i.e., "beauty," "success," "wealth," etc.), the fantasy apparatus and the constitution of the sexed subjectivities, the ideological appartus and the devices of "self-fashioning," across this vast array of the social and material network, the subject of African-American community is installed in processes of "social contagion." In fact, we might pick up the trail of one of its key manifestations in the new institutional practices that we have been alluding to all along.

For all intents and purposes, the years immediately following the publication of *The Crisis of the Negro Intellectual*—1968–69—marked the inaugural years of Black Studies as a new institutional site within the mainstream academy. At Brandeis University, for instance, the student occupation of Ford Hall, during eleven days in February 1969, had elaborated fourteen demands, one of which called for the creation of black studies, whose chief administrative officer would be chosen by the students themselves. As I recall, the initial outcome of the rebellion virtually followed the outline demanded by black student leadership. This pattern of instauration proceeded across the country so that by the mid-seventies, many of the leading predominantly white campuses either had a Black Studies program or department in place, or were putting forth some effort to establish one. The 5 May 1994 volume of *Black Issues in Higher Education*[38] calls attention to the twenty-fifth anniversary of this initiative. Two paradigms obtained: (1) an appointment in Black Studies, as some of the programs fashioned an Afrocentric/Africanist response to the traditional disciplines, heavily influenced by the American social science paradigms and their empiricist concept of "reading," or (2) an appointment in one of the traditional disciplines in the humanities or social sciences, with a complementary appointment in Black Studies. In some instances, the institutions pursued a mix of procedures, with the Black Studies protocol filled in by both disciplinary and extra-disciplinary appointments. It was not always clear, however, under the circumstances, just how an FTE in literature, say, situated in the English department, would differ in her pedagogical and "scientific" practices of the teaching of African-American literature, for example, from one situated in Black Studies, teaching the same. But there was some vague sense that the *discipline* of literary instruction, as well as a body of critical knowledge, would prevail in one case, while it was not at all certain what its opposite, or contrastive, aim or project might be from the perspective of Black Studies. It is fair to say that if the practices of reading, criticism, and theory in the field of African-American literature are an example, then Black Studies has either not yet defined its *disciplinary object, apart from* the itineraries of the traditional disciplines that converge—revised and corrected—on it, or has had a very difficult time clarifying such an object. While there doubtlessly have been, and continue to be, successful programs and departments in African-American studies (as it is called today)—the tenuring and promotion of personnel, the granting of degrees and/or certificates, even a few research centers, scattered across the country—the visionary company of African-Americanists tends to "do" the studies from the vantage of the constitutive disciplines.

What we have, then, is an interesting, complicated picture—African-American studies, as a discrete *bureaucratic unit,* often separated from (by choice) or peripheral to (by design) the main centers of the ongoing life of the institution, and African-American studies, as it is renamed and refracted through the optic of conceptual apparati located "elsewhere." Personalities working the field split along similar fault lines so that many black scholars in the humanities fields of the institution, wherever they may be *bureaucratically located* in relationship to the "Keepers," belong, by implication, if not by practice, to the African-American studies project in its dizzying replication of the issues. (One of its latest reincarnations is cultural studies, with its nexus to African-American literary studies and its sixties' political formulas.) It would appear, then, that within this economy of ways and means, the most innovative and substantial work has come from black creative intellectuals located *within* the disciplinary spaces of the traditional curricula, inasmuch as their work is directed toward intervening on a *specific thought-object* (i.e., literature, philosophy, sociology, etc.).

We must try, then, to sort out a *disciplinary object* from a layered and complex political motivation, differently understood, it turns out, by different actants, depending on location. To my mind, that object must move through a first step—to *become* a disciplinary object, or to undergo transformation of African-American studies into an "object of knowledge," rather than a more or less elaborate repertory of performative gestures and utterances. At the end of the first twenty-five years, the intellectuals have barely taken the first step, though we have had important work emerging from individuals in the disciplines, particularly in literary studies, history, and sociology.

Today, the emergence of such an object is blocked by two difficulties, which appear linked to the same regime of power that Black Studies was originally thought to impinge upon, and that is the "pimpification" and the colonization of the (non)object, worked through those attractive practices and proprieties that more or less "get" us all, one way or another. The colonizing of the new institutional spaces is rather like its pimpification, except that the personalities in the former relations are more attractive, in some cases, downright charming and seductive, and differently configured in relationship to the regime of knowledge. In other words, today's "colonialist" of the new protocols is quite a lot smarter than his predecessors and brings quite legitimate skills of accomplishment to his or her work. He *himself,* she *herself,* is not a bad fellow; in fact, one might even go so far as to say that some of her best friends are among them; but none of that, of course, is quite the point to be made: we wish to know what happens to *the investigation,* whatever soul is minding the store or when one leaves the scene. Now, what follows might be read as blank parody, with grave implications for our common future as culture workers, and if we imagine that this part of the writing is *novel-like,* we shall all have fun: it is a misfortune of our history that certain of our Black Studies programs, for reasons that will already be apparent, were left to the charge of perfectly nice people, in some cases, and not so nice at all, in some others, but who, at any rate, were not scholars and writers in the least sense, say nothing of scholars and writers of some stature. In the most offending cases, some of the black personalities who converged on black student populations, on predominantly white campuses in the late sixties, were rather sinister figures, or of shadowy character, but in the event that I am wrong about this interpretation, they had, as far as one could tell, at least no interest in scholarship and inquiry of any sort and no skills, actually, to engage them. The male figure, in almost every example I mean here, was put in place *by the institution, with the endorsement* of local student leadership, itself misinformed, often, about a proper set of aims and objectives for a Black Studies protocol and even less about an acceptable set of credentials *for a college or university.* I would call, in the worst-case scenario, which is obviously not the only possible one, the male figure of the old model the paradigm of the "pimp," because all the resources earmarked for the local black population passed through him and, quite literally, through his offices—personnel action, curricula development, course requirements, and most particularly, the dreams and aspirations of the black young, who were not and are not the children of the "Keepers." With their "man" on the job, the "Keepers" themselves could then look away, as this has been the paradigm of the "overseer" and *his* "over seer" in the life-world since time immemorial.

The next act of this development is even painful to ponder, say nothing of write about, and follows the initial deeds like night the day: Because we ourselves were not sufficiently vigilant, or experienced, or were guided, as well, by the practical objectives of career building, we could not have clearly perceived how the groundwork was laid *then* for our intellectual synthesis *now,* and that is the *commercialization* of Black Studies/African-American studies without deliberate speed. I think we must make here a slight distinction between *commercialization* and *commodification,* inasmuch as the latter is to effect, in cash nexus, an exchange of work for a salary, or wage, from a corporation; it is the money of our bread. For lack of a better word, *commercialization* is the "selling" of an "object," however we identify it, for purposes of self-aggrandizement and gain, even though it is not always clearly the case and even though the *outcome* could well benefit many others, and that is the subtlety of African-American studies *as a business,* or an enterprise, today. We are, quite simply, not certain where its *commercial* successes will take us, though it is a dead certainty right now that some of us are personally benefiting from its journey along the academic interstate. Because it was installed on the academic time line when it was, even though "Negro History," for example,[39] was introduced to the curricula of historic black institutions of higher learning decades ago, African-American studies became a mode of analysis subject to the heightening tensions of late capital and its thorough intrusion into every crevice of daily life. On the other hand, then, we could say that the commercialization of the object of inquiry is nothing more than a smart and strategic response to the occasion at hand. It is to be *enterprising* in light of opportunity; and given the American Way, this is downright *patriotic* participation in the GNP. On the other hand, however, we must point out what seem to be some of the dangers of commercial shock treatment.

Because today's academy moves farther and farther away from its educative aims and becomes an arm of what Cornel West refers to as "business civilization,"[40] it tends to be thoroughly corrupt in its measure of intellectual work, which slides, more and more, onto an interface with the performance arts. Today's black creative intellectuals, then, in responding to the provocation, are sometimes as likely to be made up in their public function by the agent and the ad man as not. The *economically* and *politically* weakest constituent groups among the college's and the university's clientele suffer the gravest damage in this case, though none of that will be apparent, since the aim, it seems, is to graduate consumers, not literate, capable persons. We risk banality in saying that today's academy, by trivializing and degrading its *critical* function in the society, has shot itself in the foot: administratively top-heavy, bogged down in the "business" of making money, "busy" with "image," "name," "rep," "public relations," the ratings game, and how to keep its professoriate the most impoverished and demoralized class of professional workers in the nation's history and conscience, today's academy has broken faith with its own most sacred duty, if we might call it that—to feed the mind-life of the civilization entrusted to it. While we cannot definitively blame the site for its various and varied products, just as the institution, at any given moment, must respond to a general economy of practices, I nevertheless see the trade in the souls of academic folk as a prime example of the context and system of values through which American culture work unfolds today. As for the impact it is having on *African-American* culture work, quite specifically, I would dare say that as a *process in intellection,* the latter verges on a state of collapse. Do we exaggerate?

While the work of individual scholars and writers goes on in a successful, often admirable, way, there is not a campus, or a single black academic person, who remains unaffected by the "morning news," let's call it. I do not wish to impose a "speed," or rate of velocity, on the change of the tune, nor am I suggesting that anyone ought to, but it does seem to me that too rapid oscillations (1) prevent careful and considered work from occurring, since one is "bopping" right along to the next latest "hit"; (2) identify African-American work in culture as a fashion, eminently, if not imminently, dis-placeable by other fashion modes; (3) feed the sole frenzy of the "Keepers" to attract students and dollars, which emphasis further debases the intellectual currency; and (4) "evacuate" graduate education, wherein lies the object's future, in the sense that our students quite sensibly flock to wherever they perceive "it" is happening. African-American studies and those disciplines arrayed around it can least afford this modality of response, since its aim is to take hold of an utter paradox, lived and conceptual, into whose midst the intellectual is hurled with considerable force, and that is her situatedness in American/Western culture as an African-descended subject. Therefore, the demand on her work seems to be, at all times, the powerful articulation of a mode of address that speaks/writes/teaches this problematic in its various theoretical inflections. In brief, it is the work of synthesis and the consoli-dation of the collective gain: at this late date in the century, we cannot prop-erly gauge, have not properly gauged, the work of DuBois, Woodson, Cruse, and Blassingame, among others, against their social context, if we no longer have a good idea why we are here.

It seems to me that we must aim farther toward improving the *quality* of African-American culture work and not simply proliferating its number of bibliographical items; in the past, detractors of the Black Studies model dis-paraged it because it was said to be an unresearched field. This criticism was not as useful as it might have been, though one got the point, inasmuch as "fields" are not provided by nature. They are founded, processional, and dynamic, and cannot be researched until they are materially situated in re-lationship to a conceptual landscape—to a repertoire of topics and in-quiries. Fields emerge from the socius as *collective* engagements, but we verge on losing this dimension of the studies because the time to *reflect* in reading and writing is truncated, not by shifts in the paradigm, or improve-ments on the question, but by the need to sound the next thing. But how do we decide? If such determination is simply market-driven, then it seems the obligation of the intellectuals to weigh the implications of this out-come. African-American studies, as a "supermarket" of notions, certainly describes one of several possibilities of form and, in fact, faithfully mimics the public relations urges of today's academy. But what does such form se-cure for the object's location?

To build institutional legacies in African-American studies, within the mainstream academy, seems entirely appropriate as one of the goals of American higher education today. But this aim must be clarified *over* and *above* the heroic personality of individual figures, and that identifies one of the central weaknesses of the academic context in which the black intellectual operates. For example, more than one institution, to my knowledge, has thrown its weight behind a single individual, in whose departure the site of African-American studies, if not, in fact, razed, is emptied out (like an abandoned building) of gesture, civil and otherwise, for those who follow. In other words, the representative figure, in the absence of commitment to a scene of instruction, in the absence of an informed *political practice,* exhausts whatever goodwill there might be—in the local case—with his departure. Without putting too fine a point on this, we could say that at least the political lesson here can be read as on a sign board: that until the dominant culture of academic life is prepared to receive black people *in the moment of their appearance,* in the moment of their person, and not as the diapason replay of "race" myth, then the decisions of individuals might well echo in the lives of others. No one ever said that this was a fair outcome, but I believe that it *is* an accurate reading.

Quite in keeping with the thought-object-become-an-object-of-capital, the institution, in some cases, has not only "domesticated" the dissent of African-American studies but has moved it "uptown." This is very fine, except that doing so appears to have induced what I called earlier the formation of a now-colonized studies, squarely installed within the central machinery of the liberal institution. But is this a contradiction? Today's black creative intellectuals in the academy are being sorted out now as two decisive *class* interests *within* an already small minority social formation, and its main determinant is drawn along lines of gender. Heads of programs and departments, of research centers and the like, are male, by and large, and, just as interestingly, with *considerable* cooperation from some of their female colleagues often enough. Even this is not entirely objectionable, except that funding agencies, administrative officials, or any other agentification of the resources tend to bunch up the working capital, let's say, at the door of the male head, just as in the old Black Studies model, the campus's sphere of (black) influence orbited its path. It needn't be as sure as sunrise that *women* intellectuals, in this order of things, are going to be declassed and "orientalized," but it is so, as a handful of males ascend to the top and females descend toward the bottom. We cannot assign fault or blame here, as there would be no justice, or accuracy, in attempting to pinpoint it. We can certainly not claim, either, that the ascendant sphere, or class, has not earned its status, deserved its various merits, but we do mean to call attention to the *systemic* and *systematic* replay of gestures of empowerment that, by definition and practice, exclude women as social subjects from whatever grouping as a matter of reflex. At some time, the black creative intellectuals must respond to this aspect of the definition of *siting* on the conceptual object. I mean, in other words, that the *position* of the speaker in discourse goes far to decide the credibility of her report.

Quite possibly a reflection of the shadowy "laws" of cross-racial male bonding, this late development in African-American studies, enabled and rewarded by college and university administrations, has impact on the entire field of inquiry: the women "teach," the men "preach," the women "follow," the men "lead," the women "nurture," the men "posture," the women "do good," the men "do well," just as the men drive "rather elegant cars," they think, while the women take the "unbearable ugliness" of their solid old Volvos down to the local mechanic's for the installation of a new airflow meter and hope that that will do. Is this nothing more than the all-too-human cackle of envy? If that is all that the complaint were, then we could dismiss it as a minor misfortune of the trivial, but I am not altogether sure that we can dispatch it so easily, because the moment of the scene that I am describing appears to have become the staging ground for the reprise of certain historic tensions that perennially surface across the life-world. Not forcefully drawn out by either feminist inquiry, or African-American theoretical work, this component of division offers one of the key reasons why an *intramural* aspect of culture analysis is both necessary *and* evaded, for it would force us to confront what is suppressed in the public discourse of the analysis, indeed, what the politics of "race" customarily require to be censored here: the *strong* line of gender, as "race" "within" runs a broken line from one actant to another, as positioning in discourse overlaps a strategic class formation. African-American "community" fractures against the broad back of this paradigmatic social configuration, mapped according to the demographies of larger cultural patterns. Mediated, in this case, by the American academy, this network of social relations reveals—in small—the incredible array of unarticulated tensions that would describe *movement* and *mobility* as decidedly *internal* features of analysis.

Thus, the academy offers the black creative intellectual his own, dear laboratory. He brings the community with him to it, bears it between his ears, so that, quite remarkably, his community must be rethought on the site of the foreign, with the learned tool. We are accustomed to hearing that the intellectuals must go back to community, but the only community there is goes forward with the objects already at hand. In fact, the "answers" that he seeks are already there, at hand, if by that we mean the willingness *to stake the inquiry.* I have placed emphasis on "inquiry" throughout this essay precisely because it is the *refused* device within a repertory of choices. I am quite frankly puzzled that this is so widely true, except that it "tears" one apart, insofar as she must now *discriminate* within a field of objects held in trust as her familiar. The rupture of certainty is exactly the stage here so that the narrative of the "sojourner" in a "strange land" is not entirely, or solely, the work of figuration. Or, we could say that if it is, then the uses to which it is put are not negligible. We have not yet quite seen, even though some notable persons—Harold Cruse, among them—once labored diligently for the *conceptual object* of an African-American studies. Still called "victim studies" by those who have no idea what its architects were aiming for and who have no interest in knowing, it is, to their mind, the sign of "Africanity"—the illegitimate issue of an unnamed and unnamable source. But that seems exactly the point—to now *name* the question that rupture evokes within the context of a specified loss—here, *imagined*. But in the game of culture, there are ways by which loss is *suspended* in gain. Is there a "science" in such a social text? At least one culture worker thought so.

Michel de Certeau highlights Freud's *Moses and Monotheism* as just such an act of suspenseful engagement—on the oxymoron, we might say. The studies in a cultural demography that I have insisted upon would at least light out for new ground with a somewhat different thought in mind. I borrow it from de Certeau:

> [*Moses and Monotheism*] has much to do with suspicion, which is rupture, doubt; and with *filiation*, which is both debt and law. Membership is expressed only through distance, through traveling farther and farther away from a ground of identity. A name still obliges, but no longer provides the thing, this nurturing land. Thus Freud must bet his place within writing. He gambles it with his cards on the table—he risks his relation with the real—in the game organized by a loss. The obligation to pay the debt, the refusal to abandon the name and the people ("Jerusalem, I shall not forget thee.") and hence, the impossibility of not writing, are built over the dispossession of all "genea-log-ical" language. The work has no hereditary soil. It is nomadic. Writing cannot forget the misfortune from which its necessity springs; nor can it count on tacit, rich, and fostering "evidences" that can provide for an "agrarian" speaker his intimacy with a mother tongue. Writing begins with an exodus. It proceeds in foreign languages. Its only recourse is the very elucidation of its travels in the tongue of the other: it is analysis.[41]

With *interrogation* to the fore, in lieu of the transparencies of "reading," perhaps we leave in place for Lois Brown, Lindon Barrett, and all their arriving company a clearer space for work.

" . . . And so, I cleaned my house."

Notes

Preface

1. These essays have been the subject of critique on two occasions now, and I have been profoundly honored and moved by them: The Center for the Study of Black Literature and Culture at the University of Pennsylvania sponsored "A 'National Treasury of Rhetorical Wealth': A Symposium on the Work of Hortense Spillers" on 28 January 2000. The event was organized by the Center's director, Professor Michael Awkward, his colleague at Penn, Professor Farah Jasmine Griffin, and Professor Saidiya Hartman, University of California, Berkeley; other participants included: Professors Nahum Chandler, the Johns Hopkins University, Gina Dent, the University of California, Santa Cruz, Ronald Judy, University of Pittsburgh, Wahneema Lubiano (snowed in in Durham that frigid winter week), Duke University, and Tommy Lott, San Jose State University.

The Program (and Center) in Comparative American Cultures at the Johns Hopkins University, under the leadership of Professor Nahum Chandler, organized a fall symposium, 26–27 October 2001, on "Intellectual Practice, Feminism, and Psychoanalysis: The Work of Hortense Spillers." Participants included Professors Chandler, Fred Moten of the Tisch School of the Arts, New York University, Riche Richardson, the University of California, Davis and a current fellow at the Hopkins Center in Comparative American Cultures, Nicole Waligora-Davis, Cornell University, Celia Brickman, psychoanalytic practitioner at the University of Chicago, Kalpana Seshadri-Crooks, Boston College, and Charles Shepherdson, SUNY, Albany. The interlocution generated by the essays was bracing in itself, but even more important than that is the work that they have partially enabled beyond them.

2. This formulation is indebted to the opening pages of Ernesto Laclau and Chantal Mouffe, *Hegemony and Socialist Strategy: Toward a Radical Democratic Politics* (London: Verso, 1985), p. 7ff.

3. "Isom," *Essence* (May 1975). Marcia Gillespie, editor at the time of this new magazine devoted to black women's issues, must be thanked here for publishing my first piece of fiction. *The Black Scholar* picked up two others, "A Day in the Life of Civil Rights" and "A Lament," respectively: vol. 9, nos. 8, 9 (May/June 1978); vol. 8, no. 5 (March 1977).

4. "Martin Luther King and the Style of the Black Sermon," *The Black Scholar* 3, no. 1 (September 1971). Rpt. in *The Black Experience in Religion,* ed. C. Eric Lincoln (New York: Anchor Books, 1974).

5. "Toward a Separate Peace: Notes on the Life of Toomer," *The Harvard Advocate* ("Odyssey: A Search for Home") 108, no. 4 (Spring 1974), and "The Politics of Intimacy: A Discussion," in *Sturdy Black Bridges,* ed. Roseann Bell, Bettye Parker, Beverly Guy-Sheftall et al. (New York: Doubleday, 1979).

6. Marjorie Pryse and Hortense J. Spillers, eds. *Conjuring: Black Women, Fiction, and Literary Tradition* (Bloomington, Indiana: Indiana University Press, 1985).

7. Mary Louise Pratt, *Imperial Eyes: Travel Writing and Transculturation* (London: Routledge, 1992).

Introduction

1. Alice Thomas Ellis, "Mayonnaise Proves the Existence of God," in *The Faber Book of Food,* ed. Colin Spencer and Claire Clifton (London: Faber and Faber, 1993), 188.

2. Ibid.

3. Ibid.

4. Francis Joannes, "The Social Function of Banquets in the Earliest Civilizations," in *Food: A Culinary History From Antiquity to the Present,* ed. Jean-Louis Flandrin and Massimo Montanari; trans. Clarissa Botsford et al.; English edition by Albert Sonnenfeld (New York: Columbia University Press, 1996), 32–37, at 35.

5. Ralph Ellison, *Juneteenth,* ed. John F. Callahan (New York: Random House, 1999); 105; 133. This posthumously published fiction entered the literary world anticlimatically, it seems, and with quite a lot less fanfare than the author of *Invisible Man* might have deserved; in any event, this novel, concocted by the editor from Ellison's notes, tells the story of a racist white senator who was actually raised in black culture by a black preacher, Rev. Hickman, one of the novel's key narrators. Food frequently appears as an organizing motif in his speeches and reminiscences. In one case, a scene of apocalyptic grotesque gives way to tall tale humor, as in another, "fifty pounds of potato salad," while fabulous, can be imagined.

6. William Faulkner, "The Bear," *Go Down Moses* (New York: Vintage International, 1990), 181–317; see especially Part IV, 247ff.

7. In 1915, Carter G. Woodson established the Association for the Study of Negro Life and History and the following year the *Journal of Negro History.* These founding events in turn engendered the Associated Publishers in 1921, "Negro History Week" in 1926, and *The Negro History Bulletin* in 1937 (*Africana: The Encyclopedia of the African and African-American Experience,* ed. Kwame Anthony Appiah and Henry Louis Gates Jr. [New York: Basic *Civitas* Books, 1999], 2020–21). While we must credit Woodson with putting down the parameters of the discipline of Negro history and related historiographies, Woodson belongs to a distinguished line of diasporan intellectuals who directly addressed the target communities in their work, including, prior to Woodson, Alexander Crummell, E. W. Blyden, and W. E. B. DuBois. These Culture workers constitute what could be called an early formation of social scientific/historiographical protocols focused on black life-worlds. See also: Wilson Jeremiah Moses, *The Golden Age of Black Nationalism, 1850–1925* (New York: Oxford University Press, 1978), as well as V. Y. Mudimbe, *The Invention of Africa: Gnosis, Philosophy, and the Order of Knowledge* (Bloomington, Indiana: Indiana University Press, 1988), especially "The Power of Speech," 44–98, and "E. W. Blyden's Legacy and Questions," 98–135; Jacqueline Goggin, *A Life in Black History: Carter G. Woodson* (Baton Rouge: Louisiana State University Press, 1993).

Recent inquiries into black intellectual formation include Ronald A. T. Judy, "Untimely Intellectuals and the University," *boundary 2,* vol. 27, no. 1 (Spring 2000, special issue, "The University"), 121–35, and Hortense J. Spillers, "Crisis of the Black Intellectual," in *The Blackwell Companion to African-American Philosophy,* ed. Tommy Lott and John P. Pittman (Oxford: Blackwell Publishers, 2001). Under a similar title, issues taken up in the latter inquiry are expanded in this volume, "*The Crisis of the Negro Intellectual:* A Post-Date." While the systematic and scientific study of black community *as a writing* specifically belongs to the post-emancipation period and the development of the social scientific disciplines in industrialized economies, we could say with a great deal of justification that this work is predicated on black writing in fiction, poetry, the essay, and the autobiography that precedes it. The Black Studies movement of the late twentieth century owes its conceptual contours to these earlier categorical alignments.

8. Harold Bloom, *The Anxiety of Influence: A Theory of Poetry* (New York: Oxford University Press, 1973); my reading of Bloom's revisionary ratios is adopted from the introduction to this influential work, 15–16. The ratios are elaborated in Bloom's *Map of Misreading* (New York: Oxford University Press, 1975).

9. Robert E. Spiller, Willard Thorp, Thomas H. Johnson, Henry Seidel Canby, and Richard M. Ludwig, eds. *The Literary History of the United States,* 3d ed. (New York: The Macmillan Company, 1963). A couple of decades later, this entire project was revised: Emory Elliott, general ed., *Columbia Literary History of the United States* (New York: Columbia University Press, 1988).

10. F. O. Matthiessen, *American Renaissance: Art and Expression in the Age of Emerson and Whitman* (London: Oxford University Press, 1968).

11. Darwin Turner, J. Saunders Redding, and Charles T. Davis are among the distinguished practitioners of the New Criticism; in their respective cases, the critical lens of close textual reading and *explication du texte* is turned toward black writers: Darwin T. Turner, ed. *The Wayward and the Seeking: A Collection of Writings by Jean Toomer* (Washington, D.C.: Howard University Press, 1980); J. Saunders Redding, *To Make A Poet Black,* with an introduction by Henry Louis Gates Jr. (Ithaca: Cornell University Press, 1988). Reissued from the 1939 publication of this work in the approach to its fiftieth birthday, *To Make A Poet Black* examines the literature from its eighteenth century forerunners through the period of the Harlem Renaissance. In his introduction to the 1988 edition, Gates calls Redding "the dean of Afro-American literary critics" (vii). Gay Wilson Allen and Charles T. Davis, eds., *Walt Whitman's Poems* (New York: New York University Press, 1968).

One of the first black professors in the history of Yale University's English Department, Davis came to the Ivy League from a distinguished career in one of the nation's first historically black institutions, Hampton Institute, Hampton, Virginia; leaving his mark on the sixties generation, Davis was posthumously honored in a publication by one of his former students, Henry Louis Gates Jr. (cf. Charles T. Davis, *Black Is the Color of the Cosmos: Essays on Literature and Culture, 1942–1981,* ed. Henry Louis Gates Jr. [New York: 1982]).

12. A survey of key moments in the development of African-American literary criticism and culture critique is provided in Winston Napier, ed., *African-American Literary Theory: A Reader* (New York: New York University Press, 2000).

13. A definitive history of the black nationalist movement in the United States (between Martin Luther King's assassination and the presidential election of Ronald Reagan) has yet to be written. Various miscellanies, however, articulate some of its most important formulations, including: *Black Fire: An Anthology of Afro-American Writing,* ed. Leroi Jones/Ameer Baraka and Larry Neal (New York: William Morrow and Co., 1968); *The Black Power Revolt: A Collection of Essays,* ed. Floyd B. Barbour (Boston: Extending Horizons Books, 1968); *The Black Aesthetic,* ed. Addison Gayle Jr. (Garden City, N.Y.: Anchor Books, 1971); Manning Marable, *Beyond Black and White: Transforming African-American Politics* (London: Verso, 1995), especially chap. 18, "History and Consciousness: The Political Culture of Black America," 216–30.

14. Perhaps no single work is more telling of the critical change I am pointing to here than the bellwether, *The Structuralist Controversy: The Languages of Criticism and the Sciences of Man,* ed. Richard Macksey and Eugenio Donato (Baltimore: The Johns Hopkins University Press, 1972). Many of the players on the developing stage appear in this volume of writing.

15. Jacques Derrida, *Of Grammatology,* trans. with preface by Gayatri Chakravorty Spivak (Baltimore: The Johns Hopkins University Press, 1976).

16. Melanie Klein, "Envy and Gratitude," in *Envy and Gratitude and Other Works 1946–1963* (New York: The Free Press, 1984), 176–236. Klein's discussion of "envy" takes us back to the "earliest object relations and internalization processes" rooted in orality and the maternal breast. The infant's primary and primordial object, the breast marks the infant's earliest emotional life and the "sense of losing and regaining the good object" (180). "Happy experiences" and "unavoidable grievances," which "reinforce the innate conflict between love and hate, in fact, basically between life and death instincts, [resulting] in the feeling that a good and bad breast exist," might be thought of as the subject's first adventure on the roller coaster. Envy, growing out of those early object relations, is the "angry feeling" that someone possesses and enjoys "something desirable" (181). Envy wants to take it away, Klein argues, to spoil it. If envy is tethered to the life-death instinct(s), then perhaps Kleinian descriptions lend it a far wider sphere of influence on human and social interaction than simply "the personal problem" of an individual alone, or even a formation of individuals.

17. Mieke Bal, *Narratology: Introduction to the Theory of Narrative* (Toronto: University of Toronto Press, 1985). I am borrowing the concept of "actant" from Bal's interrogation of the conduct of narrative; see especially "Fabula: Elements . . . Actors," 11–47.

18. Toni Morrison, *Sula* (New York: Bantam Books, 1973), 105.

19. Gwendolyn Brooks, *The World of Gwendolyn Brooks* (New York: Harper and Row, 1971); reprinted as *Blacks* (Chicago: Third World Press, 1994), Harper's *World of Gwendolyn Brooks* was, regrettably, out of print for a couple of decades and was as close as we had come, up to the moment, of a collected edition of the poetry. The orange hardcover bore a photograph of the poet on the book jacket.

20. "Maud Martha," *The World of Gwendolyn Brooks*, 125–307; in *Blacks*, 141–323. See also Mary Helen Washington, " 'The Darkened Eye Restored': Notes Toward a Literary History of Black Women," in *Reading Black, Reading Feminist*, ed. Henry Louis Gates Jr. (New York: Meridian Books, 1990), 30–44 (see "An Order of Constancy" in this volume).

21. Encompassed in the volume entitled *Annie Allen*, Brooks's "children of the poor" extends the poet's work in the sonnet form of which she was an exquisite practitioner; compare with these poems Brooks's "Gay Chaps at the Bar," *Blacks*, 64–75.

22. Mary Louise Pratt, *Imperial Eyes: Travel Writing and Transculturation* (London: Routledge, 1992).

23. This reference offers a riff, of course, on Paul de Man, *Blindness and Insight: Essays in the Rhetoric of Contemporary Criticism*, introduction by Wlad Godzich, Theory and History of Literature, vol. 7 (Minneapolis: University of Minnesota Press, 1983).

24. Teresa de Lauretis, "The Technology of Gender," in *Technologies of Gender: Essays on Theory, Film, and Fiction* (Bloomington, Indiana: Indiana University Press, 1987), 1–30.

25. Saidiya Hartman, *Scenes of Subjection: Terror, Slavery, and Self-Making in Nineteenth Century America* (New York: Oxford University Press, 1997).

26. Pierre Bourdieu, *Outline of a Theory of Practice*, trans. Richard Nice (Cambridge: Cambridge University Press, 1977); see especially chap. 4, "Structures, Habitus, Power: Basis for a Theory of Symbolic Power," 171–83.

27. Ralph Ellison, "Change and Joke and Slip the Yoke," in *Shadow and Act: The Collected Essays of Ralph Ellison*, preface by Saul Bellow, introduction by John F. Callahan (New York: The Modern Library, 1995), 100–13.

28. Helen Tunicliff Catterall, ed., *Judicial Cases Concerning American Slavery and the Negro*, 5 vols. (Washington, D.C.: The Carnegie Institution of Washington, 1926–37); vol. 1, *Cases from the Courts of England, Virginia, West Virginia, and Kentucky*.

29. John Hope Franklin, *From Slavery to Freedom: A History of Negro Americans*, 3d ed. (New York: Vintage Books, 1969). In this classic, Franklin discusses the status of the

Jamestown arrivals in chap. 6, "Servitude and Slavery in the Southern Colonies," 71–89; see also Ira Berlin for a variation on the question of black social status: *Slaves Without Masters: The Free Negro in the Antebellum South* (Oxford: Oxford University Press, 1974). The static figures landed at Jamestown take on flesh and bone in Berlin's "From Creole to African: Atlantic Creoles and the Origins of African-American Society in Mainland North America," *The William and Mary Quarterly*, 3d ser., vol. 53, no. 2 (April 1996): 251–88; qtd. 276–77. See also: Elizabeth Donnan, ed. *Documents Illustrative of the History of the Slave Trade to America*, 4 vols. (Washington, D.C.: The Carnegie Institute, 1930–35), vol. 4, *The Border Colonies and the Southern Colonies*, 2–4.

30. Catterall, *Judicial Cases Concerning American Slavery*, vol. 1, pp. 53–54.

31. Ibid., vol. 1, p. 47.

32. Edmund Morgan, *American Slavery, American Freedom: The Ordeal of Colonial Virginia* (New York: W. W. Norton and Company, 1975): "The rise of liberty and equality in America had been accompanied by the rise of slavery. That two such seemingly contradictory developments were taking place simultaneously over a long period of time, from the seventeenth century to the nineteenth, is the central paradox of American history" (chap. 1, "Dreams of Liberation," 3–24, at 4).

33. Morgan's "central paradox" here finds echo in Louis Althusser's rereading of Marx's *Capital:* Part I: "From *Capital* to Marx's Philosophy," in Louis Althusser and Etienne Balibar, *Reading Capital*, trans. Ben Brewster (London: New Left Books/Verso, 1970), 13–69, qtd. at 26.

34. Slavoj Žižek, *The Sublime Object of Ideology* (London: Verso, 1989); Žižek's discussion of the "social symptom" reverberates here: "a certain fissure, an asymmetry, a certain 'pathological' imbalance which belies the universalism of the bourgeois 'rights and duties' " (21).

35. Ibid., 21.

36. Ibid.

37. Thomas S. Kuhn's seminal examination of the career of research paradigms in the scientific fields is also instructive elsewhere: *The Structure of Scientific Revolutions*, 2d ed. International Encyclopedia of Unified Science, vol. 2, no. 2 (Chicago: University of Chicago Press, 1970).

38. Hannah Arendt, *The Origins of Totalitarianism* (San Diego: Harcourt Brace and Company, 1973); see especially chap. 12, "Totalitarianism in Power," 389–459, at 440–41.

39. For the "subject of feminism," see Teresa de Lauretis, n. 24.

40. Nahum Chandler argues quite persuasively here that the construction of the subject position is carried out *"in relationship* and not before" ("Originary Displacement," *boundary 2*, vol. 27, no. 3 [Fall 2000]: 249–83; my emphasis, at 282).

41. Houston A. Baker Jr., "A Dream of American Form: Fictive Discourse, Black (W)holes, and a Blues Book Most Excellent," in *Blues, Ideology, and Afro-American Literature* (Chicago: University of Chicago Press, 1984), 113–99.

42. Herman Melville, *Moby-Dick* (1851; Indianapolis: The Bobbs-Merrill Company, Inc., 1964). Mapple's remarkable sermon, which Ishmael takes in, constitutes chapter 9 of the novel. Describing Jonah's guilt before his God, Father Mapple adopts and arranges this scene according to the exactitude of a geometrical relationship between things: "Screwed at its axis against the side, a swinging lamp slightly oscillates in Jonah's room . . . and the ship, heeling over towards the wharf with the weight of the last bales received, the lamp, flame and all, though in slight motion, still maintains a permanent obliquity with reference to the room; though in truth, infallibly straight itself, it but made obvious the false, lying levels among which it hung" (p. 75).

43. Alice Walker, "The Child Who Favored Daughter," in *In Love and Trouble* (New York: A Harvest/HBJ Book, 1967), 35–47.

44. An explanation of the primary and secondary processes could run for pages, since the latter make up one of the central veins of Freudian inquiry. One of the best sustained engagements with these processes, however, is provided in Juliet Mitchell's *Psychoanalysis and Feminism: Freud, Reich, Laing, and Women* (New York: Vintage Books, 1975); perhaps Freud's *Interpretation of Dreams* offers the most elaborate discussion of those differences as the cornerstone of the canon: *The Standard Edition of the Complete Psychological Works of Sigmund Freud*, trans. James Strachey (London: Hogarth Press, 1953), vols. 4 and 5.

45. Frederick Douglass, *Narrative of the Life of Frederick Douglass, An American Slave Written by Himself* (1845; New York: Signet Books, 1968), chap. 5, 43.

46. Robert Stepto, *From Behind the Veil: A Study of Afro-American Narrative* (Urbana: University of Illinois Press, 1979), 20.

47. Leroi Jones, *Blues People: Negro Music in White America* (New York: Morrow Quill Paperbacks, 1963).

48. Jean Toomer, "Brown River, Smile," in *American Negro Poetry*, ed. Arna Bontemps (New York: Hill and Wang, 1963), 34–37; this poem, in its Whitsmanesque scope, reaches toward a rhetoric of democratic inclusion, toward a multicultural American scene. Perhaps in that sense, it is a kind of latter-day epic verse; its ambitions certainly seem epical in their resemblance to the sweeping design of, say, Hart Crane and Carl Sandburg and later on, William Carlos Williams.

49. James Weldon Johnson, ed., *The Book of Negro Poetry* (1922; rev. ed. New York: Harcourt, Brace and World, 1959). This landmark book of black verse, which precedes Alain Locke's *New Negro* by a few years and anticipates a period of rather stunning growth and activity on the scene of the black arts, carries no examples of Toomer's poetry. Apparently, the writer did not think of his work as "Negro" or "black."

50. One of the key critics and culture workers in the field of Latin American and Caribbean studies, Roberto Marquez takes up the question of the hierarchy of pigmentation against the backdrop of Hispanic-African cultures across the New World complex: "Raza, Racismo, E Historia: 'Are All My Bones from There?'" I express here my deep gratitude to one of my first friends for sharing this keynote address with me, delivered at the Symposium on Afro-Latinos and the Issue of Race in the New Millennium, Brooklyn College, 21 October 2000, and at the Colloquium on the Americas, at the Federal University of Rio de Janeiro, Brazil, 9–10 November 2000.

51. The concept of "Our America," borrowed from José Martí's illustrious essay on the subject, has generated a number of recent studies that include: José David Saldívar, *The Dialectics of Our America: Genealogy, Cultural Critique, and Literary History* (Durham: Duke University Press, 1991); as if in ironic, certainly oppositional, response to culture work on "race," Walter Benn Michaels calls his different project *Our America: Nativism, Modernism, and Pluralism* (Durham: Duke University Press, 1995).

52. Paule Marshall, *Soul Clap Hands and Sing* (Washington, D.C.: Howard University Press, 1988).

53. Paule Marshall, *The Fisher King* (New York: Scribner's and Sons, 2000).

54. In Marjorie Pryse and Hortense J. Spillers, eds. *Conjuring*, 151–76.

55. Abdul JanMohamed and David Lloyd, eds., *The Nature and Context of Minority Discourse* (Oxford: Oxford University Press, 1990). This important work, initiated in an issue of *Cultural Critique*, gave a name to a situation that needed a name, a "strategy." Usually adopted to describe a demographic condition within Western community, "minority" traditionally referred to groups other than the dominant; one of the genuine achievements of the JanMohamed/Lloyd volume is that it retrieved this name—which many still think of as a pejorative—for the project of systematic culture critique. Now we may think of it as a position/positionality from which discourse about specific social formations might be generated.

56. Henry Louis Gates Jr., *The Signifying Monkey: A Theory of African-American Literary Criticism* (New York: Oxford University Press, 1988).

57. Mae G. Henderson, "Speaking in Tongues: Dialogics, Dialectics, and the Black Woman Writer's Literary Tradition," in *Changing Our Own Words: Essays on Criticism, Theory, and Writing by Black Women*, ed. Cheryl Wall (New Brunswick, N.J.: Rutgers University Press, 1991), 16–38.

58. David Lionel Smith, "Black Figures, Signs, Voices: Recent Scholarship on Afro-American Literature," *Review* 11, ed. James Hoge and James L. West (Charlottesville, Va., 1989), 1–36. This review of the Baker and Gates volumes should not be missed.

59. Harriet Jacobs [Linda Brent], *Incidents in the Life of a Slave Girl Written by Herself*, ed. Jean Fagan Yellin (Cambridge, Massachusetts: Harvard University Press, 1987).

60. Toni Morrison, *Beloved* (New York: Alfred Knopf, 1987).

61. Friedrich Wilhelm Nietzsche, *The Use and Abuse of History*, trans. Adrian Collins, with an introduction by Julius Kraft, The Library of Liberal Arts (Indianapolis: The Bobbs-Merrill Company, Inc., 1957); 12.

62. Frantz Fanon, *Black Skin, White Masks* (New York: Grove Press, 1967).

63. Jacques Lacan, "The Function of Language in Psychoanalysis," in *Speech and Language in Psychoanalysis*, trans. with notes and commentary by Anthony Wilden (Baltimore: The Johns Hopkins University Press, 1968), 83.

64. Harold Cruse, *The Crisis of the Negro Intellectual* (New York: William Morrow, 1967).

65. Paul Bové, "Editor's Note," "The University," *boundary 2*, vol. 27, no. 1 (Spring 2000):. 1–6; see also Bové's excellent study of the critical intellectual in *Intellectuals in Power: A Genealogy of Critical Humanism* (New York: Columbia University Press, 1986).

66. Allan Stoekl, *Agonies of the Intellectual: Commitment, Subjectivity, and the Performative in the 20th Century French Tradition* (Lincoln: The University of Nebraska Press, 1992), 2.

67. See note 7.

68. Paul Jefferson, "Working Notes on the Prehistory of Black Sociology: The Tuskegee Negro Conference," *Knowledge and Society: Studies in the Sociology of Culture Past and Present*, vol. 6, pp. 119–51.

69. Floyd Barbour, ed., *The Black Power Revolt*. See note 13.

70. Allan Stoekl, *Agonies of the Intellectual*, 1.

71. Stuart Hall, "Cultural Studies and Its Theoretical Legacies," in *Stuart Hall: Critical Dialogues in Cultural Studies*, ed. David Morley and Kuan-Hsing Chen (London: Routledge, 1996), 262–75, at 271.

72. Anthony Bourdain, *Kitchen Confidential: Adventures in the Culinary Underbelly* (New York: Bloomsbury, 2000).

73. Wolfgang Schievelbusch, *Tastes of Paradise: A Social History of Spices, Stimulants, and Intoxicants*, trans. David Jacobson (New York: Vintage Books, 1993); in the preface, Schievelbusch notes that *Genusmittel*, in reference to "articles of pleasure," also implies that "these substances are luxuries for sybaritic enjoyment, means for creating epicurean delights and, by extension, a state of sensual bliss" (xiii).

74. Ibid., 13.

75. Andrew Dalby, "The Land of Pepper," in *Dangerous Tastes: The Story of Spices* (Berkeley: The University of California Press, 2000), 83–107.

76. Reay Tannahill, *Food in History* (New York: Crown Publishers, Inc., 1988), 222–23; hereafter abbreviated *FH*.

77. Robin Blackburn, *The Making of New World Slavery: From Baroque to the Modern 1492–1800* (London: Verso, 1997), 4.

78. Ibid., 11.

79. Diane M. Spivey, "African Foods and Culinary Heritage in Mexico and Central

America," *The Peppers, Cracklings, and Knots of Wool Cookbook* (Albany: State University Press of New York, 1999), 87–135, at 103; hereafter abbreviated *PCKW.*

80. Ivan Van Sertima, *They Came Before Columbus* (New York: Random House, 1976).

81. Donna R. Gabaccia, *We Are What We Eat: Ethnic Food and the Making of Americans* (Cambridge, Massachusetts: Harvard University Press, 1998); hereafter abbreviated *WWE.*

82. Sidney W. Mintz, *Sweetness and Power: The Place of Sugar in Modern History* (New York: Penguin Books, 1985), 9; hereafter abbreviated *SP.*

83. Alan Davidson describes haggis as "relatively large parcels of offal mixed with cereal and enclosed in some suitable wrapping from an animal's entrails, usually the stomach" (*The Oxford Companion to Food* [Oxford: Oxford University Press, 1999], 365; hereafter abbreviated *OCF*).

84. John Gilmore, *Faces of the Caribbean* (London: Latin America Bureau, 2000), 163.

85. See Reay Tannahill, *Food in History,* for an examination of the culinary infrastructure—especially the gas and electric range—and processes of food production in the modern period: Chapter 20: "The Food Supply Revolution," 306–32. For a general overview of the genesis and development of American mass culture and markets from the late nineteenth century, see Richard Ohmann, *Selling Culture: Magazines, Markets and Class at the Turn of the Century.* Haymarket series, ed. Mike Davis and Michael Sprinker (London: Verso, 1996).

86. On the wonders of the pepperpot, John Gilmore calls it a symbol of the European's knowledge of indigenous food knowhow learned from the Amerindian; the main ingredients are hot peppers and cassareep, "the concentrated juice of the bitter cassava which acted as a natural meat tenderizer and preservative, as well as giving the contents of the pot a characteristic flavor" (*Faces of the Caribbean,* 163).

87. Tzvetan Todorov reports that to the shouts of the first Spaniards, gaining landfall on the peninsula of Yucatan, the Mayans answered "ma c'ubah than," or "We do not understand your words." "Faithful to the tradition of Columbus" [read: lack of interest in communicating with the Native Americans he encountered], the Spaniards on Yucatan decide that the Mayans are telling them the name of the province where they have landed (*The Conquest of America: The Question of the Other,* trans. Richard Howard [New York: Harper Colophon Books, 1984], 99, 33). The phenomenon of aural misprision must mark one of the substantial traces of contact between widely divergent cultures and subjects. We can take such misreading as a sign of creolité and often enough of violent social congress.

88. See Ira Berlin, "From Creole to African." See note 29.

89. William Pietz, "The Problem of the Fetish, II: The Origin of the Fetish," *Res* 13 (Spring 1987): 23–47, at 23.

90. Vertamae Smart-Grosvenor, *Vibration Cooking or the Travel Notes of a Geechee Girl* (New York: Ballantine Books, 1970), 94–95.

91. Jack Goody, "Structuralism, Materialism and the Horse," in *Food and Love: A Cultural History of East and West* (London: Verso, 1998), 148–160, at 155.

92. John Gilmore, *Faces of the Caribbean,* 162.

93. Jessica B. Harris, *The Welcome Table: African-American Heritage Cooking* (New York: Simon and Schuster, 1995), 105–7; hereafter abbreviated *WT.*

94. Devinia Sookia, *Caribbean Cooking* (Secaucus, N.J.: Chartwell Books, 1994), 52; hereafter abbreviated *CC.*

95. Ntozake Shange, *If I Can Cook You Know God Can,* foreword by Vertamae Grosvenor (Boston: Beacon Press, 1998), 11.

96. Jessica B. Harris, *The Africa Cookbook: Tastes of a Continent* (New York: Simon and Schuster, 1998); hereafter abbreviated *AC.*

97. Harris notes that the "grains of paradise," a relative of cardamon, is not frequently used today, although it appears in Nigerian, Beninoise, and Moroccan dishes, especially *ras alhanout* in the latter case; the entire coastal region from Guinea to Côte d'Ivoire was known as the grain coast "in honor of the grains of paradise that were produced there" (60).

98. Andrew Dalby, *Tastes of Paradise*, 83, 86.

99. Terry Eagleton, *The Idea of Culture* (Oxford: Blackwell Publishers, 2000).

100. Dorinda Hafner, *United Tastes of America* (New York: Ballantine Books, 1997), 19.

101. Danella Carter, *Down Home Wholesome* (New York: Dutton, 1995), 163.

102. Ntozake Shange, *If I Can Cook You Know God Can*, 73.

103. Wayne C. Robinson, *The African-American Travel Guide* (Edison, N.J.: Hunter Publishing, 1998); hereafter abbreviated *AATG*.

104. Danella Carter, *Down Home Wholesome*, 157ff.

105. Farah Jasmine Griffin, *'Who Set You Flowin'?': The African-American Migration Narrative* (New York: Oxford University Press, 1995).

106. J. M. Barrie, *Peter Pan* (1904; New York: Scribner's Sons, 1980).

Chapter One

"Ellison's Usable Past: Toward a Theory of Myth" was published in *Interpretations: Studies in Language and Literature* 60, no. 1 (1977). Rpt. in *Speaking for You: A Vision of Ralph Ellison*, ed. Kimberly Benston (Washington, D.C.: Howard University Press, 1987).

1. William Gass, "Imaginary Borges and His Books," in *Fiction and the Figures of Life* (New York: Vintage Books, 1972), 120–34.

2. José Ortega y Gasset, "The Dehumanization of Art," in *The Dehumanization of Art and Other Essays*, trans. Alex Brown with intro. Phillip Troutman (New York: Norton, 1972), 65–84, at 70.

3. Kenneth Burke, "On Words and the Word," in *The Rhetoric of Religion: Studies in Logology* (Berkeley and Los Angeles: University of California Press, 1970). Of the four categories to which words belong, Burke calls this class "logology," to which literary criticism, rhetoric, poetics, dialectics, grammar, etymology, and philology have been relegated.

4. Robert Bone, *The Negro Novel in America* (New Haven: Yale University Press, 1965), 198. Subsequent references to the acceptance speech come from this source, hereafter abbreviated *NNA*, page numbers parenthetically noted.

5. The concept of the "ancestral imperative" is fully explored by Albert Murray in a study of Afro-American cultural symbols, *South to a Very Old Place* (New York: McGraw Hill, 1971).

6. Northrop Frye, "Mythical Phase: Symbol as Archetype," *Anatomy of Criticism: Four Essays* (Princeton: Princeton University Press, 1973), 106. (All references to this source come from this edition, page numbers parenthetically noted.)

7. Roland Barthes, *Mythologies*, trans. Annette Lavers (New York: Hill & Wang, 1972). All references to this source come from this edition, page numbers parenthetically noted.

8. Ralph Ellison, *Invisible Man* (New York: Random House, 1952), 437; Ellison's emphasis. All references to this source come from this edition, hereafter abbreviated *IM*, page numbers parenthetically noted.

9. Ralph Ellison, "The Art of Fiction: An Interview," *Shadow and Act* (New York: Random House, 1964), 169–87.

10. Maud Bodkin, *Archetypal Patterns in Poetry: Psychological Studies of Imagination* (London: Oxford University Press, 1963), 1.

11. Erich Auerbach, "Figura," in *Scenes from the Drama of European Literature* (New York: Anchor-Doubleday, 1959).

12. Søren Kierkegaard, *The Concept of Irony: With Constant Reference to Socrates,* trans. with intro. Lee M. Capel (Bloomington: Indiana University Press, 1965), 245. All references to this source come from this edition, hereafter abbreviated *CI,* page numbers parenthetially noted.

Chapter Two

"Formalism Comes to Harlem" was published in *Black American Literary Forum* 16, no. 2 (Summer 1982): 58–64.

1. W. E. B. DuBois, *The Souls of Black Folk* (1903; rpt. New York: Fawcett, 1961), 16–17. This seminal essay on Afro-American life and thought, with its arguments developed through the metaphors and imagery of black spirituals, the "sorrow songs," is a brilliant demonstration for this generation of scholars of the law of mixed styles—lyrical and polemic.

2. Frantz Fanon, *Black Skin, White Masks* (New York: Grove Press, 1967). I have specific reference here to Fanon's portrayal of the "Negro of Antilles." This new man's mastery of the symbols of the dominant class worries Fanon's formulations to the point that mastery itself becomes, in Fanon's view, a condition of ambivalence.

3. Jesse B. Semple, as Hughes explains it, is a composite figure drawn from many. What they all have in common, however, is a complaint about their feet. "Simple" goes back to the thirties, and Hughes brings the development forward to the period of the Supreme Court's 1954 ruling on the desegregation of public schools and the early years of the King movement. Reflecting the common experiences of the man on the street, "Simple" shows a great deal of sophistication concerning the trickery of words and those who use them unthinkingly. That he realizes that their "polyvalence" often conceals the true political nature of speech suggests Hughes's unfailing commitment to the rights of the ordinary black man. Hughes's translations of the everyday rhythms of black speech as it occurs in urban life are among the chief interests of his poetry as well. His essay, "Who is Simple?" is the "Foreword" to *The Best of Simple* (New York: Hill & Wang, 1961), vii–viii.

4. The thrust of concern for both panels is briefly captured in remarks by Darwin Turner. I make use of them here: "Despite fifty years of criticism in Afro-American Literature, criteria for criticism have not been established. Consequently, some readers judge literature by Afro-Americans according to its moral value, and too many according to their response to the personalities of the Black authors." Quoted in "Black Critic," by Don L. Lee (Haki R. Madhubuti) in *Jump Bad: A New Chicago Anthology,* presented by Gwendolyn Brooks (Detroit: Broadside Press, 1971).

5. "The Little Man at Chehaw Station: The American Artist and His Audience," *The American Scholar* 47 (1978): 25–48. Rpt. in *The Collected Essays of Ralph Ellison,* Preface by Saul Bellow, Editor's Introduction by John F. Callahan (New York: The Modern Library, 1995), 489–520. I am grateful to the late Larry Neal for first calling my attention to this essay.

6. Houston A. Baker Jr., "On the Criticism of Black American Literature: One View of the Black Aesthetic," in *Reading Black: Criticism of African, Caribbean, and Black American Literature,* ed. Houston A. Baker Jr., Monograph no. 4 (Ithaca, N.Y.: Africana Studies Research Center, 1976), 48–58, at 56.

7. "Beyond Formalism," in *Beyond Formalism: Literary Essays, 1958–1970* (New Haven: Yale University Press, 1975), 57.

8. "The Song of Toni Morrison," *The New York Times Magazine,* 20 May 1979, 56. I am grateful to Ann Leventhal for sharing this long review with me.

9. During the 1977 Bread Loaf Writers' Conference, Toni Morrison read excerpts from her latest work and lectured on the importance of African and Afro-American myth and symbolism to the novelist. *Song of Solomon* might be considered an investiga-

tion into points of contact between history and myth/folklore. I believe that there is a significant philosophical, if not structural, link between her use of the motif of flying in the new work and an earlier novel, *Sula;* in a key passage, the narrator explains that the population of Medallion, Ohio—the scene of Sula's misdeeds and subsequent victimization—never learned what to do "with the wings, a way of holding the legs and most of all a full surrender to the downward flight" ([1973, rpt. New York: Bantam, 1975], 104). In further conversation concerning *Song of Solomon,* Morrison suggested that the crucial moral problem for Milkman was the lesson of surrender, restated in the novel in figurative terms. The African myth of flying seeks a level of displacement and transformation in the novel.

10. *Song of Solomon* (New York: Knopf, 1977), 337.

11. José Ortega y Gasset, "The Dehumanization of Art," in *The Dehumanization of Art and Other Essays,* trans. Alex Brown (New York: Norton, 1972), 65–84.

12. "Bop," in *The Best of Simple,* 117–18.

13. "Commitment: Toni Cade Bambara Speaks," an interview with Beverly Guy-Sheftall, in *Sturdy Black Bridges,* ed. Roseann P. Bell, Bettye J. Parker, and Beverly Guy-Sheftall (Garden City, N.Y.: Anchor/Doubleday, 1979), 230–49.

Chapter Three

"A Hateful Passion, A Lost Love: Three Women's Fiction" was published in *Feminist Studies* 9 (Summer 1983): 293–323, and is reprinted by permission of the publisher, Feminist Studies, Inc. Rpt. in *Feminist Issues in Literary Scholarship,* ed. Shari Benstock (Bloomington: Indiana University Press, 1987).

1. Mary Helen Washington, ed. *Black-Eyed Susans: Classic Stories by and about Black Women* (New York: Anchor Books, 1975), xxxii.

2. See "'Intimate Things in Place': A Conversation with Toni Morrison," in *Chant of Saints: A Gathering of Afro-American Literature, Art and Scholarship,* ed. Michael S. Harper and Robert B. Stepto (Urbana: University of Illinois Press, 1979), 213–30.

3. Harold Bloom's by-now familiar revision on the Freudian Oedipal myth in relation to the theme of literary successions and fortunes is not applicable to the community of black American women writers, even as a necessary critical fable. Bloom speaks for a powerful and an *assumed* patriarchal tradition, posited by a dominative culture, in the transmission of a political, as well as literary, wealth; in the case of black women's writing (and women's writing without modification) the myth of wealth as an aspect of literary "inheritance" tends to be sporadic. See Bloom, *The Anxiety of Influence: A Theory of Poetry* (New York: Oxford University Press, 1973), and *A Map of Misreading* (New York: Oxford University Press, 1975).

4. Toni Morrison, *Sula* (New York: Bantam Books, 1975), 105, emphases mine. All references to this source come from this edition; page numbers noted in the text.

5. bell hooks [Gloria Watkins], *Ain't I A Woman: Black Women and Feminism* (Boston: South End Press, 1981). The particular role of Daniel Moynihan's *Report* is put in perspective here with what hooks calls "the continuing devaluation of black womanhood," 51–87.

It is with crucial deliberation that the editors of a feminist collection of scholarship call their volume *All the Women Are White, All the Blacks Are Men, But Some of Us Are Brave* (Old Westbury, N.Y.: Feminist Press, 1982). Editors Gloria T. Hull, Patricia Bell Scott, and Barbara Smith realized that public discourse—certainly its most radical critical statements included—lapses into a cul-de-sac when it approaches this community of women and their writers.

6. After this essay appeared, the *Schomberg Library of Nineteenth-Century Black Women Writers,* ed. Henry Louis Gates Jr. (New York: Oxford University Press, 1988) was published. Interestingly, these thirty volumes not only altered our view of a woman's tradi-

tion of black writing, but could only have appeared as a result of the seventies renaissance of women writers, Morrison eminent among them. That this canon was *as if* "lost" to African-American culture work goes far to suggest the role and status of gender in determining a politics of dissemination.

7. Erich Auerbach, "Fortunata," in *Mimesis: The Representation of Reality in Western Literature,* trans. Willard Trask (New York: Doubleday Anchor Books, 1957). In tracing the shift in stylistic convention and emotional resonance from the literature of classical antiquity to the modern period, Auerbach provides a definition of the change which I would consider crucial to any consideration of the problematic of "realism," "the birth of a spiritual movement in the depths of the common people, from within the everyday occurrences of contemporary life, which thus assumes an importance it could never have assumed in antique literature" (37).

8. Margaret Walker, *How I Wrote Jubilee* (Chicago: Third World Press, 1972). *Jubilee* was submitted as Walker's Ph.D. dissertation to the University of Iowa Creative Writer's Workshop. The source material for the novel is based on the life story of the author's great-grandmother, told to her by her grandmother in the best tradition of oral his/herstory. The specificities of this transmitted tale from one generation to another was researched by Walker over nearly two decades, and it anticipates another odyssey of search in Alex Haley's *Roots,* a detailed study of an African-American genealogy. Walker later on actually brought suit against Haley for the supposed plagiarizing of a theme that Walker considers special, if not unique, to her own work.

9. Paul Tillich, A History of *Christian Thought: From Its Judaic and Hellenistic Origins to Existentialism,* ed. Carl E. Braaten (New York: Touchstone, 1972). My own use of Tillich's "theonomy" is vastly simplified and lifted out of the context that the theologian establishes between the idea and its relationship to the Christian European eras of sacred theology. But I hope that we might summarize a complicated idea here without seriously violating the original intent.

10. The student of Americana will immediately recognize that "God" is manifest cause to worldly effect within a certain configuration of cultural values; Perry Miller's classic work on early New England communities renders a detailed analysis of the view; see "God's Controversy with New England," in *The New England Mind: The Seventeenth Century* (Boston: Beacon Press, 1961), 463–92.

11. Margaret Walker, *Jubilee* (Boston: Houghton Mifflin, 1966), 3–4. All references to and quotations from this source come from this edition; page numbers noted in the text.

12. Emile Durkheim, *The Elementary Forms of Religious Life,* trans. Joseph Ward Swain (New York: Free Press, 1965).

13. Robert Hemenway, *Zora Neale Hurston: A Literary Biography* (Urbana: University of Illinois Press, 1977). This important work on Hurston's life provides an exhaustive account of the writer's various relationships. Hurston herself was a lover of males, but never sustained the liaisons quite long enough for us to see any pattern in this chapter of her biography except as short-lived serial monogamies.

14. Zora Neale Hurston, *Their Eyes Were Watching God* (New York: Fawcett Premier Books, 1969), 121. All references to and quotations from this source come from this edition; page numbers noted in the text.

15. Zora Neale Hurston, "What White Publishers Won't Print," in *I Love Myself When I am Laughing . . . and Then Again When I am Looking Mean and Impressive,* ed. Alice Walker (Old Westbury, N.Y.: Feminist Press, 1979), 169–73. In discussing why white American publishers of her time would only publish the "morbid" about the lives of black Americans, Hurston suggests what is both frightening and familiar to contemplate. "It is assumed that all non-Anglo-Saxons are uncomplicated sterotypes. Everybody knows all about them. They are lay figures mounted in the museum where

all may take them in at a glance. They are made of bent wires without insides at all. So how could anybody write a book about the non-existent?" (170). But we might also consider whether or not the obscene didn't happen—if black people themselves did not come to see their lives as a very fixed, monolithic, immobile quality of human experience? Alice Walker in the dedication to this volume points out that if Hurston were a "colorist," as some of her critics have claimed, then she "was not blind and . . . saw that black men (and black women) have been, and are, colorist to an embarrassing degree" (2).

16. W. E. B. DuBois, *The Souls of Black Folk: Essays and Sketches* (New York: Fawcett Publications, 1967). Dubois' classic reading of the African-American predicament is posed in the opening chapter of this seminal piece. He writes, "one ever feels his twoness,—an American, a Negro; two souls, two thoughts, two unreconciled strivings; two warring ideals in one dark body, whose dogged strength alone keeps it from being torn asunder" (17).

17. Zora Neale Hurston, "My Folks," *Dust Tracks on a Road*, intro. Larry Neal (Philadelphia: J. P. Lippincott, 1971), 12–32.

18. The term "ancestral imperative" does not originate in Albert Murray, but his use of it is dialectical and expansive. The best demonstration of Murray's argument is his *South to a Very Old Place* (New York: McGraw-Hill, 1971).

19. Virginia Woolf, *A Room of One's Own* (New York: Harcourt, Brace and World, 1957), 61–81.

20. Professor Nellie McKay reminded me that African-American women during the era of slavery often killed their offspring in order to forestall their enslavement. Read against McKay's interpretation, Eva Peace's "intervention" is historically grounded at the same time that it does not lose its awful aspects. The convergence of historical motivation, individual willfulness, and the mother's violation of blood rites would create one of the profounder bases of tension across the work.

21. See, for example, the description of these arrangements in Dorothy Dinnerstein, *The Mermaid and the Minotaur: Sexual Arrangements and the Human Malaise* (New York: Harper Colophon Books, 1976).

22. The terms are taken from Northrop Frye, "Historical Criticism: Theory of Modes," *Anatomy of Criticism: Four Essays* (Princeton: Princeton University Press, 1971), 36–67.

23. Kenneth Burke, "The Four Master Tropes," *A Grammar of Motives*, appendix D (New York: Prentice-Hall, 1945), 503–17. Burke's refinement of a notion of dialectics in art is significant both as an image and concept of radical revision. His "perspective of perspectives"—the principle of the "modified noun"—locates an ideal against which we might try to imagine the future of Afro-American letters and our meditation concerning them.

24. "Intimate Things in Place," in *Chant of Saints*, ed. Harper and Stepto, 215.

Chapter Four

"Gwendolyn the Terrible" was published in *Shakespeare's Sisters*, ed. Susan Gubar and Sandra Gilbert (Bloomington: Indiana University Press, 1979), 233–44. Rpt. in *A Life Distilled: Gwendolyn Brooks, Her Poetry and Fiction*, ed. Maria Mootry and Gary Smith (Urbana, Ill: University of Illinois Press, 1987).

1. Gwendolyn Brooks passed in December 2001.

2. Gwendolyn Brooks, *Report from Part One: An Autobiography*, intro. Don L. Lee and George Kent (Detroit: Broadside Press, 1972.), 183.

3. Gwendolyn Brooks, *The World of Gwendolyn Brooks* (New York: Harper and Row, 1971), 315. All quotations from Brooks's poetry come from this edition, hereafter designated *WGB*, with page numbers noted in the text.

4. Brooks's reading of "We Real Cool" is somewhat different from my own. *Report from Part One,* 185.

5. Ibid., 158.

6. Northrop Frye, "Emily Dickinson," *Fables of Identity: Studies in Poetic Mythology* (New York: Harcourt Brace Jovanovich, 1963), 202.

7. Kenneth Burke, "On Words and the Word," *The Rhetoric of Religion: Studies in Logology* (Berkeley and Los Angeles: University of California Press, 1970), 14ff.

Chapter Five

" 'An Order of Constancy': Notes on Brooks and the Feminine" originally appeared in *The Centennial Review* 29, no. 2 (Spring 1985), published by Michigan State University Press.

1. In discussing the social uses to which literature may be put, Kenneth Burke identifies the art work as a strategy for naming situations for which we need a name, "for selecting enemies and allies, for socializing losses, for warding off evil eye, for purification, propitiation, and desanctification, consolation and vengeance, admonition and exhortation, implicit commands or instructions of one sort or another" ("Literature as Equipment for Living," *The Philosophy of Literary Form: Studies in Symbolic Action* [Berkeley: University of California Press, 1973], 304). The "feminine" as an embattled idea offers a single example of a mandate for strategy.

2. Adrienne Rich, "Compulsory Heterosexuality and Lesbian Experience," in *Women: Sex and Sexuality,* ed. Catharine R. Stimpson and Ethel Spector Person (Chicago: University of Chicage Press, 1980), 62–92. Rich's article is addressed primarily to the experiences of lesbian women as they are refracted through the dominant cultural patterns of heterosexuality; implicit in her argument is the idea that the heterosexual synthesis represents an aspect of the oppression of women.

3. Nannerl O. Keohane, Michael Z. Rosaldo, and Barbara C. Gelpi, eds., *Feminist Theory: A Critique of Ideology* (Chicago: University of Chicago Press, 1982).

4. For an American audience, DuBois's concept of the "double consciousness," sketched in *Souls of Black Folk* in reference to African-American cultural apprenticeship, remains the preeminent concept and icon for explicating the dual and conflicting character of the misplaced person "at home" in an alien context. Originally published three years after the turn of the twentieth century, this collection of essays has gone through a number of editions (e.g., New York: Fawcett Publications, 1963).

5. Keohane et al., *Feminist Theory,* ix.

6. Julia Kristeva, "Stabat Mater," in *The Female Body in Western Culture: Contemporary Perspectives,* ed. Susan Rubin Suleiman (Cambridge, Mass.: Harvard University Press, 1986), 115.

7. Alice Jardine, *Gynesis* (Ithaca: Cornell University Press, 1985).

8. Suleiman, *The Female Body,* 2.

9. One of the poet's "prophetic books," *Vala, or the Four Zoas* offers a preromantic view of the "fall" of human society. "Tharmas," or the human body, represents one of four characters in Blake's work, suggesting the various ordering principles of the human personality. David V. Erdman, ed., *The Complete Poetry and Prose of William Blake* (Berkeley: University of California Press, 1982).

10. The excerpts from Schiller to which I refer are taken from his "Letters" in *Critical Theory Since Plato,* ed. Hazard Adams (New York: Harcourt Brace Jovanovich, 1972). The distinction that Schiller draws between sensuality (the sensations) and the reason in "Letter 13" and their mutual reconciliation and repose in the play-drive has been considerably influential on my own thinking about this topic.

Not wishing to confine "sensual/sensuality" to the "feminine" (since I believe that the "feminine" engenders its own forms and formalities), I have, nonetheless, been struck by the evidence of the "common sense" in speculating that the woman's intimate proximity to the theme of human continuance and nature offers prime material for her cultural apprenticeship in the feelings and notions of receptivity. While I would agree with Dorothy Dinnerstein's position in *The Mermaid and the Minotaur* (New York: Harper Colophon Books, 1976) that the responsibility of human nurture must be shared by female and male, I shudder to think what might happen if the contest for "equal time" leads to women's abandonment of the site of the child, as has men's renunciaton too often, and with absolutely fatal results.

11. Virginia Woolf, *A Room of One's Own* (New York: Harcourt, Brace and World, Inc., 1957). "Perhaps a mind that is purely masculine cannot create, any more than a mind that is purely feminine. . . . Coleridge . . . meant, perhaps, that the androgynous mind is resonant and porous; that it transmits emotion without impediment; that it is naturally creative, incandescent and undivided" (102).

12. Elaine Showalter, "Feminist Criticism in the Wilderness," in *Writing and Sexual Difference*, ed. Elizabeth Abel (Chicago: University of Chicago Press, 1982), 9–37. The displacing of male bias by various evidence of female experience generates the gynocritical enterprise that Showalter elaborates in this essay.

13. Gwendolyn Brooks, *The World of Gwendolyn Brooks* (New York: Harper and Row, 1971); hereafter designated *WGB*. During the seventies, Brooks switched her publishing allegiance from the New York house to Detroit's Broadsides Press and, later on, to the Third World Press of Chicago as testimony to her commitment to the political ideas of the Black Nationalist movement. *Riot, Family Pictures,* and *Beckonings* were all volumes published under the Broadsides imprint.

The World of Gwendolyn Brooks was reprinted in the late eighties as *Blacks* under the auspices of Chicago's Third World Press, 1987; the seventh printing of *Blacks* appeared in 1994. More recent critical work on Gwendolyn Brooks's life and career includes the following: Maria K. Mootry and Gary Smith, eds., *A Life Distilled: Gwendolyn Brooks, Her Poetry and Fiction* (Urbana: University of Illinois Press, 1987); D. H. Melhem, *Gwendolyn Brooks: Poetry and the Heroic Voice* (Lexington: The University Press of Kentucky, 1987); George E. Kent, *A Life of Gwendolyn Brooks* (Lexington: University Press of Kentucky, 1990); and Susan Marie Schweik, *A Gulf So Deeply Cut: American Women Poets and the Second World War* (Madison: University of Wisconsin Press, 1991).

14. Gwendolyn Brooks, *Primer for Blacks: Three Preachments* (Chicago: Brooks Press, 1981). "Black Love," first published in *Ebony* (August 1981), appeared in 1982 under the auspices of the Brooks Press.

15. Showalter, "Feminist Criticism in the Wilderness," 30–31. Showalter's discussion and diagram of the work of British anthropologist Edwin Ardener poses a useful paradigm for perceiving the relationship between dominant and muted groups. The Ardener diagram is also a circle, reminiscent of a penumbra, in which case the y circle (muted) falls within the dominant circle x. The crescent of the y circle outside the dominant boundary might be called "wild." Showalter proposes that we can think of the "wild zone" of women's culture spatially, experentially, or metaphysically. Spatially, it stands for an area that is literally no-man's land.

In this imagined relationship between Brooks's "feminine" and "masculine," both circles bear crescents on their periphery. These equally "wild zones" are mutually exclusive, by inference, and we have no idea what the characters who live there utter. My guess is that their "wild" is a spiralling crescent to Ardener/Showalter's so that we would have to draw a far more elaborate configuration in order to address the realities of "color."

16. Woolf's central consciousness in *To the Lighthouse,* Mrs. Ramsay, provides an astonishing association for what I later explore here as a "severe privacy."

17. Frank Kermode, *The Genesis of Secrecy: On the Interpretation of Narrative* (Cam-

bridge: Harvard University Press, 1979). From Dilthey, Kermode adopts this formulation to explain the hermeneutical relationship between interpreter and work. I borrow it here to argue that *Maud Martha* punctuated a significant period of work in the poet's career and that after it Brooks seemed to turn increasingly toward the meditative poetry that we associate with *In the Mecca* and *After the Mecca*.

18. All references to *Maud Martha* refer to *The World of Gwendolyn Brooks;* page numbers noted in the text.

19. For a full discussion of Brooks's projected sequel to *Maud Martha,* the reader should consult "Update on 'Part One': An Interview with Gwendolyn Brooks," by Gloria T. Hull and Posey Gallagher, *College Language Association Journal* 21, no.1 (September 1977): 26–28. Brooks points out that the extant *Maud Martha* "has much autobiography though I've twisted things" (27).

For a complete autobiographical sketch, Brooks's *Report from Part One* (Detroit: Broadsides Press, 1973) and *Report from Part Two* (Chicago: Third World Press, 1996) are indispensable. The poet explained to Claudia Tate in an interview that she was at work on a second volume of autobiography. See *Black Women Writers at Work* (New York: Continuum, 1983), 39–48.

20. Northrop Frye, in a description of Emily Dickinson's poetic diction, takes the term "aureate" from medieval poetics: "big soft bumbling abstract words that absorb images into categories and ideas" (*Fables of Identity: Studies in Poetic Mythology* [New York: Harcourt, Brace and World, 1963], 202).

21. From *The Bean Eaters, WGB,* 313.

22. A remarkable study of the human and social body as a site of *contracted* or *expanded* ground, Elaine Scarry's *Body in Pain* (New York, Oxford University Press, 1985) offers an unusual reading of aspects of Holy Scripture and excerpts from the Marxian canon as speculative inquiry into the principles of "making" and "unmaking."

23. Gwendolyn Brooks, "The Womanhood: The Children of the Poor," *Selected Poems* (New York: Harper and Row, 1963), 53.

24. "The Egg Boiler," *WGB,* 366.

25. Richard Ohmann's discussion of narrative-prose style as the writer's "epistemic choice" offers a richly suggestive study in the behavior of the rhetoric of fiction. Ohmann, "Prolegomena to the Analysis of Prose Style," in *Essays in Stylistic Analysis,* ed. Howard S. Babb (New York: Harcourt Brace Jovanovich, 1972), 35–50.

26. Burke, "Literature as Equipment for Living," *Philosophy of Literary Form,* 293–305.

27. The term is taken from W. J. Cash's classic study of the mythic operations of the "white male mind" of the South: *The Mind of the South* (New York: Alfred A. Knopf, 1941). It is not altogether surprising that "mind" in this case is confined to the male, while the female becomes the object of investigation.

28. I have placed these typically descriptive words for two American races in quotation marks here because the terms are often inadequate for what we actually mean. As we know, "color" in America is "washable" since "black" registers along a range of genetic traits, and so does "white," or the notion of "passing" would have no value whatsoever, either as an actual deed, or trophic possibility. "Race" should be an anachronism, or dead, but it is neither. We await, in the meantime, a vocabulary that gets us through the complexities that we sometime observe.

29. *WGB,* 14.

30. Mary Helen Washington's "Plain, Black, and Decently Wild: The Heroic Possibilities of *Maud Martha,*" in *The Voyage In: Fictions of Female Development,* ed. Elizabeth Abel, Marianne Hirsch, and Elizabeth Langland (Hanover, N.H.: University Press of New England, 1983), 270–86, gives good account of the coeval critical opinions of the work.

31. Virginia Woolf, *To the Lighthouse* (1927; New York: Harvest/HBJ Book, 1955), 95.

32. "Stetson! / You who were with me in the ships at Mylae! / That corpse you planted last year in your garden, / Has it begun to sprout? Will it bloom this year? / Or has the sudden frost disturbed its bed?" from T. S. Eliot, *The Waste Land: A Facsimile and Transcript of the Original Drafts including the Annotations of Ezra Pound,* ed. Valerie Eliot (New York: Harcourt Brace Jovanovich, 1971), 136.

33. In two separate studies, I examine these historical/terministic issues with an eye to locating African-American women's community in relationship to questions of feminist investigation: "Mama's Baby, Papa's Maybe: An American Grammar Book" and "Notes on an Alternative Model—Neither/Nor" (see this volume). These pieces anticipate a longer work that examines the rift between "the body" and "the flesh" as means of social and cultural production.

34. Burke, "Literature and Equipment for Living," in *Philosophy of Literary Form,* 300.

Chapter Six

"Interstices: A Small Drama of Words" was published in *Pleasure and Danger: Exploring Female Sexuality,* ed. Carol Vance (London: Routledge, Kegan Paul, 1984), 73–101.

1. Audre Lorde, *Chosen Poems: Old and New* (New York: W. W. Norton, 1982), 49–50.

2. Calvin C. Hernton, *Sex and Racism in America* (New York: Grove, 1965), 121–68. I should point out that while the following texts actually do not specifically address the question of black female sexuality, many of their concerns intersect the issues, especially the three essays under "Sexuality and Sexual Attitudes" in Gloria I. Joseph and Jill Lewis, eds., *Common Differences: Conflicts in Black and White Feminist Perspectives* (New York: Anchor, 1981), 151–274. Other points of reference touching sex-related questions in African-American women's community include Tracey A. Gardner's "Racism in Pornography and the Women's Movement" and Luisah Teish's "Quiet Subversion" in *Take Back the Night: Women on Pornography,* ed. Laura Lederer (New York: William Morrow, 1980); Lorraine Bethel and Barbara Smith, eds., *Conditions: Five: The Black Women's Issue,* New York: 1979.

3. Dennis Wepman, Ronald B. Newman, and Murray B. Binderman, eds., *The Life: The Lore and Folk Poetry of the Black Hustler,* in The Folklore and Folklife Series, gen. ed. Kenneth S. Goldstein (Philadelphia: University of Pennsylvania Press, 1976). *The Life* provides mostly a collection of narratives in the tradition. A more comprehensive and useful perspective on the meanings and transformations of this type of oral narrative is supplied by Roger D. Abrahams in his important study, *Deep Down in the Jungle: Negro Narrative Folklore from the Streets of Philadelphia* (Hatboro, Penn.: Folklore Associates, 1964).

4. Ibid., 111–23. Different versions of "The Titanic" are given by Abrahams in demonstration of the "oikotype," the local variations that an oral narrative assumes when it reaches a specific area (10ff). The expurgated version of the narrative, reprinted in Langston Hughes and Arna Bontemps, eds., *The Book of Negro Folklore* (New York: Dodd, Mead, 1958), 366–67, might be advantageously compared with Abraham's.

5. Hernton, *Sex and Racism in America,* 166.

6. Two recent additions to the women's studies library inquire into black women's economic exploitation and its political and historical significance: Angela Y. Davis, *Women, Race, and Class* (New York: Random House, 1981); bell hooks, *Ain't I A Woman: Black Women and Feminism* (Boston: South End Press, 1981).

7. Winthrop Jordan's *White Over Black: American Attitudes Toward the Negro, 1550–1812* (Baltimore: Penguin, 1969) is virtually unique in its systematic exploration of the concept of race in its European symbolic and geopolitical origins. An analysis of cultural vestibularity in its symbolic contours is the aim of Henry Louis Gates's "Binary Oppositions in chap. 1 of *Narrative of the Life of Frederick Douglass, An American Slave*

Written by Himself," in *Afro-American Literature: The Reconstruction of Instruction,* ed. Dexter Fisher and Robert B. Stepto (New York: Modern Language Association, 1979), 212–32.

8. Alice Walker, "One Child of One's Own: A Meaningful Digression Within the Work(s)—An Excerpt," in *All the Women Are White, All the Blacks Are Men, But Some of Us Are Brave: Black Women's Studies,* ed. Gloria T. Hull, Patricia Bell Scott, and Barbara Smith (Old Westbury, New York: Feminist Press, 1981), 42–43.

9. For a recent account of this famous story from the annals of the historic women's movement, see chap. 5 of hooks's *Ain't I A Women,* 159–160. More recent work on the life and career of Sojourner Truth includes: the annotated edition of *The Narrative of Sojourner Truth,* ed. with an intro. by Margaret Washington (New York: Vintage Books, 1993); Erlene Stetson and Linda David, *Glorying in Tribulation: The Lifework of Sojourner Truth* (East Lansing: Michigan State University Press, 1994); Nell Irvin Painter, *Sojourner Truth: A Life, a Symbol* (New York: W. W. Norton, 1996).

10. Freud's notes on the "frequency with which sexual repression makes use of transpositions from a lower to an upper part of the body" were a surprising find in connection with this point. He specifically names the replacement of the genitals by the face as a dynamic "in the symbolism of unconscious thinking" ("The Dream Work," *The Interpretation of Dreams,* trans. James Strachey [New York: Avon, 1966], 422). I do not claim to know the artist's mind and might guess that she was thinking of a Freudian reading of her subjects, giving her viewers the benefit of the doubt, or that they knew their Freud. But beyond this exhibit, we might wonder, if American culture, generally speaking, is involved in an intricate calculus of sexual repressions that both identifies black personality with "wild" sex and at the same time suppresses the name in reference to her.

11. Edward Said, *Orientalism* (New York: Vintage, 1979), 28. Said adopts the term from Raymond Williams, *Culture and Society, 1780–1950* (London: Chatto & Windus, 1958), 376.

12. Alice Walker in *Take Back the Night,* ed. Lederer, 100.

13. Shulamith Firestone, *The Dialectic of Sex: The Case for Feminist Revolution,* rev. ed. (New York: Bantam, 1971), 105–26.

14. Adrienne Rich, *On Lies, Secrets and Silence: Selected Prose, 1966–1978* (New York: W. W. Norton, 1979), 275–310; Catharine A. MacKinnon, "Feminism, Marxism, Method and the State," in *Feminist Theory: A Critique of Ideology,* ed. Nannerl O. Keohane, Michael Z. Rosaldo, and Barbara C. Gelpi (Chicago: University of Chicago Press, 1982), 1–30.

15. Kate Millet, *Sexual Politics* (New York: Ballantine, 1970); Susan Brownmiller, *Against Our Will: Men, Women and Rape* (New York: Bantam, 1975).

16. Catharine R. Stimpson and Ethel Spector Person, eds., *Women: Sex, and Sexuality* (Chicago: University of Chicago Press, 1980).

17. Dorothy Dinnerstein, *The Mermaid and the Minotaur: Sexual Arrangements and Human Malaise* (New York: Harper Colophon, 1976); Nancy Chodorow, *The Reproduction of Mothering: Psychoanalysis and the Sociology of Gender* (Berkeley: University of California Press, 1978); Mary Daly, *Gyn/Ecology: The Metaethics of Radical Feminism* (Boston: Beacon Press, 1987). Audre Lorde specifically addresses those aspects of African women's culture that Lorde believes Daly has either missed altogether or misinterpreted; see Lorde, "Open Letter to Mary Daly," in *This Bridge Called My Back: Writings by Radical Women of Color,* ed. Cherrie Moraga and Gloria Anzaldúa (Watertown, Mass.: Persephone, 1981), 94–98.

18. The various positions within the gynocritical spectrum of procedure—women critics and writers at the center of the critical enterprise with women's culture as their theme—is the subject of a striking essay by Elaine Showalter, "Feminist Criticism in the

Wilderness," in *Writing and Sexual Difference,* ed. Elizabeth Abel (Chicago: University of Chicago Press, 1982), 9–37. (See above in this volume, "An Order of Constancy.") It is noteworthy that this interesting volume of essays on points of intersection between writing culture and female gender does not have a single item in it on black American women's writings. The absence is stunning to my mind in that it demonstrates precisely the sort of symbolic lapse of nerve I am identifying in the associating women of color with the intellectual and artistic project that relates to sexuality.

19. A café (where smoking is permitted!). The resonance of the line in the text is borrowed directly from T. S. Eliot's "Gerontion": "My house is a decayed house, / And the Jew squats on the window sill, the owner, / Spawned in some estaminet of Antwerp" (*The Complete Poems and Plays, 1909–1950* [New York: Harcourt Brace, 1971], 21). I intrude the image to make plain the bad taste that Firestone's emblem-making leaves in my mouth as certain aspects of Eliot's poem might do for certain other American communities; I'd assume quite a lot in thinking so and would ignore, for the sake of the point, the poem's aesthetic gestures. Doing so wrenches meaning, but the poet occasionally and the scholar more often compel a sort of resistance of reading in this case.

20. Firestone, *The Dialectic of Sex,* 119–20.

21. Ibid., 118.

22. The term is taken from W. J. Cash's *Mind of the South* (New York: Vintage, 1941).

23. The condition of the "double-consciousness" in specific reference to black Americans is first explored by W. E. B. DuBois in this early twentieth-century classic, "Of Our Spiritual Strivings," *The Souls of Black Folk: Essays and Sketches* (New York: Fawcett Premier, 1961), 15–22.

24. Michel Foucault, *The History of Sexuality, Vol. I: An Introduction,* trans. Robert Hurley (New York: Pantheon, 1978), 1–15.

25. Ibid., 4–5.

26. Kenneth Burke, *A Grammar of Motives* (New York: Prentice-Hall, 1952), 3–15. This important study by a distinguished American critic is crucial to many of the ideas in this article. Though related to the literature of the stage, Burke's notion of the "five key terms of dramatism" is applicable to any human situation that involves a structure of motives to be read and interpreted. The *agent* is the actor or performer; the *agency* is the instrument by which the act is performed; the *act* names what has occurred; the *scene* is the background of the act; and the *purpose* is the goal of the act.

27. Michele Russell, "Slave Codes and Liner Notes," in *All the Women Are White, All the Blacks Are Men, But Some of Us are Brave,* ed. Hull, Scott, and Smith, 129–40.

28. Ibid., 133.

29. Kenneth Burke, "On Words and the Word," *The Rhetoric of Religion: Studies in Logology* (Berkeley: University of California Press, 1970), 14–15. Burke proposes that of the four realms to which words may refer, the third realm—words about words—"is the realm of dictionaries, grammar, etymology, philology, literary criticism, rhetoric, poetics, dialectics."

30. Michel Foucault, *The Archaeology of Knowledge and the Discourse of Language,* trans. A. M. Sheridan Smith (New York: Harper Colophon, 1972). Foucault's discussion of fields of discourse, or the "enunciative field," is very useful in explaining continuities and discontinuities among concepts that share a common familial identity; concepts within an "enunciative field" may be related in three ways: (1) by way of a "field of presence," (2) a "field of concomitance," and (3) a "field of memory" (57–58ff.).

31. In an address at Wellesley College a few years ago, Toni Morrison provided a moving testimony to the textual silence concerning black American women. She could find on the library shelves books about virtually every community of women in the world, but precious few about her own. One of Morrison's ambitions as a writer, she said, is to supply some of the missing narrative.

32. Elaine Marks and Isabelle de Courtivron, eds., "Introduction I: Discourses of Anti-Feminism," *New French Feminisms: An Anthology* (New York: Schocken, 1981).

33. John Langston Gwaltney, *Drylongso: A Self-Portrait of Black America* (New York: Vintage, 1981), 142–76.

34. An example of reminiscence narratives is Julius Lester's *To Be A Slave* (New York: Dell, 1968); Studs Terkel, *Working* (New York: Avon, 1972).

35. Catharine A. MacKinnon, *Sexual Harassment of Working Women: A Case of Sex Discrimination*, with foreword by Thomas I. Emerson (New Haven: Yale University Press, 1979), 1.

36. Gwaltney, *Drylongso*, 146–47.

Chapter Seven

"Changing the Letter: The Yokes, the Jokes of Discourse, or, Mrs. Stowe, Mr. Reed" was published in *Slavery and the Literary Imagination: Selected Papers from the English Institute, 1987*, ed. Deborah McDowell and Arnold Rampersad (Baltimore: The Johns Hopkins University Press, 1988), 25–61. © 1988 [Copyright Holder]. Reprinted with permission of The Johns Hopkins University Press.

1. Harriet Beecher Stowe, *Uncle Tom's Cabin, with an Afterword by John William Ward* (New York: New American Library, 1966), 179–80. All direct quotations from the novel come from this source, hereafter cited parenthetically in the text.

2. Harriet Beecher Stowe, *The Key to Uncle Tom's Cabin, Presenting the Original Facts and Documents upon Which the Story is Founded Together with Corroborative Statements Verifying the Truth of the Work.* (London: Clark, Beeton, and Co., Foreign Booksellers, n.d), 45.

3. Nancy C. M. Hartsock, *Money, Sex, and Power: Toward a Feminist Historical Materialism* (New York: Longmans, 1983), 192.

4. Kenneth Burke, *A Grammar of Motives* (New York, Prentice-Hall, 1952), 122.

5. Gillian Brown, "Getting in the Kitchen with Dinah: Domestic Politics in *Uncle Tom's Cabin*," *American Quarterly* 36, no. 4 (1984): 505.

6. My notion of an intertextual eventuality between these texts is heavily influenced by Michel Foucault's *Archaeology of Knowledge and the Discourse on Language*, trans. A. M. Sheridan Smith (New York: Harper Colophon Books, 1972), 193.

7. Richard Yarborough, "Strategies of Black Characterization in *Uncle Tom's Cabin* and the Early Afro-American Novel," in *New Essays on Uncle Tom's Cabin*, ed. Eric J. Sundquist Jr. (New York: Cambridge University Press, 1986), 45–85, at 68.

8. George Eliot, Review of *"Dred: A Tale of the Great Dismal Swamp,"* in *Critical Essays on Harriet Beecher Stowe*, ed. Elizabeth Ammons (Boston: G. K. Hall and Co, 1980), 43.

9. Yarborough, "Strategies of Black Characterization," 63.

10. Foucault, *Archaeology of Knowledge*, 58.

11. Ishmael Reed, *Flight to Canada* (New York: Avon books, 1976), 29. All direct quotations from the novel come from this source, hereafter cited parenthetically in the text.

12. Umberto Eco, *A Theory of Semiotics* (Bloomington: Indiana University Press, 1979), 215.

13. Ibid., 81.

14. Stephen Greenblatt's impressive formulation of "improvisational skills" concerning Shakespeare's Iago richly informs my own thinking about intertextual possibilities between *Uncle Tom's Cabin* and *Flight to Canada*: "I shall call that mode *improvisation*, by which I mean the ability both to capitalize on the unforeseen and to transform given materials into one's own scenario" (*Renaissance Self-Fashioning: From More to Shakespeare* [Chicago: University of Chicago Press, 1980], 227).

15. Eco, *A Theory of Semiotics*, 66.

16. I refer here not very precisely to René Girard's formulation of the triangle of de-

sire in *Deceit, Desire, and the Novel: Self and Other in Literary Structure*, trans. Yvonne Freccero (Baltimore: Johns Hopkins University Press, 1965), 1–52. There is, of course, no obvious "rivalry" for Eva's affections between Uncle Tom and Augustine St. Clare, but imagining for the moment that these central figures embody wider psychocultural functions, we might say that "Little Eva" is made to represent, indeed, the gynophobic object of desire, dangerously poised between the "black" male and his freedom, essentially "held in fief" by the "white" male.

17. Ann Douglass, *The Feminization of American Culture* (New York: Alfred A. Knopf, 1977), 3–13.

18. Jane Tompkins, *Sensational Designs* (New York: Oxford University Press, 1985), 124–25. One of the most recent definitive texts on American women writers, Tompkins's work offers a brilliant paradigm of conceptualization on the issues. Although I accept her basic premises, my most significant reservations about this work have to do with the muting of "race" in this cultural analysis.

19. Elizabeth Ammons, "Heroines in *Uncle Tom's Cabin*," *American Literature* 49 (May 1977): 161–79.

20. James Baldwin, *Notes of a Native Son* (New York: Bantam Books, 1972), 13.

21. Even though one could draw on a number of sermons from black preaching tradition that subvert the discursive economies of sacrifice, I refer specifically to the Washington, D.C., pulpit of Francis Grimké, whose sermons, speeches, and letters have been edited by Carter G. Woodson: *Works of Francis James Grimké*, 4 vols. (Washington, D.C.: Associated Publishers, 1942).

22. Kenneth Burke, *The Rhetoric of Religion: Studies in Logology* (Berkeley and Los Angeles: University of California Press, 1970), 14–15.

23. Brown, "Getting in the Kitchen With Dinah," 518.

24. Sundquist, Introduction to *New Essays on Uncle Tom's Cabin*, 110.

25. Catherine Beecher, *Treatise on Domestic Economy* (1842; rpt., New York: Schocken Books, 1977).

26. Karen Halttunen, "Gothic Imagination and Social Reform: The Haunted Houses of Lyman Beecher, Henry Ward Beecher, and Harriet Beecher Stowe," *New Essays on Uncle Tom's Cabin*, 110.

27. Ammons, "Heroines in *Uncle Tom's Cabin*," 164.

28. Sundquist, Introduction to *New Essays on Uncle Tom's Cabin*, 35.

29. Ibid.

30. Tompkins, *Sensational Designs*, 137.

31. Halttunen, "Gothic Imagination," 115.

32. René Girard, *Violence and the Sacred*, trans. Patrick Gregory (Baltimore: Johns Hopkins University Press, 1977), 257.

33. Leslie Fiedler, "Harriet Beecher Stowe's Novel of Sentimental Protest," in *Critical Essays on Harriet Beecher Stowe*, 114.

34. Ibid., 115. Fiedler provides a more recent assessment of Stowe's work in "The Many Mothers of *Uncle Tom's Cabin*," in his *What was Literature? Class, Culture and Mass Society* (New York: Simon and Schuster, 1982).

35. The dynamics of the mechanism of violent reprisal are formulated in Girard's *Violence and the Sacred*.

36. This narrative is reported in Albert C. Baugh's *History of the English Language*, 2d ed. (New York: Appleton-Century-Crofts, 1957), 94.

37. I borrow this formulation from Zora Neale Hurston's celebrated ethnograpic study, *Mules and Men: Negro Folktales and Voodoo Practices in the South* (New York: Harper and Row, 1970).

38. Michel Foucault, *The Order of Things: An Archaeology of the Human Sciences* (New York: Vintage Books, 1973), xv.

39. Joe Weixlmann provides interesting speculation on the origins of Raven Quick-skill's name from the raven myth of the Tlingit community of Native Americans in "Ish-mael Reed's Raven," *The Review of Contemporary Fiction* 4, no. 2 (Summer 1984): 205.

40. Jerry H. Bryant, "Old Gods and New Demons: Ishmael Reed and His Fiction," *Review of Contemporay Fiction* 4, no. 2 (Summer 1984): 196.

41. James R. Lindroth, "From Krazy Kat to Hoodoo: Aesthetic Discourse in the Fic-tion of Ishmael Reed," *Review of Contemporary Fiction* 4, no. 2 (Summer 1984): 227.

42. Eco, *A Theory of Semiotics*, 204–5.

43. The destructive effects of the mythologizing of Afro-American personality are powerfully articulated in Deborah E. McDowell's "Boundaries: Or Distant Relations and Close Kin," proceedings from the Symposium in Afro-American Literature, convened by Houston Baker at the American College, Bryn Mawr, Pa., April 1987.

44. Eco, *A Theory of Semiotics*, 204.

45. Ibid., 205.

46. Quoted in Eco, *Theory of Semiotics*, 205.

47. Peter Nazareth, "Heading Them Off at the Pass: The Fiction of Ishmael Reed," *Review of Contemporary Fiction* 4, no. 2 (Summer 1984): 219.

48. Ibid.

49. W. E. B. DuBois, *Black Reconstruction in America, 1860–1880* (New York: Merid-ian Books, 1968), 102–3.

50. Nazareth, "Heading Them Off at the Pass," 211.

51. Oswald Ducrot and Tzvetan Todorov, *Encyclopedic Dictionary of the Sciences of Language*, trans. Catherine Porter (Baltimore: Johns Hopkins University Press, 1979), 222.

52. Yarborough, "Strategies of Black Characterization," 58.

53. The title of my essay offers a riff, of course, on Ralph Ellison's celebrated piece, "Change and Joke and Slip the Yoke," *Shadow and Act* (New York: Signet Books, 1966), 61–74.

Chapter Eight

"Mama's Baby, Papa's Maybe: An American Grammar Book" was published in *Diacritics* 17, no. 2 (Summer 1987). Reprinted with permission of The Johns Hopkins University Press. Rpt. in *Within the Circle: An Anthology of African American Literary Criticism from the Harlem Renaissance to the Present*, ed. Angelyn Mitchell (Durham: Duke University Press, 1994), reprinted by permission of the publisher; and in *African American Literary Theory: A Reader*, ed. Winston Napier (New York: New York University Press, 2000).

1. Daniel P. Moynihan, *The Negro Family: The Case for National Action* (Washington, D.C.: U.S. Department of Labor, 1965). Reprinted in *The Moynihan Report and the Politics of Controversy: A Transactional Social Science and Public Policy Report*, ed. Lee Rainwater and William L. Yancey (Cambridge: MIT Press, 1967), 47–94, at 75. All citations are from the latter edition. Hereafter, "The Moynihan Report."

2. As a result of faulty memory, I misinterpreted a crucial detail from Giambattista Vico's *New Science (Scienza nuova)*: according to Roman law, children born of prostitutes were called "monsters" because they exhibited "the nature of men together with the bestial characteristic of having been born of vagabond or uncertain unions." Because the newborn in this case were considered "monstrous," or born without the "benefit of solemn nuptials," the law of the Twelve Tables commanded that they "be thrown into the Tiber" (*The New Science*, trans. from the 3d ed. by Thomas Goddard and Max Harold Fisch [Ithaca, N.Y.: Cornell University Press], Book II, "Poetic Wisdom," section 2, "Po-etic Logic," chap. 2, "Corollaries concerning Poetic Tropes, Monsters and Metamor-phoses," ¶410, p. 118). An abridged version of the 1948 *New Science* was brought out in 1970 by Cornell University Press. In the shortened version ¶410 appears on p. 90.

This prophetic world history, first published in 1744, inquires into the rise of human institutions from the "age of gods," to the "age of heroes," to the "age of men" (1948, 18). In wrestling with this fascinating work, the reader must be prepared for a structure that is massive and, to the contemporary eye, in massive disarray, or, as Bergin and Fisch suggest in the preface to the 1948 translation, Vico "is more poet than philosopher . . . even more prophet than poet." The translators go on to point out that Vico's language is obscure, incoherent, and magnificent because it is "the language of one who holds a vision" (preface, ix) and the vision pursues its thematics in an *order* that eludes readerly expectations; for an investigator interested in Vico's conceptualizations of the family, of wives, and children, the evidence is dispersed over four books and numbered corollaries that seem to fall helter skelter in his poetic account of the rise of man, institutional growth and development, and the instauration of what the modern critic might call systems of signs, primarily rhetorical tropes. The thematic logic of *The New Science* defies one's own readerly intuitions; for example, the infants hurled into the Tiber at ¶410 might have had a different fate had they been born among the Spartans; lacking in "civil beauty" because they came through the lineage of peasants or the plebians (who were denied the connubial contract), or through unmarried noble women, these newborn were considered "ugly and deformed" and were cast down by the Spartans "from Mount Taygetus" (Book II, "Poetic Wisdom," section 4, "Poetic Economy," chap. 2, "The Families with Their *Famuli,* which Preceded the Cities, and without which the Cities Could Not Have Been Born," ¶566, p. 182).

In Vico's history, the institution of matrimony is one of the foundation stones of human order and in fact enables it through the spectrum of historical continuity.

3. Roland Barthes, "Myth Today," *Mythologies,* trans. Annette Lavers (New York: Hill and Wang, 1972), 109–59, esp. 122–23.

4. William Goodell, *The American Slave Code in Theory and Practice Shown By Its Statutes, Judicial Decisions, and Illustrative Facts,* 3d ed. (New York: American and Foreign AntiSlavery Society, 1853), 221.

5. Elaine Scarry, *The Body in Pain: The Making and Unmaking of the World* (New York: Oxford University Press, 1985), 27–59.

6. See Susan Rubin Suleiman, ed., *The Female Body in Western Culture* (Cambridge: Harvard University Press, 1986).

7. Angela Y. Davis, *Women, Race, and Class* (New York: Random House, 1981), 9.

8. William Faulkner, *The Mansion* (New York: Vintage Books, 1965), 227.

9. Olaudah Equiano, *The Life of Olaudah Equiano, or Gustavus Vassa, The African, Written by Himself,* in *Great Slave Narratives,* introduced and selected by Arna Bontemps (Boston: Beacon Press, 1969), 1–192.

10. Tzvetan Todorov, *The Conquest of America: The Question of the Other,* trans. Richard Howard (New York: Harper Colophon Books, 1984), 61.

11. Elizabeth Donnan, *Documents Illustrative of the History of the Slave Trade to America.* 4 vols. (Washington, D.C.: The Carnegie Institution of Washington, 1932).

12. Todorov, *Conquest of America,* 3.

13. Gomes Eannes De Azurara, *The Chronicle of the Discovery and Conquest of Guinea, 1441–1448,* trans. C. Raymond Beazley and Edgar Prestage (London: Hakluyt Society, 1896, 1897), in Elizabeth Donnan, *Documents Illustrative of the History of the Slave Trade to America,* 1:18–41.

14. Elizabeth Donnan, *Documents Illustrative of the History of the Slave Trade to America,* 1:42.

15. Ibid., 2:592, n.

16. Herbert S. Klein, "African Women in the Atlantic Slave Trade," in *Women and Slavery in Africa,* ed. Claire C. Robertson and Martin A. Klein (Madison: University of Wisconsin Press, 1983), 29–39, at 29.

17. See Deborah Grey White, *Ar'n't I A Woman? Female Slaves in the Plantation South* (New York: Norton, 1985), 63–64.

18. bell hooks, *Ain't I a Woman: Black Women and Feminism* (Boston: South End Press, 1981), 15–49.

19. Claire C. Robertson and Martin A. Klein, "Women's Importance in African Slave Systems," in *Women and Slavery in Africa*, 3–28.

20. Claude Meillassoux, "Female Slavery," in *Women and Slavery in Africa*, 49–67.

21. See John Blassingame, *The Slave Community: Plantation Life in the Antebellum South* (New York: Oxford University Press, 1972), 79ff.

22. E. Franklin Frazier, *The Negro Family in the United States*, rev. with foreword by Nathan Glazer (Chicago: The University of Chicago Press, 1966).

23. Davis, *Women, Race, and Class*, 14.

24. Eugene Genovese, *Roll, Jordan, Roll: The World the Slaves Made* (New York: Pantheon Books, 1974), 70–75.

25. Frederick Douglass, *Narrative of the Life of Frederick Douglass An American Slave, Written by Himself* (rpt., New York: Signet Books, 1968), 22.

26. Malcolm El-Hajj Malik El-Shabazz, *Autobiography of Malcolm X*, with Alex Haley, intro. M. S. Handler (New York: Grove Press, 1966), 21ff.

27. Linda Brent, *Incidents in the Life of a Slave Girl*, ed. L. Maria Child, intro. Walter Teller (rpt., New York: Harvest/HBJ Book, 1973), 29–35.

28. Valerie Smith, "Loopholes of Retreat: Architecture and Ideology in Harriet Jacobs's *Incidents in the Life of a Slave Girl*." Paper presented at the 1985 American Studies Association Meeting, San Diego. Cited in Henry Louis Gates Jr., "What's Love Got to Do With It?" *New Literary History* 18, no. 2 (Winter 1987): 360.

29. A. Leon Higginbotham, "The Black Experience in Colonial America—Virginia," in *In the Matter of Color: Race and the American Legal Process: The Colonial Period* (New York: Oxford University Press, 1978), 19–60, at 50.

30. Margaret Strobel, "Slavery and Reproductive Labor in Mombasa," in *Women and Slavery in Africa*, ed. Robertson and Klein, 111–30, at 121.

Chapter Nine

"'The Permanent Obliquity of the In(pha)llibly Straight': In the Time of the Daughters and Fathers" was published in *Daughters and Fathers*, ed. Lynda K. Boose and Betty Sue Flowers (Baltimore: The Johns Hopkins University Press, 1988), 157–81. Rpt. in *Changing Our Own Words*, ed. Cheryl Wall (New Brunswick: Rutgers University Press, 1990).

1. E. Franklin Frazier, *The Negro Family in the United States*, with a foreword by Nathan Glazer (Chicago: University of Chicago Press, 1966); Lee Rainwater and William L. Yancey, eds., *The Moynihan Report and the Politics of Controversy: A Transaction Social Science and Public Policy Report* (Cambridge: MIT Press, 1967), 47–94.

2. Maya Angelou, *I Know Why the Caged Bird Sings* (New York: Bantam Books, 1970); James Baldwin, *Just Above My Head* (New York: Dell Books, 1979); Gayl Jones, *Corregidora* (New York: Random House, 1975); Toni Morrison, *The Bluest Eye* (New York: Washington Square Press/Pocket Books, 1970); Ralph Ellison, *Invisible Man* (New York: Random House, 1952); Alice Walker, "The Child Who Favored Daughter," in *Love and Trouble* (New York: Harcourt Brace Jovanovich, 1982). Hereafter, all citations from these works appear in the text.

3. François Roustang, "Uncertainty," *October* 28 (Spring 1984): 91–105.

4. Angela Y. Davis, *Women, Race, and Class* (New York: Random House, 1981); William Goodell, *The American Slave Code in Theory and Practice, etc.* (New York: American and Foreign Anti-Slavery Society, 1853; rpt, New York: Arno Press, 1969).

5. Robert Manson Myers, ed., *The Children of Pride: A True Story of Georgia and the Civil War* (New Haven: Yale University Press, 1972). This rich collection of letters, writ-

ten between friends and family of the Rev. Dr. Charles Colcock Jones, from 1854 to 1860, provides sporadic information on African-American women in slavery in the United States.

6. W. E. B. DuBois, *The Souls of Black Folk: Essays and Sketches* (1903; rpt., New York: Fawcett Books, 1961).

7. Claude Lévi-Strauss, *The Elementary Structures of Kinship,* ed. Rodney Needham, rev. ed. and trans. James Harle Bell and John Richard von Sturmer (Boston: Beacon Press, 1969); W. Arens, *The Original Sin: Incest and Its Meaning* (New York: Oxford University Press, 1986). Though coming to my attention too late to inform this writing, Arens's text promises to correct our notions concerning the historic origins of incest.

8. Jacques Lacan, *Écrits: A Selection,* trans. Alan Sheridan (New York: W. W. Norton, 1982); Terry Eagleton, *Literary Theory: An Introduction* (Minneapolis: University of Minnesota Press, 1983); Sigmund Freud, *Totem and Taboo,* vol. 11 of *The Standard Edition of the Complete Psychological Works of Sigmund Freud* (London: Hogarth Press, 1981).

9. Houston Baker, *Blues, Ideology, and Afro-American Literature: A Vernacular Theory* (Chicago: University of Chicago Press, 1984).

10. Mary Douglas, *Purity and Danger: An Analysis of the Concepts of Pollution and Taboo* (London: ARK Paperbacks, 1984).

11. Frantz Fanon, *The Wretched of the Earth,* preface by Jean-Paul Sartre, trans. Constance Farrington (New York: Grove Press, 1975).

12. I borrow freely from the title of Annette Kolodny's brilliant study, *The Lay of the Land: Metaphor as Experience and History in American Life and Letters* (Chapel Hill: University of North Carolina Press, 1975).

13. Susan Suleiman, ed., *The Female Body in Western Culture: Contemporary Perspectives* (Cambridge: Harvard University Press, 1986).

14. Anthony Wilden, *The Language of the Self: The Function of Language in Psychoanalysis* (New York: Dell Publishing, 1968).

15. Harryette Mullen, "Daughters in Search of Mothers," *Catalyst* (from the Women's Research Center at Spelman College, Atlanta) (Fall 1986): 45.

16. Luce Irigaray, *This Sex Which Is Not One,* trans. Catherine Porter with Carolyn Burke (Ithaca, N.Y.: Cornell University Press, 1985).

17. Roustang, "Uncertainty," 99.

18. Ibid., 101–2.

19. Frances E. W. Harper, *Iola Leroy, or Shadows Uplifted* (rpt., New York: AMS Press, 1971); Pauline Hopkins, *Contending Forces,* afterword by Gwendolyn Brooks (Carbondale: Southern Illinois Press, 1978); Charles W. Chesnutt, *The Short Fiction of Charles W. Chesnutt,* ed. with intro. by Sylvia Lyons Render (Washington, D.C.: Howard University Press, 1978); *idem, The Marrow of Tradition,* intro. by Robert M. Farnsworth (Ann Arbor: University of Michigan Press, 1969); Claudia Tate, "Pauline Hopkins: Our Literary Foremother," in *Conjuring: Black Women, Fiction, and Literary Tradition,* ed. Marjorie Pryse and Hortense J. Spillers (Bloomington: Indiana University Press, 1985), 53–67. A general perspective on late nineteenth-century fiction by African-American women writers is provided by Barbara Christian, *Black Women Novelists: The Development of a Tradition, 1892–1976* (Westport, Conn.: Greenwood Press, 1980), 35–62. See also Hazel V. Carby, "'On the Threshold of Woman's Era': Lynching, Empire, and Sexuality in Black Feminist Theory," *Critical Inquiry* 12 (Autumn 1985): 262–78.

20. Elaine Scarry, *The Body in Pain: The Making and Unmaking of the World* (New York: Oxford University Press, 1985).

Chapter Ten

"Moving on Down the Line: Variations on the African-American Sermon" was published in *The American Quarterly* 40, no. 1 (March 1988), and is reprinted with the per-

mission of The Johns Hopkins University. Rpt. in *The Bounds of Race*, ed. Dominick La-
Capra (Ithaca: Cornell University Press, 1991).

1. One of the most significant readings by an American of European culture, reflected in the architecture of its churches, is provided in Henry Adams's classic study,
Mont-Saint Michel and Chartres.

2. I have adopted a contextual meaning of this term from Robert Plante Armstrong,
The Powers of Presence: Consciousness, Myth, and Affecting Presence (Philadelphia: University of Pennsylvania Press, 1981), 31ff. Armstrong's term "im-media/im-mediate(d)"
refers to the symbolic system that cues "through a semantic construct" an existential
analogue, that is, the literary arts "that proceed through the employments of the names
of meanings to the evocation of subsequent analogic states" (34). For my own purposes,
I use the term "immediated" to mean those recessed spaces of architecture that affect
consciousness with suggestions of mystery, inward-turning, the hidden.

3. The "Eagle" sermon is to the African-American church what the oikotype is to the
folk narrative. See Roger D. Abrahams, *Deep Down in the Jungle: Negro Narrative Folklore
from the Streets of Philadelphia* (Hatboro, Penn.: Folklore Associates, 1964). This popular
sermonic motif, usually appearing under the title "The Eagle Stirs Her Nest," is featured
in sermons preached in various regions of the country, by various preachers, over time.
Though the details of the sermon differ according to individual circumstance, the narrative essentially concerns a story of mistaken identity: an eagle turns up in a chicken
coop; acquires the behavior of its surroundings, and the farmer of the yard eventually
discovers the error. The Schomburg Collection, New York Public Library, New York City,
holds in its archives of sermons the Rev. E. O. S. Cleveland's "The Eagle Stirring Her
Nest" (1946). One of the most celebrated versions of the "Eagle" is preached by the late
Rev. C. L. Franklin of Detroit and is available on Chess Records. My family's church in
Memphis was pastored from about 1948 to the late eighties by the Rev. L. D. McGhee Sr.
Growing up, I heard this sermon preached once a year. It is obviously a piece of the
repertoire that ministers of an older generation—and apparently all of them Baptist—
kept at hand.

4. For Pennington's narrative, see "The Fugitive Blacksmith, or Events in the History
of James W. C. Pennington, Pastor of a Presbyterian Church, New York, Formerly a Slave
in the State of Maryland," in *Great Slave Narratives*, ed. and intro. Arna Bontemps
(Boston, 1969), 192–269. The impact of literacy, as the gateway to the "pre-generic
myth," is illuminated in Robert B. Stepto's "Teaching Afro-American Literature: Survey
or Tradition," in *Afro-American Literature: The Reconstruction of Instruction*, ed. Dexter
Fisher and Robert B. Stepto (New York: Publications of the Modern Language Association, 1978), 8–25.

5. *A Two Years' Absence or a Farewell Sermon, preached in the Fifth Congregational
Church by J. W. C. Pennington*, Nov. 2, 1845 (Hartford, 1845), 3–31, at 22–23. The Moorland-Springarn Collection, Howard University, Washington, D.C.

6. My work on the rhetoric of Afro-American sermons involves the study of some
three hundred manuscripts, gathered from the Schomburg Collection of the New York
Public Library, New York City, and the Moorland-Spingarn Research Center of Howard
University, Washington, D.C. This survey is confined to printed documents preached
and narrated by black religious figures from Jupiter Hammon's *A Winter Piece, Being a Serious Exhortation* (1782) up to Randall Albert Carter's "Morning Meditations and Other
Selections" (1917). The latter marks a strategic and rather arbitrary cut-off point. After
World War I, the electronically recorded sermon was possible; that media shift provides
this material with another dimension, beyond the immediate aims of my project.

7. The colonial outcome of this thematic lends shape to Sacvan Bercovitch's significant study of aspects of an American identity, *The Puritan Origins of the American Self*
(New Haven, Conn.: Yale University Press, 1975). A brilliant counterreading is pursued

in the opening chapter of Houston Baker's *Blues, Ideology, and Afro-American Literature* (Chicago: University of Chicago Press, 1984). The magisterial work of Annette Kolodny opens up the entire field of inquiry into origins of American culture to the voices of women; see Kolodny's *The Lay of the Land: Metaphor as Experience and History in American Life and Letters* (Chapel Hill: University of North Carolina Press, 1975), and *The Land Before Her: Fantasy and Experience of the American Frontiers 1630–1860* (Chapel Hill: University of North Carolina Press, 1984).

8. Though the forceful contemporaneity of these two figures requires no documentation, I would note one of the most recent studies of King's career: David J. Garrows, *Bearing the Cross: Martin Luther King, Jr., and the Southern Christian Leadership Conference: A Personal Portrait* (New York: William Morrow and Co., 1986). In addition to Alex Haley's co-written *Autobiography of Malcolm X* (New York: Evergreen, 1965), John Henrik Clarke's collection of critical essays, *Malcolm X: The Man and His Times* (New York: Collier Books, 1969), remains one of the best sources for Malcolm X studies.

9. The classic reading of the Puritan sermon in the colonial experience is provided by Perry Miller in his two-volume work, *The New England Mind: From Colony to Province* (Cambridge, Mass.: Harvard University Press, 1953), and *The New England Mind: The Seventeenth Century* (New York: Macmillan, 1939; rpt. Boston: Beacon Press, 1961). Emory Elliott's *Power and the Pulpit in Puritan New England* (Princeton, N.J.: Princeton University Press, 1975) rereads the Puritan context against current modes of literary/ theoretical analysis.

10. James Cone, *God of the Oppressed* (New York: The Seabury Press, 1975).

11. The study of Afro-American oral sermons, or the unwritten, recorded ones, has attracted a number of researchers. Among the most noted studies are Charles V. Hamilton, *The Black Preacher in America* (New York: William Morrow and Co., 1972); Henry H. Mitchell, *Black Preaching* (Philadelphia: J. B. Lippincott, 1970); William H. Pipes, *Say Amen, Brother: Old-Time Negro Preaching: A Study in American Frustration* (rpt. Westport, Conn.: Negro Universities Press, 1970). Though the following texts do not focus on sermons, they provide a historic context for reading/hearing them: James H. Cone, *Black Theology and Black Power* (New York: The Seabury Press, 1969); Arthur Huff Fauset, *Black Gods of the Metropolis: Negro Religious Cults in the Urban North,* new intro. by John Szwed (Philadelphia: University of Pennsylvania Press, 1980); C. Eric Lincoln, ed. *The Black Experience in Religion: A Book of Readings* (Garden City, N.Y.: Anchor Books, 1974); Joseph R. Washington Jr., *The Politics of God: The Future of the Black Churches* (Boston: Beacon Press, 1969). My own study of the sermon style of Martin Luther King Jr. (in *The Black Scholar* 3 [September 1971] and reprinted in Lincoln, *Black Experience in Religion*) led to the writing of my dissertation on the subject, "The Fabrics of History: Essays on the Black Sermon," Brandeis University, 1974.

12. William Hatcher, a white Virginia journalist, contemporaneous with the slave preacher the Rev. John Jasper, has left transcriptions of several of Jasper's sermons; *The Unmatched Negro Philosopher and Preacher* (New York: Negro Universities Press, 1908). See chapter 3 of Spillers, "The Fabrics of History."

13. Barbara Christian's term for "race" moves us much closer to the cultural scene that illuminates the making of "race" as a social construct; *Black Women Novelists: The Development of a Tradition, 1892–1976* (Westport, Conn.: Greenwood Press, 1980).

14. "The Life Experience and Gospel Labors of the Rt. Rev. Richard Allen, to which is annexed the rise and progress of the African Methodist Episcopal Church in the United States of America. Containing a narrative of the yellow fever in the year of our Lord 1793. With an address to the People of Color in the United States. Written by Himself and published by request," intro. by George A. Singleton; in the Schomburg Collection. Bishop Daniel A. Payne, *History of the African Methodist Episcopal Church* (Philadelphia, 1922).

15. "Chronology of St. Thomas' M. E. Church" carries a full entry on this sermon and notes the Rev. Samuel Magaw as the rector of St. Paul's Church (cataloged in the Schomburg Collection with Allen's "Life Experience").

16. Samuel Magaw, *Discourse Delivered July 17, 1794, in the African Church of the City of Philadelphia, on the occasion of opening the said church, and holding public worship in it the first time. . . . Divine service introduced with select scripture passages, and a special prayer, and then proceeding in its usual offices, having been performed by James Abercrombie* (Philadelphia: W. W. Woodward), 9–24; in the Schomburg Collection.

17. William Miller, *A Sermon on the Abolition of the Slave Trade Delivered in the African Church, New York on the First of January, 1810. . . . Published by request of the Committee* (New York, 1810), 3–16; in the Spingarn Collection.

18. Ibid.

19. Jupiter Hammon, *A Winter Piece; Being a Serious Exhortation with a call to the Unconverted: And a short Contemplation of the Death of Jesus Christ written by Jupiter Hammon, a Negro Man belonging to Mr. John Lloyd, of Queen's Village, on Long Island, now in Hartford. Published by the author with the assistance of his Friends* (Hartford, Conn., 1782); in the Moorland Collection. William H. Robinson's *Early Black American Poets* carries Phillis Wheatley's "On Being Brought to America" and several other Wheatley poems under the category "Formalist Poets" (Dubuque, Iowa: William C. Brown Co., 1969). See also M. A. Richmond, *Bid the Vassal Soar: Interpretive Essays on the Life and Poetry of Phillis Wheatley and George Moses Horton* (Washington, D.C.: Howard University Press, 1974).

20. Albert J. Raboteau, *Slave Religion: The "Invisible" Institution in the Antebellum South* (New York: Oxford University Press, 1978), 152.

21. See Robinson, *Early Black American Poets:* "On the Death of the Rev. Mr. George Whitefield." See also Samuel J. Rogal, "Phillis Wheatley's Methodist Connection," *Black American Literature Forum* 21 (Spring/Summer 1987): 85–97.

22. Sydney E. Ahlstrom, *A Religious History of the American People* (New Haven, Conn.: Yale University Press, 1972), part 3, "The Century of Awakening and Revolution," and part 6, "Slavery and Expiation."

23. An impressive array of feminist scholarship has effected powerful intervention on the assumptions that cluster around patriarchist religion. Among these are included Mary Daly, *Beyond God the Father: Toward a Philosophy of Women's Liberation* (Boston: Beacon Press, 1973); Rosemary Radford Reuther, *Sexism and God-Talk: Toward a Feminist Theology* (Boston: Beacon Press, 1983). Reuther and Rosemary Skinner Keller are also the general editors of Harper and Row's *Women and Religion in America* series. Its first volume was published in New York in 1981: *The Nineteenth Century: A Documentary History.*

24. Roland Barthes, *S/Z* trans. Richard Miller (New York: Hill and Wang 1974), 76, my emphasis.

25. See note 2.

26. Kaiser quotes from William J. Simmons in his preface to *Men of Mark: Eminent, Progressive, and Rising* (Cleveland, Ohio, 1887; rpt. New York: Arno Press, 1969).

27. In fact, modern African-American biography has become literally voluminous over a diversity of fields; a history of this research tool is provided in "Historical Research Aids and Materials," in *The Harvard Guide to African-American History,* ed. Evelyn Brooks Higginbotham, Leon F. Litwack, and Darlene Clark Hine (Cambridge, Mass.: Harvard University Press, 2001), 25–29.

28. Wilson J. Moses, "The Lost World of the Negro, 1895–1919: Black Literary and Intellectual Life before the 'Renaissance,'" *Black American Literature Forum* 21 (Spring/Summer 1987): 61–85, looks at some of the issues that contextualized the period in which Bowen preached.

29. Cornel West, *Prophesy Deliverance! An Afro-American Revolutionary Christianity* (Philadelphia: The Westminster Press, 1982), 102–3.

30. Together, the Schomburg and the Moorland-Springarn Collections carry a number of Grimké's sermons. Carter G. Woodson's *Works of Francis James Grimké,* 4 vols. (Washington, D.C.: Associated Publishers, 1942) explores, in addition to the sermons, the addresses, meditations, thoughts, and letters. Volume I provides a study of Grimké's life. Related to Sara and Angelina Grimké, on the "black" side of this white South Carolina slave-holding family, Grimké became one of the most eminent Afro-American figures of the turn of the century and beyond. Grimké preached through the 1930s and, like W. E. B. DuBois, gives the impression of having lived "forever." The intensity of Grimké's sermons burns the consciousness in a manner comparable to J. W. E. Bowen's.

31. *Who's Who in Colored America: A Biographical Dictionary of Notable Living Persons of African Descent,* ed. Joseph J. Boris (New York, 1920), 43.

32. Carter G. Woodson, *The History of the Negro Church* (Washington, D.C.: Associated Publishers, 1921), 275.

33. John Hope Franklin, *From Slavery to Freedom,* 3d ed. (New York: Vintage Books, 1969), 441.

34. J. W. E. Bowen, *A National Sermon: or A Series of Plain Talks to the Colored People of America, on their Problems* (Washington, D.C., 1902), 12–87, at 12; in the Schomburg Collection. Hereafter page numbers are cited in the text.

35. Some of the sermons of this survey are published as practice, or paradigmatic sermons, for example, James Walker Hood's *The Negro in the Christian Pulpit; or Two Characters and Two Destinies, as Delineated in Twenty-one Practical Sermons* (Raleigh, N.C., 1884); in the Spingarn Collection.

36. Coretta Scott King, *My Life with Martin Luther King, Jr.* (New York: Holt, Rinehart, Winston, 1969), 239.

37. Alain Locke's celebrated 1925 volume, *The New Negro* (rpt. New York: Atheneum, 1977), a miscellany of critical and creative work by Afro-Americans, suggests a contrast between the "New Negro" and the "Negro Problem."

38. The problematic of the analogical dimensions of art is explored in the opening chapter of Armstrong's *Powers of Presence.*

39. An illuminating inquiry into the symbolic import of the voice and the ear is provided in a fascinating narrative of conceptualization in Thomas G. Pavel, "In Praise of the Ear (Gloss's Glosses)," in *The Female Body in Western Culture: Contemporary Perspectives,* ed. Susan Rubin Suleiman (Cambridge, Mass.: Harvard University Press, 1986), 44–68.

40. Ibid., 49.

41. An examination of Douglass's "syncretic phrasing" is offered in Robert B. Stepto, *From Behind the Veil: A Study of Afro-American Narrative* (Urbana: University of Illinois Press, 1979), 20. Chapter 5 of Frederick Douglass's 1845 *Narrative* (New York, 1968), 43, gives the context for this quotation.

Chapter Eleven

"Black, White, and in Color, or Learning How to Paint: Toward an Intramural Protocol of Reading" was published in *New Historical Literary Study: Essays on Reproducing Texts, Representing History,* ed. Jeffrey N. Cox and Larry J. Reynolds (Princeton: Princeton University Press, 1993): 267–91. © 1993 by Princeton University Press.Reprinted by permission of the publisher.

1. See note 6 in "Chosen Place, Timeless People: Some Figurations on the New World," in *Conjuring: Black Women, Fiction, and Literary Tradition,* ed. Marjorie Pryse and Hortense J. Spillers (Bloomington: Indiana University Press, 1985). The dispute here primarily concerns one reading of Marshall's novel as "homophobic." My position is that "homophobia" as interpretive/critical device for this, or any other novel, represents a single constituent reading of the work, but that there are others. For me to call

the "homophobic" claim "racist" would simply proliferate the name-calling, even if I do think so. That our various readings replicate today's fractured political scene will not come as news, but as *citizens* who are also *critics*, I think we owe it to the "business" of our work to do more than simply impose our particular prejudice on forms of art. The point is to *use* one's view in a way that is rigorous, responsive and contextualized according to the *situations* of the work before us. *Not to account for the narrative positionalities* of *Chosen Place, Timeless People* is to imagine that the work was derived in a vacuum of politics and history and that we can impose whatever discursive fashions and passions of the moment reflected in our *own* historicity. It seems to me that doing so would be an error that "criminalizes" any viewpoint that is not our own.

2. Pierre Bourdieu, *Outline of a Theory of Practice,* Cambridge Studies in Social Anthropology, gen. ed. Jack Goody (Cambridge: Cambridge University Press, 1977). Articulating the relatedness between "economism" (in the narrow and traditional sense) and noneconomic topics of appeal, Bourdieu suggests that the former might be understood "as a particular case of a *general science of the economy of practices*" (183). In abandoning the dichotomy, we are in position to derive, then, a discursive practice that is "capable of treating all practices, including those purporting to be disinterested or gratuitous, and hence non-economic, as economic practices directed toward the maximizing of material or symbolic profit." Somewhat relatedly, I would contend that a "general science of the economy of practices" in its literary critico-theoretical moment might urge a more forceful articulation between, or among, divergent constituencies of cultural claims. Any reading project or discipline will, of necessity, leave something out, but its doing so need not occasion celebration, or the arrogance of a moral rightness. In fact, the abounding absences—collateral with the emergent discourse—enable a particular interpretive economy by shaping it as *this* choice and not *that* or the *other.* In short, the critico-theoretical text attempts to identify and mark its investments as a single site of contestatory urgencies and commitments (cf. Stanley Fish, *Is There a Text in This Class? The Authority of Interpretive Communities* [Cambridge, Mass.: Harvard University Press, 1980]).

3. Barbara Herrnstein Smith, "Contingencies of Value," "Canons" *Critical Inquiry* 9 (September 1983): 1–36. See also her *Contingencies of Value: Alternative Perspectives for Critical Theory* (Cambridge, Mass.: Harvard University Press, 1988).

4. The title of this essay is based on two punctualities: Joanna Field's *On Not Being Able to Paint* (Los Angeles: J. P. Tarcher, Inc., 1957) and Jean-Jacques Annaud's 1976 film, *Black and White in Color.* A film from the Ivory Coast, *Black and White,* coauthored by Annaud and Georges Conchon, bears the French title *La Victoire en chantant.* Produced by Arthur Cohn, Jacques Perrin, and Giorgio Silvagni, the film—which focuses postcolonial intersubjectivities in the Francophone sphere—won the Motion Picture Academy's best foreign film award in 1976.

5. Paule Marshall, *The Chosen Place, the Timeless People* (1969; rpt., New York: Vintage Contemporaries, 1984). All references to the novel and quotations from it are taken from this edition; page numbers noted in the text.

6. Roland Barthes, *S/Z,* trans. Richard Miller, preface by Richard Howard (New York: Hill and Wang, 1974), 22.

7. John T. Irwin, *Doubling and Incest/Repetition and Revenge: A Speculative Reading of Faulkner* (Baltimore: Johns Hopkins University Press, 1980), 31–33.

Jacques Lacan's discussion of the significance of the "mirror stage" ("stade du miroir") in the development/deployment of the cultural agent, alienated in language, is provided in "The Mirror Stage as Formation of the Function of the I," in *Écrits: A Selection,* trans. Alan Sheridan (New York: W. W. Norton and Company, 1977), 1–8.

For critique, see, among numerous other sources: Anthony Wilden, "Lacan and the Discourse of the Other," in Jacques Lacan, *The Language of the Self: The Function of Lan-*

guage in Psychoanalysis, trans. with notes and commentary by Anthony Wilden (New York: Delta Books, 1968), 157–313; and Fredric Jameson, "Imaginary and Symbolic in Lacan," *The Ideologies of Theory: Essays 1971–1986,* vol. 1, *Situations of Theory* (Minneapolis: University of Minnesota Press, 1988), 75–119.

In Lacanian epistemology, the mirror becomes the primary hodological (self-mapping) instrument of ego-identity, which arises in critical deception, in *meconnaissance.* Imbricated between and in the midst of the imaginary and symbolic dimensions of the Lacanian project, the "mirror stage" inscribes the tiny subject's "interpellation" by the self-alienating dynamics of self-image and representation. If we could risk such imprecision, we would say that the subject's involvement in the prelinguistic realm of undifferentiated objects demarcates the "beginning" of its crucial destiny in, its traverse (and travail?) through, the Symbolic Order and the Name (and the Law) of the Father. See also Julia Kristeva, *Desire in Language: A Semiotic Approach to Literature and Art,* ed. Leon S. Roudiez, trans. Thomas Gora, Alice Jardine, and Leon S. Roudiez (New York: Columbia University Press, 1980).

Marshall's characters "mimic" the "mirror stage" insofar as they register the necessary coupledness of self-gazing, a process that occurs *because* there is a witness (in Lacan's scheme, a parental caretaker) *against* whom the unknowing and primary subject "sees" itself for the first time. The characters in the novel aggressively engage parodies and illuminate the identitarian and the egoistic as a *rupture* in the apparent unity of perception and desire.

8. Among recent works of feminist theory that devote all, or some significant portion of, their conceptual apparatus to an investigation of female representability are included: Teresa de Lauretis, *Alice Doesn't: Feminism, Semiotics, Cinema* (Bloomington: Indiana University Press, 1982); Alice A. Jardine, *Gynesis: Configurations of Woman and Modernity* (Ithaca: Cornell University Press, 1985); Susan Rubin Suleiman, ed., *The Female Body in Western Culture: Contemporary Perspectives* (Cambridge, Mass.: Harvard University Press, 1986); Teresa DeLauretis, ed., *Feminist Studies/Critical Studies* (Bloomington: Indiana University Press, 1986); Teresa de Lauretis, *Technologies of Gender: Essays on Theory, Film, and Fiction* (Bloomington: Indiana University Press, 1987).

9. Julia Kristeva, "Stabat Mater," in Suleiman, *The Female Body in Western Culture,* 115.

10. Georg Simmel, *The Philosophy of Money,* ed. David Frisby, trans. Tom Bottomore and David Frisby (London: Routledge and Kegan Paul, Ltd., 1978), 61–66. Simmel's discussion of desiring subjects and objects of desire occurs within the context of his elaboration of "value" and money" in chapter 1. Independent of natural order, valuation and its conceptual apparati inscribe the "whole world viewed from a particular vantage point" (60). Over and against what Simmel calls "objective qualities and determinations," "the great categories of being and value, inclusive forms that take their material from the world of pure contents," stand arrayed (61). The sharp distinctions that Simmel draws between "objective determinations" and subjective valuation omit the intermediary stages that decide how the repertoire of value/desire arises; such a question is posed by psychoanalytic theories of language, specifically, Lacan's itinerary of the "unconscious" as that which is structured "like" a language.

Getting to money as value's signifier and signification—terms which Simmel does not specifically deploy—the author "reduces" value and the desiring ego to the same temporality, or contemporaneity (67). The latter constellation, therefore, situates the tension that disrupts and interrupts the unity of subject-effect and its lost, or receding, or interchangeable, objects and "makes us conscious of each in relation to the other." In desiring what we do not yet own or enjoy, "we place the content of our desire outside ourselves" (66). Characterized by its separation and distance from subject, object is posited as that which desire seeks to *overcome.* By way of this transitivity, object is situated, therefore, as a *value* (66).

11. Ibid., 66.

12. Toni Morrison, *The Bluest Eye* (New York: Washington Square Press, 1970), 21. Claudia MacTeer, one of the adult-as-child narrators in Morrison's first novel, comments on "desire" as oppressive imposition: "But I did know that nobody ever asked me what I wanted for Christmas. Had any adult with the power to fulfill my desires taken me seriously and asked me what I wanted, they would have known that I did not want to have anything to own, or to possess any object. I wanted rather to feel something on Christmas day . . . to sit on the low stool in Big Mama's kitchen with my lap full of lilacs and listen to Big Papa play his violin for me alone." Even though Claudia's notion of authentic desire is nonetheless as staged and melodramatic as the customary baby doll for girls at Christmas time, her narrative at least points up the adopted and adaptive *fictionality* [of] *wanting* as adults author it in this novel.

13. Robert Scholes, *Structuralism in Literature: An Introduction* (New Haven: Yale University Press, 1974), 26.

14. Basil Davidson identifies the Tiv as a West African family that moved into southern Nigeria of the Niger Delta around A.D. 1500. Grouped with the Fulani, the Tiv came into the area from distant regions to the north of Nigeria. *A History of West Africa to the Nineteenth Century* with F. K. Buah and the advice of J. F. Ade Ajayi (New York: Doubleday Anchor, 1966), 145.

Chapter Twelve

"Notes on an Alternative Model—Neither/Nor" was published in *The Year of the New Left*, Spring 1987. Rev. and rpt. in *The Difference Within: Feminism and Critical Theory*, ed. Elizabeth Meese and Alice Parker (Amsterdam: John Benjamins, 1989); reprinted with permission.

1. Winthrop Jordan, *White Over Black: American Attitudes Toward the Negro 1550–1812* (Baltimore: Penguin Books, 1969), remains one of the most thoroughgoing analyses of this subject from the point of view of the United States and its colonial antecedents. Part IV, "Fruits of Passion: The Dynamics of Interracial Sex" concerns specifically the historical context against which sexual mores, or an American behavior of sexuality, were played out. In this "cultural matrix of purpose, accomplishment, self-conception, and social circumstances of settlement in the New World, the mulatto child violated the strictest intentions of a binary racial function" (167). For Jordan, the situation of the mulatto reflects a persistent historicity: the configurations assumed by a cultural phenomenon, or structure of attention, against the perspective of time.

Barbara Christian, *Black Women Novelists: The Development of a Tradition, 1892–1976* (Westport, Conn.: Greenwood Press, 1980), looks closely at the theme of the mulatta in certain nineteenth and twentieth century fiction, including that of Frances E. W. Harper, William Wells Brown, Jessie Fauset, and Nella Larsen. See especially, "From Stereotype to Character," 3–61.

Mary V. Dearborn, *Pocahontas's Daughters: Gender and Ethnicity in American Culture* (New York: Oxford University Press, 1986), 158, explores the specific connection between the thematics of the mulatta heroine in fiction and the act of incest: the denial of paternity and of blood rite to the interracial child creates an ignorance of identity that can redound to the distinct disadvantage of certain lateral kin relations. Even though Dearborn does not employ Judith and Henry Sutpen as an instance of the fatal unknowing, I think that a case can be made for it. Because they are ignorant of the existence of Charles Bon—their "black" brother—incest becomes a distinct possibility for all of Sutpen's children. Drawing out the symbolic and rhetorical resonances of the mulatto theme, Dearborn defines both the fictive character and the historical subject, we infer, as "a living embodiment of the paradox of the individual within society." She suggestively describes the "fictional mulatto" as the "imaginative conjunction of a cultural disjunction."

Henry Louis Gates's guest-edited volume of *Critical Inquiry* 12 (Autumn 1985) does not propose to look specifically at the mulatto/a as an aspect of the problematics of alterity. But the various other issues of alterity explored in the volume are suggestive in a number of ways, specifically, Israel Burshatin's "The Moor in the Text: Metaphor, Emblem, and Silence," 98–119. Burshatin's "moor," like the "mulatto/a," might be viewed as an already inspissated identity before the particulars of context have had an opportunity to do their work.

2. The following listing of fictional texts on the mulatto/a is not offered as an exhaustive survey. We regard them as impression points that the reader achieves in tracing the career of the subject from Harper's era through the 1930s:

James Weldon Johnson, *The Autobiography of an Ex-Colored Man,* intro. Arna Bontemps (New York: Hill and Wang, 1960). Jean Toomer, *Cane,* intro. Darwin Turner (1923; New York: Liveright, 1975). The reader should see specifically the closing section of this powerful work for the tale of Kabnis. Here, the exteriority of the mulatto figure has been revised and corrected into a structure of internal, or psychic, complication.

Nella Larsen, *Quicksand* (New York: Alfred A. Knopf, 1928; rpt. New York: Negro Universities Press, 1969); idem, *Passing* (New York: Alfred A. Knopf, 1929), rpt. *Afro-American Cultural Series: The American Negro, His History and Literature,* ed. Arthur P. Davis and Darwin Turner (New York: Arno Press, 1969). It would be fair to say that Larsen criticism comes into its own with the explosive critical work of Deborah McDowell, whose introductory essay to the reprinted edition of *Quicksand* and *Passing* (New Brunswick, N.J.: Rutgers University Press, 1986) brought out features of these novels that prior readings had simply missed. For other biographical and critical work on Larsen, see: Thadeous Davis, *Nella Larsen: Novelist of the Harlem Renaissance* (Baton Rouge: Louisiana State University Press, 1994); Jacquelyn McClendon, *The Politics of Color in the Fiction of Jessie Fauset and Nella Larsen* (Charlottesville: University Press of Virginia, 1995); and Charles R. Larson, *Invisible Darkness: Jean Toomer and Nella Larsen* (Iowa City: University of Iowa Press, 1993).

Jessie Redmon Fauset, *The Chinaberry Tree: A Novel of American Life* (1933; College Park, Md.: McGrath Publishing Company, 1969); idem, *Comedy: American Style* (1931; College Park, Md.: McGrath Publishing Company, 1969).

The reader might consult the opening section of Barbara Christian's work for a more comprehensive account of the fiction of the mulatto/a. A fine study of Pauline Hopkins, contemporaneous with Frances Harper and in pursuance of the mulatto thematic, is provided by Claudia Tate, "Pauline Hopkins: Our Literary Foremother," in *Conjuring: Black Women, Fiction, and Literary Tradition,* ed. Marjorie Pryse and Hortense Spillers (Bloomington: Indiana University Press, 1985).

3. The Oxford English Dictionary on "mulatta" situates the term in Spanish. Born of a "Negra and a fayre man," "mulatta" in the English lexis appears c. 1622. Among its permutations in Portuguese is "mullato," young mule, or one of a mixed race.

4. Frederick Douglass, *Narrative of the Life of Frederick Douglass, An American Slave, Written by Himself* (1845; rpt. New York: Signet Books, 1968), 21–22.

5. Werner Sollors points out that "mulatto/a," as a term of self-reference, was recurrent in the work of certain black writers and intellectuals in the 1980s and 1990s. I am hardly aware, however, of any widespread currency of the term, now or then, either as a mode of self-reference, or a way to describe someone else. The two examples that he evinces in support of his claims are simply the exception that proves the rule; Trey Ellis's "cultural mulatto," one of the examples pressed into service by Sollors, is a different order of cases altogether from "mulatto/a" as a phenotypic designation. My whole point in the essay was to suggest that, *historically,* black people in the U.S. context— whatever their skin tone might have been—did not refer to themselves as "mulatto/a," and that the "mulatto/a" should be distinguished, *as a literary device,* from *interracial progenies and* cultural commingling. See Werner Sollors, *Neither Black Nor White Yet*

Both: Thematic Explorations of Interracial Literature (Cambridge, Mass.: Harvard University Press, 1997), 128ff.

6. William Faulkner, *Light in August* (1932; New York: Random House Modern Library, 1959), 100.

7. Girard's explosive work offers a background against which we might view the fundamental structuration of human community as the deployment of the dynamics of violence and the fear of violent reprisal. By isolating an "expendable figure," the "unanimity-minus one," community purges itself of various impurities, including guilt. Community also discovers the One Man or Woman (or the substitute) whose elimination would not generate the operations of revenge. Faulkner's Joe Christmas is perfectly placed to carry out all the requirements of Girard's sacrificial program. Essentially unfathered, Christmas is Every man/woman *before* the name of the Father "cleanses" him/her, or releases from the terrors of "unculture."

8. Tzvetan Todorov, "Typology of Relations to the Other," *The Conquest of America*, trans. Richard Howard (New York: Colophon Books, 1984), 185–201, at 185. Todorov's interesting conceptual narrative concentrates in the career of the Native American at the hands of the European explorer, but its application lays hold of a broader frame of reference.

9. William Faulkner, *Absalom, Absalom!* (1936; New York: Random House Modern Library, 1951).

10. John Irwin's brilliant structuralist reading of incest in Faulkner traces its manifestations in the agency of Quentin Compson (*Doubling and Incest/Repetition and Revenge* [Baltimore: Johns Hopkins University Press, 1975]). Overlapping *The Sound and the Fury* and *Absalom, Absalom!*, Quentin reflects his own incestuous urges toward his sister Caddy *(Sound and Fury)* in the narrative that he "repeats" concerning Charles Bon.

A critical reevaluation of Marxist theory in perspective with the contemporary scene of criticism occasions Fredric Jameson's *Political Unconscious: Narrative as a Socially Symbolic Act* (Ithaca: Cornell University Press, 1981). The opening chapter of the work questions the adequacy of a Freudian "Family Drama" as a comprehensive paradigm and theory of processes of social production. (See "Faulkner Adds Up" in this volume.)

11. The economic uses of African female personality under the onus of captivity are alluded to in Linda Brent's chapter, "Sketches of Neighboring Slaveholders," *Incidents in the Life of a Slave Girl,* ed. L. Maria Child, intro. Walter Teller (New York: Harcourt Brace Jovanovich, Harvest Books, 1973), 45–53. Not commenting specifically on the mulatta's value, the writer sounds, nonetheless, the profit connections between the female body/sexuality and the oppressive conditions of enslavement.

12. The informing conceptualization of the relevant paragraph here is suggested by the brilliantly speculative work of Gayatri Chakravorty Spivak in "French Feminism in an International Frame," *Yale French Studies*, no. 62, Feminist Readings: French Texts/American Contexts, 154–84.

13. Various aspects of female sexuality in conjunction with history and politics are examined in *Pleasure and Danger: Exploring Female Sexuality,* ed. Carole Vance (Boston: Routledge and Kegan Paul, 1984). My own essay here, "Interstices: A Small Drama of Words," looks specifically at the grammar of sexuality in relationship to African-American women's community (in this volume.) The essays in *Pleasure and Danger* are based on papers delivered by the participants at the controversial "Feminist and Scholar Conference, IX," at Barnard College, Spring 1982.

14. Foucault, re-opening the problem of Victorian sexuality, considers the discursivity of his subject. Victorian Europe was not, in his view, a sexually muted culture, but seized instead every occasion to induce and excite discourse about it. Illegitimate sexuality in the historic context he examines becomes one of the "forms of reality" subjected to a discourse that is "clandestine, circumscribed, and coded" in reference to the

brothel, the mental institution, and other spaces of marginality (*The History of Sexuality: Volume 1–An Introduction,* trans. Robert Hurley [New York: Pantheon Books, 1978], 4ff.). We would regard the site of the mulatta mistress as a marginalized class of objects erotically configured.

15. "History is what hurts" profoundly informs Jameson's sense that "History" is the "ground and untranscendable horizon [that] needs no theoretical justification." He offers its inexorability as the fundamental scene against which the critical praxis unfolds; against which we gauge the efficacy and completeness of any critical system (102).

16. Perry Miller, *The New England Mind,* vol. 1, *The Seventeenth Century;* vol. 2, *From Colony to Province* (Boston: Beacon Press, 1961).

17. The classic reading of the tensions engendered between the wish-fulfillment and its prohibitive mechanism is given in Freud's *Totem and Taboo,* vol. 13 of *The Standard Edition of the Complete Psychological Works of Sigmund Freud,* trans. James Strachey (London: Hogarth Press, 1955).

18. The codification of law that underscores the institution of slavery in the United States is sporadically examined in numerous texts of history. But a work contemporaneous with the final days of the "Peculiar Institution" provides not only a detailed reading of the code, but also an instance of a parallel and *counter* sensitivity that takes on historic appeal in its own right: William Goodell, *The American Slave Code in Theory and Practice: Its Distinctive Features Shown by its Statutes, Judicial Decisions, and Illustrative Texts* (New York: American and Foreign Anti-Slavery Society, 1853). Apparently the "runaway slave" was neither rare nor forgotten. The plentifulness of advertisements describing the *person* of the fugitive—the model, we might suppose, for the contemporary "All Points Bulletin" of the Federal Bureau of Investigation and those mug shots that grace the otherwise uniform local post office—argue the absolute solidification of captivity—the major American social landscape, in my view, for two and a half centuries of human hurt on the scene of "man's last best hope": *Runaway Slave Advertisements: A Documentary History from the 1730s to 1790,* comp. Lathan A. Windley, vol. 1, *Virginia and North Carolina;* vol. 2, *Maryland* (Westport, Conn.: Greenwood Press, 1983); on the "mulatto," see Joel Williamson, *New People: Miscegenation and Mulattoes in the United States* (New York: The Free Press, 1980).

19. Elizabeth Donnan, ed. and comp, 1932. "Accounts from an African Trade Book, 1733–1736," from the Archives of the Newport Historical Society, *Documents Illustrative of the History of the Slave Trade to America,* vol. 3, *New England and the Middle Colonies* (Washington, D.C.: The Carnegie Institute, 1932), 130.

20. Frederick Douglass, *Narrative of the Life of Frederick Douglass,* 59–60.

21. Michael Cobb, "Racial Blasphemies" (Ph.D. diss., Cornell University, 2001).

22. Frances Harper, *Iola Leroy, or Shadows Uplifted* (1893; rpt. New York: AMS Press, 1971), 281.

23. Faulkner, *Light in August,* 440.

24. Michel Foucault, *The Archaeology of Knowledge and the Discourse on Language,* trans. A. M. Sheridan Smith (New York: Harper Colophon Books, 1972), 56–64, at 58.

25. A description of the paradoxical nature of the *pharmikon* is provided by René Girard, *Violence and the Sacred,* trans. Patrick Gregory (Baltimore: Johns Hopkins University Press, 1977).

26. The dispatch, in Roman society, of the illegitimate children of unwed mothers becomes a striking item of anthropological interest. See chap. 8, n. 2.

Chapter Thirteen

"Who Cuts the Border?: Some Readings on America" was published in *Comparative American Identities,* ed. Hortense J. Spillers (New York: Routledge, Chapman, and Hall, 1991), 1–25.

1. José Martí, *"Our America": Writings on Latin America and the Struggle for Cuban Independence,* ed. with intro. and notes Philip S. Foner, trans. Elinor Randall, Juan de Onis, and Roslyn Held Foner (New York: Monthly Review Press, 1977), 94. All quotations from *"Our America"* come from this edition; page numbers noted in the text.

2. Foner, *"Our America,"* Introduction, 17.

3. Roberto Marquez, "Soul of a Continent," *America Quarterly* 41, no. 4 (December 1989): 695–704, provides a very informative review of the four English-language editions of Martí's writings. All of them translated by Elinor Randall, editorially marshaled by Philip Foner, and published by the Monthly Review Press, the other volumes are: *Inside the Monster: Writings on the United States and American Imperialism* (1977); *On Education: Articles on Educational Theory and Pedagogy and Writings for Children from the "Age of Gold"* (1979); *On Art and Literature: Critical Writings* (1982).

4. Foner's tracking of Martí's inflections of "Our," "his," and "Other America" is pointedly read on pp. 24–25 of the Introduction to *"Our America."*

5. Georg Wilhelm Friedrich Hegel, *The Philosophy of History,* intro. C. J. Friedrich, prefaces by Charles Hegel, trans. J. Sibree (New York: Dover Publications, Inc., 1956). All quotations from Hegel come from this edition; page numbers noted in the text.

6. Foner, *"Our America,"* Part III—"The Second War for Independence"—"Cuba Must Be Free of the United States As Well as Spain": A Letter to Gonzalo Quesada, New York, October 29, 1889, 244.

7. Marquez's "Soul of a Continent" (n. 3) offers a reading on Martí's life and work that would surprise any facile conclusions concerning certain of the activist's imagined loyalties. Marquez notes that Martí's attitudes about "the concept of class warfare" and "working class violence" would suggest that he did not "believe that any intrinsic or essential conflict of interest divided classes" (701).

In the Preface to *Caliban and Other Essays,* Roberto Fernández Retamar engages our deepest complexities of imagination about a figure who lived fifteen years (1880–1895) in the United states, yet forged the second of Cuba's revolutionary struggles in New York City. As a ring on the thematics of paradoxical change, Martí, for Retamar, became "not only the most advanced of our thinkers," because of the context out of which his Cuban struggle was solidified, "but a North American radical as well." Retamar goes on: "Although, on the one hand, he criticized with ever-greater lucidity the ills of North American society and the danger that one sector of it represented for Latin America and the Caribbean . . . on the other hand (as Juan Ramón Jiménez stated, thinking of his great essay on Whitman from 1887), Spain and Spanish America owe him, in large part, our poetic access to the United States" (trans. Edward Baker; foreword by Fredric Jameson [Minneapolis: University of Minnesota Press, 1989], xv–xvi]).

8. Peter Hulme, "Hurricanes in the Caribbees: The Constitution of the Discourse of English Colonialism," in *1642: Literature and Power in the Seventeenth Century,* ed. Francis Barker et al. Essex Sociology of Literature Conference, Proceedings of the Essex Conference on the Sociology of Literature, July 1980 (University of Essex, 1981), 55–56. All quotations from Hulme come from this edition; page numbers noted in the text.

9. Roberto Fernández Retamar, "Caliban: Notes Toward a Discussion of Culture in Our America," trans. Lynn Garafola, David Arthur McMurray, and Roberto Marquez, *The Massachusetts Review* 15, nos. 1/2 (Winter–Spring 1974): 7–72 (special issue, ed. Roberto Marquez).

This celebrated essay originally appeared in *Casa de las Americas* (Havana) 68 (September–October 1971).

Retamar's "Caliban" engendered a catalytic moment for a "little magazine" project in "New World Thought and Writing" that surfaced in Amherst, Massachusetts in the mid-1970s. Conceived of by Roberto Marquez, the journal was a semi-annual publication, named *Caliban,* with a trial run in the special edition of the *Massachusetts Review* that Mr. Marquez edited. David Arthur McMurray and Hortense Spillers assisted Marquez in this bilingual editorial work that featured writings by, among others, Edward Braithwaite, Jan Carew, Mario Benedetti, and Andrew Salkey (vol. 1, no. 1 [Fall–Winter, 1975]).

10. Retamar refers here to a repertory of significant texts that include Fanon's *Black Skin, White Masks,* Césaire's *Discourse on Colonialism,* and Mannoni's *Psychology of Colonialism* ("Caliban," 17–21).

11. Cited by Retamar from Columbus's Navigation Log Books ("Caliban," 11).

12. Ivan Van Sertima, *The African Presence in Ancient America: They Came Before Columbus* (New York: Random House, 1976).

13. This term offers a slight variation on "situation-specificity" which Fredric Jameson coins in his foreword to *Caliban and other Essays* (cf. n. 7) . In a discussion of Retamar's place in the mapping of culture work, Jameson speaks of a "situation-specificity" "for a positioning that always remains concrete and reflexive." Intervening on the "binary and invidious slogan of *difference*" (Jameson's emphasis), "situation-specificity" seems to get at concisely what it evokes.

14. In reviewing the career of his essay "Caliban," Retamar points to certain uses of the 1960s ("Both decades and centuries can have their uses"). He situates here the political context in which the essay was produced and cites *The 60s Without Apology* as a "noteworthy book" (Sohnya Sayres, Anders Stephenson, et. al., eds. [Minneapolis: University of Minnesota Press, 1984]). Retamar's reading of the background for his essay appears in "Caliban Revisited" in *Caliban and Other Essays,* 47.

15. I borrow freely here from Elizabeth Fox-Genovese and Eugene D. Genovese, *Fruits of Merchant Capital: Slavery and Bourgeois Property in the Rise and Expansion of Capitalism* (New York: Oxford University Press, 1983).

16. Abena Busia's illuminating discussion of the tropes and complexities of "silence" that loudly speak female "unrepresentability" in the modernist text about "Colonialism" is found in "Silencing Sycorax: On African Colonial Discourse and the Unvoiced Female," *Cultural Critique* 14 (Winter 1989–90): 81–104. I am grateful to Professor Busia for sharing this text with me prior to its publication.

17. In a fascinating study of Aristotelian catharsis, John McCumber suggests a relocation of the concept: "one which places it not in the masculine framework of the doctor's office or the equally masculine sanctuaries of Eleusis but in the infinitely more subtle and profound terrain of woman's body" ("Aristotelian Catharsis and the Purgation of Woman," *Diacritics* 18, no. 4 [Winter 1988]: 58). The quotation in the text is found on p. 55.

18. Patricia Parker, *Literary Fat Ladies: Rhetoric, Gender, Property* (London: Methuen, 1987), 140. All quotations from Parker come from this edition; page numbers noted in the text. My personal thanks to Professor Parker for this wonderful gift.

19. A close examination of the history of dramatic representations of the figure "Caliban" is provided by Virginia Mason Vaughan, " 'Something Rich and Strange': Caliban's Theatrical Metamorphosis," *Shakespeare Quarterly* 36, no. 4 (1985): 390–405; the Folger Shakespeare Library.

20. William Faulkner, *The Sound and the Fury* (New York: Vintage Books, 1956), 390–405. This edition of Faulkner's novel carries the genealogical chart of familial traits that identifies all Compson-connected characters, including house servants. The more recent Norton Edition of the work relegates this material to the appendix: Ed. David Minter (New York: W.W. Norton, 1987). Professor Minter points out that the "Appendix/Compson" was not composed until the fall of 1945 for Malcolm Cowley's *Portable Faulkner* (224). Even though not a part of the novel per se, this trace inaugurated in the invocation of "Ikemotubbe" hounds the reader from beginning to end. It appears to

pose the same kind of problematics of reading that Eliot's "appendix" to "The Waste-land" generates.

21. *Absalom, Absalom!* (New York: The Modern Library, 1951). All quotations from the novel come from this edition; page numbers noted in the text.

22. This phrase is "lifted" from David Krause's close reading of aspects of *Absalom, Absalom!* in his citation of Denis Donaghue's *Ferocious Alphabets* (London: Faber, 1981), in Krause, "Reading Bon's Letter and Faulkner's *Absalom, Absalom!,*" PMLA 99, no. 2 (March 1984): 225–41.

23. Krause, following Donaghue, distinguishes "epireading" and "graphireading": "Graphireading," on the other hand, "'deals with writing as such and does not think of it as transcribing an event properly construed as vocal and audible'" (226). One might think of "epireading," given Krause's translation, as "speech on the human tongue," as Hugh Kenner once described it—without recourse to the dictionary, etc. But the de-constructionist project has rendered such distinction, perhaps, less easy to formulate. It seems to me that Faulkner's canon straddles this debate in quite astonishing ways, inas-much as his syntactical protocol seems dominated by the anxieties of revision and a se-vere oppositional movement to the uncertainties of "improvised" speech. More exactly, Faulkner's narrative devices appear to generate speaking-as-repentance, in which case, whatever one might speak at one moment becomes, on second thought, inadequate, as the latter is not effaced so much as "improved" upon and "essayed" over and over again. This seems the dominant semiotic burden of *Absalom, Absalom!* as characters "listen" to themselves talk and appear to revise and correct, aggrandize and elaborate in the moment.

24. Current critical inquiry generates quite appropriately, I think, regard for "race," "gender," "class," "sex/sexuality," as key terms of our social fabulations. But like my colleague, Professor Amy Lang, I weary (somewhat) of the 3–4 step language device that fractures the fabulous social subject into a few Big Moments. This problem is partially addressed in "Sieving the Matriheritage of the Sociotext," by Myriam Diaz-Diocaretz in *The Difference Within: Feminism and Critical Theory,* ed. Elizabeth Meese and Alice Parker (Amsterdam: John Benjamins Publishing Company, 1989), 115–49. I am suggesting "socionom" as a shorthand for those Big and small "moments" of the biotext that are both proclaimed and ignored, that loudly intrude, or slip away into the margins of the evasive. One is "also . . . " as the real and historical situation dictates, as choice seems available, and in connection with a complicated repertoire of means that Barbara Christian has identified under the head of "natal commu-nity."

25. Portions of Faulkner's letter to Malcolm Cowley, in answer to a question about *Absalom, Absalom!* have become a heady piece of Faulkneriana. Cited in Krause: "I am telling the same story over and over, which is myself and the world. Tom Wolfe was try-ing to say everything, get everything, the world plus 'I' or filtered through 'I' or the ef-fort of 'I' again, into one volume. I am trying to go a step further . . . I am trying to say it all in one sentence, between one Cap and one period . . . I am still trying to put all mankind's history into one sentence" (cf. 240, n. 22).

26. C. L. R. James, *The Black Jacobins: Toussaint l'Ouverture and the San Domingo Rev-olution* (New York: Vintage Books, 1963), from preface to the first edition (ix).

27. Like the "Appendix/Compson," the Modern Library edition of *Absalom, Absa-lom!* carries sketches of the Faulkner character. We learn from this source, for instance, that "Shreve McCannon" (Shrevlin McCannon) is a citizen of Edmonton, Alberta, Canada. This "Chronology" begins with Thomas Sutpen, "born in West Virginia moun-tains. Poor whites of Scottish-English stock."

28. The concept of "paralogism" is discussed in Fredric Jameson's foreword to Jean-François Lyotard, *The Postmodern Condition: A Report on Knowledge,* trans. Geoff Ben-

nington and Brian Massumi, Theory and History of Literature, vol. 10 (Minneapolis: University of Minnesota Press, 1984), xix.

29. Lillian Hellman, *Pentimento: A Book of Portraits,* (Boston: Little, Brown, 1973). The "pentimento" seems to be a slightly different concept from the "palimpsest," exquisitely configured as a background idea in *Civilization and Its Discontents*. The mind as a "Rome" of impressions shows depth and layering, or dimensionality, in contrast to the surface of the "pentimento."

30. This term is taken from Sartre's *Being and Nothingness: An Essay on Phenomenological Ontology,* trans. Hazel Barnes (New York: Philosophical Library, 1956). From "hodos," Sartre's use of "hodological" concerns one's "everyday pragmatic level of existence." We form a hodological map of the world "in which pathways are traced to and among objects in accordance with the potentialities and resistances of objects in the world" (from the translator's introduction, xiv). The reader will also recognize symptoms of Sutpen's "stroke" from the gaze as elements compatible with Sartre's "Look," Part III, chap. 1, IV. I am suggesting here that mirrors, like maps, constitute the "hodological" equipment—the way by which we establish who/where we think we are.

31. Second Annual Retreat in African-American Literature and Culture, "Sites of Colonialism." Convened by Professor Houston Baker and the Center for the Study of Black Literature and Culture at the University of Pennsylvania; March 15–17, 1990.

32. One of the most persuasive interventions on the traditional mythos of the American scene is provided in the second chapter of Houston Baker's *Blues, Ideology, and Afro-American Literature*, "Figurations for a New American Literary History: Archaeology, Ideology, and Afro-American Discourse" (Chicago: University of Chicago Press, 1984.)

Chapter Fourteen

This is an excerpt from "Faulkner Adds Up: Reading *Absalom, Absalom!* and *The Sound and the Fury*," published in *Faulkner and America*, ed. Joseph Urgo (Oxford, Miss.: University of Mississippi Press, 2001), 24–45.

1. Gertrude Stein, *The Autobiography of Alice B. Toklas* (New York: Vintage Books, 1960); excerpts from *The Making of Americans* in *Selected Writings of Gertrude Stein,* ed. with introduction and notes by Carl Van Vechten and with an essay on Gertrude Stein by F. W. DuPee (New York: Vintage Books, 1962); all quotations from *The Making of Americans* come from this edition, page numbers noted in the text. The entire work was republished in 1995, with a Foreword by William Gass (Normal, Ill.: Dalkey Archive Press, Illinois State University).

2. William Faulkner, *Absalom, Absalom!* The Corrected Text (New York: Modern Library, 1993). All quotations from the novel come from this edition, page numbers noted in the text.

3. The psychoanalytic method that Jacques Lacan was devoted to inaugurating was based on a revision and correction of Freudian theory and practice. Incorporated in Anthony Wilden's text, Lacan's "Rome Report," delivered to an international forum of psychoanalysts after a split within the French circle during the 1950s, elaborated what Wilden has called "the new terminology"—which sought to integrate the Levi-Straussian hypothesis about the interrelatedness of linguistic and social structures with psychoanalysis (Jacques Lacan, *Speech and Language in Psychoanalysis,* trans. with notes and commentary by Anthony Wilden [Baltimore: the Johns Hopkins University Press, 1981], xiv.) In "The Empty Word and the Full Word," which appears in Wilden's translation, Lacan speaks of the subject's verbalizing of the event as the way by which the latter passes into the *verbe* "or more precisely into the epos," when the subject "brings back into present time the origins of his own person" (17).

Wilden points out that the *verbe*—"more or less synonymous with *mot, parole, logos,* and the *Logos*"—maintains a flavor of its own. In its early acceptations, the term was "reserved for religious and ecclesiastical contexts" (104, n. 41). In reference to Faulkner's character, I am taking it to mean the Word, "in so far as the Word confers a meaning on the functions of the individual; its domain is that of the concrete discourse; insofar as this is the field of the transindividual reality of the subject; its operations are those of history, insofar as history constitutes the emergence of Truth in the Real" (19).

"Ownmost" is borrowed from the Heideggerian canon, as Lacan's work is braided from philosophical elements that trace back to Hegel and the influential teachings of Alexandre Kojève in *Introduction to the Reading of Hegel: Lectures on the Phenomenology of Spirit,* assembled by Raymond Queneau, ed. Alan Bloom, trans. James H. Nichols Jr. (Ithaca: Cornell University Press, 1980).

4. William Faulkner, *The Sound and the Fury,* ed. David Minter, a Norton Critical Edition (New York: W. W. Norton, 1987). All quotations from the novel come from this edition, page numbers noted in the text.

5. In his magisterial study of Faulkner's life and work, Joseph Blotner points out that only the southern third of the state of Mississippi was inhabited by whites when the state was admitted to the Union in 1817. The remainder of the state was occupied by the Choctaw and Chickasaw communities; by way of the Treaty of Dancing Rabbit Creek, "a large part of North Mississippi running eastward from the Mississippi Delta" was ceded to the United States in 1830 (Joseph Blotner, *Faulkner: A Biography,* 2 vols. [New York: Random House, 1974], 1:11). Belonging to the era of President Andrew Jackson's coercive policies toward Native Americans and the notorious "Trail of Tears," the Treaty of Dancing Rabbit Creek, as well as others, was little short of unilateral surrender (Jeffrey P. Brain and Frank W. Porter III, *The Tunica-Biloxi,* Indians of North America Series [New York: Chelsea House Publishers, 1990], 10). The guilt that ensued left its fictive trail through Faulkner's work, particularly in the instance of Ike McCaslin and the repudiation of the land.

6. For a full discussion of "diegesis," from its Platonic origins, to its career in the hands of modern writers, see Gérard Genette, "Frontiers of Narrative," *Figures of Literary Discourse,* trans. Alan Sheridan, intro. Marie-Rose Logan (New York: Columbia University Press, 1982), 127–44. Migrating into film theory, "diegesis" is defined by one pair of cinéastes as the film's "recounted story," "the total world of the story action," over and against its plot: David Bordwell and Kristin Thompson, *Film Art: An Introduction,* 3d ed. (New York: McGraw-Hill Publishing Company, 1990), 56–57.

7. The "one" of the Lacanian project runs parallel to the "individual" of liberal property, but is far more complicated, insofar as his/her subjectivity arises elsewhere, not only in the sense of other subjects who precede him on his own stage, but also regarding the subject's relationship to his "unconscious." If the particular aim of psychoanalysis is "historically defined by an elaboration of the notion of the subject," then the "Ich"—"the complete, total locus of the network of signifiers, that is to say, the subject, *where it was,* where it has always been, the dream"—must be mapped. And *"where it was,* the *Ich*—the subject, not psychology—the subject must come into existence" (Jacques Lacan, *The Four Fundamental Concepts of Psychoanalysis,* ed. Jacques-Alain Miller, trans. Alan Sheridan [New York: W. W. Norton, 1981], 44–45, 77.

8. The paradigm of repetition in the poetics field rests in poetry itself. When such strategies appear, as they inevitably do, in works of prose fiction, we usually recognize them as image clusters, or other configurations of figures that add up to kinds of patterning, more or less predictable. But the repetitive in Stein's work, for example, does not produce an image or a visual field. From *The Making of Americans,* the following passage, among others, seems to defy traditional repetitive practices and expectations: "It is a very difficult thing to know it of any one the being in them, it is a very difficult

thing to tell it of any one what they are feeling, whether they are enjoying, whether they are knowing that they are hurting some one, whether they had been planning doing that thing. It is a very difficult thing to know these things in anyone, it is a difficult thing if that one is telling everything they can be telling, if that one is telling nothing" (287). The effect of the repetitive here might be described as *tickling,* though I can detect no humor in it. The self-conscious manipulation of signs, however, is somehow pleasurable at the same time that it makes the reader *herself* self-consciously engaged in the act of reading.

Søren Kierkegaard's 1843 novel *Repetition* bears the subtitle "An Essay in Experimental Psychology" and is narrated under a "symbolic pseudonym"—"Constantine Constantius." An excerpt from it appears in *A Kierkegaard Anthology,* ed. Robert Brettal, trans. Walter Lowrie (New York: The Modern Library, 1946), 134–52. The entire novel, alongside *Fear and Trembling,* appears in *Fear and Trembling; Repetition,* vol. 6 of *Kierkegaard's Writings,* ed. and trans. with intro. and notes by Howard V. Hong and Edna H. Hong (Princeton: Princeton University Press, 1983). In flight to Berlin after disappointment in love, Kierkegaard remained captive to his desire to marry Regine Schlegel. The possibility of a "repetition" of this affair, as well as the theme of repetition from other experiences in his life, is said to have suggested the plot of Kierkegaard's novel (Brettal, 135). Constantine's pursuit of repetition on aesthetic grounds is supposed to be a failure "just because it is an *attempt* and because it is *pursued*" (136, my emphasis). In this case, repetition consists in an action—the return on a scene in four dimensional space; but perhaps it has in common with repetition on a literary surface the idea of *fixation,* and "in so far as fixation is to be understood as an 'inscription' . . . regression might be interpreted as the bringing back into play of what has been inscribed" ("Regression," *The Language of Psychoanalysis,* ed. J. Laplanche and J.-B. Pontalis, trans. Donald Nicholson-Smith [New York: W. W. Norton, 1973], 386–88, 388).

9. Freud offers the paradigmatic model of repetition in "Remembering, Repeating and Working Through," *The Standard Edition of the Complete Psychological Works of Sigmund Freud,* trans. James Strachey in collaboration with Anna Freud, assisted by Alix Strachey and Alan Tyson, 24 vols. (London: The Hogarth Press, 1958), 12:147–56. Contrasted with "remembering," repetition, or the compulsion to repeat, becomes a major aspect of the transference; not only a transference onto the person of the doctor, but "also on to all the other aspects of the current situation," repetition "now replaces [in the patient] the impulsion to remember." The patient "repeats under the conditions of resistance" (151).

10. Citation appears on the dust jacket of *William Faulkner Reads: The Nobel Prize Acceptance Speech, As I Lay Dying* (excerpts), *A Fable* (excerpt), and "The Old Man" (excerpt). Classic Literature. Caedmon Audio (New York: HarperCollins Publishers, Inc., 1998).

11. See chap. 13, n. 25 above.

12. Gérard Genette, *Figures of Literary Discourse,* 133ff. Problems of narrative, as an instrument of cross-disciplinarity, as well as a recurrent theme in literary criticism and theory, have been recently taken up in the following sources, among others: Patricia Yaeger, *Dirt and Desire: Reconstructing Southern Women's Writing, 1930–1990* (Chicago: University of Chicago Press, 2000); Martin Kreiswirth, "Tell me a Story: The Narrativist Turn in the Human Sciences," in *Constructive Criticism: The Human Sciences in the Age of Theory,* ed. Martin Kreiswirth and Thomas Carmichael (Toronto: University of Toronto Press, 1995), 61–87; idem, "Merely Telling Stories? Narrative and Knowledge in the Human Sciences," *Poetics Today* 21, no. 1 (Summer 2000): 293–318; James Phelan, *Narrative as Rhetoric: Technique, Audiences, Ethics, Ideology* (Columbus: Ohio State University Press, 1996).

13. Genette, "Principles of Pure Criticism," 69.

14. I take up this problematic in greater detail in "Who Cuts the Border?" in this volume.

15. For a full discussion of deictic markings, see Jonathan Culler, "Poetics of the Lyric," *Structuralist Poetics: Structuralism, Linguistics, and the Study of Literature* (Ithaca: Cornell University Press, 1975), 161–88.

16. My notions about the uses of the "ornamental epithet" are reanimated and informed by Bernard Knox's introduction to Robert Fagles's translation of *The Odyssey* (New York: Viking, 1996), 3–64; "The Language of Homer," 12–22.

17. Deflecting, somewhat, Althusser's discussion of sightings on a theoretical object, I mean, in the specific instance of Faulkner's fiction, that his characters "see" by the lights of their positionings and investments. In explaining how Marx, in the project of *Capital*, begins with the question of "labor" and ends with an answer whose question had not been posed yet, even by Marx—that of the "labourer"—Althussser argues that the faculty of vision becomes "the act of its structural conditions." Once grasped as part and parcel of such "conditions," "vision then loses the religious privileges of divine reading: it is no more than a reflection of the immanent necessity that ties an object or problem to its conditions of existence, which lie in the conditions of its production" (Louis Althusser and Etienne Balibar, "From 'Capital' to Marx's Philosophy," *Reading Capital*, trans. Ben Brewster [London: New Left Books, Verso, 1986], 13–69, at 25).

18. This formulation is indebted to René Girard's *Violence and the Sacred*, trans. Patrick Gregory (Baltimore: The Johns Hopkins University Press, 1977).

19. Jacques Lacan, *The Four Fundamental Concepts of Psychoanalysis*. In "Tuché and Automaton," Lacan takes up the problematic of repetition by focusing on the startling dream of a father, who loses his sick child by fire; assigned the responsibility of watching over the child while its father took a rest, the attendant fell asleep, upsetting a candle at the child's bedside, setting the bed aflame. The father dreams the child's saying to him: "I'm burning . . . Father, don't you see?" (cited from Sigmund Freud, *The Interpretation of Dreams, Standard Edition*, 5:509–10); in this case, the burning child is running a fever—Lacan asks whether or not the father's remarkable dream of the situation is "an act of homage to the missed reality—the reality that can no longer produce itself except by repeating itself endlessly, in some never attained awakening?" (58). If, as Freud argued, the dream fulfills a wish, then the father's dream would appear to directly contradict such a conclusion. But as Lacan reads it from Freud, the dream signals that the father wants to continue sleeping, in which case his son, the dream's co-protagonist, is still alive.

20. Deborah Tannen, *Talking Voices: Repetition, Dialogue, and Imagery in Conversational Discourse*, Studies in Interactional Linguistics 6, general editor John L. Gumperz (Cambridge: Cambridge University Press, 1989).

21. Ibid., p. 37.

22. Roman Jakobson and Morris Halle, "The Twofold Character of Language," *Fundamentals of Language* (The Hague; Mouton, 1975), 72–76.

23. Tannen, *Talking Voices*, 95.

24. "The fragile thread" provides the title of Donald Kartiganer's moving study of Faulkner's works, from *The Sound and the Fury* to his last novels: *The Fragile Thread: The Meaning of Form in Faulkner's Novels* (Amherst: The University of Massachusetts Press, 1979). A post-1960s interpretive gesture, Kartiganer's work, among others, belongs to a repertoire of readings that launches what I would call the maturation of Faulknerian criticism and marks, for sure, a project decidedly distinct from an earlier critical phase by strict attention to Faulkner's *poetics*, his language: see also Arthur F. Kinney, *Faulkner's Narrative Poetics: Style as Vision* (Amherst: The University of Massachusetts Press, 1978), and John T. Matthews, *The Play of Faulkner's Language* (Ithaca: Cornell University Press, 1982), among others. Excerpts from both Kartiganer's and Matthews's mono-

graphs appear in the Norton *Sound and Fury* (see note 4 above), alongside other essays which reflect changes on the critical landscape of Faulknerian criticism over the last three decades.

25. W. E. B. DuBois, *The Souls of Black Folk,* ed. Henry Louis Gates Jr. and Terri Hume Oliver, Norton Critical Edition (New York: W. W. Norton and Company, 1999). One of the most well-known formulations in American social critique, DuBois's concept of "double consciousness" is tersely stated in these lines: "It is a peculiar sensation, this sense of always looking at one's self through the eyes of others, measuring one's soul by the tape of a world that looks on in amused contempt and pity. One ever feels his two-ness,—an American, a Negro, two souls, two thoughts, two unreconciled strivings; two warring ideals in one dark body, whose dogged strength alone keeps it from being torn asunder" (11).

Dickson Bruce's "W. E. B. DuBois and the Idea of Double Consciousness," which essay appears in the Norton edition (236–44), examines some of the philosophical and figurative precedents for the term; for example, Emerson's 1843 essay "The Transcendentalist" provides one such link. In the essay, Emerson proposes a conflictual relationship between "the demands of daily life" and the "transcendental perspective on self and world" (237). But the term, according to Arnold Rampersad in his work on DuBois, initially emanated from the field of medicine and appeared, eventually, in the emergent territory of psychology with reference to cases involving split personality (237). While DuBois's application of the concept was specifically adopted to the circumstances of African-Americans in the aftermath of the failures of Reconstruction, its potential use across a wider expanse of meaning is noteworthy: Sutpen's subaltern status as "po' white trash" assigns him, for all intents and purposes, to another "race" from that of the master *class*. In this fictional instance, the latter is profitably "confused" with the former, which dynamics boy Sutpen cannot be said to have fully understood. But the insult, nonetheless, constituted a trauma, or break in whatever unitary consciousness we imagine he might have intuited as belonging to the system *moi*.

26. The career of the concept of "libido/hunger," or of the "instincts," across Freud's work offers a rich itinerary of evolutionary development; in the *Three Essays on the Theory of Sexuality,* Freud opens with these lines: "The fact of the existence of sexual needs in human beings and animals is expressed in biology by the assumption of a 'sexual instinct,' on the analogy of the instinct of nutrition, that is of hunger. Everyday language possesses no counterpart to the word 'hunger,' but science makes use of the word 'libido' for that purpose" (*Standard Edition,* 7:135). In Part III of the *Introductory Lectures on Psycho-Analysis,* Lecture 20, "The Sexual Life of Human Beings," Freud again stresses an analogous relationship between the self-preservative and reproductive instincts: "On the exact analogy of 'hunger,' we use 'libido' as the name of the force (in this case of the sexual instinct, as in the case of hunger that of the nutritive instinct) by which the instinct manifests itself" (*Standard Edition,* 16:313.) Pointing out that he is following the popular view that distinguished between "love" and "hunger," Freud, in *An Infantile Neurosis,* elaborates: "The force by which the sexual instinct is represented in the mind we call 'libido'—sexual desire—and we regard it as something analogous to hunger, the will to power, and so on, where the ego-instincts are concerned" ("A Difficulty in the Path of Psycho-analysis," *Standard Edition,* 17:137). Approximately a decade later, however, the analogous association has yielded a new dialectical force in his thinking; in pursuit of a solid foundation for a theory of the instincts, Freud notes that he began the project "by drawing a contrast between the ego-instincts (the instinct of self-preservation, hunger) and the libidinal instincts (love), but later replaced it by a new contrast between narcissistic and object-libido." This "single class of instincts," insufficient as well, pressed on to greater speculation on Freud's part: "I have combined the instincts for self-preservation and for the preservation of the species under the con-

cept of Eros and have contrasted with it an *instinct of death* or *destruction* which works in silence" ("An Autobiographical Study," *Standard Edition*, 20:57).

27. Eve Kosofsky Sedgwick, *Epistemology of the Closet* (Berkeley: University of California Press, 1990). One of the founding and seminal texts of lesbian-gay-bisexual studies, Sedgwick's work proposes that "an understanding of virtually any aspect of modern Western culture must be, not merely incomplete, but damaged in its central substance to the degree that it does not incorporate a critical analysis of modern homo/heterosexual definition" ("Introduction: Axiomatic," 1). The reader of Faulkner's *Absalom, Absalom!* is so struck by elder Compson's insistence on Charles Bon's "orientalist" performance of self-presentation and fashioning that it is not at all out of the question that he harbors homoerotic desire in his own version of fantasy life; Sedgwick's readings enable our speculation that this character may bear not only a profound secret, but for him an unspeakable one.

28. Freud, "Screen Memories," *Standard Edition*, 3:321.

29. Kenneth Burke, *The Philosophy of Literary Form: Studies in Symbolic Action*, 3d ed. (Berkeley: University of California Press, 1973).

30. Ibid., 360.

31. Winifred Bryan Horner, *Rhetoric in the Classical Tradition* (New York: St. Martin's Press, 1988), 316.

32. Ibid., 317.

33. Martin Luther King, "Letter From Birmingham Jail," *Why We Can't Wait* (New York: Signet, 1964), 76–96.

34. Richard A. Lanham, "A Brief Glossary of Rhetorical Terms," *Analyzing Prose* (New York: Charles Scribner's Sons, 1983), 254.

35. Kartiganer, *The Fragile Thread*, 22.

36. Ibid., 9.

37. Burke, *The Philosophy of Literary Form*, 261.

38. Ibid.

39. Jakobson, "The Metaphoric and Metonymic Poles," *Fundamentals of Language*, 90–96.

40. Ibid., "The Twofold Character of Language," 73.

41. Reading Faulkner against Nietzsche and Freud, John Irwin provides a seminal study of the novels by way of the "Quentin Compson" configuration. Irwin places the double and the theme of the uncanny at the center of the oscillations of his argument between texts (*Doubling and Incest/Repetition and Revenge: A Speculative Reading of Faulkner* [Baltimore: The Johns Hopkins University Press, 1975]).

Other important psychoanalytic inquiries into aspects of the Faulknerian canon include: Carolyn Porter, "Symbolic Fathers and Dead Mothers: A Feminist Approach to Faulkner" and Jay Watson, "Faulkner's Forensic Fiction and the Question of Authorial Neurosis," in *Faulkner and Psychology,* ed. Donald M. Kartiganer and Ann J. Abadie (Jackson: the University Press of Mississippi, 1994), 78–123, 165–89; Doreen Fowler, *Faulkner: The Return of the Repressed* (Charlottesville: University Press of Virginia, 1997).

42. Walter Benjamin, "The Work of Art in the Age of Mechanical Reproduction," *Illuminations: Essays and Reflections,* ed. with intro. Hannah Arendt, trans. Harry Zohn (New York: Schocken Books, 1968), 217–53. Benjamin proposes that in the age of mechanical reproduction the aura of the art work withers, as "the technique of reproduction detaches the reproduced object from the domain of tradition. By making many reproductions it substitutes a plurality of copies for a unique existence" (221).

The 1954–55 Jacques Lacan seminar features several interlocutors on the "Freudian Schemata of the Psychic Apparatus." In the course of the exchange, Lacan elaborates the Freudian distinction between *reminiscence,* which may analogize with Benjamin's eviscerated "aura of art," and *repetition,* which matches his "age of mechanical reproduction." In Lacan, these differences are designated as "structurations of human expe-rience": on the one hand, *reminiscence* presupposes "agreement, harmony between man and the world of his objects, which means that he recognizes them, because in some way, he has always known them," and on the other, "the conquest, the structura-tion of the world through the effort of labour, along the path of repetition" (100). Inso-far as what appears to him "corresponds only partially with what has already gained him satisfaction," the subject engages and repeats the quest "indefinitely until he re-discovers his object." Structured along the path of repetition, the object is never the "same object which the subject encounters. In other words, he never ceases generating substitutive objects" (100). *The Seminar of Jacques Lacan,* Book 2: *The Ego in Freud's The-ory and in the Technique of Psychoanalysis, 1954–1955,* trans. Sylvana Tomaselli, ed. Jacques-Alain Miller, with notes by John Forrester (New York: W. W. Norton and Com-pany, 1991), 93–161.

43. Burke, *The Philosophy of Literary Form,* 260.

44. Ibid., 191.

45. Though Lacan's triangulation of the psychic web is foundational to his own vast contributions to the psychoanalytic field and is, therefore, woven throughout his work, a concise definition of the Imaginary/Symbolic/Real concatenation is offered in the "Translator's note" to *Écrits: A Selection,* trans. Alan Sheridan (New York: W. W. Nor-ton and Company, 1977), vii–xii.

46. Lacan, *The Four Fundamental Concepts of Psychoanalysis,* 20, 21.

47. Jacqueline Rose, *Sexuality in the Field of Vision* (London: Verso, 1986), 55. Ele-ments of this work appear in Jacqueline Rose's introduction to *Feminine Sexuality: Jacques Lacan and the École Freudienne,* ed. Juliet Mitchell and Jacqueline Rose, trans. Jacqueline Rose (New York: W.W. Norton and Company, 1982), 27–59; the "moment of fundamental and irreducible division" initiates, in Lacan, entry into the "order of lan-guage," or the Symbolic sphere, whereas "that of the ego and its identifications" belong to the "imaginary (the stress, therefore, is quite deliberately on symbol and image, the idea of something which 'stands in.')" The Real is Lacan's term "for the moment of im-possibility onto which both are grafted, the point of that moment's endless return" (*Feminine Sexuality,* 31).

48. Ibid.

49. This powerful concept is elaborated by Wahneema Lubiano, "Like Being Mugged By a Metaphor: Multiculturalism and State Narratives," in *Mapping Multicultur-alism,* ed. Avery F. Gordon and Christopher Newfield (Minneapolis: University of Min-nesota Press, 1996), 64–75.

50. Rose, *Sexuality in the Field of Vision,* 54.

51. Ibid., 55.

Chapter Fifteen

"'All the Things You Could Be by Now, If Sigmund Freud's Wife Was Your Mother': Psy-choanalysis and Race" was published in *boundary 2,* vol. 23, no. 3 (Fall 1996): 75–143, and is reprinted by permission of Duke University Press. Rpt. in *Female Subjects in Black and White: Race, Psychoanalysis, Feminism,* ed. Elizabeth Abel, Barbara Christian, and Helene Moglen (Berkeley, University of California Press, 1997). Shorter version pub-lished in *Critical Inquiry* 22 (Summer 1996); rpt. *African American Literary Theory: A Reader,* ed. Winston Napier (New York: New York University Press, 2000).

Unless otherwise stated, all translations are my own.

1. Perhaps the long-awaited thaw in the recognition of a collective and cooperative interest among African-American women in the academy is only now coming about. During the month of January 1994, several hundred black women and women of color converged on the campus of the Massachusetts Institute of Technology for four days of

meetings devoted to inquiry concerning a range of issues. Organized by MIT Professors Robin Kilson (history) and Evelyn Hammond (the history of science), "Defending Our Name, 1984–1994," its title taking its cue from the *New York Times* advertisement in support of Professor Anita Hill, was keynoted by three leading figures: Dr. Johnetta Cole, then president of Spelman College, now president of Bennett College; Professor Angela Davis, of the History of Consciousness Board, University of California, Santa Cruz; and law Professor Lani Guinier, at the time of the University of Pennsylvania Law School, now at Harvard. Prior to the MIT conference, however, black women graduate students in English and African-American studies at the University of Pennsylvania convened a smaller conference of similar design at the Philadelphia campus during the spring of 1993. The MIT symposium was modeled on this idea.

2. Mark Seem, introduction to Gilles Deleuze and Félix Guattari, *Anti-Oedipus: Capitalism and Schizophrenia,* trans. Robert Hurley, Mark Seem, and Helen R. Lane, preface by Michel Foucault (Minneapolis: University of Minnesota Press, 1983); originally published as *L'Anti-Oedipe* (Les Éditions de Minuit, 1972). Seem identifies the project in this way: "What it attempts to cure us of is the cure itself. Deleuze and Guattari term their approach 'schizoanalysis,' which they oppose on every count to psychoanalysis" (xvii).

3. For a recent examination of the problematics of "race," in aspects of its loose and strict construction, see Dominick LaCapra, ed., *The Bounds of Race: Perspectives on Hegemony and Resistance* (Ithaca: Cornell University Press, 1991).

4. Frantz Fanon, *Black Skin, White Masks,* trans. Charles Lam Markmann (New York: Grove Press, 1967), 151; originally published as *Peau Noire, Masques Blancs* (Paris: Éditions du Seuil, 1952). This work is hereafter cited parenthetically as *BS,* page numbers noted in the text.

5. This particular cluster of historical motives provides the framework of reading the project of historiography in Michel de Certeau, *The Writing of History,* trans. Tom Conley (New York: Columbia University Press, 1988); originally published as *L'Écriture de l'histoire* (Paris: Gallimard, 1975).

6. de Certeau, *The Writing of History,* preface, xxv.

7. This line of argument is fruitfully pursued in Patricia Parker's *Literary Fat Ladies: Rhetoric, Gender, Property* (London: Methuen, 1987), 141ff. Parker's "feminized New World" offers the ground for the convergence of diverse human interests: male gaze, real estate, and the operations of rhetoric. See also "Who Cuts the Border?" my introduction to *Comparative American Identities: Race, Sex, and Nationality in the Modern Text,* ed. Hortense J. Spillers, English Institute Essays (New York: Routledge, 1991), in this volume.

8. Jacques Lacan, *Écrits: A Selection,* trans. Alan Sheridan (New York: W. W. Norton, 1977); selected from the original *Écrits* (Paris: Editions du Seuil, 1966). In the translator's note to the English version, the three Lacanian dimensions are defined together: Sheridan points out that the "imaginary" was the first to appear, prior to the Rome Report of 1953, in which writing the notion of the "symbolic" surfaces. The "real" was initially "of only minor importance, acting as a kind of safety rail." Gradually developing, its impact shifted over time, from a "function of constancy" as that "which always returns to the same place," to that "before which the imaginary faltered, that over which the symbolic stumbles"—thus, the "impossible" (x).

9. Jacques Lacan, *The Four Fundamental Concepts of Psychoanalysis,* ed. Jacques Alain Miller, trans. Alan Sheridan (New York: W. W. Norton, 1981); originally published as "Les quatre concepts fondamentaux de la psychanalyse," in *Le Seminaire de Jacques Lacan,* Livre XI (Paris: Éditions du Seuil, 1973). In the translator's note on this text, Sheridan points out that, though linked to the symbolic and the imaginary, the "real" stands for neither and "remains foreclosed from the analytic experience, which is an experience of speech." In any case, the "real" comes about prior to the subject's assumption of

the symbolic and "is not to be confused with reality, which is perfectly knowable: the subject of desire knows no more than that, since for it reality is entirely phantasmatic" (280).

10. J. Laplanche and J.-B. Ponatalis, *The Language of Psychoanalysis*, trans. Donald Nicholson-Smith, with intro. by David Lagache (New York: W. W. Norton, 1973); originally published as *Vocabulaire de la psychanalyse* (Paris: Presses Universitaires de France, 1967). No discussion is found here of the "real," but there are entries on the "Reality Principle" and "Reality-Testing"; on the "Imaginary" (210); on the "Symbolic" and its contrastive uses in Freud and Lacan (439–41).

11. This fourth register would be nothing more or less than "reality," constructed in relationship to the Lacanian Schema R (see Anthony Wilden, trans., and commentary, *Speech and Language in Psychoanalysis: Jacques Lacan* [Baltimore: Johns Hopkins University Press, 1968], 294–98). If we think of this encodation as a psychic totality of "one," it might be analogized in accordance with genetic structure as the "socionom."

12. Lacan, "Excommunication," in *The Four Fundamental Concepts*, 8–12.

13. One such project did in fact appear with the *Journal for the Psychoanalysis of Culture and Society*, edited by Mark Bracher and inaugurated in 1995–96.

14. Pierre Bourdieu, *Outline of a Theory of Practice*, trans. Richard Nice, Cambridge Studies in Social Anthropology, gen. ed. Jack Goody (Cambridge: Cambridge University Press, 1977); originally published as *Esquisse d'une théorie de la pratique, précédé de trois études d'ethnologie kabyle* (Paris: Librarie Droz, 1972). See especially "Structures, Habitus, Power: Basis for a Theory of Symbolic Power," 159–97, which makes a case for the "perfect interconvertibility of economic capital . . . and symbolic capital" in his study of Kabyle anthropological structures, and in which Bourdieu argues an explicit link between forms of capital and modes of circulation (177). I am borrowing his notion toward different ends, however, by contending that a revised African-American culture critique would seek to place the subject in the "totality" of his/her surround, *including* the interior. Bourdieu's context is specifically this: "Thus, homologies established between the circulation of land sold and bought, the circulation of 'throats' 'lent' and 'returned' (murder and vengeance), and the circulation of women given and received, that is, between the different forms of capital and the corresponding modes of circulation, oblige us to abandon the dichotomy of the economic and the non-economic which stands in the way of seeing the science of economic practices as a particular case of a general science of the economy of practices, capable of treating all practices, including those purporting to be disinterested or gratuitous, and hence non-economic, as economic practices directed towards the maximizing of material or symbolic profit" (183).

15. Robert Stepto, *From Behind the Veil: A Study of Afro-American Narrative* (Urbana: University of Illinois Press, 1979). Readdressing Victor Turner's "ritual topography" to specific, other narrative matters at hand, Stepto seeks a paradigmatic concept that would be capable of identifying "the requisite features or tropes of any ritualized journeys or pilgrimages in Afro-American narratives, whether they be of ascent [the journey North, actually and symbolically, toward freedom in the historical outline] or of immersion [the reversal of direction, back toward the matrix or cradle of the South]" (67). Stepto's "symbolic geography" "focuses on the idea that a landscape becomes symbolic in literature when it is a region in time and space offering spatial expressions of social structures and ritual grounds on the one hand, and of *communitas* and *genius loci* on the other" (67). Stepto's "moments in and out of time" that would also entail the imaginary and the phantasmal, as I see it, provide a basis for a more generous application of the principle of *communitas*.

16. A good introduction to a study of the social context of emergent psychoanalytic theory is offered in Juliet Mitchell, *Psychoanalysis and Feminism: Freud, Reich, Laing, and*

Women (New York: Vintage, 1975), especially the appendix, "Psychoanalysis and Vienna at the Turn of the Century," 419–35. Peter Gay's biographical study of Sigmund Freud exhaustively articulates the life with the career, and both within the context of Freud's era, in *Freud: A Life for Our Time* (New York: W. W. Norton, 1988), see especially chaps. 5–7, 197–361.

17. A number of important works—both monographs and essay collections—in feminist interventions on the psychoanalytic object have emerged within the last decade and a half, including, among others: Charles Bernheimer and Claire Kahane, eds., *In Dora's Case: Freud-Hysteria-Feminism,* Gender and Culture Series (New York: Columbia University Press, 1985); Mary Jacobus, *Reading Woman: Essays In Feminist Criticism,* Gender and Culture Series (New York: Columbia University Press, 1986); Teresa Brennan, ed., *Between Feminism, and Psychoanalysis* (New York: Routledge, 1989); and Richard Feldstein and Judith Roof, eds., *Feminism and Psychoanalysis* (Ithaca: Cornell University Press, 1989).

18. Delineating the four realms or regions of linguistic reference, Kenneth Burke speaks of the "paradox of the negative" in that context: it "is simply this: Quite as the word 'tree' is verbal and the *thing* tree is nonverbal, so all words for the non-verbal must, by the very nature of the case, discuss the realm of the non-verbal in terms of *what it is not.* Hence, to use words properly, we must spontaneously have a feeling for the *principle of the negative" (The Rhetoric of Religion: Studies in Logology* [Berkeley: University of California Press, 1970], 18). For all intents and purposes, the classic distinction between sign and thing gained primacy via the field of modern linguistics and one of its most influential teachers of the early twentieth century, Ferdinand de Saussure (*Course in General Linguistics,* ed. Charles Bally and Albert Sechehaye in collaboration with Albert Riedlinger, trans. Wade Baskin [New York: McGraw-Hill, 1966]). Overlapping Freud's era, Saussure's researches were posthumously introduced to a wider audience of readers by some of his former students.

On this side of the Atlantic, however, philosopher Charles Sanders Peirce carried out innovative work on semiotics and a theory of signs during the late nineteenth and early twentieth centuries; see "Logic as Semiotic: The Theory of Signs," *Philosophical Writings of Peirce,* ed. with intro. Justus Buchler (New York: Dover Publications, 1955), 98–120.

19. Juliet Mitchell offers what appears to be an unobjectionable, perhaps even inevitable, response to notorious penis envy, for example, one of the reportorial items that renders feminist theories and indeed some feminists edgy about the entire Freudian protocol: "but I think the main problem arises because the suggestion is taken outside the context of the mechanisms of unconscious mental life—the law of the primary process (the laws that govern the workings of the unconscious) are replaced by these critics by those of the secondary process (conscious decisions and perceptions), and as a result the whole point is missed" ("Freud: The Making of a Lady I: Psychoanalysis and the Unconscious" in *Psychoanalysis and Feminism,* 8).

20. Irene Gendzier, *Frantz Fanon: A Critical Study* (New York: Vintage, 1974). Fanon's early adulthood and medical training in Lyon, France, instead of Paris—"to avoid too many blacks"—provide the background for the opening chapter of this study, "Biographical Notes to 1952," (3–21, passage cited from 16). Gendzier claims that Fanon maintained some reluctance to engaging himself in the process of psychoanalysis (19). In fact, he appears to have held psychoanalysis "in disdain." Working as a resident during the summer of 1952, under the direction of one Professor François Tosquelles, at the Saint Alban Hospital, Fanon performed "with enthusiasm and . . . learned his lessons well." According to Gendzier, French psychoanalytic training did not require at the time that "potential psychiatrists be analyzed" (19). It is not clear to me that this mode of bypass still operates in the French psychoanalytic community, but given Lacan's persistent concern for the training of the analyst and the apparently retortionary en-

tanglements embroidered through his troubled relationship with the French establishment and, furthermore, his attentiveness to Freud's ethical dimension, we should be
surprised if at least Lacan himself had not urged the protégé to an analytic course. For
more recent work on Fanon's life and career, see *Fanon: A Critical Reader,* ed. Lewis R.
Gordon, T. Denean Sharpley-Whiting, and Renee T. White (London: Blackwell Publishers, 2000); Paget Henry, *Caliban's Reason: Introducing Afro-Caribbean Philosophy* (New
York: Routledge, 2000); and David Macey, *Frantz Fanon: A Life* (London: Granta Publications, 2000).

21. Frantz Fanon, *The Wretched of the Earth,* preface by Jean-Paul Sartre, trans. Constance Farrington (New York: Grove Press, 1968); originally published as *Les Damnés de
la terre* (Paris: François Maspero, 1961); also published in *Présence Africaine,* 1963. Sartre
appears to have been, singlehandedly, the stellar one (white)man imprimatur of Francophone intellectuals—those students from "France Overseas"—in "introduction" to
proper French culture. He had also "fronted" for an earlier generation of black intellectuals, including Aimé Césaire, by way of his introduction to the anthology of poets of
négritude, *Black Orpheus,* trans. S. W. Allen (Paris: Presence Africaine, [1963]). Are we
correct to see in such a move an analogy on Frederick Douglass's *Narrative* (1845) and
the role wielded by a couple of famous New England intellectual-abolitionsists, William Lloyd Garrison and Wendell Phillips? (See *Narrative of the Life of Frederick Douglass
an American Slave Written by Himself* [New York: Signet, 1968].)

22. Frantz Fanon, *Toward the African Revolution—Political Essays,* trans. Haakon Che-
valier (New York: Grove Press, 1967); originally published as *Pour la révolution africaine*
(Paris: François Maspero, 1964). See especially chap. 2, "West Indians and Africans,"
17–29, and chap. 19, "Blood Flows in the Antilles under French Domination," 167–
70.

23. Famous Senegalese novelist-filmmaker Ousmane Sembene has garnered a significant repertory of films to his credit and as a pioneer in the emergence of the field of
West African cinema. One of Sembene's latest films, *Guelwaar,* played the U.S. circuit
during 1993 (see *New York Times,* Living Arts, Thursday, 29 July 1993, B5). For sustained
commentary on Sembene's films, see Roy Armes, *Third World Film Making and the West*
(Berkeley: University of California Press, 1987); "An Interview with Sembene Ousmane," with Nourreddine Ghali, in *Film and Politics in the Third World,* ed. John D. H.
Downing (Brooklyn, N.Y.: Autonomedia, 1987); and Manthia Diawara, *African Cinema:
Politics and Culture* (Bloomington: Indiana University Press, 1992).

24. I wish to thank here Ms. Yolanda Pierce, a member of my Cornell graduate seminar "On Minority Discourse" (Fall 1995; now a professor of English at the University of
Kentucky, Lexington), and Professor E. Ann Kaplan, Director of the Humanities Center,
SUNY-Stony Brook, for taking issue with my reading of this chapter. The opportunity to
give a version of "Psychoanalysis and Race" at the SUNY campus (Fall 1995) and to follow it up with a seminar the next day, suggested a reading strategy to me that I had simply not considered: that Fanon's "Negro of the Antilles" imagines that he is French,
which I am prepared to accept, steps off the deep end when it modulates into his thinking that he is "white." This was also Ms. Pierce's observation. In fact, the reading accords with the fine print of a footnote that Fanon works out in the course of the
chapter, but, in a way, by no means as transparently as I have stated it just now: the
twenty-fifth footnote of the chapter in question runs about four pages, and in it, Fanon
explains how the imaginary appears to work in the European subject (on the basis of Lacan's "mirror stage") and how the imaginary of the Antillean complicates the picture.
For the white man, "the Other is perceived on the level of the body image, absolutely as
the not-self—that is, the unidentifiable, the unassimilable." For him, there can be no
further doubt, Fanon offers, "that the real Other . . . is and will continue to be, the black
man" (*BS,* 161). The black as a "phobogenic object, a stimulus to anxiety" (*BS,* 151 n. 4),

may be read against this elaboration, as the black person begins the biological cycle in the white imaginary as the "destructuration" of the body of the latter. But Fanon appears to draw a distinction at this point between "visual perception" as the "elaboration of the imago" and "the level of the imaginary" (*BS*, 163). He contends that "in the Antilles perception always occurs" on that level, as "it is in white terms that one perceives one's fellows"—people will say, for instance, that "thus and so" is "very black." In other words, the Antillean is seeing his fellows as a white man would see him. When he adds "that every Antillean expects all the others to perceive him in terms of the essence of the white man" (*BS*, 163), is he saying that every Antillean expects to be seen as a white man, or as a white man might see him? The confusion lies here—the extent to which the activity of seeing/being seen, or "visual perception," as Fanon would have it, is already a product of the *imaginary* and what the black person sees when he/she stands before the mirror. Taking this problematic on its crudest terms, I should think that it would be difficult for the black person *not* to see himself as he is, but Fanon must be asking, What is he?

25. I am referring to the following passage from Freud's "Question of Lay Analysis": "We know less about the sexual life of little girls than of boys. But we need not feel ashamed of this distinction; after all, the sexual life of adult women is a 'dark continent' for psychology" (*The Standard Edition of the Complete Psychological Works of Sigmund Freud*, trans. James Strachey [London: Hogarth Press and the Institute of Psychoanalysis, 1959], 20:212).

26. Ernesto Laclau and Chantal Mouffe, "Beyond the Positivity of the Social: Antagonisms and Hegemony," *Hegemony and Socialist Strategy: Towards a Radical Democratic Politics* (London: Verso, 1985), 146, n. 19. Laclau points out here that capitalist accumulation in Marx's protocol "is presented as a *strictly social* logic which only imposes itself through establishing a relation of equivalence among materially distinct objects" (my emphasis). The writers not only insist on the discursive relations between materialism and discursive positionality, but argue the priority of the latter.

27. Marie-Cécile and Edmond Ortigues, *Oedipe Africain* (Paris: Éditions L'Harmattan, 1984), 9. The translations from this work are my own and come from this edition, which hereafter is cited parenthetically as *OA*, page numbers noted in the text.

28. See note 25. An important new reading of Fanon and the "querelle de femme" is offered by Gwen Bergner, "Who Is That Masked Woman? or, The Role of Gender in Fanon's *Black Skin, White Masks*," in *Special Topic: Colonialism and the Postcolonial Condition*, ed. Satya P. Mohanty and Linda Hutcheon, *Publications of the Modern Language Association of America* 110, no. 1 (January 1995): 108–19.

29. "It thus seems that the West Indian, after the great white error, is now living in the great black mirage" (Fanon, *Toward the African Revolution*, 27).

30. Jürgen Habermas, *Knowledge and Human Interests*, trans. Jeremy J. Shapiro (Boston: Beacon Press, 1968); appendix, 310; originally published as *Erkenntnis und Interesse* (Frankfurt am Main: Suhrkamp Verlag, 1965); reprinted as *Technik und Wissenschaft als "Ideologie"* (Frankfurt am Main: Suhrkamp Verlag, 1968).

31. The value of the synecdochic figure rests in its commutability—Kenneth Burke speaks of the "noblest synecdoche" entailed in the identity of "microcosm" and "macrocosm." In this "noblest instance . . . the individual is treated as a replica of the universe, and vice versa . . . since microcosm is related to macrocosm as part to whole, and either the whole can represent the part, or the part can represent the whole" (*A Grammar of Motives* [New York: Prentice Hall, 1952], appendix D, "The Four Master Tropes," 508).

32. The speaking subject of enunciation marks two distinctions: The "I" of the enunciation is not the same thing as the "I" of the statement (Lacan, "Analysis and Truth," *The Four Fundamental Concepts*, 138–39). Alan Sheridan translates *énoncé* as the

statement, or the "actual words uttered," whereas *énonciation* refers to "the act of uttering them" (*Écrits*, translator's note, ix). The "I" who makes "the statement is the subject of the enunciation *(sujet de l'énonciation)*," or what I am calling here the "speaking subject of the enunciation," whereas the "I" that constitutes "the grammatical subject of the statement itself is the subject of the statement *(sujet de l'énoncé)*" (Mikkel Borch-Jacobsen, *Lacan: The Absolute Master*, trans. Douglas Brick [Stanford: Stanford University Press, 1991], 260 n. 20; hereafter, this work is cited parenthetically as *LAM*). Now, the consciousness who "counts" is the one who speaks his position, whereas the statement does not uniquely define him by virtue of the shifter "I" that establishes his relation in grammatical context—a position in discourse.

33. Jean-Paul Sartre's "bodies" exist in three-dimensional space—the "body-for-me," or one's relations with objects of the world; the "body-for-the-other"; and the "body-as-seen-by-the-other" (*Being and Nothingness: An Essay on the Phenomenological Ontology*, trans. with intro. Hazel E. Barnes [New York: Philosophical Library, 1956], x1i). Lacan and Sartre might have shared a teacher in Alexandre Kojève, whose lectures on Hegel's *Phenomenology* were delivered at the École des Hautes Études between 1933 and 1939 (Wilden, *Speech and Language in Psychoanalysis*, 192–93); these lectures became the influential *Introduction to the Reading of Hegel: Lectures on the Phenomenology of Spirit*, assembled by Raymond Queneau, trans. James H. Nicols Jr., ed. Allan Bloom (Ithaca: Cornell University Press, 1980). This passage of the essay is much indebted to the Sartrean body and "look": "What I constantly aim at across my experiences are the Other's feelings, the Other's ideas, the Other's volitions, the Other's character. This is because the Other is not only the one whom I see but the one who sees me. . . . [F]inally in my essential being I depend on the essential being of the Other, and instead of holding that my being-for-myself is opposed to my being-for-others, I find that being-for-others appears as a necessary condition for my being-for-myself" (228, 238).

34. See Freud, *The Interpretation of Dreams*, in *Standard Edition*, vols. 4 and 5; specifically, "Regression," 5:533–49.

35. Freud, *The Interpretation of Dreams*, 5:578.

36. Jacques Lacan, *The Four Fundamental Concepts*, 77.

37. W. E. B. Du Bois, *The Souls of Black Folk* (New York: Bantam Books, 1989).

38. DuBois, *The Souls of Black Folk*, 2–3: "After the Egyptian and Indian, the Greek and Roman, the Teuton and Mongolian, the Negro is a sort of seventh son, born with a veil, and gifted with second-sight in this American world,—a world which yields him no true self-consciousness, but only lets him see himself through the revelation of the other world. It is a peculiar sensation, this double-consciousness, this sense of always looking at one's self through the eyes of others."

39. The locution "talking cure" was attributed to one of Freud's colleague's patients—"Fräulein Anna O"—whose case history is sketched out by Dr. Joseph Breuer in *Studies in Hysteria*, in *Standard Edition*, vol. 2. Freud opened his Clark University lectures, on the occasion of the twentieth anniversary of the founding of the Worcester campus (September 1909), with an examination of the progression toward psychoanalytic procedure from hypnosis and the "talking cure": The hypnotized patient "relives," in the presence of the doctor, the occasion, the connection, and the accompanying affect of the first appearance of the symptom of disorder (12–13). The patient is also said to have jokingly referred to the treatment as "chimney sweeping." In any case, the point was to get the patient to talk along the mnemic traces of the traumatizing event in a reverse chronological order, starting with the latest manifestation of the symptom and working back in time. Because Freud came to think of hypnosis as a "mystical" and an "arbitrary" ally, he ditched it in favor of the technique of "free association," combined with the interpretation of dreams. He called this method of treatment "psychoanalysis" (28).

When I refer here to "talking," or more exactly "speaking," I am far closer to meaning the plain speech of everyday encounter than the particularized discourse of the psychoanalytic hermeneutic. For example, during the long televised ordeal of the O. J. Simpson murder trial, CNN reported on events surrounding the news phenomenon with unrelieved regularity; one of the stories that the cable outlet carried for the customary twenty-four hour cycle of coverage was that of a black doctor (M.D.) in Los Angeles, who had turned the site of his practice, for a few hours a day, into a sort of neighborhood den, open to members of the community, where talk about the trial occurred. In the footage I saw, the scene was arranged like a classroom, as the doctor himself both talked and listened to what his interlocutors had to say. That is exactly the sort of protocol I would mean for the "talking cure" as a metaphor for *exchange* that occurs quite a lot less often in black communities than we might imagine. I see no reason, again, why black church congregations cannot convert pulpit and altar into a public forum at least once a week for the exercise of discourse related to events that touch the lives of the congregants. It seems to me that a few valuable lessons might be conveyed this way, in the undramatic informal analysis of the Event. As the last standing independent organ in black communities, black churches, in my opinion, have the stellar occasion to teach attention (as a function of determining how one is situated), criticism (as a function of seeing), and articulation (as a function of saying what is on the mind and the heart). We do not need psychoanalytic training for these tasks, but the simpler will to communicate.

40. Toni Morrison, *Beloved* (New York: Knopf, 1987).

41. In *La Culture au pluriel* (Paris: Christian Bourgois Éditeur, 1980), Michel de Certeau makes a distinction between discourse as work and discourse as the mark of activity in getting at the problematic of "culture" (225).

42. For a systematic investigation of various positions on property, see C. B. MacPherson, ed., *Property: Mainstream and Critical Positions* (Toronto: University of Toronto Press, 1978).

43. I am borrowing this notion from Louis Althusser and Étienne Balibar, *Reading Capital,* trans. Ben Brewster (London: Verso, 1979), see especially part 1, "From *Capital* to Marx's Philosophy."

44. See note 14 above.

45. During the winter 1995 convocation of the Rainbow Coalition, the Reverend Jesse Jackson emphatically addressed the question of "personal responsibility": "We cannot give up any more ground on that word." His remarks were contextualized, indeed necessitated, by what the pundits have called a political "tsunami"—an earthquake at sea—that stunned the nation in November 1994, when less than 43 percent of the national electorate reporting brought us a Republican majority in Congress and the so-called revolutionary leader of the new majority for the first time in more than four decades, Newton Gingrich of Georgia, newly ascendant Speaker of the House of Representatives. The winter meeting of the Rainbow Coalition had been called as a signal to the American "Lib/Lab/Left" (to borrow a term from Britain's Paddy Ashdown) coalition to mark this moment as a crucial realignment of the sociopolitical landscape and to think again, as a result, the uses to which the idea of alliance might be put. Jackson's remarks also signaled that he was alert to the question of agency and the imperative to refashion a notion of it. ("Defending the Family: Strategies for Economic Justice and Hope," 5–7 January 1995, Washington, D.C., Friday, 6 January 1995, C-SPAN).

46. This powerful text, to which the title of the quoted passage refers, has become a classic tool of thought about the insurgent aims of education. Paulo Freire, *Pedagogy of the Oppressed,* trans. Myra Bergman Ramos (New York: Herder and Herder, 1970). Specifically grounded in the Brazilian situation, Freire's work, in applying the thinking of Fanon and Marx, might be suggestive for other localities.

47. Anthony Wilden's *Speech and Language in Psychoanalysis* addresses the 1966 edition of *Oedipe Africain* as an instance of the anthropological uses of psychoanalysis (303–6). See also note 11 above.

48. Ibrâhîm Sow, *Les Structures anthropologiques de la folie en Afrique noire* (Paris: Payot, 1978), 48, hereafter cited parenthetically as *SA;* trans. Joyce Diamanti, as *Anthropological Structures of Madness in Black Africa* (New York: International Universities Press, 1980), 53, hereafter cited parenthetically as *AS;* trans. mod. The translations from *SA* are mine.

49. Professor Valentin Mudimbe's work on the African problematic has been rich and steady; among other titles, his *Surreptitious Speech: Présence Africaine and the Politics of Otherness 1947–1987* (Chicago: University of Chicago Press, 1992) is not to be missed.

50. One of the most exciting works in African-American culture studies over the last couple of decades has been John Gwaltney's *Drylongso: A Self-Portrait of Black America* (New York: Vintage, 1981), a veritable mine of black talk on every conceivable subject, from sex to the economy. *Drylongso* foregrounds ordinary "members of the tribe," as Ralph Ellison might have put it. I am uncertain of the origins of the locution, "drylongso," but it was well known in my household and neighborhood in Memphis: when some character had not shown particular flair or aplomb in carrying out some task, my mother, for example, would describe his/her behavior as "just drylongso." This was not simply an explanation but was accompanied by kinetic gestures and a trill of the voice whose register a musician could identify with accuracy. My mother, whose every gesture exudes more or less passion of one sort or another, could "collapse" her voice and posture with great skill in telling what a "drylongso" looked like. In Gwaltney's book, however, the characters are anything but uninteresting, as they make no pretense, as far as we can tell, to any particular competence or "expertise." I believe that Gwaltney was driving home that exact point. (See chap. 6, this volume.)

51. This sentence alludes to a wonderful collection of short stories by the Barbadian Canadian writer, Austin Clarke, *When He Was Free and Young and He Used to Wear Silks* (Toronto: House of Anancy Press, 1971).

52. For a lucid reading of Jacques Lacan's indebtedness to Hegelian philosophy by way of Alexandre Kojève, see Borch-Jacobsen, *Lacan: The Absolute Master.*

53. Compare Roland Barthes, "Myth Today," in *Mythologies*, trans. Annette Lavers (New York: Hill and Wang, 1975).

54. Sigmund Freud, quoted in Lacan, *The Four Fundamental Concepts*, 44. (See chap. 14, this volume.)

55. For the "boomerang" effect and an inquiry into it, see Ralph Ellison, *Invisible Man* (New York: Modern Library, 1992), in particular, the Prologue, 3–14.

56. Fanon, *Black Skin, White Masks*, 150: "Then there is the unconscious. Since the racial drama is played out in the open, the black man has no time to make it unconscious." Yes, *but* one wonders along a repertoire of unanswered, inchoately posed questions—how to explain intramural "colorism," as Alice Walker called it, which embarrassing trend did not die out, I recently discovered, with the black nationalist sixties? Exactly how does one think about, though it is not particularly her business, the mind-boggling tendency of black men of virtually any generation and a certain profile of "success" (or even not "success") to include any and all women, if he is heterosexually defined, as potential love objects, *except* black women? It is not so much that "the black man" ought to love "the black woman" as that he apparently might love anyone but . . . At the moment, this question is posed as the "black man/black woman thang," which the African-American popular press covers with notable frequency. Why do we pose it over and over again? Perhaps we might say that if "the black man" does "not have time" for the unconscious penetration of the "race" question, then he ought to

make time and the "black woman" right along with him, inasmuch as "she" has some work to do here as well.

57. Wilden, *Speech and Language in Psychoanalysis,* 303.

58. "En décrivant dans ce chapitre la situation d'un psychanalyste travaillant dans une civilisation étrangère à la sienne, nous n'avons fait en définitive qu'illustrer un caractère essentiel de l'attitude analytique puisqu'aucun propos ne peut se comprendre sans référence au contexte familial, social, culturel" (*OA,* 57).

59. "Faudrait-il en conclure qu'une information sociologique poussée doit précéder le travail clinique? Nous répondrons que, si un minimum d'informations est nécessaire, ce qui importe avant tout c'est l'attitude analytique qui cherche à comprendre la place du sujet *dans ce qu'il dit*" (*OA,* 57, my emphasis).

60. "Et, en effet, ici, la maladie n'est pas une entité clinique. Pour les maladies mentales, il n'y a de classification que par la causalité magique ou le destin voulu par Dieu. . . . On se réfère soit à une action contrariante des *rab,* soit à 'l'amour' possessif de *rab* liés à une famille, etc." (*OA,* 40).

61. "L'élément de cohérence dans la réprésentation de la maladie c'est le *rab.* . . . C'est pourquoi nos consultants sont déroutés par nos interrogatoires" (*OA,* 40).

62. At the time of the work's publication, the author was apparently a researcher and lecturer at the Laboratoire de Psychopathologie at the Sorbonne, Université René Descartes (Paris V), after having practiced psychiatric medicine in his native Senegal.

63. The French text reads: "En sa lecture la plus profonde, la folie est 'signe'; elle indique d'emblée que le sujet affecté exprime un conflit: conflit entre lui et les instances constitutives de sa personnalité qui lui sont extérieures, selon la conception traditionnelle" (*SA,* 42).

64. "En effet, on pourrait dire que le signifié du névrosé est enfoui dans son individualité et, au bout du compte, 'double' son désir narcissique qui fonctionne comme s'il était, en lui-même, sa propre finalité; alors que le signifié de l'homme face au sacré, c'est le Verbe, la Loi, la Tradition, en un mot: l'Origine, dans le sacrifice de l'Ancêtre fondateur, créateur de la Loi, garant de la paix et de la coexistence entre les humains actuels" (*SA,* 162).

65. " . . . coupé de ses instances constituantes par 'l'agresseur.' Ainsi, tout d'abord, il faudra transformer l'affection en structure de communication" (*SA,* 42).

66. " . . . parmi les moyens du rapprochement, il y a la parole, la prière et le rêve . . . mais, comme toujours en Afrique, le dialogue entre Dieu et les hommes passe par l'intercesseur privilégié qu'est l'Ancêtre" (*SA,* 164 n. 27).

67. "Factors that are often cited are . . . effective psychological—in effect, cultural—defenses, such as the externalization of conflict, with precise group identification with a persecutor" (*AS,* 38). [On souligne souvent, en effet . . . des défenses psychologiques—en fait, culturelles—efficaces telles que extériorité du conflit avec nomination collective précise d'un persécuteur (*SA,* 36).]

68. "Le matériel de la psychothérapie montre qu'arrivé au seuil d'un affrontement assumé personnellement, Samba . . . situe l'image paternelle et la castration dans la rapport aux ancêtres: le baobab de la vision initiale, lors d'un rêve (il figure dans de nombreux rêves), réclame que l'on enterre 'le mort' à son pied et non au cimetière; le personnage terrifiant des hallucinations s'est mué en un homme au regard bon qui prononce ces seuls mots: 'C'est le père des pères' " (*OA,* 101).

69. "Les troubles de Samba ont commencé le jour où, passant sous un grand baobab en revenant de l'école, il entendit une voix qui l'appela trois fois par son nom de famille. Heureusement, il ne répondit pas car 'quand on répond c'est mauvais, on devient fou, ou on est sale et seul dans la brousse' (comme un homme que Samba a vu jadis); il ne s'est pas retourné non plus. Il a eu très peur et est rentré chez lui en courant, s'est couché tremblant et a vomi dans la nuit. Depuis ce jour et des mois durant, Samba

tient ses paupières closes comme s'il redoutait une vision terrifiante: 'comme des enfants, quelque chose de gros, un diable.' Il souffre de céphalées intenses, refuse de s'alimenter et en aucun cas ne porte lui-même à ses lèvres le peu de nourriture ou de boisson qu'il absorbe. Il reste inerte, prostré, le dos voûté, en geignant. Ses gémissements peuvent, des heures durant, s'amplifier en de longues plaintes monotones. Les quelques mots que l'on parvient à lui arracher sont murmurés, à peine audibles et accompagnés d'un mouvement de négation de la tête.

"Ce tableu persistant plusieurs mois, au dire des parents, Samba est conduit à la consultation de neurologie et hospitalisé. Tous les examens pratiqués sont négatifs. Son état étant inchangé trois semaines plus tard, Samba sort sur sa demande insistante, après de quotidiennes tentatives de fugues. Il est hospitalisé peu après en psychiatrie. En un an il y sera hospitalisé à trois reprises et suivi entre-temps à titre externe. A chaque hospitalisation une série d'électro-chocs est pratiquée parallèlement à la psychothérapie. Un traitement par neuroleptiques est poursuivi également.

"Dans le cas de Samba, il est légitime de parler de psychothérapie psychanalytique au sens le plus classique du terme. La demande de l'enfant est claire: il vient 'parler pour être guéri.' Une relation transférentielle riche s'établit rapidement. A ce jour le traitement dure depuis un an et a comporté 51 séances. Samba est intelligent et cherche à verbaliser tout ce qu'il vit" (*OA*, 96–97).

70. "(. . . [D]es enfants ou un serpent ou un homme noir très, très grand, viennent lui faire peur, comme un diable. . . .), il dit de l'homme noir: 'Il me faisait peur. Il m'a montré le bonheur. . . . ' [D]es serpents sont dans son corps, sur son corps, ils vont le mordre, ils boivent son sang, il va mourir dans l'instant" (*OA*, 97–98).

71. "Pour le père et la mère de Samba, pour tout l'entourage, l'existence des djiné et saytané est une évidence quotidienne depuis l'enfance; chacun a une ou plusieurs expériences personnelles les concernant" (*OA*, 98).

72. "Dans ses fantasmes le personnage du diable, monolithique au départ, terrorisant et fascinant, s'est progressivement dédoublé puis scindé en un groupe de 3 ou 4 personnes, ce qui permettait à Samba un jeu de plus en plus souple où il se projetait dans des positions variées à l'égard de son désir et de son anxiété" (*OA*, 99).

73. " . . . mais cela ne peut empêcher de se demander si la culture qui est celle de Samba ne lui impose pas ou ne lui propose pas de manière privilégiée la solution de la psychose hallucinatoire à thème de persécution" (*OA*, 99–100).

74. "Il est en effet bien difficile d'imaginer Samba guéri grâce à un traitement psychanalytique, après avoir intériorisé ses tensions, les avoir résolues 'personnellement.' Cela supposerait que, seul de son milieu, de sa famille, il se désolidarise des croyances communes, qu'il se singularise d'une manière telle qu'il deviendrait comme étranger chez lui, qu'il aurait accédé à un niveau de conscience personnelle qui le situerait bien 'en avant de ses pères' (il se trouve que l'on ne peut attendre aucune évolution du groupe familial). Est-ce possible? Est-ce souhaitable?" (*OA*, 100).

75. "Ici l'accent est davantage mis sur l'affirmation d'un statut, d'un prestige. Il s'agit plutôt de montrer aux autres, aux 'frères,' une certaine image de soi-même, de faire qu'ils y croient pour pouvoir soi-même coïncider avec cette image. . . .

"Pour les jeunes Dakarois que nous avons vus, les projets d'avenir, le 'quand je serai grand,' ne portent guère sur des performances ou des activités personnalisées: il est peu question d'inventer quoi que ce soit, ou de dépasser qui que ce soit, *sinon en se donnant à regarder*. On dira que l'on veut porter de beaux vêtements, que l'on veut avoir une bonne situation, mais l'activité précise, disons le métier, que suppose la bonne situation ou l'acquisition des beaux vêtements, est peu considérée pour elle-même. Le voeu est moins celui d'une activité plus intéressante ou plus efficace que d'une place plus en vue, d'une raison sociale plus éminente. Le fantasme sous-jacent est d'imaginer ce que les autres pensent en vous regardant. Pour se valoriser on dira autant: 'J'ai fait ceci ou cela,' que: 'Un tel m'admire . . . Un tel a dit que j'étais intelligent . . . Un tel a dit que j'étais un grand' (ce sont là paroles d'étudiants). Si l'on dit: 'J'avais plus de succès féminins que mes camarades,' ce sera moins pour évoquer ses relations avec les filles que pour renvoyer à l'admiration ou à la jalousie des camarades" (*OA*, 101–2).

76. See note 38.

77. "Chez tous nos sujets la référence au père ou à l'oncle a le caractère d'un spectacle, d'un témoignage offert au regard des autres. . . . L'enfant se sent en puissance de père, aimé du père, quand il est bien habillé, quand il imagine les autres le regardant bien habillé" (*OA*, 102–3).

78. "Chez nous, selon son âge, un garçon pensera: 'Mon père est plus fort qu'un lion . . . mon père a la plus grosse voiture . . . mon père est riche et commande . . . ' Ici, l'enfant pense: 'Mon père va m'acheter une belle chemise, un beau costume'" (*OA*, 103).

79. "Le désir d'habits meilleurs, plus beaux, est le premier désir exprimé par les jeunes garçons, désir de montrer leur père. Et chez ceux qui souffrent de son indifférence ou de son éloignement, il n'est pas rare de rencontrer un souci obsédant de leur apparence jusqu'à évoquer l'homosexualité dans la recherche apportée aux colifichets" (*OA*, 104).

80. "La fréquence avec laquelle le déclenchement de sensations douloureuses, perçues au niveau de la peau ou de la musculature superficielle, est attribué au regard des autres. Dans bien des cas, l'angoisse paraît être secondaire à la douleur perçue, à la crampe, comme si l'éprouvé corporel était directement modelé par le regard d'autrui. . . . L'attention portée au regard dans les descriptions de comportement qui nous sont faites: il a un regard formidable; il a un regard méprisant; il est masqué; il a un regard détourné; il ne te regarde pas; il tient les yeux de côté; il regard et il rit, ce n'est pas l'enfant réglementaire; il garde *la tête baissée*" (*OA*, 104, my emphasis).

81. Wilden, *Speech and Language in Psychoanalysis*, 305.

82. Ibid., 304.

83. I am referring here to the very influential and suggestive writing by Laura Mulvey, "Visual Pleasure and Narrative Cinema," *Visual and Other Pleasures* (Bloomington: Indiana University Press, 1989), 14–26.

84. "Dans le modèle européen du complexe d'Oedipe, le fils s'imagine tuant le père. Ici la pente typique serait plutôt: le fils se référant par l'intermédiaire du père à l'ancêtre déjà mort donc inattaquable et constituant ses 'frères' en rivaux. C'est pourquoi les représentations que nous avons utilisées, phallus collectif, ancêtre inégalable, ne peuvent se comprendre qu'en fonction du terme où elles conduisent, le jeu de la rivalité-solidarité entre les frères. . . .

"*La rivalité nous paraît tout d'abord être systématiquement déplacée sur les 'frères' qui polarisent les pulsions agressives. . . . L'agressivité s'exprime principalement sous la forme de réactions persécutives.* . . . L'ensemble des rapports interpersonnels est fortement coloré par le fait que chacun se perçoit facilement comme persécuté. On pourrait dire qu'une partie de l'énergie qui, dans un autre contexte, serait employée à s'affirmer en agissant, est ici consommée à se défendre. En toutes circonstances, il convient de se protéger des intentions menaçantes. . . .

"La culpabilité est peu intériorisée ou constituée comme telle. Tout se passe comme si l'individu ne pouvait pas supporter de se percevoir divisé intérieurement, mobilisé par des désirs contradictoires. Le 'mauvais' est toujours situé à l'extérieur de moi, il est du domaine de la fatalité, du sort, de la volonté de Dieu" (*OA*, 79, 92, 93, 94).

85. " . . . dans la mesure où les pulsions agressives ne sont pas projetées, on peut constater qu'elles sont conscientes mais réprimées, contrôlées, non exprimées. Les fantasmes ou émois agressifs sont présents comme une longue souffrance, sourde et secrète, écrasante, inavouable, qu'il convient de taire 'pour ne pas décourager mes

parents.' . . . 'parce qu'ils comptent sur moi' et aussi pour ne pas se montrer vulnérable. Bien souvent des somatisations apparaissent comme le moyen d'inhiber dans l'instant l'expression des fantasmes ou impulsions agressives. Le comportement de ces sujets est de méfiance dissimulée sous une imperturbable gentillesse visant à ne pas donner prise aux attaques. . . . A moins qu'ils ne recherchent la solitude pour se protéger des contacts devenus trop anxiogènes, les jeunes gens décrivent tous comment ils sont poussés irré-sistiblement à aller avec les amis, comment pour eux être 'bien' (heureux, dynamique) c'est être partie d'un groupe, d'une foule. Peu importe souvent qu'il s'agisse d'une réu-nion sportive, dansante, de palabres interminables ('faire la nuit blanche'). . . . La présence des autres est rassurante, nécessaire; elle désamorce ou repousse à l'arrière-plan les fantasmes agressifs latents" (*OA*, 95–96).

86. Claude Meillassoux, *Maidens, Meal, and Money: Capitalism and the Domestic Community* (1975; rpt., New York: Cambridge University Press, 1981), 79.

87. Ibid., 47.

Chapter Sixteen

"*The Crisis of the Negro Intellectual: A Post-Date*" was published in *boundary 2*, vol. 21, no. 3 (Fall 1994): 65–116, and is reprinted by permission of Duke University Press.

1. Recently reissued, *The Crisis of the Negro Intellectual* bears the subtitle *From Its Origins to the Present* (New York: William Morrow and Company, Inc.,1967). All citations from the text come from the 1967 edition, with page numbers parenthetically noted.

2. Robert L. Allen's *Black Awakening in Capitalist America: An Analytic History* (Garden City, N.Y.: Anchor Books, 1970) examines *The Crisis* against the backdrop of the Black Power movement. See "Black Power and Bourgeois Black Nationalism," 171–80.

Contemporaneous reviews of Cruse's work are too numerous to list here, even par-tially, but I would call brief attention to two of them from the period: Michael Thelwell, "What is to Be Done?" *Partisan Review* 35, no. 4 (Fall 1968): 619–22; and Ernest Kaiser, "Review," *Freedomways* 9, no.1 (Winter 1969): 24–41. Thelwell finds abundant ironies riddling Cruse's posture toward the intellectuals, among them, that Cruse, while lam-basting others for their pursuit of integrationist social practices, had had himself to go "downtown" for the publicaton of *his* book. Furthermore, just as Cruse had held black intellectuals culpable to charges of intellectual timidity and self-ostracism, he himself, Thelwell implies, had reenforced such a stance by appealing to them as a separate and distinct class interest or formation; "Even the title of this book constitutes a kind of heresy in that liberal tradition which maintains that the community of 'intellectuals' is raceless and shares only work-related problems of methodology, analysis, craftsman-ship, for it sets up a 'class' of black intellectuals with common problems not shared by nonblacks" (619). Thelwell finds the intent of *The Crisis* "obscure," its focus "blur[red]," and its reading of the role of communist ideology overdetermined in Cruse's assess-ment of integrationist distortions. (I would point out another small irony of ironies: that Thelwell himself would appear as one of the essayists in a collection of responses to William Styron's controversial novel of 1968, *The Confessions of Nat Turner. Ten Black Writers Respond* published pieces on Styron's work that ranged in view from outrage to subtler critical signatures. The point is that if Thelwell himself does not mean the open-ing sentence of his review as tongue-in-cheek, then he will have missed the political im-plications of both the collection of essays and many of the essayists' anger at what they felt to be aggressive presumptuousness on Styron's part. Need we point out that black intellectuals as a social formation sprout teeth precisely because the liberal view, itself a *political* position, sutures power differences that conceal the moves it performs as a nat-ural "innocence"?)

Ernest Kaiser reviews *The Crisis of the Negro Intellectual* against the perspective of African American intellectual history, noting that several of its early reviewers, many of them Anglo-American reviewers for mainstream journals and newspapers, had produced a hodgepodge of incoherence in addressing this work, precisely because they were ignorant of its predecessor texts. Kaiser's review is valuable, because it examines several positions on *The Crisis* and the ways in which they are flawed. The *Journal of Ethnic Studies* devoted a third of its contents to a reappraisal of Cruse's work in vol. 5, no.2 (Summer 1977): 1–69.

3. Pastor of Dorchester, Massachusetts's Azuza Christian Community, the Reverend Eugene Rivers addressed an open letter to Boston's black intellectuals entitled "On the Responsibility of Intellectuals in the Age of Crack," published in the *Boston Review* 17, no. 5 (Sept/Oct 1992): 3–4. The letter elaborates its concerns against the background of Noam Chomsky's essay, "The Responsibility of Intellectuals," which appeared in a 1967 issue of the *New York Review of Books*. Chomsky, in turn, had been inspired by a series of articles written by Dwight MacDonald, appearing in the journal, *Politics*. The question was whether intellectuals have any special moral responsibility, and Rivers quotes from Chomsky's piece: "Intellectuals have a 'responsibility . . . to speak the truth and to expose lies' and a duty 'to see events in their historical perspective'" (3). Calling directly on the Boston/Cambridge intellectuals by name, Rivers reminds his readers that a black elite is "not exempt" from the current crises facing African American communities across the country. Rivers's call was answered on two separate occasions, at fora sponsored both times by the *Boston Review*. The first exchange took place on 30 November 1992, at the Arco Forum at Harvard University's Kennedy School of Government; hosted by Anthony Appiah of Harvard, speakers included Rivers himself, Cornel West, bell hooks, Henry Louis Gates Jr., Glenn Loury, and Margaret Burnham. The transactions from the initial symposium were published in the *Boston Review* 18, no. 1 (Jan/Feb 1993): 22–28.

The second round of talks was convened at MIT, again under the auspices of the *Boston Review*, with complementary sponsorship provided by MIT's Department of Politics; hosted by Margaret Burnham of the Department of Politics, the program's speakers included the Reverend Rivers, Regina Austin, Randall Kennedy, Selwyn Cudjoe, and bell hooks. This second forum occurred nearly a year later on 17 November 1993. The *Boston Review* published the transactions in volume 19, no. 1 (Feb/Mar 1994): 3–9. Glenn Loury, whose illness prevented him from attending the second meeting, published a companion piece, "The Poverty of Reason," 10–11, in the same issue of the journal.

4. I broadly allude to one of the definitive works on the postmodernist encounter provided by Fredric Jameson in *Postmodernism, or, the Cultural Logic of Late Capitalism* (Durham, N.C.: Duke University Press, 1991).

5. A useful collection of essays on positions on property, beginning with the seventeenth-century doctrine of liberal property, espoused by John Locke, is provided in *Property: Mainstream and Critical Positions*, ed. C. B. MacPherson (Toronto Press, 1978).

6. Mike Davis offers a stunning reading of the nation's socioeconomic crisis by way of one of its major inner-city formations—South Central Los Angeles—in "Who Killed LA? A Political Autopsy," *The New Left Review* 197 (Jan/Feb 1993): 3–29. Davis trails the tax base to the suburban context and discusses its implications for presidential politics 1992. But against his broad strokes, we espy the larger fate of the American people in light of post–Cold War labor surpluses.

7. A piece of work that I would consider required reading for a fuller understanding of the political conjuncture in which we are currently located, "Manufacturing the Attack on Liberalized Education," by Ellen Messer-Davidow, *Social Text* 36 (Fall 1993): 40–81, unfolds the sources and the stage of right-wing U.S. political formation in the Reagan/Bush era.

8. Cruse felt that such groups should aim beyond "the goals of mere anti-poverty

welfare state programs such as HARYOU-ACT" (The Harlem Youth Rehabilitation Program-Harlem Youth Unlimited).

9. Dorothy Sterling, *We Are Your Sisters: Black Women in the Nineteenth Century* (New York: W. W. Norton, 1984). See especially Part 2, "Free Women, 1800–1861" (85–235), on the early work by African-American women's community.

10. Interestingly enough, a decade might make a notable difference: between the time that this essay was written and the appearance of this volume, Harlem's fortunes have been apparently reversed. The good news is that it "is reviving," according to Rob Gurwitt; but the question for Harlem-watchers and aficionados is whether or not this rediscovered site for vigorous capitalist investment can sustain Harlem's age-old "sense of place," "as a spiritual home" for African-Americans. This query has recently been conducted by Rob Gurwitt, "Up in Harlem," *Preservation: The Magazine of the National Trust for Historic Preservation,* July/August 2002: 40–47, 82, at 42, 43.

11. One of the most important works on paradigm formation and its impact on scientific research is provided by Thomas S. Kuhn, *The Structure of Scientific Revolutions,* International Encyclopedia of Unified Science, vol. 2, no. 2 (Chicago: University of Chicago Press, 1970).

12. Louis Althusser and Etienne Balibar, *Reading Capital* (London: Verso Books, 1986); see especially Part 1, Louis Althusser, "From *Capital* to Marx's Philosophy," 11–71. All quotations come from this edition and are cited parenthetically in my text as *RC.*

I obtained a copy of Althusser's posthumously published autobiography, *The Future Lasts Forever* (*L'Avenir dure longtemps*), ed. Olivier Corpet and Yann Moulier Boutang, trans. Richard Veasey, with an intro. by Douglas Johnson (New York: The New Press, 1993), too late to examine for this writing. Its revelations will inevitably alter our reading of "Althusserianism," as Douglas Johnson calls it, though I would not attempt to predict in what ways. If, as Johnson suggests, the autobiography, "is filled with details which one can read, irrespective of the destiny of the Althussers," then I would conjecture that "Althusserianism" offers an "intellectual adventure" that we might pursue, as well as the "histoire à sensation" (Introduction, xvii). In any case, I am not shy to press a point borrowed from his theoretical scaffolding in order to advance the building at hand. Althusser died in 1990, of a heart attack at seventy-two years of age after a long regimen of psychiatric treatment and sporadic confinement in various French hospitals. One of them was Paris's Sainte-Anne, a site which provided the occasion for Michel Foucault's studies in madness—which would lead him to *Madness and Civilization*—when Foucault, along with Johnson and Althusser, was an agrégé candidate at the École Normale Supérieure. The autobiography features two pieces, "The Facts" ("Les Faits," 1976) and the longer confessional discourse that names the book. It tells the story that Althusser did not pass on to the French courts for reasons of insanity—euphemistically called, we might guess, the "non-lieu," the "no grounds," or the magistrate's "refusal to order prosecution": On 16 November 1980, Althusser, apparently overwhelmed by severe confusion and derangement, strangled his wife/companion of some thirty years, Hélène Légotien/Rytman, in their apartment on the grounds of the École. Immediately consigned to doctors' care at Sainte-Anne, Althusser was interned there for three years. Released after that time, he lived alone in northern Paris until his death seven years later. Althusser never stood trial for what was designated a "voluntary homicide," as the public variously attributed this outcome to a French "ole boy" network and/or the French government's vaunted respect for left intellectuals ("Introduction," *The Future Lasts Forever,* vi–xviii).

13. See "Changing the Letter," chap. 7 in this volume.

14. Cornel West and bell hooks, *Breaking Bread: Insurgent Black Intellectual Life* (Boston: South End Press, 1991), see especially "The Dilemma of the Black Intellectual,"

137–47. One of the clearest, and most compassionate, voices of our time, Cornel West would supplement the Marxist and Foucaultian paradigms of knowledge with the habit of insurgency as the required *repositioning* of the black creative intellectual. While I agree with him that the insurgent feature of black intellectual life must be recovered in its critico-theoretical efficacy, I take fairly strong objection to the route that his conclusion traverses: Firmly rooted in the romantic ground of organicity, this argument conduces to the two most powerful (and predictable) motifs of African-American cultural life: *"the black Christian tradition of preaching and the Black musical tradition of performance"* (136). Compared to the "richness, diversity and vitality" of these great forces, "black literate intellectual production" is impoverished, etc. Not only is "black literate intellectual production" *another order of cases,* with which the current generation of black creative intellectuals is not consistently engaged, but the analogy itself, which actually collapses those *differences on the bottom line,* induces invidious distinction. One could say, on the one hand, that black preaching shows no commensurate achievement to John Coltrane's discography, while, on the other, no musical artist, one might contend, can claim an accomplishment equal to the Reverend Martin Luther King's— in actual and pragmatic outcome (i.e. Civil Rights legislation, etc.). Either way, such an interpretation would be absurd, wrongheaded, and incapable of providing the subject the means by which to justly gauge either black preaching or black musical performance. Just so, I would suggest that the way to intellectual "greatness," if we must put forth a cattle show here, will *not* consist in the oral, improvisational, and histrionic modes of production, but in the risks, *in writing,* in the systematic wager to expose the gaps in Western writing economies. I would submit that the historic *conceptual/enunciating* impoverishment of African and diasporic social formations is equal, at every step, to their "concrete oppression" and, in fact, *names* its twin force. What, then, is black creative intellectual production when *not* oral improvisational, and histrionic? We already know what it is as the latter, if the real legacy that we fashioned during the late sixties tells us anything and signals exactly where we have landed today. We might say, finally, that the work of the intellectual is to make her reader/hearer *discomfitted, unoriented* and, therefore, *self-critical.* She is not in fact a "Dr. Feelgood" or "Mr. Goodbar."

15. West and hooks, *Breaking Bread,* 144.

16. As the "experience of Necessity," Fredric Jameson argues, as the refusal of masterful encodation to be dismantled, "History is what hurts." See "On Interpretation," in *The Political Unconscious: Narrative as a Socially Symbolic Act* (Ithaca, N.Y.: Cornell University Press, 1981), 102.

17. The "signifying" process comprises one of the rich semiotic practices of the lifeworld and has been the subject of seminal investigation in Geneva Smitherman's *Talkin and Testifyin: The Language of Black America* (Detroit: Wayne State University Press, 1977) see especially chap. 5, "'The Forms of Things Unknown': Black Modes of Discourse," 101–67. In *The Signifying Monkey: A Theory of Afro-American Literary Criticism* (New York: Oxford University Press, 1988), Henry Louis Gates Jr. magisterially bridges Smitherman's vernacular "signifyin/siggin" and literary theory's signification to construct a contemporary interpretive model of black tradition theorizing "about itself."

18. Jonathan Culler's work includes two indispensable texts that introduced a wider audience to the propositions and methodologies of linguistic/structuralist literary procedure: *Structuralist Poetics: Structuralism, Linguistics, and the Study of Literature* (Ithaca, N.Y.: Cornell University Press, 1975); *The Pursuit of Signs: Semiotics, Literature, Deconstruction* (Ithaca, N.Y.: Cornell University Press, 1981).

19. *The Structuralist Controversy: The Languages of Criticism and the Sciences of Man,* ed. Richard Macksey and Eugenio Donato (Baltimore: The Johns Hopkins University Press, 1972). This work is hereafter cited in my text as *SC.*

20. One of the earlier anthologies of cross-disciplinary readings in linguistic method

starts its chronology with excerpts from Marx, through the canons of Michel Foucault and Jacques Lacan. *See The Structuralists from Marx to Lévi-Strauss,* ed. Richard and Fernande deGeorge (New York: Anchor Brooks, 1972).

21. In 1997, the School of Criticism and Theory changed venues again and is currently hosted by Cornell University, under the directorship of Dominick LaCapra.

22. Paul Bové, *Intellectuals in Power: A Genealogy of Critical Humanism* (New York: Columbia University Press, 1986).

23. In his germinal work on romanticism, M. H. Abrams, as one of the school of the late New Criticism critics, discusses the poem "as heterocosm." Marking one of the stages of literary historiography that Abrams evolves from the mimetic, to the objective, traditions of the literary art, the heterocosmic replaces "the speculative metaphor of poem as mirror" (*The Mirror and the Lamp: Romantic Theory and the Critical Tradition* [New York: Oxford University Press, 1953], 272).

24. For a "different" Derrida, Rodolph Gasche's *Tain of the Mirror: Derrida and the Philosophy of Reflection* (Cambridge: Harvard University Press, 1986) takes the philosopher askew the field of literary theory per se and reads him against the grain of post-Hegelian discourse.

25. Jacques Derrida, *Of Grammatology,* trans. with into. Gayatri Chakravorty Spivak (Baltimore: Johns Hopkins University Press, 1976). Originally published as *De la Grammatologie* (Paris: Seuil, 1967).

26. One of the controlling metaphors by way of which Ellison's protagonist descends into a deep reading of the historical narrative is supplied by the figure of Louis Armstrong and the Blues. See the Prologue, *Invisible Man* (New York: The Modern Library, 1992).

27. Imamu Amiri Baraka, *Home: Social Essays* (New York: William Morrow and Co., Inc., 1966); see especially "The Myth of a Negro Literature," 105–15. A writer himself of considerable power and range, Imamu Baraka/Leroi Jones anguishes the reader about what he calls "Negro literature." One is afraid that he meant nothing much more than that the "Negro" writers—those of "impressive mediocrity," in his opinion—were quite simply the ones who came *before* him and his generation of black/American writers. The point, however, is that, once again, literary intellection/production among African-Americans is abject before the towering accomplishments of the musical artists: "Only in music, and most notably in blues, jazz, and spirituals, i.e. 'Negro music,' has there been a significantly profound contribution by American Negroes" (106). On prediction, we read that the writers' quite "spectacular vapidity" is due, in large part, to their membership in the "Negro middle class" that goes "out of its way to cultivate *any* mediocrity" in the interest of showing that it is not what it is—Negro. Thirty years down the line, perhaps it is time for the intellectuals to revise and correct the question of "middle-class" status *in/and* black music/art?

28. In this wonderful interview with Robert Stepto, Toni Morrison, shortly before the publication of her third novel, *Song of Solomon* (1977), can at least imagine an "enormous space" of possibility for all the black arts/creativity. Speaking of an "open," "freer" moment for literature in the post-sixties period, she observes, "I think of it in terms of the one other art form in which black people have always excelled and that is music, an art form that opens doors, rather than closes them, where there are more possibilities, not fewer." See "'Intimate Things in Place': A Conversation with Toni Morrison," in *Chant of Saints: A Gathering of Afro-American Literature, Art, and Scholarship,* ed. Michael S. Harper and Robert B. Stepto (Urbana, Ill.: University of Illinois Press, 1979), 213–30.

29. "Twelve Years A Slave: Narrative of Solomon Northup," with a preface by David Wilson, in *Puttin' On Ole Massa,* ed. Gilbert Osofsky (New York: Harper Torchbooks, 1969), 324. Northup penned his narrative in the 1850s.

30. Karl Marx, *Capital: A Critique of Political Economy,* vol. 1, intro. by Ernest Mandel, trans. Ben Fowkes (New York: Vintage Books, 1977).

31. Althusser quotes this passage of *Capital,* vol. 1, from the Éditions Sociales version.

32. Ernesto Laclau and Chantal Mouffe, *Hegemony and Socialist Strategy: Towards a Radical Democratic Politics* (New York: Verso Books, 1989), 7.

33. Ibid., 3.

34. See note 3 above. In an attempt to interpolate, on the spot, one of the layers of analysis that tends to be elided in public discussion about the duties of black intellectuals, Harvard law professor Randall Kennedy, in response to moderator Margaret Burnham's request, during the second Cambridge symposium, that he clarify some earlier remarks that he had made, asked: "Do black people have more of a responsibility towards black people who are in misery *than their white counterparts who are sitting next to them?* [my emphasis]. My answer was: *no* [Kennedy's emphasis]; we all have a very high responsibility towards those who are in misery" (*Boston Review* 19, no.1 [Feb/Mar 1994]: 5–6). Reading the question again for this transcription, I now see that the italicized portion of the sentence *could* just as well mean "white counterparts" to the black helper-intellectuals, as "white counterparts" to misery's helpees. If the former then the question is worth asking, inasmuch as non-blacks occasionally believe, it seems, that blacks can solve their "Problem" all by themselves since "It" is their "fault." At any rate, my question would be rather different from Kennedy's (and would include, for example, who is going to "help" the intellectuals?), though *who* is asking the question, as I had inferred that Kennedy meant—*when, where, how, why*—is dropped from the inquiry, as a rule, and should be restored. Further, one conjures a question that is never asked: What is the obligation of white intellectuals to *their* people? And why is the question never posed in that way, linking the white intellectual subject to "race"/ethnicity, since there seems to be incredible need for *someone* to tend this field? Or did 1968 take care of that?

35. Apologies to Professor Deborah McDowell for "misreading" the title of one of her essays, "The Changing Same," on African-American women writers. See "The Changing Same: Generational New Literary History," *New Literary History* 18, no. 2 (Winter 1987): 282–302. In this context, I mean the exact opposite from McDowell's "changing same."

36. Robert Stepto has created a stunning interpretive device by way of a demographic topos—ascent and immersion thematics—in his examination of select narratives from African-American writing. He reads his "symbolic geography" against several canonical works, including that of DuBois, and Hurston, in *From Behind the Veil: A Study of Afro-American Narrative* (Urbana: University of Illinois Press, 1979).

37. See "All the Things You Could Be by Now, If Sigmund Freud's Wife Was Your Mother," chap. 15 in this volume.

38. Mary-Christine Phillip, "Of Black Studies: Pondering Strategies for the Future," *Black Issues in Higher Education* 11, no. 5 (5 May 1994): 14–19.

39. One of the country's early black eminences, Carter G. Woodson, along with DuBois, can arguably be said to have established the discipline of African-American historiography, both as a profession and as a conceptual itinerary. With George Cleveland Hall, W. B. Hartgrove, Alexander Jackson, and J. E. Stamps, Woodson founded the Association for the Study of Negro Life and History and established the *Journal of Negro History* in 1916. Complementary to this effort, Woodson also initiated "Negro History Week," which slowly evolved into "Black History Month." For the academic year 1919–1920, he served as dean of the School of Liberal Arts and head of the graduate faculty at Howard University; from 1920 to 1922, Woodson functioned as dean at what would later become West Virginia State College, retiring from teaching at the end of this stint.

Born in 1875, Woodson edited the Journal and directed the Association until his death in 1950. His prolific output includes archival work on education and the church, his most well-known texts, perhaps, *The Negro in our History* and *The Miseducation of the Negro*. Though a difficult personality, apparently, Woodson seems to have cultivated a talent for what Susan Sontag called "appreciation": Four volumes of the Reverend Francis K. Grimké's sermons, speeches and addresses were edited by Woodson, as well as a volume of letters written by enslaved persons. (See the Introduction to this volume.)

40. See note 3 above. At the first Cambridge symposium, Cornel West made an incisive point in observing that one of the black intellectual's difficulties was the sustaining intellectual life in a "business civilization." The problem seems so severe that one wonders if the entire problem of the intellectual subject and ethical responsibility is itself an anachronism, if we have in fact entered the first stages of a post-intellectual period, as the thought-object is packaged like the self-serve food item? In such a culture, West goes on, the intellectuals "actually surface precisely when they are experts . . . but experts aren't intellectuals. Some are. But most aren't" (*Boston Review* 18, no. 1 [Jan/Feb 1993]: 25). West offers that the Reverend Rivers, perhaps, had invited his interlocutors to be *experts,* rather than *intellectuals,* a distinction West insisted upon. Might we add to his carefully stated objection the "fallacy of authority," in which case the subject-who-is-supposed-to-know is *assumed* to know everything?

41. Michel de Certeau, *The Writing of History,* trans. Tom Conley (New York: Columbia University Press, 1988), 318–19.

Index

abnormal, 389, 390, 392

Absalom! Absalom! (Faulkner): and mulatto/a, 302, 305–12, 313, 315–17; and narrative, 336–39, 340, 341–56, 357–60; and New World, 32–33, 327–34; and return, 375; and sexuality, 238–39, 282

academy: and African-Americans, 430, 449–50; and Black Studies/African-American studies, 30–31, 37–40, 462–64; and colonization, 468; and feminism, 11, 12, 158; and not-mother, 460; paralysis in, 433–34; and public relations, 465–67; and society, 466; and structuralism, 446–49. *See also* education

aesthetics, 6, 9, 85, 103

Africa: Bowen and, 271; Dubois and, 397; and family, 218–19; Faulkner and, 312; and food, 43–44, 47, 51–55; Marshall and, 295, 296, 297; Miller and, 260; and psychoanalysis, 405, 409–25; and slavery, 206, 217, 425

Africa Cookbook (Harris), 53, 54, 61

African, 392–93, 410

African-American: analysis of, 433; Bowen and, 270–76, 275; and capitalism, 437–38; and culture, 377; and domesticity, 249; and economy, 383–84; Fanon and, 390; and father, 230; and feminism, 153–54, 301; Gwaltney and, 169; image of, 196–97; and individual, 394, 395; Magaw and, 259; and mulatto/a, 302, 503n.5; and name, 232; and one, 394, 395; as phobogenic object, 379, 390, 397, 519n.24; problems of, 430–31; and psychoanalysis, 376–77, 384, 385; and race, 395; and sexuality, 164, 165, 488n.10; and shadow, 302; as term, 25; and thingness, 318; and wounding, 276. *See also* blacks; Negro

African-American critics, 81–83

African-American intellectual: C. West on,

529n.14, 533n.40; conversion of, 434; crisis of, 428–29; culpability of, 431; and culture, 441–42, 462; and gender, 468–69; and history, 444–45; and individualism, 461; and knowledge, 440–41, 456; and music, 450–51; and one *vs.* many, 461; and politics, 433; and quality, 467; representative figure of, 468; successes of, 430; and theory, 441, 456, 457, 461

African-American men, 193, 205, 228, 266, 269–71. *See also* men; *specific male characters*

African-American Studies. *See* Black Studies/African-American Studies

African-American Travel Guide (Robinson), 58–60

African-American women: and African-American men, 205; as agents, 154–55; and body, 20–21, 171, 172, 189; Brooks and, 122, 123, 135; and commodification, 155; and difference, 20–21, 312–13; and empowerment, 156; and feminism, 153–54, 156, 158, 174; Firestone and, 159; and gender, 228–29; Gwaltney and, 169; Hernton and, 154, 155; as human, 155; and inferiority, 156; and language, 156; and matriarchy, 204, 205, 218, 228; and men, 174, 205; mulatto/a, 312–13; and naming, 168, 169; non-being, 156; as other, 155; and psychoanalysis, 203; and rape, 207; and reproduction, 227; and self-image, 167; and sexuality, 12–14, 30, 154–64, 165–68, 169–75; and slavery, 19, 155, 212, 220, 221–24, 313; as split subject, 203; Stowe and, 189; and symbolic power, 159, 161; and torture, 207, 208; and white families, 170; and white women, 158, 161, 170, 172–73; as whores, 162, 164, 165. *See also* black women; female; feminine; women; women of color

535

culture: and abandonment, 406; and Africa,
410–12; African-American, 34, 406, 440,
460, 462; and African-American intellectual, 462; and African-Americans, 377;
American, 85, 195; analysis of, 462; Bowen
and, 265, 270; Brooks and, 136, 140–41;
cannibalism, 322; and democracy, 443;
and differentiated identity, 414–15; dispersion of, 460; Ellison and, 5, 67, 72, 84;
Fanon and, 387, 390; Faulkner and, 311–
12, 345; and female body, 134; and food,
53, 56, 61; and gender, 22; Harlem, 436,
438–39; Kristeva and, 288, 290; M. Walker
and, 103; Marshall and, 289, 296, 297,
298, 300; mulatto/a, 27, 28, 302; nationalism vs. integrationism, 440; Ortigueses
and, 417; and psychoanalysis, 34, 384,
401; and race, 22, 378–81, 410; and the
sermon, 254; and sexuality, 157; and slavery, 215, 314; Sow and, 412; Stowe and,
189, 192
culture worker, 391, 404
Cunnigham, J. V., 7

daily life, 137, 169, 401, 402
Dallas, 62
Daly, Mary, 160
Dante, 71–72
daughter: A. Walker and, 242, 244, 245, 247,
248; Ellison and, 237, 239, 240, 241; and
father, 23, 204–6, 230, 231, 234, 237–38,
240–43, 245–50; and mother, 237
Davidson, Alan, 48, 57, 64
Davidson, Cathy, 26
Davis, Angela, 218
death: A. Walker and, 247; and African-Americans, 385; Bowen and, 265; Brooks and,
150, 151; Faulkner and, 344, 370–71, 374;
M. Walker and, 100, 101, 103; Marshall
and, 280, 285, 289
"Decay of Lying, The" (Wilde), 198
de Certeau, Michel, 381, 385, 399, 470
deconstruction, 448, 449
de Courtivron, Isabelle, New French Feminisms,
168
dehumanization, 65, 66
Delany, Martin R., 435
delay, Faulkner and, 342, 348
Deleuze, Gilles, 134
democracy, 32; and the Bible, 268; Brooks
and, 129, 139; Cruse and, 435; and culture, 443; Hughes and, 82; and potential,
403; and slavery, 20; of the specular, 280;
and the transcendent, 407
Democratic Party, 430
deracination, 99, 107, 304
Derrida, Jacques, 82, 134

description, 141, 341, 342
desire: and African-Americans, 385; and consciousness, 399; Faulkner and, 345; Marshall and, 291; and speaking/talking, 400;
Stowe and, 185, 191, 192–93. See also sexuality
destiny, 99, 104, 382
detachment, 358, 403
Dialectic of Sex, A (Firestone), 159–60, 161–64,
167
difference: A. Walker and, 248; and African-
American women, 312–13; as arbitrary,
380; and community, 461; Ellison and,
248; Faulkner and, 328, 330, 364; and
flesh, 327; Gaddis and, 90; Marshall and,
289; Morrison and, 9; and mulatto/a, 313;
and race, 380; and slavery, 213, 314; and
stigma, 425
differentiation: and African-American literature, 83; failures of, 14; and identity, 414–
15; and incest, 23; Marshall and, 285; and
slavery, 214
Dinnerstein, Dorothy, 160; The Mermaid and
Minotaur, 167
disalienation, 391. See also alienation
"Disciplinary Character of Affliction, The"
(Bowen), 270–76
discourse: access to, 425; colonization of, 278;
and community, 459; first order, 172; first
vs. second order, 168; and literary studies,
448; materiality of, 7; public, 153; and sexuality, 152–53, 168, 172; of slavery, 179,
181, 182, 183
discursive/imaginative project, 96
discursivity: and Caliban, 326; conditions of,
446; Faulkner and, 339; tyranny of, 183
"Disloyal to Civilization" (Rich), 160
distancing, 402, 403, 462
doll, 285, 291, 293, 294
domesticity: A. Walker and, 248; and African-
Americans, 249; Brooks and, 136, 138;
Faulkner and, 351; and gender, 214; and
incest, 233–34; Jacobs and, 223; and slavery, 176, 178–79. See also home; house
domination: Bowen and, 272; consensus vs.
compromise, 382; cooperation vs. complicity, 382; Faulkner and, 305, 308, 309,
310; and feminist sexuality, 158; Firestone
and, 163; Foucault and, 448; Lacan and,
386; Marshall and, 300; and outsider, 382;
and psychoanalysis, 35; and symbol, 173–
74. See also slavery
Donato, Eugenio, The Languages of Criticism
and the Sciences of Man, 446
Donnan, Elizabeth, 210–11, 213–15, 314
double, 281, 283, 302, 346, 398, 404, 406. See
also repetition

peer, 418, 422, 423
Pennington, J. W. C, 252–53, 254, 258–59
Peppers, Cracklings, and Knots of Wool Cookbook, The (Spivey), 43–44
perception: Brooks and, 147, 148, 150; Faulkner and, 350–52, 512n.17; of self, 397, 398
perceptual cramp, 198, 391
performance, 347, 355, 397, 450, 451, 466
Person, Ethel Spector, *Women: Sex and Sexuality*, 160
persona, 416, 417
personhood, 212
personnalité, 413
personne, 413
Peter Pan (Barrie), 64
phallogocentrism, 188, 234
phallus, 248, 304, 318, 330, 337
phatic dimension, 294
Philadelphia, 438
Phillips, Paul, 137, 139–40, 141, 146, 150
Philosophy of Literary Form, The (Burke), 367–68
photography, 349, 350, 356, 360. *See also* film/cinema
Pietz, William, 47
pigmentocracy, 27, 30. *See also* skin color
Plum, 112, 113
Poe, Edgar Allen, 343
political economy: Althusser and, 453; Marshall and, 287, 288; and materiality of discourse, 7
politics: and activism, 3–4; African-Americans and, 83, 84, 429, 433; and American society, 430, 433; and black nationalism, 6; and Black Studies/African-American studies, 39–40; Bowen and, 275; Cruse and, 437, 441; and culture worker, 404; and democracy, 403; Ellison and, 76; of enunciation, 199; and formalism, 85; of identity, 21; integrationist *vs.* nationalist, 435, 436; Marshall and, 292, 296; and race, 380, 394; and sentimental novel, 184; and sermons, 254, 261, 269; and theology, 267; women and, 8
Pontalis, J.-B., *Language of Psycho-analysis*, 381
Portrait of a Lady (James), 116
Portugal, 211
possession, 105, 106
possibility, 200, 215, 456
postmodernism, 36, 161
postmodern society, 431
post-structuralism, 339, 371
potentiality, 79, 258, 407, 408
Powell, Adam Clayton, Jr., 319, 435, 439
power: African-American men and, 266; African-American women and, 159, 161;

Foucault and, 448; and human value, 314; Hurston and, 105; Marshall and, 277; Morrison and, 95; and sexuality, 157
Praisesong for the Widow (Marshall), 377
Price, Leontyne, 451
Princess Quaw Quaw Tralaralara, 194
private, 176, 179

property: African-Americans and, 385; and America, 325, 327; and family, 218; Faulkner and, 331; and human, 20; and incest, 246; men and, 204; and slavery, 217, 218, 220, 225, 226, 314–15, 324; Stowe and, 185; use rights, 400
prostitute. *See* whore/prostitute
psyche: Brooks and, 149; Hurston and, 108; mulatto/a, 302; primary process, 24, 396; secondary process, 24, 385. *See also* consciousness; unconscious
psychoanalysis: and Africa, 405, 409–25; and African-Americans, 203, 376–77, 384, 385; and culture, 384; and Duboisian double, 398; and family, 384; Fanon and, 386–94; Faulkner and, 339; and incest, 231, 233; Jacobs and, 223; and language, 371, 375, 404–5; and literature, 372, 373–74; and pathology, 427; and race, 33–34, 376, 378–407, 425–26; and racism, 394; and slavery, 22–23; and speaking/talking, 400; universality of, 384. *See also* consciousness; Freud, Sigmund; Lacan, Jacques; madness; neurosis; psyche; psychosis; unconscious
psychocultural, 397, 398
psychology, 103, 125, 142
psychosis, 418, 420. *See also* neurosis; psychoanalysis
public forum, 459, 460
public relations, 466, 467
public sphere, 397, 405

Quickskill, Raven, 185, 195
Quimbo, 181

Raboteau, Albert, 261
race: and academic feminism, 12; African-Americans and, 395; and America, 26; blankness of, 385; and body, 21; Bowen and, 270, 271; Brooks and, 125–26; and culture, 22, 378–81, 410; and difference, 380; Ellison and, 72; as fallacy, 28–29; Fanon and, 388–93; Faulkner and, 304, 305, 312, 329–31, 333–45; Freud and, 386; and God, 394; and hierarchy, 380; and history, 394; and the irrational, 378; Lacan and, 381; and language, 396; Marshall and, 30, 277, 297, 298; and meaning,